America
Forge of Freedom

Volume Two: From 1865

First Edition
Second Printing

Edited by

KENNETH B. CLARK

SETON PRESS

About the Cover

The front cover of Volume 2 features a photo of the moon landing. In the photo, astronaut Buzz Aldrin salutes the flag of the United States flying on the surface of the moon.

The back cover is a photo of the Cathedral Basilica of St. Louis, Missouri.

 **SETON PRESS**

© 2023 Seton Press
All rights reserved.
Printed in the United States of America.

Seton Press
1350 Progress Drive
Front Royal, VA 22630
Phone: (540) 636-9990

ISBN: 978-1-60704-212-9

For more information, visit us on the web at www.setonpress.com
Contact us by e-mail at info@setonpress.com

20240605

Table of Contents

(Page numbers resume from Volume 1.)

The Lincoln Memorial, Washington D.C.

Reconstruction   1865-1877

On the last day of his life, Abraham Lincoln pardoned a Union soldier charged with desertion. Lincoln's death changed the course of the nation for decades to come.

Lincoln's Assassination

On April 14, only five days after General Lee's surrender, **John Wilkes Booth**, a Southern sympathizer, shot President Lincoln. Lincoln and his wife Mary had been attending a play at **Ford's Theater** in Washington D.C. Booth snuck into the president's unguarded theater box on the balcony and shot President Lincoln. Shouting "*Sic Semper Tyrannis*" ("*Thus Always to Tyrants*"), Booth leapt from the balcony onto the stage below, breaking his leg in the fall. In the confusion, he limped away, escaping to Virginia. Lincoln died from his wound early the next morning.

The authorities found and arrested three conspirators in the assassination plot the same week. On April 26, sheriffs cornered John Wilkes Booth in a barn on Garrett's Farm. When Booth refused to surrender, the barn was set on fire. Booth died from a gunshot, whether self-inflicted or from his pursuers, no one knows for certain. However, many historians believe that **Thomas "Boston" Corbett,** a sergeant in the Union Army, shot Booth. The other conspirators were quickly tried and hanged.

Abraham Lincoln's murder deprived our badly splintered nation of a leader who earnestly sought to "bind up the nation's wounds" and build a bridge of understanding and assistance. In his second Inaugural Address, Lincoln had spoken in true Christian charity of working "with malice toward none" and "with charity for all." His death meant that rebuilding the war-devastated South would be the work of other men. It would fall to Lincoln's vice-president, **Andrew Johnson**, to oversee the reconstruction of the South.

Andrew Johnson Succeeds Abraham Lincoln

If President Lincoln had lived, his desire to engineer a righteous peace between North and South, coupled with his political ability, might well have bound "up the nation's wounds." The awesome burden of national leadership after his death became the responsibility of President Andrew Johnson. Historians have not generally rated Johnson high among U.S. presidents, but since he led the nation in a time of such suffering and strain, his choices deserve careful consideration.

President Andrew Johnson

Born in Raleigh, North Carolina, in 1808, Andrew Johnson became a tailor's apprentice at a young age. After his apprenticeship, he worked as a tailor in dozens of villages, in return for food and lodging. He finally settled in Greeneville, Tennessee, married and raised a family. Johnson lacked a formal education and his young wife tutored him in math and writing. One of the sources she used to teach him to read was the U. S. Constitution.

Friendly, but also cautious and shy, Andrew Johnson was resolute in the tasks he set for himself as a young man. Those who knew him, respected him for his determination to learn and his honesty. For these reasons, his friends asked him to run for public office. Over time, Johnson served as an alderman and a mayor before being elected to Tennessee's House of Representatives. Eventually, he served in the United States House of Representatives, as governor of Tennessee, and as a United States senator.

President Andrew Johnson did his best to fulfill Lincoln's plan of reconciliation, not punishment, with the South. President Johnson began by issuing a proclamation pardoning all the states and everyone responsible for seceding from the Union, with the exception of the Confederacy's most prominent leaders and anyone who had mistreated black Union troops. He urged the former Confederate states to elect officials and organize governments that would repeal the Declarations of Secession, repudiate the Confederate war debt, and ratify the **Thirteenth Amendment**, which had been adopted on December 6, 1865, abolishing slavery.

Johnson and the Congressional Republicans

Andrew Johnson had been chosen to run as vice-president in 1864, even though he was a Democrat. Nevertheless, his relationship with the Republicans in Congress had always been quite friendly. The moderate Republicans liked Johnson because he had always favored small farmers over large plantation owners. Johnson also wanted to improve public education. The moderate Republicans saw him as a "man of the people." When Johnson issued amnesty to the Confederates, something the moderates felt that Lincoln

Columbia, South Carolina in 1865. The photograph has been taken from the steps of the capitol building. The once beautiful city, one of the jewels of the South, has been almost completely destroyed.

certainly would have done, they felt Johnson had acted properly and they supported him. They wanted the former states to re-enter the Union as full members as soon as possible. The former Confederate states should hold elections for congressmen and senators and send them to Washington.

However, another group of Republicans, called the **Radical Republicans**, expected Johnson to act more harshly toward the South. They too recalled that Johnson had supported small farmers over plantation owners, whom Johnson had once called "traitorous aristocrats." The leader of the Radical Republicans, a congressman from Pennsylvania named **Thaddeus Stevens**, felt that the federal government should confiscate large Southern plantations and divide this newly-acquired land among the recently freed slaves.

Johnson could not support both plans. A clash with the Radical Republicans seemed inevitable. The confrontation would be historic!

Congress Rejects Johnson's Plan for Reconstruction

By the end of 1865, the Thirteenth Amendment, which abolished slavery, had been ratified by three-fourths of the states and became part of the U.S. Constitution. Despite slavery's official abolition, many Southern states passed laws called **Black Codes**, which state officials designed to restrict the social and economic conditions of freed slaves. While the Codes gave freed blacks some rights, such as the right to own property, overall the Black Codes reduced black Americans to an almost slavery-like situation. For example, the Codes in some states, such as South Carolina, prohibited freed blacks from working at any occupations other than farming or household work, that is, the same jobs they performed as slaves, unless they paid a tax. Because some Southerners were extremely concerned about freed blacks "getting into trouble," the black codes in many states required black Americans to sign yearly labor contracts. If they refused, or broke a signed contract, they could be arrested or sentenced to perform unpaid labor. The black codes also treated vagrancy among blacks very harshly. Blacks who could not provide evidence of employment could be arrested and sentenced to unpaid labor to pay the fine.

Sunday Morning in Virginia by Winslow Homer (1877). Set in a former slave cabin, Homer depicts a nicely dressed teacher instructing three black children to read using the Bible.

Of course, Northerners found these Black Codes reprehensible. It appeared that the South had passed the Thirteenth Amendment, but did not mean to implement it. Southern elections to Congress did little to assuage Northern concerns.

President Johnson and the moderate Republicans had encouraged Southerners to send representatives to the U.S. Congress. However, the Republicans perhaps did not expect that the people of the South would elect the same men to Congress who had just led the Confederacy. For example, in 1866, Georgia elected **Alexander Stephens**, the former Vice-President of the Confederacy, to the U.S. Senate. The Senate refused to seat him. (A few years later, Stephens wrote a book defending the South's right to secede and denouncing the North's aggression.) In fact, the members of Congress refused to seat the senators and representatives elected in the former Confederate states. The Radical Republicans, who controlled Congress, were adamant that it was Congress, not the president, who had the authority to decide how and when the Southern representatives to the Houses of Congress would be readmitted. Many congressmen resented what seemed to them as President Johnson's infringement on their own congressional right and lawful power. Consequently, members of Congress refused to recognize the "Reconstruction" state governments that had been organized at the president's command. They rejected Johnson's plan for Reconstruction of the South. Moreover, because the Republicans had won the 1866 congressional elections in a landslide, they controlled more than three-fourths of the House seats. As a result, they could override any presidential veto. President Johnson was virtually powerless before the Republican Congress.

Congress Reconstructs the South

Having rejected President Johnson's plan of Reconstruction, the Republicans in Congress now implemented their own vision of Southern Reconstruction. In March 1865, President Lincoln, in an effort to support former slaves and alleviate their desperate plight, had established the **Freedmen's Bureau**.

Administered by the U.S. army and managed by Union soldiers, the Freedmen's Bureau sought to supply food, clothing, and shelter to Southerners, both black and white, who the war had impoverished. Efforts were made to find jobs for the destitute and open schools for the children. The Bureau was empowered to relocate people to new locations where their opportunity to gain worthwhile employment was greater. The Bureau proved very successful at negotiating work contracts between freed blacks and their new employers. The Bureau also gave public land to former slaves and opened a number of "care centers" to assist the feeble and the elderly.

Probably the Bureau's finest achievement was providing funds to various private missionary societies which allowed them to establish primary and secondary schools to educate freed blacks. By 1870, perhaps as many as 250,000 black students had received the benefit of an education sponsored by the Freedmen's Bureau. Of the nearly two dozen black colleges started with the support of the Freedmen's Bureau, the most famous is undoubtedly **Howard University** in Washington, D.C. Founded in 1867, it was named in honor of Oliver Otis Howard, the Bureau's commissioner and the university's president from 1869 to 1874.

Congress had created the Freedmen's Bureau as a temporary fix to the war's problems. They authorized its existence only until one year after the war ended. Thus, in early 1866, Congress passed a bill *re-authorizing* the Freedmen's Bureau. President Johnson vetoed the bill. He said that he agreed with Congress in wishing to grant more opportunities and independence to black people However, he had serious concerns about

The Thankful Poor by Henry Ossawa Tanner. Despite the efforts of numerous good people after the Civil War, too many blacks lived in a condition of semi-slavery and terrible poverty. Here a grandfather and his grandson give thanks for the meager meal they are about to eat.

using the Bureau to achieve those results. In vetoing the bill, he noted that it made inappropriate use of the military during peacetime. He also felt it unconstitutionally infringed on states' rights and gave assistance to freed blacks that were not provided to poor whites. Finally, he said he felt that continuing to assist freed blacks in this way would discourage them from becoming self-sufficient. Despite his arguments, Congress overrode his veto.

In April 1866, Congress passed a **Civil Rights Act**. This act sought to make black people citizens of the United States, thus overturning the Supreme Court's *Dred Scott* decision. The act also prohibited states from treating blacks differently than whites, especially in areas such as employment. Thus, the Civil Rights Act would negate the Black Codes.

Once again, President Johnson chose to veto the bill. In his lengthy explanation to Congress for his veto, he wrote that "*the policy of the (U.S.) Government, from its origin to the present time, seems to have been that persons who are strangers to and unfamiliar with our institutions and laws, should pass through a certain probation; at the end of which, before attaining the coveted prize, they must give evidence of their fitness to receive and to exercise the rights of citizens as contemplated by the Constitution of the United States.*" Thus, Johnson argues that blacks need to go through a time of probation before they can be granted citizenship. During this probation period – a period immigrants undergo – the former slaves would learn about the customs, laws, and institutions of the United States.

The Republicans, with their super majority in both Houses of Congress, easily overrode Johnson's veto. On April 9, 1866, the **Civil Rights Act of 1866** became law. Johnson became less popular with Congress.

The Fourteenth Amendment

Next Congress sent what would become the Fourteenth Amendment to the Constitution to the states for ratification. Congress had four goals in creating the Fourteenth Amendment. First, it granted blacks citizenship and all the rights that accompany citizenship. Second, it proclaimed that any state which denied blacks the right to vote would have its representation in Congress reduced. Third, it denied the leaders of the Confederacy the right to hold public office unless pardoned by Congress. Finally, it forbade federal payment of the Confederate war debts or any reimbursement for the loss of slaves.

President Johnson's home state of Tennessee promptly approved the Fourteenth Amendment, and Tennessee representatives were admitted to Congress. However, the other Southern states refused to ratify the Fourteenth Amendment. In reprisal, Congress passed a series of new bills, over President Johnson's veto. One of these new laws was the **Reconstruction Act of 1867**. It required that the ten "rebel states" which had not ratified the Fourteenth Amendment would be divided into five military districts. Each district was placed under a military commander. In order to become free of military rule, the states would have to create new state constitutions which guaranteed black men the right to vote and ratify the Fourteenth Amendment.

Despite the pressure of the Reconstruction Act of 1867, the Southern states refused to comply. Congress passed three more Reconstruction Acts, each more onerous than the last, in an attempt to compel the Southern states to comply. Finally, between 1868 and 1870, the Southern states did agree to Congress' demands.

The Fourteenth Amendment to the United States Constitution was adopted on July 9, 1868. It guaranteed that: "*All persons born or naturalized in the United States, and subject to the jurisdiction thereof, are citizens of the United States and of the State wherein they reside. No State shall make or enforce any law which shall abridge the privileges or immunities of citizens of the United States; nor shall any State deprive any person of life, liberty, or property, without due process of law; nor deny to any person within its jurisdiction the equal protection of the laws.*" Thus, blacks became citizens of the United States, no matter in which state they lived.

However, neither the **Fourteenth Amendment**, nor the **Fifteenth Amendment** (ratified in 1870), which guaranteed black men the right to vote, abolished racial segregation. White Southerners, many of them former slave-owners, governed the Southern states. While these state governments restored order and stability, they also slowed down attempts to create greater equality for blacks. Between 1865 and 1870, the Reconstruction Congress in Washington successfully added the 13th, 14th, and 15th Amendments to the Constitution. However, when "home rule" governments were reestablished in the South, the spirit and the good intentions of these amendments were not fully implemented. Racial equality would not come into full fruition in the South until almost 100 years later with the enactment of the Civil Rights Act of 1968.

The Impeachment of Andrew Johnson

By early 1868, what had started as a promising relationship between President Johnson and the Republican Congress had turned bitter. Johnson's vetoes of Congressional attempts to aid former slaves had begun the process. He had vetoed bills that he knew would be overridden by vast margins. Congress rightly blamed Johnson for the Southern states' refusal to ratify the Fourteenth Amendment. Johnson had urged the states not to ratify. Because of this confrontation between the Congress and President Johnson, in February 1868, the Radical Republicans decided to take the amazingly aggressive act of removing Andrew Johnson from office by impeaching him.

Under the U.S. Constitution, the House of Representatives, by a majority vote, can bring charges against a president. This act of bringing charges is called **impeachment**. Once charges have been brought, the president is tried before the Senate. The Chief Justice of the Supreme Court acts as the presiding judge over the trial. The Senate acts as the jury. Two-thirds of the Senators must vote affirmatively to convict. If convicted, the president is removed from office.

The Founders created the ability of the Congress to impeach the president as part of the balance of powers. Both Houses must agree to remove the president, the House must bring the charges and the Senate must convict. The Founders also expected that impeachment would involve only serious matters. For example, the president might commit perjury, or sell secrets to a foreign power, or in some other way commit treason. The Founders did not intend impeachment to be used because Congress did not like the president's policies. That is the purpose of elections.

Nevertheless, the Radical Republicans brought eleven charges against President Johnson. Almost all of them lacked any validity. However, one charge had some substance. The House accused Johnson of violating the **Tenure of Office Act of 1867** when he fired Secretary of War **Edwin Stanton**. Under the Tenure of Office Act, the president could not fire cabinet officers without the approval of Congress. Johnson, believing the law was unconstitutional, had intentionally fired Stanton to challenge it. Johnson wanted the Supreme Court to hear the case and rule on the law, which seemed to infringe on the president's power. Thus, even this charge had little validity.

In 1868, the Senate consisted of fifty-four members. This meant that thirty-six senators would need to vote "guilty" to convict Johnson and remove him from office. As the historic roll call vote began, Radical Republicans were certain of thirty-five votes.

Secretary of War Stanton

If one of the nineteen uncommitted senators voted guilty, Johnson would be ousted from the presidency. The roll was called, and thirty-five guilty votes were recorded as expected, as were the expected eighteen "not guilty" votes. President Johnson's fate rested on the decision of a "replacement" senator from Kansas.

The replacement senator was **Edmund G. Ross**. He had become a member of the Senate because Senator Jim Lane of Kansas had died unexpectedly. Edmund Ross was not a professional politician, but a businessman who had invested a great deal of money in the Atchison, Topeka, and Santa Fe Railroad, and became one of that railroad's directors. He was also a Republican. Had he voted "guilty," he might have had a bright political future. However, he cast a vote for what he honestly believed to be just and right. His "not guilty" vote kept President Johnson in office. Ross' willingness to stand up for what he believed, against the wishes of his own Party, has earned the respect of many since then. However, when he ran for re-election two years later, he lost, as did all the Senators who voted to acquit Johnson.

Although President Johnson had avoided being removed from office, his administration had been badly damaged. He remained in office until March 1869. However, he accomplished nothing during his last months as president.

Interestingly, the people of Tennessee still respected Johnson. In 1875, they elected him to the U.S. Senate. However, his political triumph was short-lived. He died of a stroke on July 31, 1875.

The Election of 1868

In 1868, the Republicans held their presidential nominating convention in Chicago, Illinois, the state in which General **Ulysses S. Grant** had lived much of his adult life. Three unsteady and troubled years had passed since Lincoln's death. Andrew Johnson had been unpopular with the Radical Republicans. General Grant was the logical man to resume his role as the "savior" of the Union--this time in the Oval Office rather than on horseback. The Radical Republicans, who were at the peak of their power, favored Grant, who tended to agree with their policies. Therefore, it was not surprising when the Republicans nominated Grant on the first ballot at their Convention. To strengthen the ticket, the Speaker of the House **Schuyler Colfax** became the vice-presidential nominee.

Edmund G. Ross

President Ulysses S. Grant

The Democrats struggled to find someone to oppose the wildly popular Republican candidates. Eventually, they settled on a two-time governor of New York, **Horatio Seymour**, who refused the honor as strongly as possible. His vehement protests have earned Seymour the label "The Great Decliner."

Although some Northern states prohibited black men from voting, federal troops stationed in the Southern states ensured that blacks in those states were permitted to vote. Not surprisingly, blacks voted almost unanimously for the Republican candidate: Ulysses Grant. As a result, although the popular vote was close, Grant won a landslide victory in the Electoral College: 214 to 80.

The Fifteenth Amendment

Following the election of 1868, the Republicans spent time carefully analyzing the results, after which they reached some interesting conclusions. They noticed that blacks who had been allowed to vote had voted almost unanimously for Grant. However, almost no blacks had been allowed to vote in Northern states. Had blacks in the North been allowed to vote, they almost certainly would have voted for Grant. Thus, Grant's margin of victory in the North would have been much greater. Republican politicians realized that granting blacks the vote throughout the nation would mean massive black support for Republicans for decades. (**Note**: Blacks voted Republican until the 1960s.)

To ensure that black men could vote, in early 1869, the Republican-controlled Congress drafted what would become the **Fifteenth Amendment**. The Amendment states, "*The right of citizens of the United States to vote shall not be denied or abridged by the United States or by any State on account of race, color, or previous condition of servitude.*" The states ratified the amendment on February 3, 1870.

Governments in the Southern States

Had Lincoln lived, a more lenient and gentle approach to the post-war South might have occurred. However, with the Radical Republicans in charge, and the U.S. Army occupying the former Confederate states, harsher policies had been imposed. Still, the presence of the army did create some positive aspects. For example, the army ensured that blacks were allowed to vote. The army also made it possible for blacks to hold office in Southern governments, although mostly just at the local, that is, city and county, level.

The Congressional Republicans also created numerous problems for Southerners. First, because most of the South's brightest and most capable leaders had governed the Confederacy, the U.S. government would not permit them to run for office in the new state governments. As a result, many of the men who were elected were far less qualified and lacked leadership and fiscal ability. Consequently, corruption and inefficiency beset many Southern state governments.

White Republicans in the South

Radical Republicans controlled most of the governments of the newly re-admitted Southern states. Although the large number of newly freed black voters kept them in power, most of these Republican politicians were white men. White Republicans who had moved to the South from Northern states were called **Carpetbaggers** by their political enemies. This nickname painted an image of unscrupulous men who carried all their possessions in a traveling bag made of carpet rushing down south to take advantage of the South's

Senator Hiram Rhodes Revels became the first African-American to serve in the U.S. Congress when he was elected to the United States Senate as a Republican from Mississippi in 1870.

weakened political situation for their own personal gain. White Republicans from the South received the label **Scalawags**, which means rascals, from their political opponents.

White Republicans were despised by many white Southerners who objected to the harsh Republican reconstruction policies, as well as the change in the social order which allowed former slaves to rise to positions of power and to vote. Many white Southerners regarded Scalawags as traitors to the Southern cause. Although some corruption existed among Republican politicians, many of the so-called carpetbaggers and scalawags sincerely tried to rebuild the South and create a more just society for people of all races. They helped rebuild bridges, roads, and other infrastructure that the war had damaged and destroyed. They built railroads and began investing in public education.

Probably the most well-known scalawag was former Confederate general James Longstreet, who fought with Robert E. Lee in many of the most important battles of the war, including Gettysburg. Despite the hatred of many of his former comrades, Longstreet remained in the South, living much of his post-war life in New Orleans. In that very Catholic city, James Longstreet underwent a conversion experience and, in 1877, converted to Catholicism.

The Ku Klux Klan

Resentment in the South to the North's concepts of Southern reconstruction grew increasingly intense. When legal means to halt Reconstruction, such as the Black Codes, failed, a few Southerners turned to secret organizations to stop Reconstruction through terrorism and violence. The most influential and horrible of these secret societies was the **Ku Klux Klan (KKK).**

The principal purpose of the Klan was to discourage blacks from voting by subjecting them to a "reign of terror." Klan members, dressed in flowing white robes and hoods, claimed to be the ghosts of dead Confederate soldiers. They galloped along roads and village streets at night, only stopping to burn an occasional cross beside the home of a black family. Shrieks accompanied the blaze, warning blacks that if they voted, they better leave town or prepare to suffer. The Klan favored beating or whipping "wrong-doers." Blacks were not the only victims. Klan members often whipped white men who tried to help their black neighbors.

To curb the Klan's brutal and outrageous criminal activities, the U.S. Congress passed the Force Act, and the Klux Klan Act, in 1870 and 1871. These Acts empowered the president to use martial law when and where the rights and the lives of blacks were endangered. By 1871, these laws had checked the power of the Klan. Federal troops were sent to areas where violence occurred. Although the Klan was not destroyed, its power was lessened. The existence of the Ku Klux Klan is a horrible blight on the history of America and has resulted in a deserved bitterness by many blacks even today as they remember their ancestors being beaten or murdered.

President Grant's Scandals

In 1869, shortly after Ulysses S. Grant assumed the presidency, a pair of unscrupulous speculators named **Jim Fisk** and **Jay Gould** set out to corner the *gold market*. They quickly gained access to President Grant through one of his relatives. The clever pair dazzled Grant, who believed them when they showed him why it would be dangerous if the Treasury Department continued to sell gold. When other gold traders heard that the Treasury was stopping gold sales, the price of gold skyrocketed. When more honest and wiser men soon convinced President Grant that he had been misled, he ordered the Treasury to begin selling gold again. The price of gold then dropped, which caused a national financial panic on September 24, 1869. This day was remembered as "Black Friday."

The next scandal under President Grant involved the *transcontinental railroad*. The Union Pacific was one of two companies responsible for building the railroad across the country. However, the Union

Schuyler Colfax (c. 1865). Colfax denied involvement in the *Credit Mobilier* scandal and testified before Congress in January 1873 that he had never received a bribe. Evidence later revealed that in 1868 he had taken at least two bribes.

Horace Greeley

Pacific hired a company called *Credit Mobilier* to do the construction. Credit Mobilier actually was owned by a small group of Union Pacific stockholders who intended to cheat the other stockholders by charging $94,000,000, instead of the real price of $50,000,000. To buy goodwill from the most influential Republicans and Democrats, Credit Mobilier sold these men shares of stock for very little. Evidence eventually implicated eight members of Congress, as well as Vice President Colfax, in the dishonest financial scheme.

The Election of 1872

President Grant's term had been marked by virtually no accomplishments and many humiliations. Although Grant was personally honest, he had become the victim of numerous scandals. While he had been an excellent general and personally heroic, he was a poor president. During the early 1870s, the Republican Party became weaker and weaker.

Thus, it was inevitable that a new anti-corruption group or "wing" would be added to the Republican Party. It was called the **Liberal Republican Party**, and included powerful, well-known journalists, such as **Horace Greeley**, the fiery publisher of the *New York Tribune*. The Liberal Republican Party nominated Horace Greeley as a third party candidate. This put the Democrats in a tricky political position. Fearing that the third party might split the vote and allow Grant to win the election, the Democrats nominated Greeley as their candidate. Although it seemed politically wise to back Greeley, he turned out to be a poor campaigner and unpopular. Despite his scandals, Grant remained well-liked with the people and won the election with more than 55% of the popular vote.

The New South Rises from the Ashes of the Old

By 1872, the end of the Reconstruction Era was visible on the political horizon. Congress enacted legislation giving amnesty to most former Confederates, thus permitting them to vote and to hold public office. 1872 also spelled the end of the Freedmen's Bureau. Termination of the Bureau provided visible proof that Radical leaders were losing their power in Congress. The supporters of the Freedmen's Bureau, as well as many others who had zealously worked to improve the lives of former slaves, had discovered that the task they had allocated for themselves was far more tedious and difficult than they had imagined. The situation had been made more difficult because Northern businessmen realized that investing in the South's recovery was a losing proposition as long as the South was saddled with inept and/or corrupt Reconstruction governments.

As a new *modern* South began to emerge from Reconstruction, Northern investors began to look past the South's deficits and examine the many assets it had to offer. The South's total dependence on "King Cotton" as its main export was over. However, the Southern states still grew cotton. In fact, by 1875, the amount of cotton produced equaled the level of twenty years earlier. Rather than exporting the raw cotton, investors had built textile mills which dotted the landscape of the South, manufacturing clothing and every other manner of cloth for export. Factories also produced cottonseed oil, an oil extracted from the seeds of cotton plants. Cottonseed oil was used for cooking and the production of cosmetics.

In addition to these manufacturing enterprises, the rich soil in the South had always proven ideal for growing many types of plants, vegetables, and fruits. By the late 19th century, tobacco, always a cash crop, had become even more profitable to the South. In the 1870s, a machine was invented that automated the creation of cigarettes. Within about a decade, the *American Tobacco Company*, located in North Carolina, became the largest cigarette manufacturer in the world. The forests of the South were rich in pulpwood and hardwood. Lumber mills could service a growing list of customers throughout the South. Southern factories, and small shops, could construct furniture and a rich assortment of other wood products.

Southerners recognized the bounty of fish that the ocean and the Southern rivers offered to industrial fishermen, as well as to sport fishermen. More than any other enticement to investors were the available workers, the millions of men desperately in need of jobs, who comprised the workforce. All this and more, wise business entrepreneurs foresaw. That is why and how these investors financed the development of the New South.

Before the war, the South relied almost entirely on agriculture; but now a plethora of industries, including iron and steel manufacturing mills, emerged. Since coal and iron ore were plentiful in Alabama, **Birmingham** soon became known as the "Pittsburgh of the South." Hundreds of cities and towns in the South grew larger, and many new towns were established. Mostly, honest men ran these operations, seeking to make a profit for themselves and make life better for their workers. Unfortunately, there were others who charged high prices to keep workers in debt to them. Sadly, few factories employed black workers. Racial equality was still a dream in progress.

However, many Southerners, especially men like Henry Grady, the editor of the Atlanta *Constitution*, dared to dream that dream. In December 1886, Grady addressed an audience in New York City. He spoke of the New South. He opened his speech by quoting Georgia Senator Benjamin H. Hill who said, "There was a South of slavery and secession - that South is dead. There is a South of Union and freedom - that South, thank God, is living, breathing, (and) growing every hour."

The Questionable Election of 1876

After sixteen years of Republican presidents, Democrats felt confident that they would win the presidency in 1876. Grant's two terms had produced perilous economic times and wholesale scandals, which had implicated many of his appointees as well as his relatives. In fact, Grant's second term might possibly have been even worse than his first.

Shortly after Grant's second term began, the **Financial Panic of 1873** swept across the nation. A number of factors caused the Panic, including out of control government spending, government waste, and inflation. Large banks went bankrupt and about 100 banks across the country failed. Railroads and associated industries also went bankrupt, resulting in serious unemployment across the nation. The Panic lasted for almost six years. The public blamed Grant and the Republicans for the Panic. As a result, in the 1874 congressional elections, the Democrats gained control of the House of Representatives.

As if the most serious Panic in American history up to that time had not caused Grant enough problems, scandals continued to plague his administration. In 1873, the Republican-controlled Congress decided to raise their salaries by 50% and President Grant's by 100%. Observers nicknamed it the **Salary Grab Act**. [In fairness, the president's salary had not been raised since George Washington was president, and congressmen were not that highly paid. The bill just did not look good to the general public.]

The next scandal involved tax collectors in the Treasury Department and whiskey distillers. Known as the **Whiskey Ring**, hundreds of federal tax agents and whiskey-makers conspired to defraud the government of taxes. Over two hundred people were indicted in the bribery scheme, including Orville Babcock, President Grant's private secretary. Babcock was tried, but acquitted in February 1876.

Another scandal in Grant's administration occurred between 1870 and 1876. During the so-called "Trader post scandal," Secretary of War William Belknap, who had authority to appoint and license traders on U.S. military forts, began accepting bribes in return for the licenses. In 1876, Congress discovered his dishonorable conduct. Belknap resigned as Secretary of War, becoming a private citizen. However, Congress, enraged at his actions, decided to impeach him anyway. The impeachment failed as the senators who voted against conviction realized that the Senate had no authority to attempt to convict a private citizen of a crime.

The Panic of 1873 and Grant's scandals seriously damaged the Republican Party. Not surprisingly, Republican popularity had dropped dramatically. By 1876, the Republican Party only controlled three southern states: Louisiana, South Carolina, and Florida. Democrats had good reason to be confident of victory in the upcoming presidential election.

In 1876, the Democrats selected **Samuel J. Tilden** to champion their cause. Tilden had been governor of New York, the nation's most populous state. During the campaign, the Democrats often reminded voters that Tilden had been responsible for ending the political corruption in New York City and the state of New York. He was known for his honesty and integrity as well as his ability to organize and run a government efficiently. After eight years of President Grant's scandals and mismanagement, Tilden seemed the kind of man Americans would want as their next president.

The Republicans convened in Cincinnati that sweltering summer and nominated Ohio Governor **Rutherford B. Hayes**. Although Hayes was not the Republicans' first choice (that was James Blaine of Maine), Hayes had much to

The Rush from the New York Stock Exchange on September 18, 1873, by Howard Pyle

Samuel J. Tilden. Should he have been president of the United States? Almost 4.3 million voters thought so.

recommend him. He had left a promising political and legal career at the beginning of the Civil War to enlist in the Union army and was quickly commissioned a major. Hayes served with distinction, suffering five wounds in battle, and ultimately achieved the rank of major general. Following the war, he served in Congress from 1865 to 1867, then twice as governor of Ohio from 1868 to 1872. Re-elected in 1876, he was the current Ohio governor when he sought the Republican presidential nomination. During his time as governor he helped reform the state's mental hospitals and school system. Additionally, he worked zealously to promote suffrage for African-American men. To many voters, Rutherford B. Hayes also presented a refreshing change from Grant.

On Election Day, 4,289,000 men voted for Tilden and 4,036,000 men voted for Hayes. Tilden won his home state of New York, a few other Northern states, and all of the Southern states. Since Tilden received 253,000 more popular votes than Hayes it seems that this should have made Samuel J. Tilden America's nineteenth president—but it did not. **American elections are decided in the Electoral College, not according to the popular vote.**

Samuel Tilden had amassed 184 Electoral College votes. However, he needed **185** to claim victory. Tilden needed only one more vote and seemed to have an excellent chance to obtain it, since twenty Electoral votes were being challenged. One disputed vote, from Oregon, was quickly reconciled and awarded to Hayes. That left 19 Electoral College votes in Louisiana, Florida, and South Carolina, all of which the Republicans controlled.

The Compromise of 1877

The issue of declaring a victor in the election became even more difficult when the matter fell to the states. Each state had *two* election boards, one Republican and the other Democrat. Not surprisingly, each state election board asserted that their candidate had won. A situation like this had never occurred before, so there were no guidelines or precedents upon which to rely.

It seemed that in such a predicament, Congress – the representatives of the people - should decide the outcome. However, Congress was also divided. The Republicans controlled the Senate and the Democrats the House. Congress decided to appoint an Electoral Commission. Five members of the Commission would come from the House of Representatives, five from the Senate, and five from the Supreme Court. Seven Democrats and eight Republicans formed the Commission. The fifteenth member was Supreme Court Justice **Joseph Bradley**, who, although a Republican, was considered the most impartial of the five Justices and politically moderate.

The Commission launched an investigation and heard evidence. Proof of voter fraud from both Republicans and Democrats emerged. Of course, when the Commissioners voted, they did so along party lines. All votes ended 8 to 7 with Justice Bradley voting to give the election to Hayes.

The outcome caused a great deal of bitterness. Rioting and wholesale civil disobedience lurked in the near future. Realizing that serious violence lay close at hand, the leaders of both parties reached a compromise. Under the **Compromise of 1877**, the Democrats reluctantly agreed to support the election of

Rutherford B. Hayes. In exchange, the Republicans and President Hayes declared he would withdraw all federal troops from Southern states that had been stationed there since the end of the Civil War. Also, Hayes agreed to appoint a Southerner to his Cabinet. The new president would also approve funds to repair and extend Southern railroads from Texas to California. On March 5, 1877, Rutherford B. Hayes was publicly inaugurated America's 19th president in a very peaceful ceremony.

Hayes' Election

Hayes' election by one vote, 185 to 184, in the Electoral College remains the closest election in American presidential politics. Although no one can ever know for certain, the result seems to be the fairest one. Tilden had won the popular vote in all the Southern states. However, Mississippi, which had a majority black population, would most likely have voted Republican had there not been violence and intimidation against blacks. Hayes might have lost Florida's four electoral votes, but would have received Mississippi's eight. Thus, he would have had 189, more than enough to elect him president.

Because of the questionable way he won the election, Democrats nicknamed Hayes "His Fraudulency."

The Hayes Administration

Once elected, President Hayes continued his efforts at reform. He did his best to end the "spoils system" in the federal government that had been in vogue since Jackson's administration. Hayes favored a *Merit System* that would award government jobs to applicants who achieved the best scores on a test. Hayes achieved only partial success because he could not convince the members of Congress that this reform of government was long overdue. However, President Hayes succeeded in filling many positions based on the person's ability rather than his or her political influence or wealth.

Reconstruction Ends

The Compromise of 1877 officially ended the Reconstruction Era. The squabbling continued for a while, but most of the long-held animosity between North and South had mellowed a bit. The hideous practice of slavery was over. Blacks were citizens who could vote, but because of local conditions in many parts of the South, their voices were silent. However, they had taken the first step on the long, uphill road to racial equality. It was not the end of their struggles, or even the beginning of the end; but as British Prime Minister Winston Churchill said so eloquently of another situation, "It was perhaps, the end of the beginning."

Black Voters in the South

The road to equality for blacks was made more difficult by the Southern states that constantly seemed to put roadblocks in their path. Although violence against African-Americans trying to vote continued sporadically, the more insidious tactics were those "lawfully" enacted to suppress their rights. Among the most common obstacles employed to deprive blacks of the right to vote were the **poll tax** and **literacy tests**.

A poll tax is simply a state-imposed tax to vote. Poor people often did not have the money to pay the tax. Thus, they could not afford to vote. The poll tax affected blacks and poor white people. The right to vote has always been held as a fundamental right in the United States, and the notion of charging people to exercise that right is truly monstrous.

A literacy test affected blacks and whites who could not read. Often, blacks who could read, had to read a very complicated passage about the law and explain its meaning. It is doubtful that the white test administrator could have read and explained the complicated passage, but it meant that the black man could be refused his right to vote. While the Southern states sometimes made allowances for illiterate whites, they did not for blacks.

Despite the impact of the poll tax and the literacy tests, these tools did not violate the Fifteenth Amendment because they were not based on race, color, or previous condition of servitude. Nevertheless, the states clearly intended to disenfranchise black voters. Tragically, these laws had the desired effect. By 1900, few blacks voted in Southern states.

Segregation Becomes the Law of the Land

To a certain degree, segregation existed in the United States before the Civil War because of economic conditions, not as a result of an active attempt to segregate American society. The more affluent members of society simply did not interact that frequently with the poorer elements. Most free blacks tended to be poor. Thus, they did not patronize the same establishments, like hotels, restaurants, theatres, or even churches, that middle class and wealthy families did. Nevertheless, free blacks and whites did interact in the decades before the Civil War.

In fact, based on census data, there were approximately as many free blacks living in the South before the Civil War as there were in the North. Free blacks tended to live in large cities, either in the North or South, because they could find work in these cities. Most free blacks in the "South" lived in the border states, e.g. Delaware, Maryland, Virginia, and Tennessee, rather than the "Deep South."

In 1875, Congress had passed the **Civil Rights Act of 1875**, which provided that blacks were entitled to the same treatment as whites in theaters, restaurants, hotels, trains, and other public accommodations. However, after the election of President Hayes in 1877 and the withdrawal of federal troops, people in the Southern states began to ignore the Civil Rights Act of 1875. Racial segregation became increasingly common.

Over the next several years, blacks were turned away from theaters, were not allowed to stay in hotel rooms, and were denied travel in first class railroad carriages. To redress these grievances,

In *His First Vote* (1868) by Thomas Waterman Wood. The artist depicts a bearded African-American man holding a folded white paper (ballot) in his right hand. Wood painted the image in 1868, anticipating ratification of the Fifteenth Amendment. Wood shows a middle-aged man with worn hands and rumpled clothing. Yet his expression is hopeful as he prepares to vote for the first time in his life. Sadly, because of poll taxes and literacy tests, few blacks were able to vote in the South until the 20th century.

Justice John Marshall Harlan. Justice Harlan, whose family had owned slaves, was the only Justice to dissent from the decision in *Plessy*. He wrote that in time *Plessy* would "prove to be quite as pernicious" as the *Dred Scott* decision. He went on to write that "our Constitution is color-blind, and neither knows nor tolerates classes among citizens." Sadly, Harlan not only held the minority opinion on the Court, his belief was in the minority among most white Americans.

a number of black plaintiffs brought a series of cases before the United States Supreme Court. In 1883, the Supreme Court ruled in these Civil Rights Cases that the **Civil Rights Act of 1875 was unconstitutional.** The majority of the Court wrote that when the Congress and the states ratified the 14th Amendment, they sought to limit the authority of *state governments* to practice racial segregation. The Court reasoned that nothing in the 14th Amendment addressed the actions of private individuals. Thus, private individuals had the right to practice racial segregation if they wished. It was not unconstitutional for them to do so.

In 1896, the Supreme Court handed down its landmark decision on segregation, *Plessy v. Ferguson*. In *Plessy*, the Court ruled that even segregation by the states was permissible as long as the states made a **"separate but equal"** accommodation for blacks. The "separate but equal" language of *Plessy* made segregation the law of the land. Blacks would be forced to ride in the back of buses. They would have their own bathrooms, water fountains, and even cemeteries. Blacks would have separate facilities, but those facilities would never be equal.

CHAPTER 20   REVIEW QUESTIONS

Answer the following questions:

1. Who killed Abraham Lincoln? Where did it happen?
2. Who became president after Lincoln was killed?
3. Who were the "Radical Republicans?" Who was their leader?
4. What were the "Black Codes?"
5. What did the 13th Amendment do?
6. What did the 14th Amendment do?
7. What did the 15th Amendment do?
8. What was the "Freedmen's Bureau?" What were its major goals?
9. Explain some of President Grant's scandals.
10. Who were "carpetbaggers?" Who were "scalawags?"
11. Why was the Presidential election of 1876 "questionable?"
12. What was the Compromise of 1877?
13. What officially ended the "Reconstruction Era?"
14. What was a poll tax? What was a "literacy test?"
15. What is the significance of *Plessy v. Ferguson*?
16. Why did Andrew Johnson overturn a Civil Rights Act which sought to make black people citizens of the United States?
17. What did Rutherford B. Hayes do before he was elected president? What did he do as president?

Identify the following:

1. Andrew Johnson
2. Impeachment
3. Ku Klux Klan
4. Horace Greeley
5. Samuel J. Tilden
6. Edmund G. Ross

The United States Continues Expanding Westward 1850-1900

The Last of the Buffalo is Albert Bierstadt's final, massive, western painting. Bierstadt incorporates many geographical features typical of the Great Plains: large stretches of flat open land with few trees; a river gently winding its way back into the horizon; the snowcapped peaks. He has also filled the scene with the animals of the plains, including a fox and some elk who run among the immense buffalo herd. The painting, with its focus on the Native American warrior locked in mortal combat with a charging buffalo, is simultaneously heroic and tragic. The viewer appreciates the heroism of a warrior, armed only with a lance, facing a massive attacking buffalo, for all intents and purposes, nature's battle tank. Yet, the tragedy of the painting is far greater. Innumerable buffalo lie dead across the plain. Bones and skulls bleach in the sun. We know that when Bierstadt created this painting in 1888, buffalo had been hunted almost to extinction. Fewer than 1,000 buffalo remained alive. Thus, he truly was depicting the last of the buffalo in an attempt to draw attention to a serious issue. In time, the government worked to preserve the population and introduced buffalo to the National Zoo.

Immigrants and Southerners Move West

The Civil War's devastating effects on the people of the South made the western states attractive places to relocate after the War. People who had lost their homes, farms, and businesses turned their backs on their ruined lives and seized the opportunity that a fresh start afforded them. In the West, most people discovered that the harder they worked, the better life became.

In addition to displaced Southerners, the western frontier drew factory workers and other low-income laborers living in the overcrowded tenements of Northern cities. During the latter three decades of the nineteenth century, trans-Atlantic ships brought thousands of eager immigrants to America's major port cities. New York City acted as a beacon for Irish, German, and Italian families who thought they had left the hard times behind them. Sadly, anti-Catholic prejudice made their lives miserable. "No Irish" signs too often greeted them. The West meant a chance for a better life that only freedom and fresh opportunity offered. By moving out of an eastern city to the West, many realized their American dream.

In 1865, America's westward expansion, which the Civil War had interrupted, surged onward once again—this time with a bit more determination not to turn back. These brave men, women, and children drew on the pioneering spirit of the Pilgrims and the early colonists. They daily fought against danger and hardships, heat and cold, hunger and sickness ... and they won. However, as they carved out new homes and new states on the Great Plains, they, like the early colonists, soon realized that someone already lived there.

The Great Plains

The region known as the "Great Plains" extends from western Texas north through Oklahoma, up through the Dakotas and most of Montana, and continues into Canada. **Plains** are generally flat grasslands. One feature of the Great Plains is the lack of trees. Trees not only provide welcome shade on blistering hot days, but serve as the source of wood for houses, barns, sheds, and fences which protect the crops from the wandering herds of cattle and sheep that graze on the Great Plains. The dearth of trees caused many problems. For example, the flat barrenness of the Plains meant that in winter, arctic winds sweep down from Canada, freezing the region. In summer, hot winds from Mexico baked the Plains.

The lack of rainfall, which was far less than the amount which fell east of the Mississippi River, also made life on the Great Plains a struggle. One alternative to scarce rainfall was a well. However, on the Great Plains, a well often had to be dug for more than a hundred feet before striking water. Most families could not afford the drilling equipment necessary to sink such a deep shaft. Moreover, water located hundreds of

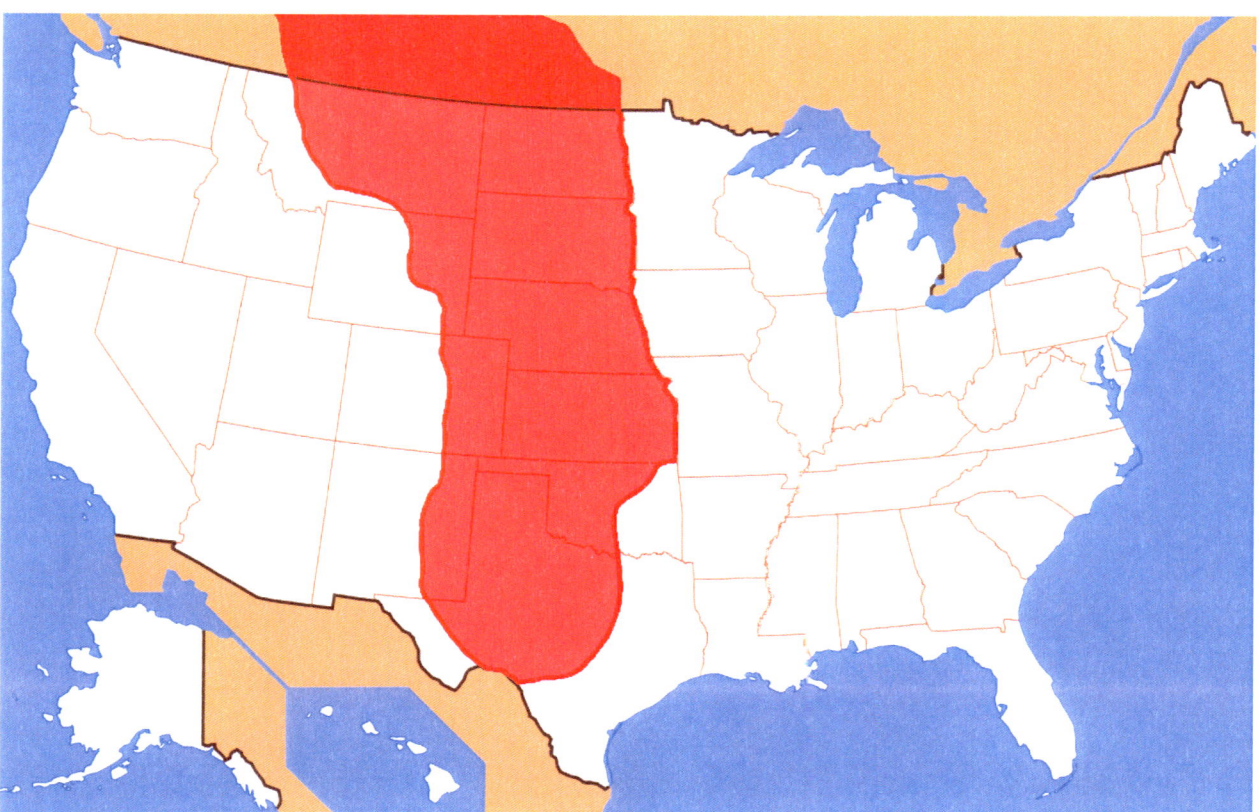

The Great Plains

feet underground must be pumped up to the surface by a power source—usually a windmill. Some families could not afford a windmill.

Most farmers did not believe in **windbreaks**, that is, a line of trees, bushes or shrubs planted around the edges of both plowed and unplowed fields to protect the crops and the topsoil from erosion. The windbreak both reduces the wind's energy and forces it over the windbreak and away from the precious topsoil and even more precious growing crops. Fierce wind storms often stripped the topsoil from the ground, covering every building, animal, and human with a layer of dust that crept into their noses, ears, eyes, and throats.

Numerous insects spawned by the prairie provided a constant nuisance. During a period of three years, in the mid-1870s, astonishing numbers of grasshoppers swarmed over the land like clouds of disaster. They consumed every plant leaf and blade of grass. When they could not find anything green, the grasshoppers satisfied their appetites with the wood in farm implements and the leather in straps and harnesses.

Since little wood existed for houses, the Plains families used what else was available. To provide shelter from all of the extremes they faced, some enterprising settlers dug a deep shelter-home in the side of a hill. Then they chopped squares of sod, solid hard ground, from about half an acre of prairie, and built a sod hut, appropriately called a "soddy."

To survive, settlers on the Great Plains adopted **dry-land farming**, a method of farming that **Hardy W. Campbell**, a Dakota farmer, developed. Dry-land farming required at least twelve inches of soil and an annual rainfall of fifteen inches or more. Campbell also planted certain varieties of wheat that required less water. Dry-land farming allowed farmers to raise crops even in years when droughts occurred. The situation for western farmers did not become easier or more productive until the invention of modern farm equipment and scientific advances in agriculture.

Native American women move the tribe's camp. Painting by Charles M. Russell.

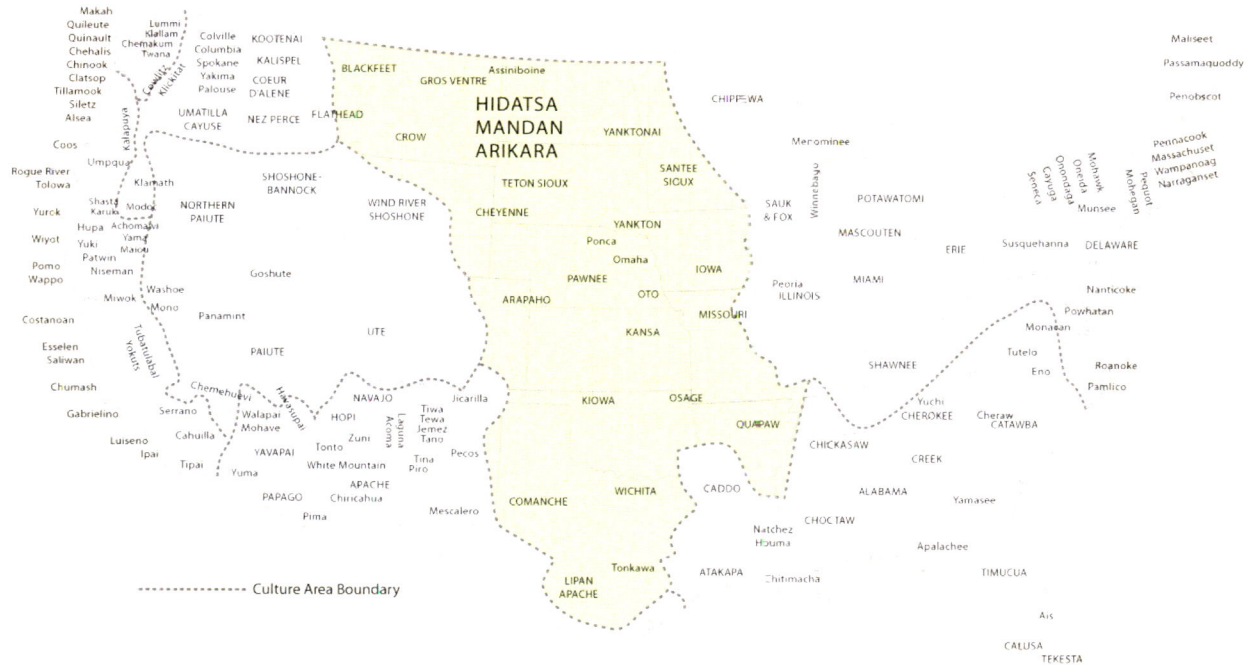

Map showing the Native American tribes in the United States, especially those living in the Great Plains region, along with their cultural area boundaries

Native American Tribes of the Great Plains

Long before the arrival of white settlers, more than thirty nomadic tribes roamed the Great Plains, roughly the area between the Mississippi River and the Rocky Mountains. Although these tribes are collectively known as "Native Americans," each tribe possessed its own language and customs. Thus, the tribes were as unique to each other as people from European nations are to one another. Based upon the census of 1860, there were probably about 250,000 Native Americans living on the Great Plains in 1850.

The largest of the Native American tribes included the **Comanche**, **Lakota**, **Pawnee**, **Cheyenne**, and **Arapaho**. The Comanche, who lived in eastern New Mexico and Texas tended to be more warlike and often took captives from weaker tribes, whom they sold as slaves. In the Dakotas, the Lakota Sioux were the dominant tribe. Like the Comanche, the Lakota were known for a culture based on hunting and warfare. The **Pawnee**, a tribe located in Kansas and Nebraska, had been one of the largest and strongest of the Great Plains tribes. However, numerous wars with enemy tribes greatly reduced their numbers and influence. The final two major tribes, the **Cheyenne** and their allies the **Arapaho**, historically lived in Colorado, Wyoming, Nebraska, and South Dakota. The cultures of all these tribes were based to varying degrees on hunting and warfare. The Great Plains tribes moved in the wake of the enormous buffalo, or more accurately *American bison*, herds.

When European explorers brought the first horses to America, Native American culture underwent a massive change. Native Americans captured some of these horses and tamed them. Quickly, Native American tribes developed into a **horse culture**, that is, a society which revolves around the breeding and herding of horses. Almost overnight, horses became the most prized possession of any Native American. Tribes launched raids to steal horses from other tribes as well as white settlers. A Native American measured his wealth in the number of horses he owned. In a real sense, horses became currency. A man could buy and sell items based on the value of a horse he was willing to exchange.

The Buffalo Hunt by Charles Marion Russell. Amazingly, Charles Russell, known as America's "Cowboy Artist" for his western art, never actually saw a buffalo hunt. By the time he arrived in Montana from St. Louis in 1880, the bison had been hunted nearly to extinction. He would have seen only individual buffalo. Yet his paintings are incredibly realistic.

Native Americans became expert horsemen. Where once they had had to track the buffalo herds on foot, they could now chase down the buffalo on their speedy ponies. Tribes could cover great distances in a short amount of time with horses. Life with horses became immeasurably better.

Native Americans became some of history's finest cavalry soldiers. The Plains warrior carried an ash bow about three feet long, along with a quiver of steel- or bone-tipped arrows. Others carried spears (lances) and shields made from buffalo hides. The shields had been hardened with glue made from buffalo hooves to the point where they were so tough that bullets often bounced off them. Armed with their bows and arrows, a warrior on horseback could fire five or six arrows in the time it took a white soldier to fire one shot from his muzzle-loading rifle. The arrows hit with devastating and deadly impact.

Life for the Plains Tribes

Following the movement of migrating buffalo and other game animals meant that Native Americans needed to transport their possessions and their tent-homes to the animals' next feeding-ground. In most cases, the tent-home was a structure of long poles, the bottom ends of which rested on the ground around the perimeter of a large outer circle. The top ends of the poles leaned inward and were tied together near the top at the point where they intersected, thus forming a cone. Women then attached various animal skins to the outside of the poles from the ground to the top. Two short poles, fastened to skins, controlled the ventilation system. The structure was usually referred to as a **teepee** or a **lodge**.

Interior of a Mandan chief's lodge

Once the family had finished constructing their teepee, they moved their "furniture" inside. This often consisted of sleeping couches and comfortable benches with backrests. The family had warm buffalo robes, weapons, and eating utensils. If the father had won honors in battle, his wife and children painted the tanned animal skins and hides to commemorate his valor.

Whites and Native Tribes Compete for the West

For thousands of years, Native American tribes roamed the Great Plains at will. They hunted and enjoyed great freedom. For the most part, the various tribes respected the hunting areas of other tribes. The land over which they traveled belonged to everyone and no one. It was, in a sense, public land that extended from ocean to ocean.

Nineteenth-century Americans moving west did not understand this concept of sharing land. They dreamed of owning a farm with a little log cabin and a big barn. Because of high prices for land, these dreams seemed impossible in the East. But land in the west was there for the taking! All that was needed was the desire to work hard and build a life. So, men packed up their families and headed west to California and Oregon. Before the 1850s, settlers traveling to Oregon and California rarely had trouble with the Plains tribes. Most settlers simply avoided them. The few white trappers and hunters who did interact with the Plains tribes tended to do so in a friendly manner.

However, after 1850, the situation changed. That was the year that settlers began moving into Kansas and Nebraska. The passage of the Kansas-Nebraska Act in 1854 increased the number of settlers in these territories. By 1860, most Native Americans had been forced out of these Plains states.

The Oregon Trail by Albert Bierstadt. Most settlers traveling to Oregon simply avoided the Plains tribes.

The Transcontinental Railroad

The 19th century saw the creation of many incredible inventions: the locomotive, the repeating rifle, the revolver, the telegraph, the telephone, iron ships, and the electric light bulb. For a nation as vast as the United States, railroads and the telegraph brought people together and made expansion into the west possible.

Prior to the Civil War, railroad companies had built about 9,000 miles of railways throughout the Eastern United States, most in the North. However, as more and more Americans made their way West, Congress realized a **transcontinental** railroad linking east with west was a necessity if America truly were to be *united* states. Therefore, in 1862, Congress passed the **Pacific Railway Act,** which granted the Union Pacific Railroad Company permission to begin building a railroad west from Omaha, Nebraska to the Pacific and the Central Pacific Railroad the right to begin building east from Sacramento, California. The two lines of track would meet somewhere in the middle of the country.

The federal government provided the railroads with millions of acres of public land upon which to construct the track. This included land adjacent to the tracks which the railroads could sell to generate income for construction. The railroads also owned the mineral rights on the land they received. Because they owned the land over which they laid track, the two companies were incentivized to lay track as quickly as possible to produce as much revenue as possible. Finally, the government issued bonds, basically low interest loans, which also provided cash to the railroads.

Charles Crocker ran the construction crews for the Central Pacific Railroad. Crocker, who had trouble hiring white laborers, finally decided to hire Chinese immigrants to build the Central Pacific Railroad. Tens of thousands of Chinese had come to the West Coast during the Gold Rush, and despite the anti-

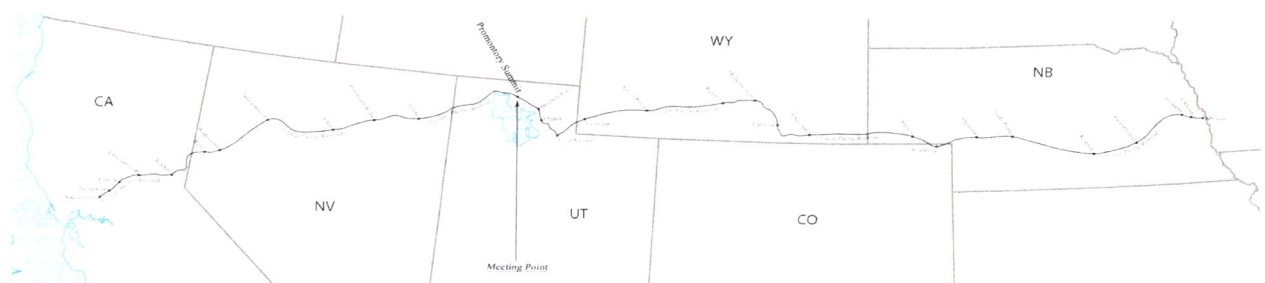

The route of the transcontinental railroad from Omaha, Nebraska in the East to Sacramento, California, in the West.

Chinese attitudes of many whites, Crocker found them to be excellent workers. On the other hand, the Union Pacific's workforce, under the management of former Union Generals **Grenville Dodge** and **John Casement**, consisted mainly of Irish immigrants and Civil War veterans.

The two rail companies faced enormous difficulties during construction. First, of course, were the natural obstacles that had to be overcome, e.g. mountains, rivers, snowdrifts. At one place along the railroad, a bridge 700 feet long and 125 feet high had to be constructed. Secondly, Omaha, Nebraska was not connected by rail with the east railroads. All the building materials had to be shipped by boat or hauled overland to the construction site. The many problems the builders had in obtaining their supplies demonstrated the desperate need for the railroad they were building! Third, Native Americans, who saw their lands and way of life being threatened by the encroaching white men, attacked the railroad workers. Fourth, feeding and housing thousands of workers proved no easy task. Railroad companies hired professional hunters to keep the construction workers supplied with buffalo meat for the hard-working men laying railroad track. The most famous of these hunters, **William F. Cody**, killed thousands of these animals, earning the nickname "Buffalo Bill."

The ceremony for the driving of the golden spike at Promontory Summit, Utah on May 10, 1869. In the center, Samuel S. Montague of the Central Pacific Railroad (left) shakes hands with Grenville M. Dodge of the Union Pacific Railroad (right).

Finally, on May 10, 1869, the two railroad lines met at **Promontory Summit, Utah**. The Central Pacific had laid 689 miles of track and the Union Pacific had laid 1,086. **Leland Stanford**, one of the Directors of the Central Pacific, had the honor of driving home the final spike which connected the two railroads. With great ceremony, Stanford drove a golden spike with a silver hammer into the track. The news went out across the nation: the transcontinental railroad had been completed!

Before long, railroad companies built other transcontinental railroads. Eastern cities were connected with the Northwest and Southern California. People could travel from the Eastern seaboard to Seattle, Sacramento, Los Angeles, and San Diego in a week. Before the railroads, it had taken three months aboard a fast clipper ship to sail from New York to San Francisco.

The expansion of the railroads created incredible economic opportunities for almost every American. However, for one group, the railroads spelled the end of their way of life. For Native Americans, railroads meant more and more settlers would be coming west – coming into land formerly inhabited almost exclusively by them.

The Plains Tribes Lose Military Dominance

Native American warriors generally were superb horsemen. When they overtook and surrounded a wagon train, many warriors kept their horse's body between the men firing at them from the circle of wagons, by clinging to the animal's back with only one foot exposed to enemy fire. Many warriors could shoot their own weapons from under their horse's neck. Many of the soldiers who opposed them called the Plains Tribes the

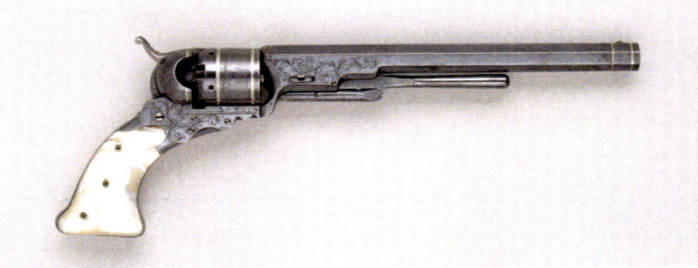

The Colt Revolver

finest light cavalry in the world. Their superior horsemanship and fighting skills created an advantage for Native Americans in the early years of their conflicts with white settlers and the U.S. army.

Two factors ended the military superiority of the Plains tribes. The initial factor involved the advent of new weapons. The first new weapon, which reached the frontier a short time after **Samuel Colt** patented it in 1836, was a revolver (a pistol), known as the **Colt Revolver**. Colt's pistol held six bullets in a cylinder, which, as the name suggests, revolved. This weapon evened the fight a bit, since a soldier or settler could shoot six times before reloading. The Native American, of course, with his bow and arrows, could shoot many times. However, the pistol's accuracy was limited to a short range.

Then, in 1860, **Benjamin Tyler Henry** invented, patented, and produced the **Henry Rifle**. The Henry rifle could fire sixteen rounds before reloading. In 1866, the Winchester Arms Company improved the Henry rifle, renaming it the "**Winchester Rifle**." Finally, in 1873, Winchester marketed a very accurate repeating rifle that held 15 cartridges in a spring-loaded, tubular magazine. It has been called "The Rifle that Won the West." Bows and arrows proved no match for a man with a Winchester. The Winchester rifle would become one of the most famous guns in American history.

The Winchester Rifle. The Rifle that won the West.

However, even more devastating to the Plains tribes than these new weapons, which they actually were able to obtain in small numbers, was the **extinction of the bison**. Historians estimate that in 1800, between fifty to sixty million buffalo roamed the Great Plains. These large, lumbering beasts meant the difference between life and death for Native Americans. With the construction of the railroads and their penetration of the Great Plains, the day of the bison herds and the Native Americans' nomadic way of life were coming to an end. Not only were professional hunters like Buffalo Bill Cody killing bison to feed railroad workers, but by the mid-1870s, frequent railroad excursions transported trainloads of "hunters" out to the Great Plains, where they shot bison from train windows. In some cases, the rifle muzzles actually touched the animals as the shots were fired. These shootings were purely for amusement; the mountain of meat the "hunters" left behind, which was so precious to Native Americans, was left to rot on the prairie. Between 1872 and 1874, over five million bison were killed. By 1884, between natural disasters such as droughts and fires, as well as the relentless hunting, the American bison had become nearly extinct. Probably fewer than 1,000 bison existed in the United States by 1890.

The "Indian Wars" Erupt

Beginning in late 1849, when most Americans became aware of the gold strike in California, ever-increasing numbers of Easterners traveled west. All of the optimists were California-bound, but many sensible traveling families saw opportunity beckoning to them in the rich farmland over which they crossed. These families found beauty, water, land, and opportunity as they put down roots beyond the Mississippi in the traditional hunting territories of the Great Plains tribes. By the time the Kansas and Nebraska territories were created in 1854, there were so many settlers spread throughout the Great Plains that Colorado, Wyoming, Idaho, Montana, and Dakota all became territories. It signaled the beginning of the end of the nomadic existence the Plains' tribes had long enjoyed.

In 1858, gold was discovered near Pike's Peak in Colorado. Quickly, over 100,000 men became Colorado gold miners. Aware of the imminent threat this horde of gold-crazed men posed, Native American tribal elders had to make a choice: run or fight. The Northern Cheyenne and Arapahoe tribes, joined by their loyal allies, the very powerful Sioux, decided to fight.

Three years later, in 1861, the Northern Cheyenne and Arapahos were forced off the land which a U.S. treaty had awarded to them! Soldiers took them to southeastern Colorado. To protest the broken treaty, a band of Native Americans, led by Roman Nose and Black Kettle, made raids on several white settlements between 1861 and 1864. These raids gave Colorado Militia **Colonel John M. Chivington** an excuse to raid the village where the Cheyenne had been relocated by the U.S. Government.

The American militia's brutal attack on the Cheyenne encampment at **Sand Creek**, Colorado, began at dawn on November 29, 1864. Most of the Cheyenne slept as the first cannonballs ripped through their teepees. **Chief Black Kettle** tried to surrender by raising a white flag, but Chivington ignored it. Chivington's sneak attack took a heavy toll on the

Sand Creek Memorial. In 2007, the federal government designated the site of the massacre as a National Historic Site

Early Dawn Attack by Charles Schreyvogel. The artist depicts the brutal attack on a peaceful Cheyenne village during which several unarmed women and children were killed.

Cheyenne. Chivington and his men murdered as many as five hundred Cheyenne, less than one hundred of whom may have been warriors. In a later court investigation, many soldiers admitted wrongdoing in the killing of unarmed women and children. The **Sand Creek Massacre** stands as one of the most inexcusable acts perpetrated by whites against Native Americans in U.S. history. (**Note**: In 2007, the federal government designated the site of the massacre as a National Historic Site.)

The Cheyenne and Arapahoe responded to the Chivington Massacre with attacks on white settlements. In November 1868, at Washita River (present-day Oklahoma), a sinister tableau played out. Lieutenant Colonel George Armstrong Custer and his cavalry attacked the peaceful village of Cheyenne leader Black Kettle, who had escaped Chivington's raid. Custer's troops ran down and killed Black Kettle. During the raid, Custer's men also killed 38 unarmed women and children. Custer's scouts had followed a trail of Cheyenne and Arapahoe warriors who had earlier attacked a white settlement. Apparently, the raiding party had only passed through Black Kettle's village but not been part of it.

Meanwhile, in order to protect settlers traveling west, the U.S. Army began constructing a series of forts along the **Bozeman Trail**. This trail, first followed by John Bozeman, a Georgia prospector, began in Fort Laramie, Wyoming and proceeded north into Montana. Unfortunately, it cut through the Big Horn mountains, the Lakota hunting grounds. The Lakota chief **Red Cloud** warned the government that the Lakota would fight to protect their hunting grounds. He warned against use of the Bozeman Trail. Beginning in 1865, Red Cloud, true to his word, began attacking white settlers and prospectors using the Bozeman Trail. The army responded by building the string of forts.

In 1868, the Lakota and the federal government signed a peace treaty at Fort Laramie. Under the treaty, the Lakota received permanent ownership of the Black Hills, a sacred place to them. The government agreed to abandon the forts that it had constructed along the Bozeman Trail. The Lakota would stay on their land and the whites would not trespass upon it. Both sides hoped that this would lead to peace, but sadly, fighting broke out almost immediately. Over the next several years, despite the **Treaty of Fort Laramie**, hundreds of attacks occurred between Native Americans and army units.

The Government Moves Native Americans onto Reservations

Under the Treaty of Fort Laramie, the federal government granted the Lakota ownership to land in the Black Hills. [Native Americans have argued they always owned the land.] This land became known as the Great Sioux Reservation. By creating **reservations**, that is, tracts of land set aside for particular tribes, the government hoped to reduce the violence between the Native Americans and the white settlers. Of course, living on a reservation meant that the natives would relinquish their nomadic life-style and either rely on the government for sustenance or become farmers.

Over the next decades, several more reservations were formed. Most tended to be away from white settlers and the railroads. Unfortunately, most Native American tribes were either coerced or tricked into signing treaties that moved them onto reservations. Many Native Americans, unhappy at their treatment, continued to fight the U.S. Army.

One particularly violent episode of relocation to a reservation occurred in 1874 in Texas. On June 27, 1874, three hundred Comanches attacked a buffalo hunting lodge at Adobe Walls in the Texas panhandle. When the attack failed, the Comanches launched additional attacks on white settlers. However, these attacks caused the U.S. Army to launch a campaign to remove not only the Comanche but also the Kiowa, Southern Cheyenne, and Arapaho tribes from the Southern Plains and forcibly relocate them to reservations in "Indian Territory," most of present-day Oklahoma. During the *Red River War*, which was fought mainly during the summer of 1874, most of the Native Americans on the Southern Great Plains were relocated to reservations.

Gold is Discovered in the Black Hills

The animosity between whites and the Lakota Sioux heated up in 1874 when **George Armstrong Custer** was ordered to lead an expedition into the Dakota territories to explore the Black Hills, in direct violation of the Fort Laramie Treaty just a few years before. Custer had been ordered to find a location for a fort and search for mineral deposits. While Custer and his troopers spent the summer of 1874 tramping in woods rich with game and angling in the streams choked with trophy-sized fish, some of the miners who traveled with Custer saw more than fish in the streams. The newspaper reporters who accompanied the expedition wrote articles trumpeting the news that rich gold deposits had been found in the Black Hills.

Such headlines acted as an invitation for miners who began sneaking into the Black Hills despite the cavalry's "effort" to rebuff them.

Various members of the peace chiefs in 1877. Chief Red Cloud is seated second from the left.

In 1875, an impressive "Peace Chiefs" contingent of representatives, led by Red Cloud, traveled to Washington to ask President Grant to enforce the Treaty of Laramie and to stop the increasing number of miners from entering the Black Hills. The chiefs met with President Grant and the Commissioner of Indian Affairs. The white leaders offered the Native Americans $25,000 if they left the Black Hills and relocated elsewhere. The chiefs refused the offer.

Despite the Lakota's adamant refusal to relinquish any of their Black Hills territory, increasing numbers of American gold seekers continued to invade the Black Hills. To accommodate them, mining camps such as Custer City and Deadwood sprang up in many nearby valleys. Government agents tried to purchase the Black Hills from Lakota Chief **Sitting Bull**. He adamantly refused. Near the end of 1875, cavalry troops raided several Cheyenne camps.

In December, President Grant issued a far-reaching proclamation. Grant's proclamation stated that white miners and settlers would be free to mine or settle on open land west of the Black Hills. The document implied that federal enforcement agents would ignore anyone who mistakenly crossed the boundaries and trespassed on tribal lands. Additionally, the federal government sent agents to all of the "hostile" Lakota and Cheyenne informing them that anyone who did not report to a reservation or army post on or before January 31, 1876, would be sought out and driven to such a location. In January, these tribes were snowbound in the middle of a fierce winter. Also, they did not understand the concept of an ultimatum from the U.S. government. Even if it meant life or death, they could not have complied with the unreasonable demand in mid-winter.

On January 31, 1876, the Secretary of the Interior declared that any Native American who failed to comply with Grant's proclamation would be considered a dangerous enemy. The Secretary of War now was called upon to institute appropriate action. He ordered General Sheridan to subdue all dangerous renegades as quickly as possible. Sheridan ordered General Nelson Miles and General George Crook to prepare for extensive maneuvers against hostile native insurgents, led by Sitting Bull.

Custer's Last Stand

One of the soldiers ordered to subdue the "dangerous renegades" was George Armstrong Custer. Custer, a West Point graduate, had served with distinction as a cavalry commander during the Civil War, fighting at Bull Run and Gettysburg. In July 1866, he was appointed a lieutenant colonel in the 7th Cavalry and sent west to fight Native Americans. Of Custer, most historians agree on two facts. Firstly, he was flamboyant. Custer had long blond hair and a blond mustache. He wore buckskin trousers, red-topped boots, and a wide-brimmed hat, often at a jaunty angle. Secondly, he had tremendous personal bravery, almost to the point of recklessness. As a result, he sometimes led his men into dangerous situations that a more prudent officer would have avoided. Ultimately, his reckless bravery proved his undoing.

George Armstrong Custer

On June 25, 1876, Custer decided to attack what he thought was a small Sioux village with his troop of about 700 cavalry soldiers and scouts. However, Custer had erred in calculating the size of the village on the Little Big Horn river. Instead of a small village, Custer's men faced about 1,800 warriors commanded by Crazy Horse and Sitting Bull.

Custer, believing he faced a small force, split his command into three parts. Per standard practice of the U.S. Cavalry of the time, his men dismounted and formed a skirmish line, with every fourth soldier holding his and three other horses. By splitting his force and dismounting, Custer lost the battle even before the first shots were fired. The Lakota warriors on their ponies surrounded the soldiers. A hail of bullets and arrows rained down upon the 7th Cavalry. Men and horses died swiftly during this hail of death. Within thirty minutes, the 7th Cavalry had been wiped out.

The defeat of Custer at the **Battle of the Little Big Horn** may have been the greatest victory for Native American warriors. However, Custer's defeat could not change the inevitable and overwhelming force that bore down on the Sioux: the federal government. Though Crazy Horse and Sitting Bull continued to fight, their time was drawing to a close.

The Last Stand of Crazy Horse and Sitting Bull

On January 8, 1877, Crazy Horse and his warriors fought their last major battle against the U.S. Cavalry at Wolf Mountain (Montana). With his people weakened by hunger during the terribly cold winter, Crazy Horse felt he had no choice but to surrender if he wanted his people to survive. In May, he surrendered to the U.S. Army at Fort Robinson, Nebraska. Four months later, in September 1877, a military guard bayoneted and killed Crazy Horse as he allegedly defied an order.

Chief Sitting Bull

Sitting Bull had a much more interesting career after the Battle of Little Big Horn. He led his people into Canada where they remained for several years. However, by 1881 hunger forced Sitting Bull to surrender to the Army. In 1884, the government allowed Sitting Bull to leave his reservation. In March, he met sharpshooter **Annie Oakley** with whom he formed a deep, lifelong friendship. The following year, he performed for several months with Buffalo Bill's *Wild West Show*. In 1890, fearing that Sitting Bull would flee the reservation, local authorities issued orders for his arrest. On December 15, police officers approached Sitting Bull's house where they attempted to arrest him. When Sitting Bull refused to comply with their orders, two officers shot and killed him.

Chief Joseph of the Nez Perce

The Indian Wars spread across the Rockies to the Pacific Coast, where settlers felt the sting of tribes on the warpath in Idaho and Oregon. The most famous Native American tribe in this region was the **Nez Perce**. The Nez Perce, known as a peace-loving people, had the reputation of never having killed a white man. During the early 1870s, **Chief Joseph** led the Nez Perce.

In 1877, the federal government demanded that the Nez Perce leave their ancestral lands to make room for white settlers. Chief Joseph decided to yield to this demand, but during the march to the new land, some Nez Perce killed some white settlers. The federal government sent troops to capture the Nez Perce. Joseph decided that instead of going to the reservation, he would lead his people to Canada.

For months, Chief Joseph and his ragged group of Native Americans led the U.S. Army on a wild hunt. Time and again they evaded the pursuing soldiers. In September 1877, they reached the Bear Paw Mountains, less than 30 miles from safety in Canada, where the U.S. Army could not follow. On the brink of escape, with many of his people sick and hungry, Joseph called a halt. Suddenly the cavalry attacked. For four days, Joseph and his warriors held off the Army. Finally, sick, hungry, and without ammunition, Joseph asked for a parley. He told the Army that he was tired of fighting. He said that he had no more ammunition and that his people were starving. Finally, Chief Joseph vowed: "From where the sun now stands I will fight no more forever."

The government settled the Nez Perce in Oklahoma, far from their beloved mountains. Chief Joseph eventually got permission to move closer to a reservation in Washington state, but they were never allowed to return to their homeland. He died in 1904. His doctor listed his cause of death as "a broken heart."

Geronimo

The last Native American "renegade" to be captured was an Apache named **Geronimo**. Geronimo outran and out-smarted his American and Mexican military pursuers for several years. In the final years, before he surrendered, his band consisted of only 34 men, women, and children. After his final surrender in 1886, he and his family were moved around to various reservations. They were considered prisoners of war for the rest of his life. Though a prisoner, Geronimo gained a celebrity status among the American public and was allowed to attend many events, including the 1905 Inaugural Parade of Theodore Roosevelt. He died in 1909 without ever being allowed to go home to the land he loved.

Promoters of Native American Rights

The treatment of Native Americans by whites during the 19th century represents a blight on America's history. Too often treaties were broken almost before the ink had dried. Many Americans during the time were shocked when they learned of the government's treatment of the various tribes.

One of the leading proponents of the rights of Native Americans was the author **Helen Hunt Jackson**. In 1881, she published her nonfiction work *A Century of Dishonor*, in which she describes the way in which the U.S. government has treated Native Americans from colonial times to the time of the book's

Helen Hunt Jackson

publication. Her book addressed the treaties broken by the government, the forced removal of tribes to unsuitable land, and the massacres of Native Americans by white people. The book, perhaps ahead of its time, failed commercially.

In 1884, Jackson published her novel *Ramona* to great critical and popular success. Set in California shortly after the Mexican-American War, the novel tells the story of a mixed-race Native American orphan girl who suffers racial discrimination. Jackson had hoped to create a novel that would have as powerful an impact as Harriet Beecher Stowe's *Uncle Tom's Cabin*, thus doing for Native Americans what Stowe's book did for the slaves. Though *Ramona* proved immensely popular, and remains so even today, it failed to have the impact that Jackson sought.

Government Policy Fails Native Americans

In 1887, Congress enacted the Dawes Act, named for its leading sponsor Senator Henry Dawes of Massachusetts, the Chairman of the Committee on Indian Affairs. The Dawes Act represented an attempt by Congress to assimilate Native Americans into mainstream American society. The Dawes Act broke the reservations into individual family units which they could use as farms. To protect the families from land speculators, they could not sell the land for twenty-five years.

While Congress enacted the Dawes Act with the best of intentions, it failed. Sadly, white Americans did not understand Native Americans and their culture. Most Native Americans did not wish to abandon their tribal culture and live as white people, especially as farmers. Additionally, the tribal lands were located in places, like Arizona and Oklahoma, that are not conducive to farming. Most Native Americans suffered terrible hardships and ultimately had to sell their land. From 1850 to 1900, the Native American population declined from about 350,000 to about 250,000.

The Cattle Kingdom

When the Spanish settled what would become the Southwestern United States, they imported cattle from the Canary Islands and Portugal. Over the decades, many of these cattle became feral, that is, they wandered about the land and became wild, and eventually drifted north and east into the area of the Great Plains. Only the hardiest cattle survived the rampant diseases, the violent winter storms, the scorching summer heat, the floods, and the droughts. These cattle learned to defend themselves and their calves from the attacks of wolves and other predators. They developed into lean, tough animals, known as **longhorns** because their horns could span as much as seven feet from tip to tip. Their legs were longer than those of most other cattle, which provided them with speed and mobility. Living in the wild made them rather aggressive animals. Most people considered the meat from the longhorns to be too tough to eat, so their only value lay in their hides, which sold for very little. By 1860, perhaps as many as five million wild Texas longhorns grazed the Texas grasslands unattended by anyone.

After the Civil War, the lush grasslands east of the Rocky Mountains, where buffalo had grazed for hundreds of years, became the "cattle kingdom." Adventurers found wild cattle wandering around the Texas prairie. Almost all of them knew that the grass-covered Great Plains, which stretched all the way from the Rio Grande in the south to Canada's border in the north, was owned by the government, which did not charge for the use of the land. Consequently, wandering cowboys had a **free pasture** available to them bigger than most foreign countries. This free pasture induced enterprising men to invest in thousands of cattle and employ cowboys to care for their herds. Since the cattle kingdom had no fences, owners **branded** their cattle so there could be no mistake about ownership. Branding involved marking each steer with a unique symbol. A hot iron seared the mark into the hide of the cattle. During the spring roundup, local

In *The Herd Quitter*, noted American artist Charles Marion Russell depicts a group of cowboys roping a steer trying to "quit" the herd. Note the rather large brand on the side of the longhorn.

cattle owners branded unbranded cattle, like newborn calves, with their brands and these became a part of the herd.

Following the Civil War, demand for meat in the East increased dramatically. Cattle worth four dollars in Texas sold for ten times as much in New York, Boston, and Philadelphia. The problem involved transporting thousands of head of cattle from Texas to the east. The dilemma was finally solved when an entrepreneur named **Joseph McCoy**, an Illinois meat packer, decided to construct a new railroad shipping location in western Kansas at the town of **Abilene**, which lay in low rolling hills covered with lush grass. Abilene provided an accessible mid-point where eastern cattle buyers could meet with western cattle sellers. McCoy built large corrals, stock pens, and loading chutes to load cattle in railroad cars. He even built a rooming house for the cowboys and a hotel for the eastern cattle buyers. Then he negotiated with the Kansas Pacific Railroad to build a track from Abilene to Chicago. Before long, Chicago became known as a leading meat packing city—because of all the beef and pork processed there. Still, the longhorns had to be driven from Texas to Abilene.

The Cattle Drive

During the first cattle drives, as well as during the early years of cattle ranching in the Southwest, the men who tended those herds were Mexicans called *vaqueros*, which means "cattle tender" or "cowboy." The era of the American Cowboy really began after the Civil War and lasted until the outbreak of World War II. When the Cowboy era began, the inexperienced American cowboys asked the *vaqueros* for guidance in handling cattle, as well as advice about the type of clothing and equipment that they should use. These cowboys also learned about the special training horses could be given to make the cowboy's jobs easier. Some of the most athletic horses, those that were quick and nimble of foot, were trained as "cutting horses." Cowboys used these horses to select, or "cut out," a single steer from a herd. Once the cowboy had focused the horse on the chosen animal, the cutting horse, without further direction from the cowboy, stopped every attempt the steer made to rejoin the herd.

The Stampede by Frederick Remington shows some of the dangers of a cattle drive.

To move the cattle to Abilene and the other "cattle towns," cowboys drove herds north to the railroad centers in eastern Kansas, along the **Chisholm Trail**, named for Cherokee fur trader **Jesse Chisholm**. Cowboys used the **Goodnight-Loving Trail** to move herds west from Texas across an arid desert with blast-furnace temperatures. This included an eighty-mile stretch of waterless desert. The cattle drive turned north along the Pecos River, then skirted along the edge of "Comanche Country," where Comanche warriors kept a deadly patrol. They hunted down and killed every white man they could who crossed their land. Comanches mortally wounded rancher and cattle driver **Oliver Loving** who, together with **Charles Goodnight**, developed the trail that bears their names. The Trail crossed through New Mexico and Colorado before finally ending in Cheyenne, Wyoming where the Union Pacific Railroad had a major junction.

During the two-month drive, cattle grew fat from grazing on the buffalo grass of the Great Plains. Cowboys drove them at a slow pace to Abilene where they arrived nice and fat. From there, the cattle were shipped to the great meat packinghouses in Chicago.

Between 1866 and 1886, cowboys drove 20 million cattle from Texas to the rail heads in Kansas. During those years, "cow-towns" like **Dodge City**, Kansas, the "Cowboy's Capital," were welcome sights for saddle-weary Texas cowboys who had spent a hundred or more days on the trail herding cattle. Tales about marauding Comanches or outlaw gangs intent on stealing herds, as depicted in pulp fiction and early western movies, often swelled to unbelievable proportions. However, serious dangers did exist. Every river crossing posed a perilous adventure. An unwary cowboy could be injured or killed. Even after the herd had been bedded down for the night, the mournful howl of a coyote or a loud snap from a piece of wood in the embers of the dying cooking fire might start a stampede.

The Cowboy

During the day, the cowboy spent as much as fourteen hours in the saddle during a cattle drive. While the horse he rode belonged to the cattle rancher who employed him, the saddle was his own, so the cowboy

In *Smoke of a .45*, Charles Marion Russell depicts a violent episode as a group of men exchange gun fire from their .45's outside a gambling casino, The Palace. While the scene is incredibly dramatic, such violent events were actually rather rare.

typically spent up to a month's wages on a good saddle. He used a **western saddle**, which has a **pommel** that he used to help him control cattle. He could rope a steer, then tie the rope to the saddle's pommel. At night that saddle became his pillow, as he slept by the campfire on a blanket roll, laid on the cold, hard ground of the sun-scorched prairie.

When the cowboy reached the rail-head and loaded the cattle into the train's boxcars, the time had come to collect his money. He wanted to recover from the physical hardships he had endured on the long trail up from Texas. In town, after a few days of well-earned rest, many cowboys took some time to spend some of their money before heading back to Texas. Many bought fancy new clothes and discarded their worn ones. Then, clad in their new clothes, they wanted to celebrate and "let off some steam," which often included drinking whiskey at a dimly-lit saloon. Saloon girls received a small portion of the money they enticed from the cowboys to spend in poker games and other games of chance.

Nat Love

Historians estimate that between 20% to 25% of all cowboys were African-American. After the Civil War, the West provided many opportunities to blacks. In fact, many of the top wranglers were black. **Bill Pickett**, became well known for inventing the technique known as "bull dogging," a means by which the cowboy grabs a steer by the horns and wrestles it to the ground. Pickett eventually became a rodeo star and Wild West performer. Perhaps the most famous African-American cowboy was **Nat Love**. Love was born a slave, but unlike most slaves was taught to read and write. Love wrote an autobiography in which he described his exploits on cattle drives, confrontations with Native American warriors, and encounters with numerous Western celebrities including Pat Garrett and Billy the Kid. Thousands of black cowboys, like Love and Pickett, played a significant role in helping build the cattle kingdom.

The Peace Keepers

To maintain order when trail herds arrived, the cow-towns hired sheriffs to "ride herd on the drovers." However, these peace keepers did not interfere unless lives were threatened. Some of the most famous frontier lawmen were the **Earp Brothers**: **Wyatt**, **Virgil**, and **Morgan**. Outlaws killed Morgan with a shotgun blast and seriously injured Virgil, who lost the use of his right arm. Wyatt Earp, the most famous peacekeeper, seemed to attract trouble in every place he lived. However; he lived until 1929 and died in Los Angeles at the age of 80, never having even been scratched in a gunfight. At his funeral, silent film star Tom Mix, who played a cowboy, acted as one of Wyatt Earp's pallbearers.

Brothers **Bat** and **Ed Masterson** also served as frontier sheriffs. A drunken cowboy murdered Ed, but Bat died at the age of 67 as a result of a heart attack. At the time, he was composing an article for the regular newspaper column that he wrote for the *New York Morning Telegraph*.

James Butler "Wild Bill" Hickok wore two guns, but an enemy also murdered him. Hickok was playing poker when a man snuck behind him and shot him in the back of the head. At the time, Hickok held a pair of aces and a pair of eights, a hand that has gone down in history as a "dead man's hand."

Wyatt Earp did not shoot rowdy cowboys, but rather "buffaloed" them, which means hitting a disruptive man on the head hard enough to knock him out. Earp once explained, "My job is to keep the peace, not to kill paying customers." Pulp fiction writers and Hollywood have produced books and films that portray cow-towns as excessively violent and brutal. While violence existed, most professional peace keepers disarmed the cowboys while they were in town. Consequently, cow-towns averaged only one-and-a-half fatal shootings per year! This is far less than the number of killings in almost any American city today.

The Era of the Open Range Comes to a Close

By the 1880s, the era of the open range began to decline. The cattle kingdom had succeeded because ranchers allowed their herds to roam the prairies, where they thrived on the free grass of the open range. However, by the mid-1880s, good grass became harder to find as five million cattle grazed on the land. There were simply too many cattle!

Free-range cattle-raising faced another problem in the 1880s when an influx of sheep owners moved west. Cattlemen believed that the sheep ruined the open range land for cattle. Sheep eat the grass much closer to the ground, which made it harder for cattle to find the "shorter" grass. It also meant that the grass took longer to grow back. Several vicious local "range wars" erupted between sheepherders and cattlemen, and many good, honest men lost their lives.

Additionally, more farmers moved into the Great Plains. They also competed with the ranchers for the land. The herds often trampled the farmers' crops, sometimes accidentally and sometimes not so accidentally. Also, cattle caught diseases which could spread. Farmers feared the spread of diseases to their farm animals.

The final blow to cattle ranchers was dealt not by other men, but by nature. During the winters of 1885 to 1887, terrible blizzards hit the Great Plains. When spring 1887 finally arrived, nearly all the cattle had been killed. The age of the open range had ended. Cattlemen could no longer risk letting their herds wander free on the grassy plains.

The concept of free-grazing cattle ranches gave way to smaller ranches that ranchers could more easily operate and control. They built fences and rounded up their herds. The days of longhorns wandering over the open range came to an end. Other breeds of beef cattle, such as **Herefords**, provided better and more usable meat. On small ranches, cattle men could maintain the purity of their breeds more easily. Ranchers could inspect for diseases more easily than on the open range. Overall, the product improved.

By the mid-1920s, longhorns had become an endangered species. To preserve them from extinction, in 1927, the federal government gathered a large herd of longhorns at the Wichita

A Hereford

Wildlife Refuge in Oklahoma. The *Texas Longhorn Breeders Association of America* was founded in 1964. Consequently, Longhorn became a breed. Lean beef lovers rank Longhorn steaks as the best eating of all.

Private ranches still hold an important place in the beef industry. Feed lots in states far from cattle country are raising beef cattle on such things as cottonseed meal. More than a million tons of the meal are currently fed to livestock annually. Beef remains an important item on America's meat list as well as a major part of our foreign trade.

The Comstock Lode

In the twenty-five years following the original 1849 California Gold Rush, similar "rushes" occurred in Colorado, Idaho, Montana, Wyoming, New Mexico, Arizona, and Utah. Gold was but one of the valuable minerals being sought. God blessed the Western United States with rich deposits of copper, lead, zinc, coal, oil, and iron. During these years of "strikes" and "rushes," the Rocky Mountain region became dotted with mining towns.

In 1859, a California Gold Rush veteran discovered the **Comstock Lode**, the largest silver mine in the world, in Virginia City, Nevada. Second in importance only to the discovery of gold at Sutter's Mill, the Comstock Lode was the first major discovery of silver in the United States. This massive silver discovery effectively ended the California Gold Rush.

Centered in Gold Canyon on the slopes of Mount Davidson (Nevada), **Henry Comstock**" originally sought for gold. When their initial panning in the stream failed to develop any "flake," the two men looked for other places to dig for gold in Gold Canyon. Meanwhile, in the spring of 1859, two other miners, named **Peter O'Riley** and **Patrick McLaughlin**, began digging on the northern slope of Six-Mile Canyon, a ravine on the northern slope of Mount Davidson. By June, they *seemed to have discovered gold*. When Comstock learned of the discovery, he rode over and falsely told O'Riley and McLaughlin that they were working on land that he and Fennimore owned. Afraid that they might lose their claim, O'Riley and McLaughlin agreed to give the lying Comstock and his partner an interest in the gold find.

Soon the four men began digging at the claim but found little gold, only bluish sand and bluish-gray quartz. Discouraged, they discarded the seemingly valueless rock in a pile next to their diggings. Meanwhile, another miner took the pile of junk rock and had it tested. It proved to be rich in silver and worth a fortune! Over the next few months, 15,000 men rushed to the **Comstock Lode**, named for the man who tricked his way into the partnership.

"Bonanza Ore" from the Comstock Lode. Note the bluish-grey quartz.

Although the Comstock Lode proved incredibly valuable, it was incredibly difficult to mine. The silver was buried deep in the quartz veins and required experienced mining engineers with specialized equipment to remove it. None of the four partners had the skill for the task or the money to purchase the necessary equipment. Comstock sold his share of the mine, which eventually yielded silver and gold worth more than 700 million dollars, for $11,000.

Railroads Stimulate Growth in the Northern Plains

In 1864, Congress approved construction of the Northern Pacific Railroad, a transcontinental railway intended to connect the western Great Lakes region to the Pacific Ocean. When the railroad was completed in 1883, it ran from the western tip of Lake Superior to the Pacific running across the Northern United States. Once travel became available on the Northern Pacific, thousands of Northern European immigrants by-passed the East Coast and rushed to the Dakota Territories. Some of them prospected for gold, but a vast majority of Germans and Scandinavians came to farm the land. A few were able to acquire land very quickly. Others had to work for other farmers until they were able save enough money to purchase their own land. The land proved to be well-suited for the production of wheat, which rapidly became a principal crop. In 1889, the Dakota Territory was divided, and on November 2, the states of North and South Dakota entered the Union. It is interesting to note that the capital city of North Dakota was named Bismarck to honor the German Chancellor, and to lure German settlers into the new state.

West of the Dakotas, the state of Montana joined the Union less than a week later on November 8, followed swiftly by Washington state on November 11. In 1890, Idaho (July 3) and Wyoming (July 10) were admitted to the Union. With the exception of Washington, these states have grown slowly and all have small populations. Montana became a new home for many miners. Cattle and sheep ranching became a principal occupation in Wyoming. Agriculture and tourism remain important industries in South Dakota. Farming has played a major role in North Dakota; however, in the 21st century oil production became a leading industry. Washington became a leader in lumber production, agriculture, and commercial fishing.

The Oklahoma Land Rush

At noon on April 22, 1889, the federal government opened a large portion of Oklahoma to settlement. The "Indian Territory" had been located in Oklahoma. This was an appropriate name since "Oklahoma," in the Choctaw language, means "red people." The territory had originally been assigned to the five major tribes that had been removed from the southern United States. These tribes had allied themselves with the Confederacy during the Civil War and during Reconstruction had been forced to make large land concessions. The Native Americans had been bought out and then relocated. On that April morning, over 50,000 eager pioneers waited at the starting line, anxious to farm on good water-fed land. For quite some time, cavalry patrols had been clearing out people who had snuck into their claims before the starting gun was fired. These people were called "Sooners" because they entered the land "sooner than they should have" to stake their claims. They gave Oklahoma its nickname, the "Sooner State."

The Oklahoma Land Rush Monument. Created by sculptor Paul Moore, the monument in Oklahoma City is one of the largest sculptures in the world. It contains forty-seven individual statues which include 38 people, 34 horses, three wagons, and a cannon.

The 50,000 contestants for the most valuable land prepared to rush forward in very different ways. Along the crowded starting line, affluent men sat astride expensive thoroughbred horses from England or Kentucky. Other men rode smaller, sturdier mustang ponies. Families in slow-moving covered wagons, filled with all their worldly possessions, hoped for a decent plot of land. Other contestants had hired stagecoaches for the race. Three confident riders waited patiently on camels! They staked their futures on their belief that their camels could outrun horses over short distances. The most bizarre form of transportation was a small, low, lightweight wagon with a front end that looked like the prow of a sailing ship. The "prairie schooner" held a mast that supported a large white sail that billowed in the wind.

Precisely at noon, the starting gun was fired and the mayhem began. When one of the settlers wanted to claim a plot of land, he drove a **claim identification stick** into the ground, indicating that the land was now taken. However, many settlers were surprised to discover that many of the best locations were already taken. The cavalry had failed to discover some of the "Sooners" who seized the choicest land. In addition, a number of brigands and thieves simply tossed away the original claim identification sticks and substituted stakes of their own. These people hunkered down on their stolen property and chased away or even killed the original claimants.

The town of Guthrie did not exist when the starting gun sounded at noon that day. Before thousands of campfires were lit that evening, soon-to-be Guthrie had ten thousand residents! People staked out streets and town lots. They took steps toward creating a municipal government. Literally overnight, a large number of happy people came to live in the fastest growing town in American history.

Oklahoma became the 46th state in 1907. New Mexico was admitted to the Union in 1912. One month later, Arizona became the last of the forty-eight continental states.

America's Breadbasket

In the 1850s, farming on the Great Plains seemed nearly impossible. Farmers had to resort to extreme measures such as dry-land farming. The Great Plains might have been called the Great American Desert. Yet in forty years, this desert had become America's breadbasket. Technological improvements and mechanization caused this wonderful change.

Man plowing with a team of four horses in North Dakota circa 1890. By the 1890s, farming on the Great Plains was no longer impossible.

In 1868, inventor and manufacturer **James Oliver** began producing the latest in a line of steel plows. This new plow was vastly superior to his previous versions as well as other plows on the market. The plow easily cut through the tough sod of the Great Plains. Over the next decades, Oliver's company began producing specialized models for different kinds of soil.

The use of **steam threshers** and **automatic twine binders**, for example, meant that work that had once taken farmers and their helpers weeks to accomplish could be done in a few hours. As the 1880s dawned, more and more farmers, using the new machines and technology, began producing massive amounts of food in places where once only wild animals roamed. By 1890, about five million people lived on the Great Plains, which had become the greatest wheat-producing region in the world! This former desert had become America's breadbasket. It would one day feed the world.

CHAPTER 21   REVIEW QUESTIONS

Answer the following questions:

1. Why was the buffalo so important to Native Americans?
2. Why was the Native American society described as a "horse culture?"
3. How did the federal government encourage construction of the transcontinental railroad?
4. How did the transcontinental railroad change the nation?
5. Where did the companies building the transcontinental railroad join up to complete the railroad?
6. What was the Sand Creek Massacre?
7. Where did George Custer die?
8. How did Crazy Horse die?
9. What was the Cattle Kingdom?
10. What city might have been nicknamed "Pork Hamlet" or "Beefburg" and why?
11. What factors ended the "open range?"
12. What is the Comstock Lode?
13. Who are the Sooners? How did they earn that name?
14. What inventions and techniques turned the Great Plains into America's breadbasket?
15. Who was Helen Hunt Jackson? How did she work to aid Native Americans?
16. Why did Southerners move West after the Civil War?
17. What were some of the larger Native American tribes to live on the Great Plains?
18. Why did the federal government move Native American tribes onto reservations?

Identify the following:

1. Red Cloud
2. Chief Joseph
3. Buffalo Bill Cody
4. Battle of the Little Big Horn
5. Black Hills
6. Nat Love
7. Range Wars
8. Geronimo
9. Bill Pickett

CHAPTER 22

America's Second Industrial Revolution

1860-1900

Men of Progress (1862) by Christian Schussele. In 1857, the inventor of a coal-burning stove, Jordan Mott, commissioned Schussele to paint a group portrait of eighteen American scientists and inventors who "had altered the course of contemporary civilization." The group portrait did not depict a real event but was intended to honor the achievements of American industry. Men of Progress visually documents the start of America's second Industrial Revolution as it celebrates the inventions and innovations pioneered by men such as Cyrus McCormick, Samuel Colt, and Samuel Morse.

Introduction

From 1860 to 1900, the United States underwent an industrial and technological revolution that would not be seen again until the late 20th and early 21st centuries. In 1860, America was still primarily an agricultural and rural nation, as nearly 80% of the population lived on farms. Only about 5% of the population, about 1.5 million people, worked in factories. Over the next three decades, that number more than tripled. By 1900, America had become an industrial superpower with manufactured goods worth nearly as much as all of Western Europe!

Where in 1860, only a few thousand miles of track had existed, by 1900, an entire railroad network spanned the nation. The oil and steel industries, which barely existed in 1860, had become massive industries in 1900. New inventions revolutionized the communications industry. Truly, America was undergoing a second Industrial Revolution even more dramatic than its first.

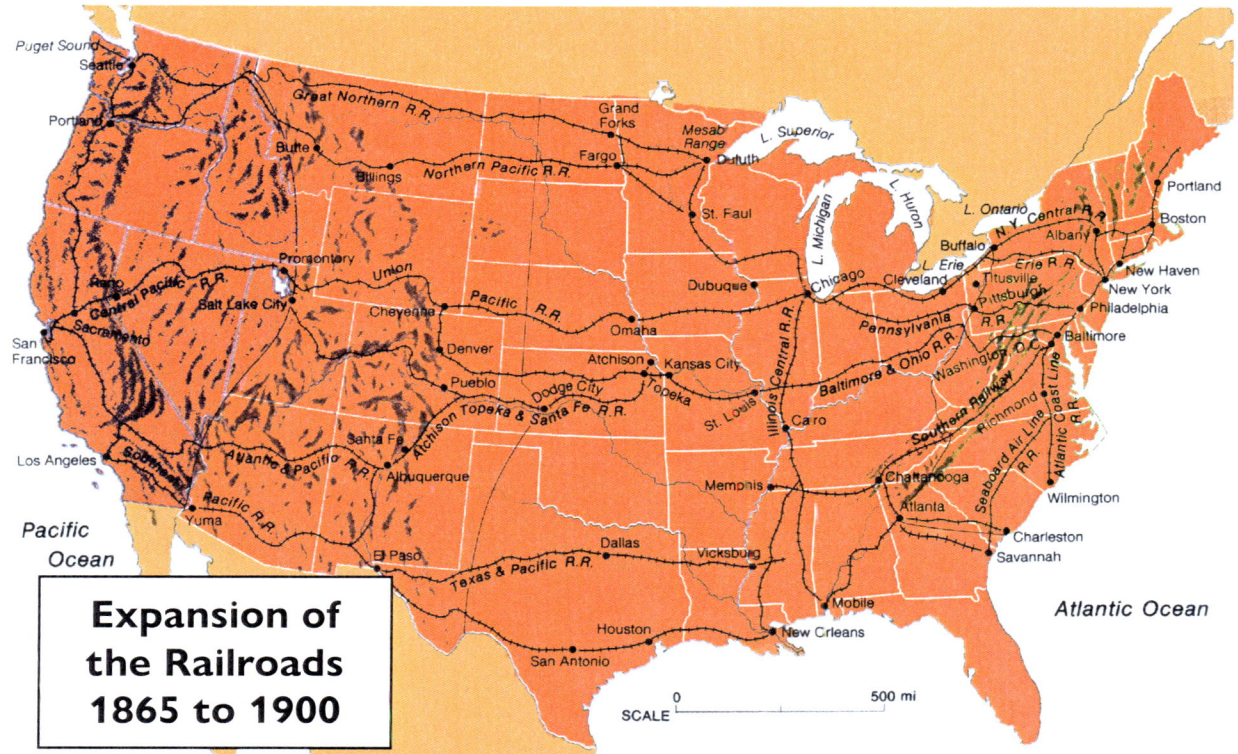

Expansion of the Railroads 1865 to 1900

By 1900, almost 200,000 miles of railroad tracks, nearly one-third of all the track in the world, crisscrossed the United States!

The Expansion of the Railroads

The Improvement of Rail Travel

More than anything else, to Americans living in the latter half of the 19th century, the railroads represented not only progress but also the greatness of America. Once rails had been laid between cities, personal and commercial travel flourished. Even today, many American businesses depend on the railroad to transport their goods and tens of millions of Americans use the railroads to travel for business and pleasure.

In 1830, workers laid railroad track for America's first railroad in Baltimore, Maryland. For the next twenty years, the development of railroads progressed rather slowly. Only ten thousand miles of track had been laid by 1850. No rails extended west beyond the Appalachian Mountains. By the beginning of the Civil War, thirty thousand miles of track existed.

These early railroads differed greatly from modern railroads. For example, many ran for only twenty to thirty miles. The builders simply wished to connect their city with one nearby with which they did business. Another problem existed because railroad builders varied track width, or gauge, from three and a half feet in some places to five feet in others. As a result, the cars of one railroad could not run on the tracks of another.

Before 1860, only a handful of people thought of connecting big cities and even fewer of creating a national network. One of these forward thinkers was Erastus Corning, who, in 1853, merged ten railroads across the state of New York to create the New York Central Railroad, one of the largest railroads in the nation. Corning ran trains between Albany and Buffalo. In 1850, it had taken about two weeks to travel from New York City to Chicago. Because of the New York Central Railroad, and others, by 1860, the time had been reduced to about two days to travel by train from New York to Chicago. However, it required a passenger to make *10 separate connections!* While it was a great improvement, railroad owners realized they needed to provide better service.

In 1886, the railroad companies in the South agreed to conform to a common gauge of four feet nine inches that was used in the North. Beginning on May 31, 1886, and continuing for the next 36 hours, tens of thousands of men pulled out every rail spike on one side of track that was five feet apart, and then moved it three inches closer to its neighbor. Then they hammered the spikes back into the rail ties. Railroad tracks were finally compatible throughout America!

Railroad tracks also improved during this period as brittle iron rails were replaced with stronger steel rails. Steel rails made travel far safer. In addition, the stronger steel could support heavier trains. This allowed for larger, more powerful locomotives which could pull bigger freight and passenger cars. Bridges made of steel made it possible to construct routes across chasms impossible with the weaker iron girders. New, faster routes became possible. The railroads opened more of the nation to business and opportunity.

The appearance of early rail cars indicated the limited comfort they provided. Early passenger cars were basically stagecoaches chained together and equipped with wheels that fit the tracks. Early trains had no sleeping accommodations. Smelly kerosene lamps or candles lit the smoke-filled cars. Wood or coal burning stoves provided little heat. Constantly changing from one railroad to another and bumping up and down over rough roadbeds, in a noxious environment of soot and cinders, made train travel extremely uncomfortable. Nevertheless, in terms of speed and convenience, railroad travel surpassed all other forms of transportation at the time. Moreover, as the railroads expanded, the railroad companies made improvements to their passenger cars and to their freight cars.

Turn of the century train car. The incredible luxury rivals anything available even 125 years later.

In 1854, **George Pullman** constructed the first railroad sleeping car, the Pullman sleeper which added substantially to the comfort of rail travel. Pullman's sleeping car had an upper and lower berth. During the day, the upper berth was pushed back and up against the wall, and the lower berth could be used as a seat. In 1865, President Lincoln's body was carried from Washington, D.C. to Springfield, Illinois on a Pullman sleeper. Although the Pullman sleeper was five times more expensive than a regular train car, the publicity from carrying the assassinated president generated national attention and the company became incredibly successful. After the Civil War, Pullman began hiring freed slaves to work as porters on his sleeping cars. For almost one hundred years, the Pullman Company hired only African-Americans as porters.

In 1867, Pullman introduced a new type of rail car: the dining car. He hired top chefs and waiters so that the food and service matched the nation's finest restaurants. It was then possible to dine as well as sleep on a trip by rail.

In 1869, **George Westinghouse** invented an important safety feature: the air brake. This increased the comfort and the security of rail travel. Before the air brake became available, the brakes on each car were applied separately. The air brake allowed all the brakes to be set at once by compressed air. This made it possible to stop the train more quickly and safely.

George Pullman

Around 1880, inventors discovered various means to ship **perishable** food in **refrigerated boxcars**. Perishable foods, like fruits and butchered meats, could be shipped long distances. Produce from California could ship to the Eastern states. Meat from Chicago's packing plants could ship anywhere in the nation. Refrigeration then became "air-conditioning," a giant step forward in making travelers comfortable, and far more eager to take trips even in warm weather. A system using steam from the engine was employed to heat the passenger cars and replaced the old wood and coal burning stoves. Tourists and businessmen could plan trips knowing they could travel safely, quickly and comfortably.

Creation of a National Railroad Network

In 1860, two tasks faced the nation's railroad builders. First, construct a transcontinental railroad that would link east and west. Although the Civil War slowed construction, by 1869, only four years after the close of the War, rail crews had constructed a transcontinental railroad. The two crews met at Promontory Point, Utah where Leland Stanford drove a golden spike into the tie that connected the rails. The first transcontinental railroad system stretched across three thousand miles and, at last, united the East with the West.

Yet one transcontinental railroad did not connect all of the nation's cities. A second task faced the railroad companies. They needed to build a railroad network that would connect all the existing railroads as well as many others. This network would link all the parts of the nation so a person could travel from New York to Chicago easily and in comfort. The men who ultimately built this railroad network became known as **railroad barons**. Among the most well-known barons was **"Commodore" Cornelius Vanderbilt**.

Although not well-educated, Cornelius Vanderbilt possessed a keen mind and a shrewd intelligence. He quickly realized that railroads were America's future. Thus, he invested the money that he had made in shipping – hence the honorific "Commodore" – into railroads. By 1869, he controlled three railroads that linked New York City with Buffalo and Albany. The following year he purchased the *Lake Shore* and *Michigan Southern* railroads, which linked his first three railroads with Cleveland, Toledo, and Chicago. On Vanderbilt's railroads, a passenger could travel between New York City and Chicago in less than twenty-four hours without having to change trains! Over the next seven years, until his death in 1877, he acquired more than 4,500 miles of railroad.

Among Vanderbilt's most well-known competitors was **Jay Gould**. Gould, a ruthless individual, became involved in railroads in 1859 when he was in his early twenties. Gould also partnered with **James Fisk** and the two men began working with "Boss" Tweed in New York City. In 1869, Gould and Fisk were involved in the "Black Friday" Scandal that embarrassed President Grant. Over the years, Gould built up a system of railroads in the West and Midwest. In 1873, he gained control of the Union Pacific Railroad, one of the two companies that had constructed the first transcontinental railroad. During the next years,

Cornelius Vanderbilt began his career in the rough world of New York City's port. He parlayed small shipping ventures into larger ones eventually dominating the New England trade and seaborne travel to San Francisco. He next moved into railroads, eventually gaining a major control of the industry. A ruthless businessman, Vanderbilt helped organize America's fragmented transportation system into an efficient national network.

Gould gained control of several more railroads. Although many people personally disliked him, Gould ran his railroads efficiently. Businesses and people could depend on them. He became one of the richest men in America. He died in 1892.

Between 1870 and 1873, more railroads were constructed in the United States than had existed in 1855. Because the South had fewer railroads than the North, and those that existed before the Civil War had almost all been destroyed, railroad construction in the South proceeded more rapidly than anywhere else in the nation. Of the approximately 19,500 miles of track laid, about 2,500 were built in the South.

During the late 1860s and 1870s, various other lines were established which linked more and more of the nation. The *Pennsylvania Railroad* linked Philadelphia to Chicago and St. Louis. The old *Baltimore and Ohio RR* (B & O) tied Baltimore into Philadelphia and then into Chicago. Chicago became a major midwestern hub, rivaling New York City, and linked to the Pacific Northwest, California, and New Orleans. Chicago quickly became America's "Second City."

The railroads also created national time zones. Because people were traveling across the nation, a standardized schedule system needed to be introduced in order to make traveling easier. On November 18, 1883, the railroads devised four time zones, eastern, central, mountain, and western. These replaced a myriad of time zones that existed in individual states. For example, Illinois had twenty-seven different local time zones. In 1918, Congress formally adopted the system which is still used today.

Many people objected to the sometimes-ruthless way in which the railroad barons operated. The railroad barons made millions of dollars for themselves, but they also created hundreds of thousands of jobs for American workers. For example, in 1891, the Pennsylvania Railroad had over 110,000 employees. By contrast, the U.S. Post Office, the largest federal employer, had 95,000 employees.

Of course, this direct employment does not even count the number of jobs the railroads created indirectly by stimulating the national economy. Railroads needed iron, steel, and coal, thus creating jobs in those sectors. Railroads could ship heavy materials at very reasonable prices. Wood from Oregon could be sold in Boston. Oranges from California could be sold in New York City. The number of jobs and the wealth the railroads created is incalculable. They represented the greatness and power of the growing nation. It is no wonder that poets sang their praises:

Jay Gould was one of the most successful yet controversial businessmen of the 19th century.

Limited by Carl Sandburg

I am riding on a limited express,
one of the crack trains of the nation.
Hurtling across the prairie into blue haze and dark air
go fifteen all-steel coaches holding a thousand people...
I ask a man in the smoker where he is going
and he answers:
"Omaha."

The Beginning of *Corporate* America

The Corporation

Building railroads was probably the most expensive endeavor that private individuals undertook in American history up to this time. In fact, it was so expensive that one person, or even a group combining private funds, simply could not afford to do it. Some other means of raising the huge amount of money necessary was required. Thus, the railroad builders formed **corporations**.

The people who establish corporations sell **shares**, called **stock**, in the corporation. Everyone who buys a share of stock owns a percentage of the corporation. Because the railroads had to generate millions of dollars, they would sell hundreds of thousands of shares of stock. Each share might cost only a few dollars, but thousands of people could buy shares. Thus, the corporation could finance the cost of the construction of the railroad.

When the corporation makes a profit, the **board of directors**, the men and women who run the corporation, usually pay a **dividend**. Each stockholder receives a percentage of the profit based on the amount of stock that they own. If the corporation makes a million dollars and a stockholder owns 10% of the stock, he or she would receive a $100,000 dividend.

The stockholder can sell his shares at any time. The value of the stock will rise or fall depending on the value of the company. A stock that might be inexpensive when it is first issued will increase in price if the company succeeds. On the other hand, a stock might become worthless if the company fails. For example, Apple Computers began selling shares on December 12, 1980, for $22 per share and generated over $100 million. On August 19, 2020, Apple shares sold for about $467, making Apple worth $2 trillion. However, even if Apple went bankrupt, the shareholders would only lose the value of their shares, they would not be responsible for the debts of the corporation. Also, corporations have perpetual existence, making them reliable business entities. Thus, when Apple founder Steve Jobs died in 2011, the corporation continued to function.

Over time, for financial and legal reasons, more and more Americans chose to form corporations as their choice of business entity. It was the beginning of corporate America. It also meant that the state and federal government would eventually step in and begin regulating corporations.

America's Steel Industry

Of all of America's great industries, none can rival the steel industry. In fact, many other industries, such as the construction and railroad industries, depended on the steel industry for their very existence. For example, in the early days of the railroads, builders constructed tracks from iron. However, although it is very strong, steel is fifteen times stronger. Trains could not travel as fast nor be as heavy as builders would have preferred because of iron track. Unfortunately, the cost of steel rails prior to the 1870s made steel track too expensive to use.

The problem that steel manufacturers faced involved the long, expensive process that turned iron into steel. Beginning in 1850, an English inventor named **Henry Bessemer** began working on a method that would inexpensively turn iron into steel. In 1856, he publicly revealed his **Bessemer Process** by which a blast of hot air directed at melting iron in a furnace burned out the iron's impurities. These impurities made the

Henry Bessemer. Note the statue in the background of an iron worker.

iron weak. The hot air blasted out the impurities in a shower of fiery sparks. Bessemer then added carbon to the molten wrought iron. When the metal cooled, it had been converted into steel. This remarkably simple method remained the primary means for making steel for the next 100 years! Not only could steel be made cheaply, it could also be made quickly. Five tons of iron could be converted into steel in just a few minutes. In a very real sense, Henry Bessemer was one of a handful of men who almost single-handedly created the Second Industrial Revolution.

Of all the nations in the world, none benefited from the Bessemer Process more than the United States, a nation blessed with the abundant natural resources of iron ore and **coal**, the fuel needed to fire the great furnaces that would **smelt**, that is, burn away, the impurities in the iron. In 1866, prospectors discovered one of the greatest iron ore fields in the world in the **Mesabi Range** in Minnesota, near Lake Superior. Barges

Although Adolph Menzel's *The Iron Rolling Mill* (1875) portrays a German mill, his representation is precise in its realistic depiction of a late 19th iron-producing factory.

carried the ore across Lake Superior to cities in the Midwest. Almost overnight, cities like Toledo, Youngstown, and Cleveland, Ohio became major steel-producing centers. Pittsburgh, with its great coal fields, became the greatest steel-producing city in the world.

Because of its strength, steel naturally became the primary construction material for tall buildings during the Second Industrial Age. In New York and Chicago, tall commercial buildings made from steel, called *skyscrapers*, began to appear. In 1885, the **Home Insurance Building**, the first skyscraper, a ten-story building, opened in Chicago. From that date forward, architects built taller and taller buildings.

The man most responsible for building the American steel industry was **Andrew Carnegie**. Carnegie's story truly is that of the American dream. Carnegie emigrated to the United States from Scotland while a teenager, arriving on these shores almost penniless. Carnegie took a job as a telegraph messenger boy in the Pittsburgh office of the Ohio Telegraph Company. Though he had no

Andrew Carnegie

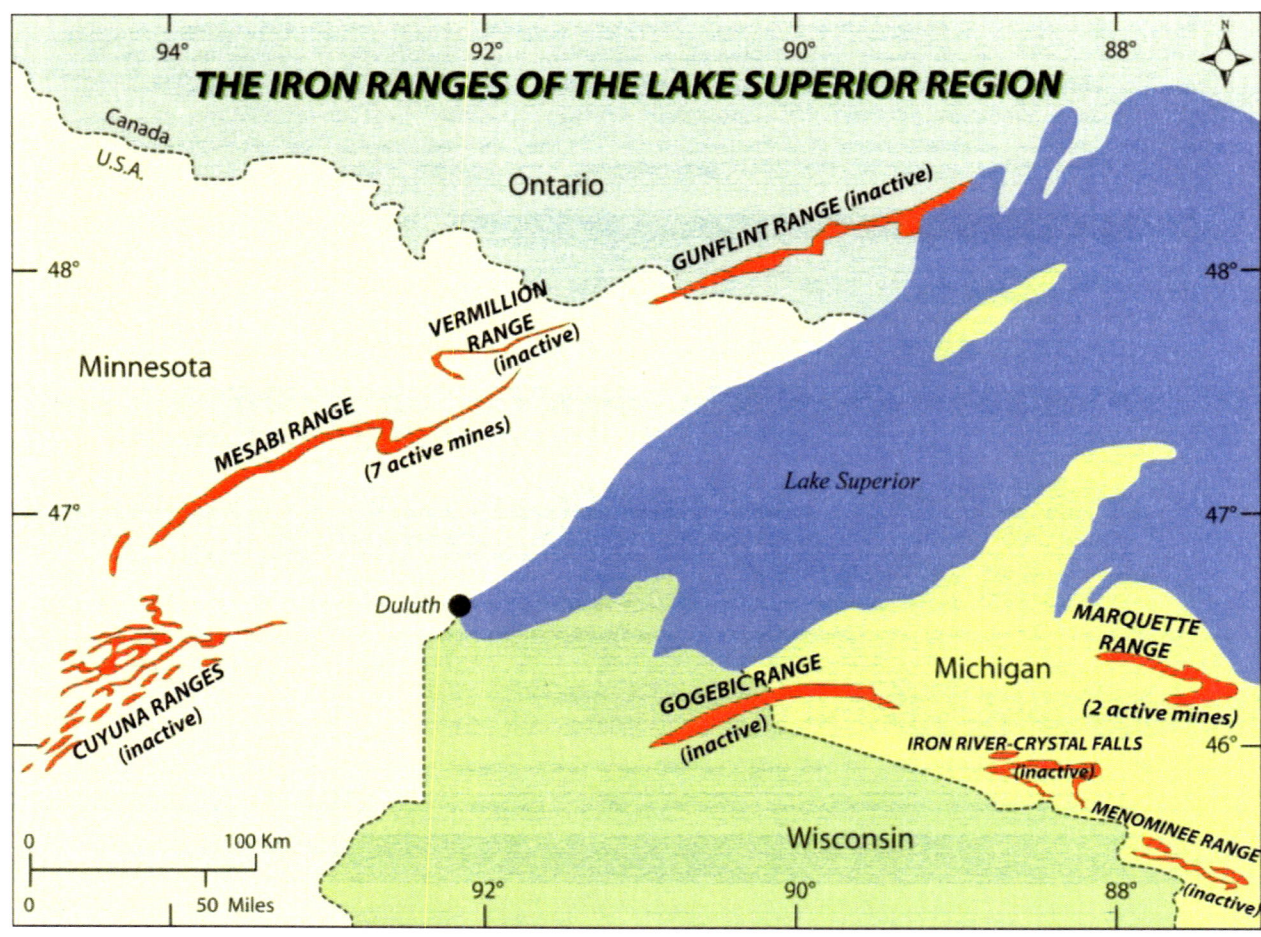

THE IRON RANGES OF THE LAKE SUPERIOR REGION

formal education, he borrowed books from friends and became well educated. His hard work earned him a promotion at the Telegraph Company. However, he realized that railroads were the future and he left to take a job at the *Pennsylvania Railroad Company*.

Carnegie became friends with the president of the *Pennsylvania Railroad Company*, became his personal assistant, and advanced rapidly. He also invested in railroads. His investments paid off and he reinvested, always wisely, constantly increasing his fortune. During the Civil War, he worked as a Union railroad superintendent, assuring that military supplies reached the Union forces. After the war, Carnegie focused on the steel industry, which became the source of his immense fortune. He met Henry Bessemer in Europe and adopted the Bessemer Process for his steel mill. In 1873 built the **J. Edgar Thomson Steel Works**, the largest Bessemer steel plant in America. The railroads ordered massive quantities of steel rails from him and he became the largest manufacturer of steel in the world. In 1889, the United States became the world's leading steel manufacturer, surpassing Great Britain.

By 1900, *Carnegie Steel Company* provided about 75% of all steel produced in the United States. The following year he sold his company to the United States Steel Corporation (U.S. Steel), at the time, the largest corporation in the world. During the remaining nineteen years of his life, Andrew Carnegie gave away his money. Recalling how he had borrowed books, he endowed thousands of libraries. He donated to numerous universities in the United States and in Britain. He also endowed a number of museums. At his death, Andrew Carnegie had given away about $350 million, about 90% of his immense fortune.

The Communications Industry Sounds Off

Introduction

Internet, cell phones, Twitter, Facebook. These are the means of communications of the 21st century—instantaneous! People can send and receive electronic messages from around the globe in mere seconds. Amazingly, only a century and a half ago, the fastest and most reliable means of communication involved riders on horseback!

The Pony Express

On April 3, 1860, in St. Joseph, Missouri, a young man named Johnny Fry leaped astride his horse and galloped off on the first leg of an arduous 1,966-mile journey! Johnny was the first **Pony Express** rider to ride westward. A little later that day, in Sacramento, California, another young man named James Randall became the first eastbound rider for the Pony Express. The Pony Express was the brainchild of **William Russell**, a businessman who owned a stagecoach company. Russell hoped to provide a mail delivery service between St. Joseph and Sacramento in ten days or less. Each ounce of mail cost $10.00.

The average Express rider was in his teens and weighed no more than 120 pounds. Riders were strong, wiry fellows, willing to risk riding through dangerous territory for $100 per month. In the nineteen months the Pony Express operated, over 180 pony riders were hired. About 160 mail stations ran along the route where station keepers tended the horses. Each horse was ridden between 10 and 15 miles, depending on the difficulty of the "road," that is, uphill or downhill, rocky or smooth. A rider averaged 75 miles as his part of the route, so each rider switched horses about five or six times.

The riders carried the mail in a **mochila**, a leather blanket that fitted over the saddle. Mochilas had four pouches. One pouch held "local mail," for which station keepers had a key. The other three pouches were

In this painting the Pony Express rider prepares to defend himself.

opened at the end of the route. Each rider had a "home station," where he stayed between rides. The riders carried a rifle and a pair of pistols, which testify to the danger they could expect along the way.

The last ride occurred on October 26, 1861. On that day, a telegraph line connecting East and West was completed, thus ending the days of the Pony Express. However, the nineteen months of the Pony Express symbolize the ingenuity, courage, and determination so common to Americans of that era.

The Telegraph

Developments in railroads and steamships made it possible for travelers to reach their destinations more quickly, safely, and comfortably. Advances in communication made it possible to transmit messages faster and more reliably. A new era in communications began when Samuel Morse invented the **telegraph**. Samuel Morse's telegraph sent steady electrical current through special wires between two terminals. Then he interrupted the current for short or long intervals that he called dots and dashes. Various combinations of these dots and dashes spelled out words. For example: three dots, followed by 3 dashes, followed by 3 dots (… --- …) spells SOS. In 1844, after years of experimenting, Samuel Morse sent the first historic message by telegraph wire from Washington, D. C. to Baltimore. The message read, "What hath God wrought?"

Foolish people ridiculed the telegraph; wiser people saw the merit of rapid communication. Entrepreneurs soon strung telegraph lines and established communication centers across the country. 1862 saw telegraph communications reach California. By 1866, the **Western Union Telegraph Company** operated a national telegraph network. The telegraph became a vital link in American communication. Newspapers printed news from distant parts of the country almost as soon as it occurred. Railroads found the telegraph useful in reporting train movements, establishing schedules, and improving safety. Businesses could plan the delivery of products and better prepare inventory. Managers could determine the price of products throughout the nation. The telegraph improved commerce, health and safety, as well as personal life.

Samuel Morse, *Self-Portrait* (1812). Morse was originally and primarily an artist. Around 1832 he became fascinated with the idea of sending messages over electrical wire. Despite not possessing a scientific background, Morse created a revolutionary machine that sent coded messages by opening and closing an electrical circuit, the telegraph.

The Transatlantic Cable

Many people began to wonder if a communications cable could be laid across the Atlantic Ocean. Any sort of cable would need to be protected in some sort of waterproof material before it could be laid on the bottom of the ocean. Mark Twain is credited with saying that because a person did not know that something was impossible, he went ahead and did it. **Cyrus W. Field** was such a person. He was the New York businessman mainly responsible for installing the first transatlantic cable, partly because the United States and England provided ships to Cyrus Field.

Due to the tremendous distance and depth of the ocean, laying the transatlantic cable proved to be a massive undertaking. After several unsuccessful attempts, the two ships carrying portions of the cable met in mid-ocean. Engineers spliced the ends of the cable together, then one ship sailed for Ireland while the other set sail for Newfoundland. Each ship carried huge spools of cable on their sterns. As the vessels sailed away from each other, the cable played out and sank to the bottom of the ocean. Once the ships reached their destinations, they had succeeded in laying the transoceanic cable from Ireland to Newfoundland. Another, shorter cable then connected Newfoundland with the mainland of North America.

On August 16, 1858, England's Queen Victoria used the cable to send a congratulatory telegram to President James Buchanan. Unfortunately, three weeks later, the cable, which had shown signs of deterioration during its installation, was destroyed when someone applied too much voltage while trying to send out a series of messages. Undaunted, Cyrus Field continued his efforts. However, the outbreak of the Civil War diminished American interest in laying cable. Only after the War ended in 1866, was Field successfully able to lay a stronger cable capable of handling the quantity of telegraph traffic between England and the United States. In the following years, engineers laid more such cables, which effectively provided the United States with communications all over the world.

Cyrus Field in 1863. He holds cable in one hand and plans in the other. He dared to dream a great dream and then made it come true.

The Telephone

Alexander Graham Bell provided the next step forward in the communications revolution when he invented the telephone. Even as a teenager in Scotland, Bell had an interest in the sciences, especially those dealing with sound and electricity. When he was about twelve, his mother began to lose her hearing. His mother's deafness profoundly affected young Bell, and he began his life-long study of elocution and acoustics, the science of sound. Moreover, Bell, having developed certain techniques to communicate with his mother, began a career teaching other deaf people. In October 1872, Bell moved to Boston, where he began teaching the deaf and became a professor at Boston University. Meanwhile, he continued his experiments with sound.

By late 1873, the demands of his teaching and his private tutoring were consuming almost all of Bell's time. He had no time to work on his sound experiments. Therefore, he made a decision which changed not only his life, but that of the future of mankind. Bell determined to devote most of his time to his sound experiments. With financial assistance

Alexander Graham Bell

from the parents of his two remaining students, Bell hired **Thomas Watson** as his assistant. Although the investors held little hope of getting their money back, they were grateful to Bell for the work he had done to help their children. Bell and Watson began working on a device that would turn sound waves into an electric current, which would pass through a wire and then change back into sound waves at the end of a receiver—the telephone. On March 7, 1876, the U.S. Patent Office granted Alexander Graham Bell a patent for the first telephone. History records that Bell spoke the first words into the phone when he said, "Mr. Watson, come here, I want to see you." Watson, in the next room, heard the words clearly.

Bell offered to sell the telephone to *Western Union*, but the president of the company, failing to see its incredible value, turned him down. In 1876, Bell demonstrated the telephone publicly at the Centennial Exposition in Philadelphia. The public was enthralled and the telephone became an overnight success. In 1877, Bell established the **American Bell Telephone Company**, which later took the name AT&T. Before long, telephone lines and telephone poles crisscrossed the nation. Women soon comprised the majority of the workforce who operated the switchboards to connect calls. They soon affectionately became known as "hello girls."

On July 11, 1877, only a few days after Bell established his telephone company, he married Mabel Hubbard, one of the two students he continued teaching and whose father had invested in Bell's company. As a wedding present, he gave Mabel all but ten of his shares in the new company. Bell continued to invent the rest of his life, even developing an early airplane. Alexander Graham Bell was 75 when he died on August 2, 1922.

Thomas Alva Edison: History's Greatest Inventor

In all of history, probably no individual (with perhaps the exception of Steve Jobs, the founder of Apple) has had such a lasting and widespread influence on technology that has changed and enhanced the quality of human life as **Thomas Alva Edison**. During his life, the U.S. Patent Office granted him more than 1,000 patents! Yet it is not simply the number of Edison's patents but the incredible impact that they have had on the world. His electric light, phonograph, motion picture machine, and microphone all created new industries. Even today, more than 80 years after his death, Edison's inventions continue to affect billions of people around the world… almost entirely for the better.

Thomas Edison was born on February 11, 1847, in Milan, Ohio. In 1854, the family moved to Port Huron, Michigan, where Edison attended public school for three months. As he was hyperactive and prone to distraction, his teacher classified him as "difficult" (or ADD in today's terminology). His mother, herself a teacher, decided to homeschool him. At age 11, Thomas Edison showed an exceedingly inquisitive mind and a voracious appetite for knowledge, which he nourished by reading books on a wide range of subjects. He learned how to adjust his knowledge absorption level to the difficulty level of the material that he was studying. Using this method, Edison developed a process for self-education and independent study, which included experimentation, that served him throughout his life.

At twelve, Thomas Edison developed an interest in chemistry and gathered items for his experiments. To earn enough money for laboratory materials, he sold candy and newspapers on the local trains that ran from Port Huron. Three years later, he took a job as a telegraph operator to earn additional money for books and laboratory materials. In fact, some of his first inventions dealt with telegraphy.

By age twenty-two, Thomas Edison had become a professional inventor. On June 1, 1869, the Patent Office granted him his first patent, which was for the **electric vote recorder**. In 1872, Western Union hired Edison to improve their telegraph system. Through a clever use of electricity, Edison developed his first major invention, **quadruplex telegraph**, which could send four messages over one wire simultaneously. Western Union became much more efficient and profitable. In 1876, Edison established a research and development laboratory in **Menlo Park**, New Jersey using the money he made from the sale of his quadruplex telegraph.

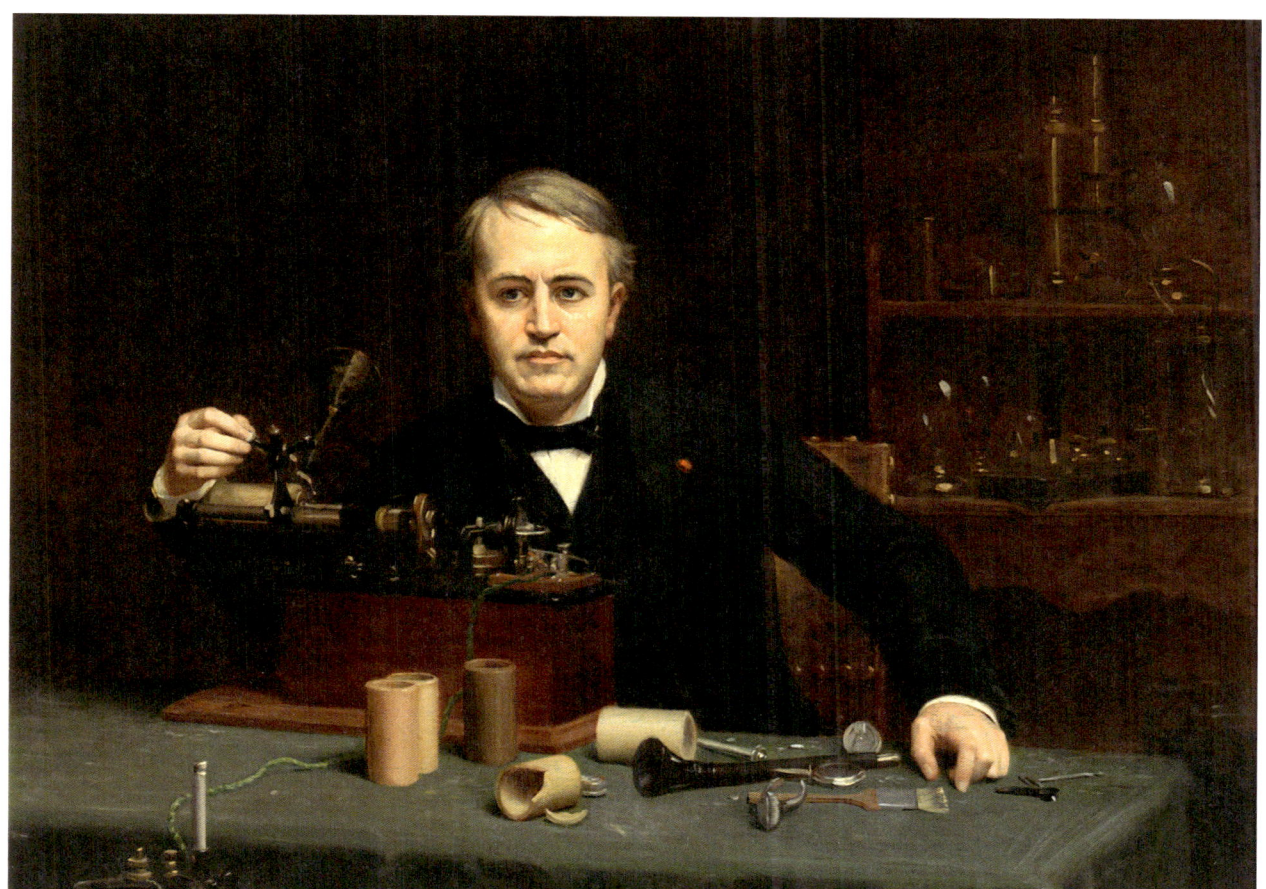

Thomas Edison. Painted in 1890 during Edison's visit to Paris for the Universal Exposition, the portrait depicts him at the height of his career. Visitors to the Exposition were especially interested in Edison's phonograph, the recent improvement of which is shown in the painting.

In his Menlo Park lab, Edison would discover the inventions that would change the world and earn him the nickname, the **"Wizard of Menlo Park."**

In 1877, Edison created the first in a line of historic inventions: the phonograph. He followed this with his most ground-breaking invention, the electric light bulb. In 1878, electric lighting was not new. Many cities used arc lights for outdoor lighting. While arc lights burned very brightly, they possessed numerous issues. For example, they produced a loud annoying buzzing sound; the heat created serious fire hazards; and – most seriously - they emitted carbon monoxide. As a result, they could literally be fatal if used indoors. An alternative light needed to be used indoors. Edison had the notion that an electric current could be run through a fine wire inside a vacuum inside a glass globe. The electricity would cause the wire to burn very hot and very brightly, but because *there was no oxygen inside the glass globe*, the wire would not catch fire. The wire would only become hot and bright!

For Edison, the problem involved finding a type of metallic wire that would burn for a prolonged period. Other inventors had tried to solve this problem but had failed to create an *inexpensive* light that *lasted a long time* and *did not use a tremendous amount of electricity*. For two years, Edison sought the right metal, or combination of metals, that would solve these three problems. Finally, he created a light bulb that used a carbon filament. It burned for 1,200 hours! On New Year's Eve 1879, he demonstrated his new light bulb to the world. Of his new bulb he said, "We will make electricity so cheap that only the rich will burn candles." Over the next years he created power companies around the country and sold millions and millions of light bulbs.

Other electric companies also formed. In 1885, George Westinghouse formed Westinghouse Electric and engaged in the so-called *War of the Currents* with Edison. The two men "fought" over whether Westinghouse's alternating current model for lighting homes or Edison's direct current model was safer and more efficient. Ultimately, Westinghouse, with his alternating current proved victorious. Alternating current could travel over longer distances and retain its higher voltage.

In 1860, the electrical industry, that is, the selling and creation of electrical power and the equipment which used electricity had not existed. In a few decades, men like Thomas Edison and George Westinghouse had created a massive industry that employed thousands of workers and changed the face of the nation. Thousands of electrical power stations were built between 1882 and 1900, yet they still powered only a small fraction

George Westinghouse in 1906

of America's manufacturing plants. Millions and millions of incandescent light bulbs were sold.

Edison would also go on to invent the **motion picture camera** and establish a motion picture studio. Between 1894 to 1918, his studio would create over 1,000 films. These were mostly black and white films lasting less than fifteen minutes. In 2016, the motion picture industry generated about *$40 billion* worldwide.

Thomas Edison continued working almost until the day of his death on October 18, 1931.

The Oil Industry Gushes Forth

Before 1860, most people considered oil to be a nuisance. It was a dark, thick ooze that ruined farmland, seeped into wells, and got all over animals and people. No one had done much good with it. In the 1850s, **Samuel Kier**, an entrepreneur in Western Pennsylvania, began collecting the oil that had seeped to ground level. The thick goop was interfering with his salt mine. Apparently, Kier dumped barrels of the collected oil into a nearby canal which caught fire one day when a worker threw away a lit match. Suddenly, Kier realized that the "goop" might be worth something!

At first, Kier just burned the **crude oil** to light the lamps at his salt mine. However, the burning oil produced thick, smelly, black smoke. He realized that the oil might have value if he could **refine** it, that is, remove the impurities from it. He refined the crude oil into kerosene which burned much cleaner. In time, **kerosene** replaced whale oil in lamps because it was less expensive and provided better light. Before long, the demand for kerosene rose. In 1853, Samuel Kier established America's first oil refinery in Pittsburg and earned the title, "The Father of the American Petroleum Industry."

In one of the most unselfish acts in history, Samuel Kier, who had invented the oil refining process, never patented his ideas. He believed that no single person should own such an important innovation because of the great good that it could do for society. As a result, other men freely utilized his ideas and processes. For this reason, most people, sadly, have never heard of Samuel Kier.

Kier's discovery that oil was a valuable commodity caused a demand for more. In 1859, **Edwin Drake** drilled the first successful oil well in Titusville, Pennsylvania. Many people thought he was crazy and called his well "Drake's Folly," mostly because he seemed to be drilling into a dry hole. However, Drake persevered. First, he developed a method for drilling that involved attaching pipes to each other to extend the drill. He attached ten-foot sections of iron pipe to each other so that he could drill his well deeper and deeper. At seventy feet, Drake struck oil. His crew collected the oil in a bathtub! The well proved viable and began to produce about 25 barrels of crude oil per day.

When others heard of Drake's "strike," prospectors rushed to Pennsylvania. By 1860, **"wildcatters"** (oil prospectors) were drilling wells all over western Pennsylvania. The "Black Gold" of Pennsylvania's oil fields made many men oil tycoons. Within two years, the region was producing about 16,000 barrels of oil per day!

Initially, the oil tycoons shipped their product in barrels carried by horse-drawn wagons. This proved slow and inefficient. The oil companies next built special railroad tanker cars to ship the oil. The tanker cars were better than the wagon barrels, but still unsafe and inefficient. In the 1870s, the oil tycoons began constructing pipelines from their wells to their refineries. Pipelines, most buried underground, proved to be the most safe and efficient means to transport oil. Pipeline construction proceeded relatively slowly until the end of the century. However, in the 1890s, automobile inventors realized that oil could be refined into gasoline and used as a fuel source. With the advent of the automobile industry in the early 20th century the demand for oil skyrocketed. In 1911, for the first time, more gasoline was sold than kerosene. In 2020, the United States had 2.6 million miles of pipelines to satisfy America's daily consumption of 400 million gallons of gasoline.

Of all the oil tycoons, none achieved more wealth than **John D. Rockefeller**. In 1859, Rockefeller made a great deal of money in the food industry in Cleveland, Ohio. However, he quickly realized that the real fortunes in America would be made in the oil industry, not in the drilling of oil,

Edwin Drake, in top hat, stands in front of one of his wells.

John D. Rockefeller in 1914

but in its refining. Therefore, in 1863 he and his partners built their first oil refinery in Cleveland. In 1870, they formed the **Standard Oil Company**. At this point, he expanded into drilling and selling oil-based products. Remarkably, **by 1879, Rockefeller controlled 90% of all the oil production in the United States!**

John D. Rockefeller was a man of great personal contradictions. Although religious and philanthropic, he was also ruthless and unscrupulous. For example, he was a devout Baptist who read the Bible daily and donated hundreds of millions of dollars to churches, colleges, and medical research. Yet he forced railroads to give him special prices. He forced other refineries to sell to him or face bankruptcy. He conducted what today is known as "industrial espionage," by spying on his competitors.

Despite his ruthlessness, even his enemies agreed that John D. Rockefeller was an exceedingly good businessman. He hated waste so insisted that his refineries be incredibly well managed. One reason that he could undercut his competition was because he managed his business better than they did. Another reason was his ability to obtain special prices from the railroads which undercut his competition. Finally, Rockefeller ultimately gained control of every aspect of the oil business from the drilling, to the refining, to the distribution. Moreover, he did achieve his goal of combining all the oil refineries into one company.

Rockefeller was determined to monopolize the oil industry. In 1870, Cleveland had twenty-five oil companies. During the next two years, Standard Oil purchased twenty of them. To establish an oil monopoly, Rockefeller created a **trust**, that is, an entity in which all the stockholders of all the separate companies give control of their stock to a board of directors called "trustees." The federal government did not like the notion that so few men could hold such a vast amount of power in the nation. The government would not sit quietly by as one man took control of almost all of the nation's oil. The time had come to regulate big business.

Regulating Big Business

Men like Rockefeller and Carnegie had created incredible new industries as well as tens of thousands – perhaps hundreds of thousands - of new jobs. They had managed their companies efficiently and contributed to the nation's overall economic growth. However, they possessed enormous power to impact the nation and the economy. For example, huge corporations were so efficient that they produced goods at very low costs by producing in large quantities and reducing waste. This gave buyers the benefit of better prices and manufacturers higher profits. Unfortunately, it forced many small businesses to close since they could not compete with these giants. This still is true today. In thousands of towns across America, family businesses are being forced to close when a national chain store opens in the community. Such power in the hands of a few, concerned many, especially people in government. The government began to consider ways in which the power of big business, despite the good it might be doing for the economy, would be controlled.

Large corporations can control the economy in various ways. The first method is **collusion**. Collusion occurs when two or more corporations in the same business agree to control their production and divide the available markets. For example, railway officials in a specific area agree on the percentage of the business they will each control. Then they agree to set prices on freight and passengers at the same rates. Secondly, big businesses can control markets by **mergers**. Mergers happen when the strongest corporation in an area buys all of its competitors. Vanderbilt and Gould used this method to build their railroad empires. They merged many companies into one. Thomas Edison merged his electric company with several others to form General Electric. Thirdly, businesses create **trusts**, the method John D. Rockefeller used to establish the Standard Oil Company. Unlike collusions and mergers, trusts can control an entire industry and completely eliminate competition.

As American business headed toward the 1890s, businessmen saw how successfully Rockefeller's Standard Oil Trust operated. They naturally wanted to emulate his model. As a result, American businessmen organized trusts that encompassed a wide variety of products, ranging from shipbuilding to whiskey production. Of course, this alarmed the nation's small business owners, who could not compete with the powerful trusts. "The trusts are destroying the free enterprise system," many small merchants asserted. Many consumers also feared the trusts. Although prices might be low now, what happened once all competition had been abolished? The trust could increase prices and customers would have to pay, having no other place to purchase their goods. As trusts became more powerful and more prevalent, demand for government regulation increased.

Americans feared that trusts held too much power and were becoming **monopolies**, that is, one company with total control of an industry. In the case of Standard Oil, which controlled over 90% of the nation's oil, this belief was accurate. The first industry to face government regulation was the railroads.

The Interstate Commerce Act

Since the construction and equipment needed to run a railroad was so expensive, usually only a single railroad company serviced many parts of the Western United States. In the 1870s, western farmers, who had no alternative means of shipping their products to market, began to complain that the rates the railroads were charging were too high and thus unfair. The farmers urged the federal government to pass laws regulating the railroads.

In response to the farmers' request, in 1887, Congress passed the **Interstate Commerce Act**. The Act required that all rail charges had to be "just and reasonable." Second, it prohibited collusions, special rates, and rebates for select customers. Third, the railroads had to charge all customers the same rates for similar distances and similar types of freight. Fourth, all shipping rates were to be made public. Finally, railroads were required, upon request, to submit their schedules, shipping documents, and accounting ledgers for government inspection. To ensure enforcement of the Interstate Commerce Act, Congress created the **Interstate Commerce Commission**, a regulatory agency.

Enacted exactly one hundred years after the framing of the Constitution, the Interstate Commerce Act was the federal government's first step toward regulating business. Prior to this, a state government would have enacted this type of regulation, if the state felt it needed to act. However, most railroads operated across many state borders. No single state could possibly have dealt with the problem. The Constitution grants the federal government the authority to regulate interstate commerce. However, as with any government regulation, *it should be limited to burden Americans and restrict freedom as little as possible*. The Interstate Commerce Act, although necessary, immediately began to show why such regulations can cause as many problems as they seek to remedy.

The Interstate Commerce Act required that all charges be "just and reasonable." However, what did that mean? That phrase is so vague that the law itself is probably unconstitutional. Yet the Interstate Commerce Commission had to enforce it. Problems always arise when the government tries to tell businesses what to charge for something. Government often has little or no knowledge what something costs, and thus no idea of what is "just and reasonable." The other parts of the Act are more specific, that is, charging the same amount for the same products to everyone; not giving rebates; publishing rates so everyone knows ahead of time what they will pay.

In passing the Interstate Commerce Act, Congress basically sought to ensure that the railroads did not cheat the American people. However, in a sense, the Act was too specific, aimed as it was at just the railroads. In the late 1880s, dozens of trusts existed—e.g. oil trust, tobacco trust, sugar trust—which operated as monopolies. It seemed the only way to stop these trusts from controlling prices was to break them up and make the individual companies compete with each other. After years of complaints from the public and failed attempts by the states to prohibit trusts, Congress finally began enacting **anti-trust legislation**.

The Sherman Anti-Trust Act

In 1890, Congress passed the **Sherman Antitrust Act**. Aimed at destroying monopolies and trusts, the Act declared that anyone who "shall monopolize or attempt to monopolize" commerce could be fined or even jailed. Moreover, it declared any "contract, combination, or conspiracy" that restrained trade was illegal. Unfortunately, like the Interstate Commerce Act, the Sherman Anti-Trust Act failed to specifically define important terms such as "monopoly" or "restraint of trade." The trusts found loopholes in the law and when the government took the trusts to court, the courts sided with big business.

In one of the most important cases dealing with the Sherman Act, the federal government charged the E.C. Knight Company with being a trust in violation of the Act. Everyone agreed that E. C. Knight controlled *over 98%* of the sugar-refining in the United States! In 1895, the U.S. Supreme Court decided the case (*U.S. v. E. C. Knight* (1895). The court wrote that because E. C. Knight refined their sugar in just one state, they had not engaged in "interstate commerce." The Court decided the case along a very narrow line. They said that the Sherman Anti-Trust Act was constitutional, but that *it did not apply to manufacturing*. The Court said that manufacturing was not commerce. Thus, even though E.C. Knight had a sugar monopoly, the Court found no violation of the Anti-Trust Act because refining only involved *intrastate* commerce. The trust did not lead to

In 2012, Chief Justice John Roberts wrote the Supreme Court opinion which declared that Congress had the authority under its taxing power to compel Americans to purchase insurance.

control of interstate commerce which was only affected "incidentally and indirectly." Thus, while the Court did not declare the Act unconstitutional, it stripped it of any real meaning and power.

As a result of its ambiguous language, the loopholes it created, and the Knight case, the Sherman Act had little effect on the trusts. However, the federal government had given notice to business: government would regulate business. Although the Interstate Commerce Act and the Sherman Anti-Trust Act proved both feeble and clumsy attempts, Big Business would soon feel the pressure from Big Government. Before long, the federal government would consider virtually every piece of commerce and trade, no matter how small, to be part of "interstate commerce." In the 21st century, the federal government would go so far as to claim that the *failure* to buy a product, i.e. insurance, affected interstate commerce.

Most Americans favored some regulation of big business in the 1890s because they felt that monopolies and trusts were perversions of the *free enterprise system*, the economic system upon which America had been built and thrived. Under the free enterprise system, businesses compete with each other to sell products and/ or goods to the public. Competition results in better products at lower prices which benefits the purchaser. The individual purchaser can decide which product to purchase based on the factors most important to them. Perhaps a less expensive product is more important than a costlier, but sturdier version. Competition also leads to innovation. Cell phones, personal computers, in fact, nearly all the technology of the past twenty years, demonstrate the value of the free enterprise system. On the other hand, a monopoly forces a customer to purchase from one company and often discourages innovation. Americans tended to oppose government regulation because it increased prices and diminished the value of a product often without benefit to the customer.

Changes in Southern Agriculture and Industry

The emancipation of the slaves dramatically changed farming practices in the South. Virtually all former slaves had worked on farms or plantations. Farming was the only work that they knew. After the War, most continued on farms although many traveled westward and others sought employment in the cities. While some freed slaves remained with their former owners, many did not want to work for someone who had once owned them. In the years immediately following the Civil War, the former slaves worked for cash. However, the taxes that the government levied during the Reconstruction period proved too high for impoverished white planters to pay. Many farmers lost their land. Others paid the tax, but did not have enough funds to hire either white laborers or freed slaves. Fields lay fallow. A new system had to be devised. The new system was **share-cropping**.

As the name implies, share-cropping simply means that the crop is shared between the worker and the landowner. The land owner would provide the worker with tools, seeds, and fertilizer to grow the crops. The worker provided the skill and labor necessary to grow and harvest the crop. The worker was incentivized to produce the largest harvest possible both to reimburse the land owner and to provide a better life for his family. However, many people point out that under this system, most sharecroppers were bound to the land with little hope of ever being more than sharecroppers. High interest rates, bad harvest, and dishonest landowners often kept sharecroppers in debt nearly all their lives. Many laws forced the sharecropper to sell only to the landowner or to try to relocate if they owed the landowner money. Although sharecropping is usually associated with freed blacks, *approximately two-thirds of all sharecroppers were poor white families.* Sharecropping would be practiced in the United States until the 1940s.

As unfair as some of the elements of sharecropping sound to many modern Americans, it did provide poor black and white families with the opportunity for a chance at a decent life. The family had their own plot of land to cultivate and they had a small house. Most importantly, for many poor families, they had hope that if they worked hard and saved, they could buy their own plot of land and their own house. They could participate in the American Dream. Share-cropping caused many plantations to be broken up into small farms that ultimately were sold to black farmers, which is how many small farms came into existence throughout the South.

Sadly, in the post-war South, many whites treated black sharecroppers unfairly. As a result, black farmers struggled to purchase their own farms. Also, prices in the South after the war were very high. Storekeepers charged more for products because they were hard to get in the South. These prices affected whites as well as blacks. Prejudice and financial pressures meant that most blacks lacked the resources to buy their own farms.

Crop-sharing and the growth of small farms were not the only changes in Southern agriculture during the latter half of the 19th century. Southern farmers realized the inefficiency of the one-crop system of farming. Consequently, they began diversified farming. Cotton, tobacco, rice, and indigo remained the main crops, but Southerners also began to raise oranges, peaches, grapefruit, and a variety of fruits and vegetables. Improvements in rail transportation and the introduction of refrigerated train cars made fruit and vegetable production profitable. Thus, the agricultural system of the South gradually changed.

After the Civil War, the South began to industrialize. Southerners left the farms for the big cities where they devoted their efforts to industry and commerce. In addition to the burgeoning textile industries, Southerners tapped the regions' rich natural resources. Miners developed coal and iron mines. In 1901, wildcatters discovered oil in Texas and Louisiana. That discovery spawned an industry that became widespread over the next hundred years. Exploration and development of vast oil fields in Texas, Louisiana, Kansas, and Oklahoma provided tens of thousands of jobs. Lumberjacks commercialized the extensive forests in the South and lumbering became a significant industry in those areas.

Blacks in Business and Education

The emancipation of the slaves and the passage of the Civil Rights Amendments allowed black men and women to achieve successes they never imagined possible. Two of the more important black leaders of the latter half of the 19th century were **Booker T. Washington** and **George Washington Carver**. Though both men were born into slavery, they achieved remarkable accomplishments. In the words of Booker T. Washington: *"Success is to be measured not so much by the position that one has reached in life as by the obstacles which he has overcome."*

Booker T. Washington

Booker T. Washington was born to a slave woman named Jane about 1856, on a farm in western Virginia. Of his father, he knew nothing. In his autobiography, *Up From Slavery*, he recalls the joy the slaves felt on the day that they were emancipated: "As the great day drew nearer, there was more singing in the slave quarters than usual. It was bolder, had more ring, and lasted later into the night." After emancipation, Jane took Booker to West Virginia and joined her husband Washington Ferguson, who had earlier escaped slavery. In West Virginia, the illiterate nine-year-old boy began to teach himself to read. He also adopted his stepfather's name, as well as the middle name his mother had given him at birth, "Taliaferro," although he almost never used it, being called Booker T. Washington from that moment forward.

Booker T. Washington

Washington went on to attend **Hampton Institute**, one of the earliest schools for freed blacks. Hampton was devoted to providing an industrial education. Washington would use Hampton as the model upon which he based his own **Tuskegee Institute**. On July 4, 1881, Washington became the first director of the Tuskegee Institute, a trade school for blacks in Alabama.

Washington's experiences had convinced him that black people could succeed if they worked hard and accepted the prejudices of powerful people, that is, white people. He had seen first-hand what happened to black people, especially in the South, who fought against white prejudice. Blacks who fought violently against prejudice were often **lynched**, that is, hanged by a mob. He worked with whites, especially Northern whites, who donated money to the Tuskegee Institute, which prospered. By 1890, Washington had become the acknowledged leader of America's black community.

In 1895, Washington delivered a talk that became known as the "**Atlanta Compromise**," in which he advocated **racial accommodation**. Although privately he wished for equality, he publicly told blacks to accept the notion of the "separate but equal doctrine," but to learn a skilled trade that would improve their lives. Through work and education rather than the political process, blacks would improve their situation. He told his audience it was "folly" for blacks to expect whites to truly treat them equally. In turn, Washington asked that whites treat blacks fairly.

Today, many African-Americans feel Booker T. Washington too easily accepted the policies of segregation. After his death, most black leaders abandoned his positions. Even during his life, his opponents, most notably W. E. B. DuBois, a history professor at Atlanta University, created the **National Association** for the **Advancement of Colored People** (NAACP) to work for political change. DuBois favored a more aggressive political approach, preferring "agitation" over "accommodation." However, Washington was a *pragmatist* who sought to maintain the gains that blacks had made in the decades immediately after the Civil War. Moreover, Washington's views on economic self-reliance should inspire not only blacks but also whites. As he once said, "There is as much dignity in tilling a field as there is in writing a poem."

George Washington Carver

Perhaps the greatest success of the Tuskegee Institute was **George Washington Carver**, a brilliant botanist and inventor who earned worldwide fame. Born into slavery in the early 1860s in Missouri, he was owned by a family named Carver. After the abolishment of slavery, the Carvers raised George as one of their own children.

In spite of many hardships resulting from poverty and racial discrimination, Carver worked his way through school and graduated from Iowa State Agricultural College with a degree in botany and a brilliant academic record. Carver remained at Iowa State to obtain his master's degree as well as conduct ground-breaking agricultural research. He eventually became the first black professor at Iowa State.

In 1896, Booker T. Washington invited Carver to head Tuskegee Institute's Agriculture Department. Carver taught at Tuskegee for the next 47 years, developing the department into a strong center for

George Washington Carver

agricultural research. George Washington Carver gave lectures before humble farmers as well as influential congressional committees in an effort to improve Southern farming. Through his efforts, the people of the South learned to grow a variety of crops that helped replenish the nutrients in the soil, so that various crops could be alternated and a crop could be produced each year. These included vegetables, peanuts, and sweet potatoes. Amazingly, George Washington Carver developed over two hundred products from the little peanut. Peanut products included instant "coffee," soap, and ink. Sweet potatoes were used to make shoestrings, flour, candy, and dozens of other useful products.

George Washington Carver died on January 5, 1943. He is buried next to Booker T. Washington at Tuskegee University. Carver's tombstone reads: *"He could have added fortune to fame, but caring for neither, he found happiness and honor in being helpful to the world."*

The Birth of Organized Labor

The success of big business depended on two elements. The first was money or **capital**. Business needed capital to purchase equipment like railroad cars, steel, or machines for digging coal or drilling oil. Business also needed **labor**, that is, people to run the machines. As more and more machines did more and more work, more and more people were needed to run them. In fact, as the type of machines became more **specialized**, workers needed to learn specific jobs.

As businesses grew larger, the number of workers increased. Some manufacturing plants had thousands of people working in them. To function efficiently, these plants had to be run like armies. Plants had managers, who had assistants who supervised various departments, which had groups of workers. As national employment grew, individual workers came to believe that they had become little more than tiny cogs in gigantic industrial wheels. Sadly, many employers treated their employees less like people and more like machines. Of course, the employees resented this. They began to seek a way to have a larger influence over their own livelihoods and working conditions.

Because one person would have little power against a large corporation, workers had to band together, in a sense, become a large corporation themselves, in order to have any influence. After the Civil War, workers, especially skilled workers, began uniting in unions. In 1869, a group of tailors, led by Uriah Stephens, founded the **Knights of Labor** in Philadelphia. At first, the Knights of Labor were a secret society, but they quickly realized the importance of a large and varied membership. In 1879, Uriah Stephens resigned and **Terence Powderly** became head of the Knights. He opened membership to blacks, women, and unskilled workers.

Under Powderly, the Knights pressed for an eight-hour work day, the regulation of trusts, and the exclusion of Chinese immigrants who Powderly believed would take American jobs and reduce wages. Powderly, who was Catholic, also worked with Bishop James Gibbons to allow Catholics to join the Knights. In 1879, when Powderly became leader of the Knights,

Terence Powderly in 1915. At the time the photograph was taken, Powderly was working as Chief of the Division of Information in the Bureau of Immigration.

they numbered about 9,000 members. By 1885, they had more than 700,000 members, due mostly to the Knights' ability to win concessions from the railroads as a result of **strikes**, that is, work stoppages. It seemed that the Knights would be America's strongest and most important union as the nation entered the new century. However, in May 1886, a terrible incident known as the **Chicago Haymarket Affair** effectively ended the Knights.

On May 4, 1886, workers gathered in Chicago's Haymarket Square for a rally to support the eight-hour work day. When police entered Haymarket Square to disperse the crowd, someone threw a bomb at the officers. The explosion and the ensuing gunfire killed seven police officers and four civilians. Dozens of other people were wounded. Although no evidence indicated that the Knights were responsible, public opinion turned strongly against the union. Over the next few years, hundreds of thousands of members left the Knights. By 1890, the Knights numbered fewer than 100,000 members. Although the Knights of Labor continued until 1949, it had lost its power as a labor union. A new organization was poised to become the leader in the American labor movement.

The American Federation of Labor

Labor unions fall into two categories: craft unions and industrial unions. Craft unions consist of skilled workers in a specific trade, e.g. carpenters, masons, or musicians. Industrial unions accept all the workers in a particular industry, whatever their trade within that industry. For example, an industrial mining union would have members who work in mines extracting metals and minerals; plus, workers who work in smelters and mills; as well as workers engaged in processing and distributing these materials.

In December 1886, craft union leaders, unhappy with the Knights of Labor, met in Columbus, Ohio. Under the leadership of **Samuel Gompers**, the head of the cigar-makers union, these men formed the **American Federation of Labor (AFL)**. Gompers would serve as the AFL's president, except for one year, until his death in 1924.

Unlike the Knights of Labor, the AFL restricted its membership to skilled workers. Gompers believed that this would allow the individual unions to negotiate better on behalf of their members. Because membership was restricted to skilled workers, the AFL contained few blacks or women, since they tended not to work in the skilled-craft industries.

Gompers felt that AFL should focus on the core issues most important to its members like higher wages, improved working conditions, an eight-hour work day, and job security. Gompers believed that the way to obtain the union's goals was through **collective bargaining**, that is, the union would negotiate on behalf of all the workers. When the AFL bargained with owners, it could negotiate better salaries, more benefits, and improved working conditions. However, workers needed to be prepared to strike if bargaining failed. Yet Gompers never saw business as his enemy. Rather, he believed in capitalism and realized that it gave his members the best opportunity to succeed. By 1904, the AFL became America's leading union and claimed to have over 1.7 million members.

Jobs Attract Immigrants

America's second industrial revolution had turned America into a land of opportunities like no other. America had jobs, jobs, and more jobs. Men like Andrew Carnegie had come to America with almost nothing and become fabulously wealthy. It is no wonder, then, that about 14 million immigrants rushed to these shores between 1860 and 1900 – all seeking the American Dream! Most settled in the big cities, which grew even bigger.

Prior to 1880, America had experienced several "waves" of immigration. However, most of the migrants had come to America from either Great Britain, Ireland, or Germany. For example, in the mid-1840s and 1850s a wave consisting mainly of Irish and German Catholics had immigrated to the United States. Immigration stopped in the 1860s only as a result of the Civil War. Immigrants from England and Ireland spoke English, which gave them an advantage in the English-speaking United States. Germans tended to be well-educated and knew a trade which gave them an advantage over unskilled laborers. Most of these immigrants experienced some prejudice, as people in America feared that the newcomers would take their jobs. The Irish and Germans, being Catholics, experienced somewhat more prejudice than the others. While the Irish tended to remain in the East, Germans moved to the "German triangle," whose three points were Cincinnati, Milwaukee, and St. Louis. In general, most of these immigrants became part of the "melting pot" that formed late 19th-century America.

The Dedication of the Statue of Liberty by Edward Moran. For many immigrants arriving in America, the Statue of Liberty in New York harbor was their first glimpse of their new home. The Statue, a gift from France, remains a symbol of freedom and opportunity after more than 130 years.

Between 1870 and 1900, about eleven million people immigrated to the United States from Europe. Of these, about eight million came from northern and western Europe. However, in the late 1880s a new batch of immigrants began arriving in America. These families came from eastern and southern Europe. They did not speak English and had little education. They had no money and no skills. Most were Catholic, Russian Orthodox, or Jewish. In Europe, they had lived in rural areas quite different than the big cities in which they now found themselves. As a result, once in a big city like New York, they tended to live in ethnic neighborhoods, like "Little Italy." In these neighborhoods, they found people who believed and spoke like they did and ate the same food as they did. (**Note**: Even today these neighborhoods exist in New York City.)

The new wave of immigrants caused a resurgence in the Nativist movement. Nativists called Catholics from Poland or Hungary "mentally inferior," not because few people could understand their language, but because these immigrants would work for a very low wage. The Nativists began demanding immigrants pass a literacy test which they knew would keep most of these poor illiterate people out of the country. In 1897, Congress passed a law requiring immigrants to pass a literacy test. However, President Grover Cleveland vetoed the bill. The veto came as good news to many large employers, who continued to employ these hard-working eastern Europeans at very low wages.

No Chinese Need Apply

Sadly, perhaps because they were so culturally and ethnically different, the Chinese were the one immigrant group that Congress did legally exclude. By 1880, over 100,000 Chinese immigrants lived in the United States, many in California. However, unlike European immigrants, the Chinese made almost no effort to assimilate into American society. In 1882, Congress passed the **Chinese Exclusion Act** which prohibited Chinese laborers from entering the United States for ten years. The ban proved effective as the Chinese population in America declined by about 15% between 1880 and 1900. Congress finally repealed the Act in 1943 after the U.S. and China became allies during World War II. However, Congress did not lift the ban until 1965.

The Urban Explosion

In 1860, only one American city had a population in excess of one million people: New York City. The only other city with a population over 500,000 was Philadelphia. Yet over the next forty years, three cities topped one million in population: New York (3.4 million), Philadelphia (1.3 million), and Chicago (1.7 million), which had had just over 100,000 people in 1860. In 1900, Boston, St. Louis, and Baltimore each had over 500,000 people. San Francisco, the most populous western city, topped 300,000. New Orleans, the most populous Southern city, had just under 300,000. The South remained generally less

City	1860	1880	1900
New York City	1,174,800	1,912,000	3,437,000
Philadelphia	565,500	847,000	1,294,000
Boston	177,800	363,000	561,000
Baltimore	212,400	332,000	509,000
Cincinnati	161,000	255,000	326,000
St. Louis	160,800	350,000	575,000
Chicago	109,300	503,000	1,698,000

Chart showing the growth of America's largest cities

densely populated, but one other Southern city, Memphis, had a population over 100,000. By 1900, over fifty cities had populations with more than 100,000 people.

The growth of manufacturing had drawn people to America's cities, which had exploded with population. America in 1900 was no longer an agricultural nation; it was a nation of city-dwellers, factory workers, and businessmen. In forty years, America had undergone rapid change. The people of 1860 had lived much like their parents and grandparents. By 1900, Americans were beginning to live more like people of the 21st century.

America's Golden Age

America's second industrial revolution created a *golden* age for some but a *gilded* age for others. The nation saw rapid economic growth as old businesses flourished and new ones appeared as the result of technological advances. The increase in industrialization led to more, better-paying jobs for nearly everyone. At the same time, trusts and monopolies remained strong, often with the protection of corrupt politicians. This new industrial age brought prosperity to many. However, many still suffered. That suffering would again cause reformers to seek to improve America. They would use the federal government as their means. The 1890s would launch a period of social and political reform known as the Progressive Era.

CHAPTER 22 REVIEW QUESTIONS

Answer the following questions:

1. How did the creation of a network of railroads change the American economy?
2. What is a monopoly? Why are they problematic?
3. What is a trust? Why were some Americans concerned about trusts?
4. Name three improvements in rail travel other than expansion of service.
5. Name at least two men responsible for the creation of the national railroad network.
6. What is a corporation? Why were they formed in the 19th century?
7. What is the Bessemer Process?
8. Who invented the telegraph?
9. Who is known as the Wizard of Menlo Park? What are some of the things he invented?
10. Who started the Standard Oil Company?
11. How were the Interstate Commerce Act and the Sherman Anti-Trust Act supposed to regulate big business?
12. What is "share-cropping?" Why was it a good idea in the South after the Civil War?
13. What was the Chicago Haymarket Affair?
14. Why did some Americans oppose immigration in the last decades of the 19th century?
15. Who were the one ethnic group that Congress legally excluded from immigrating to the United States in the 1880s?
16. How did Nativists attempt to keep Catholics from Poland and Hungary from immigrating to America at the end of the 19th century?
17. How did the Interstate Commerce Act try to regulate the railroads?

Identify the following:

1. Booker T. Washington
2. George Washington Carver
3. Cornelius Vanderbilt
4. Samuel Kier
5. Andrew Carnegie
6. Samuel Gompers
7. Terence Powderly
8. John D. Rockefeller
9. Alexander Graham Bell
10. American Federation of Labor
11. Pony Express
12. Mesabi Range
13. Cyrus Field
14. W.E.B. DuBois

American Politics in "The Gilded Age"

1870-1896

Breezing Up or *A Fair Wind by Wind* by Winslow Homer. Painted in 1876, the 100th anniversary of America's independence, in many ways it symbolizes the optimism of the Gilded Age. The boys gaze into the limitless horizon, their futures and that of America yet to be written. In the bow, we see an anchor, the symbol of hope. As the boys sail forward, hope leads their way. The Gilded Age was one of enormous prosperity and opportunity. Homer has filled his painting with freedom, hope, and optimism, reflecting not gilt, but real gold.

Introduction

Historians often refer to the period from about 1870 to 1896 as a "Gilded Age" in American history. Mark Twain had coined the term to refer to the late 19th century. *Gilding* involves putting a thin layer of gold over a base metal like lead or iron. Thus, Twain meant that while events during the period might appear attractive on the surface, in reality they were corrupt underneath. Although Twain ranks among America's finest authors, perhaps his condemnation of the time period is a bit overstated.

While the United States had problems during these years, they were a time of economic growth and opportunities. Most Americans had better lives than they had before 1860. With the exception of the battles with Native Americans in the West, the nation was at peace. In fact, other than the four-months long Spanish-American War in 1898, the United States remained at peace from 1865 until 1917, the longest period of peace in American history. During this period, America also celebrated its 100th birthday. Thus, the period from the end of the Civil War to the beginning of America's involvement in

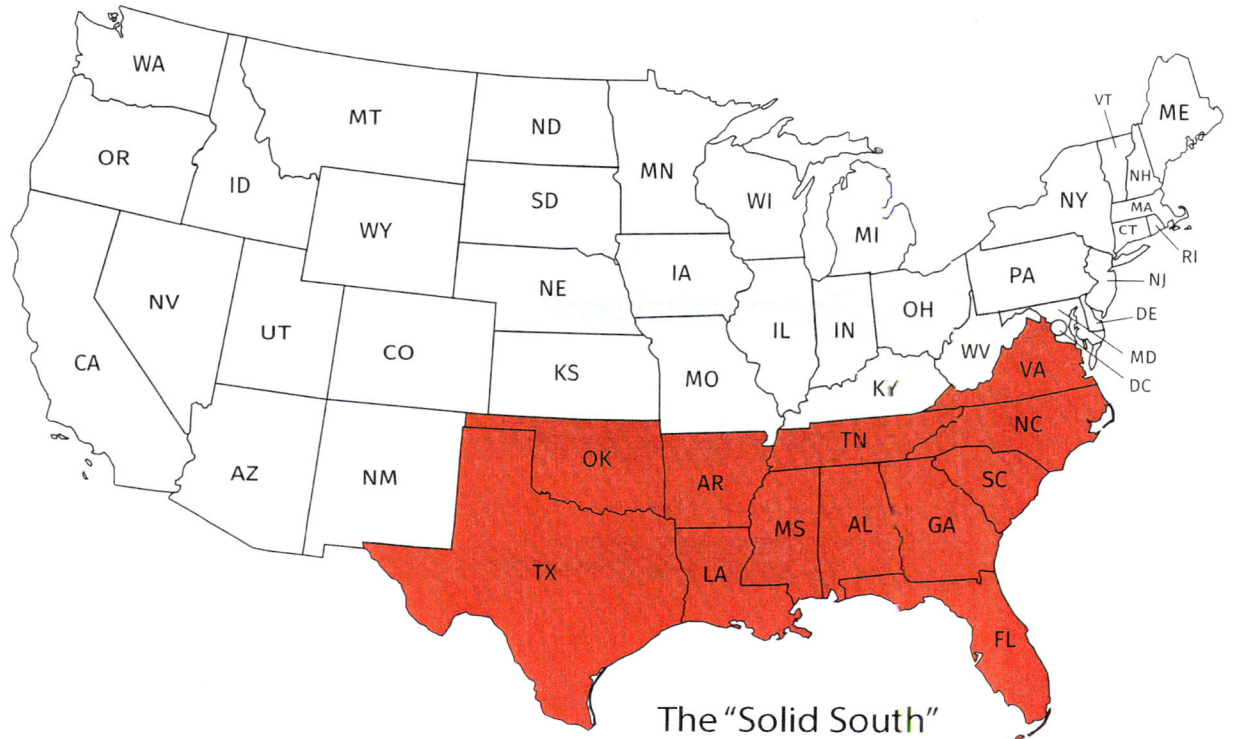

The "Solid South"

World War I might rightly be called America's "*Golden Age*." However, even a Golden Age has problems. During this period, the North and South were reunited—but they struggled to come together. Millions of nearly freed African Americans had a chance for unprecedented opportunities - that unfortunately went too often unrealized. A serious Depression struck the country and political corruption reached extraordinary levels. And a second president was assassinated.

The "Solid South" and the "Swing" States

Most Southerners had become Democrats in the years preceding the Civil War, because that had been the pro-slavery party. The way that the Republicans in the North had treated the South during Reconstruction had caused many hard feelings among Southerners. As a result, after the War and the end of Reconstruction, most white Southerners remained Democrats for political as well as personal reasons. From 1880 until 1928, every former Confederate state cast its electoral votes for the Democratic presidential candidate. Because Republicans had no chance to win elections in the South, the block of Southern states became known as the "**Solid South**," or in other words, solidly Democratic.

On the other hand, by 1860, in the North and the West, the Republican Party became dominant. This remained the case for nearly the next seventy years. In fact, the Republican Party held such national power that between 1860 and 1928, only two Democrats were elected president. Many people viewed the Republicans as the Party that had saved the Union and the Democrats as the Party that tried to destroy it. So long as the Civil War remained in the memories of voters, Republicans had an edge.

However, Republicans could never count on a "Solid North," or a "Solid West," like the Democrats could in the South. Republicans could generally rely on the West as well as New England for support;

however, New York and Connecticut, as well as the Midwestern states of Ohio, Indiana, and Illinois, would hold close elections. Because voters in these states did not always vote for the same party, they would later be called "**swing**" states, because their votes swung between the parties.

After the Civil War, the presidential candidate who won the majority of these "swing states" won the elections. The two parties understood that choosing candidates from these swing states improved their chances of winning the popular vote in these states. Between 1876 and 1920, of the 35 men the Democrats and Republicans nominated as either president or vice-president, 25 of them were from Ohio, Indiana, or New York. Every president elected between 1876 and 1908 came from either Ohio, Indiana, or New York. The two major parties did not even nominate a Southerner during those thirty-two years.

As political opinions hardened over the years, the swing states increased in importance. More and more, the presidential candidates spent the majority of their time campaigning in swing states. Of the three critical 19th-century swing states, today only Ohio remains in that category, as New York is reliably Democratic and Indiana reliably Republican. Since 1900, Ohio, a **bellwether state** (one that indicates trends), has voted for the winning president in every election but three: 1944, 1960, and 2020. It is reasonably fair to say that "as Ohio goes, so goes the nation."

The Rise of the Political Machine

Elections in Northern industrial states like New York, Ohio, Indiana, and Illinois tended to be close because of the presence of large numbers of immigrants and of "political machines," that is, party organizations. Most immigrants came to America seeking jobs, which were most plentiful in industrial cities like New York City, Cleveland, and Chicago. When these immigrants arrived, the Republican Party should have done more to encourage them to become Republicans. However, the Republicans, being in the majority, felt that they did not need these poor and uneducated people as members and so made little effort to enlist them. As a result, new immigrants tended to support the Democrat Party in the large cities.

Democrats, eager for voters, took advantage of the immigrants to build up "political machines" which were run almost exclusively by the Democrat party and by party "bosses." The party boss created voter loyalty, especially among immigrants, by performing favors for the immigrant and his family. Often that favor meant giving the man a job or housing or even buying groceries if an immigrant lost a job. In a sense, it might appear as if the Party performed a social welfare function; however, the price of the boss's generosity was a vote. Sometimes bosses just gave people money to vote the way they wished.

Through strict discipline and an almost military hierarchy, in cities with hundreds of thousands of people, the bosses ran their machines with remarkable efficiency. In fact, the term "party machine" refers to the **mechanical efficiency** with which the party could elect their chosen candidate. The political machine nominated candidates upon whom they could rely. Then, on election day, the machine would "turn out" large numbers of "reliable" voters to support their candidates.

The most infamous political machine was **Tammany Hall** in New York City, run by **William M. "Boss" Tweed.** One of the most corrupt politicians in American history, before he died in 1878, Boss Tweed may have stolen more than $50 million. Eventually, convicted of corruption, he died in jail.

Of course, winning elections meant power. Once in office, corrupt politicians could sell city contracts for constructing public roads and buildings. They could demand bribes for just about anything. They could reward their friends and punish their enemies. Moreover, they could even sway presidential elections in a state like New York. Although Republicans ran a few small political machines, the Democrats ran nearly all the big city machines, and ran them with frightening efficiency.

Thomas Nast drew this political cartoon in 1871 to draw attention to Tammany Hall's corrupt practices. In this cartoon, Tammany Hall presides over the New York City elections. Note the signs in the back. The one on the left promises "Rewards" like "Fat Offices" for those who vote for Tammany Hall's men. The sign on the right offers a $100 reward for anyone informing on an anti-Tammany voter. The corruption is so rampant that even the police, who should be maintaining law and order, are ensuring the men vote "the right way," that is, for Tammany.

The Tariff Question

During the Gilded Age, the nation needed to address two financial questions. The first involved tariffs. The issue of tariffs had affected the United States almost from its inception. In the early 1800s, those who favored a high tariff argued that as a young, struggling, industrial nation, America needed a high protective tariff to defend its own manufacturing from foreign competition, whose lower prices would cripple domestic manufacturing. Although Americans would have to pay more for foreign goods, the nation would ultimately benefit by becoming a strong industrial nation. By 1865, those who had argued for the protective tariff had been proven correct. America had become an industrial superpower.

After the Civil War, the Republican Party supported the high tariff to protect the new industries which emerged during America's second industrial revolution. Industrial workers tended to make more money in these "protected" industries. This made the Republicans popular with voters in the industrial northwest and Midwest. On the other hand, Democrats tended to oppose the tariff. People in the South had never liked it and many in the West also opposed it because it raised the prices that farmers and ranchers paid for manufactured goods. When Grover Cleveland, a Democrat, became President, he tried to reduce the tariff because he thought it provided a benefit to big manufacturers at the expense of consumers. However, Congress would not support him.

Following Cleveland's re-election defeat, Congress passed the highest tariff in history. With the election of Republican presidents, Congress enacted extraordinarily high protective tariffs. In 1894, Congress passed the *Wilson-Gorman Tariff*, which reduced the rate somewhat, but it still remained among the highest in history. In 1897, Congress enacted the *Dingley Tariff*, the highest in American history.

The "Greenbacks" Question

The second financial question Congress needed to address involved the resolution of the "**greenbacks**" issue. Prior to the Civil War, all Americans knew that they could take their paper money to the bank that printed it and that that bank would exchange the paper currency for gold or silver. By 1862, the war had become so expensive that the Union, despite its great economy, could not pay for it through taxes or by borrowing. As a result, in 1862 and 1863, Congress enacted two pieces of legislation which allowed the federal government to print $450 million worth of paper currency known as "**greenbacks**" because they were printed with green ink. However, unlike other papery currency *this paper money could not be exchanged for hard currency*. It was only backed by the credit of the federal government. As a result, the value of the currency fluctuated throughout the war, as did the Confederate currency which also had no hard currency backing. Thus, when the Union won a major battle, the greenback's value rose. When something dire happened, like Lincoln's assassination, the value fell. Although people initially feared having to accept greenbacks, they became standard currency.

At the time the federal government issued the greenbacks, it intended that they be redeemable for their face value. However, that did not happen. By the time the War ended, a greenback was worth about sixty-seven and a half cents.

After the War, the question of how to deal with the greenbacks posed a serious national financial question that affected millions of Americans. On the one hand, if the government exchanged the greenbacks for gold or silver, the people who held them could make a huge profit because the greenbacks were worth less in hard currency than their face value. Some people had purchased the greenbacks for as little as $40. These *speculators* were betting that the Union would win the war and redeem the greenbacks for their face value. Even people who had taken the notes based on their sixty-seven-cent value would benefit.

On the other hand, the government could withdraw the greenbacks from circulation. The government routinely burns old money and reprints new money. In this case, it would destroy, but not replace the greenbacks. This would result in less money being in circulation. When less money circulates, it can cause **deflation**. Deflation causes the price of goods to fall, which means that money buys more. Businessmen and bankers supported the withdrawal plan because having loaned a dollar, they did not want to be repaid sixty-seven cents. On the other hand, the people to whom they had loaned the money favored the plan because they would have to use hard currency to repay loans made in greenbacks. They would have to use $150 of hard currency to repay a $150 greenback loan. Debtors demanded that the greenbacks not be retired. They actually favored **inflation**, which caused the price of goods to rise, because it would make it easier for them to pay off their debts.

Farmers were especially hurt by the greenbacks issue. They had borrowed money to purchase land during the Civil War to grow more crops. After the war, many were heavily in debt. They increased production to pay their debts, but this meant lower prices because there was more product on the market.

Clearly, whichever plan the government implemented, Americans would be injured. The best answer seemed to be some form of compromise. Thus, the government decided to retire the greenbacks *gradually*. Therefore, in 1866, the federal government started slowly retiring the greenbacks. The government hoped that by gradually withdrawing the greenbacks from the money supply, it could control deflation and keep the public from becoming alarmed. However, many people did become alarmed as the economy began to falter. Therefore, in 1868, Congress halted the retirement of the greenbacks. For the next several years, it debated the issue but took no action. Finally, in January 1875, Congress passed the *Specie Resumption Act* which declared that as of January 1, 1879, the greenback would be treated like all other paper money, that is, convertible into hard currency.

America's Centennial Celebration

In 1876, Americans celebrated our nation's one hundredth birthday with a grand Centennial Exposition in Philadelphia attended by over 10 million visitors from the United States and dozens of foreign countries. The Exposition gave Americans a chance to greet the future, as they gazed in awe upon such wonders as Alexander Graham Bell's telephone; a large, powerful machine called the Corliss Steam Engine; and a special preview of a gift of friendship from France – the huge arm and torch of a statue that would be erected on Bellows Island: The Statue of Liberty. The statue was dedicated on October 28, 1886. In a *first* for the times, the Centennial Exposition featured a *Women's Pavilion* dedicated to highlighting the work and accomplishments of women. Other than some design work on the Pavilion, women managed and constructed the entire Pavilion and its exhibits.

The arm and torch of The Statue of Liberty on exhibit at the Centennial Exposition

The Presidential Election of 1880

Rutherford B. Hayes had been elected in 1876 in one of the closest and most controversial elections in American history. Yet after becoming president, he announced that he would serve just one term and not seek re-election. Therefore, the Republicans needed to find another candidate. Once again, they looked to Ohio for their candidate. They nominated **James Abram Garfield**, who had served nine terms in the U.S. House of Representatives.

The Democrats nominated one of the finest army officers ever to serve this nation: **General Winfield Scott Hancock**. Hancock had served with distinction for four decades, including service in the Mexican-American War and the Civil War. His leadership at the Battle of Gettysburg, where his men broke Pickett's Charge, stands as perhaps the brightest moment in his illustrious career. During the Confederate bombardment of Cemetery Ridge that preceded the charge, Hancock could be seen astride his horse

General Winfield Scott Hancock

encouraging his men. When one of his subordinates objected that a corps commander should not risk his life in such a fashion, Hancock replied, "There are times when a corps commander's life does not count." In fact, he was wounded but refused to leave the field until the outcome of the battle had been determined. As a result of his personal bravery, even his enemies admired him.

For these reasons, the Democrats believed Hancock to be an excellent presidential candidate. Moreover, as he was a beloved Union war hero, the Republicans were loath to attack him. The only issue in the campaign was the high protective tariff, which the Democrats opposed. Using that issue, the Republicans emphasized in their campaign that the Democrats were against Northern industrial workers. The strategy worked. The Republicans narrowly carried almost all the Northern states. In an election with almost nine million votes, Garfield won the popular vote by less than 2,000.

President James A. Garfield

Hayes and Garfield Attempt to Reform the Government

One reason that President Hayes decided to serve only one term was in order to make serious reforms in the federal government which he believed would be more likely if he could focus on the reforms rather than on his re-election. Since the time of Andrew Jackson's presidency, both parties had employed the *spoils system* to fill government jobs as rewards to loyal party members or as a way to increase their own political power. However, it was arguably the worst way to choose a person for a job and Hayes hated it. He decided to dedicate his presidency to improving the way government workers were hired.

Rather than appointing a person because of their connection to a party leader or as a favor, Hayes wished to use a merit-based system in order to hire the most qualified person for the job. Under his plan, job applicants would all take a test. The people who scored the highest on the test – a civil service examination – would be hired *regardless of their political affiliation*. Also, no one hired would be fired unless they performed their job poorly. This effort to improve the government was known as **civil service reform**.

Hayes' call for civil service reform was not new. After the Civil War, people began advocating for reform. These reformers argued that other than jobs that set national policy, like Cabinet officers and their assistants, all other government positions should be based on merit. They pointed out that the government was growing larger and that government jobs were becoming more complex. For example, in 1830, the entire federal government employed fewer than 24,000 people. By 1880, more than 24,000 people worked in just the Treasury Department! Also, unlike five decades earlier, in 1880, there were fewer unskilled government jobs. The government was employing scientists, lawyers, and accountants. Many jobs required some training and some jobs required a great deal of training.

By 1878, the spoils system had become unworkable. Every time a new president was elected, tens of thousands of federal employees were fired and tens of thousands of new employees had to be hired and trained. This took months to accomplish and wasted time and money. Moreover, qualified people would never take a government job. They would not give up a good job in private business to take a government job, knowing that in four or eight years they might be fired – even if they had done an excellent job. Imagine if Booker T. Washington, a Republican, takes a position with a Republican administration, does a wonderful job finding work for black men and women, but is then fired when a Democrat is elected president.

A merit-based civil service system should have appealed to both parties and everyone interested in better, more efficient government. However, many in the government, like Republican Senator Roscoe Conkling of New York, believed that the spoils system was necessary and a legitimate prerogative for Congressmen. These politicians opposed a merit-based system for personal financial and political reasons. However, over time, more and more people began to see the necessity of reform.

President Hayes spent his entire presidency working to reform the Civil Service. Unfortunately, Congress refused to act to abolish the spoils system. It seemed it would take something almost unprecedented to move Congress. Tragically, that "something" occurred on a hot July day in 1881.

The Assassination of James A. Garfield

Like his predecessor, President Garfield sought to reform the Civil Service and believed that the federal government should use a merit-based hiring system. Unfortunately, thousands of job-seekers, who opposed hiring the most competent applicants, besieged the government demanding jobs. While most of these men simply went home unhappy and sought employment elsewhere, on July 2, 1881, one man went much too far.

The second of July was a typical mid-summer day in the nation's capital: devastatingly hot in the shade and even more so in the sun. To escape the broiling heat, President Garfield decided to take a train to the New Jersey shore where he would enjoy a few vacation days. As he walked across the train station lobby, nodding pleasantly to travelers who recognized him, a half-crazed man wielding a pistol suddenly confronted him. The man, later identified as **Charles Guiteau**, a lawyer who had unsuccessfully sought employment

in the State Department, pointed his weapon at Garfield, who stood less than two feet away, and pulled the trigger. The thunderous shot echoed around the walls of the cavernous train station. Miraculously, the bullet merely grazed the president's arm. However, Guiteau fired again. The echoes were the same, but the results tragically different. The second bullet struck the president's abdomen. President Garfield slumped slowly to the marble floor in excruciating pain.

President Chester A. Arthur

The bullet wound did not immediately kill Garfield. In the weeks that followed, doctors tried to find and extract the bullet using probes and fingers. In a time when doctors did not fully understand proper sterilization, the many unsterilized probes and improperly cleaned hands almost certainly contaminated Garfield's wound. He developed a high fever and a rampant infection. He finally died on the night of September 19, 1881. **Chester A. Arthur**, a New York politician, became America's twenty-first president.

The jury convicted Charles Guiteau of Garfield's murder. His attorneys argued that he should only be convicted of assault. They tried to blame the president's death on the doctors whose unsanitary hands probably did more to kill Garfield than the bullet. One attorney also argued that Guiteau had been **temporarily insane**, one of the first times an attorney presented such a defense in an American court. However, although 19th-century attorneys proved more able than doctors, the argument failed to convince the jury. They found him guilty. He was hanged on June 30, 1882.

The Pendleton Act

Tragically, President Garfield may have accomplished in death what he might have been unable to accomplish in life. His death aroused the whole nation and brought the evils of the spoils system into sharp focus in a national conversation. An outraged public demanded *immediate* reform. Newspapers and churches united to force Democrats and Republicans to end the spoils system.

Congress finally passed the **Pendleton Civil Service Act** in 1883, two years after President Garfield's assassination. In addition to creating the **Civil Service Commission**, the Act specified the manner by which appointments to federal government service positions would be made. Civil Service Commission representatives would screen each applicant who applied and administer **exams** to determine the applicant's capabilities and fitness for office. The Civil Service Commission established a **merit system:** an applicant's rank on the jobs list depended on his **grade on the exam**. Under the protection of the **Civil Service Act**, no one appointed under the terms of the Act can be removed from office, with the exceptions of neglect of duty or improper conduct on the job.

At first, only about 15,000 jobs fell under the Civil Service Act. However, by 1900, almost half of all jobs in the federal government had been classified as being part of the civil service system. Over time, civil service reform has been extended to include many more federal government jobs, as well as spreading to state and local governments. In 1940, on the recommendation of President Franklin D. Roosevelt, Congress passed the Ramspeck Act, which allowed the president to add many more government employees to the civil service classified list.

Like many laws, the Civil Service Act also had negative effects. While it initially provided more qualified men and women for government jobs, it started today's mammoth federal bureaucracy. People work for the government for years and years because it has become so difficult to fire them even when they are negligent or act improperly on the job.

The Presidential Elections of 1884, 1888, and 1892

The presidential elections of 1884, 1888, and 1892 pitted Democrat Grover Cleveland against Republicans James Blaine, Benjamin Harrison, and then Benjamin Harrison again. Although Republican Chester Arthur was the sitting president and thus the presumptive nominee, Arthur suffered from serious health problems. He made only a token effort at securing the nomination. In fact, after leaving the presidency, he almost immediately retired from public life. He died November 18, 1886, at the age of fifty-seven.

With Chester A. Arthur as non-viable, the Republicans chose **James Gillespie Blaine** as their candidate in the 1884 election. Blaine had a long and distinguished record. He had served in the U.S. House of Representatives from 1863 to 1876, then in the Senate from 1876 to 1881. He had also served twice as Secretary of State. In many ways, Blaine was an excellent candidate. However, he was not from Ohio, New York, or Indiana, but from Maine. On the other hand, Blaine's opponent, **Grover Cleveland**, had spent his life in New York politics, including a term as mayor of Buffalo and governor of New York. Despite this, Cleveland barely carried New York, winning by just over 1,000 votes. Had he lost New York, he would have lost the election. With New York's 36 electoral votes, Cleveland defeated Blaine 219 to 182 in the Electoral College. Cleveland also received 48.85% of the popular vote, beating Blaine by only half a percent.

Four years later, Cleveland, now the *incumbent*, faced **Benjamin Harrison**. Initially, the Republicans favored James Blaine, who had so narrowly lost to Cleveland four years earlier. However, Blaine had no interest in running again. Harrison was nominated.

Benjamin Harrison, the grandson of President William Henry Harrison, had spent his life in Indiana politics and served during the Civil War, reaching the rank of brigadier general. As so often happened during this period, the election focused on the swing states of New York and Indiana, which Harrison won. Although Cleveland received more popular votes (48.6% to 47.8%), he narrowly lost his home state of New York and its 36 electoral votes. Harrison carried the Electoral College 233 to 168.

The **Presidential Election of 1892** was unique in American politics for two reasons. First, for the only time prior to the 21st century, two presidents faced off against each other: former President Grover Cleveland and incumbent

Benjamin Harrison

THE REPUBLICAN SOUVENIR.

James Blaine Campaign Poster. Blaine reminds voters that Republicans had preserved the Union, emancipated the Black race, created universal suffrage (at least to men) and had established a free public school system.

President Benjamin Harrison. Second, Cleveland won re-election, *becoming the only man to serve two non-consecutive terms as president.* However, once again, Cleveland failed to obtain a majority of the popular vote. He received 46% to Harrison's 43%.

Third Party Candidates

From the election of 1880 to that of 1896, no presidential candidate received a majority of the popular vote, because of the presence of "third party" candidates. While the Republican and Democratic candidates in those elections tended to hold nearly identical positions on the issues, third party candidates had specific issues that concerned them. For example, in 1880 and 1884, the **Greenback Party** ran candidates who favored *more* rather than *fewer* Greenbacks in circulation. In 1888, the **Prohibition Party**, which proposed a national ban on alcoholic beverages, managed to win about 250,000 votes. Finally, in 1892, the **Populist Party**, a party that supported western farmers and the labor movement, carried five western states, received over 1,000,000 votes, and captured 22 electoral votes.

Grover Cleveland by Swedish artist Anders Zorn. Zorn painted Cleveland in 1899, two years after he completed his second term. The sittings took place at Cleveland's home in New Jersey. Apparently, the two men became quite friendly. Commenting on the painting, Cleveland declared, "As for my ugly mug, I think the artist has 'struck it off' in great shape."

With so many close elections in which the president failed to obtain a majority of the popular vote, no president really had the power to make substantive changes. In Congress, the House and Senate split between Republicans and Democrats for most of this period. The two majority parties had neither the will to address serious issues nor the power to make real changes.

The Populist Party

Although the lives of most Americans improved during the Gilded Age, *farmers* were one group that struggled. The protective tariff, which raised the price of manufactured goods, and deflation, which lowered the price of their produce, both hurt them. When neither of the two major political parties would help them, the farmers sought other means to help themselves.

One of the first actions farmers took was to organize themselves. Founded in 1868, the **Grange** was a fraternal and social organization that encouraged farmers to band together to promote their communities and each other. Somewhat ahead of its time, it included women as members. By 1875, the Grange had over 800,000 members.

Very quickly the Grange became a political organization as well as a "social" one. However, it tried to remain **non-partisan** in its politics, choosing instead to focus on those issues that affected farmers, most notably the prices railroads charged. Farmers believed that the railroads, because they held a monopoly over the transport of farm products, charged higher than reasonable prices. The Grange leaders demanded that state legislatures act to curtail these prices. Many states passed **Granger Laws** which set prices. The railroads challenged these laws in court, but in 1877 the U.S. Supreme Court ruled the Granger Laws constitutional. However, in 1886, the Supreme Court overturned its earlier ruling. The following year, the U.S. Congress passed the Interstate Commerce Act. By the 1880s, the Grange began losing members because it proved incapable of actually solving farmers' economic problems. However, farmers realized that political action was the means to achieve reform.

In 1876, another organization, similar to the Grange, was formed in Texas. Known as the **Farmers' Alliance**, it was created to end the sharecropping system in the South. Originally, the Farmers' Alliance worked to help its members by forming co-ops that would sell produce at better prices as well as purchase farm material in bulk to obtain better prices for members. However, soon, like the Grange, the Farmers' Alliance became a political organization promoting a variety of issues including regulation of the railroads and banks. Unlike the Grange, the Farmers' Alliance also began to run candidates for political office, who promised to help farmers if elected.

In 1890, the Farmers' Alliance managed to elect several candidates to

Grange Poster

local offices as well as eight men to the United States House of Representatives. Moreover, the Alliance had supported many Democrats for office, mainly because of their opposition to the tariff. Alliance-supported Democrats won more than forty House seats and several Senate seats. Earlier, the Alliance had contacted Terrence Powderly of the Knights of Labor. Encouraged by their election victories, in February 1892, members of the Farmers' Alliance, along with farmers from the Grange and members of the Knights of Labor decided to form a political party and run a candidate for president in 1892. They named their new party the **People's Party**, although it is usually called the **Populist Party** and its members simply **Populists**.

The Populists held their nominating convention in July 1892 in Omaha, Nebraska. Their ticket represented one of the most intriguing in all of American history. For president they nominated **James Weaver** of Iowa, a former Union General. For vice-president, they nominated **James Field** of Virginia, a former Confederate General.

Unlike the Democrats and Republicans, whose political platforms failed to address the controversial issues of the day, the Populists declared their positions with bold specificity! Today, the Populist platform would be called very **liberal** or **left-wing**. Comprised mainly of farmers and union members, the populists advocated "reforms" that appealed to their members. The Populists called for government ownership of the railroad lines. Likening the telephone and the telegraph systems to the Post Office, they also called for government ownership of these industries. In support of the labor movement, they wished to restrict immigration because the current laws allowed in "the pauper and criminal classes of the world" while crowding out American wage-earners. The Populists also "sympathize[d] with the efforts of organized workingmen to shorten the hours of labor," and demanded an eight-hour work day.

In addition to these "liberal" demands in support of the Labor movement, the Populists also proposed a few "conservative" ideas. Notably, they favored the legislative reform known as the "initiative and referendum." (This will be discussed in a later chapter.) They also favored "a constitutional provision limiting the office of president and vice-president to one term." Finally, they also proposed a few ideas that eventually did become laws: the federal income tax and the direct election of senators.

As third-party candidates, Weaver and Field polled rather well. They received over a million votes – about 8.5% of the total cast – and won five states. The Populists also won many local elections. However, their positions were too radical for too many Americans. Although the Populists expected to sweep into the White House in 1896, they would be disappointed. In the midterm elections of 1894, the Populist candidates fared badly and their allies, the Democrats, lost over 100 seats in the House. In 1896, the Populists would nominate the Democrats' presidential candidate as their candidate as well, essentially becoming a part of the Democratic Party.

The Depression of 1893, aka The Panic of 1893

Shortly after Grover Cleveland's election, the United States was hit with the worst Depression in its history up to that time. Historians estimate that national unemployment **may have been as high as 18% by 1894.** Thousands of businesses, especially railroads (including the Union Pacific), went bankrupt. About twenty percent of all factory workers lost their jobs. As people, fearing that their paper money would become worthless, exchanged their paper money for hard currency, banks became insolvent. Hundreds of banks closed, as people panicked and began hoarding gold. Hundreds, perhaps thousands, of families lost their homes when the banks failed. Hundreds of farmers lost their farms.

Many factors, both domestically and internationally, caused the Depression of 1893. One cause had been the long period of deflation. Democrats blamed the high tariff which they

Populist Party 1892 presidential campaign poster

Panic scene in the New York Stock Exchange on the morning of Friday, May 5, 1893.

said decreased income from custom duties. Regardless of the causes, the American people blamed Grover Cleveland. Grover Cleveland blamed America's *bi-metal* economy, that is, one based on the two metals, gold and silver. He felt that people had become uncertain about the currency, especially America's reliance on silver, and that had caused the Depression. In 1893, he convinced Congress to limit minting silver.

Cleveland's plan failed to improve the Depression. During the following year, the economic situation worsened. Furthermore, he lost the support of many Democrats who favored minting both silver and gold.

The Pullman Strike

Whoever is president during bad economic times receives much of the blame. To many Americans it seemed that President Cleveland simply had not done enough to alleviate the Depression. Moreover, what he had done appeared to have failed. To be fair, neither party seemed to know how to fix the economy or aid farmers and workers. Unfortunately, the poor economy persisted for the remainder of Cleveland's presidency. President Cleveland became even less popular when workers at the **Pullman Company** went on strike in May 1894.

George Pullman had achieved incredible success with his Pullman Company which manufactured sleeping and dining cars for the railroads. Sadly, he too often failed to do good, as he did well. For example, he hired freed slaves to work as porters in his company, but paid them very little. The Pullman Company ultimately became the largest employer of African-Americans in the United States, yet most of his porters needed to rely on tips from passengers to make a living. Concerned about the workers in his factory, in 1880 Pullman bought 4,000 acres of land fourteen miles south of Chicago. He hired a leading architect to design not only the Pullman factory, but an entire "company town" (named Pullman) with homes, stores, parks, theatres, and a church. Pullman believed that people living in the country would lead happier lives free from the vices of the city, as well as union "agitators," and be more efficient workers. However, Pullman charged his workers rents that were about 25% higher than those paid in nearby communities. Although George Pullman did not force anyone to live in Pullman, those workers who did not were fired.

When the Depression hit in 1893, Pullman cut wages by about 25%, but he did not cut rent by the same amount. As a result, most workers could barely feed their families. On May 11, the nearly 4,000 workers at the company went on strike over the reduction in their wages. On June 26, the 150,000 members of the **American Railway Union** (ARU), a union composed of engineers, conductors, and other railroad workers, led by **Eugene V. Debs**, in solidarity with the Pullman strikers, agreed not to handle trains to which Pullman cars were attached. By the end of June, the effect on the railroads and the already fragile national economy was devastating.

At this point, the railroad owners devised a clever plan. They determined to attach Pullman cars to trains carrying mail. Interfering with the delivery of the mail is a federal offense. However, the strikers still refused to attach the Pullman cars.

A federal judge ordered the workers to return to their jobs, but they refused. Based on the federal power to deliver the mail, Cleveland ordered federal troops into Chicago to break the strike. When the soldiers entered the Chicago rail yards, fighting broke out between the military and the strikers. Ultimately, the strike left 30 strikers dead and 57 wounded. Property damage reached nearly $100 million. The police arrested Eugene Debs, who would ultimately be defended by **Clarence Darrow**, one of the most famous attorneys in American history. The court sentenced Debs to six months in prison. Federal troops were recalled from Chicago on July 20 and the strike was declared over in early August. The violence turned the public against the union and the strikers. Cleveland had broken the strike, but he had paid a price.

As a Democrat, Cleveland realized he needed to maintain good relations with the labor movement and did try to keep them with him. At the height of the strike, Congress enacted legislation creating a national holiday recognizing the contribution that the labor movement had made to America. On June 28, 1854,

Federal troops called in to break the Pullman strike

President Cleveland signed the bill into law, thus making *Labor Day* a national holiday. While the holiday would be very popular, Cleveland no longer was.

By the end of the summer 1894, Cleveland had lost the support of most Americans. As a Democrat, he had little support among Republicans. His use of the army to break the Pullman strike had alarmed many Democrats. The governor of Illinois, a Democrat, had bitterly objected to sending in the army, claiming that the Chicago police were well-equipped to handle the situation. The governor's comments, as well as Cleveland's own actions, turned Democrats and Union members against him.

In the congressional election of 1894, Republicans gained 130 seats in the House of Representatives, one of the largest swings in American history. The House contained 254 Republicans and 93 Democrats, mostly in the "Solid South." The stage had been set for the Presidential Election of 1896.

The Election of 1896: The Candidates

The Presidential Election of 1896 would be one in which the members of the two major parties would realign and both parties knew it. President Cleveland, who had run three times and been elected twice, was wildly unpopular and therefore not really an option for the Democrats. In their stronghold, the South, the Populists were calling for the free coinage of silver. The Democrats knew that they could not nominate someone who, like Cleveland, supported only the gold standard. If they did, they might lose the South to the **Populists.**

On the other hand, for the first time in decades, the Democrats felt that they had a good chance to win a number of Western states. This was because the Republicans had chosen **William McKinley** of Ohio as their candidate. McKinley had served in the U.S. House of Representatives and as governor of Ohio before his nomination. In the House, he had helped enact the "McKinley Tariff" in 1890, one of the highest tariffs in American history, to protect domestic - especially Ohio - industries. The Republican platform of 1896 also firmly "opposed the free coinage of silver" insisting rather that the "existing gold standard be maintained."

While McKinley's positions appealed to people in the industrial North and Midwest, who saw them as pro-business and job-protection measures, they were less popular in other areas of the nation. Between McKinley's stand on the tariff and the Republican plank on silver, both western farmers and miners, who traditionally voted Republican, had reasons to vote Democratic in the 1896 election if the Democrats favored silver coinage. Nebraska, Wyoming, Montana, South Dakota, and Washington had all voted Republican in the 1892 election. The issue for the Democrats was finding a man who could swing those states Democratic.

The Democrats met in July, 1896 in Chicago to nominate a candidate to run against William McKinley. Eight men stood as candidates. Prior to the nomination vote, they debated the merits of the gold standard versus free coinage of silver.

William McKinley

The final speaker was **William Jennings Bryan**. At thirty-six years of age, he was just one year older than the Constitutionally established age to run for president. His youth meant that Bryan had a slim resume. He had served two terms as a U.S. Representative from Nebraska, but outside of Nebraska almost no one knew who he was. However, Bryan was an exceptionally brilliant orator. The Democratic convention provided him the opportunity of a lifetime. He grabbed it with both hands.

Bryan delivered what historians have labeled his **"Cross of Gold"** Speech, one of the most magnificent pieces of oratory in American history. He compared those who favored coining silver to the "crusaders who followed Peter the Hermit" and freed Jerusalem from the Muslims. Of farmers he spoke eloquently, calling them "hardy pioneers who have braved all the dangers of the wilderness, who have made the desert to blossom as the rose… who rear their children near to Nature's heart, where they can mingle their voices with the voices of the birds…" He continued: *"Now, my friends, let me come to the*

William Jennings Bryan (c. 1902) about ten years after he delivered his "Cross of Gold" speech.

great paramount issue. If they ask us here why it is that we say more on the money question than we say upon the tariff question, I reply that protection has slain its thousands, the gold standard has slain its tens of thousands…. You come to us and tell us that the great cities are in favor of the gold standard. I tell you that the great cities rest upon these broad and fertile prairies. Burn down your cities and leave our farms, and your cities will spring up again as if by magic; but destroy our farms and the grass will grow in the streets of every city in this country." Bryan concluded his speech by likening the forces of labor to Our Lord: *"You shall not press down upon the brow of labor this crown of thorns. You shall not crucify mankind upon a cross of gold."*

As Bryan spoke his last words, he extended his arms out from his body and held this Christ-like pose for about five seconds before descending from the stage. In silence, he walked back to his seat. In later years, Bryan would recall that in those painful seconds as he walked back to his seat, he felt that he had failed. However, the silence lasted only a few seconds before the convention erupted into thunderous applause. For thirty minutes the crowd cheered Bryan. Had a vote been taken at that moment, he might have been unanimously nominated by acclamation. It is a tribute to his character that Bryan refused to allow a vote immediately after his speech.

Nevertheless, Bryan's speech had the desired effect. Free silver became the position of the Democrats. William Jennings Bryan, "The Nebraska Cyclone," a man of high morals and deeply held religious beliefs, became the Democratic nominee for president.

After much debate, the Populists also nominated Bryan as their candidate, thus ending their party's existence as well as the Populist movement. They basically became part of the Democratic Party. The Populists felt that if they nominated their own candidate, they would split the "free silver" vote, thus ensuring McKinley's victory.

The Election of 1896: The Campaign

To a great extent, the campaign of 1896 was one of perception more than reality. To the men who ran businesses and industries, McKinley represented "sound money" policy. They believed that free silver would destroy their businesses and ruin the nation. This perception was largely inaccurate. The gold standard had not saved the nation nor a bi-metal economy destroyed it. Nevertheless, businesses and industries strongly backed McKinley.

Though never considered a great political thinker, William McKinley had several positive personal qualities. He was a hard worker and a gifted politician, two qualities that can never be underestimated. He also had a brilliant friend and adviser, the wealthy Ohio businessman **Mark Hanna**, who for twenty years helped McKinley. They made an impressive team. During the 1896 campaign, Hanna became McKinley's campaign manager. In addition to giving much of his own money to McKinley's campaign, Hanna raised enormous sums of money from other individuals, especially wealthy businessmen, many of whom were Democrats.

Hanna used the money he raised brilliantly. He sent Republicans all over the nation to speak on the issues and printed hundreds of millions of pamphlets explaining the Republican position on the issues which he had distributed around the country. Many of these pamphlets addressed the all-important money question. Hanna set up special committees aimed at winning various ethnic voters, e.g. Blacks, Italians, Germans, etc. Under Hanna's leadership, the Republicans were well funded and well organized.

Ida McKinley

Meanwhile, William McKinley himself ran what was known as the **"Front Porch Campaign."** He stayed at home and campaigned from his "front porch" in Canton, Ohio. He ran this type of campaign for two reasons. First, he wanted to be close to his wife Ida, who suffered from epilepsy. Second, it was easier for groups of people to travel to Canton to meet with him than for him to travel around the nation meeting with them.

Each delegation of visitors would arrive at the Canton railroad station, where a mounted reception committee would greet them and escort them down a flag-lined street to McKinley's home. McKinley, often accompanied by Ida, would come out on his front porch to greet his guests. Depending on the group, McKinley gave a speech addressing their particular concern. To business owners and factory workers, he talked about the protective tariff and the importance of the gold standard. The newspapers covered his speeches and reprinted or reported on their content. Thus, from his porch in Canton, his message spread across the country.

While McKinley, Hanna, and the Republicans seemed to be completely in agreement, the Democrats seemed completely confused and in utter disarray. Unlike the Republicans, they had little money, mainly because many wealthy, normally Democratic donors, were supporting McKinley. Secondly, they had no one like Mark Hanna, so their party

William Jennings Bryan's 1896 presidential campaign poster. Bryan emphasizes his youth, his family, and his support for American workers. He also reprints his "Cross of Gold" Speech.

organization was also poor. Moreover, in many of the industrial states, individual Democratic candidates, afraid of losing their own elections, would not support the free silver movement. Many of these "Gold Democrats" split from the main Democrat party and created the National Democratic Party which supported the gold standard. They nominated John M. Palmer, a 79-year-old senator from Illinois who had served as a general in the Union Army and Simon Buckner of Kentucky, a former confederate general, as their vice-presidential candidate. The two had fought against each other at the Battle of Chickamauga during the Civil War. The Gold Democrats bitterly opposed Bryan. They felt that he and his supporters were anarchists and compared them to the French Revolutionaries. Hanna supported them financially because they drained votes from Bryan.

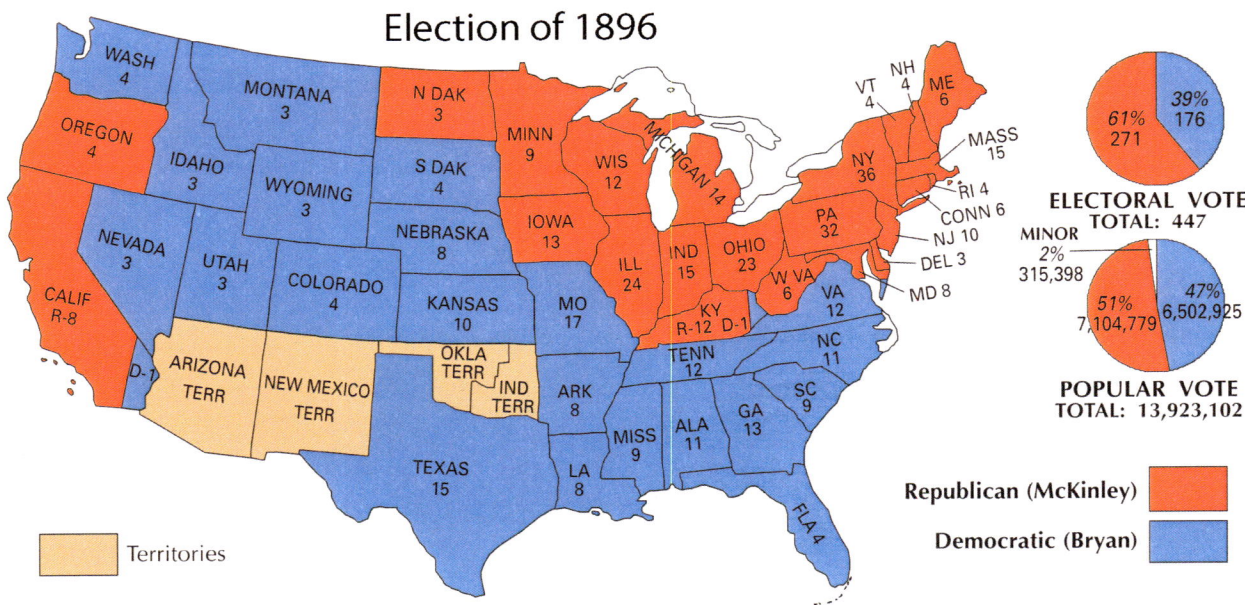

Election of 1896

ELECTORAL VOTE
TOTAL: 447

POPULAR VOTE
TOTAL: 13,923,102

Republican (McKinley)
Democratic (Bryan)

Territories

In fact, during the campaign of 1896, the Democrats had only one asset: William Jennings Bryan. However, he was a formidable asset indeed. Bryan possessed several qualities indispensable for success in politics. First, he had remarkable strength of character. This became apparent early on when, as a virtual unknown, he chose to seek the presidency against apparently overwhelming odds. Second, he seemed to have endless energy. During the campaign, he made over 600 speeches between August and Election Day in November! He spoke to large auditoriums filled with people as well as small groups from the back of his railroad car. Third, he may have been the most brilliant orator in American presidential history. Although only the content of his speeches from that time remains, other recordings of his speeches do exist, although in rather poor quality. Fourth, contemporaries describe Bryan as having a magnetic personality. All of these qualities made him a fantastic campaigner.

Although most major newspapers supported McKinley, they did accurately report Bryan's speeches. Thus, like McKinley, Bryan's message spread across the country. By Election Day, any voter who wished could read numerous speeches by both candidates on a variety of issues.

The Election of 1896: The Results

The Election of 1896 caused a major shift in voting patterns - with a few exceptions. The "Solid South" remained solidly Democratic and voted for Bryan. However, the West, usually so reliably Republican, went overwhelmingly for Bryan. Only Oregon (4 electoral votes) and California (8 electoral votes) went for McKinley by razor-thin margins. Of the nearly 300,000 votes cast in California, McKinley won by less than 2,000! But thousands of men who had voted for Democrat Grover Cleveland four years earlier changed allegiance and voted for Republican William McKinley in 1896. McKinley won all the midwestern states and all the Northeastern states. He had convinced factory workers in these industrial states that the protective tariff and the gold standard would protect their jobs. In big cities with strong unions that had voted Democratic in 1892, men voted for McKinley. He won 51% of the popular vote compared with Bryan's 47%, a margin of more than 600,000 votes. In the Electoral College, he won 271 to 176.

The election was a decisive Republican victory. Although McKinley won Indiana by less than 3% and his home state of Ohio by less than 5%, he carried New York by almost 20%. Even if Bryan had won the close contests in Oregon and California, it would not have been enough to overcome McKinley's massive victory in the Northeast and Midwest.

The End of the Gilded Age

Many historians mark the election of William McKinley as the end of the Gilded Age. It certainly marked the end of much of what had preceded it. William McKinley was the last man elected to the presidency who had served in the Civil War. The election of 1896 had resulted in a major political realignment. Farmers and miners had voted Democratic, while big city factory workers in unions had voted Republican. Even the "Solid South" had seen sections of Tennessee, Texas, and Georgia vote Republican.

CHAPTER 23 REVIEW QUESTIONS

Answer the following questions:

1. Why might the years between 1865 and 1917 be termed a "Golden Age?"
2. What events tarnished the Gilded Age?
3. What is meant by "The Solid South?"
4. Why is Ohio known as a bellwether state?
5. What were political machines? How were they corrupt? Why did immigrants become involved with them?
6. What was the political machine in New York City at this time? Who ran it?
7. Who assassinated President Garfield? Who succeeded Garfield as President?
8. Why did Chester A. Arthur choose not to run for re-election?
9. What groups supported the Populist Party?
10. What was the Grange? Why did it become popular?
11. What was the Pullman strike? How was it resolved?
12. What is the "Cross of Gold Speech?"
13. What is the "Front Porch Campaign?" Was it effective? Why or why not?
14. Why is the election of William McKinley seen as the end of the Gilded Age?
15. How were "greenbacks" different from other currencies?
16. Who coined the term "Gilded Age?"
17. What made the Centennial Exposition in Philadelphia unique for the time period?
18. What caused the Depression of 1893?
19. What made William Jennings Bryan a great candidate for president?
20. What were some issues of the Populist Party platform?

Identify the following:

1. Benjamin Harrison
2. Swing State
3. Winfield Scott Hancock
4. Civil Service Reform
5. Eugene Debs

CHAPTER 24 | The Church in the Second Half of the 19th Century

John Neumann discusses construction of a Catholic school.

Introduction

During the second half of the 19th century, the Catholic Church in the United States faced many of the same issues that it had encountered since colonial times, e.g. providing the Sacraments to the faithful, educating Catholics in their Faith, evangelizing non-Catholics, and dealing with anti-Catholic bigotry. The latter half of the 19th century did not present new challenges *per se*, but rather presented these old challenges in new ways. America's Catholic bishops sought to address these issues as the Catholic Church grew larger and became a larger part of American society.

Thus, America's bishops focused on strengthening and improving the Catholic school system; increasing the number of American priests and nuns; establishing Catholic newspapers; evangelizing non-Catholics, especially Black and Native Americans; and fighting anti-Catholic bigotry. Later in the century, with the growth of corporations and "big business," the Catholic Church also took a strong stand in favor of the family and the working man. Moreover, as the Church grew, she became the largest private social welfare organization in the nation, creating hospitals, orphanages, soup kitchens, and associations like the St. Vincent de Paul Society, which provides clothes and food to the needy.

The Growth of the Church from 1800 to 1850

In 1800, there were probably less than 25,000 Catholics living in the United States. This represented an insignificant percentage of the overall population. Fifty years later, the number exceeded 1,000,000 and represented about 5% of the total population. While Catholics tend to have large families, immigration from Ireland and other Catholic nations was the main cause of this massive increase.

While most Protestants in 1800 had probably never even met a Catholic, by 1850 tensions between Catholics and Protestants, always an underlying current in American society, began to flare. These tensions were enhanced by Protestant preachers delivering anti-Catholic sermons from their pulpits, as well as by teachers in the Protestant public schools seeking to "save" Catholic school children. By 1850, America's Catholic bishops felt that they needed to hold a national conference to establish national policies, especially concerning the education of children. In 1851, Pope Pius IX granted permission for the Catholic bishops in the United States to hold their first national, or **Plenary Council**.

The First Plenary Council

The First Plenary Council was convened in Baltimore in 1852. Six archbishops and twenty-six bishops attended. Archbishop **Francis Kenrick** of Baltimore presided as the Apostolic Delegate. The assembled bishops approved the Acts of all the previous seven Provincial Baltimore Councils.

Archbishop Francis Kenrick

The Council's main focus was the creation of a Catholic school system. The bishops saw how Protestant teachers in the public schools worked to convert Catholic students. For the bishops, this posed a threat not only to the Church, but also to the parents of these children. The Council directly addressed the role of the Church in education when it declared that "bishops are exhorted to have a Catholic school in every parish and the teachers should be paid from the parochial funds." Bishops should "begin these schools whenever possible in their dioceses, since Catholic boys and girls are in grave danger in educational institutions which are not directed by [Catholic] religious motives." Thus, the national parochial school system was born.

The Council also adopted various rules for parish and diocesan governments. The Council discouraged marriages between Catholics and non-Catholics. It also warned against lay interference in Church affairs, which was becoming a problem in the United States. Lay Protestants always had leading roles in their churches' operations. Protestants had the right to choose their pastors as well as to fire them. Some Catholics in the United States were beginning to believe that they too had this "right."

The primary and lasting significance of the First Plenary Council was its impact on Catholic education. Although Catholic school systems existed on a city-wide basis, especially in Philadelphia and New York City, no attempt had been made by the bishops to create a *national* system or unify the local systems.

Stained glass window of St. John Neumann from his shrine in Philadelphia

St. John Neumann, who became Bishop of Philadelphia in March 1852, took the few existing Philadelphia Catholic schools and organized them into the first **diocesan** school system. He increased a handful of parochial schools to 200. For this reason, he is sometimes called the "Father of the Parochial School System."

The Second Plenary Council

In 1852, Massachusetts, under the influence of Horace Mann, the "Father of the American Public School System," passed a compulsory education law. Seemingly a rather benign law, it required that students between the ages of 8 and 14 attend public school for at least twelve weeks per year. "Seemingly benign," because although children could attend "approved" private schools, most immigrants, that is, Catholics, could not afford these schools, which meant they were forced, under penalty of law, to attend public schools. Three years later, in 1855, Massachusetts took its "benign" law to the next step when it required that the Bible be read in school. Of course, this meant the Protestant, *King James*, version of the Bible. In 1852, the Plenary Council had specifically called for priests to openly oppose the use of the *King James Bible* in the public schools. Massachusetts, though acting at the state level, reflected the actions being taken at the local level in communities throughout the United States.

In response to the compulsory attendance laws, Catholics, in fairness, sought public funding for Catholic schools. **John Hughes**, the Bishop of New York from 1842 to 1864, led this movement. Although he failed to obtain state funding for Catholic schools, he did convince New York's governor to allow Catholic students in the public schools to be allowed to use the Catholic Bible rather than the Protestant version.

Even such small concessions inflamed the anti-Catholic bigotry of the Nativist movement. By the 1850s, the Nativists had become even more violent. However, Bishop Hughes, who would now earn the nickname "Dagger John," refused to sit idly by while Nativists burned his churches and murdered his parishioners. The bishop armed 1,000 Irishmen with rifles. They defended Old St. Patrick's Cathedral in New York City against the Nativist mob.

Happily, in addition to these negative events, the Church received several blessings between 1852 and 1866. The huge increase in immigration during the 1850s doubled the Catholic population in the United States. The number of parishes multiplied from 1,411 in 1852 to 3,366 in 1866. However, the massive

Bishop John Hughes

increase in population, as well as the serious social, educational, and political issues facing the Church after the Civil War, caused the bishops to appeal to Rome for permission to convene a second Plenary Council.

Granted permission by the Holy See, the Second Plenary Council of Baltimore met in 1866. Seven archbishops, thirty-eight bishops, three abbots, and more than one hundred and twenty priests attended the Council. To demonstrate that one could be a good Catholic *and* a good American, the bishops invited President Andrew Johnson, who also attended.

As with the First Council, the Second Council focused strongly on education. Among its mandates, the Council issued decrees that Catholic teachers working in public schools should be hired to work in Catholic schools when possible. Second, every parish should build a parochial school. Third, parents who send their children to public school should send their children to Sunday catechism classes at their local church for doctrinal instruction and sacramental preparation, especially for First Holy Communion and Confirmation. The Council Fathers also recommended that a Catholic university be built in the United States.

With the end of slavery, the priests and bishops at the Council recognized that the Church had a duty to minister to freed slaves. Among its decrees, the Plenary Council passed a resolution asking priests to dedicate as much time as possible to the service of helping educate Blacks, especially Black children.

Once again, the attempts by Catholics to create their own school system and raise their children in their faith inflamed the passions of anti-Catholic bigots in the United States. Nevertheless, the drive on the part of priests and bishops to build Catholic schools could not be stopped. Determined to raise a generation of children taught in Catholic schools, these leaders began to build, and build, and build!

The Third Plenary Council

In 1866, about 2.5 million Catholics lived in the United States. By 1884, that number had more than doubled. Once again, immigration accounted for the huge spike in Catholic population. Once again, the bishops feared that children not attending Catholic schools would fall prey to the evangelization efforts of teachers in the public schools. In 1875, some bishops, concerned with low attendance in the parochial schools, even wrote to the Vatican office responsible for the propagation of the Faith, seeking advice on increasing Catholic school enrollment. Rome responded by directing the bishops to build schools where there were none and to improve the existing ones so that they were equal to the public schools. With this directive, the bishops did just that. This directive became an important guide for the bishops' educational apostolate in the years that followed.

Interestingly, the political machines of the late 19th century did much to help the Catholic school system. In their desire to "woo" immigrants, most of whom were Catholics, the Democratic bosses gave millions of dollars of public money to parochial schools. Of course, this enraged Protestants who viewed any attempt, licit or not, to fund Catholic schools as nothing less than an attack on the very foundations of American democracy.

James Blaine

The furor over Catholic schools receiving state funds reached its peak in 1875 when President Grant called for a Constitutional amendment banning any state or federal funds being given to any religiously-based school. Of course, since nearly all of the religiously-based schools were Catholic, the target of the amendment was quite clear to everyone. After Grant's speech, Maine Congressman **James Blaine**, the future Republican nominee for president, proposed that such an amendment be added to the Federal Constitution. Although Blaine's amendment passed almost unanimously in the House of Representatives, it narrowly failed in the Senate. Supporters of the **Blaine Amendment** then turned to the states, where a majority of state legislatures passed Blaine's Amendment.

In 1883, the Vatican summoned a number of American archbishops to Rome to discuss the status of Catholic education in the United States. After meeting with the archbishops, the Vatican officials urged Pope Leo XIII to approve a third plenary council.

The Third Plenary Council was held in Baltimore in November 1884. It was presided over by **James Gibbons**. In addition to Archbishop Gibbons, fourteen archbishops, sixty-one bishops, and numerous priests and theologians also attended. In fact, it was one of the largest Church councils held since the Council of Trent adjourned in 1563. Once again, the Council focused on education. However, this time, the Council Fathers took much stronger positions on the issues. For example, they now *mandated*, rather than *requested*, that priests establish Catholic schools in their parishes within two years of the close of the Council. The Council also took a firmer stand with Catholic parents. In its own version of compulsory attendance, the Fathers wrote that *"we not only exhort Catholic parents...but we command them with all the authority in our power, to procure a truly Christian education for their dear offspring...[and] send them to Catholic schools."* The Council also expressed the desire that the parochial schools be free. In order to be excused from attendance at Catholic school, parents had to obtain permission from their local *bishop*! Believing that Catholic schools needed to be more competitive with the public schools, the bishops considered implementing a nationally standardized curriculum. The Third Plenary Council also appointed a commission to prepare a catechism for use in the schools, which became the famous *Baltimore Catechism*.

The Council also addressed the need for **Catholic high schools**, which the previous Councils had not even mentioned. Over the next fifteen years, the Church would build one hundred Catholic high schools in the United States. By 1920, there would be 1,500!

Caldwell Hall, the first building of the Catholic University of America. Named in honor of Mary Gwendoline Caldwell who pledged $300,000 to establish the University.

The Council also felt that it was time to found a Catholic university. They created a commission to begin planning its construction. In 1887, the cornerstone of the first building of the **Catholic University of America** was laid in Washington, D.C.

The Third Council also stressed the education of the clergy and the importance of founding seminaries as well as the curriculum that they should teach. In addition, the Council decreed that there should be six holy days of obligation. The bishops also created a commission to aid the missions to the Native American and Black populations.

The Third Plenary Council took a giant step forward by removing the mission status of the American Church. It prepared the Church in the United States for the move from a missionary project to a mature part of the Body of Christ ready to provide for its own support. In fact, the United States would become the Catholic Church's largest financial supporter in the following century. Under the influence of this Third Plenary Council, Catholic education was reorganized in the United States. The amazingly successful national system of Catholic parish schools began because of the strong support of the bishops throughout the United States.

Mother Katharine Drexel

One of the decrees issued by the Third Plenary Council of Baltimore had been to appoint a committee to aid the missions to help Blacks and Native Americans. Among the Catholics working to help Blacks and Native Americans, **Mother Katharine Drexel** took a leading position.

Katharine was born in 1858 to a wealthy Philadelphia family, who used their wealth to help the poor as well as Blacks and Native Americans. Always concerned with the underprivileged, Katharine was one of those few people upon whom Helen Hunt Jackson's *A Century of Dishonor*, detailing the plight of Native Americans, had the desired effect. In 1884, on a journey to the West, she personally saw the tragedy of the Native Americans of which she had only read. She determined to dedicate her life to bettering theirs.

The following year her father died, leaving her a vast fortune. She also began contemplating the religious life. In May 1889, she became a Sister of Mercy, determined to dedicate her life and fortune to assisting the Black and Native American missions. In 1891, Katharine Drexel, along with thirteen other women, founded a new religious order, the **Sisters of the Blessed Sacrament.** As leader of the order, she would be known as "Mother" Drexel.

During her long life, Mother Drexel founded sixty-three schools for Blacks and Native Americans across the United States. In 1925, Mother Drexel founded her most famous school, **Xavier University of Louisiana**, in New Orleans, Louisiana. Xavier is the only *historically black*, co-educational Catholic university in the United States.

Mother Drexel died in 1955. Pope St. John Paul II declared her a saint in October 2000. The Sisters of the Blessed Sacrament continue to work with African Americans and Native Americans.

Mother Katharine Drexel

The Church and the Labor Movement

In addition to the vital spiritual issues facing Catholics during the late 19th century, priests and bishops also faced a number of political and social issues. One of the more important social issues with which they dealt involved the question of the Catholic Church's relationship with the Labor Movement. Amazingly for a religion that represented such a small segment of the population, the Church would play a large role in the Labor Movement.

Most Catholics lived in the large Northern cities, rather than on farms, in rural communities, or in the South. Thus, although Catholics represented a small part of the national population, they represented a larger percentage of factory workers, many of whom were unskilled or low-skilled immigrants. As a result, as the labor movement began to form unions, Catholics joined. Moreover, even Catholics who did not work in factories likely attended Mass alongside parishioners who did. Consequently, the Church has had close ties to the labor movement almost from its inception.

Most priests and bishops supported the improvements called for by the unions which affected the welfare of Catholic families. Among the leaders for social reform was the first bishop of Peoria, Illinois, **John Lancaster Spalding** (1840-1916). Bishop Spalding championed the cause of better social conditions as well as safer working conditions. He advocated that employers pay their workers a "**living wage**." To Spalding, a "living wage" meant a salary that allowed workers to live a decent physical existence, in which they could have a family and live under conditions favorable to mental, moral, and religious improvement. For the bishop, the issue of a living wage was one of justice. The role he played in the American labor movement was such that in 1902, President Theodore Roosevelt appointed him to the **Anthracite Coal Strike Commission** to help judge claims of striking miners. Bishop Lancaster helped the two sides reach a compromise settlement.

Bishop John Spalding

Cardinal Gibbons and The Knights of Labor

The staunchest friend that American workers had in the Catholic Church was **Cardinal James Gibbons** (1834-1921), the Archbishop of Baltimore. Under his leadership, the Church gave new importance to the cause of labor and the rights of workers to organize. In 1887, Cardinal Gibbons journeyed to Rome to meet with Pope Leo XIII. He wished to inform the Pope generally about the American labor movement and specifically to defend the **Knights of Labor**.

The Knights of Labor was a semi-secret organization committed to defending the interests of workers. It became the nation's leading union in the second half of the 19th century. The leaders of the Knights of Labor believed secrecy was necessary to protect their members from harassment or loss of employment for belonging to the union. However, because the Knights was a secret organization, many Church leaders opposed Catholics becoming members. These leaders believed that they had valid concerns, since many *anti-Catholic* societies held secret rituals and had secret memberships. **Elzéar-Alexandre Cardinal Taschereau**, the Archbishop of Quebec and Canada's first cardinal, forbade Catholics from joining the Knights and threatened Catholics who did with excommunication. Although Taschereau's excommunication

James Cardinal Gibbons (1904) (detail of a somewhat larger portrait)

would only affect the Knights in his diocese, and none in the United States, his threat and condemnation of the Knights were causing them immeasurable harm, both in Canada and the United States. That the Knights' leader, Terrence V. Powderly, was a Catholic compounded the problem.

Cardinal Gibbons knew the issue needed to be addressed, so he investigated all of the charges against the union. In 1887, Cardinal Taschereau advised Pope Leo XIII to consider barring Catholics from joining the Knights. In response, Cardinal Gibbons went to Rome and also spoke to Pope Leo XIII. He defended the Knights' right to organize a union that opposed oppression and unfair tactics by employers. As a result of his spirited defense, the Holy Father decided that prohibiting membership in the union was unwarranted. It is possible that Cardinal Gibbons' strong defense of labor caused Pope Leo XIII to issue his famous encyclical on labor: *Rerum Novarum*.

The Impact of *Rerum Novarum* in the United States

Pope Leo XIII (1878-1903) was the first pope to write a papal encyclical on modern social issues. In 1891, in his encyclical, **Rerum Novarum** (*On capital and labor*), Leo XIII emphasized the moral principles of justice and charity, the principles that should regulate the relationship between capital (managers and investors) and labor (workers). He proclaimed that laborers are entitled to a **living wage**, which he defined as a salary that would allow a working man and his family to live decently. Leo also declared that workers had the right to organize unions to secure better wages and to improve working conditions.

Most bishops in the United States fully supported the ideas in *Rerum Novarum*. However, many years passed before people began to widely accept its message. In 1891, a right to unionize and to bargain for wages still seemed to be a dangerous idea to many people. However, beginning in 1919, American bishops began to promote *Rerum Novarum* more strongly. Some bishops issued pastoral letters that supported and helped strengthen its teachings. In the first half of the 20th century, Congress enacted laws that followed many ideas similar to the ones in Leo's encyclical.

Leading Churchmen of the Late 19th Century

As further evidence of the growth of the Church in the United States, in the late 19th century, the Holy Father elevated two men, **John McCloskey** and **James Gibbons**, to the College of Cardinals.

John McCloskey

John McCloskey was born in New York City, to Irish immigrant parents, in 1810. He attended Catholic grade school and Mount St. Mary's College, from which he graduated in 1826. The following year, a tragic accident seriously injured him. During his recovery, McCloskey determined that he had a vocation and returned to Mount St. Mary's, where he began studying for the priesthood. On January 12, 1834, Bishop John Dubois ordained John McCloskey a priest for the diocese of New York.

John Cardinal McCloskey (1875)

Over the next years, McCloskey served as a priest in New York in addition to furthering his studies at Catholic colleges and universities in Europe. In 1843, Pope Gregory XVI appointed McCloskey Coadjutor Bishop of New York. [**Note**: A coadjutor bishop is a bishop who assists the diocesan bishop in governing the diocese and automatically replaces him when he dies or retires.] Bishop "Dagger" John Hughes presided at his consecration as bishop.

On May 21, 1847, Pope Pius IX named John McCloskey Bishop of the newly created Diocese of Albany. During his tenure as Bishop of Albany, he built a cathedral, more than quadrupled the number of parishes, and almost tripled the number of priests. He also attended the First Plenary Council of Baltimore and, in keeping with its exhortation that every parish have a school, he built fifteen parochial schools. He also built a seminary.

Following the death of Archbishop John Hughes in 1864, Pope Pius IX named John McCloskey New York's second archbishop. He resumed construction of the new St. Patrick's Cathedral, which Bishop Hughes had started. He dedicated the magnificent cathedral in May 1879. In 1866, he attended the Second Plenary Council of Baltimore. Three years later, he journeyed to Rome where he took part in the First Vatican Council, voting in favor of the Doctrine of Papal Infallibility.

As the Diocese of New York represented a microcosm of the Catholic Church in America, John McCloskey focused on those issues that concerned all bishops dealing with a rapidly growing Church. During his twenty-one years as Archbishop of New York, he increased the number of parishes by eighty-eight as well as creating one specifically for black Catholics. He also more than doubled the number of priests in his diocese to four hundred. Bishop McCloskey also increased the number of children attending the parochial schools in his parishes.

In March 1875, Pope Pius IX elevated him to the Sacred College, making him the United States' first cardinal. Even non-Catholics celebrated the news that an American had become a Prince of the Church. Although eligible to vote in the election of Pius IX's successor, Cardinal McCloskey arrived in Rome too late to participate in the 1878 Conclave that elected Pope Leo XIII.

After a lengthy illness, John Cardinal McCloskey died on October 10, 1885. He was buried in St. Patrick's Cathedral. The man who delivered the eulogy at Cardinal McCloskey's funeral was his good friend, **James Cardinal Gibbons**, America's second cardinal.

James Gibbons

James Gibbons was born in Baltimore, Maryland on July 23, 1834 to Irish immigrant parents. In 1839, his father moved the family back to Ireland for health reasons. However, his health failed to improve and he died in 1847. In 1853, James' mother returned to the United States, settling the family in New Orleans.

Believing that he had a vocation, in 1855, James entered St. Charles College in Maryland before entering St. Mary's Seminary in Baltimore, two years later. During his time in the seminary, his health diminished so severely that it appeared he would not be ordained. Yet, by the grace of God and the strength of his own will, he completed seminary. On June 30, 1861, Archbishop Francis Kenrick ordained him at Baltimore Cathedral.

Over the next years, Fr. Gibbons served at various parishes, eventually becoming secretary to Baltimore's archbishop, **Martin John Spalding**, in 1865. In that capacity, he helped Bishop Spalding prepare for the Second Plenary Council of Baltimore, which met in 1866. During the Council, Spalding recommended that the state of North Carolina be made an **apostolic vicariate** (a type of mission diocese) and that Fr. Gibbons be placed in charge. The Council agreed.

In March 1868, Pope Pius IX made Fr. Gibbons the Apostolic Vicar of North Carolina as well as a bishop. At only thirty-four years of age, James Gibbons was one of the youngest bishops in the world. North Carolina, while geographically large, is located in the **Bible Belt**, that predominantly Protestant section of the South. Thus, then – as now – it had a tiny Catholic population, probably less than seven hundred Catholics. Gibbons' main mission, in addition to ensuring that his few parishioners had access to the Sacraments, was to evangelize the Protestants in his territory.

As Bishop Gibbons engaged in his conversion efforts, he found that all existing apologetics books failed to meet his needs. Not deterred, he wrote his own book, *Faith of Our Fathers*. Published in 1876, it would become one of the best-selling religion books in history. By 1917, *Faith of Our Fathers* had sold over 1.4 million copies, an incredible figure for those times, ranking it with the Bible and *Uncle Tom's Cabin* among the best-selling books of the 19th century. Moreover,

Bishop Martin John Spalding

Bishop James Gibbons in 1872

Faith of Our Fathers made Bishop Gibbons a celebrity. His sermons even began to attract non-Catholics who appreciated his perspective on Christianity.

During his life, Bishop Gibbons would write several more books, including *Our Christian Heritage* (1889), *The Ambassador of Christ* (1896), *Discourses and Sermons* (1908), and *A Retrospect of Fifty Years* (1916). He also wrote numerous articles for various magazines. Because his writing style was simple, straightforward, and engaging, even Protestants read his books and magazine articles, especially on controversial issues.

In 1869, along with Bishop John McCloskey, Bishop Gibbons attended the First Vatican Council in Rome, where he also voted in favor of Papal Infallibility. In July 1872, Pius IX named James Gibbons bishop of Richmond, Virginia. He served as bishop of Richmond until the Pope named him bishop of Baltimore in May 1877. In 1886, Leo XIII elevated James Gibbons to the rank of cardinal, making him the second American to be so honored.

The following year, Cardinal Gibbons, who had been one of the leading voices at the Third Plenary Council to advocate for the creation of a Catholic University of America, became its first Chancellor. In 1903, he had the honor to participate in the papal conclave that elected Pope Pius St. Pius X, the first American ever to vote for the pope.

Cardinal Gibbons' greatest efforts lay in the social arena, where he worked tirelessly on behalf of the rights of working men and women. Through Gibbons' efforts, Catholics were allowed to join the Knights of Labor. In 1887, Gibbons presented a letter to Pope Leo XIII explaining why Catholics should be allowed to join the Knights of Labor, or any other labor union. Basically, the letter sought to explain how the labor and political situation in the United States differed from that in Europe. Gibbons pointed out that in American labor unions, Catholic workers held no animosity toward the Church, unlike so many European unions, run by Communists who saw the Church as their mortal enemy. As a result of his excellent explanation, the Pope allowed Catholics to become union members.

Cardinal Gibbons' influence extended well beyond the Church. Many American presidents sought his advice. Some became his close friends. In 1917, former President Theodore Roosevelt said of Cardinal Gibbons: "Taking your life as a whole, I think you are the most respected, venerated, and useful citizen of our country."

James Cardinal Gibbons died on March 24, 1921. He was buried in Baltimore Cathedral, where he had been baptized eighty-six years earlier. Five years before his death, the *Baltimore Sun* newspaper had written of him, "The Catholic Church has given many distinguished prelates and priests to its work in this country, but none who has inspired the same general confidence and the same earnest esteem."

Cardinal Gibbons embraces Theodore Roosevelt

Catholic Social Programs

Bringing aid and comfort to the less fortunate is a vital part of the Catholic Faith and the Catholic Church. Since the days of the Apostles, the Church has been concerned with people's spiritual welfare as well as their physical welfare. Catholic history is filled with many wonderful examples of men and women who have expressed their love of God and of neighbor by aiding needy people, especially families. The Church in America has always tried to help the poor, the disabled, immigrants, the homeless, the sick, and the neglected. Various types of Catholic agencies provide care for them all. As part of that work, the Church has diligently spread the Gospel, as more and more Catholic organizations have been established to care for people in every kind of need.

Of the various Catholic social service organizations, the **Society of St. Vincent de Paul** is one of the best-known. **Bl. Frederic Ozanam** and a group of his friends founded the Society in Paris, France in 1833. The Society of St. Vincent de Paul in America came to Saint Louis in 1845. By the end of the century, it had grown into a major Catholic service organization. It is still very active, especially in large cities. The Society is staffed by men and women who visit distressed and indigent families in their own parishes. If physical aid is required, families are given food, clothing, and shelter. If spiritual help is needed, the case is always referred to the local pastor. Inspired by their patron, who was a model of Christian charity, Vincentians duplicate the works of St. Vincent de Paul and have become living examples of the charity of Christ.

The Third Plenary Council had created a commission to study evangelization of America's Black and Native American populations. The commission determined that a national association was needed that would more efficiently coordinate the Church's activities among Native Americans and Blacks. In 1874, a Bureau of Catholic Indian Missions was established. Later on, the Bureau established the **Black and Indian Mission Office**.

In 1882, **Fr. Michael McGivney** founded the **Knights of Columbus**, which began as a way to help working men pool their resources to help each other and their families. However, the Knights soon began helping anyone in need. Today, the Knights of Columbus support a wide range of activities, such as promoting vocations and pro-life activities. They especially help the handicapped and needy families, and have helped pay for Catholic education of children, whether in the local parish, at a high school, or in home schooling. The Knights were instrumental in adding the phrase "under God" to the Pledge of Allegiance in the 1950s.

The **National Society for the Propagation of the Faith** was organized in the United States in 1897 under the direction of the Holy See. It performs two principal functions. First, it serves as the Church's main source of increasing awareness of her worldwide missions. Second, it generates financial support for those missions. The work of the Society is so vital that each diocese has a director. Their duty is to collect funds for the foreign missions and to educate the faithful in the value of these missions.

As our nation grew, so did the need for charity. At the turn of the century, it became clear that charitable activities had to be better organized to meet the needs of modern society. In 1910, Cardinal Gibbons created the **National Conference of Catholic Charities**, now called **Catholic Charities, U.S.A.** It has become the major service organization of the Church in the United States, serving

Portrait of Fr. McGivney

a network of more than 1,200 agencies and institutions. As their website says, they support "a wide range of programs and services that protect, strengthen and empower the most vulnerable people in our society." They accomplish this goal by providing food, shelter, and counseling services to teenagers, parents, the elderly, and many others.

The Catholic Church at the Turn of the Century

By 1900, about 11 million Catholics lived in the United States, representing about 14% of the entire population. Most lived in the industrial Northeast. Following the decrees of the Three Plenary Councils of Baltimore, America's Catholic bishops had dedicated themselves to creating a robust parochial school system that rivaled the government-run public school system. By 1900, about 3,500 parochial schools operated in the United States. The bishops could say, "Mission Accomplished." In the next century, America's Catholic schools would become the envy of the world, attracting even leading non-Catholics to send their children for an education.

By 1900, the United States no longer had the status of "mission territory." It had one cardinal, over ninety bishops, and more than 12,000 priests. The Church in America was not merely financially independent, but becoming wealthy. In the next century, the United States would become the leading financial supporter of nearly all Catholic projects worldwide. Meanwhile, Catholic social service organizations sought to help America's needy through a variety of programs.

The Mustard Seed by Vincent Van Gogh

Although Catholics still faced prejudice, by 1900 they were increasingly accepted into American society. Terrence Powderly, a Catholic, led the Knights of Labor. Numerous Catholics joined labor unions. Both major political parties sought the "Catholic vote."

As the 20th century began, the Church would continue to face the same challenges it had in the previous century. However, it was larger, better funded, and better prepared for the challenges. To paraphrase St. Matthew (13:31-2): In 1800, the Church in America was like a mustard seed that a person took and sowed in a field. It is the smallest of all the seeds. However, when full-grown it is the largest of plants. It becomes a large bush, and the birds of the sky come and dwell in its branches. By 1900, the American Church had become a large bush. In the next century, it would become larger still.

CHAPTER 24   REVIEW QUESTIONS

Answer the following questions:

1. What were some of the issues the Church faced in the second half of the 19th century?
2. What was the main focus of the First Plenary Council of Baltimore?
3. Who presided over the First Plenary Council of Baltimore?
4. Who is known as the "Father of the Parochial School System?" Why does he have that honor?
5. During his time as Archbishop of New York, how did John Hughes work to improve the Catholic schools in his diocese? How did he deal with the "Nativists?" What was his nickname?
6. What were some of the mandates the Second Plenary Council issued regarding education?
7. What is the "Blaine Amendment?" How did it originate?
8. Who presided over the Third Plenary Council? What was its main focus? What very famous book did the Council instruct be written?
9. What was the name of James Gibbon's best-selling book? Why did he write it?
10. What was the relationship between Cardinal Gibbons and the Knights of Labor? How did Cardinal Gibbons help the Knights?
11. Who was America's first cardinal? Who was the second?
12. Who was the first American to vote in a papal election?
13. Where is the Catholic University of America located?
14. Who founded the Knights of Columbus?
15. Why was the original purpose of Knights of Columbus? What is its current purpose?
16. Who founded the National Conference of Catholic Charities?
17. Why did the Catholic Church have close ties to the Labor Movement during the 19th century?
18. Why is John McCloskey such an important figure in the history of the Church in the second half of the 19th century?

Identify the following:

1. Mother Katherine Drexel
2. John Lancaster Spalding
3. *Rerum Novarum*
4. Bible Belt
5. Xavier University of Louisiana

America on the World's Stage

1865-1914

In this painting "*A Word to the Kaiser*," President Roosevelt meets with the German ambassador, Dr. Von Holleben. Because Venezuela had not paid its debts, Germany threatened to occupy one or more Venezuelan ports in clear violation of the Monroe Doctrine. Roosevelt called Von Holleben for a meeting where he told the Ambassador that unless Germany agreed to the arbitration that Roosevelt would send Admiral Dewey and the American navy to interfere with Germany's plans. In light of Roosevelt's threat, the Germans chose to arbitrate. The Kaiser, the German King, learned that the Monroe Doctrine was to be taken seriously.

America's Early Isolation Policy

In his *Farewell Address* of 1796, George Washington said, "*The great rule of conduct for us, in regard to foreign nations, is, in extending our commercial relations, to have with them as little political connection as possible. So far as we have already formed engagements, let them be fulfilled with perfect good faith. Here let us stop.*" Washington's warning was straightforward. America should be a great business partner with all foreign nations, especially European nations, but should avoid any involvement in European politics. His *Address* set the tone for the next seventy years of American foreign policy.

For the first several decades of its history, the United States did not have the military strength to become involved in foreign affairs, even had our leaders so desired. In 1823, when James Monroe proclaimed the "Monroe Doctrine," it more represented America's *determination* to create a policy than a real *ability* to enforce one. Nevertheless, the Monroe Doctrine was a direct outgrowth of George Washington's warning. America was telling Europe that, while we would not involve ourselves in their affairs, we expected them not to involve themselves in the affairs of North and South America.

Until the Civil War, European nations adhered to the Monroe Doctrine. However, during the Civil War, Great Britain provided blockade runners to the Confederacy and even considered entering the War as a Confederate ally. However, even more offensive to Americans were the actions of France. In October 1863, Austrian Prince Maximilian, the brother of the Holy Roman Emperor, accepted the offer of the pro-

George Washington set American foreign policy for seventy years. In this painting by Gilbert Stuart, the artist portrays Washington as both a military man (holding a sword) but also a man of peace, gesturing to the quill pen and parchment, symbolic of peace treaties.

Catholic and pro-monarchist forces in Mexico to become Emperor of Mexico. The conservative Mexican forces were at war with anti-Catholic leader Benito Juarez. With the help of Napoleon III, who provided French troops, Maximilian began his rule in late May 1864. The French and the forces of Benito Juarez fought continuously for the nation.

Although the United States viewed the French intervention in Mexico as a direct violation of the Monroe Doctrine, at the time, with the Civil War going on, nothing could be done. However, once the Civil War concluded, the United States put serious diplomatic pressure on France to withdraw its troops. America also moved 50,000 troops to the Mexican border. The threat of an American invasion and war with the United States caused Napoleon III to withdraw his soldiers. Many of Maximilian's followers also abandoned his cause. By spring 1866, his cause was clearly lost. Almost any other man would have abdicated and fled. Napoleon III urged him to do so. Nevertheless, Maximilian was the son of the Hapsburg family, the great ruling family of Europe for almost 1000 years. He was an Austrian naval officer. He remained at his post, unwilling to desert his remaining followers. On May 16, 1867, Benito Juarez's troops captured him after a lengthy siege. They executed him the following month.

In 1823, had America tried to force France to leave Mexico through a show of military strength or diplomatic pressure, it might not have worked. America may simply not have been strong enough. However, by 1866, America possessed the strength to stand up to any European nation – if it had need to do so. Yet most Americans preferred to remain isolated from the problems of other nations. By 1866, most nations saw that America could defend itself, so they realized that she should be left alone.

By 1890, America had become incredibly prosperous and an economic superpower. American industry produced twice the industrial goods of the next largest economy, Great Britain. Moreover, America not only sold goods domestically, but also sold its products all over the world.

However, the United States was not yet the world's foremost *military* superpower. That title still belonged to Great Britain. Great Britain possessed an army many times larger than America's and its navy was ten times larger than the U.S. Navy. The United States had not built up large armed forces for two reasons. First, it did not anticipate war in the foreseeable future. It had the natural defenses of the Atlantic and Pacific oceans, immense obstacles for potential European or Asian aggressors; and it enjoyed friendly relations with its North American neighbors, Canada and Mexico who posed no military threat. Second, prior to the latter part of the 19th century, America had no interest in military involvement outside of the Western Hemisphere.

However, after the end of the Civil War, America began to step onto the world's stage as a major actor. For the first time, the United States was going to expand beyond its natural North American borders. America would look north to Alaska, west to the Pacific, and south to the Caribbean.

The Alaska Purchase

America's first land purchase beyond its continental borders occurred in 1867, when the United States bought nearly 600,000 square miles of largely barren tundra called **Alaska** from the Russian Empire. Since the 1790s, Russia had claimed Alaska, or "Russian America," as it was known in 1867. However, despite efforts by Russian fur trappers and merchants, the territory had never been a commercial success. Moreover, by the late 1850s, Russia also realized that it could not protect Alaska against an invasion from British Canada. Russia decided to sell the huge area rather than spend any more on development or risk its loss to the British. The United States seemed the logical purchaser.

The Russians initially began negotiations for the sale of Alaska in 1857, but with the pressures mounting that would lead to the Civil War, America felt the time was not right to make such a purchase. However, after the war, Secretary of State **William H. Seward** resumed talks. Eventually the parties agreed America would pay $7,200,000, or about 2 cents per acre, for Alaska.

Secretary of State Seward

Americans had two reactions to the idea of purchasing Alaska. Some people, including members of Congress, criticized the notion of buying the seemingly endless miles of Arctic wasteland. They called Alaska "Seward's Folly" and "Seward's Icebox." They joked that cows in Alaska would give ice cream, not milk! However, they were in the minority. Most people, like powerful senator Charles Sumner, agreed with Seward that Alaska had immense value. They pointed out that the lumber, fur, and fishing industries would generate more than the $7.2 million asking price. They noted that having control of such a vast territory would give the United States greater influence in the Northern Pacific and provide access to Asia. Newspapers and public opinion supported Seward. On April 9, 1867, the Senate voted 37 to 2 to confirm the treaty and purchase Alaska.

Seward was correct. The land quickly proved to be worth many, many times its purchase price. Natural resources include gold, silver, copper, lead, tin, gypsum, platinum, coal, and tungsten. During the last few decades, Alaska has become one of the world's top producers of natural gas and petroleum. Billions of barrels of crude oil have been discovered. The petroleum industry has made Alaska and her citizens wealthy.

Signing of the Alaska Treaty by Emmanuel Leutze. From left to right are portrayed: diplomat Robert Chew; Secretary of State William Seward; diplomat William Hunter Jr.; Russian diplomat Waldemar de Bodisco; Russian ambassador Eduard de Stoeckl; senator Charles Sumner, Chairman of the powerful Senate Foreign Relations Committee; and Assistant Secretary of State Frederick Seward.

Commercial fishing is another important industry in Alaska and has been for more than a hundred years. Alaska salmon, snow crabs, and king crabs number among the more lucrative catches. Some of the best sport fishing in the world is found off the Alaska Peninsula. Sport fishermen from around the globe travel to Alaska to test their skill with a rod and reel against the various trophy-class fish that lurk in the abundant lakes and rivers, in water so clear that anglers can easily see fish twenty or more feet below the surface.

Although the United States had purchased the massive land, few Americans chose to live there during the next thirty years. However, in 1898, gold was discovered in the Klondike region of the Yukon River Basin, in lower Canada. The frenzied eagerness characteristic of California's gold-seeking "Forty-Niners" was reborn! Hopeful men and women rushed north to the new gold fields. Soon thereafter, prospectors discovered more gold farther along the Yukon River in Alaska. Boom towns sprang up in Alaska virtually overnight.

In the 1920s, discussion began about building a highway to connect Alaska to the lower 48 states. However, it was not until the outbreak of World War II and the Japanese threat to the West Coast that Congress approved construction. Highway construction began in March 1942, proceeded quickly, and was finished by the end of October. The 1,500-mile **Alaska Highway** runs through northern Canada and Alaska. It traverses some of the world's most rugged terrain, including swamps and rivers. This highway still remains the only land route linking the lower forty-eight states with Alaska. In 1959, Alaska joined the Union as the 49th state. America had a new group of "49ers" after all.

The Hawaiian Islands

If anywhere on Earth is more unlike the cold tundra of Alaska, it must be the warm, tropical islands of Hawaii. The **Hawaiian Islands** are an *archipelago*, or island group, consisting of eight major islands, plus many smaller islands, located about 2,500 miles off the coast of Northern California. By the late 19th century, the United States had become very interested in the Hawaiian Islands.

British explorer Captain **James Cook** discovered Hawaii in January 1778. He found about 300,000 Hawaiians frolicking about in the thundering surf and the golden sands without serious issues or cares. However, these natives were pagans who worshiped many gods and idols. He named his discovery the **"Sandwich Islands"** in honor of the First Lord of the Admiralty, the Fourth Earl of Sandwich. Cook anchored off the coast and traded with the Hawaiians for food and water. When he returned the following year, a dispute with the natives ended in his death.

The first Americans to reach Hawaii were New England whalers and traders. Like Cook, they stopped in Hawaii for fresh food and water. Whaling would remain an important industry in Hawaii until the oil boom in Pennsylvania in the late 1850s. Kerosene would replace whale oil, crippling the industry.

In 1820, the first shipload of Protestant missionaries arrived in Hawaii. Led by Hiram Bingham, they came to Hawaii to convert the pagan natives. Calvinists from Massachusetts, Bingham and his missionaries were aggressive and relentless in their determination to convert Hawaii to Christianity. Within three years, he had managed to convince Hawaii's queen to be baptized and enact laws stressing a more moral lifestyle. However, Bingham proved excessively hostile to the evangelization efforts of Catholic missionaries who arrived in Hawaii in 1827. The Catholic mission had some small success before the government ordered it off the islands in 1831.

Unknowingly, the missionaries and whalers brought with them measles, smallpox, and other diseases unknown to Hawaii and for which Hawaiians had no immunity. Although many of these were simple "childhood illnesses" to white Americans, the effects upon Hawaiians proved devastating. By the end of the 19th century, the native Hawaiian population may have numbered fewer than 40,000.

In order to support themselves, the missionaries had become involved in Hawaii's sugar industry. Hawaiians had raised sugar cane since the first Polynesians had settled Hawaii. They chewed the cane for its sweetness and its nutritional value. It had been one of the items favored by whalers and traders. The first mill to refine sugar cane was established in 1835.

By the 1840s, the missionaries became more involved in the sugar industry. Over the next two decades, the white missionaries, who had ostensibly come to convert the natives, had slowly taken over the islands' economy and government. By 1860, sugar, sold mostly in the United States, had become the islands' most important export. Unfortunately, European diseases had decimated the native Hawaiian population and few natives wanted to work on the sugar plantations. Therefore, the planters began importing tens of thousands of inexpensive laborers, first from China and then from Japan, to work in the sugar cane fields.

King Kamehameha III

Since the time of Captain Cook, Hawaii had been ruled by a series of kings. However, in 1840, **King Kamehameha III** issued Hawaii's first constitution which created a constitutional monarchy. Hawaii's new government would have separate executive, legislative and judicial branches. The king acted as the executive branch. A house of nobles acted as the upper House (Senate) with membership based on heredity, but an elected lower House of Representatives was added. A supreme court would adjudicate legal questions.

In 1875, the United States and Hawaii signed a **Reciprocity Treaty** that allowed sugar and other Hawaiian products to enter the United States free of tariff. In return, the government of Hawaii gave the United States land in Hawaii for what would become the **Pearl Harbor** naval base and agreed not to give land or other special privileges to any other nation. For decades, Hawaii's sugar planters had sought to abolish the sugar tariff. The Reciprocity Treaty caused a massive increase in sugar production.

The sugar planters became fabulously wealthy and the Hawaiian economy grew several times larger. In 1861, Hawaii shipped about 2 million pounds of sugar to the United States From 1875 to 1890, Hawaii's sugar exports to America jumped from 25 million pounds to over 224 million pounds. However, in 1890, Congress passed the **McKinley Tariff** which imposed a high protective tariff on *all* sugar imported into the United States, including Hawaii's sugar. Starting in 1890, Hawaii had to compete with all world-wide sugar production. Sugar from other markets was being sold more inexpensively than Hawaiian sugar in America. The price of sugar fell and Hawaii plunged into a major economic depression. The sugar planters - mostly white Americans - realized that if they became part of the United States they would not be subject to the tariff and their sugar problems would dissolve. As Hawaii faced this serious economic crisis, the Hawaiian government confronted grave political issues.

In 1874, the dynastic rule of the Kamehameha family ended with the death of William Lunalilo. Following his death, the legislature elected David Kalākaua, king. In 1887, King Kalākaua proclaimed a new constitution which stripped him of most of his power and granted more power to the legislature, which had come under the control of the wealthy non-Hawaiian landowners. Since he signed it under threat of violence, it has become known as the "**Bayonet Constitution**." In 1891, Kalākaua died and his sister **Liliuokalani** became Queen of Hawaii. Liliuokalani came to power during a time when Hawaii faced many serious crises.

Queen Liliuokalani had many fine qualities. She was intelligent and patriotic. Moreover, she wanted to protect her nation and its people. She realized that Americans had gained too much power over her country. She also knew that the Bayonet Constitution had been illegally promulgated and had been the instrument by which the wealthy American landowners had gained their power. In her mind, it was the root cause of many of Hawaii's problems.

In January 1893, Liliuokalani proposed a new constitution which would replace the Bayonet Constitution. Among its provisions, the new constitution restored the monarchy's power. It decreased the property requirements for voters, thus increasing the number of Hawaiians eligible to vote. Thirdly, American and European residents, who received the right to vote under the Bayonet Constitution, would lose that right. Her new constitution expressed her desire for greater Hawaiian sovereignty.

Sadly, the notion of Hawaii being governed by Hawaiians proved unacceptable to the wealthy American landowners. Once they learned of the proposed constitution, a group of them, led by **Sanford Dole**, staged a coup and overthrew Liliuokalani. **John L. Stevens**, the American representative to Hawaii, supported the rebels. He ordered U.S. Marines ashore in Honolulu, the kingdom's capital. On January 24, 1895, under the threat of the American troops, Liliuokalani was forced to abdicate the Hawaiian throne. Sanford Dole became president of the Hawaiian government.

Stevens then announced that Hawaii was under America's protection. He sent a treaty to Washington D.C. that would annex Hawaii to the United States; thus, resolving the tariff issue. In February 1893, President Harrison sent the treaty to the Senate for ratification. However, President-elect Grover Cleveland, to his everlasting credit, asked the Senate not to vote on the treaty until he could consider it. The Senate agreed to wait. On December 18, 1893, President Cleveland issued his "Message about Hawaii." He determined that the "military demonstration upon the soil of Honolulu was of itself an act of war." Therefore, he decided "to withdraw the treaty from the Senate for examination."

In the meantime, Cleveland sent former Georgia Congressman **James H. Blount** to Hawaii to examine the situation. Blount's investigation revealed that the native Hawaiians did not want to be annexed to the United States.

Queen Liliuokalani

Sanford Dole. Because of Sanford, the Dole family would become incredibly wealthy and of course Dole products, such as Dole Pineapples, can be found in virtually every store in America.

He further determined that John Stevens had not only exceeded his authority but in fact had been part of a revolution to overthrow a sovereign government! President Cleveland ordered Stevens to return to the United States and sent a new representative in his place. Cleveland also canceled the annexation treaty. America's new minister urged Sanford Dole to resign and re-instate Queen Liliuokalani. Dole flatly refused. On July 4, 1894, Dole and his followers proclaimed Hawaii a republic, with Dole as president.

However, Dole's goal remained annexation. If Hawaii were part of the United States, it would not have to pay tariffs. In 1897, William McKinley became president. Unlike Cleveland, McKinley favored annexation. On July 7, 1898, the United States annexed Hawaii. The formal annexation ceremony was held at Iolani Palace on August 12, 1898. Almost no native Hawaiians attended. On February 22, 1900, the Hawaiian Islands became the **Territory of Hawaii**, a part of the United States. Sanford Dole was appointed the first territorial governor.

Other Pacific Islands: Coaling Stations

The Civil War battle between the "ironclads" *Monitor* and *Merrimac* had shown that steel ships were the fighting vessels that would command the seas of the late 19th century. As a result, the United States began replacing its wooden ships with steel ones. Three decades later, America had a modest naval fleet but was on the way to becoming a leading naval power. Ships of this era were propelled by steam, which was produced by large, coal-fueled boilers. Many tons of coal were stored in large coal bunkers. Of course, when ships sailed to foreign lands, they needed to have access to strategic ports around the globe where they could be serviced and refueled. This meant obtaining naval bases and coaling stations.

In 1867, the United States began acquiring islands in the Pacific Ocean that would become important naval stations. That year, the U.S. took possession of **Midway Island**, which lies about 1,200 miles northwest of Hawaii. **Wake Island**, lying 2,300 miles west of Hawaii, was acquired in 1898. **Guam**, about 2,000 miles south of Japan and west of Wake Island, was captured by the U.S. in 1898. Finally, in 1899, the U.S. acquired part of the **Samoan Islands**, northeast of Fiji in the southern Pacific.

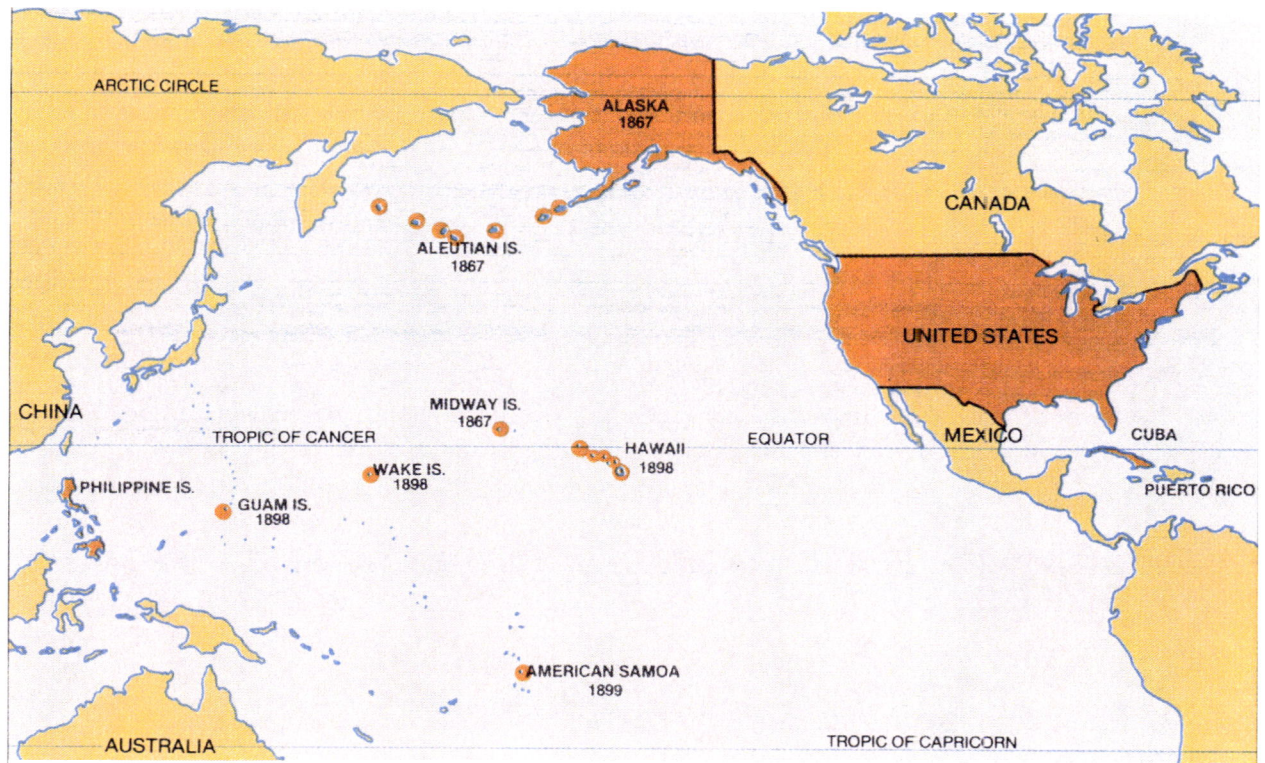

Pacific island coaling stations

The Spanish-American War

America

Before 1867, Americans had shown little interest in expanding beyond the United States' "natural borders:" the Atlantic Ocean in the East, Canada in the North, the Pacific Ocean in the West, and the Rio Grande River in the South. Americans had not expanded for two reasons. Then, as now, they believed that Democracies should not own colonies, as this violated the most basic principle of self-determination. Moreover, Americans had no practical desire to govern people of other lands. However, by the end of the 19th century, America underwent a change in attitude.

Attitudes changed for two reasons. First, as the "Progressive Era" began, Americans started more and more to believe that America truly was a "city on a hill," which meant that not only was the United States exceptional, but it had a duty to export that which made America great to the rest of the world. Some Americans believed that the United States had a moral duty to lift up "backward societies" and bring them American culture. Even today, while the U.S. does not normally impose its will *militarily*, American culture and values, both good and bad, permeate the world. Unfortunately, American culture was Protestant, and to many 19th-century Americans, "backward nations" meant *Catholic* nations.

The second cause of the shift in American attitudes, involved the European nations involvement in a new period of *imperialistic expansion*. During this period, the major European nations raced against each other to acquire colonies in Africa and Asia. From 1870 to 1900, the largest European powers seized 10 million square miles of land in Africa and Asia, bringing nearly 150 million people under colonial control. The massive landgrab by America's rivals caused great concern. Although most Americans had no desire for colonies, business and government leaders feared America would lose the raw materials available in Africa and Asia. Also, by this time America's factories and farmers were producing more than Americans could purchase or consume. Americans wanted to establish markets throughout the world where they could sell these "surplus" goods. They feared that Europe's competition for colonies would cost them opportunities to sell various products in overseas markets.

As a result of a change in both domestic feelings and international politics, the United States became more involved in international affairs in the late 19th century. For example, in 1889, Secretary of State James Blaine invited representatives from Latin American nations to attend a Pan-American conference in Washington D.C. In 1891, the United States became involved in a civil war in Chile. In 1895, the United States became entangled in a serious border dispute between Venezuela and Great Britain. For a time, it seemed that Great Britain and the United States might even go to war over America's enforcement of the Monroe Doctrine. However, in 1899, the parties settled the dispute amicably. On the other hand, just a year earlier, America was unwilling to settle its conflict with Spain amicably.

Spain

In 1492, Spain defeated the Muslims and captured the Muslim stronghold of Granada, ending history's longest war, 770 years. Spain's rulers, Ferdinand and Isabella, took a chance on an Italian sailor who claimed that he could reach India by sailing west. They financed the voyages of Christopher Columbus. With the wealth generated from its New World colonies, for the next 156 years, Spain remained the dominant power in the world. In 1648, with its defeat during the Thirty Years' War, Spain began a slow but inevitable decline.

By the early 19th century, Spain reflected a mere shadow of her former glory. Napoleon conquered Spain, installed his brother as king, and sold Louisiana to the United States. Meanwhile, with the mother country in turmoil, Spain's colonies in Latin America began revolting and seeking independence. By the end of the century, Cuba, the "Ever Faithful Isle," remained Spain's last important possession in the New World. The Philippines, her colony in the Pacific Ocean, remained Spain's only other important colony. Spain herself, once the world's mightiest empire, had been reduced to the status of a third-rate power.

The Battle of Rocroi by Augusto Ferrer-Dalmau (2011). The Battle of Rocroi (May 19, 1643) marked the end of Spain's time as Europe's leading power.

Cuba

Since the 1860s, the United States had had a strange relationship with the island of Cuba. On the one hand, Cuba's strategic location at the entrance to the Gulf of Mexico made it valuable as a military outpost and refueling station. The United States did not want it to fall into the hands of a potential enemy. Also, Cuba produced a vast amount of sugar so it possessed economic value. For these reasons, Secretary of State William Seward had considered purchasing Cuba. On the other hand, Cuba still practiced slavery. Seward could make no progress as long as slavery existed on the island. [**Note**: Slavery was not abolished in Cuba until October 1886, making it one of the last two nations in the Western Hemisphere to end the vile practice.]

In 1868, the Cubans, seeking independence, rebelled against their Spanish rulers. During the uprising, a Spanish warship captured a rebel ship and executed the people on board as "pirates." Among those executed were several Americans. War with Spain was narrowly averted when Spain apologized and paid reparations to the families of the Americans who were killed. However, Cuba, which seemed so far from God but so close to the United States, remained a potential problem – and opportunity - for America.

In 1895, the Cubans - for the sixth time in fifty years - again revolted against Spain. Applying guerrilla tactics, the skillful and determined Cuban fighters would burn sugar cane fields or ambush small squads of Spanish soldiers before disappearing into the mountains. By the end of 1896, the rebels controlled much of the Cuban countryside. It became more and more evident that the Spanish soldiers could not stop the Cubans' guerrilla tactics, at least while General Campos, the Spanish commander in Cuba, remained in charge.

In 1896, with Cuba in a full-blown rebellion, General **Valeriano Weyler** was named governor of Cuba, replacing General Campos. Weyler's orders were to suppress the rebellion and restore order to Cuba. To reestablish order, General Weyler incarcerated about 500,000 Cubans, whom he accused of aiding the rebels, in detention camps. He forced them out of their homes and into the camps. Weyler believed that the

One of the less offensive "Yellow Kid" cartoons. Written at the end of the 19th century, the cartoons apparently intended to offend every religious and ethnic group in the world. In this cartoon the artist has begun promoting Cuban independence.

detention camps would prevent people incarcerated in the camps from providing food, supplies, or other aid to the rebels. However, the camps had an effect that Weyler did not expect.

The Spanish detention camps were unsanitary, filthy, and disease-ridden. By 1898, as many as 200,000 Cubans may have died from disease and malnutrition in the camps. Americans, who naturally supported any group seeking independence, became enraged when they learned of the camps. American newspapers began an all-out campaign against General Weyler, calling him a "butcher." They demanded that Spain immediately recall him. Some proposed that an American army be dispatched to Cuba to free the Cubans as well as protect Americans in Cuba.

As events in Cuba became more explosive, some newspapers in America launched a campaign pushing for American intervention in the Cuban conflict. While some truth existed for the charges against General Weyler, the American newspaper campaign exemplified **yellow journalism** which was becoming extremely popular in America. At the time, two New York newspapers, one run by **William Randolph Hearst** and the other by **Joseph Pulitzer**, were competing for readers. Rather than ensuring the accuracy of their news stories, they ensured the stories contained *exaggerated headlines*, *overemotional cartoons*, and *shocking details* in order to sell more newspapers than their rival. The term "yellow journalism" was derived from a comic strip character called the "Yellow Kid" who appeared in Joseph Pulitzer's paper. Hearst and Pulitzer, who both supported the revolution and American intervention, published stories exaggerating the real atrocities and inventing atrocities where none existed. They sent reporters to Cuba who often "reported" on events that they had not witnessed. In one legendary event, Hearst sent renown painter Frederic Remington to

Cuba to paint scenes from the war. Remington, unable to find any violent scenes, telegraphed Hearst for instructions. Hearst is said to have replied, "You furnish the pictures and I'll furnish the war." Hearst and Pulitzer convinced many Americans that the United States should become involved in Cuba. These two multimillionaires had no real concern for the Cubans, but they knew that the news from a war would sell more papers!

Despite Hearst and Pulitzer, President McKinley did not want war with Spain. The Monroe Doctrine stood as a pledge that the United States would not interfere with existing European colonies in the Western Hemisphere. Obviously, Cuba was such a colony of Spain. Consequently, the United States felt obliged to maintain a neutral stand toward the disorders in Cuba. Nevertheless, many American businessmen saw large potential profits if Cuba gained her independence from Spain.

The Battleship *Maine*

President Cleveland and then President McKinley tried to convince the Spanish government to grant Cubans a greater role in their own rule. Their pleas fell on deaf ears. As tensions increased, President McKinley ordered the battleship *Maine* to Havana, Cuba's capital city, in January 1898. Havana had been the scene of violent riots, and McKinley felt that an American naval presence was needed to protect Americans in Havana. The *Maine* remained at anchor in the Havana harbor until the night of February 15, 1898, when the *Maine* exploded. Two hundred and fifty enlisted men and two officers died during the explosion while another fourteen sailors later perished as a result of their injuries. It ranks among the navy's worst peacetime catastrophes. Although investigations in the latter part of the 20th century determined that the explosion was an *accident* occurring *within* the ship, an American court of inquiry convened immediately after the sinking blamed the explosion on an underwater mine, thus implicating Spain in the sinking. On the other hand, a Spanish inquiry conducted at the same time correctly concluded that an internal explosion sank the *Maine*. However, the American press never reported on the Spanish findings.

1898 Photograph of the *Maine*.

Logically, Spain had no reason to go to war with the United States and every reason to avoid a war. Thus, logically, there was no reason for the Spanish to have blown up the *Maine*. However, in 1898, logic was in short supply in the United States. Spain did not want to go to war nor did President McKinley, who having fought in the Civil War knew the horrors of war first-hand. Yet Spain's government felt it could not grant complete independence to Cuba and still remain the ruling government of Spain. Losing Cuba could mean the overthrow of the Spanish government, possibly even of the monarchy. McKinley, under pressure from the newspapers, the public, and the Congress, felt that he could not accept anything less than Cuba's complete independence. The insistence that he declare war had simply become too great.

On April 20, President McKinley demanded Spain withdraw from Cuba. The next day, Spain broke off diplomatic relations with the United States and the U.S. Navy started a blockade of Cuba. On April 23, Spain stated that it would declare war if the United States invaded Cuba. On April 25, Congress declared that a state of war had existed between Spain and the United States since April 21, the day the blockade began and the official start of the Spanish-American War. Almost overnight, Americans adopted the slogan: *"Remember the Maine, and to hell with Spain."*

Remember the *Maine* propaganda poster. Top left image shows Havana harbor and the top right shows the recovery of the bodies. The bottom caption details the history of the Maine and its crew and armaments as well as the number of dead. The center image, with its graphic representation of bodies being blown into the air, served to incite American feelings against Spain.

The Battle of Manila Bay

Despite its alleged determination to free Cuba, the United States launched its first attack of the War against the Spanish-held islands of the Philippines. The Philippines had come under Spanish control in 1521, when Magellan, during his voyage around the world, had claimed them for Spain. However, almost forty years elapsed before Spanish colonists, missionaries, and conquistadors arrived to settle the islands. In 1571, the Spanish established Manila as the nation's capital city. For the next three hundred years, under Spanish rule, the Philippines became Catholic, prosperous, educated, and a generally good place to live and raise a family. During that time, Spain defended the islands from aggression from pirates, Muslim countries, and European nations seeking to extend their influence in Asia. Spain also quelled a number of indigenous revolts. However, by the end of the 19th century, more Filipinos began demanding independence from Spain. The internal resolution of these conflicts would never occur because on May 1, 1898, the American navy attacked the Spanish fleet in Manila Bay.

Commodore George Dewey

Commodore George Dewey, the commander of America's **Asiatic Squadron** naval forces stationed in Hong Kong, had been alerted weeks earlier by Assistant Secretary of the Navy Theodore Roosevelt to be ready for battle. When war was declared, Dewey received orders to immediately "capture or destroy the Spanish fleet," which was reported to be concentrated close to the Philippines. Dewey instantly steamed across the China Sea for the Philippines.

The American fleet of four cruisers and two gunboats entered Manila Bay on the night of April 30, 1898. The following morning, Dewey gave his famous command, "You may fire when ready, Gridley." The **Battle of Manila Bay** was more of a slaughter than a real battle. The fighting began at 5:41 AM and lasted for almost exactly seven hours, during which time the American ships withdrew to check their ammunition supplies. By 12:40 PM, the Spanish surrendered, as all of their ships had been sunk or scuttled. At the time, Commodore Dewey reported that he had lost only one American sailor who had died of a heart attack.

Although Dewey had destroyed the Spanish fleet, he did not have any Marines to capture the city of Manila or any other part of the Philippines. Thus, Dewey established a blockade of the harbor and waited for reinforcements. On August 13, American Marines went ashore and, in conjunction with the navy, captured the city of Manila.

Americans Volunteer to "Liberate" Cuba

The American navy achieved success through preparation and training. That could not be said about the American **army**, which was not prepared for war. At the outset of the Spanish-American War, President McKinley called for volunteers. Within two months, 200,000 men had enthusiastically volunteered, due largely to the yellow journalism of Hearst and Pulitzer. The most prominent volunteer was the Assistant Secretary of the Navy **Theodore Roosevelt**. In world history, certain men, once they stride upon the world's stage, force the spotlight of history to shine upon them. Theodore Roosevelt was such a man.

Theodore Roosevelt had *charisma*, that is, a compelling charm that can inspire devotion in others. Even his enemies said that you had to hate him a lot not to like him a little. Born in 1858, into a wealthy New York family tracing its roots back to the Dutch settlers of New Amsterdam, Theodore Roosevelt had been a skinny and sickly child with asthma and poor eyesight. However, he refused to allow his physical limitations to hinder him. He exercised and built up his body. He became a boxer and a skilled athlete. He grew to love the outdoors and spent time hunting and hiking. An intelligent boy, he loved history and politics. While at Columbia Law School, he wrote a well-received book on the history of the naval War of 1812. Published in 1882, it is still considered a definitive work.

Also, in 1882, Theodore Roosevelt, a Republican, was elected to the New York State Assembly. He began to make a name for himself fighting corruption, especially some of Jay Gould's schemes. In 1886, Roosevelt ran for, but failed to be elected, Mayor of New York City. In 1894, he became a

Theodore "Teddy" Roosevelt, the leader of the "Rough Riders"

police commissioner for New York City. He implemented various reforms, including merit-based hiring practices, as well as annual physicals for his police officers and firearms training. In many ways, he helped modernize the NYPD. In 1897, President McKinley appointed the up-and-coming Roosevelt Assistant Secretary of the Navy. As the Secretary of the Navy was in poor health, Roosevelt was *de facto*—that is, for all practical purposes—Secretary of the Navy. Roosevelt called for an increase in naval power, especially the construction of more battleships.

When the Spanish-American War broke out, Theodore Roosevelt, despite being forty years old, resigned from his position in the government and called for volunteers to join his unit, the **1st U.S. Volunteer Cavalry**, nicknamed the "**Rough Riders**." Amazingly, 23,000 men answered his call – such was his charisma! Of these thousands, he chose several hundred. Most were cowboys that he had known from the time he owned a ranch; a few were policemen from his days as police commissioner; and some were former soldiers. All the men were good horsemen, good with guns, and good athletes.

Meanwhile, tens of thousands of volunteers had to be organized into an efficient fighting force. However, the army had more men than it could organize. The volunteers were sent to Tampa, Florida for training prior to embarkation for Cuba. However, the situation at Tampa was dreadful and confusing. War had been declared before the men were ready to fight or the U.S Army had time to prepare. The army issued soldiers spoiled food which made them sick and winter woolen uniforms which made life in the tropical weather unbearable.

The Fall of Cuba

Before the soldiers in Tampa could be transported to Cuba, the U.S. Navy needed to ensure that it had control of the seas. Therefore, the navy was tasked with finding and destroying the Spanish navy under the command of **Admiral Pascual Cervera**. Although the American fleet patrolled the Caribbean in hopes of catching the Spaniards, the Cervera managed to sneak his ships past the Americans and sail into the harbor of Santiago, a city on the southern coast of Cuba. On May 29, the American navy discovered Cervera's

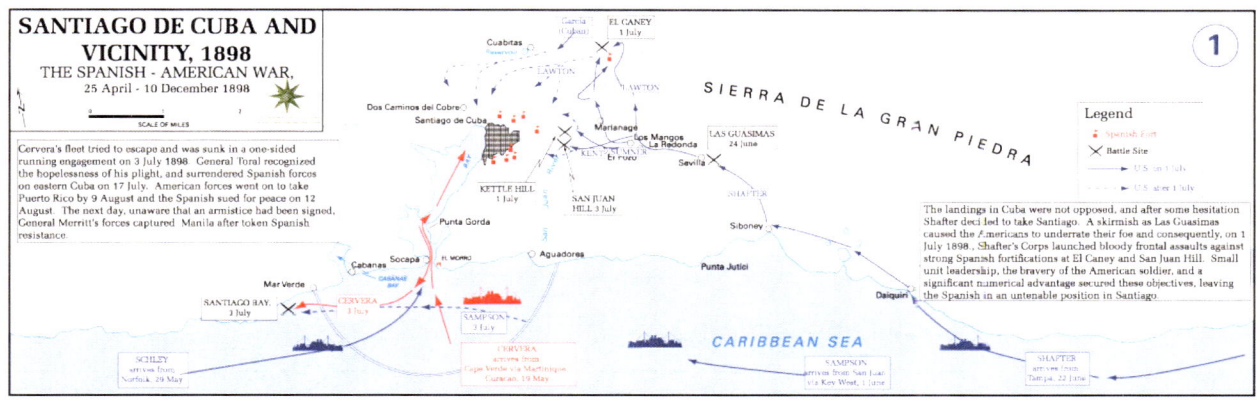

fleet and immediately began blockading the harbor. With the Spanish navy bottled in the harbor, the U.S. soldiers could sail for Cuba.

On June 14, 1898, the American expeditionary force numbering 17,000 men sailed for Cuba. The plan was to capture Santiago and, once captured, install artillery on the heights overlooking the harbor and bombard Admiral Cervera's fleet. The American troops, under the command of Major General William R. Shafter, landed at Daiquiri, a town east of Santiago. Over the next few days, the American forces pushed towards Santiago, encountering tough Spanish resistance along the way.

Finally, on July 1, the two armies fought a decisive battle at **San Juan Hill**, a hill about a mile east of Santiago. The most famous conflict of the war, it provided the greatest victory for Theodore Roosevelt and his Rough Riders, who proved instrumental in capturing these heights. Although vastly outnumbered, the Spanish fought fearlessly, resisting the American efforts to take the hill for hours. During the battle, Roosevelt galloped back and forth urging his men forward. Finally, Roosevelt led the Rough Riders, supported by African-American infantry and cavalry units, to the top of the hill, taking it by storm. His role in the battle made Theodore (Teddy) Roosevelt a national hero.

The fall of San Juan Hill meant that the Spanish navy could no longer rely on the Santiago's harbor guns for protection. In fact, once the Americans moved in their own artillery pieces to the top of San Juan Hill, the army could bombard the Spanish navy. With Santiago harbor no longer a safe haven but a death trap, Admiral Cervera had no choice but to try to escape.

On July 3, Cervera ordered his ships out of the harbor in hopes of running the American blockade. The **Battle of Santiago Harbor** began at about 9.30 am. Cervera sought only to escape. The U.S. Navy wanted to sink the Spanish fleet. As a result, the "battle" turned into a chase rather than a fight. The Spanish fleet had no chance, a reality Cervera must have realized. First, he was outnumbered. Second, the American ships were bigger with bigger guns. Third, the Americans had better commanders utilizing superior

Teddy Roosevelt (center) and his Rough Riders atop San Juan Hill.

naval tactics. By 1:30 pm the battle was over. The entire Spanish fleet had been destroyed. The U.S. Navy suffered almost no casualties.

Meanwhile, after the Battle of San Juan Hill, the attack on Santiago had stalled. The US army began to besiege the city. On July 13, 1898, the city surrendered. Almost 400 years of Spanish reign in Cuba had come to an end. Although a formal peace treaty remained to be signed, the war was essentially over.

By the end of July, a group of army officers asked Theodore Roosevelt to send a letter to Washington asking that the army be evacuated. More soldiers were dying from yellow fever and typhoid than had ever died in battle. On August 7, the army began evacuating its soldiers. Only after the war did Dr. Walter Reed and a staff of scientists prove that mosquitoes spread these often-deadly diseases.

The Paris Peace Treaty

After her defeat at Santiago, Spain asked for peace terms. Representatives from the United States and Spain met in Paris, where they drew up a treaty with four key provisions. First, Spain recognized Cuba as an independent nation under the protection of the United States. Second, Spain gave the island of Puerto Rico to the United States. The United States had nearly captured Puerto Rico during the war, although some small resistance remained. Third, Spain surrendered the island of Guam, in the Pacific, to the United States. On June 20, 1898, the Spanish defenders of Guam rowed out to welcome the crew of the U.S. cruiser *Charleston*, unaware that war had been declared. They quickly surrendered. Fourth, the United States demanded the Philippines. Spain vehemently objected to surrendering islands that they had ruled for more

Signing of the Peace Treaty Between Spain and the United States. President McKinley stands on the left, observing the signing. Seated are Secretary of State William R. Day and, shown in the act of signing, French Ambassador to the United States Jules Cambon, who represented Spain and acted on her behalf. [Note: William Day served as Secretary of State for less than five months in 1898 before John Hay replaced him.]

than 300 years, especially to a Protestant nation like the United States. However, Spain really had no choice. To make this demand more palatable, the United States agreed to pay Spain twenty million dollars for the Philippines.

In the treaty, the United States agreed to Cuban self-government as soon as order was restored. Three years later, Cuba, with a constitution modeled after that of the United States, became an independent nation, but remained under the guardianship of the United States. During the early 20th century, America intervened in Cuba periodically to preserve peace and order. In 1934, the United States gave Cuba its complete freedom. The two nations enjoyed friendly relations until Communist dictator Fidel Castro came to power in 1959.

Spain and the United States signed the Treaty of Paris on December 10, 1898, only ten months after war was declared. Of course, most of the treaty had nothing to do with America's proclaimed aim of "liberating Cuba." The Philippines, Guam, and Puerto Rico were not part of Cuba. Shortly after the war, McKinley's Secretary of State **John Hay** called the Spanish-American War "a splendid little war." Thankfully, most Americans have never believed that any war was *splendid*. Certainly, the Spanish would not have agreed with Hay's assessment. In fact, Hay was about to learn that most Americans did not agree with him either.

John Hay

Opposition to the Treaty of Paris

By 1898, as a result of John Hay's "splendid little war," the United States possessed a colonial empire. However, most Americans opposed the idea of being a colonial empire. They felt it violated America's fundamental values as a republic. Americans had no desire to enter the race to become an imperialist empire like England or Germany. Moreover, they had no great desire to rule a tiny island ninety miles off the coast of Florida – Cuba – and very much opposed the notion of ruling an island chain half a world away – the Philippines.

In fact, Commodore Dewey, once he had defeated the Spanish at Manila Bay, had returned the leader of the Filipino resistance movement, **Emilio Aguinaldo**, to the Philippines and encouraged him to continue his fight for independence against Spain. Believing that the American navy would support him, Aguinaldo did as Dewey suggested. On June 12, 1898, Aguinaldo issued the **Philippine Declaration of Independence**, which proclaimed the Philippines' independence from Spanish rule.

Emilio Aguinaldo in 1919. He had led the Filipinos against Spain and then the U.S. and served as the first president of the Philippines.

All seemed to be well, but on February 4, 1899, fighting broke out in Manila between Filipino and American forces, thus beginning the **Philippine-American War**. The Filipinos, upon learning that the United States would not grant them independence but instead had chosen to retain control of the islands, in the words of President McKinley, "to educate… uplift… civilize… and Christianize…" them, had chosen to oppose his kind offer. Instead, they chose independence rather than American domination. The war lasted until July 2, 1902 when America finally defeated the Filipinos. The United States suffered between six to eight thousand dead and wounded. The Filipinos suffered far greater casualties. Although about twenty thousand soldiers died or were wounded, almost 250,000 civilians perished during the war as a result of disease or famine. The Philippines would not be recognized as an independent nation until after World War II in 1946.

Meanwhile, as the Treaty of Paris made its way through the U.S. Senate, it seemed in grave danger of being rejected. Firstly, many Democratic senators were willing to vote against the Treaty simply to embarrass President McKinley and the Republicans. However, many other senators had strong moral objections to voting for a treaty that essentially made the Philippines an American colony without the consent of the Filipino people. The Senate was scheduled to vote on the treaty on February 6, 1899. Just days before the vote, it seemed that the opponents of the treaty had the votes to kill it. Then, the unexpected events that make history so exciting happened.

First, William Jennings Bryan, who had run for president as a Democrat in 1896, and planned to do so again in 1900, urged Democratic senators to vote for the Treaty. Bryan opposed the annexation of the Philippines and had been an outspoken critic of any imperialistic expansion. However, Bryan made a shrewd political calculation. He believed that the majority of Americans opposed the annexation. He also thought that annexing the Philippines would cause the United States trouble. During the 1900 election, he could blame the Republicans for the Treaty and the trouble. Bryan did intend that, if he were elected, he would grant the Filipinos their independence, so his calculations were not totally cold-hearted. Although Bryan probably did not sway many Democrats, in a close vote, his influence might have swayed enough that it made a difference.

Second, on February 4, 1899, the Philippine-American War erupted. During the initial fighting, 60 Americans were killed and more than 270 were wounded. News of the battle caused some senators to change their minds about the Treaty. They felt that no nation could treat America this way.

The Treaty of Paris needed 56 "aye" votes to pass. The final vote was 57 "aye" and 27 "nay." Only two Republican senators voted "nay." The Treaty had passed – just barely.

The Election of 1900

For the presidential election of 1900, the Democrats once again nominated William Jennings Bryan. The Republicans chose the incumbent president, William McKinley. However, in this election, McKinley's running mate would be Theodore Roosevelt, as McKinley's former vice-president, Garret Hobart, had died in November 1899. After returning from Cuba, Roosevelt had been elected governor of New York and planned to run for re-election in 1900. Initially, Roosevelt had no interest in becoming vice-president, feeling that the office had little power and preferring to serve as governor of New York. However, when the Republican convention nominated him, he took the position.

The nomination of Roosevelt caused Bryan's Philippine strategy to fail. First, Roosevelt proved as vigorous a campaigner as Bryan, traveling all over the country giving speeches. Bryan did make the Philippines a campaign issue, arguing that annexing them made America an imperialist nation; however, Roosevelt, the war hero, made the counter-argument that the annexation would make the Philippines a better, more stable country.

The final election results of 1900 nearly mirrored those of 1896. Bryan won the Solid South. McKinley won almost every state he had in 1896 as well as several Western states. McKinley received 292 electoral votes to Bryan's 155.

On September 6, **Leon Czolgosz** shot President McKinley in Buffalo, New York. McKinley died from the attack on September 14 and Theodore Roosevelt was sworn in as the nation's twenty-sixth president. When Theodore Roosevelt became president, no Constitutional provision existed for filling the office of

THE ADMINISTRATION'S PROMISES HAVE BEEN KEPT

1896   1900

Gone Democratic.   Gone Republican.

BANK   INTEREST PAID ON DEPOSITS

SAVINGS BANK

run on the Bank   A run to the Bank

THE AMERICAN FLAG
"HAS NOT BEEN PLANTED IN FOREIGN SOIL
TO ACQUIRE MORE TERRITORY
BUT FOR
HUMANITY'S SAKE"

Spanish Rule in Cuba.   American Rule in Cuba.

The Republican campaign poster argues that America is in foreign nations to help them not enslave them.

vice-president. Therefore, Theodore Roosevelt served his first term without a vice president.

The "Open Door Policy"

America had shown a serious interest in the Far East since the middle of the 19th century, when **Commodore Matthew Perry** had opened Japan to American trade. However, it was not until the United States annexed the Philippines that America became seriously involved in the political and economic issues of the Far East, particularly those of China. For most of the 19th century, European nations saw that China, which for many centuries had controlled a vast, powerful empire, was now helpless. Great Britain, Russia, Germany, Japan, and France rushed into China and forced the Chinese government to grant them "**spheres of influence**," which gave them control over huge regions of China. In their spheres of influence, the European powers developed valuable harbors, railroads, and mines, and exploited an untapped wealth of raw materials. With its massive population and huge, undeveloped natural resources, China presented an almost limitless financial opportunity to Japan and the Western European powers.

The rather touching poster issued to commemorate the death of President McKinley. He is pictured with his wife on the left and his mother on the right. His birthplace of Niles, Ohio is shown in the top left and his home in Canton, Ohio is shown on the right. The bottom quotes his final words: "God's will, not ours, be done."

Painting depicting the first landing of Matthew Perry and his men in Japan

As the great nations divided China among themselves, they established trade policies that benefited their spheres of influence. By 1889, America became more and more concerned that this policy would cause the United States to lose its trade benefits with China and even eventually lead to the breakup of China. To forestall this, in 1899, Secretary of State John Hay sent a note to the nations with spheres of influence in China. In his note, Hay established what became known as the **"Open Door Policy."** Hay asked Japan and the Europeans to agree not to close their doors to trade and allow all nations to trade with China equally. Of course, Hay sought to protect the United States' interests, not those of the Chinese.

Hay initially received the conditional approval of the British and Japanese governments. Next, France agreed. With England, Japan and France on board, Germany and Russia felt pressured to accept. Although none of the great powers fully agreed with Hay's note, none openly opposed it. Thus, Hay could declare that all the powers had accepted his Open Door Policy. However, the Open Door Policy nearly failed before it began, as weeks after Hay's letter, China broke into open warfare.

The Boxer Rebellion

A short time after Secretary John Hay sent his Open Door Note, members of an anti-foreign, anti-Christian group launched an uprising. Known in Chinese as the "*Yihequan*" or in English as the "Righteous and Harmonious Fists," the group practiced certain martial arts. Thus, their rebellion became known as the **"Boxer Rebellion."** The Boxers wished to rid China of all foreigners. They saw Christians, especially Catholics, as being most worthy of death. The Boxers murdered thousands of *Chinese* Catholics!

In the face of the Boxer menace, foreigners fled to Beijing, the Chinese capital where the various foreign nations had their embassies. The people waited there, virtually prisoners, hoping for rescue. In an effort to quell the vicious revolt and protect the lives and the business interests of their citizens living in China, an international army of 20,000 soldiers, including 2,500 Americans, was rushed to China. The strong army quickly overwhelmed the Boxers and saved the besieged civilians.

The victor nations required China to compensate each nation whose citizens had lost their lives or property during the Boxer rebellion. China paid the United States twenty-four million dollars in reparations. However, when our government discovered that its losses totaled only eleven million dollars, Congress voted to return thirteen million dollars to the Chinese, if they used the money to establish an education fund for Chinese nationals studying in the United States. This act of justice and charity greatly impressed the Chinese.

The Panama Canal

By the time that the Spanish-American War ended, the idea of building a canal that would connect the Atlantic and Pacific Oceans was probably almost four hundred years old.

In 1513, the chief of a Central American tribe offered to lead Balboa across the Isthmus of Panama to a great body of water with "gold" on its beaches. After hacking his way through fifty miles of machete-resistant jungle, Balboa reached the mighty ocean he named "Pacific." He did discover beaches of golden sand, but strewn with gold they were not. Disappointed, Balboa may have been the first man to envision a canal across the Isthmus of Panama. Shortly after his discovery, Spanish mariners began urging construction of a canal. In 1534, Emperor Charles V ordered a survey to determine if a canal could be built. However, his surveyors determined construction was not possible.

When prospectors discovered gold in California, interest was again rekindled in the notion of constructing a canal across Panama because of the long, hazardous ocean voyage around Cape Horn. The alternative meant the dangerous journey across America's prairies and mountains, facing extreme heat, oppressive cold, and often hostile natives. A canal also interested Great Britain, since it would shorten the sailing time of ships carrying cargoes and passengers from the Atlantic to the Pacific. In 1850, the United States and Britain signed the **Clayton-Bulwer Treaty**, which stated that if either nation built a canal, they would share equal rights. However, when America completed the transcontinental railroad, the United States government lost interest in the canal project.

In 1881, a French company began constructing a canal across the Isthmus of Panama under the direction of **Ferdinand de Lesseps**. Ferdinand de Lesseps had successfully constructed the Suez Canal in Egypt, and by 1881 it was generating huge profits. The French believed that a canal in Panama, which would be much shorter than the Suez, could be constructed and also generate great profits. However, from the beginning, the French workers encountered serious problems. Scorching heat made the work almost unbearable. Most of the construction ran through swamps infested by mosquitoes which transmitted malaria and yellow fever. Thousands of men died each year from these diseases. After five years operating under these terrible conditions, the company went bankrupt and suspended work on the project.

Ferdinand de Lesseps managed to build the Suez Canal almost through the sheer force of his will alone. However, in 1879 when it was decided to build the Panama Canal, he was 74 years old, perhaps a bit too old to undertake a project that he estimated would take more than eight years to complete.

The Spanish-American War once again revived America's interest in building a canal to connect the Atlantic and Pacific Oceans. During the War, the battleship *Oregon* had taken 68 days traveling at top speed to travel from the West Coast around Cape Horn to reach Cuba to fight in the battle of Santiago. A canal would have cut that time by two-thirds!

Although the Panama Canal was primarily constructed for its military value, Roosevelt was aware that since the United States and England had signed the Clayton-Bulwer Treaty in 1850, American and English businesses had sought to build such a canal to facilitate the transport of merchandise more quickly and less expensively between the two oceans. Thus, before the United States could act, the Clayton-Bulwer Treaty had to be addressed. While the treaty had been a smart one in 1850 before the expansion of the railroads, major industries, and the nation's economy in general, it was woefully outdated in 1901. The United States did not need—nor want—a partner for such an undertaking. Thus, Secretary of State John Hay met with Great Britain's ambassador to the United States and drafted a new treaty, the **Hay-Pauncefote Treaty**. Under the Hay-Pauncefote Treaty, Great Britain abandoned its rights under the Clayton-Bulwer Treaty and agreed to give the United States full control over the proposed canal. In keeping with the philosophy behind the "Open Door Policy," America would allow all nations to use the canal.

Choosing a Canal Route

As American engineers looked at maps of central America, two viable canal routes presented themselves. The first route ran through the **Republic of Nicaragua**. This route was somewhat level and part of the canal could use Lake Nicaragua for passage. Although the longer of the two routes, because it was at sea level, it seemed easier to build and operate. The second alternative ran across the **Isthmus of Panama**, following the route Balboa had taken almost four hundred years earlier. While shorter than the Nicaraguan route, this path ran across mountainous jungles. Moreover, the French company that had tried to build a canal along this line had failed.

By 1902, President Theodore Roosevelt and the United States Senate had decided on the Panama route, provided that a deal could be arranged with Colombia, the nation that owned the Isthmus of Panama. On January 22, 1903, Secretary of State Hay and Colombian Minister Herran signed the Hay-Herran Treaty. Under the Treaty, the United States would pay Colombia $10 million as well as $250,000 per year as rent on the land. The United States Senate quickly ratified the treaty, but the Colombians did not, instead pressing for more money.

When Colombia rejected the treaty, President Roosevelt encouraged the Colombian province of Panama to secede. Panama had rebelled to gain its independence in the past, but Colombia had easily suppressed these revolts. However, this time the Panamanians had the support of the United States. When the Colombians sent troops to quash the rebellion, they were met by the American warship *Nashville* which had landed marines in Panama to maintain access across the isthmus in accordance with a treaty the United States had signed with Colombia in 1846! The Colombians had to retreat.

Map of Central America. Note that cutting a canal across Panama is shorter but going across Nicaragua allows the use of Lake Nicaragua.

Shortly thereafter, Panama declared its independence. On November 3, 1903, only three days later, the United States quickly recognized the independence of the **Republic of Panama**, which prevented Colombia from attempting to recover her lost province. (In 1921, after Roosevelt died, the United States paid Colombia twenty-five million dollars to atone for Roosevelt's part in Panama's war of independence.) On November 18, the Republic of Panama's representative, Phillipe Bunau-Varilla, signed a treaty with Secretary of State John Hay on behalf of the United States. Phillipe Bunau-Varilla, had served as general manager of the bankrupt French canal company. He had actively worked to convince the United States to choose the Panamanian route and then planned the Panamanian revolt. In return, the new government made him ambassador to the United States. The **Hay-Bunau-Varilla Treaty** granted the U.S. government a strip of land ten miles wide with all desired rights and privileges. In return, Panama received ten million dollars and an annual payment of $250,000.

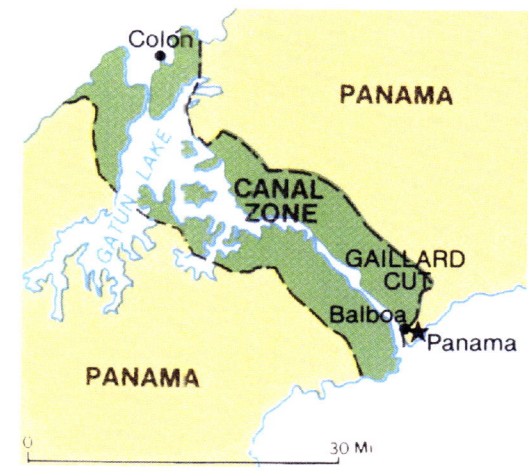
Route of the Panama Canal

Construction of the Panama Canal

Construction of the Panama Canal began in May 1904, with a projected completion date of 1916. John Frank Stevens, a railroad designer, became the chief engineer. He abruptly resigned in 1907, saying that he simply was not able to complete the task. Roosevelt appointed **Colonel George W. Goethals** as chief engineer. Unlike Stevens, the West Point-trained Goethals was a civil engineer who had experience building canals.

Perhaps the most important person on the project was **Colonel William C. Gorgas**, the chief sanitary officer. Colonel Gorgas was a superb doctor who knew that mosquitoes carried yellow fever and malaria. To protect the canal workers, Colonel Gorgas ordered the swamps drained and all areas sprayed in an effort to kill the dangerous mosquitoes. He installed mosquito netting and protected public water systems. Dr. Gorgas protected the health of the workers, which played a major part in the completion of the Panama Canal. Despite his efforts, thousands of workers still died from tropical diseases during the construction.

The Panama Canal today. View of a cruise ship transiting the Canal.

Trenching and cutting a canal ranks among the most incredible and impressive feats of engineering. Nothing comparable to the Panama Canal had ever been attempted. Thirty-five thousand men toiled for ten years on this massive project! At the Culebra Cut, engineers leveled an entire mountain. Engineers built another mountain as a dam between the Chagres River and the great Gatun Lake. Since the Pacific Ocean is eighty-five feet higher than the Atlantic Ocean, builders had to construct several locks at increasing levels to raise or lower the heavy ships on their passage through the canal.

On August 15, 1914, American engineers completed the fifty-mile Panama Canal and opened it to shipping traffic. What Spain had dreamed of and France had failed at, America accomplished in ten years, two years ahead of schedule. Sea travel between New York and San Francisco was now 7,000 miles shorter! America guaranteed all nations equal access. The United States reserved the right to close the canal only in time of war. The Panama Canal remains one of the most amazing engineering triumphs in history.

The construction of the canal greatly increased America's prestige throughout the world. The need to protect the canal gave the American president an important voice in any Caribbean activity. It gave the United States the "power" to "speak softly, but carry a big stick" as President Theodore Roosevelt proclaimed in 1900.

Despite the good that the United States did in building and maintaining the Canal, many Panamanians felt resentful. Their resentment was based in large part on wounded national pride caused by America owning what they considered to be "their canal." On January 9, 1964, this bitterness erupted into a series of bloody riots which caused the deaths of more than twenty Panamanians. The situation became so dangerous that the American embassy in Panama City had to be evacuated. The crisis escalated when Panama broke off diplomatic relations with the U.S. and demanded a new canal treaty. Negotiations began under President Johnson and continued under Presidents Nixon, Ford, and Carter. Finally, President Carter signed a new treaty with Panama in 1977 which the Senate ratified the following year. Under the treaty, Panama pledged to keep the Canal open to ships of every nation.

Today, the Panama Canal enjoys fantastic success and provides Panama one of its chief sources of income. Although the nature of ships and shipping has changed since its creation, the Canal remains a vital part of world trade. More shipping than ever transits the canal. In addition to cargo ships, cruise ships take passengers through the Panama Canal simply for the experience. To provide for its upkeep, vessels passing through the canal pay a toll. In 2014, a cruise ship paid the largest toll ever collected for passage through the canal.

The Roosevelt Corollary

On December 6, 1904, in his fourth message to Congress, Theodore Roosevelt announced a rather controversial position which came to be known as the **Roosevelt Corollary** to the Monroe Doctrine. Roosevelt announced that he wanted European nations not to interfere with Latin American nations, per the Monroe Doctrine. However, he also recognized that many Latin American nations were poor and often borrowed money from European nations. He said that in fairness, these debtor nations had to pay their debts. However, if a nation in the Western Hemisphere did not pay its lawful debts, the Europeans should not intervene; rather, the United States would make the debtor pay. Thus, Roosevelt was declaring that to keep the Europeans from intervening, the United States would intervene instead. Many Americans, including future presidents, felt that America should not be so involved in the relations of other nations. Nevertheless, Roosevelt's position of interventionism as the Western Hemisphere's "policeman" remained American foreign policy for the next thirty years.

When Roosevelt announced his new doctrine, the United States had many interests in Latin America. The United States had annexed Puerto Rico after the Spanish-American War. In 1901, the Congress enacted the Platt Amendment which gave the United States permission to intervene in Cuba and lease land for a naval base at Guantanamo Bay. Generally, the United States tended to intervene in Latin American nations to protect the financial interests of American companies.

For example, in 1916, American troops invaded the Dominican Republic when an American-owned sugar cane plantation was attacked during a revolt. Marines remained in the Dominican Republic until 1924. Unrest in Nicaragua caused a similar situation as Marines occupied that central American nation from 1912 until 1933. Honduras, another central American nation, saw several military interventions between 1903 and 1925 to protect the interests of American fruit companies. Threats to American financial interests as well as a civil war caused the United States to send Marines into Haiti to keep the peace in 1915. The situation in Haiti remained violent for the next nineteen years despite the presence of the peace keepers. These incursions caused Latin Americans to distrust the United States. Some Latin American leaders believed that the United States was more concerned with protecting its financial interests than with promoting justice.

Starting in 1928, the United States began to reject the Roosevelt Corollary and embrace what came to be known as the "**Good Neighbor Policy**." In early November 1928, Herbert Hoover was elected president. On November 19, two weeks after his election, he took a ten-week tour of South and Central America visiting with leaders in ten nations. Hoover specifically meant to convey the friendship of "one good neighbor to another."

Official White House portrait of President Theodore Roosevelt (1903) by John Singer Sargent, the leading portrait painter of the time

Yet, Hoover did not intend for the visit to serve as a mere symbolic gesture. Hoover delivered twenty-five speeches in which pledged to decrease America's involvement in Latin America. Hoover believed that the Roosevelt Corollary was not only bad foreign policy, but also probably a violation of international law, thus he moved to reject and replace it.

President Hoover proved as good as his word. On January 2, 1933, he removed the last American troops from Nicaragua. Later, after an anti-American rebel, who Hoover called "a bandit," attacked and killed Americans in Nicaragua, Hoover refrained from sending in troops. In fact, despite more than twenty uprisings in Latin America during his presidency, he refrained from military intervention.

In early 1930, Hoover began trying to find a way to remove troops from Haiti, which still faced numerous economic and social problems. Hoover signed a treaty with Haiti by which the parties agreed American troops would be removed by January 1, 1935. The last contingent of Marines departed on August 15, 1934. When President Hoover left office in 1933, America's relations with Latin America had improved immeasurably and the Roosevelt Corollary no longer played a role in American foreign policy.

In 1933, Franklin D. Roosevelt became president and further solidified the "Good Neighbor Policy" into American foreign policy. In his first inaugural address, Franklin Roosevelt pledged to "dedicate this nation to the policy of the good neighbor." Later that year, his Secretary of State, Cordell Hull, told the Pan-American Conference in Uruguay that the United States would end her policy of armed intervention in Central and South America. He added that in the foreseeable future, the Monroe Doctrine would benefit every nation in the Americas, not just the United States. To prove his "neighborliness," the United States canceled the Platt Amendment and did not intervene in 1933 when rebels overthrew a Cuban government. During the Franklin Roosevelt Administration the last American troops left Haiti.

The final repudiation of the Roosevelt Corollary occurred in 1945 in Mexico City. Since 1933, the United States and the nations of Latin America had been working towards closer financial and military cooperation. The United States had reduced tariffs for nations in the Western hemisphere to increase trade. In 1945, nations in the western hemisphere agreed on a military defense pact in which they declared that an attack on one would be considered an attack on all. From Theodore Roosevelt to Franklin Roosevelt, America's foreign policy had evolved from armed intervention to a policy completely opposed to armed intervention. America now declared that, "No state has the right to intervene in the internal or external affairs of another."

CHAPTER 25 REVIEW QUESTIONS

Answer the following questions:

1. Who discovered the Hawaiian Islands? What did he name them?
2. During the second half of the 19th century what was Hawaii's most important crop?
3. What was the Bayonet Constitution?
4. What role did Sanford Dole play in the annexation of Hawaii to the United States? How did native Hawaiians feel about the annexation? How can historians tell how they felt?
5. Why did the United States begin acquiring islands in the Pacific Ocean in the late 1860s? Name at least two islands or island chains the U.S. acquired.
6. How did the battleship *Maine* explode?
7. Where did the first conflicts of the Spanish-American War occur?
8. What is the significance of the Battle of Manila Bay?
9. Who were the "Rough Riders?" Who was their leader?
10. What was the significance of the Battle of San Juan Hill? Why was it important to Theodore Roosevelt?
11. Why did so many people oppose the peace treaty that ended the Spanish-American War?
12. How did Theodore Roosevelt become president? What positions did he hold in government prior to becoming president?
13. What was the Roosevelt Corollary? Why did Roosevelt create this policy?
14. Why did the United States decide to build the Panama Canal?
15. How did President Roosevelt ensure the Panama Canal would be built after Colombia refused to sign a treaty?
16. What is the "Good Neighbor Policy?"
17. What was America's foreign policy during its first seventy years? Why did most Americans favor this policy?
18. What was known as "Seward's Folly?"

Identify the following:

1. Queen Liliuokalani
2. Valeriano Weyler
3. George Dewey
4. John Hay
5. Yellow Journalism
6. Joseph Pulitzer
7. William Randolph Hearst
8. Boxer Rebellion
9. Battle of Santiago Harbor
10. Pearl Harbor
11. Emilio Aguinaldo
12. "Open Door Policy"

The Lone Tenement (1908) by George Bellows. Like many American artists during the Progressive Era, George Bellows was interested in realistically portraying the social problems that confronted society. The Lone Tenement represents the nearly finished Blackwell's Island Bridge that passes over Blackwell's Island (modern Roosevelt Island), linking Manhattan with Queens. However, instead of focusing on the magnificent feat of engineering, Bellows emphases an old, abandoned tenement building and a group of figures warming themselves by a fire. Such tenements were associated with a host of social ills because of their impoverished residents. The progressives sought to improve places like New York City so that everyone had better working conditions, better living conditions, and better government.

Introduction

Historians have dubbed the period from about 1897, when William McKinley took office, until about 1920, or the end of Woodrow Wilson's second term as president, as the **Progressive Era**. These years saw widespread social activism and political reform across the United States. Since the days of the Pilgrims, Americans had always sought to improve their world and their standard of living. From colonial days, Americans had believed that "progress" was a positive goal, whether it was westward progress, scientific progress, or progress in business.

However, progress, or change, simply for its own sake, is not always a good or desirable goal. G. K. Chesterton wrote, "Progress should mean that we are always changing the world to suit the vision. Progress

Gilbert Keith Chesterton

does mean (just now) that we are always changing the vision." He meant that a society must have fundamental, immutable rules by which it is organized. True progress means that society improves, but these rules, the vision, remain the same. In the Christian Western world these rules and the vision have always been based on natural law. Thus, for example, *the right to life* cannot be legislated away or abolished by a Supreme Court decision. Unfortunately, too many progressives believed that by changing the vision, they would improve the world. Thus, **progressivism**, as it developed over the 20th century and the 21st century, became the enemy of conservatism, which sought to keep the vision.

Although progressivism was more of a *political philosophy* than a *political party*, over time, it became more closely associated with the Democrat Party. President Woodrow Wilson, a Democrat, was among the early progressive leaders. However, in the beginning, progressive reformers could be found on both sides of the political spectrum. Theodore Roosevelt, a Republican, is considered the first progressive president. These early reformers wanted America to be a better place where everyone had better working conditions, better living conditions, and better government.

The Progressive Agenda

Like most movements and political philosophies, the Progressive Movement did not suddenly erupt upon America. The issues that concerned progressives had existed long before the beginning of the 20th century. The government had addressed the growth of the Trusts. People in government had tried to improve living and working conditions. Reformers had fought the corrupt political bosses and big city political machines. With the turn of the century, Americans, as they often do at the beginning of a new year, took stock of the status of the United States and resolved to address the problems that confronted the nation. In their view, more could be done to improve America.

The progressives believed that if individual Americans, who were basically honest and hardworking, knew what needed to be done to improve government, they would do it. So first, people had to be made aware of what needed to be done to improve the nation. Second, corruption had to be eliminated so that an individual's vote mattered. Democracy did not exist if bosses and machines bought and sold votes. Third, government had to be efficient and honest. This meant that voters needed the power to remove inefficient, dishonest government workers and officials and replace them with people who would work hard and honorably, striving to serve the public good and improve society rather than line their own pockets.

Spreading the Progressive Message

As part of their agenda, the progressives felt that people needed to be informed of the problems that faced America. They believed that once the people knew what was wrong, *the people would work to fix it*. The progressives pointed out the problems, and offered what they believed would be solutions.

In order to inform Americans of the problems the nation faced, thousands of **investigative reporters** began to look into almost every aspect of public life. They talked to police officers, immigrants, business leaders, and factory workers. In fact, they interviewed just about everyone. They also went through city and state records and files looking for corruption. Then they published their stories in the newspapers around the country. Theodore Roosevelt called these men and women "**muckrakers**," because they were raking up muck (dirt). In fact, they were exposing the corruption of the political bosses, the awful living conditions in the slums, the dreadful working conditions in many of the factories, and the atrocious treatment of children who worked in factories. The recent ability of newspapers to print photographs added to the potency and drama of these horrific accounts. Many of the muckraker books became best-sellers and part of the American literary canon. Arguably the most significant book is Upton Sinclair's *The Jungle* which exposed the dangerous and unhealthy conditions in Chicago's meat-packing plants.

Interestingly, in a time when most women still worked at home, one of the leading muckrakers was a woman, **Ida Tarbell**. Before becoming one of America's foremost journalists, Tarbell had been an outstanding biographer, writing biographies of Lincoln and Napoleon. However, her most influential work was her 1904 book, *The History of the Standard Oil Company*, which was published as a series of nineteen articles in *McClure's Magazine* between 1902 and 1904. Still considered one of the masterpieces of investigative journalism, *The History of the Standard Oil Company* detailed the methods John D. Rockefeller used to build and expand the Standard Oil Company. Her book would ultimately cause Standard Oil to be broken up as a monopoly as well as lead to other federal regulation of big business.

Ida Tarbell in 1904. Tarbell had personal reasons to investigate John D. Rockefeller. In 1872, Rockefeller forced dozens of small oil producers in Ohio and Western Pennsylvania, including her father, to sell their businesses to the Standard Oil Company. Rockefeller left Cleveland owning about 85% of the city's oil refineries.

Reforming City and State Government

Once the muckrakers had informed the people of the problems confronting society, the next step in the progressive agenda was the reformation of city and state government. To bring about this reform, the progressives believed that people had to have more control of government. Thus, they developed several new ideas.

Secret Ballots

Of all the governmental reforms implemented during the Progressive Era, arguably none was more significant than the institution of the secret ballot or the "Australian ballot," so-called because in 1856, South Australia became the first state to introduce secrecy into the ballot. The system spread to England by the 1870s and to the United States after the presidential election of 1884.

The lack of secrecy in balloting had caused widespread corruption, intimidation, violence, and bribery. The secret ballot would soon become an integral part of American politics and tradition. In 2009, Congressman Darrel Issa said that, "The secret ballot is the cornerstone of how our democracy works. It is the right to vote your conscience - without fear of retribution, intimidation or bribery."

Prior to enactment of the secret balloting system, voters received their ballots from the representatives of the various political parties, then placed them in a ballot box in full view of everyone at the polling place.

AT THE POLLS.

At the polls. This political cartoon appeared in Harper's Weekly on November 7, 1857. It portrays the chaotic, violent, yet enjoyable 19th century voting process. Because each candidate had a color specific ballot, everyone knew for whom each man was voting. This created an exciting and sometimes violent election day. On the other hand, the political parties often brought barrels of whiskey for their voters. So, the election turned into a giant party.

Since the political parties handed out ballots of different colors and sizes, everyone could tell how a man voted. Ostensibly, the parties printed their ballots to be easily distinguishable to aid the less well-informed voter to find the ballot he wanted. However, this allowed for innumerable problems. Honest voters could be intimidated with threats of violence to "vote the right way" or for "the right candidate." Dishonest voters could sell their votes or be bribed to vote a certain way. Because everyone could see and identify a man's ballot, the political boss's agents watched, or bullied, to ensure the man voted "the right way." As a result, corruption reached staggering levels. The lack of secrecy allowed the parties' political machinery to grow so strong that local bosses became virtual dictators.

In 1867, states began enacting laws to curb the abuses these easily distinguishable ballots created. By 1881, fifteen states had regulations specifying how ballots should be printed. Generally, ballots had to be printed with black ink on plain white paper without anything to distinguish one ballot from another except the name of the candidate. By the end of the decade, only Kentucky had not implemented ballot reform, but would do so the following year.

In 1888, Massachusetts became the first state to adopt the secret ballot. Over the next decades, the remainder of the states also implemented the Australian system. Under this new system, voters received their ballots directly from neutral election officials stationed at polling places on Election Day. Voters then entered a voting booth where they secretly marked their ballots. Since all of the ballots were the same size, color, and shape, no one could be coerced into voting against his will.

Interestingly, the secret ballot faced significant opposition, and not just from the party bosses and the political elites. One group who opposed them argued that having to vote in a booth in a relatively short period of time detracted from the voter's ability to think and consider his vote. Previously, he had been given a ballot that he could take to the polls. This allowed him time to consider his vote. In response, supporters of secret ballots noted that voters could still consider their vote before entering the polls. [Modern elections provide a vast amount of time and information to voters, so this argument has lost all relevance.] Another group suggested a second, more nefarious reason, to oppose the secret ballot: voter suppression. They argued that it disenfranchised anyone unable to read the ballot, which at the time had an especially disproportionate impact on black voters, many of whom were unable to read. These people favored the pre-written ballot as a means of enabling black voters.

Nevertheless, implementing secret ballots created a culture of voter freedom and helped abolish much of the corruption in elections. Recently, most government entities have reduced the probability of voter fraud by installing electronic and computerized voting machines. However, voter fraud can still infiltrate America's elections, making constant vigilance a necessity.

The Direct Primary

The secret ballot greatly lessened, but did not eliminate, the power of political bosses. Bosses continued to control party conventions in their local, state, and national elections. Consequently, while voters could cast a secret ballot to choose a candidate, powerful bosses chose the candidates whose names appeared on those ballots. In some cases, honest voters were forced to vote for dishonest politicians because they had no other choice.

In 1896, **Robert La Follette** sought the Republican Party's nomination to run for Governor of Wisconsin. He lost the nomination, he claimed, because the eventual nominee had bribed delegates at the party's nominating convention. As a result, La Follette began advocating that the old system of conventions be replaced with a **direct primary** in which the voters would choose the nominee, rather than the party bosses. La Follette failed to win the nomination again in 1898, but won both the Republican nomination and the race for governor in 1900. La Follette would eventually serve as governor of Wisconsin from 1901 to 1906 and as U. S. Senator from Wisconsin from 1906 until his death on June 18, 1925.

From the time he entered the governor's mansion in 1901 until his death, La Follette earned a reputation as a champion of the Progressive movement and the "common man." He was a dedicated opponent of the bosses and their political machines. As such, he was the leading advocate of the direct primary system as the way to give average voters a voice in choosing a party's candidates. In the direct primary system, any member of any party may run for their party's nomination. The party then holds an election, called a Primary, in which all the members decide who the party's candidate will be. Each registered party member votes for the person they want to be the candidate for an upcoming election. Therefore, the party's nominees for office are chosen by popular vote, not by a convention filled with the political cronies of a powerful boss. In 1903, Wisconsin adopted the direct primary. As a result, La Follette's program came to be known as the **Wisconsin Idea**.

Robert M. La Follette

Over the next ten years, nearly all the states had adopted the direct primary. In 1910, Oregon expanded the idea to include a "Presidential Preferential Primary." Party members chose "preferred presidential candidates," and the state's presidential electors "pledged" to vote for that candidate at the national conventions. Other states also began to use the Oregon plan. Today, the major political parties in every state rely on direct popular voting to nominate their choices for president.

The Initiative, Referendum, and Recall

In addition to the secret ballot and direct primaries, three other major reforms also emerged at this time which gave voters direct power over their government and elected officials: the **referendum**, the **initiative**, and the **recall**.

Under the **Referendum**, voters have the right to vote on certain laws the state legislature enacts. Usually this applies to new taxes, but it can apply to any law. A certain percentage of voters, usually about 10%, must sign a petition challenging a particular law. If the petition receives the required signatures, the law is placed on the ballot. If the majority of voters reject the law, the law must be repealed.

The **Initiative** gives voters powers to initiate, that is, introduce, laws or even amend their constitution. Obtaining signatures from a specified number of voters who favor the proposed law is the first step. Then any voter may demand that the proposed law or amendment be voted upon, either by the state legislators or by the people at the polls. In either case, if the proposed bill receives a majority vote, it becomes a law.

In 1898, South Dakota became the first state to implement the referendum and initiative. In 1900, Utah followed and over the next twenty years more than 30 states adopted these reforms. However, most initiatives never get to the ballot box. In fact, people vote on only about 20% of initiatives, of which about half are actually enacted.

The **Recall** strengthens the control voters possess over their elected officials. Recall provides that if the required number of signatures to a petition is secured, an official may be forced to stand for a new election at any time during his term. If the official receives a majority of the votes at the new election, he retains his office. If he does not, he is recalled, or dismissed from office.

The power to recall harkens back to colonial times. The laws of the General Court of the Massachusetts Bay Colony of 1631 contained the right to recall. In 1908, Oregon enshrined the recall in its state constitution and other states followed suit such that by 2022, forty states allow for recall of certain elected officials at the local and/or state level. About seventy-five percent of recalls occur at the city council or school board level. Although nineteen states permit the recall of governors, since 1921, only four have been subject to recall and only two, Lynn Frazier of North Dakota (1921) and Gray Davis of California (2003) have actually been voted out of office. Thus, it seems that voters, at least on the state level, tend to stay with the person they elected and generally do not wish to remove them before their normal term in office expires.

The Popular Election of U.S. Senators

Bolstered by the increase in influence that voters had recently achieved, reformers sought another important voter empowerment measure: the direct election of U.S. Senators. The framers of the U.S. Constitution had decided that *the state legislators* would select the two senators from each state. Since voters elected members of the states' legislatures, voters played an indirect part in the process of choosing their senators. However, some citizens supported the **direct election of senators** because they believed that all power must come directly from the people. Others supported direct election in an attempt to limit the power of political machines.

One by one, states began to allow the voters to indicate, in the primary elections, their choice of candidates for the United States Senate. The states also required the members of the state legislatures to pledge to vote for the men the voters chose. As a result, by 1910, most states had direct election of senators.

In response to the overwhelming desire of the American people, the U.S. Congress passed the **Seventeenth Amendment**, which went into effect in 1913. The Seventeenth Amendment, which allows for the direct election of U.S. Senators, supersedes Article I, §3, Clauses 1 and 2 of the Constitution, under which state legislatures elected U.S. Senators.

Women Gain the Right to Vote

At the end of the 1840s, a new crusade began dedicated to the principle of **equal rights for women** in political matters. In 1848, a "Declaration of Sentiments" was drawn up at a Woman's Rights Convention, in Seneca Falls, New York, which proclaimed that all men and women are created equal. The implication of such a statement is that women, like men, should have the right to vote. During the next decade, the women's rights movement faced great opposition but nevertheless gained momentum. However, the Civil War focused the public's attention on slavery and the terrible suffering and death resulting from the War.

After the war, the movement to grant women the vote started to have success. In early 1869, Congress proposed what would, in 1870, become the Fifteenth Amendment, which guaranteed black men the right to vote. Seeing the opportunity presented by the Fifteenth Amendment's ratification process, **Susan B. Anthony**, a teacher and reformer, proposed that the Constitution be amended to grant women the right to vote. This right was soon labeled "**women's suffrage**." Many men greeted her proposal with hostility and derision. In 1869, Anthony and **Elizabeth Cady Stanton** formed a group called the **National Woman Suffrage Association** and began to fight for a universal suffrage amendment to the U.S. Constitution.

Susan B. Anthony in 1895 at 75 years of age.

Over the next years, Susan B. Anthony worked tirelessly, giving speeches around the country in support of women's suffrage. She even became the first woman to vote in a presidential election when, in 1872, she voted illegally. She was tried, convicted, and fined $100, but never paid the fine. She continued to fight for the right to vote until she died in 1906. Though she did not live to see a universal suffrage amendment, her work was not in vain.

In the fall of 1869, the Wyoming Territory passed a bill which gave women over the age of 21 the right to vote. The governor signed the bill into law on December 10, 1869. **Wyoming thus became the first government in the world to grant full voting rights to women.**

In 1890, when Wyoming became a state, its constitution granted women the right to vote. This proved to be the opening salvo that would eventually lead to the adoption of the **Nineteenth Amendment**. By 1896, Colorado, Utah, and Idaho had joined Wyoming and became suffrage states. By 1919, fifteen states, all but two west of the Mississippi River, had granted women full voting rights. Many others had granted partial suffrage, such as the right to vote in presidential elections. Only a handful of states had no women's suffrage. The Nineteenth Amendment was adopted in 1920. It granted women throughout the United States the right to vote in all elections. They finally had achieved the same political rights as men.

Just four years after ratification of the Nineteenth Amendment, Texas and Wyoming elected women governors. **Frances Perkins** became the first woman to serve in the U. S. president's cabinet, when she became the Secretary of Labor in President Franklin D. Roosevelt's cabinet. In 1932, **Hattie Caraway** of Arkansas became the first woman elected to the United States Senate.

Social Reforms

In addition to political reforms which made government more democratic, progressives also sought social reforms which made living and working conditions better. Reformers made major efforts to improve the health and housing conditions of the poor, especially those living in the inner cities. In New York City, for example, laws were passed at the turn of the century requiring that tenements have appropriate plumbing and ventilation. Older buildings had to be remodeled and "brought up to code." Other cities followed New York's example.

Frances Perkins

Conditions in America's factories varied across the country. Some owners, like Samuel M. Jones of Toledo, applied the Golden Rule ("Do unto others as you would have them do unto you") in their factories. However, too many other owners cared only for the gold. The oppressive working conditions became more apparent after the tragic **Triangle Fire** of 1911. On Saturday afternoon, March 25, 1911, a fire broke out on the upper floors of the **Triangle Shirt Company** in New York City. By the time the fire ended, 146 women, some as young as 14 years old, had died. Most had died either from the flames or from smoke inhalation. Others died as they leapt from the factory's ninth floor windows in an attempt to avoid burning to death in the raging inferno. The Triangle Fire tragedy caused New York State to pass several new safety regulations, including many requiring inspections. Several other states followed New York's lead and passed stronger laws requiring safer factory working conditions.

Hattie Caraway, Democrat Senator from Arkansas

States also began to regulate the number of hours that children could work. Most states already prohibited the employment of pre-teen children. During the progressive era, states began to limit the number of hours that women and older children could work. However, most people believed that in a free society, the state had no right to regulate the number of hours that an adult male worked. They contended that such laws impinged upon individual freedom. In response, the progressives argued that individual freedom was not absolute and that the state could enact legislation that protected people even if they did not want that protection. They argued that laws that shield people from unhealthy and dangerous working conditions safeguard not only the workers, but also their families and society in general.

The Courts Intervene

As so often happens in America when parties are unable to resolve their disputes, it falls to the Courts to decide. In 1905, the United States Supreme Court decided the case of *Lochner v. New York*. In 1895, the state of New York passed a law which prohibited bakers from working more than ten hours per day. Joseph Lochner, who owned a bakery in Utica, New York, had been convicted of breaking the law. He ultimately appealed his conviction to the United States Supreme Court. The Court in *Lochner* declared the New York law to be unconstitutional, declaring that it was a "meddlesome interference with the rights of the individual."

Interestingly, the Supreme Court, reflecting the feelings of the times that the government could regulate women and children, came to a different conclusion in the case of *Muller v. Oregon* (1908). The *Muller* case involved an Oregon law which prohibited women laundry workers from working more than ten hours,

Justice Louis Brandeis

although permitting men to work more than ten hours. The court distinguished *Muller* from *Lochner* simply by distinguishing women from men. The court ruled that the state had the duty to protect women because a woman's "physical structure and a proper discharge of her maternal functions —having in view not merely her own health, but the well-being of the race —justify legislation to protect her from the greed as well as the passion of man."

The *Muller* case also became significant for one of the **briefs**, or arguments, that were submitted. One of the lawyers for Oregon was a young attorney named **Louis Brandeis**. Brandeis' brief was groundbreaking because it did not focus on the law. Instead, his brief concentrated on the social, scientific, and economic impact that long working hours had on the health of women. The *Muller* court found Brandeis' arguments, which showed that long hours injured individual women and thus the public health in general, to be compelling. In 1916, Louis Brandeis became a member of the U. S. Supreme Court. A **Brandeis Brief** came to be known as one containing social and scientific data rather than legal citations.

Not Everyone Benefited from the Reforms

Although the reformers generally acted with the best of intentions, they tended to be white middle-class Protestants who lived in the big cities, so they tended to address the problems they saw in the big cities. Thus, they addressed issues of slums, political corruption, and social injustice, largely because they encountered these issues. Numerous New Yorkers actually *saw* the Triangle Shirt Fire. However, sadly, as Protestants, they retained much of the prejudice that their parents had towards Catholics and immigrants. Most immigrants during this period were Catholics. The Catholic Church, more than the government or any other organization, welcomed Catholic immigrants and found them jobs and homes while Protestants often excluded them from secular opportunities. Nuns taught children in Catholic schools and priests worked to protect political interests.

Sadly, black Americans also did not benefit much during the progressive period. After the removal of federal troops from the South in 1877, Southern governments enacted so-called **Jim Crow laws**, named after a character in a black minstrel (musical) show. The Jim Crow laws marginalized blacks in the South by forcing them to use separate restaurants, hospitals, railroads, streetcars, even water fountains. Tragically, the progressive era had almost no impact on these laws.

However, the progressive era did see a shift in the attitude of many Black Americans toward a greater political activism in addressing racial injustice. Booker T. Washington had advocated a passive approach to gaining racial equality through policies of accommodation. Yet with the dawn of the progressive age, a new group of leaders had emerged in the Black community. Led by **W. E. B. Du Bois**, they *actively* sought racial and economic equality. They specifically demanded an end to racial segregation and protection of voting rights for Black Americans.

To facilitate their goals, in 1905, Du Bois and thirty other prominent Black leaders met in Niagara Falls, Canada. Although the group failed to achieve much, members of the group, including Du Bois, three years later established the **National Association for the Advancement of Colored People (NAACP)**. According to its charter, its goals were, *"To promote equality of rights and eradicate caste or race prejudice among citizens of the United States; to advance the interest of colored citizens; to secure for them impartial suffrage; and to increase their opportunities for securing justice in the courts, education for their children, employment according to their ability, and complete equality before the law."*

Photograph of W. E. B. Du Bois in 1907

Jewish Americans also failed to benefit during the progressive era. Although not a large segment of the population, members of the Jewish faith had been an important part of the fabric of America since early colonial days. Many were merchants and teachers, highly respected for their capabilities, education, and forthrightness. By the end of the 1870s, there probably were less than 250,000 Jews in America. However, during the 1880s, Jewish immigrants began to arrive in substantial numbers such that by 1900, more than two million Jews had immigrated to America, most fleeing from religious and political discrimination in Russia.

Like most other Europeans, Jews were welcomed into their own ethnic neighborhoods in large cities. Many of the Jews, like their ancestors for thousands of years, were scholars who cherished education. Jewish children quickly seized on all the educational opportunities in their new world. In fact, many Jewish communities were able to build Jewish Temples and schools.

Theodore Roosevelt: America's First "Progressive" President

In 1901, following the assassination of President William McKinley, Theodore Roosevelt became the twenty-sixth president of the United States and America's first progressive president. Roosevelt was a committed reformer, who believed in public safety, a strong democracy, and fair trade. As a result, he favored laws that promoted individuals over big business.

Theodore Roosevelt's Domestic Policy

President Theodore Roosevelt believed in strong government involvement and strong government control. He felt that a strong central authority, like the president, was the best person to make decisions. Congress was too slow and inefficient. In 1902, he demonstrated his belief in a strong president when he became involved in a national coal strike that threatened to disrupt the nation's economy. No previous president had ever become involved in such a dispute. However, Roosevelt threatened the mine owners with a federal takeover unless they settled the strike. He also appointed a commission to resolve the strike. Both sides actually benefited from the intervention, but Roosevelt had set a precedent. Today, presidents routinely become involved in such disputes.

Because Theodore Roosevelt strongly believed that the government should exercise more control over corporate trusts to keep them in line, he became known as a **trust buster**. Under his administration, the federal government brought many lawsuits against businesses thought to be violating the Sherman Antitrust Act. One of Roosevelt's first targets was the Northern Securities Company, which controlled three railroads. These three railroads carried most of the rail traffic between Chicago and the Pacific Northwest. Roosevelt contended that the Northern Securities Company was so powerful in its ability to control rail traffic that it had to be broken up.

In 1904, in the *Northern Securities Case*, the United States Supreme Court agreed with Roosevelt. The Court ordered the Northern Securities Company dissolved. Roosevelt went on to bring suits against Trust after Trust, including the Standard Oil Trust, which ultimately was broken up.

In 1906, Roosevelt convinced Congress to pass the **Hepburn Act**, which increased the power of the Interstate Commerce Commission (ICC). With its new powers, the ICC could inspect the records of the railroads and set prices for freight charges for the railroads. Although Roosevelt saw these actions as a way to ensure people were fairly treated, this increase in the power of government frightened many people.

Establishing strong public health codes became a national concern when it became known that some of the food and drug manufacturers employed unsanitary procedures. In 1904, muckraker **Upton Sinclair** went undercover and worked several weeks in Chicago's meatpacking plants gathering information for his book, *The Jungle*. Published in 1906, *The Jungle* caused

Justice John Marshall Harlan who wrote the opinion in the *Northern Securities Case*

a national panic with its claims of unspeakable health violations and unsanitary practices as people feared they would consume tainted meat. President Roosevelt sent government agents to Chicago to investigate Sinclair's claims, which, for the most part, proved accurate! Other deadly cases involved a company adding impure ingredients to foods and medicines. To bring an end to these dangers, President Roosevelt championed national regulation through the passage of a pure food and drug law. The **Pure Food and Drug Act**, passed in 1906, provided for accurate labeling on all foods and drugs, as well as many other similar precautions. Passed on the same day as the Pure Food and Drug Act, the **Federal Meat Inspection Act** required that government health inspectors thoroughly examine meat packing plants. These federal meat inspectors certified that the meat had been processed under sanitary conditions and was fit for human consumption.

As an avid outdoorsman and hunter, Theodore Roosevelt felt a special connection to the land. As president, he was dedicated to protecting and preserving America's natural resources. The Roosevelt conservation program had four well-defined purposes. First, preserve American forests. Second, reclaim unused lands. Third, develop inland waterways. Fourth, care for America's water sites and mineral lands.

The Theodore Roosevelt Dam

In 1902, Congress passed the **Newlands Reclamation Act**. It provided for irrigation projects in western deserts, to make the land more hospitable and easier to farm. The Act included the construction of the **Theodore Roosevelt Dam**, built between 1905 and 1911, north of Phoenix, Arizona. Next, Roosevelt appropriated one hundred and fifty million acres as national forests and instituted the **Bureau of Forestry**. Now called the **Forest Service**, it works to prevent forest fires and protect valuable timber from destruction. No president ever worked harder to conserve our nation's natural resources. However, over time, some Americans feel threatened as the government takes more and more land, leaving less available for those who would like to purchase more land. Today, the federal government owns a little less than 30% of all the land in the United States, more than 90% of it in western states.

Theodore Roosevelt's Foreign Policy

President Roosevelt's predecessors had been isolationists, determined to stay out of the affairs of other countries. Roosevelt, however, so willing to become involved in Cuba, had a more *flexible* attitude towards foreign interaction. Roosevelt's foreign policy was strong yet patient. Unlike Roosevelt the "Rough Rider," *President* Roosevelt usually acted prudently, practically, and at times, surprisingly conciliatory in his international decisions. He demonstrated this capacity when he firmly opposed members of Congress who wanted America to take possession of Cuba and the Dominican Republic. In 1905, he was awarded the Nobel Peace Prize for his efforts mediating an end to the Russo-Japanese War. His firm leadership in the Algeciras (Spain) Conference of 1906 may well have delayed the outbreak of World War I until 1914. The Algeciras Conference met to decide who was to control Morocco in North Africa. Both France and Germany sought control, but President Roosevelt showed unusual mediation skills to settle a serious international dispute.

In December 1907, towards the end of his second term, President Roosevelt sent the entire U. S. Naval Fleet on an around-the-world voyage. With their hulls painted white, the Navy's peacetime color, and decorated with a red, white, and blue banner on their bows, these ships would come to be known as the **Great White Fleet**. The purpose of the mission was ostensibly peaceful: visiting friendly nations

The Great White Fleet by John Charles Roach

and paying America's respects to other sovereign nations. But the mission also had another purpose: demonstrating that America had a strong navy that could enforce American foreign policy. At the time, relations with both Germany and Japan had begun to falter. The fleet's visit to Japan proved especially successful, as thousands of Japanese school children sang "The Star-Spangled Banner" when the fleet visited. Relations with both nations improved and Roosevelt felt that the voyage had enhanced world peace.

The Great White Fleet's mission embodied Theodore Roosevelt's foreign policy motto, "*Speak softly and carry a big stick.*" Roosevelt believed that the United States should never seek out trouble, it should "speak softly," but by being well prepared for trouble, "and carry a big stick," it would prevent trouble from happening. Overall, President Roosevelt's strength and foresightedness played a major part in U. S. foreign relations for many years.

The Election of 1908

Theodore Roosevelt had been elected president in 1904 by a landslide. He had received more than 56% of the popular vote, carried 32 out of 45 states, and won 336 of 476 votes in the Electoral College. His opponent, Democrat Alton B. Parker of New York, had won the thirteen states that comprised the Solid South. In 1908, Theodore Roosevelt remained widely popular and likely could have easily won re-election. However, he had served nearly two full terms, and, like every president before him, chose not to seek a third term. Instead, he used his considerable influence to ensure that his good friend **William Howard Taft** of Ohio received the Republican nomination.

William Howard Taft had served successfully in government for many years before receiving the Republican nomination. He began his career as a federal judge in Cincinnati. After the Spanish-American War, Taft had been named Governor General of the Philippines. In 1904, Theodore Roosevelt had named him Secretary of War.

For the election of 1908, the Democrats once again ran William Jennings Bryan, for the final time. Once again, the seemingly indefatigable Bryan ran an aggressive campaign. While he improved on the Democrats' performance of 1904—by carrying a few Western states—he still lost to Taft.

President William Howard Taft

History has shown that to be effective as a president, a man—or woman—needs an almost inexhaustible supply of energy, very high intelligence, charisma, and the ability to "make a deal." Taft only had one of these qualities. Firstly, when he was elected, Taft was seriously overweight. He weighed over three hundred pounds. This meant he tired quickly and lacked the energy a person needs to be a successful president. Although Taft was likable, he lacked the charisma of Teddy Roosevelt, the man who preceded him, and who was still very much in the public eye. Third, presidents need to be able to work with their political opponents to pass legislation, that is, make deals. Taft struggled to work with both his friends and his opponents.

President Taft

Although Taft continued many of Roosevelt's policies—for example, he attacked the Trusts and claimed more land for the federal government in the name of conservation—he also failed to manage his own cabinet. The most serious issue arose over what became known as the **Ballinger-Pinchot Controversy**. Soon after his inauguration in March 1909, Taft replaced Roosevelt's Secretary of the Interior with his own man, Richard Ballinger. Many conservationists saw this replacement as a change in policy by Taft. When Ballinger returned 3,000,000 acres of land to private citizens, they became even more alarmed. One of the people alarmed was Gifford Pinchot, who had been the head of the U.S. Forestry Service since 1898. Pinchot publicly accused Ballinger of mismanagement and even illegal activities. Taft investigated the allegations, cleared Ballinger, and tried to mollify Pinchot. However, Pinchot refused to be placated and instead became publicly insubordinate towards Taft, who had no option but to fire him.

After his dismissal, Pinchot, a close friend of Theodore Roosevelt's, convinced the former president that Ballinger and Taft opposed conservationism. The controversy destroyed the friendship between Taft and Roosevelt. The firing also alienated many progressives within the Republican Party. So destructive was the result that it would cause the Republican Party to split in the 1912 presidential election.

The Rise of the Progressive Party

To his credit, Theodore Roosevelt, still massively popular, did his best not to interfere with Taft's presidency, at least at first. As soon as the inauguration was over, Roosevelt went to do what he loved best, hunt big game in Africa. However, once he returned to the United States in 1910, he began to feel that Taft was making mistakes in running the nation. Roosevelt believed that Taft was mishandling the environment and the Trusts. By 1911, conservatives and progressives had convinced Roosevelt that Taft would not win re-election in 1912. They convinced him to seek the Republican nomination.

In 1912, for the first time in a presidential election, a portion of the delegates to the Republican national convention were elected in presidential primaries as a way to curb the power of the party bosses. Roosevelt entered and won nine of the twelve primaries, including the primary in Ohio, Taft's home state. However, most states still had professional politicians, that is, party bosses, choose their delegates, and Taft received the support of most of those. Thus, when the Republican convention met in Chicago in June 1912, it nominated William Howard Taft. However, if the Republicans thought that settled the matter, they had never met Teddy Roosevelt.

At this point, members of the two wings of the Republican Party came together. Many conservatives *and* even more progressives urged Roosevelt to run for president as a Third Party candidate. He gladly accepted. Roosevelt's supporters convened in Chicago and formed a **Progressive Party** which nominated Theodore Roosevelt as its candidate. When asked by reporters about the campaign, the ever-enthusiastic

Theodore Roosevelt and his family in 1908 as they prepare to leave the White House. Roosevelt would travel to Kenya for a safari he had planned with the Smithsonian Institution to collect specimens for the museum. He took his nineteen-year-old son Kermit (second from left), as he wanted to toughen up the fragile young man. His eldest son, Theodore, Jr. (left of Theodore) would have a distinguished military career and die during World War II in France of a heart attack. His youngest son, Quentin (third from left), joined the Army Air Service during World War I and was shot down and killed. To date, he is the only child of a president to die in combat.

Roosevelt answered that he felt "as strong as a bull moose." The quote resonated with reporters and cartoonists who began to use the bull moose as the symbol of the Progressive party along with the Republican elephant and the Democratic donkey. In fact, the bull moose became so associated with the Progressive Party that people began to refer to it as "**The Bull Moose Party**."

Progressive Party "Bull Moose" campaign button

The Progressive platform contained many ideas that, though controversial for the time, have since become widely accepted. For example, the Progressives called for limits on political campaign contributions and the registration of lobbyists. They called for a minimum wage, social security, a federal income tax, and workers' compensation. Roosevelt also supported primary elections for state and federal office holders, the recall, the referendum, and the initiative. He supported women's suffrage and the direct election of senators. One of his most interesting and innovative notions was the idea of **judicial recall**, which would allow citizens to overrule a decision by a court which declares a law unconstitutional. The people could override that ruling by popular vote. If judicial recall became the law of the land, the Supreme Court would not have the power it does today.

Roosevelt called his plan the **New Nationalism**. He meant that the federal government should have more power and take a more active role in the daily lives of American citizens. He said the government needed to do "whatever… the public welfare may require." Yet who decides what the public welfare is? Roosevelt had good intentions. He wanted a strong government to protect people who struggled to protect themselves. Yet these goals would lead to the "welfare" or "nanny state" and the loss of individual liberty.

The Election of 1912

Since 1860, Democrats had only won two presidential elections, in 1884 and 1892, both by Grover Cleveland. The election of 1912 looked like a chance for a third victory. Although Theodore Roosevelt was running as the Progressive candidate, he had been a lifelong Republican. While he hoped to draw some Democrats to his cause, most of his votes would likely come from Republicans, thus splitting the Republican vote between himself and Taft. The result would be an almost certain Republican defeat. As former Republican Senator Chauncey Depew of New York, bitterly put it, "The only question now is which corpse gets the most flowers." As long as the Democrats nominated a reasonable candidate, they had an excellent chance of winning the White House.

In this painting, newly elected president Woodrow Wilson, seated, holding a book, appears more like the president of a college than of the United States. Yet, he has a look of determination as he gazes at the viewer.

The Democrats met in June 1912, in Baltimore, where they held one of the most contentious conventions in American history. Because the nomination required a two-thirds majority of delegates, the voting went back and forth as no one could achieve the necessary goal. Finally, William Jennings Bryan, who still led the party's liberal and progressive wing, threw his support behind New Jersey Governor **Woodrow Wilson**. Bryan's endorsement caused more and more delegates to give their support to Wilson. Finally, on the 46th ballot, Wilson received his party's presidential nomination.

In many ways, Woodrow Wilson seemed unsuited and unqualified to be president. He had been born in Virginia in 1856. He attended Princeton University, where he studied law and political science. He then became a professor and finally, in 1902, president of Princeton University. In 1910, Wilson resigned as president of Princeton to run for governor of New Jersey as a Democrat. Upon his election as governor, he began implementing a number of Progressive ideas. Two years later, he was nominated to be President of the United States. Thus, unlike most men who had run for president, Wilson had almost no political experience. He had no business experience. Woodrow Wilson had spent his entire adult life as an academic at Princeton. He lacked what many people would call "real world" experience. Compared to Taft and Roosevelt, Wilson's resume was a little thin.

Yet Woodrow Wilson and Theodore Roosevelt, because they were both progressives, shared many of the same goals. If they differed, it was in the means by which those goals would be achieved. Roosevelt had been boisterous and cajoling. Wilson was much cooler and calculating. Wilson called his progressive agenda the **New Freedom**.

When the votes were counted, Woodrow Wilson won a landslide victory in the Electoral College, receiving 435 votes to Roosevelt's 88 and Taft's 8. Wilson also carried 40 of the 48 states. However, Wilson received less than 42% of the popular vote. Almost 51% of the country had voted for a Republican (Taft) or a former Republican (Roosevelt). On the other hand, more than 69% of the nation had voted for a progressive: Wilson or Roosevelt. Clearly, the electorate was undergoing a change.

The Sixteenth Amendment

Democrats had done well in the 1912 election, winning not only the White House, but also control of both Houses of Congress. Thus, Woodrow Wilson felt confident that he could enact much of the legislation that comprised his New Freedom agenda. With the aid of Congress, he quickly set about completely changing the American economy.

First, on February 3, 1913, the Sixteenth Amendment became part of the United States Constitution. **This amendment allowed Congress to directly tax a person's income.** Prior to the ratification of the Sixteenth Amendment, the Federal government had raised money indirectly through tariffs or by placing taxes on manufacturers. People who bought either foreign or domestically produced products paid a tax, but the tax depended on what they purchased. They were not taxed directly and they certainly were not taxed on the money that they made. The idea of an income tax had been discussed as early as the War of 1812 when the government needed extra money for the war. However, nothing had come of it. In 1861, as the nation fought for its very existence during the Civil War, the Union did enact an income tax because of the incredibly high cost of the War. The income tax ended in 1872, but proved extremely successful in generating revenue. In the decades preceding ratification of the Sixteenth Amendment, the Populist Party and the Democratic Party continually called for an income tax. Congress had attempted to impose an income tax in 1892. However, in 1895, the U. S. Supreme Court ruled that a tax on income was unconstitutional. An amendment to the Constitution, permitting such a tax, had to be approved.

Congress passed the resolution for the proposed Sixteenth Amendment and sent it to the states for ratification on July 12, 1909. The amendment had its strongest support in the South and West because these were the poorer areas of the nation. The Northeast, the more wealthy section of the nation, strongly opposed the income tax, realizing that its citizens would be the ones to bear its burden. The Republican Party led the opposition to the Amendment which had the support of the Democrats and the Progressives.

Those who argued in favor of the Sixteenth Amendment pointed out that it was a more effective way of raising money than indirect taxes. They recalled the success of the Civil War taxes. They noted that as the federal government continued to grow, it needed more money. Even some Republicans began to support the notion of the income tax as they saw the growing military of certain European nations and Japan. Opponents of the amendment feared that the federal government would continue to grow if it received more money. Like Thomas Jefferson, they feared a strong central government at the expense of the states and the individuals. They also feared, correctly, that this would increase the power of government to tax income at higher and higher rates. Many people feared the government would spend the money foolishly and inefficiently. Years later Ronald Reagan would cleverly summarize this position when he declared that, "Government is like a baby. An alimentary canal with a big appetite at one end and no sense of responsibility at the other." However, the country was in a Progressive mood. Alabama became the first state to ratify the Sixteenth Amendment and on February 3, 1913, Delaware ratified, thus attaining the three-fourths necessary to amend the Constitution. The federal income tax was now the law of the land.

The Federal Reserve

In 1913, President Wilson and Congress completely re-created the American banking and monetary system when they passed the **Federal Reserve Act**. The United States had moved into the Twentieth Century with a serious monetary problem. Money was not circulating in many parts of the country. Most of the nation's working capital could be found in New York City and other Eastern banking centers, but very little money was circulating in the rest of the country. Some farmers and planters in the West and the South found themselves heavily in debt and unable to obtain enough money to pay those debts.

In an overdue effort to correct the national money shortage and other financial problems, a group of America's leading bankers proposed a large central bank that would be under the bankers' control. However, President Wilson advocated a central bank under federal government control. After a long, tedious, and often bitter debate, Congress passed the Federal Reserve Act in 1913.

Among other enactments, the Federal Reserve Act divided the country into twelve districts, or regions, and created a Federal Reserve Bank in each region. These Banks were to regulate the distribution of money, that is, to either increase or decrease the amount of currency in the economy, and consequently, ease many financial difficulties, such as the shortage of currency in some states. The goal was to ensure that the economy remained stable so as to avoid depressions and recessions. To guarantee that the Federal Reserve System would work, the government required all national banks to become members and urged state banks to join.

The Federal Reserve banks are not normal banks. In a sense, they are banks for banks. They lend money to other banks and set the *interest rate* that they charge for the money they lend. This rate is passed on to individual lenders who pay a higher or lower rate for items like a home or car, depending upon the rate that their local bank has charged them. Over time, a high interest rate can cost an individual many thousands of dollars.

The Federal Reserve Act also created a **Federal Reserve Board** which controls the interest rate. This Board is incredibly powerful, because it controls the interest rate, it controls the economy. By raising or lowering the rate of interest that the Federal Reserve (often called "The Fed") charges, it can speed up or slow down the American economy. This takes the economy out of the hands of the business people who are running their businesses and puts it in the hands of a small group of "experts." If these experts decide the economy is growing too fast, they raise interest rates. When banks raise their interest rates, businesses tend not to borrow or borrow less. They hire fewer people, or do not build another factory or expand their existing one. On the other hand, if economic times are slow, the Fed lowers the rates. Banks lower interest rates which incentivizes businesses to borrow money to expand, hire more employees, and grow the economy. But who decides when the economic times are too good or too bad? Should the market decide on its own? Should a small handful of experts?

The Federal Reserve Building in Washington D.C.

By 1913, the banking system that had been in place since the 19th century had become outdated. By the turn of the century, the United States did not have, and probably needed, some form of central banking system to provide for a massive national and international economy. However, the issue remains: did the Federal Reserve Act put too much power in the hands of a select few?

Big Business

President Wilson faced many issues during his first term in office. He considered the abolition of business monopolies among his top priorities. Wilson believed businesses should operate on a competitive basis and that everything possible should be done to stamp out unfair business practices. Under President Wilson's influence, Congress passed the **Clayton Antitrust Act** in 1914. The Clayton Antitrust Act clarified the Sherman Antitrust Act by defining unfair business practices in detail. It also made it illegal for a director of one corporation to be on the board of directors of another corporation in the same business. In other words, a person could not be on the board of directors of two railroad companies. Labor unions were not to be considered as acting to restrain trade under anti-trust laws. To empower the Clayton Antitrust Act, Congress also created the **Federal Trade Commission** (FTC). The FTC was composed of five members who had the authority to investigate "big business," in order to expose unfair business practices and help well-intentioned corporations to follow the law.

Lasting Effects of Woodrow Wilson's Presidency

In the first two years of Woodrow Wilson's presidency, he achieved results that have lasted more than one hundred years. The Federal Reserve and the Federal Income tax are part of American life today. The progressive movement is as strong today, perhaps stronger, than it was in 1914. Perhaps Wilson could have done even more, and the Progressive Era, and his time in office, would last another six years; but events in Europe were about to change the lives of tens of millions of men and women. For a time, the progressive agenda would have to wait.

CHAPTER 26 REVIEW QUESTIONS

Answer the following questions:

1. When did the progressive era begin and end?
2. What three items formed the early progressive agenda?
3. Who coined the term "muckraker" and what did it mean? Who was an early muckraker?
4. How did the implementation of the secret ballot change elections?
5. Who is most responsible for implementing the direct primary? How did it change elections? How did it lead to a change in the Constitution?
6. Explain the initiative, the referendum, and the recall. How did they change elections and government?
7. Which amendment granted women the right to vote? Who were two women instrumental in working for women's suffrage? Who was the first woman to vote in a presidential election?
8. What is a "Brandeis Brief?"
9. What were some laws President Theodore Roosevelt helped pass to ensure safer food products?
10. What did President Theodore Roosevelt do to promote conservation?
11. What is the "Great White Fleet?"
12. What slogan did President Theodore Roosevelt use to express his foreign policy? What does it mean?
13. Who succeeded Theodore Roosevelt as president? Was he successful? Why or why not?
14. What was the "Bull Moose Party?" Why did it come into existence? How did it get its name?
15. What did Woodrow Wilson call his progressive agenda?
16. The Sixteenth Amendment allows direct taxation. How is this very different from all taxes that had preceded it? What did those who favored the Amendment argue? What did those who oppose it say?
17. Why was the Federal Reserve created? Simply put, what is the Federal Reserve? Why is the Fed so powerful?
18. What did Woodrow Wilson do before becoming president?
19. What groups did not benefit from the reforms of this period?

Identify the following:

1. Ida Tarbell
2. Frances Perkins
3. Hattie Caraway
4. Triangle Fire
5. Forest Service
6. Ballinger-Pinchot Controversy
7. Judicial Recall
8. Federal Trade Commission

The War That Nearly Destroyed Western Civilization   1914-1918

Sunk Without a Trace by Jean-Leon Ferris. In this graphic representation of Germany's policy of unrestricted submarine warfare, the German submarine has torpedoed the (passenger) ship which is burning and sinking. Despite this, the crew fires its deck gun, lower right, at the doomed ship. Meanwhile, passengers flee in lifeboats, although because at least one lifeboat hangs damaged from the ship, not everyone will survive. In the lower left, one lifeboat attempts to rescue drowning passengers, while one stalwart woman shakes her fist in impotent rage at the vicious submariners.

Woodrow Wilson's Foreign Policy

Issues of foreign policy had played very little part during the 1912 presidential election campaigns. The United States had generally followed the advice of George Washington in his *Farewell Address* and avoided foreign entanglements. With the exception of the Spanish-American War, the annexation of the Philippines, and the construction of the Panama Canal, the United States had shown no desire for territorial expansion. Moreover, the U.S. had friendly relations with Canada and Mexico.

Like most presidents, Woodrow Wilson believed that Democracy was the best form of government. However, his hatred of monarchies ran deeper than most. Like most Americans, Wilson felt that the United States should try to help the people in other nations better their lives. However, Woodrow Wilson failed to understand that he did not always know what was best for other nations. He did not understand that some nations had cultures different than the United States. As a result, he tended to try to impose his notion of what a good government should be upon others. Wilson had spent most of his life as an academic teaching students. Foreign leaders did not appreciate being lectured.

Furthermore, Woodrow Wilson had two serious character flaws that had developed over time and would cause devastating results in American foreign policy. First, Wilson became convinced that he had a unique ability to see the correct path of history and that he possessed the ability to convince others to follow his vision. For many politicians, this belief in their own abilities is a necessity, but it must be tempered with the ability to compromise.

Wilson's second character flaw, and the one most distressing for Catholics in the United States and abroad, was his *anti-Catholicism*. In 1882, in a letter to a North Carolina newspaper, Wilson described the Catholic Church as "*an organization which, whenever and wherever it dares, prefers and enforces obedience to its own laws rather than to those of the state*." He objected to Catholic immigrants coming into the country. In 1901, he wrote that the more intelligent Protestants of Northern Europe were being replaced by "*men of the lowest class from the south of Italy and men of the meaner sort out of Hungary and Poland, men out of the ranks where there was neither skill nor energy nor any initiative of quick intelligence*." Wilson's anti-Catholicism was apparently well-known to most Catholics at the time. During the 1912 campaign, a poll of 2,300 Catholic priests in major inner-city Catholic strongholds revealed that 90% of the Italian and 70% of Polish priests intended to vote for Theodore Roosevelt.

In June 1919, John Christen Johansen made portraits of the leaders during the negotiations for the Treaty of Versailles. This sketch, which he made for a larger group portrait, shows Wilson just months before his stroke.

Wilson's election did nothing to moderate either his anti-Catholic bias or his belief in his own infallibility. If anything, his character flaws were magnified. He would impose *his* vision of American democracy on millions – whether they wanted it or not. In March 1913, only days after he became president, Woodrow Wilson launched his first, ill-fated venture into foreign affairs when he became involved in the Mexican Revolution.

Wilson's First Venture into Foreign Affairs

The Mexican Revolution began in 1910, when long-time dictator **Porfirio Diaz** imprisoned his political rival **Francisco Madero**, then won a rigged election as he had for the past thirty-five years. This time, however, Madero, when released from prison, led a rebellion which forced Diaz into exile in May 1911. In November 1911, elections were held and Madero was elected president of Mexico. However, Madero, who seemed to genuinely want to reform the Mexican government and work with the Catholic Church, faced opposition from bandit leaders like **Emiliano Zapata** and **Pancho Villa**. In order to control these vicious bandits, Madero had to rely on army officers like General Victoriano Huerta, a Diaz supporter.

In February 1913, Diaz supporters launched a coup, backed by Huerta, against Madero. Huerta ordered Madero arrested and later assassinated. Huerta assumed the "presidency," really a military dictatorship. When President Wilson learned of the assassination and seizure of power, he called the Huerta government a bunch of "butchers" and refused to recognize Huerta as the legitimate ruler of Mexico.

President Wilson certainly had the moral right and probably the duty to inform Huerta that he believed that his government was illegitimate. As president, Wilson had the legal authority to recognize any government that he wished and to declare any government he wished illegitimate. Certainly, the President of the United States needed to make a statement when the new ruler of Mexico comes to power through the assassination of his predecessor.

The assassination of Madero raised the level of violence of the Mexican Revolution. For a time, Huerta maintained order and even worked with the Catholic Church. However, the forces arrayed against him, led by the governor of the State of Coahuila, **Venustiano Carranza**, as well as Villa and Zapata, caused him to begin murdering his political enemies. In late 1913, Huerta began arresting leading Mexican Catholics and suppressing Catholic newspapers wherever he could. To remove Huerta, President Wilson began supplying Venustiano Carranza and Pancho Villa with guns and supplies.

Meanwhile, various American companies with interests in Mexico urged President Wilson to intervene in Mexico to protect their investments. They noted that the uprisings throughout Mexico endangered the lives of Americans in Mexico as well as Mexicans. Bandits destroyed property and attacked the Catholic Church. Wilson continued to try to intervene diplomatically until April 1914, when a group of American sailors were arrested while on shore leave in Tampico, Mexico. They were quickly released and the government apologized. However, in the interim, Wilson had learned that a German supply ship was due to deliver weapons to Huerta at Vera Cruz. Wilson used the incident as an excuse to order the U.S. Marines to occupy the city of Vera Cruz. Nineteen Americans and about 130 Mexicans died in the attack on Vera Cruz.

The American attack on Vera Cruz lacked any legal standing. The sailors had been released and no Americans were in jeopardy. By this time, President Wilson clearly desired to assist the anti-Huerta forces in deposing Huerta. The loss of Vera Cruz, Mexico's most important port, meant that Huerta's days in power were numbered. In July 1914, Huerta resigned from office and fled Mexico. He was arrested in the United States and imprisoned. He died in January 1916. After Huerta's resignation, the American forces withdrew from Vera Cruz, where they had been for seven months.

Following Huerta's abdication, Carranza, **Alvaro Obregon**, Zapata, and Villa, met to try to end the civil war. However, Carranza and Obregon hated Zapata and Villa, who returned their feelings. Thus, the civil war continued, with those who had fought to remove Huerta now fighting each other.

At this point, Woodrow Wilson faced an impossible choice. These four were some of history's most vicious and violent men. All were murderers and all were anti-Catholic to a certain extent. Given his

Venustiano Carranza

Pancho Villa

terrible choices, Wilson initially chose to support Villa's faction. Wilson seemed to believe that he could control Villa more easily than Carranza, who had not followed Wilson's advice. (Pancho Villa was probably the least anti-Catholic leader of the four.) Wilson also believed that Villa would try to help the people of Mexico.

In April 1915, the armies of Villa and Obregon met at the **Battle of Celaya**. Villa had a reputation for being a fierce general. However, he was not a smart general. Obregon was probably the finest Mexican general of his time. Although outnumbered, Obregon defeated Villa through the use of superior battle tactics. The battle made Carranza the leader of Mexico. Villa was forced to retreat north. In October 1915, Wilson realized that Carranza, not Villa, would be the President of Mexico and recognized the Carranza government.

After supporting Villa for almost two years, Wilson now refused to supply him with more weapons and had recognized his enemy as the President of Mexico. Not surprisingly, Pancho Villa felt that Wilson had betrayed him! In reprisal, in January 1916, some of Villa's men stopped a train in Northern Mexico and murdered seventeen Americans. In March 1916, Villa and his men crossed into the United States and attacked the town of Columbus, New Mexico, killing some of the citizens before setting the town on fire. Over the next four months, Villa attacked several Texas towns and murdered more Americans. President Wilson then sent **General John "Black Jack" Pershing** into Mexico with an army. Wilson ordered Pershing to capture Villa, "dead or alive."

General John Pershing was an excellent choice for the mission to capture Villa. A West Point graduate, as a young soldier Pershing had fought in various campaigns against Native Americans during the late 1880s, earning citations for bravery. He earned his nickname "Black Jack" while in command of the 10th Cavalry Regiment, the so-called "Buffalo Soldiers," which consisted of only African-American enlisted men. At the beginning of the Spanish-American War, Pershing served in Cuba, where he was again cited for bravery. From 1899 until 1901, Pershing fought in the Philippine-American War.

General Pershing and the army crossing into Mexico to capture Pancho Villa.

He was assigned the task of suppressing the insurrection and again he was cited for his bravery. Over the next decade, Pershing continued to rise through the ranks while serving at various posts around the world. On March 15, 1916, under orders from Woodrow Wilson, Pershing led an expedition into Mexico to capture Pancho Villa. Unlike the attack on Vera Cruz, this mission had justification; Wilson had every legal right to defend Americans from Villa's vicious raids.

From March 1916 until February 1917, the American army chased Villa but failed to capture him. Nevertheless, the army ended the raids on the United States by locating and defeating the main part of Villa's army. These men had been responsible for the raid on Columbus, New Mexico.

War Erupts in Europe

In 1914, Emperor Franz Joseph of Austria was 83 years old. He had become emperor at the age of 18, in 1848, the year of revolution in Europe. His life had been dedicated to the Catholic Church, his people, and his family. In order to preserve the Church, he had granted it freedom and protection in his kingdom. In order to preserve his kingdom and his people, he had created the dual monarchy of Austria and Hungary – the Austro-Hungarian Empire. But he could not save his family from the revolutionaries that sought to destroy it. Mexican revolutionaries had killed his younger brother Maximilian in June 1867. In 1887, under the influence of revolutionaries, his son Rudolf committed suicide. In 1898, another revolutionary had murdered his beloved wife on the shores of Lake Geneva. Finally, on June 28, 1914, his nephew and heir to the throne, **Archduke Franz Ferdinand**, along with his

Emperor Franz Joseph in 1905

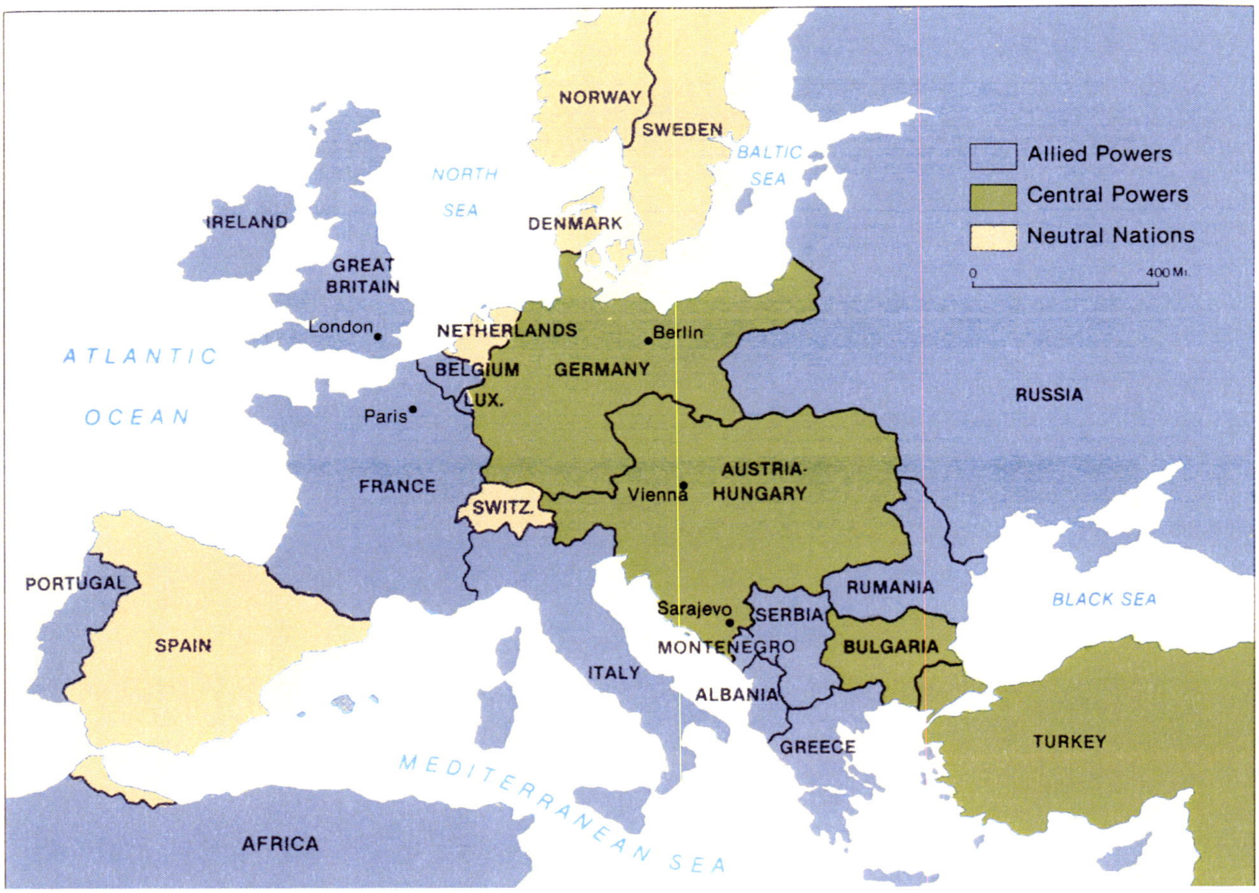

Europe in 1914

wife, was murdered in Sarajevo by a Serbian assassin named Gavrilo Princip, with the help of the Serbian government.

That two murders should lead to one of the two greatest wars in human history seems impossible, yet in 1914, that is precisely what occurred. By 1914, the nations of Europe were bound together in two great alliances created by a series of treaties. One alliance, known as the **Triple Entente**, consisted of Great Britain, France, and Russia, known during the war as "**The Allies**." The second alliance, known as the **Central Powers**, because they controlled central Europe, was composed of Germany and Austria-Hungary. Once war broke out, the Ottoman Empire (which included modern Turkey and much of the Middle East) and Bulgaria joined the Central powers. By treaty, each nation pledged to assist its partners in the event of an attack.

In justice for the murder of his nephew, Franz Joseph issued an ultimatum to Serbia—which he considered a nest of assassins—that essentially allowed Austria-Hungary to take over Serbia. When Serbia rejected the ultimatum, Austria-Hungary declared war on Serbia and attacked the city of Belgrade on July 28, 1914. Czar Nicholas II, the leader of Russia, felt that he had to aid Serbia. Although he knew it meant world war, he ordered his armies to mobilize. On August 1, in response to the Russian mobilization, Germany declared war on Russia. What otherwise might have been a small war in Serbia soon raged out of control! By the middle of August, most of Europe was at war.

The Calls for Peace

As the world tumbled into war, two men did call for peace. The first was **Pope Benedict XV**. Though he pleaded with the nations of the world, neither Catholics nor Protestants would listen. During the war, Pope Benedict XV adopted a policy of strict neutrality for the Vatican. His only involvement was publishing appeals for peace to both sides. World War I set a new precedent for the Vatican. It was the first major European conflict in which the Catholic Church did not support one of the protagonists. Pope Benedict's example has been followed by all of his successors.

Pope Benedict XV

The second voice calling for peace belonged to Woodrow Wilson. Although Wilson offered mediation, most European leaders had no desire for peace. Nationalistic feelings were running too high. European leaders had made too many mistakes, e.g. thinking that the war would be over quickly, and millions of men and women would pay the price for their miscalculations.

America's "True Spirit of Neutrality"

The outbreak of World War I caught President Wilson and the rest of America by surprise, although perhaps it should not have. Since 1815, and the defeat of Napoleon, European nations had constantly been fighting wars, either civil wars or national wars. In 1853, the *Crimean War* involved France, Britain, and the Ottoman Empire fighting with Russia in Crimea. In 1870, the *Franco-Prussian War* involved France and Prussia. France would remember their defeat in that war for decades. In 1904, Russia and Japan had gone to war over Manchuria. Yet, with the exception of the Crimean War, which involved many nations, Europe had not had a continent-wide war for one hundred years. Most European leaders believed that economic prosperity and intellectual progress made the thought of war simply too "uncivilized." As they would soon learn, this was another miscalculation.

During the Progressive Era, as a means to avert war, the United States, had signed **arbitration treaties** with many nations. Wilson and his Secretary of State, **William Jennings Bryan**, believed very strongly in these treaties and signed them with about thirty other countries. The concept was that both nations pledged to submit issues of contention to a panel that would mediate the issue in the hope of reaching a mutually satisfactory and peaceful resolution. Many of the treaties also provided for one-year cooling-off periods, during which additional talks could be held but neither nation would take any other action until the time expired. Only after the year would a nation decide whether it was in their best interests to go to war.

George Bernard Shaw, the author of such famous plays as *St. Joan* and *Pygmalion*.

When the war broke out, most Americans favored Great Britain, France, and their allies. Britain and America were on friendly terms and were strong trade and business partners. This was not surprising, since they are, as George Bernard Shaw once humorously observed, "two nations divided by a common language." However, people of German descent favored Germany and Austria-Hungary. Also, large numbers of Irish-Americans favored the Central Powers because they hoped that a British defeat would mean freedom for Ireland. In fact, in 1916, during the height of the war, Irish patriots seeking independence rebelled against the British government. While Americans may have differed on which side they supported, almost everyone agreed on one thing: America should stay out of the war and remain neutral! European conflicts did not affect the United States and this one was no different.

On August 4, 1914, shortly after World War I had started, President Wilson declared that the United States would remain "impartial in thought as well as in action." On August 19, Wilson appeared before the United States Senate. He offered to mediate the conflict but also officially proclaimed – and expressed the feelings of most Americans – the nation's **policy of neutrality**. In his short address to the Senate, Wilson declared, *"The effect of the war upon the United States will depend upon what American citizens say and do. Every man who really loves America will act and speak in the true spirit of neutrality..."*

The German Strategy to Win the War

When Russia mobilized its armies, Germany instantly implemented the **Schlieffen Plan**, its strategy for winning a general European war. Developed in 1905 by the chief of Germany's general staff, **Count Alfred von Schlieffen**, the plan called for swift and decisive action. In the first phase of Schlieffen's plan, the German army would attack northern France through Belgium, thus outflanking the strong French forces arrayed against Germany on their shared border. The German army would then swing south and envelope and capture Paris, thus knocking France quickly out of the war. With France defeated, the German armies could turn their attention east to face the Russian armies. Germany believed that Russia, because of its vast size and the poor quality of its transportation system, would take months before it could launch an attack on Germany's eastern border. Germany had no doubt that the poorly equipped Russians would prove no match for the German army. With the Russians defeated, Germany would be the strongest continental power. Of the Triple Entente, only the British would remain, and while the English had overwhelming naval power, they could not match Germany's army. Germany believed that, standing alone, Britain would sue for peace.

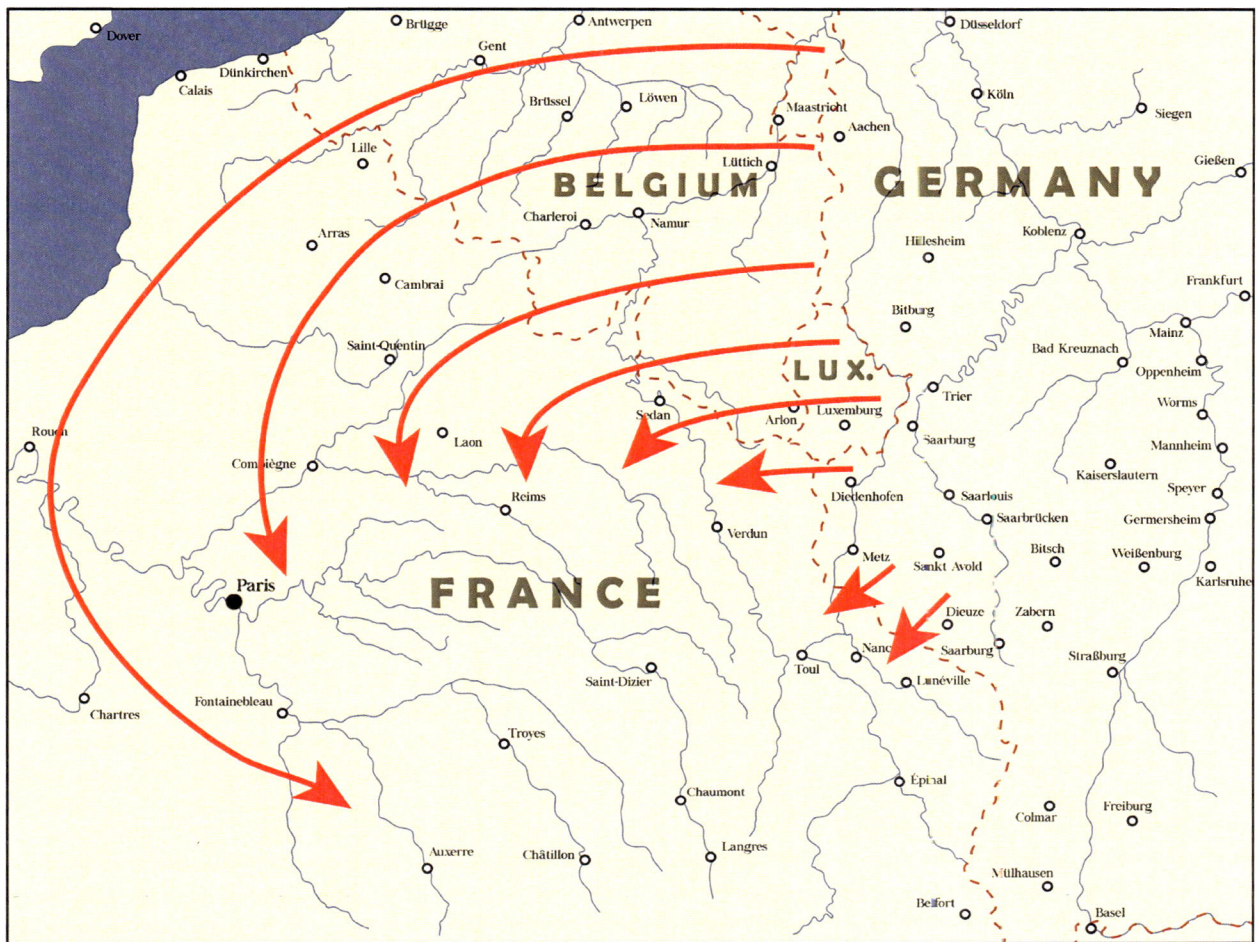

The Schlieffen Plan.

The Schlieffen Plan was bold but also incredibly dangerous if it failed to achieve its goals quickly. As renowned military historian John Keegan writes, "it was a plan pregnant with dangerous uncertainty; the uncertainty of the quick victory it was designed to achieve, the greater uncertainty of what would follow if it did not attain its intended objective." Although the Germans believed the Schlieffen Plan presented the greatest prospect for a victory, it did, however, contain at least two serious problems. The first issue was a moral one. The Germans would have to invade Belgium, a neutral nation that had offended no one. In the history of warfare, the German invasion of Belgium at the start of World War I ranks as one of the most immoral acts ever committed. However, the Germans, willing to overlook the immorality of the invasion, failed to foresee a more serious tactical issue that eventually caused the plan's failure. Since the dawn of warfare, offensive weapons and defensive counter-measures had been more or less equally matched; that is, for the sword, there was the shield. However, in 1914, the strength of the defensive weapon, the machine gun, far exceeded the strength of any offensive weapon. (The offensive answer to the machine gun, the tank, was still many months in the future. The machine gun was too heavy to carry and wield in combat, making it a purely defensive weapon.) The result of this miscalculation on the part of the Germans led to the ultimate failure of von Schlieffen's plan.

Count von Schlieffen retired in January 1906 and was succeeded by German general **Helmuth von Moltke**. Thus, it fell to Moltke to implement von Schlieffen's plan. Moltke invaded Belgium on August 4, 1914, according to plan, thus violating Germany's 1870 treaty with Belgium, international law, and every concept of morality. Almost immediately, Moltke encountered unexpected problems. His first problem occurred when the Belgian forces, led by King Albert, surprised the Germans with a steadfast, strong, and unexpected resistance. Because the German army could not attack France as quickly as planned, the French had more time to prepare for the German attack, a second problem.

The Ditches of Death

Despite the brave resistance of the Belgians, by September, the German army was within about 20 miles of Paris. Since the German army had slowed down, the French army was able to stop their enemies' advance a short distance north of Paris in September 1914. The battle became known as the **First Battle of the Marne** (the Marne River). French reinforcements were rushed into the battle by 1200 Paris taxicabs! Since their attempt to conquer Paris had been halted, the German High Command decided to march westward

British soldiers waiting in their trench

toward the English Channel. The Germans believed that if they could establish and hold a landing site on the English Channel, they would have access to the sea, which meant an opportunity for their ships to land reinforcements and additional supplies faster than over land. For the next two months, the Belgians, French, and British fought desperately to stop the Germans from reaching their objective. The casualties were catastrophic. A British Expeditionary Force, which began the battles with 100,000 men, was down to less than half that number after just two months of fighting.

By the end of September, any further advance became impossible. To protect themselves from the artillery and bombs, the two armies dug trenches and put up mazes of barbed wire in front of their positions. "**Trench Warfare**" began. The rival armies stayed in ditches that crossed the heartland of Europe. Beginning in Belgium, ditches stretched through Northern France south to Switzerland's border. The killing ground between the trenches which would be raked by machine gun fire was called "no man's land," for neither side could control it nor could any man survive in it. After only a few months of warfare from August to December 1914, World War I had become one of the bloodiest wars in human history.

Meanwhile, the Schlieffen Plan had encountered another fatal flaw. Russian forces had mobilized much faster than the Germans had anticipated. On August 17, Russian forces invaded East Prussia. Moltke, believing he had no choice, weakened his army on the western front by moving some of his soldiers to confront the Russians on the **Eastern Front**. The Germans pushed the Russians back into Poland and over the next year managed to achieve a stalemate which lasted until 1917.

The war took on an international dimension as fighting also took place in the Ottoman Empire and Serbia. In Africa, where Germany had four colonies, Allied troops fought German colonial forces along with native militia. Fighting was especially brutal in German East Africa where tens of thousands of soldiers and hundreds of thousands of civilians died. The Allies also managed to capture Germany's colonies in China and various Pacific islands, generally without the loss of life.

Italy had originally been a member of the alliance with Germany and Austria-Hungary, but when war broke out, decided to remain neutral. However, the Italians saw the war as a chance to obtain certain Italian-speaking regions of the Austro-Hungarian Empire. On April 26, 1915, Italy negotiated a secret treaty with England and France by which they promised these areas to Italy in exchange for her support in the war. On May 23, Italy declared war against Austria-Hungary. She entered the war on the side of the Allies and attacked Austria-Hungary from the south.

After September 1914, the war on the **Western Front** remained a deadly stalemate for the next three years. Occasionally, a weary company of muddy men, whose constant companions were rats and lice, were ordered to attack the nearest enemy unit. Soldiers would then flood from the safety of their trenches, their ditches of death, and "*go over the top*" into "*no man's land.*" On the far side of no man's land, enemy soldiers behind machine guns poured a withering fire onto the oncoming troops. Few survived the terrible machine guns. As a result, every warring nation fed more men into the deadly fray. At the end of those three years, the battle lines had moved less than a few miles. On October 25, 1917, at Flanders Field, the British army gained 700 yards against a German force. Every advance of two inches cost one man's life because generals could think of no answer to the machine gun but suicidal frontal assaults!

Part of the reason for the terrible slaughter of the soldiers lay in the remarkable incompetence of both the military commanders and the civilian leadership on both sides. One might argue that never in all of human history have so many incompetent individuals had so much power over so many at one time. Moreover, leaders on both sides were committed to a policy of "victory or death." Note however, for example, that on Christmas Eve 1914, the men in the trenches stopped fighting each other, began to sing Christmas carols together, and some even played soccer together. These men realized that they had no real quarrel with each other. Sadly, with a tiny handful of exceptions, their leaders failed to see that.

An artist's impression of the Christmas Truce between the German and English soldiers. It appeared in the January 9, 1915 edition of The Illustrated London News.

England Violates American Neutrality

International laws strictly regulated and protected wartime trade between nations during World War I. First, neutral ships carrying any cargo other than war supplies could sail wherever they wished. Second, neutral ships suspected of carrying military supplies could be searched and even seized if war supplies were found on board. Third, it was illegal for a country at war to stop a ship in mid-ocean. Fourth, in war zones, peaceful merchant ships, whether sailing under enemy or neutral flags, could not be destroyed until the safety of the crew and passengers had been ensured. Finally, warring nations could lawfully blockade enemy ports, but only under very specific conditions. Thus, warships were required to take up positions at the harbor mouth and along the coasts leading to the harbors they intended to blockade. Then, under international law, neutral countries had to respect the lawful blockade. If they attempted to send ships through a lawful blockade, they did so at their own peril, and their ships could be captured or destroyed.

At the outset of the War, Great Britain controlled the seas, as she had for more than three hundred years. Britain easily blockaded the ports of Germany and the other Central Powers. In addition to these blockades, the British navy tried to prevent Americans from trading with any neutral nation, reasonably arguing that neutral nations could resell American goods to Germany.

Britain had valid concerns. American goods *were* being resold to Germany by America's "neutral" trading partners. Denmark alone purchased *thirteen* times more American products than they had before the war. Clearly, the Danes were reselling American goods to warring nations. In an effort to stop U.S. trade with neutral nations like Denmark, Great Britain began blockading neutral ports. However, in doing so, Britain was violating international law.

In a published list of items that neutral countries were prohibited from selling or sending to the Central Powers, Britain included articles that are useful in war, such as rubber, cotton, leather, wool, chemicals, wheat, and other grains. To implement this embargo, British warships forced American merchant ships bound for Europe to enter British ports first. Once in a British port, the ship's cargoes were searched. Despite repeated protests from the United States, Great Britain did not decrease its seizure of American merchant ships. As a result, eventually America was trading mostly with the Allies.

Germany Violates American Neutrality

Germany also violated American neutrality; however, Germany's violation proved far more serious than Britain's because it caused many deaths. Early in 1915, Germany declared all of the seaway around Great Britain a war zone. That meant German vessels would sink every ship they caught around Great

The Sinking of the Linda Blanche by Willy Stower (1915). In this painting the German artist depicts the attack of a U-boat on the British ship *Linda Blanche* on January 30, 1915. The U-boat captain allowed the passengers to disembark the sinking ship, a procedure technically required but not always implemented.

Britain. Since the British **surface fleet** was much too powerful for the Germans to oppose, they attempted to impose a blockade against Britain with **submarines**, which they called "Undersea ships" or "**U-boats.**" U-boats were small, slow vessels. In fact, most naval experts considered them ineffective weapons. However, U-boats were the only naval weapons the Germans had, so they really had no choice but to use them. Yet, like the invasion of Belgium, employing U-boats had a serious moral objection.

German leaders believed they could not always observe the law that required attacking vessels to assure the safety of an enemy ship's crew and passengers. The U-boat's only real advantage was surprise. A U-boat fired its torpedoes from beneath the surface of the ocean while it remained undetected. A submarine that surfaced to assure the safety of an enemy's crew and passengers lost the advantage of surprise. Also, because U-boats were relatively small, large merchant ships could ram surfaced submarines or, in some cases, fire upon them from hidden deck guns. The submarine also faced the possibility that the merchant ship could call for help from an Allied warship which might be able to race to the scene and sink the submarine while the U-boat crew examined the merchant ship's cargo. Because the submarine attacked without warning, passengers and crewmen aboard the targeted ships lacked the time to launch their lifeboats and evacuate their ship before it sank. Many lives were lost, including American lives. In the effort to win the war at all costs, the German military abandoned the moral consideration of killing unarmed passengers and crews.

President Wilson Responds to the Violations of American Neutrality

President Wilson strongly protested both the British and the German violations of international law. By 1915, England could not have survived without American supplies. Had Wilson insisted that Britain cease its violations, they would almost certainly have complied. However, Wilson did not want to force the issue for at least two reasons. First, because the United States was engaging in a very profitable trade with England and her allies. Second, many Americans favored the Allied cause.

On the other hand, in February 1915, Wilson warned Germany that she had to stop her submarine attacks or risk the wrath of the United States. Despite this and protests from other countries, Germany continued the submarine warfare. U-boats sank many British freighters, killing many sailors. However, one U-boat attack changed the war dramatically.

On May 7, 1915, a tragic event occurred that shocked and infuriated American citizens. The Germans knew that the British luxury liner *Lusitania*, which sailed between New York and England, carried war supplies. In fact, the British government chose the *Lusitania* to transport guns and ammunition because she was the fastest ocean liner afloat and could easily outrun any U-boat. Moreover, because the *Lusitania* was transporting war materials, she had supports for deck cannons to defend herself, but the actual guns had yet to be installed. Thus, despite being a passenger liner, these factors made the ship a legitimate military target. In an effort to avoid U.S. reprisals, the German consulate paid fifty American newspapers, including the New York newspapers, to print large warnings not to sail on the *Lusitania* or other ships flying a British flag. Despite the warnings, American citizens boarded the ship.

Lusitania warning

The *Lusitania* entering New York Harbor.

A few miles off the coast of Ireland, the submarine *U-20* sighted the *Lusitania*. *U-20* fired a torpedo, and in eighteen minutes, the ship went down. Of the 1,962 passengers and crew aboard *Lusitania* when she sank, 1,198 died, including 128 Americans. A wave of resentment and anger swept across the United States. Americans began to demand war against Germany. Most Americans likely did not know the *Lusitania* carried war materials, despite the German newspaper warnings.

Most historians agree that the extreme carelessness of the *Lusitania's* captain contributed to his ship's sinking. In 1915, a submarine captain had to fire a torpedo ahead of the ship he intended to sink. Because the torpedo traveled in a straight line, the U-boat captain had to "lead" the ship the way a duck hunter leads a duck in flight. Had *Lusitania's* captain zigzagged his ship, no torpedo could have hit it because it would have been out of the torpedo's path. *Lusitania's* captain failed to take this simple precaution.

At this point, had President Wilson asked Congress for a declaration of war, he may very well have received it. Many Americans felt like Theodore Roosevelt who called the sinking an act of piracy and murder. Nevertheless, Wilson remained dedicated to his position of neutrality. He only asked that Germany apologize, make reparations to the families of those killed, and promise to cease its attacks on passenger ships.

U-boat attack

Over the next several months, the United States and Germany tried to resolve this issue. However, in March 1916, another U-boat torpedoed the French passenger vessel *Sussex* in the English Channel, killing eighty, and injuring several Americans. The U-boat commander thought, incorrectly, that the *Sussex* had been laying mines. When Wilson learned of the attack on the *Sussex*, he sent a note to the Germans which essentially threatened to declare war if they did not immediately abandon their "present methods of submarine warfare against passenger and freight-carrying vessels." In what became known as the **Sussex pledge,** Germany finally agreed to cease attacking merchant ships without forewarning them.

The Presidential Election of 1916

The presidential election of 1916 was the most important since 1860 and one of the three or four most important in all of American history. The fate of the nation and, in fact, of the entire world rested on the outcome. With war raging in Europe, the central issue of the campaign was America's position of neutrality.

By 1916, a small but vocal segment of the population, including Theodore Roosevelt, believed that America should enter the war on the side of the Allies. A larger portion of the population believed that the nation should at least *prepare for the possibility of war* by mobilizing its army and increasing its navy. However, *a slight majority of Americans still favored remaining neutral.* Wilson and the Democrats realized that his stand on neutrality was his strongest position, so his main campaign slogan was "He kept us out of war."

Nevertheless, many liberal Democrats and many progressives felt that Wilson had not done enough during his first term to push the Progressive Agenda. He had failed to pass women's suffrage, causing some women not to favor his re-election. He had not worked for the rights of Black Americans, and in some instances worked against them; thus, Black Americans were very unhappy with him. Wilson's weak popularity made Republicans believe that they had a good chance to win back the White House if they could nominate the right candidate.

A group of Republican Party leaders approached Theodore Roosevelt about accepting the nomination. Roosevelt was eager to accept, but the majority of Republican leaders concluded that since he had abandoned the Republican Party in the 1912 election, they would not support him. Instead, for the first and only time in American history, a major political party nominated a Supreme Court Justice, **Charles Evans Hughes**, who had been serving on the court since 1910. Party leaders saw Hughes as a compromise candidate who would appeal to both progressive and conservative Republicans.

The Progressive Party tried to nominate Theodore Roosevelt. However, he declined. He telegraphed the nominating convention that he intended to support Hughes. As a result, the Progressives ran no candidate.

Charles Evans Hughes (1921). Hughes was one of the most remarkable men to serve on the Supreme Court, a task he accomplished twice. First appointed an associate justice in 1910, he resigned in 1916 to run for president. After his defeat, he returned to private law practice until 1921, when Warren G. Harding named him secretary of state. Following the Senate's rejection of the Treaty of Versailles, Hughes helped forge a separate treaty with Germany, which formally ended the war between the two nations. In 1930, Herbert Hoover nominated him again to the Supreme Court, this time as Chief Justice, a position he held until 1941.

In a sense, the 1916 presidential election was one of the closest in American history. Although Wilson defeated Hughes by nearly 600,000 votes (49.2% of the popular vote), he received fewer electoral votes than in 1912. Wilson won 30 states including the reliably Democratic Solid South as well as winning several states by very narrow margins. In fact, on election night, Justice Hughes went to bed believing he had won the election. However, when the last California votes were finally tallied, Woodrow Wilson was declared the winner. Wilson won California by just 3,773 votes; had he lost California, he would have lost the election. Wilson won 277 electoral votes to Hughes's 254. California cast 13 votes for Wilson. Had just over half those 3,773 people voted for Hughes, he would have won 267 to 264. With his narrow victory, Woodrow Wilson became the first *incumbent* Democratic president to win re-election between 1832 and 1936.

President Wilson realized that his victory had been based on his refusal to accede to the demands of those who had sought a declaration of war. His re-election slogan, "*He kept us out of war*" had made the difference. However, Wilson knew that if Germany kept sinking merchant ships, that might be a promise he would not be able to keep very much longer.

Germany Implements Unrestricted Submarine Warfare

In 1915 and again in 1916, President Wilson sent his close friend and adviser, **Colonel Edward House**, to try to negotiate an end to the war, but his missions came to nothing. In December 1916, Wilson sent a private message to the combatant countries, asking each side to submit their requirements before they would sign a peace treaty. The terms suggested by each side were totally unacceptable to the other, making a peaceful solution impossible. On January 22, 1917, Wilson called for **peace without victory**. He said that peace must be based on justice, not on hatred. Neither side would agree.

On January 31, 1917, German diplomats officially warned the American government that every ship within areas designated by Germany as war zones would be a target of U-boat attack. German military leaders had decided that as of February 1, 1917, they would begin **unrestricted submarine warfare**, that

is, *attacks without warning*. They believed that this policy would enable them to win the war within four months by keeping food and munitions from reaching Great Britain. They also knew that sinking U.S. ships and killing the passengers and crews would provoke America's anger and cause it to enter the war on the side of the Allies. However, by early 1917, German leaders realized that they had no hope of winning the war unless they stopped America from providing Great Britain with critically needed supplies and materials. The German High Command gambled that U-boats could destroy enough American supply ships that England could be starved into surrendering before America could mobilize her troops into battle against Germany.

When the German chief of naval operations explained this immoral plan to the new Austrian emperor, the thirty-year-old **Karl**, he was appalled and strongly objected. (Emperor Franz Joseph had died November 21, 1916.) The German admiral told him that the orders had been given and dismissed his objections. For the remainder of the war, Emperor Karl and Pope Benedict were among the very few leaders who constantly worked to end the war as soon as possible.

Emperor Karl of Austria (1887-1922)

The United States Enters the Horror

In early February, the United States dissolved diplomatic relations with Germany. Faced with the certainty of U-boat attacks, President Wilson announced that the United States should no longer be considered a "strict neutrality" nation, but would now be an "armed neutrality" nation. Wilson ordered that America's merchant ships be armed with naval cannons and serviced by U.S. Navy sailors.

In late February, the British government deciphered a coded telegram sent by German Foreign Minister **Arthur Zimmerman** to Mexico. Zimmerman proposed that, if the United States entered the war on the Allies' side, Mexico should form an alliance with Germany. In exchange for the alliance, Germany offered to help Mexico reclaim the territory it had lost in Texas, New Mexico, and Arizona. Although nothing came of the **Zimmerman Telegram**, its publication further inflamed American passions against Germany and confirmed that they would stop at nothing to win the war. (**Note**: Zimmerman sent the telegram on the U.S. State Department cable which President Wilson had allowed Germany to use for peace negotiations!)

Woodrow Wilson was sworn in for a second term on March 4, 1917. During March, U-boats continued to sink merchant vessels and passenger ships. On Monday, April 2, 1917, Wilson called Congress into a special session. Woodrow Wilson had many faults. He was a racist. He was anti-Catholic. However, he truly and passionately did not want to go to war. Yet, he could see no alternative and he had tried every way to avoid war.

On the evening of April 2, Wilson stood before a wildly cheering Congress and asked for a declaration of war against Germany. He presented two justifications for his request. First, Germany was making war on the United States with its unrestricted submarine warfare. In fact, a German submarine had sunk an

Woodrow Wilson asking Congress to declare war on Germany

American ship just the previous day. Second, and more important to Wilson, America had to "*make the world safe for Democracy*." It sounded like a noble goal, but Wilson's idealism and his vision of Democracy would cause a great deal of harm. For example, he refused to deal with any government that was not democratically elected, i.e. Germany and Austria. However, Wilson acted in good faith, realizing the fateful choice that he had made. He concluded his speech by saying, "*It is a fearful thing to lead this great peaceful people into war, into the most terrible and disastrous of all wars, civilization itself seeming to be in the balance.*"

On Good Friday, April 6, 1917, Congress declared war against Germany, *but not her allies*, bringing the United States into the horror from which it had been previously spared. (Congress declared war on Austria-Hungary on December 7, 1917, but never declared war on the other Central Powers.) After three years of costly and deadly trench warfare, every European nation's soldiers were exhausted. They had all reached the point of maximum commitment. There were no more men to fight the enemy. America brought fresh, young, healthy soldiers into a war that had been at a stalemate. The entry of the United States proved to be decisive in winning the war.

The United States Prepares for War

The task of raising, training, and supplying an army was enormous. In order to facilitate production and organization, President Wilson put many sectors of the American economy under government oversight. For example, to move goods more quickly, Wilson placed the railroads under the management of the Secretary of the Treasury William McAdoo. Wilson created a **War Industries Board** to oversee the production and distribution of manufactured goods. Most companies, eager to help win the war, worked willingly with the War Industries Board. President Wilson appointed **Herbert Hoover** to the position of United States Food Administrator. Hoover was to ensure that there was enough food and that it was distributed fairly. He pleaded with farmers to increase production and asked the American people to observe both "Meatless Tuesdays" and "Wheatless Wednesdays" when people would eat no meat or no wheat. On bulletin boards, in newspapers, in magazines, and on radio, people were reminded that "Food will win the war!" Efficient organization, higher production by farmers, and the Hoover campaign turned America into "the breadbasket of the world." The United States produced enormous quantities of food for the Allied nations, the American Armed Forces, and the citizens at home.

World War I poster reminding Americans not to waste food.

Americans responded enthusiastically to the declaration of War, and thousands of young men volunteered to fight. However, to create a sufficiently strong military force, a civilian draft had to be implemented. In 1917, Congress passed a **Selective Service Act** that required men between the ages of twenty-one and thirty to register at the nearest voting site. Local draft boards selected men they deemed physically fit for military service. About four million American soldiers served on active duty with the armed forces overseas during the war.

The Selective Service System drafted both black and white men. Although the army remained segregated, blacks received better treatment than they had during the Spanish-American War. About 1,000 black men became officers. Women, of course, were not drafted, although thousands of women volunteered and served as army nurses overseas.

With millions of men serving in the army, women had more opportunity to work in factories and other jobs that would not have been available to them only a few months earlier. By 1917, women had become a vital part of the American work force. In recognition of their role, Wilson established a **Women's Bureau** in the Department of Labor.

Russia Faces Serious Perils

After its initial success during the war's first months, the conflict had turned increasingly grim for Russia, which numbered among Europe's poorest nations. Russians suffered more severely than the other participants in the war. Immense loss of life and shortages of food and other vital commodities had triggered violent riots and strikes in Russia's major cities. When a new government came to power in Russia in February 1917, replacing Czar Nicholas II, the United States quickly recognized this Russian government, because it claimed to be democratic. The presence of a democratic government in Russia made it easier for President Wilson to join the Allies, since one of his partners would no longer be a nation ruled by a king. The United States urged the new Russian government to remain in the war and the Russian leaders agreed. However, the new Russian leaders made a fatal mistake by continuing to wage war because a small group of violent and dangerous radicals, called **Bolsheviks**, promised to make peace with Germany if they gained control of the government.

Karl Marx

The Bolsheviks were dangerous because they believed in an evil system of government called **Communism**. The German philosopher, **Karl Marx**, founded Communism in 1848 when he wrote a pamphlet entitled *The Communist Manifesto*. In this and other publications, Marx outlined a philosophy that diametrically opposed the Catholic Faith in nearly every way. Communists do not believe in God, Heaven, or any unchanging moral laws. They oppose individual freedom and believe that people are merely the tools of the state. Karl Marx thought that a small group of dedicated communists should totally control the government. The Communist government would completely control every aspect of the citizens' lives in the country they ruled. Communism, the most devastatingly evil plan to control nations, afflicted millions of conquered people throughout the world.

Vladimir Lenin

By 1917, the war had been stalemated for over two years. Members of Germany's high command desperately sought a new strategy to end the stalemate and create an advantage for their troops. The Germans realized that Russia was the weakest Allied nation. If Russia surrendered, the German troops on the Eastern Front could be transferred to the Western Front. German strategists believed that by concentrating their forces on the western front, they could win the war.

Germany knew that the Bolsheviks wanted to end Russia's involvement in the war. Therefore, in April 1917, in an effort to replace the Russian government, Germany transported the Bolshevik leader, **Vladimir Lenin**, to Russia from his exile in Switzerland. When Emperor Karl learned of the plan, he vigorously opposed it. Karl realized that if Lenin gained control of Russia, he would spread communism all over the world. By November 1917, only six months after he arrived, Lenin and his supporters seized control of the Russian government. On March 3, 1918, Lenin's government signed the peace **Treaty of Brest-Litovsk** with the Central powers, ending Russia's participation in World War I.

Germany's Last Offensive

With Russia out of the war, Germany moved its troops from the eastern front to the western front as quickly as possible. With its forces strengthened, the German High Command believed its armies on the western front could launch hard-hitting attacks to win the war before fresh American troops could arrive to swing the tide of battle. Thus, in the spring of 1918, Germany launched two great offensives. The first was intended to break the Allies' battle lines, forcing the Allied troops to retreat back to the English Channel. The second involved moving farther into France in an attempt to capture Paris. On March 21, 1918, Germany launched their offensives. For a few weeks they gained ground and pushed back the Allies; however, by late April the offensive had stalled.

"Lafayette We Are Here!"

The first contingent of American troops, under the command of General John Pershing, arrived in France in June 1917. Their arrival bolstered the other Allied armies while decreasing the morale of the German troops. American soldiers had received only basic military training before being transported to Europe. They would acquire additional military expertise in the deadly combat which lay ahead. Despite their lack of extensive training and battlefield experience, the American soldiers and their commanders possessed an unshakable confidence.

The eagerness of the American troops impressed **Marshall Foch**, the French supreme commander of the Allied armies. Marshall Foch planned to use the American soldiers as replacements for Allied units that had suffered a large number of casualties, that is, *integrate them into the armies of the Allied nations*. Foch soon

American troops in battle in France. The above quote in the header is from a speech given by General John Pershing's aide, Colonel Charles Stanton. On July 4, 1917, Pershing and Stanton visited Lafayette's tomb where he said, "Lafayette, we are here!" not only to honor Lafayette for his assistance during America's War of Independence, but also as a way of telling the French people that the United States had come to France to repay its 140-year-old debt to Lafayette and France by assisting them during World War I.

discovered, however, that President Wilson had ordered General John Pershing to see that the American forces fought as an independent army and not allow them to be used as replacements.

The Germans learned about American combat skill on May 28, 1918, when American soldiers routed German troops out of **Cantigny**, a strategic town located about fifty miles from Paris. After their defeat at Cantigny, on June 1, the Germans tried to punch their way through the French lines at **Belleau Wood**, but were repulsed by the U.S. Marines. Holding the German initial advance created an advantage for the Allied soldiers, since the Allied troops' strength and morale was increasing while the German strength and morale was declining. On June 28, the Marines attacked and drove the Germans from Belleau Wood.

On July 15, the Germans launched their last major offensive of the war at the **Second Battle of the Marne.** For the next three weeks the two sides fought a series of battles, including the famous **Battle of Chateau-Thierry** on July 18, 1918, one of the first major battles the American army fought during the war. On July 18, the Allies launched a large-scale counter-offensive. By the end of July, the Germans had been pushed back to the positions they held before they launched their offensive.

On August 8, 1918, at Amiens, Marshall Foch began a maximum effort to defeat the Germans and end the war. Known as the **Hundred Days' Offensive,** it would finally end the war. The **Battle of Amiens** is notable for being one of the first major battles that involved tanks, as well as for the number of German soldiers who surrendered rather than continue fighting.

In September, the United States army played a leading role in driving a strong German military force out of the French city of **Saint-Mihiel**, which the Germans had controlled since the early days of the war. The victory, however, was dearly bought: after four days of heavy fighting, 4,500 American soldiers' lives were sacrificed before they wrested control from the German occupiers.

Casualties would have been even higher at Saint-Mihiel had it not been for the aircraft pilots who spotted German artillery emplacements and strafed the German positions with deadly machine-gun fire.

Frank-Earle Schoonover depicts the Marines' savage fight for Belleau Wood.

Capt. Eddie Rickenbacker, winner of the Congressional Medal of Honor

This was one of the first important uses of air-to-ground support in the history of warfare. The planes belonged to Great Britain and France, but many were flown by young American pilots commanded by **Colonel Billy Mitchell**. The leading American "ace" was **Captain "Eddie" Rickenbacker**, who shot down 26 German planes. Other "aces" included Rene Fonck, a Frenchman who shot down 75 enemy planes; Edward Mannock, an Englishman, who shot down 73 planes; and Germany's "Red Baron," Manfred von Richthofen, who claimed 80 kills.

(**Note**: As an example of the "criminal negligence" of the military leaders during World War I, neither British nor American pilots were issued parachutes because their superiors, most of whom had never flown a plane, believed that the availability of a parachute would cause pilots to jump from their planes at the first sign of danger, thus losing too many valuable planes. After the fatal collision of two American pilots he knew, Eddie Rickenbacker noted in his journal that he believed that parachutes would have saved his friends' lives. He wrote "*that it was criminal negligence on the part of those higher up for not having exercised sufficient forethought and seeing that we were equipped with parachutes for just such emergencies.*")

Following the action at Saint-Mihiel, the American army was assigned to take part in an offensive in an area between the Argonne Forest and the Meuse River. A million Americans participated in this mammoth offensive, which began on September 26, 1918. In the Argonne Forest, the trees and undergrowth grew so densely that vision was limited to a few yards in any direction. From September 26 until mid-October, American soldiers crawled over barbed wire that the Germans had laid beneath the dense ground cover.

Once out of the Argonne Forest, the Allies advanced towards the **Hindenburg Line**, a series of three trenches spaced several miles apart, guarded by machine guns and barbed wire. On November 7, the Allies

The Breaking of the Hindenburg Line, by James Beadle (1918)

Eugenio Pacelli (the future Pope Pius XII) (center), Benedict XV's envoy, meets with members of the Germany High Command with a peace proposal from the pope.

broke through the Hindenburg Line and pushed on towards Belgium. Meanwhile, French and British armies all along the western front were driving the Germans back. Finally on November 11, 1918, the Germans signed an **armistice**, agreeing to end hostilities.

The War's Terrible Cost

The end of the war brought blessed joy and relief to the people of the belligerent nations, but the war had taken a terrible toll. The exact number of dead and injured will never be accurately known. The total number of military and civilian casualties is estimated to be about 40 million. About 10 million soldiers and 8 million civilians died. Another 20 million suffered wounds. After the war an even larger number of people died from the **1918 Spanish influenza pandemic**, also known as the Spanish Flu. This worldwide epidemic killed somewhere between 20 and 50 million people, making it one of the worst natural disasters in world history.

The United States had suffered less than other nations. About 53,000 American soldiers were killed in battle, another 63,000 suffered "non-combat" related deaths from the Spanish Flu, while 230,000 were wounded. The war cost the United States twenty-eight billion dollars.

Pope Benedict XV During the War

Because Pope Benedict XV was neutral, many people, notably President Wilson, did not trust him. On August 12, 1917, Benedict presented a seven-point peace plan to the warring nations, but they ignored it. President Wilson would use some of the Pope's ideas in his **Fourteen Points**, which became the guide for the United States during the peace talks. However, at the time Wilson responded by saying, "What does he want to butt in for?" When Wilson traveled to Europe for the peace conference, he visited Benedict XV in Rome—the first time a sitting president visited a pope.

During the war, Pope Benedict XV mobilized the Church's resources to aid the war's victims. Never in history had so many noncombatants been dispossessed and forced to leave their homes. Perhaps the greatest service the Vatican performed was establishing a missing-persons bureau that aided prisoners of war in reuniting with their families as well as supervising prisoner of war exchanges. The Vatican established orphanages for children whose parents had died or were missing and arranged housing for the sick and wounded. The Pope's charitable efforts and appeals for peace increased the Church's moral prestige after the war.

Unfortunately, Pope Benedict's neutrality negated his influence to help plan vital political events in the post-war world. He was not invited to attend the peace conference. His presence and counsel might have curbed the harsh provisions of the Versailles Treaty.

CHAPTER 27 REVIEW QUESTIONS

Answer the following questions:

1. What were Woodrow Wilson's major character flaws?
2. Who did Woodrow Wilson send to capture Pancho Villa? Was he successful?
3. What event caused the start of World War I?
4. What were the two European alliances called and what nations were members of each?
5. What was the name of the German strategy to win World War I? Explain how it worked. Why was it an immoral plan? Why did it fail to succeed?
6. How did England violate American neutrality?
7. How did Germany violate American neutrality? Why was Germany's violation more serious?
8. How did Woodrow Wilson respond to the violations of American neutrality?
9. Why did the sinking of the *Lusitania* infuriate Americans? Why could the Germans argue the *Lusitania* was a legitimate military target? How could the sinking have easily been avoided?
10. Why was the presidential election of 1916 so important? Who were the two major candidates? What was the major issue of the election? Why was Theodore Roosevelt not nominated as a candidate for the election by any Party?
11. What is the Zimmerman Telegram?
12. How did Germany cause Russia to surrender? What was the name of the surrender treaty?
13. When did the first contingent of American troops arrive in France?
14. Who commanded the American troops in Europe during World War I?
15. Name at least two important battles in which American troops fought.
16. When did World War I end?
17. Why was John Pershing a good choice to command American soldiers in Europe?

Identify the following:

1. Marshall Foch
2. Charles Evans Hughes
3. Unrestricted submarine warfare
4. Captain Eddie Rickenbacker
5. Selective Service Act
6. Pope Benedict XV
7. Battle of the Marne

CHAPTER 28

The "Roaring" Twenties

1918-1929

Steel from *America Today* (1930–1931), mural cycle consisting of ten panels by Thomas Hart Benton). In *America Today*, Benton portrays a panorama of American life in the 1920s. He shows people in both heavy industry and on the farm. He depicts people from high society and the lower classes. He renders both black and white Americans working hard and enjoying jazz and dance clubs after work. He presents people from all parts of the nation, from a banker in New York to an actress in Hollywood. This mural reflects Benton's fascination with the production of steel and its uses. Of steel he wrote, "All that was romantic and aspiring in the American Spirit found its expression in steel. The outreaching railroad lines, the great bridges, the engines, the ships of that expanding exploitative period were converging when I reached Chicago, towards its final expression, the skyscraper." Interestingly, the mural "Steel" is one of the few that does not contain any means of transportation.

Winning the War, Losing the Peace

When the United States entered World War I, Woodrow Wilson had proclaimed that America's goal was to "make the world safe for Democracy." However, this goal was entirely contrived by Wilson. No other nation on either side was fighting for this goal or would have understood what it meant, at least as Wilson understood it. Wilson's insistence on imposing this transcendent, Messianic goal would have terrible consequences in both the short and long-term history of Europe and the United States. America had won World War I, but Wilson's character flaws would cause it to lose the peace.

President Wilson's "Fourteen Points" for Peace

On January 8, 1918, President Wilson presented fourteen points to the U.S. Congress describing his plans for peace. He believed these points would lead to international peace and avoid war among the nations of the world. Though his points were discussed during the Peace Treaty talks, England, France, and Italy generally rejected them.

Because secret treaties had helped cause the Great War, Wilson's first point stressed that the peace treaty must not contain any secret provisions. He maintained that nations must negotiate openly and publicly and sign *open treaties*. He insisted that there be no secret international understandings of any kind. Secondly, he called for *absolute freedom of navigation upon the seas*, outside territorial waters, in peace and in war. Thirdly, Wilson called for the removal of all economic barriers and the establishment of *free trade* among the signers of the peace treaty. Fourthly, Wilson called for an *arms reduction* to the lowest point consistent with domestic safety. Wilson's fifth point called for colonial populations to be given equal status with those of the "mother country," or the ruling power.

Allies Day by Childe Hassam (1917). A patriotic whirlwind swept mid–town Manhattan when America entered World War I. On Fifth Avenue, American, British, and French flags were prominently displayed during parades to honor America's allies. Inspired, Hassam painted this picture which was first exhibited in November 1918, four days after the armistice was declared. Thus, the painting originally created to signal America's entry into the war, served to commemorate its victory.

Several of Wilson's Fourteen Points addressed *redrawing the boundaries of European nations*. This notion would have immensely destructive consequences for the people and nations of Europe – most of whom Wilson did not know nor understand. It would cause virtually the entire map of Europe to be redrawn after the war, destroying nations and creating ones that had not previously existed. He based his idea on the notion of *self-determination*. This meant that areas where people considered themselves Italians should be part of Italy. People who considered themselves Polish would be part of Poland, and so forth. Two of these final Points are of particular interest. In one, Wilson rightly insisted that *Belgium must be evacuated and restored to the Belgians*. In another point, Wilson suggested that Alsace-Lorraine, which France had lost to Germany during the Franco-Prussian War of 1871, should be returned to France. Interestingly, most of the people in this region spoke German.

Of the Fourteen Points, the last was the most important to Wilson: create a general association of nations. The purpose of this **League of Nations**, as it was soon known, was to afford mutual guarantees of political independence and territorial integrity *to great and small states alike*. The League would settle disagreements between nations to avoid wars like the one that had just torn the world apart. The League would only use force when absolutely necessary to enforce its rulings.

To people around the world who had suffered through the unimaginable horrors of the Great War, Wilson's idealism sounded wonderful. They believed that with the power and wealth of the United States behind him, Wilson could bring about real changes to the world. They believed that under his leadership, a new era of peace and prosperity was about to begin.

The 1918 Midterm Elections

Although Woodrow Wilson was wildly popular in the Allied nations of Europe, he was not so popular in the United States. During the 1918 midterm elections, President Wilson asked Americans for a vote of confidence, by which he meant electing enough Democrats to control both the House of Representative and the Senate. However, when the votes were tallied, Republicans obtained control of both Chambers of Congress. This meant that two-thirds of a Republican-controlled Senate would have to ratify any treaty that Wilson negotiated.

As the time to depart for the peace talks approached, Wilson, utterly certain of his own unique ability to see the correct path of history, began making a series of mistakes that would eventually doom the treaty and the League of Nations that he so dearly loved. First, President Wilson planned *personally* to travel to Paris to attend the peace talks, which would draft the Peace Treaty. Many Americans did not believe that Wilson should leave the United States while he was president, mainly because no president had ever done so. Also, in an age before air travel, Wilson would be gone for months. Second, and more importantly, *Wilson did not select a single Republican to be part of the official American Peace Delegation.* Many people accused him of allowing only Democrats to share in the honor of what they hoped would be a historic peace treaty.

However, the answer is perhaps more fundamental. Wilson believed that he could convince people to accept his vision of history. He simply did not understand that a treaty as complicated as the Versailles Peace Treaty would contain elements that displeased various segments of the population, both Democrat and Republican. He made his third, and ultimately most critical, mistake by failing to realize that he needed the support of both parties, which meant that he would need to compromise. **Yet Wilson, once the treaty had been written,** *refused to compromise or accept any changes*.

The loss of the House and Senate to the Republicans did not seem to deter President Wilson as he sailed across the Atlantic. On the way to Paris, he visited Pope Benedict. Roman citizens hailed him as a conquering hero. When Wilson reached Paris, hundreds of thousands of French citizens jammed the streets to cheer him. Wounded soldiers from various nations reached out to touch him as he passed by them. The adulation from Europe further convinced President Wilson that the Senate would ratify any treaty he presented to them.

Wilson and King Victor Emmanuel in Rome. Wilson later met privately with Pope Benedict XV for about 20 minutes.

The Versailles Peace Conference

In January 1919, the representatives of the victorious nations met at the Palace of Versailles, just outside of Paris, for a Peace Conference to determine the conditions of the formal peace treaty. Although twenty-seven nations were represented at the Peace Conference, most issues were decided by the Allied leaders known as the **"Big Four:"** President Wilson; French Premier **Georges Clemenceau**; the Prime Minister of England, **David Lloyd George**; and the Prime Minister of Italy, **Vittorio Orlando**. Very quickly, Wilson discovered that the other three leaders held his "Fourteen Points" in low regard.

French Premier **Georges Clemenceau**, called "the Tiger of France," was seventy-seven years old in 1919. Premier Clemenceau had seen German troops invade his nation in 1870 and then again in 1914. Most of the fighting during the Great War had occurred in France. The northwestern part of France, where Germany had invaded, had been reduced to a barren wasteland. In addition to the physical damage, nearly 1.5 million French soldiers (almost 5% of the entire population) had been killed in battle, not to mention the number of civilian casualties. Understandably, Clemenceau wanted to punish Germany and ensure that it could not invade France for a third time. He planned to do that by reducing Germany financially and militarily to the status of a third-class nation.

The third member of the "Big Four" was Great Britain's Prime Minister **David Lloyd George** who had no patience with Wilson's lofty but unrealistic goals. Often when Lloyd George and Clemenceau were alone, they ridiculed Wilson and his lack of understanding of Europe. On one occasion, Clemenceau remarked to Lloyd George, "Wilson thinks he has written the Fourteen Commandments." Lloyd George replied, "The Almighty had only ten!"

The "Big Four" May 27, 1919. (L-R) David Lloyd George, Vittorio Orlando, Georges Clemenceau, Woodrow Wilson

The last "Big Four" member was the Italian premier, **Vittorio Orlando**. Orlando's principal objective was to ensure that Italy received the territories that the Allies had secretly promised him as an incentive to join them against Germany in 1915. In the final treaty, Italy received Trieste, part of the Austro-Hungarian empire

The Versailles Peace Treaty

Realizing that most Americans did not wish to punish the already destitute nation, the Germans agreed to the armistice, hoping the final peace treaty would be more favorable to Germany than the armistice had been. However, after months of talks, the Treaty of Versailles turned out to be as punitive as the armistice. Clemenceau was so angry at Germany that he insisted that the treaty contain a provision stating that Germany alone had caused the war.

However, even more devastating, the French insisted that Germany pay **reparations**, that is, compensation, for all the damage that had been done during the war to the Allies. The amount of reparations would eventually exceed $33 billion, an amount Germany could not hope to pay. The demand for reparations created universal resentment among the Germans and quickly destroyed their economy.

Wilson's insistence on "self-determination" caused the creation of several new European nations and the destruction of others. **Poland** once again became a nation. **Finland**, which had been part of Russia, became a new nation. The Baltic States, **Lithuania**, **Latvia**, and **Estonia**, which had been part of the Russian Empire, also became independent nations.

No nation suffered from Wilson's self-determination as much as the Austro-Hungarian Empire, which ceased to exist. **Austria** and **Hungary** each became new nations, and the Hapsburg family, which had ruled

Europe in 1919. Compare this map with the one in chapter 27. Entire nations have disappeared and others have appeared.

the Holy Roman Empire since 1273, was sent into permanent exile. Wilson would have no kings ruling his new Europe! Parts of the Empire, including Bohemia and Slovakia, became part of the newly-formed nation of **Czechoslovakia**. Other parts, notably Galicia, were given to Poland. Many smaller regions, such as Bosnia-Herzegovina, Slovenia, Croatia, and Serbia, were combined to form the new nation of **Yugoslavia**. Other parts of the Empire went to Italy and Romania.

The Ottoman Empire also ceased to exist. In November, a French army occupied Constantinople. A new nation known as **Turkey** soon came into existence and in 1923 Constantinople was renamed **Istanbul**. However, in order to defeat the Ottoman Empire during the war, the British had made several promises that have caused trouble even today. They promised to help the Arabs establish a nation in the Middle East. They also promised to help the Jews establish a homeland in the Middle East.

The League of Nations

Wilson agreed to many provisions in the Versailles Treaty which he personally disliked because it contained the one provision that he desperately wanted. This was the creation of the **League of Nations**. President Wilson believed the League of Nations would bring about lasting peace in the world. Members of the League of Nations would pledge assistance to one another should aggression threaten any of the members.

Woodrow Wilson was not alone in his effort to establish a League of Nations. Years before the Great War began, other leaders had talked about forming an organization of nations that would try to arbitrate disputes without resorting to war. The outbreak of the war, and the reality of its incomprehensible horror, rekindled the interest in establishing a League of Nations. The Versailles Conference gave President Wilson an opportunity to meet with other world leaders to discuss a constitution for the League of Nations. It was from these proposals that the final structure for a League of Nations, as it appeared in the Peace Treaty, was drafted. Any nation which ratified the Versailles Treaty automatically gained membership in the League of Nations. Later, other nations that wished to join could be admitted by a two-thirds vote of the existing members.

The League of Nations had a General Assembly and a Council. The Assembly would be composed of member nations, each of whom would have one vote. The Council would include delegates from the United States, Great Britain, France, Italy and Japan. These nations would hold permanent seats. Delegates

Signing of the peace treaty in the Hall of Mirrors in Versailles. Woodrow Wilson (middle left) agreed to several provisions he disliked because he desperately wanted the League of Nations to become a reality.

from four other nations, chosen by the Assembly, would hold temporary seats. The Council would settle disputes between member nations. Nations that did not follow the League's decisions could be punished. Punishments depended on the severity of the violation, but ranged from trade bans to military intervention.

Woodrow Wilson absolutely believed that the League of Nations would end war and create a lasting era of peace and prosperity. He knew that the Versailles Treaty had many flaws, but he thought that the League could address and fix those flaws. He believed the United States *must* adopt the Versailles Treaty, which would automatically make it a member of the League. In July 1919, Wilson submitted the Treaty to the United States Senate, believing that passage would be a mere formality. Woodrow Wilson had made a great many mistakes in his life; however, this one would literally break his heart.

Opposition to the Versailles Treaty

When Woodrow Wilson introduced the Versailles Treaty to the U. S. Senate, it never occurred to him that senators would reject it *because of* the League of Nations. Various senators asserted that League membership would negate the Monroe Doctrine and Congress' right to declare war. They wondered if a League controlled by foreign nations would have the power to send American soldiers to war when America itself had not been threatened.

In 1919, the Senate was comprised of forty-nine Republicans and forty-seven Democrats. As the Treaty came up for debate, most Democratic senators expressed support for the League and the Treaty. However, the Republicans, who controlled Congress, were split into various factions.

One group of about ten Republican senators was known as the **mild reservationists**. They actually seemed to favor approval of the Treaty but had some minor concerns about the League. They were willing to vote for the Treaty if certain changes were made.

Senator **Henry Cabot Lodge**, from Massachusetts, led the largest group of Republican senators and were known as the "**strong reservationists**." These senators were willing to approve the treaty but demanded that *major* changes be made to the Treaty. In a bit of a personal tweak at Wilson, Lodge introduced fourteen reservations (in direct contradiction to Wilson's Fourteen Points), called the **Lodge Reservations**, that listed his group's objections and the changes that they demanded. The most crucial Lodge Reservation insisted that the League of Nations not be allowed to send American troops into combat without the prior approval of the American Congress. The strong reservationists would vote to approve the treaty *only* if these changes were made. Many people wondered if Lodge's objections had more to do with his personal animosity toward Wilson than his patriotism.

Henry Cabot Lodge

Finally, there was a third group of about sixteen senators led by **Robert LaFollette** of Wisconsin. These Republicans (and two Democrats), labeled "**The Irreconcilables**," refused to accept the Treaty under any circumstances. The Irreconcilables either personally and/or politically hated Wilson and his policies or opposed membership in any international organization that might exercise control over the United States.

If Wilson had been willing to accept the changes sought by the "mild reservationists," he probably could have won the two-thirds votes needed to ratify the treaty. Even some of the strong reservationists

President Wilson and his wife Edith. Here Edith holds a document for her husband's signature. After Wilson's stroke Edith became extremely protective of her husband. Many historians have questioned whether or not during his illness she actually acted as president. Always one of his closest advisors, Edith accompanied Wilson to Paris where she consulted with him on the Versailles Peace Treaty.

Edith Wilson

might have been won over. However, President Wilson was adamant about his treaty. He would not accept changes. He refused to negotiate. Wilson told the Senate to take it or leave it.

Wilson, as a Progressive, appears to have believed that America should be part of the international community and sacrifice its sovereignty for the international good. Later Democratic presidents would make that same argument and push internationalism over nationalism, and many would support them. However, in 1919, the majority of Americans still felt that the United States was an exceptional nation, not simply one among many. Wilson was asking Americans to do what George Washington had warned against in his *Farewell Address* and Thomas Jefferson had warned against in his *First Inaugural Address*, that is, entangling alliances.

By 1919, the United States had become a world leader, if not yet the dominant world power. Wilson was asking too much too soon. Had he been willing to make some small concessions, the Senate would have easily ratified the treaty. However, *perhaps he physically could not have made the concessions.*

At the time of the Treaty debate, President Wilson was in extremely poor health. During the Versailles peace conference, he had suffered a mild **stroke**. A stroke occurs when the blood supply to part of the brain is interrupted or reduced, depriving brain tissue of oxygen and nutrients. Every stroke is incredibly serious because **strokes kill brain cells**. Doctors in 1918 did not understand brain chemistry or medicine like they do today, so his doctors failed to diagnose the stroke. The stroke, because it killed some of President Wilson's brain cells, almost certainly affected his judgment. Perhaps his objection to treaty concessions lay in his personality flaws, that is, his belief in his power to persuade others. Perhaps the stroke had affected his ability to recognize that he was acting irrationally in believing that he could convince the Senate to accept his vision of history. For whatever reason, Wilson refused to budge on the treaty. Instead, he determined to take his case to the American people.

The Peace Treaty is Defeated

To rally support for the peace treaty, President Wilson, against the advice of his doctors, determined to take a railroad trip across America where he would personally take his case to the American people. As he traveled, however, his usual gracious personality began to slip away. The constant travel, the numerous speeches, and his failing health wore him out. His wife and his doctors all pleaded with him to end the tour and rest. "I will not be called a quitter by my opponents," he told them. However, in late September, Wilson suffered another stroke. Even doctors in 1919 realized what had happened. His left side was partly paralyzed. Realizing that he could not continue, he returned to the White House.

In the two months that followed, his wife kept the president in seclusion. Only doctors and a few of his closest friends saw him. As Wilson recovered, his advisers pleaded with him to make a deal with the mild reservationists. He still refused. He said he would rather go down fighting than be called a quitter.

On November 19, 1919, the Senate finally voted on the Versailles Treaty with the Lodge Reservations attached. The Democrats defeated it. Then the Senate voted on the Treaty without the Lodge Reservations. This time the Republicans defeated it. In March 1920, the Senate again voted on the Treaty with reservations. Despite Wilson's urging to the contrary, some Democrats switched their positions and voted to ratify the treaty. However, not enough Democrats voted to ratify, so the treaty failed to obtain the necessary two-thirds majority. For a third time the treaty failed. It would be 1921 before the war with Germany officially ended.

The Election of 1920

As the 1920 presidential election approached, Woodrow Wilson hoped that he might run for a third term. However, he had become rather unpopular, so Democratic party leaders were unwilling to nominate him. The Republicans had originally considered nominating the sixty-year-old Theodore Roosevelt. However, Roosevelt died unexpectedly in his sleep in January 1919. Woodrow Wilson's vice president, Thomas Marshall, summed up the love and respect that all Americans had for Teddy Roosevelt when he said, "Death had to take Roosevelt sleeping, for if he had been awake, there would have been

a fight." With no obvious candidates, both parties made a political calculation and nominated two little-known candidates from Ohio – the mother of presidents.

The Democrats chose Ohio Governor **William Cox** for their presidential candidate and **Franklin D. Roosevelt**, a distant cousin of Theodore Roosevelt, for their vice-presidential candidate. Both men supported the Versailles Treaty and the League of Nations. The Republicans chose Ohio Senator **Warren G. Harding** for president and Massachusetts governor **Calvin Coolidge** as his running mate. Harding, though not a particularly brilliant man himself, ran one of the most brilliant campaigns in all of American history.

In 1919, President Wilson, a Democrat, had become unpopular. His foreign policy was unpopular as more and more Americans opposed the League of Nations. The tide of feeling that had brought progressives into office in the first decades of the twentieth century had swung against them. The year 1919 saw riots break out across the nation. The economy fell into a depression. Workers staged

Warren G. Harding

large-scale strikes in the meatpacking and steel industries. The Communist Revolution in Russia caused even greater alarm in the United States, especially when Communists launched terrorist attacks on Wall Street.

Harding and the Republicans sensed that Americans wanted to return to the "good old days" before America became embroiled in a terrible foreign war and all these tragedies had befallen the nation. Thus, Harding did not run against Cox, whom he basically ignored. Rather, he ran against Wilson and his policies. Harding's campaign slogan called for a "return to normalcy." In a speech in Boston, Massachusetts, on May 14, 1920, Harding explained that, *"America's present need is not heroics, but healing; not nostrums, but normalcy; not revolution, but restoration; not agitation, but adjustment; not surgery, but serenity; not the dramatic, but the dispassionate; not experiment, but equipoise; not submergence in internationality, but sustainment in triumphant nationality."* In other words, what the country needed was not to be involved in international schemes or other grand projects, but rather to take time to settle down and fix what had been damaged.

Harding's strategy paid off as he won the election in a massive landslide. Cox failed even to carry the reliably "Solid South," losing Tennessee. Harding received just over 60% of the total popular vote to Cox's 34%. Harding's 26% margin of victory is one of the highest in all presidential elections. In 1919, the states had ratified the **Nineteenth Amendment** to the Constitution, guaranteeing women the right to vote. As a result, the total popular vote dramatically increased from 18.5 million in 1916 to 26.8 million in 1920. Most women apparently voted for the Republican, Harding.

American Foreign Policy During the 1920s

During the 1920s, American presidents attempted to steer a path between America's traditional **isolationism** and its new-found **internationalism**. On the one hand, most Americans would have preferred to remain isolated from the foreign affairs of other nations. They would have preferred to follow George Washington's advice to engage in foreign commerce but stay out of foreign politics. On the other hand, by 1920, America was an international power. America had lent $13 billion to its Allies. American soldiers had died in Europe. The United States, regardless of the feelings of its people and leaders, could no longer remain completely isolated. Therefore, during the 1920s, American presidents worked to improve America's economic relations while decreasing military power around the world.

The Washington Disarmament Conference

In an effort to promote lasting peace, in the summer of 1921, President Warren G. Harding invited nine powerful nations to send delegates to Washington, D. C., where they would discuss world **disarmament**, that is, reducing and limiting the weapons of war. This **Washington Disarmament Conference** involved all the world's great **naval powers**, including the United States, England, France, Italy, and Japan. The nations discussed reducing the size of their navies as well as issues affecting the Far East.

The conference resulted in two treaties. In the **Five-Powers Naval Treaty**, the United States, England, France, Italy, and Japan agreed to destroy 1,878,000 tons of naval vessels. They also agreed not to build any new battleships for ten years. This "naval holiday" was scheduled to end in 1936. A second treaty, signed by all nine nations, provided for regulation of trade in China in accord with the Open Door Policy.

The Kellogg-Briand Pact

In 1927, the Prime Minister of France, **Aristide Briand**, proposed that France and the United States sign an agreement outlawing war. U. S. Secretary of State, **Frank Kellogg**, suggested that all of the leading countries of the world sign such a treaty. Secretary Kellogg arranged a treaty that was acceptable to all of the great nations. The treaty was simple. Signing nations renounced war as an instrument of state policy and resolved to settle disputes by peaceful means.

All the great powers of Europe signed the Kellogg-Briand Pact. The U.S. Senate ratified it in 1928. Due to the large number of leading nations that approved the Pact, it was considered a major step toward outlawing war. In reality, while well-intentioned, the Pact had no real effect.

Post-War Domestic Problems

Many Americans faced difficult problems in the days following the end of the Great War. There seemed to be disorder in industry, business, agriculture, and society in general. A main contributor to the unrest was the three million soldiers who had served in the armed forces and were now returning to civilian life and looking for jobs.

Most factory owners had expanded production to meet the demands of the war. After the war, they began to cut their factories' production. Cutting back from high wartime demands to a far smaller peacetime level necessitated serious reductions in the number of workers they needed. Many people lost jobs. Suddenly, unemployment became a serious national problem.

Frank Kellogg

During the war, President Wilson had asked farmers to increase production. Therefore, on the day the war ended, farmers had overflowing storage bins but no markets to sell their produce. With a great supply but smaller demand, prices dropped as farmers looked for buyers of food that would spoil quickly. In 1919, a bushel of wheat sold for over two dollars. In 1921, a bushel sold for only fifty cents.

During the war, workers pledged not to strike over salary demands. Once the war ended, however, factory workers, some of whom had worked seventy-hour work weeks during the war, demanded a reduction in hours and an increase in wages. By 1919, rampant inflation had caused the cost of living to nearly double. To obtain their demands, workers went on strike. During 1919, there were 4,000 strikes across the nation and many turned violent.

For example, on September 9, 1919, Boston's policemen went on strike demanding better working conditions and higher salaries. The police strike meant that Boston, for a time, had no law enforcement. Consequently, thieves and looters began smashing store windows and stealing whatever they could. To quell this widespread theft, Boston's mayor asked Governor Calvin Coolidge for assistance. Coolidge responded by sending a National Guard force comprised of college students and war veterans to patrol the streets and restore order in Boston.

Calvin Coolidge received national attention for his management of the Boston police strike. President Wilson summed up his thoughts on the strike by saying, "There is no right to strike against public safety by anyone, anytime, anywhere." The president congratulated Coolidge's strong stand, calling it "a triumph for law and order."

Two other notable strikes occurred around this time. The first began at a United States Steel manufacturing plant in Indiana, where workers wanted to become a part of an industrial union which would represent them in labor relations with management and ownership. This strike, which eventually involved more than 350,000 workers, failed. However, similar strikes led to more worker-friendly work hours and higher wages.

Photo of a riot on Boston Common during the 1919 police strike. Criminals attempt to take over the city during the strike. In this photo, National Guard troops subdue the rioters.

John L. Lewis, the chief executive of the United Mine Workers, organized the second strike. The miners walked out, demanding safer working conditions and higher pay. A federal court ordered them back to work. Nevertheless, most of the miners' concerns were eventually eliminated through arbitration between owners and workers.

Although the American economy slowed during the years immediately after the war, by the beginning of the new decade American merchants began exporting their products to European nations that were rebuilding. As a result of these exports, American businesses rebounded and began making a great deal of money. In addition, because of improving and updating technologies, new industries were becoming popular. Automobiles, radios, and movies, as well as a plethora of new consumer goods, became available to shoppers in the 1920s. Instead of a crisis, the post-war decade became a time of great wealth and luxury in the United States.

A Return to Normalcy

The history of America's presidents demonstrates that men who have served as state governors are better prepared to become president because of their executive experience. In other words, governors run states. Managing the United States is similar to managing an individual state. Warren G. Harding had served in the Senate, but had not been a governor. He validated history's record by being a poor leader.

Warren Harding had been elected because he promised to return the nation to its pre-war normalcy. As part of his program, he supported the traditional Republican positions of high tariffs and low taxes to create jobs and stimulate the economy. Yet after the war, Harding, and the nation, faced serious problems including growing unemployment. Though Harding was personally a decent man he probably should never have run for president. Even he realized that he lacked the intelligence and qualities of leadership necessary to succeed. As a result, he tried to surround himself with more capable men. However, Harding proved to be a poor judge of character. While some of his cabinet appointments such as his Secretary of State, Charles Evans Hughes, showed themselves incredibly able and honest, others lacked these qualities. Harding, probably unwittingly, appointed men to positions of high trust who dishonored him by stealing from the public. Many of these appointments were longtime Harding associates who became known as the "Ohio Gang." As a result of these men, a number of scandals surfaced during the Harding administration. The most famous of these was the **Teapot Dome Scandal**, during which the Secretary of the Interior, Albert Fall, accepted more than $400,000 in bribes for permitting illegal oil drilling on public lands at Teapot Dome, Wyoming.

President Harding avoided a terrible public humiliation by dying while in office. Vice-president Calvin Coolidge was vacationing on his father's Vermont farm when news of Harding's death reached him. On August 3, 1923, the presidential oath of office was administered to Calvin Coolidge by his father, a justice of the peace.

Calvin Coolidge was certainly one of America's finest presidents. A former Massachusetts governor, Coolidge was scrupulously honest and steadfast, as well as a careful spender. In other words, he was the exact opposite of Warren G. Harding. Coolidge's high sense of duty compelled him to bring to justice everyone who had been guilty of fraud in Harding's administration. As a result, the Democrats failed to gain any political advantages from the Harding scandals. President Coolidge was pro-business and favored tax cuts and limited government. He provided respectability and stability for the fast-paced, modern nation that America had become.

Secretary of the Interior Albert Fall

Calvin Coolidge

Although Coolidge was a skillful and effective public speaker, in private he seemed uncomfortable at "fashionable" parties, so he seldom spoke. This habit earned him the nickname "Silent Cal." A story is told that at a Washington society dinner, he was seated next to an elderly woman. The woman engaged

Coolidge in conversation by saying, "I made a bet today that I could get more than two words out of you." He replied, "You lose."

The Election of 1924

For the election of 1924, the Republican convention quickly chose the incumbent, Calvin Coolidge. Coolidge had turned around the economy and resolved many of the domestic problems that had beset the nation. Moreover, America was at peace.

However, the Democrats struggled for seventeen days at their convention to choose a candidate. Democrats in the Eastern part of the nation favored **Alfred (Al) Smith**, the governor of New York. Convention delegates from the West and the South favored **William McAdoo**, who had been President Wilson's Secretary of the Treasury. Both McAdoo and Smith had problems with elements in the Democratic Party. McAdoo had been tied to some suspicious land deals and some people believed he favored segregation. McAdoo also favored prohibition which the eastern convention delegates did not. On the other hand, Smith opposed prohibition and condemned segregation. Yet at its core, the objection to Smith was more hateful. Al Smith was a Catholic. In 1924, there were Americans who simply would not vote for a candidate because he was a Catholic, regardless of the position he held on a particular issue. Some ignorant people even believed that a Catholic president would follow orders from the Pope in administering the country.

Al Smith

However, other delegates to the Democratic convention, especially those in the South and West, opposed Smith for more valid reasons. Smith had been born, raised, and lived his whole life in New York City. In fact, he lived his entire life on the Lower East side of Manhattan, one of the most urban areas in all of the United States. Some people in the South and West, especially those who lived in rural areas, distrusted "city slickers" and disliked what Smith, a New Yorker, represented. For most of American history, people had lived in rural areas and farmers constituted a large percentage of the population. By the 1920s, America had shifted from a rural to an urban nation. Most people lived in cities. Farmers and people who lived in rural areas no longer comprised the majority. To them, Al Smith represented this change in American life - their way of life – from farm to city, and they did not like it. Thus, it was not Smith the Catholic whom they particularly opposed, but Smith "the man from Manhattan."

John William Davis

Under the rules of the Democratic convention, a candidate had to receive a two-thirds majority to become the party's nominee. The convention delegates voted over and over again for days and days, but neither Smith nor Cox could obtain the two-thirds necessary. Because the Democrats could not agree on one of the two leaders, on the 103rd ballot, they nominated **John W. Davis** of West Virginia, who had actually finished third on all the previous ballots. Davis had been an attorney in West Virginia before joining President's Wilson's administration as

Solicitor General of the United States (the attorney who represents the U.S. before the Supreme Court) and America's ambassador to the Court of St James's (England). For vice-president the Democrats chose Charles W. Bryan, the governor of Nebraska and the younger brother of William Jennings Bryan.

Robert LaFollette of Wisconsin ran as a third party candidate. LaFollette found Coolidge and Davis to be too conservative, so he formed a new Progressive Party. LaFollette called for more government control of business, stronger support for unions and the rights of workers, and higher taxes.

When the votes were counted, Calvin Coolidge had won in a landslide, receiving 54% of the popular vote. Coolidge carried all of the states outside of the Solid South with the exception of Wisconsin, LaFollette's home state. After almost twenty years of progressive presidents, the nation had swung back to a more conservative position, at least politically. *Socially*, the United States was undergoing some radical changes.

The "Roaring" Twenties

The 1920s has received the appellation "roaring" because of the changes that occurred in American society during that decade. For the first time, large numbers of Americans openly began to reject traditional Judeo-Christian values. Although by the standards of the 21st century, these rejections seem tame, in 1920 they were anything but tame. The war was over. Life was good. Many people decided a little immorality wouldn't hurt. In a sense, the seeds planted in the 1920s are still bearing fruit today, as more and more Americans continue to reject traditional morality or any morality.

With a strong economy, people in the Twenties had more leisure time. Thus, they looked for new ways to enjoy this free time. New leisure industries sprang up as Americans began going to jazz clubs, the movies, sporting events, and listening to the radio.

The Golden Age of Jazz

During the 1920s, the most popular type of music was called **jazz**. While jazz was not a new type of music, *it was a particularly American form of music.* Unlike other genres of music, which had their origins in Europe, jazz had been developed by black musicians in New Orleans around 1890. Jazz had grown out of an American musical genre known as the **blues**, which originated in the Deep South during the 1870s. The blues reflected the difficult lives that blacks living in that time and place endured. **W. C. Handy** of Alabama is generally considered the "father of the blues." In 1914, Handy wrote his most famous piece, and arguably the most famous blues composition in history, "St. Louis Blues."

Although most jazz musicians had no formal musical training, they possessed an immense natural talent. One of the leaders of the jazz movement was bandleader, composer, and pianist **Edward Kennedy "Duke" Ellington**, who began his career in 1923 in New York City. Over the

William Christopher Handy

next fifty years, "Duke" Ellington would play for kings and presidents. Another leading jazz musician was trumpet player **Louis Daniel Armstrong**, nicknamed *Satchmo*.

Armstrong also had a career spanning fifty years and achieved fame both as a trumpet player and as a singer. During his career Armstrong appeared in about fifteen movies, usually playing himself or a bandleader, as well as singing the sound tracks for others.

Because the early jazz musicians lacked formal training, they tended to **improvise** their music. They played a tune and followed it up and down the scale, listening for the sounds that felt right to them. Jazz vocalists also developed "**scat singing**" which is improvisation with nonsense words, e.g. "do bop wop dee bop." The singer improvises melodies using his or her voice as the instrument. Louis Armstrong and **Ella Fitzgerald** were considered great scat singers.

Jazz quickly moved from New Orleans to jazz clubs in Chicago and **Harlem**, a black neighborhood in New York City. **The Cotton Club** in Harlem featured performances from the leading jazz artists of the 1920s, including Duke Ellington and Louis Armstrong. From Chicago and New York, jazz artists took their music all over the world, not only in person but also by means of their recordings. White musicians also began performing jazz. Thus, music began to bring black and white Americans closer together and break down some obstacles to better relations as everyone could enjoy jazz.

Duke Ellington

New Roles for Women

The 1920s proved to be a turning point for women politically, economically, socially, and even fashionably. Certainly, the greatest moment for the women's rights movement occurred in 1920 with the ratification of the landmark Nineteenth Amendment. Women gained the right to vote and took their place as politically equal Americans. During the 1920s, women began taking active roles in politics. In February 1920, a small group of women founded The League of Women Voters and began working to help women exercise their voting rights. Although initially a non-partisan organization, the League has become a very progressive political organization, which, while not endorsing candidates, supports abortion and other liberal positions.

Women also began taking their place alongside men in the workforce. During the Great War, many women had taken various industrial jobs to aid the war effort. A significant number of them continued to work after the restoration of peace. During the 1920s,

Ella Fitzgerald

a variety of jobs and occupations, which had been previously deemed "men's work," began to accept capable women – although somewhat slowly.

The freedom that women achieved politically and economically became more obvious in new fashion trends that occurred over the course of the decade. With a new sense of freedom, women began to change the way that they dressed. They abandoned uncomfortable corsets and heavy petticoats for looser (freer) clothing.

They also began wearing shorter skirts. Following the example of Hollywood actresses, they began cutting their hair short and wearing lipstick and makeup.

Women also began changing their social behaviors. They began going to nightclubs where they smoked and drank in public. Both young women and young men began doing a new dance called the **Charleston**. This behavior shocked many older people, who believed that these young women were acting in a gravely immoral manner. They began calling young women who cut their hair short and wore short dresses **flappers** because during the Charleston they flapped their arms like birds. While most of these young women (and men) were not making a political statement in their dress and behavior, they tended to behave with looser morals than their parents and grandparents had. Of course, many of these young people were doing nothing more serious than just enjoying good music and a good time dancing.

Hollywood actress Gloria Swanson in the 1920s. Swanson and other actresses' short hair, called a "bob cut," would influence millions of young women to wear their hair short as well. The "bob" would become a major fashion trend during the 1920s.

The Golden Age of American Sports

Sports underwent a rebirth in the Roaring 20s for women as well as men. Professional baseball, which had begun in 1869, became extremely popular during the 1920s. In 1922, New York's Yankee Stadium was built. It soon became known as the "House That Ruth Built," due to **George Herman "Babe" Ruth's** ability to hit home runs. In 1927, Ruth hit 60 home runs. By the end of his career he had hit 714 home runs. As of May 2022, his total remains the third highest in baseball history.

Although baseball was America's national pastime, Americans dearly loved football as well. The most famous coach of the 1920s, and one of the greatest college coaches of all time, was **Knute Rockne,** who coached the University of Notre Dame's "Fighting Irish." The Fighting Irish began the 1920s with an undefeated season. From 1918 to 1930, Rockne coached Notre Dame to 105 victories, three national championships, and five undefeated seasons. His .881 winning percentage is the highest for any major college football coach with more than ten years coaching.

Babe Ruth in 1927, the year he hit sixty home runs.

From 1919 to 1926, "**Jack**" **Dempsey** reigned as the heavyweight boxing champion of the world. In July 1921, 91,000 boxing fans paid more than $1 million to see Dempsey knock out Frenchman Georges Carpentier. It was the first time a boxing match had earned a million dollars.

Dempsey's main rival was "Gene" Tunney. Tunney held the world heavyweight title from 1926 until 1928. Tunney also defeated Carpentier and defeated Dempsey twice. In 1926, Tunney defeated Dempsey by a unanimous decision of the judges. A year later, the two men met in a rematch. The rematch, known as the *Long Count Fight*, remains one of the most famous fights in boxing history. Dempsey knocked Tunney down, but because Dempsey failed to go to a neutral corner, the referee delayed counting out Tunney, who eventually recovered and won again by unanimous decision. Tunney eventually retired as an undefeated champion the following year.

During the 1920s, **Bobby Jones**, arguably the greatest golfer of all time, dominated golf. In 1930, he became the only person to win the **Grand Slam** of golf, that is, winning all four majors in one year. (In 2001, Tiger Woods won all four majors in a row, but not in the same year.)

From 1912 to 1929, William "Big Bill" Tilden ruled the world of men's international tennis, winning 138 of 192 tournaments. The greatest female tennis player of the time, and arguably of all time, was **Helen Wills Moody**. Helen Wills Moody won an incredible thirty-one Grand Slam titles during her career, including nineteen singles titles. As of January 2019, only four people have won more singles titles than she did. Only seven people have won more total titles. Helen Moody was the first American female athlete to become an international celebrity. She changed the fashions of tennis, playing in knee-length skirts rather than the longer ones players had previously worn.

Charles Lindbergh

Although the term "hero" is often applied to sports figures, and certainly many of the accomplishments of the athletes of the 1920s were in some respects heroic, on May 20, 1927, America got a taste of true heroism.

In June 1919, two British aviators, **John Alcock and Arthur Brown**, had made the first nonstop transatlantic flight, flying a modified World War I bomber from Newfoundland to Ireland. However, no one had made a *solo* transatlantic flight. A hotel owner in New York offered a $25,000 prize to the first pilot that succeeded.

On May 20, 1927, **Charles Augustus Lindbergh**, a veteran U.S. mail pilot, climbed into the cockpit of an aircraft called *The Spirit of St. Louis*, which was named for the financial backing he received from a group of St. Louis businessmen. His small plane overloaded with fuel for the long flight, Lindbergh was forced to

Bobby Jones. Between 1923 and 1930, Jones won thirteen major golf titles, all as an amateur. His best year was 1930, when he won golf's Grand Slam. Later that year, he retired from tournament play at age 28. He returned to Atlanta to practice law but never completely left the sport he loved. He made films and wrote books about golf. He also helped found Augusta National Golf Club and the annual tournament known as the Masters which has become one of golf's "Majors."

Helen Wills Moody. Beginning in 1923, when she won her first American singles title, she dominated women's tennis for more than a decade. Between 1927 and 1933 she won an astonishing 180 straight matches! This photo shows her playing an early match in the 1933 United States Open. She lost in the finals to Helen Jacobs.

taxi close to the end of the long, muddy airstrip at **Roosevelt Field** on New York's Long Island before he coaxed the plane off the ground and into the air. Some of the fuel was contained in two large gas tanks that obstructed his forward view. He carried a canteen of water and a brown bag with five sandwiches. For the next 33½ hours, the determined pilot fought his three enemies: snow, sleet, and sleep. *Flying without navigation equipment* because of the weight, he landed in Paris, at **Le Bourget Airport**, where he was given a well-deserved hero's welcome. He had become the first pilot to fly alone from America to Europe.

America's newspapers called him the "Lone Eagle" and "Lucky Lindy." However, it was not luck that allowed him to fly for more than thirty-three hours across the Atlantic. It was determination, courage, and skill.

When he returned home, Lindbergh was given a massive ticker tape parade in New York City, as four million people lined the streets to cheer him. President Coolidge awarded him the Distinguished Flying Cross and on March 21,1929, the nation's highest honor, the Congressional Medal of Honor. Lindbergh's flight grabbed the attention of every American. Almost single-handedly, Charles Lindbergh opened the Aviation Age.

The Golden Age of Radio

Many Americans first learned of Lindbergh's incredible accomplishment when they heard about it on their radios. During the 1920s, radio became a massive industry affecting almost every aspect of American society from politics to entertainment. Because so many people wanted a radio, huge companies began manufacturing radios and broadcasting equipment. For example, in 1919, the **Radio Corporation of America** (RCA) was founded. RCA manufactured radio receivers. Once radios were built, they had to be sold. Radio stores sprang up all over the nation. Department stores had entire floors dedicated just to the sale of radios. Of course, even the finest RCA radio would break down. This meant an entire industry dedicated to the *repair* of radios.

In the 1920s, radio was the leading form of entertainment. Radio had many advantages over other

Charles Lindbergh standing beside his plane

Lindbergh's ticker tape parade in New York City. The Float included a model of Lindbergh's plane and the Eiffel Tower.

forms of entertainment. First of all, it was free. People did not need to leave their homes to see a baseball game, attend a concert, or listen to a jazz band, because these events were broadcast over the radio. Also, unlike pre-recorded shows of today, the events on the radio were taking place at the moment they were broadcast. For example, on November 2, 1920, the results of the presidential election were broadcast live.

In 1920, the first **commercial** radio station, that is, one that took advertisements, began broadcasting in Pittsburgh. The station, KDKA, was operated by the Westinghouse Electrical Company. Two years later, more than 500 radio stations were operating across the United States. As the number of stations increased, companies formed to create **radio networks**. On September 13, 1926, RCA founded the **National Broadcasting Company** (NBC), the first national radio network, by combining local stations across the country. People all over the United States could hear the same program at the same time on the NBC network when it began broadcasting on November 15. The following year, the **Columbia Broadcasting System** (CBS) was formed. Under the leadership of William S. Paley, CBS would quickly rival NBC for listeners.

Because people wanted to hear something on the radio besides news and sports, a new entertainment industry was born as first radio stations and then networks created radio programs. The 1920s through the 1940s are considered the "**Golden Age of Radio**." Millions of Americans listened to programs of every genre: comedies, dramas, quiz shows, and mysteries—in other words, all the shows Americans watch today on television.

Of course, while listening to the radio was free, someone had to pay for the programs. In those days that meant a **sponsor**, that is, the company paying for the advertising. Sponsors might be *Jello* on the *Jack Benny Show* or *Dove Soap* on *Burns and Allen*. Radio entertainers became wealthy and sponsors fought for the chance to advertise on the most popular shows to get their message into consumers' homes.

Radio also began America's enduring love affair with technology. In 1922, radio sales were about $60 million. In 1929, sales had increased to more than $840 million. As new technologies emerged, Americans would embrace them with equal passion, e.g. television, personal computers, cell phones, etc.

George Burns and Gracie Allen

Jack Benny

The Rise of the Motion Picture Industry

During the 1920s another industry also came into its own, and, unlike radio, has never looked back. This is the motion picture industry. In the 1920s, the movies became one of America's ten largest industries and one of the most influential cultural forces in the world.

Movies had been popular since the mid-1890s, when Thomas Edison had invented the motion picture camera. In fact, by 1918, Edison's film company had made over 1,000 short films, including the famous "Great Train Robbery," in 1903. Around 1905, people began watching movies in empty stores and warehouses that entrepreneurs had converted into **nickelodeons**, so-called because the normal price of admission was five cents. Although these early black and white, silent motion pictures were of poor quality, people flocked to see them. Over the next ten years, nickelodeons spread across the nation.

Beginning around 1915, large movie theatres began to be constructed in America's major cities. Films became longer, around ninety minutes, and told stories. By 1920, there were about 15,000 movie theatres in America, some so large that they could seat over three thousand viewers. Yet these palatial venues were needed as America had fallen in love with the movies. In 1920, about 40 million people per week attended the movies. By 1930, that number had jumped to 100 million.

Movies had originally been produced in the East. For example, Edison Films had shot the legendary western *The Great Train Robbery* in New Jersey! However, filmmakers quickly realized that the almost constant sunshine of southern California provided the perfect environment for outdoor filming. Hollywood, California became, and remains, the movie-making capital of the world.

In the beginning, all movies were silent. Usually a pianist would play music during the movie. Cards appeared on the screen at times with important dialogue. However, on October 6, 1927, Warner Brothers, a leading motion picture company, released the first "talkie," a movie with a sound track that contained the actors' voices. The film, entitled *The Jazz Singer*, starred **Al Jolson**, one of America's most popular entertainers. The following year, **Walt Disney** released the landmark *Steamboat Willie*, the first sound cartoon and the first appearance of *Mickey Mouse*. The addition of sound to films was a monumental improvement and the beginning of a national popular entertainment.

Although Mickey Mouse is more well-known today, the biggest star of the 1920s was **Charlie Chaplin**. Chaplin wrote,

Poster for *The Jazz Singer*

Scene from "The Kid," a 1921 silent film written, directed, and starring Charlie Chaplin as The Tramp and co-starring Jackie Coogan as his adopted son. It is considered not only one of the greatest silent films but one of the best films of all time.

directed, and starred in his own films. In 1915, he created an iconic character, the **Little Tramp**. The Little Tramp was a sad but funny little man who wore baggy pants, a battered derby hat, overly large shoes, and carried a cane. The Tramp would cleverly – and hilariously – escape the authorities who did not appreciate his eccentric actions. For nearly his entire career, Chaplin played the Tramp or some version of him. In one of his most famous roles, in *The Great Dictator* (1940), Chaplin, who also wrote and directed the movie, plays a dual role of a Jewish barber, who is a version of the Tramp, and an Adolf Hitler-like character.

As motion pictures became more and more popular, their influence on American and international culture grew almost beyond a point of understanding. People then, as now, nearly worshiped Hollywood stars. People began to dress like them. Women began to wear their hair in their styles. Actors endorsed products and people purchased them. Hundreds of magazines, radio shows, and newspaper columns were devoted to their lives. Beneath the glamor, however, many of these men and women were living very immoral lives. While Hollywood covered up much of the immorality during the 1920s, the days were coming when Hollywood would no longer care about covering it up, but would embrace it.

Henry Ford and The Automobile

Radio and motion pictures changed American culture, but nothing in the 1920s changed the way Americans *lived* more than the automobile. Although inventors had been tinkering with self-propelled vehicles for many centuries, most historians point to 1886, when German inventor **Karl Benz** patented his Benz Patent-Motorwagen as the year when the modern automobile was born. The Benz Motorwagen was the first car powered by an *internal combustion engine*. In the United States, one man stands as the leading figure in the automobile industry. His name is **Henry Ford**.

Henry Ford was born July 30, 1863, on a farm in Greenfield, Michigan. Although his father expected him to run the family farm, Henry hated farming. When he was sixteen, Henry moved to Detroit, where he became an apprentice machinist.

Henry Ford in 1919

In 1891, Ford became an engineer with the Edison Illuminating Company, rising to the position of Chief Engineer two years later. While at Edison, Ford began working in his spare time on designing and building gasoline engines and automobiles. Over the next few years, Ford built a number of successful prototypes, including a race car which he drove himself, setting several speed records. Ford also built a famous racing car, the "999," which legendary racer **Barney Oldfield** drove to victory in a race in 1902. His success enabled Ford to retire from the Edison Company and attract investors in his own company. In 1903, Henry Ford founded the **Ford Motor Company**. Detroit, Michigan would become the center of the automobile industry for decades.

At the turn of the century, only the extremely wealthy could afford an automobile. Ford wanted to manufacture cars so inexpensively that almost everyone could purchase one. In 1908, Ford manufactured his first **Model T Ford**, which sold for only $850, a price that almost everyone could afford. (Adjusted for inflation, that amounts to $23,847.58 in 2020 dollars.) However, unlike most businesses, Ford continued to *reduce* the price of his cars. By 1916, Ford had reduced the price of the Model T to $345! ($8,524.90 in

1916 Model T Ford

2020 dollars.) Unbelievably, he cut the price to $260 in 1925, the lowest in company history! Despite these price reductions, Ford paid his employees well and became one of the world's richest men - and arguably the greatest manufacturer in the history of the world.

Ford's critics often said that he overpaid his employees. In fact, he was paying more than double what his workers could earn in other places. Yet he insisted that his business model was a good one. Certainly no one could argue with the results.

One might think Ford had some great secret, but he did not. His company was simply very efficient. Ford mass produced cars on a moving assembly line. Each worker or group of workers assembled one part of the car which then moved down to the next station. Ford also kept prices down by making fairly basic cars; that is, they did not have a lot of "frills." For example, Ford only built Model T's in one color, black. He also kept prices down by making basically the same car year after year. In fact, Ford did not change the Model T in any significant way until 1928, when he replaced it with the **Model A**.

Of course, in any industry, once entrepreneurs see that money can be made, they follow the leader. In short order, other automobile companies began copying Ford's mass production model. Ford's paradigm appealed to customers seeking the most basic car. However, other companies sought a wider clientele. They built bigger, more expensive, more luxurious cars. By the end of the 1920s, the **General Motors Company** had surpassed Ford Motors as the largest manufacturer of automobiles.

In 1911, there were about 667,000 automobiles registered in the United States. By 1920, because of Ford and other car companies, Americans owned about eight and one half million automobiles. By the end of the decade, Americans owned more than twenty-three million cars and the automobile industry had become America's largest. General Motors started to introduce a new model every year. Owning a new car became a status symbol, not just a "means of transportation."

The Automobile Affects Other Industries

The effect that the automobile industry had on the nation simply cannot be overstated. In fact, one might argue that since 1900, no other industry has had as dramatic an effect on America. The wealth created by the automobile industry, and the tangential industries associated with it, created is incalculable. Cars require steel, glass, paint, and dozens of other products for construction. All these industries massively increased production to supply the auto industry. Cars ride on tires. A rubber industry sprang up virtually overnight from nothing. However, the automobile affected three industries more than others.

The first is the **petroleum** or **oil industry**. To a great extent the modern petroleum industry began in 1886 when Carl Benz began the first commercial production of motor vehicles with internal combustion engines which ran on gasoline. Before 1910, petroleum was still refined mostly for its kerosene. However, once Ford made the Model T, a gas-powered car available, the market changed. People wanted gasoline for their cars. In response, petroleum refineries began refining gasoline and the demand for gasoline soared incredibly. Gasoline consumption climbed from less than three billion gallons in 1919 to approximately fifteen billion gallons in 1929. Consumption has climbed ever since. Today, the government estimates that automobiles account for approximately 90% of the energy used for travel in the United States.

Oil exploration also increased dramatically. One of the largest oil strikes occurred on January 10, 1901 in Beaumont, Texas at the Spindletop oil field. Spindletop turned Texas into America's largest oil producer and helped the United States become the world's leading oil-producing nation.

The second business to see incredible growth from the expanding auto industry was **road construction**. Prior to 1920, America's roads were of poor quality and had been constructed to carry horses or wagons. However, horses and wagons travel rather slowly. Passengers in cars traveling at 50 miles an hour – the average speed a car traveled in 1920 – could not endure the bumps, ruts, and holes of 19th century roads. New and better roads had to be built and maintained. The United States is a massive country. Hundreds of thousands of roads had to be built. This meant that asphalt and concrete had to be manufactured, which created new jobs and new industries. New machines were created to facilitate building nice, *smooth* roads. Tens of thousands of jobs were created in these industries. The United States became the greatest road-building nation in the world as the number of miles of paved roads doubled during the 1920s!

Of course, decent roads meant more freedom to travel, and Americans did just that. The United States developed a booming **tourist industry**, the third great industry to benefit from the automobile. Prior to 1920, tourism depended almost entirely on the railroads. However, railroads, by their very nature, are limited. They go where the tracks go. Cars are nearly unlimited. Americans could get into their Fords or General Motors cars and go for a drive for business or for pleasure. As people drove, they passed gas stations and restaurants which had sprung up to serve travelers. They also passed something new called **motor hotels**, or **motels**, where people on long trips could spend the night.

The Automobile Changes Society

In addition to its effects on industry, the automobile also had profound effects on society and the way that people lived. Today, every day, nearly every American rides in a car. For young people, their sixteenth birthday looms large as that magic date when they become eligible for a driver's license. During the late 19th century, people had moved into the cities because that was where the jobs were. People *had to live in the cities* because it was virtually impossible to live in the country and travel to and from their city jobs every day. However, by 1920, a car made such travel possible.

In 1920, almost everyone could afford a car. A new Model T cost about $400 and a used Model T in good condition might cost around $50 (about $650 in 2020). Even teenagers could own cars. People no longer had to live in crowded city tenements; they could live outside the city in communities called **suburbs** and drive into work. These residential districts outside the city were far more rural. Homes tend to be on large lots with gardens, grass, and trees. Neighborhoods have tree-lined streets and parks and far less congestion than the cities. Living in the suburbs meant a better, often safer, lifestyle for many families as they moved away from some of the violence and corruption of the big city.

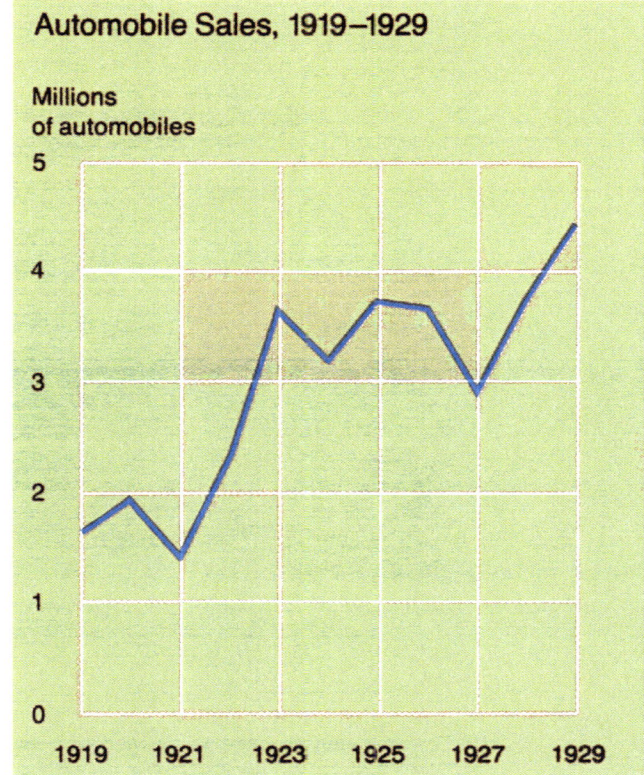

Car sales more than doubled during the 1920s.

However, the automobile also had some negative effects on society. In one sense, the freedom cars granted caused a bit of the break-up of the family. Before the car, families tended to live close to one another even after children married and had families of their own. Also, not being able to travel as quickly made it harder to spend great amounts of time away from home. Now, because cars were so inexpensive, teenagers could take their car and be with their friends. Many teenagers began spending more time with friends than with family. In some cases, these young people spent so little time at home that their house became little more than a hotel where they stopped in to sleep before heading out the next day.

As more cars appeared on the roads, traffic jams and congestion on the roads became more common. Driving to work from the suburbs took longer, causing parents to be away from their children more often. This also contributed somewhat to the breakup of the family. More cars on the roads for longer periods also added to air pollution.

The saddest consequences of the automobile on society were the inevitable deaths caused by car accidents. From 1901 to 1910, about 5,100 people died in automobile accidents. The following decade, that number jumped to over 71,000 people. In the 1920s, the number of deaths increased again – to 219,000. The number increased every single year. In 1930, car crashes accounted for more than half the accidental deaths in the United States. The number of auto deaths would continue to increase until the 1970s, when better safety features such as seat belts and air bags made driving safer.

Henry Ford and his Model T had changed the nation in a way that few, if any, men ever had. He had created new industries, helped expand existing ones, and made America a better place to live. America would go farther because of him.

Prohibition

Since the 1820s, advocates of temperance had been preaching about the evils of "demon rum," as well as all other types of intoxicating beverages. They declared that alcohol made men and women lose control of themselves and become a menace to themselves and to others. They demanded that the purchase, sale, and consumption of alcohol be prohibited. By 1913, nine states had a complete prohibition on alcohol, while another thirty-one states had some limited form of prohibition. As a result, some historians estimate that about fifty percent of the nation lived under prohibition.

In 1919, the states ratified the **Eighteenth Amendment**, which banned the manufacture, sale, or transportation of "intoxicating liquors." To enforce the Amendment, Congress passed the **Volstead Act**. However, neither the Eighteenth Amendment nor the Volstead Act *prohibited the consumption of alcohol*, only its sale, manufacture, and transportation. In fact, the Eighteenth Amendment failed even to define the words "intoxicating liquors."

Despite being politically divisive, the Eighteenth Amendment was ratified rather quickly. Barely a year elapsed between January 7, 1918, when Mississippi became the first to ratify, and February 25, 1919, when Pennsylvania became the forty-fifth. Californians dragged their heels a bit

New York City Deputy Police Commissioner John A. Leach (right) watches agents pour liquor into a sewer after a raid.

and did not ratify until three years later in March 1922. Only two states, Connecticut and Rhode Island failed to ratify.

Nationwide Prohibition did have some positive effects. First, the number of deaths associated with drunkenness declined. The number of people arrested for public drunkenness also declined. Some evidence exists to suggest that because alcohol was harder to obtain, fewer people drank, thus increasing various health benefits associated with the heart and liver. However, on the whole, most historians feel that the negatives far outweighed the positives.

For example, Prohibition caused a terrible crime wave, producing open lawlessness. Gangsters grew rich and powerful through **bootlegging**, the illegal making, selling, and transporting of alcohol. Gangsters opened nightclubs called "**speakeasies**," secret places where alcoholic drinks were illegally sold in teacups. The income was so plentiful that the nightclub owners hired top musical entertainers to perform every night. Crime grew almost uncontrollable as gangsters waged deadly wars against each other to gain territorial control in major cities to supply illegal liquor. They killed many innocent civilians in their turf wars.

In Chicago, for instance, two rival gangs fought for control of the city and its affluent suburbs. George "Bugs" Moran led one gang while "Scarface" Al Capone controlled the other. On February 14, 1929, Capone arranged to have Moran murdered at a building on Clark Street. A member of Moran's gang, who dressed and looked like Moran, was mistaken for his boss. Consequently, Capone's executioners acted before Moran arrived. Dressed as police officers, they gunned down seven men with machine guns and shotguns. The vicious attack became known as the **St. Valentine's Day Massacre**. Bugs Moran left Chicago soon after this. Al Capone was eventually sentenced to eleven years in prison for income tax evasion. Capone died in 1947.

The automobile greatly increased the gangsters' mobility. They could quickly move liquor from state to state. This made it difficult for the police in any single state to fight crime as they had done in the past. However, interstate crime brought the new **Federal Bureau of Investigation (FBI)** into the fight. In 1924, these federal police were organized under the outstanding leadership of twenty-nine-year-old

J. Edgar Hoover. Hoover told his FBI agents that letters "FBI" also stood for Fidelity, Bravery and Integrity. The FBI eventually arrested or killed everyone on the Who's Who list of Prohibition Era Outlaws.

Prohibition also created great disrespect for the law, especially for Congress. Large numbers of people thought the Volstead Act was ridiculous because it did not outlaw the *consumption* of alcohol. Thus, people started making liquor at home, so-called "bathtub gin." During Prohibition, the sale of grapes skyrocketed, not because people suddenly began to love grapes, but because they were making wine. Also, people visited speakeasies and bought liquor from bootleggers.

Prohibition remained in effect until 1933, when the **Twenty-first Amendment** was ratified. It repealed the Eighteenth Amendment. This is the only time an amendment has been repealed.

J. Edgar Hoover, the FBI's first director, a position he held for 37 years until his death in 1972.

The Threat of Communism

The Bolshevik victory in the Russian Revolution and Russia's subsequent adoption of communism rang warning bells for observant Americans in 1917. Those alarms reached higher pitches as communism spread its ever-reaching political tentacles into other post-war nations. In 1919, Communists controlled Berlin for several days and Hungary for several months. Thousands of pro-communist supporters in Western Europe, and even in the United States, hailed and celebrated these Communist successes in Central Europe.

Because they maintained secrecy, no one knows for sure how many communists were in the United States after World War I. By 1919, there were probably less than 100,000, but perhaps as many as 70,000. They soon acquired the nickname "**Reds**," after the Bolsheviks, who had been known as the Reds in Russia. Concerned Americans labeled supporters of communism as "anti-American," fearing that these people wanted to destroy the capitalist system and the American way of life through violent revolution or terrorist acts. They had seized power in Russia this way and would do so in other nations.

In 1919, as millions of workers were going on strike, the nation also suffered from a series of terrorist acts, some associated with communists. Because people felt that communists were behind the strikes and violence, a "red scare" swept the nation. The first victim of these violent acts was Seattle's mayor, **Ole Hanson**, who had asked for troops to end a strike by shipyard workers in February. Soon thereafter, someone sent Hanson a bomb in the mail. Fortunately, the bomb was discovered and disarmed before anyone was injured. Overall, thirty bombs were mailed to anti-communists, men who opposed organized labor, and people against unrestricted immigration. Then, on September 16, 1920, a bomb exploded on Wall Street, killing more than thirty people and injuring hundreds more. Because communists likely planted the bomb, U. S. Attorney General **A. Mitchell Palmer** proclaimed that "communists were preparing to rise up and destroy the government in one fell swoop."

Mitchell Palmer

Attorney General Palmer quickly backed up his strong words with decisive action. He mobilized law enforcement agencies that arrested over 6,000 suspected communists during the **Palmer Raids**. Nearly 600 were deported. In New York, five socialists who had been legally elected in 1920 were not allowed to take their seats in the legislature, in a clear violation of election laws, as well as the U. S. Constitution. A small number of Americans began to question such total disregard of the nation's legal process. For the most part, fear of the "red scare" overrode fair treatment. This lack of due process became even more clear in the case of Sacco and Vanzetti.

In 1921, a pair of known anarchists named **Nicola Sacco** and **Bartolomeo Vanzetti** were arrested. They were charged with murdering two uniformed guards while committing a payroll robbery near Boston. After a nationally publicized murder trial that was heavily reported on the radio and in the newspapers, the two men were found guilty and sentenced to death. After the trial, many legal authorities agreed that their trial had been unfair, since the prosecution lacked enough verifiable evidence to support a guilty verdict. Thousands of people held mass demonstrations to protest the guilty verdict and the death sentence. They believed that Sacco and Vanzetti had been condemned to death because they were well-known anarchists, not because they were murderers. Others believed they had been justly convicted and sentenced. They were executed in 1927.

Immigration Acts

Bowing to political pressure, in 1921, Congress passed **The Emergency Quota Act**. This act set forth two limitations on immigration into the United States. First, it capped the total number of immigrants allowed entrance annually and it capped the percentage of immigrants of a particular nationality that would be allowed to immigrate. Thus, for example, initially, no more than 350,000 immigrants would be allowed to enter each year. One reason the Act had been passed was to limit the number of immigrants from eastern and southern Europe, who tended to be less skilled, and considered less desirable as America entered an age where it needed more skilled workers. As a result, the quota for these immigrants was set rather low.

The debate over the Act raged for the next three years. Then, in 1924, Congress passed the **National Origins Act**. This Act further reduced immigration of "undesirable" unskilled laborers. No Asians would be permitted. However, no limit was placed on immigrants from Canada or Latin America. In 1927, the total number of immigrants allowed to enter the United States was reduced to 150,000.

Racial Tensions Flare in Post-War America

According to the Department of Defense, more than 380,000 African-Americans served in the Army during World War I. About 200,000 were sent to Europe where the vast majority served in support battalions building roads, bridges, and trenches in support of combat troops. However, a handful of African-Americans did see combat where they fought bravely and with distinction, earning several medals. After the war, they returned home, filled with pride in their accomplishments and hopeful that their lives might be better. Sadly, for many, that would not happen.

During the war, as many as five hundred thousand black workers, who lived in the South, moved north to work in the factories that were producing war materials. Many of these workers took jobs—now available—from the men who joined the army and went to fight in Europe. When the war ended, these soldiers returned home to discover that their jobs had been filled by black workers. At the same time, black soldiers returning from the war began demanding better treatment, better jobs, and better pay. Sadly, in this period of financial insecurity, racial tensions flared.

The summer of 1919 saw some of the worst race riots in American history. In more than two dozen cities ranging from New York to Arizona, hundreds of black and white Americans were injured and many were killed. One of the worst incidents occurred in Chicago, where the struggle for jobs between blacks and whites had caused feelings to become especially passionate. The spark that ignited the week-long

Chicago riots occurred on July 27, 1919, when an African-American teenager drowned in Lake Michigan. The young man had been swimming in the lake when he either drifted onto or intentionally swam onto an area of the beach that was "unofficially" reserved for whites. A group of white teenagers stoned him, causing him to drown. Despite eyewitness identifications, the police reprehensibly refused to arrest even a single member of the group who murdered him. This refusal, and the young man's death, caused a week of rioting between black and white Chicagoans. When the riots ended, 15 white and 23 black people had been killed, more than 500 people were injured, and over 1,000 African-American families had had their homes burned down.

"The Business of America is Business"

During the 1920s, the federal government largely created policies that encouraged business. Calvin Coolidge summed up his economic philosophy and the role of government when he said that "the business of America is business." This pro-business philosophy caused businesses to invest and grow. After companies switched back to pre-war production, they continued to prosper. During the 1920s, both old and new industries thrived.

For example, the electronics industry, in its infancy during the 1880s and 1890s, exploded during the 1920s. While the radio ranks as the probably the most beloved electronic device of the 1920s, it was only one of many devices that gained wider usage during this period. For example, between 1915 and 1930, the number of Americans who owned telephones doubled. Companies improved telephones and other equipment that increased the speed at which calls could be placed as well as reducing the price. As power companies ran electrical lines into more homes, the electric lighting and electrical appliance industries thrived. Labor-saving devices like electrical washing machines, vacuum cleaners, and refrigerators, made life better and reduced the drudgery of housework.

By 1925, about fifty percent of the population had access to electricity. However, more people in the cities had access than in rural areas. In 1936, Congress enacted the Rural Electrification Act which led to about 85% of American homes having electricity. Blessed with abundant, inexpensive electricity, the United States quickly became the world's leading consumer of electricity.

The 1920s also saw the growth of the "**chain store**," that is, stores that one company owns and that sell the same products. One of the most successful of the chain stores was **Woolworth's**, a "five and ten" store (also called "dime stores"), which meant all the products cost either five or ten cents. As America grew and became more urban and suburban, the chain store became a great convenience – a "one stop shop" for food and clothes. It is difficult to estimate the impact the *dime store model* had upon America, but people certainly appreciated the concept of discount shopping that Woolworth provided. By 1979, Woolworth's 100th anniversary in business, it had become the largest chain store in the world.

Despite the generally good economy, not all industries thrived during the 1920s and some suffered greatly. Those industries hardest hit included coal mining, textiles, and farming. As America began using more oil, electricity,

Woolworth store in Ann Arbor, MI. At its height, Woolworth had 5,000 stores in the U.S. and overseas.

and natural gas, the coal industry suffered massive declines. In the 1920s, owners shut down over 1,000 coal mines, which cost over 200,000 coal miners their jobs. The rise of new **synthetic textiles** (man-made fibers) such as rayon and nylon, which were made from chemicals, cost jobs in the natural textile industry. Also, as fashions changed and skirts became shorter, they used less material. The cotton and wool industries, which had been major industries in America since the late 18th century, began to decline. Sadly, these manufacturers also had to begin firing their employees.

Farmers suffered terribly in the 1920s. During the war, the government had asked farmers to produce crops not only for America but also war-torn Europe. After the war, European farmers began growing and selling crops again. Europeans no longer needed vast quantities of American food. The price of wheat and other farm products fell, which meant that farmers saw a decline in their income. However, many farmers had invested in new equipment, e.g. tractors and harvesters, and expanded their farms to meet the increased wartime demand. They now faced the prospect of paying off loans with less money than expected.

Meanwhile, events seemed to have conspired to hurt the farmers. Prohibition decreased the market for barley and hops (for beer), grapes (wine), and all manner of grains (alcoholic beverages) hurting farmers who grew those products. Cotton farmers lost business to short skirts and synthetics. All farmers lost market share to European and Canadian farmers. In response, Congress enacted a tariff to protect the farmers. However, other nations responded with tariffs of their own so little was actually accomplished.

The Election of 1928

From the end of the Great War to 1928, the United States arguably experienced the most prosperous decade in her entire history. Americans were earning more money and working less than they ever had. Technology had made their work and leisure time far better. The future seemed like it would be even better than the past. For most of this time, Republicans had been president and run the government. Most people credited the Republicans for America's success.

Herbert Hoover

Although extremely popular, and almost certain of victory, Calvin Coolidge chose not to run for re-election in 1928. He had already served for six years. Had he been re-elected, he would have been president for ten years. Coolidge would later write of the immense drain the Presidency placed on a man. He wrote that "it is hazardous to attempt what we feel is beyond our strength to accomplish." As a result, the Republicans had to find another candidate. They chose **Herbert Hoover**.

Herbert Hoover had been a successful businessman and mining engineer before entering politics. During the Great War he had served as head of the U. S. Food Administration, where he had launched the national ad campaign that encouraged farmers to increase production and civilians to reduce consumption. President Harding appointed Hoover Secretary of Commerce, and he remained in that position under President Coolidge.

The Democrats nominated Al Smith, making him the first Catholic nominated for president by a major party. However, Smith, or any Democrat, would have had little chance at victory. Most Americans believed that the Republicans were responsible for the nation's booming economy and general prosperity. They saw no reason to change leadership.

Herbert Hoover won in one of the most lopsided victories in American history, with 58% of the popular vote. Al Smith even lost his home state of New York. Hoover even managed to crack the "Solid South" by winning a number of Southern states. In the Electoral College, Hoover won 444 to 87. In 1928, most Americans believed that Herbert Hoover would oversee at least four more years of prosperity. They could not have been more wrong.

The Great Crash

Since the organization of the first corporations, Americans had invested their money in the stock market. During the 1920s, as the economy boomed, more and more Americans invested more and more money. They believed that times were good and that money invested would return dividends. By 1929, most companies were making money. They were paying their stockholders dividends. In fact, by 1929, the companies listed on the New York Stock Exchange were paying three times the dividends that they had in 1920!

However, all economists agree that business is cyclical. That is, it has ups and downs, or adjustments. Economic booms do not last forever. In August, the American economic boom reached its peak. In September, the economy began to shrink.

On October 24, 1929, people began selling their stocks rather than buying. Suddenly everyone wanted to sell and no one wanted to buy. Investors flooded their brokers' offices demanding that their shares be sold. Of course, when there are many sellers but few buyers, the price of the item, whatever it is, falls. In this case, the price of stocks began to fall – dramatically! In September 1929, General Electric, one of the strongest and best companies in America, traded at $396 per share. On October 24, shares of General Electric fell from $315 to $283. Still, the worst lay ahead.

On October 29, **Black Tuesday**, investors, fearing that they would lose all their money in the stock market, began to sell everything! Panic ensued. The Great Stock Market Crash of 1929 occurred as investors sold and sold and sold. Over the next two weeks the situation continued to decline. By the middle of November, General Electric shares were selling for $168. In September 1929, AT&T, another great company, traded at $304 per share. By November 1929, AT&T traded at $222 per share. Fortunes had been lost. Families had been bankrupted. The great economic boom of the 1920s had ended in a great crash. Yet worse times lay ahead. The Great Depression had begun.

One of the most famous headlines in American history. On the day after Black Tuesday, Variety, the newspaper of the entertainment industry published the headline: Wall St. Lays an Egg. To lay an egg is a colloquial expression meaning "to produce a flop." This "egg" would have enormous consequences.

Answer the following questions:

1. What was Wilson's Fourteen Points Plan? Why did he consider the League of Nations the most important point?

2. Who were the "Big Four?" How did their views affect the Versailles Treaty?

3. How did Wilson's policy of self-determination cause the map of Europe to be redrawn?

4. Explain the opposition to the Versailles Treaty in the United States? Who were the three groups who opposed it?

5. What might be the reason(s) that Wilson refused to compromise on the Versailles Treaty?

6. Why was Warren Harding's 1920 presidential campaign particularly effective? What was his campaign slogan?

7. What was American foreign policy during the 1920s?

8. What is meant by the Jazz Age? Who were some of the great Jazz musicians?

9. Why is the 1920's considered the "Golden Age of Sports?" Who were some of the great American sports men and women?

10. Why are the 1920s known as the "Roaring Twenties?"

11. How did the roles of women change during the 1920s?

12. How did the movies and radio become big businesses during the 1920s?

13. How did Henry Ford and the automobile change American society? What other industries did he directly affect? What negatives did the auto have on society?

14. How did Ford produce cars that everyone could afford?

15. What was Prohibition? How did it positively and negatively impact America?

16. What were the "Palmer Raids?" What caused them?

17. Who said "the business of America is business?"

18. Why did Calvin Coolidge choose not to run for re-election in 1928?

19. Who was the first Catholic nominated for president by a major political party?

20. Who won the presidential election of 1928? Why did he win?

Identify the following:

1. Henry Cabot Lodge
2. Tea Pot Dome Scandal
3. Knute Rockne
4. Charles Lindbergh
5. Charles Chaplin
6. Red Scare
7. Babe Ruth
8. W. C. Handy
9. Bobby Jones
10. J. Edgar Hoover

The Great Depression

1929-1939

American Gothic by Grant Wood (1930). One of the most famous paintings in all of American history, the painting depicts a farmer and his daughter standing in front of their farmhouse with their barn off to the right. Painted at the onset of the Great Depression, the two figures stoically face an uncertain future. Yet Wood explicitly intended the image to be a positive statement about the solid, traditional values represented by middle America. Although the future may be uncertain, their faith will see them through to the better times ahead. For Woods, these two are an image of reassurance. They will survive the Great Depression as will America.

The Crash of 1929 Heralds the "Great Depression"

The Crash of 1929 heralded what historians would call the "Great Depression" because this depression lasted longer and affected more people than any other depression in American history. Depressions had occurred in the United States as far back as the late 18th century. However, in every case, the depression or "panic" had been relatively short-lived, usually lasting only about three years. Thus, most Americans saw such economic downturns merely as part of the **normal business cycle**, which had both good and bad economic times.

In good economic times, businesses produced more goods and services and hired more employees. People purchased more and prices rose. When the economy experienced a downturn, businesses produced less as people had less to spend. Prices also decreased as businesses often had a surplus of goods. Needing to produce less, businesses had less need of workers, so they hired fewer workers and in very bad times had to let some of their current employees go. When that happened, the economy could be said to be in a **depression**.

However, throughout American history, these depressions tended to correct themselves without government intervention. When supplies ran low, businesses produced more. Companies hired more employees and expanded their production facilities. People once again had money and purchased more goods, which caused prices to rise. The economy recovered. For most of America's history, the economy was good and Americans were prosperous. For example, the 1920s were a time of incredible prosperity.

The Great Depression was Different

Prior to the Great Depression, a normal business cycle in America might include twenty years of prosperity and one or two years of depression. For example, in 1837, the United States had a major real estate panic which caused a large number of banks to fail. However, the panic lasted only about a year. The next panic occurred in 1857, affected mostly the North, and lasted about a year as well. In 1873, the economy again experienced a serious downturn. Over the next two years, thousands of businesses failed and unemployment rose to almost 15%. Twenty years later, in 1893, the United States experienced the worst depression in its history up to that time. The **Panic of 1893** *lasted for five years*, during which thousands of businesses and banks failed and unemployment reached 10%. Yet this disaster ended naturally as the others had. The Great Depression was different.

First, unlike the other depressions, *the Great Depression lasted almost 12 years!* From the Crash of 1929 until the winter of 1932-33, the economy experienced a steep and dramatic decline. Nothing seemed to be able to make the economy recover. Second, unlike in previous depressions, *the economy failed to recover on its own*. The Great Depression finally ended with the beginning of World War II, history's most devastating war. Had it not been for World War II, the Depression might have dragged on significantly longer.

Third, *the Great Depression was more severe than previous depressions*. During the Great Depression, 10% of the workforce was unemployed. However, at its peak in 1933, 25% of the workforce was unemployed! This meant that Americans were unable to buy food, clothes, and medicine. The suffering that most Americans experienced can be seen in the amount of food they consumed during the Depression. In 1929, at the start

of the Depression, the U.S. population was about 122 million, and Americans purchased about $11 billion of groceries. Although the population grew by more than eleven million, Americans did not purchase that amount of food again until 1941.

Unemployment spread throughout America like a virulent plague. Millions of desperate people were forced to withdraw their life savings just to buy food. However, the vast majority of banks did not have enough cash on hand to meet their depositors' demand. Banks normally invest their depositors' money in various safe money-making

The Employment Agency by Isaac Soyer (1937).

Soup kitchen in Chicago (1931). This soup kitchen was run by notorious gangster Al Capone.

ventures and keep only enough cash on hand to cover anticipated daily or weekly needs. As the depression engulfed more and more Americans, millions of borrowers who had been granted loans on the strength of their good credit history were now unable to make their repayments in a timely manner. This failure to repay caused thousands of banks to fail and eventually to close. It also meant that the banks could not repay their depositors, who lost all of their money.

Even those who still had jobs suffered greatly. In 1929, the average annual income for a working man or woman was about $700. That fell to $375 in 1933. The middle-class and wealthy suffered as well, but not as much. Doctors and lawyers saw their income reduced by 40%. Their wives often had to fire their household staffs, causing these women to become unemployed. More people began using public transportation as the cost to maintain an automobile became prohibitive.

Because of its severity and length, a depression of spirit and a soul-wrenching loss of hope accompanied the Great Depression in a way not seen in other depressions. Although churches, private charities, and state and local governments did what they could to help, the need proved too great. In almost every city and town, **soup kitchens** and long **bread lines**, where hungry people could get free food, told the same sad story of frustration, hunger, unemployment, and hopelessness. Various charities also set up **lodging houses,** where the unemployed and homeless might spend a night indoors. Sadly, despite these efforts, some people starved to death.

President Herbert Hoover

Herbert Hoover took the presidential oath on March 4, 1929, becoming America's thirty-first Chief Executive. In his Inaugural Address, President Hoover projected hope when he said, "*Ours is a land of rich resources and we are blessed with comfort and opportunity. In no nation are the fruits of accomplishment more secure. I have no fear for the future of the country.*" In many ways, Herbert Hoover was the ideal man to be president during the Great Depression. First, before entering politics, he had been a successful businessman and understood economics better than most politicians. Second, he had aided Belgium after the German invasion had devastated that nation. Then, after the U.S. had entered the war, Hoover had successfully run the American food program. After the war, he had served as Director of the American Relief Administration which provided food to the people of Europe. Warren Harding appointed him Secretary of Commerce, a position in which he performed very effectively from 1921 to 1928. Based on his record of accomplishments, there seemed few men or women in America more qualified to deal with a great depression than Herbert Hoover.

However, in other ways, Hoover's beliefs may have extended the Depression. For example, President Hoover believed the economy functioned best when government did not interfere. Hoover also believed in a small federal government and that the federal government should not extend its authority even in difficult times. He reasoned that once the federal government took power from state and local governments, it would never be returned. (A belief that the unfolding of history has affirmed.) Even when he saw that more and more cities could not care for the unemployed and homeless, because he believed in small government, Hoover opposed congressional programs to provide for relief to the homeless and unemployed. He believed such aid would destroy the freedom of individual Americans and turn their lives over to the control of the federal government.

Instead, Hoover believed that the President could improve the lives of Americans by encouraging **volunteerism**, that is, voluntary cooperation between the public and private sectors. As a result, once the Depression began, Hoover met with business leaders to encourage them not to fire employees or cut wages. He urged farmers, who had been devastated by the Depression, to form co-ops and raise smaller crops to cause prices to rise. To encourage the people, he gave speeches telling the public that prosperity was "just around the corner."

Volunteerism had worked during the war, when Hoover had called on the patriotic spirit of the nation to make sacrifices with his "Meatless Monday" campaigns. However, during the war, Americans clearly saw the enemy and understood how not eating meat would make a difference in the war's outcome. In 1930, Americans were depressed and afraid. They did not see prosperity waiting "just around the corner." They did not see it at all.

However, Hoover was not heartless. He favored government loans to banks and businesses. This money would be used to hire people and produce goods. He saw this as a good investment of the government's money. While Hoover would not have *given* a farmer money, he favored loaning the farmer money so that the farmer could invest in better equipment. Then the farmer could grow more crops which he could sell to pay back the loan. Hoover believed that the federal government should not be in the charity business. In 1930, charity was the job of the churches and private organizations as well as state and local government.

Hoover also favored lowering taxes and spending money on public works programs. These ideas would allow people to keep more of their own money and create jobs. The money could be spent on goods and services which would cause more people to return to work which would create more jobs and services. The business cycle would "reboot," and the depression would end. Unfortunately, while these policies work most of the time, the Great Depression was different.

In late 1931, the continually worsening crisis forced Hoover to intervene. He tried to restore people's confidence and trust in America's economic system by setting up the **Reconstruction Finance Corporation (RFC)** in January 1932. The RFC made loans to banks, insurance companies, railroads, and mortgage companies that were close to failing. Although the RFC saved many businesses, it did not significantly affect the Depression.

Until his very last hour in office, President Hoover believed that the Depression would be of short duration. He opposed large-scale federal relief, believing that it would further damage the economy. Many people wanted government work programs, but the Republicans viewed that as a socialistic solution that would not work.

The 1932 Election

As the Great Depression dragged on, with no end in sight, Herbert Hoover became more and more unpopular. Perhaps he could have done more to alleviate the sufferings of the people; however, this would have caused him to violate his beliefs in small government and the nature of charities. Hoover had not caused the Depression, but by 1932, almost everyone in America held him responsible for it. Homeless people lived in shanty towns they called "**Hoovervilles**."

Despite his wild unpopularity, the Republicans nominated Herbert Hoover for a second presidential term. A case can be made that the Republican Party, anticipating an overwhelming defeat because of the Depression, simply decided to sacrifice Hoover, rather than tarnishing

Franklin Delano Roosevelt -- one of the most charming and charismatic politicians in history

another Republican. In 1932, about 25% of the workforce was unemployed, somewhere between 13 and 16 million workers. Income had fallen by half from 1929 to 1932. Thousands of banks had failed. The American electorate would try anyone other than Herbert Hoover.

The Democrats nominated **Franklin Delano Roosevelt** of New York, who came from a privileged and wealthy family. Franklin Delano Roosevelt, often referred to as **FDR**, was home schooled by private tutors until he was fourteen. In 1904, he graduated from Harvard College and went on to receive his law degree from Columbia University. In 1905, he married his distant cousin, **Anna Eleanor Roosevelt**, with whom he had six children. He went on to practice law and became involved in New York state politics. In 1920, he ran as vice-president with James Cox, who lost to Warren G. Harding.

On August 9, 1921, while vacationing at his summer home in Campobello, New Brunswick, Canada, Roosevelt fell into the cold waters of the Bay of Fundy. The next day, he had a vigorous outing with his children, but that night he went to bed early, feeling very tired, and soon burned with fever. By the next day, his arms and legs were paralyzed. While he regained the use of his arms, his legs remained paralyzed for the rest of his life. At the time, his doctors diagnosed him with polio, which was an epidemic where he lived. Polio was mostly a childhood disease which few adults contracted, yet it was one of the few diseases known to cause paralysis. However, Roosevelt's symptoms are more typical of Guillain-Barre Syndrome, e.g. the progression of his paralysis, the numbness, and the way he recovered from the paralysis. Whether from polio or Guillain-Barre Syndrome, Roosevelt would walk the rest of his life with the aid of canes and metal braces. More often he rode in a wheelchair. Always concerned with his public image, for the remainder of his life, Roosevelt carefully avoided being photographed in a wheelchair.

After the attack, some of his friends and family suggested that he retire from politics. Roosevelt refused. In fact, in 1928, he ran for governor of New York when former governor Al Smith ran for president. Although Hoover defeated Smith in New York, Roosevelt won the governor's race. In 1930, Roosevelt was re-elected governor in a landslide. His popularity in New York made him the front-runner for the Democratic nomination for president in 1932.

When the Democrats met in Chicago in 1932, they nominated Franklin Roosevelt on the fourth ballot. In accepting the nomination for president, Roosevelt declared, "*I pledge you, I pledge myself to a new deal for the American people...*" When the Democrats met in Chicago in 1932, they nominated Franklin Roosevelt on the fourth ballot. In accepting the nomination for president, Roosevelt declared, "*I pledge you, I pledge myself to a new deal for the American people...*" Although Roosevelt did not explain what he meant by "a new deal," it sounded promising. Many Americans probably knew that Roosevelt, as governor of New York, had aided the unemployed in his state. Many Americans wanted a president who seemed at least to be doing *something*. In contrast to Hoover, who seemed to be a careful thinker, Roosevelt seemed more intent on just getting something done.

Moreover, whereas Hoover appeared reserved and aloof, Roosevelt possessed that compelling attractiveness known as *charisma*, and he used it in the campaign. Despite his physical limitations, Roosevelt possessed apparently unlimited energy. He was an excellent speaker and campaigner. Also, he had an infectious optimism at a time when the voters were desperate for optimism. Roosevelt won the 1932 presidential election in one of the greatest landslides in history, carrying 42 of 48 states. He received 57% of the popular vote and won 472 of 531 electoral votes.

Americans blamed not only Herbert Hoover personally, but the Republican Party in general for failing to alleviate the Great Depression. As a result, they lost their majority in Congress. Republicans lost one hundred and one seats in the House of Representatives and eleven seats in the Senate. The Democrats controlled the White House and both Houses of Congress.

The 1932 election would prove to be one of the most pivotal in American history. Prior to 1932, the Democrats rarely controlled Congress and had won only four of seventeen presidential elections. Over the next forty-seven years, the federal government would be in the hands of the Democratic Party, as they would often control Congress and the presidency.

Roosevelt's Inaugural Address

Franklin Roosevelt was scheduled to be inaugurated on March 4, 1933. However, on February 3, another bank panic hit, as people from all over the country began withdrawing what money they had from their banks. Even the most secure banks had to shut down in the face of this run on their cash reserves.

March 4, 1933, was a cold, dreary day in Washington D.C. In many ways, the weather reflected the mood of the nation. The people in the audience and those listening on the radio waited anxiously for President Roosevelt to assure them that the future would be better. He did just that. With his usual optimism he declared, "*This great Nation will endure as it has endured, will revive and will prosper. So, first of all, let me assert my firm belief that the only thing we have to fear is fear itself—nameless, unreasoning, unjustified terror which paralyzes needed efforts to convert retreat into advance. In every dark hour of our national life a leadership of frankness and vigor has met with that understanding and support of the people themselves which is essential to victory. I am convinced that you will again give that support to leadership in these critical days.*"

Roosevelt continued: "*This Nation asks for action, and action now. Our greatest primary task is to put people to work. This is no unsolvable problem if we face it wisely and courageously. It can be accomplished in part by direct recruiting by the Government itself...but at the same time, through this employment, accomplishing greatly needed projects to stimulate and reorganize the use of our natural resources.*"

Franklin Roosevelt's first inauguration

In these few sentences, Franklin Roosevelt set forth in the broadest strokes *part* of what would be his "New Deal." First, he would take immediate action in order to put people back to work. With unemployment at nearly 25%, this was a critical concern. Second, the federal government would begin hiring people. This would, of course, make the federal government far larger than it had ever been. Third, Roosevelt would begin massive building projects across the nation.

Roosevelt's speech, carried by radio into millions of homes, sparked hope in the hearts of many. His promises meant that the federal government would assume responsibility for every person's welfare on a scale never contemplated by any prior American president. In the first hundred days of his administration, Congress passed a series of laws that Roosevelt proposed which profoundly changed life in America.

Roosevelt's First Hundred Days

In his Inaugural Address, Roosevelt had addressed three pressing tasks he believed were necessary to alleviate the depression: putting people to work, helping farmers, and resolving the banking crisis. He dealt with the banking crisis first. Because drastic action was needed to repair the badly broken banking system, President Roosevelt immediately declared a "bank holiday." He ordered every bank in the country to be closed. The four-day bank holiday gave the federal government time to investigate the banks to ensure that depositors' money was safe. Roosevelt then gave a radio address promising the American people that their money was indeed safe. His actions stopped the runs on the banks by frightened depositors.

Roosevelt's Inaugural Address had also included a request that the new Congress meet in special session to begin working on the various tasks he had detailed. On March 9, Congress convened. Although no one had any specific plans, Congress stayed in session until June 16, exactly one hundred days. During those one hundred days, Congress passed an enormous amount of new legislation. (Because of this, future presidents would be gauged by what they accomplished in their first 100 days.) Roosevelt had spoken of a New Deal during his campaign, and it seemed that within his first 100 days, a new deal, if not a new era, had come to America.

Among the New Deal legislation, Congress passed several new banking laws to correct current banking problems and to forestall future problems. The most important of these acts was the **Banking Act of 1933**, which created the **Federal Deposit Insurance Corporation (FDIC)**. The FDIC provided insurance on deposits for member banks of the Federal Reserve System as well as state banks. This protected the money that people deposited in FDIC insured banks. This law stopped bank runs, because depositors knew that even if their bank failed, they would get their money from the government. The law establishing the FDIC was one of the most important ever passed in bolstering public confidence in the American banking system.

Bank run on the American Union Bank, New York City, April 26, 1932.

Another congressional act completely reorganized the **Federal Reserve System** and strengthened the control of its Board of Governors. The Board was given extensive authority to regulate banks. The Federal Reserve Board also was authorized to regulate the buying and selling of government bonds through the Federal Reserve Banks. This meant that the Board of the Federal Reserve System controlled the nation's money and the use of bank deposits. Congress passed two other Acts dealing with the stock market, which offered greater protection to stock market investors, by providing more effective federal supervision of the stock exchanges. These Federal Acts also required that all issues of stocks and bonds be filed with a government commission known as the **Securities and Exchange Commission**.

In June 1933, Congress passed a series of new laws aimed at job creation. The most far-reaching was the **National Industrial Recovery Act (NIRA)**. However, the NIRA was incredibly controversial. In the law itself, Congress said that the purpose of the NIRA was "to authorize the President to regulate industry for fair wages and prices that would stimulate economic recovery." However, other people felt that the law actually enabled the federal government to seize and control companies. The NIRA unquestionably increased the power of the federal government.

For example, the NIRA allowed businesses to establish codes of fair competition. These codes essentially abolished free enterprise and allowed businesses to create monopolies. Businesses could agree on the amount of goods produced in order to avoid surpluses which flooded the market and remained unsold. Businesses could also agree to set prices. The NIRA also encouraged union membership. It guaranteed collective bargaining, a minimum wage, and a maximum number of work hours. The key provision to the codes of fair conduct, however, was their approval by the federal government through the **National Recovery Administration (NRA)**, the government agency that had been created to administer the NIRA. While

President Franklin Roosevelt signs the Agricultural Adjustment Act into law.

the NRA certainly worked to stimulate job growth, people who favored small government could claim that the federal government had begun to take over business.

While the NIRA and its accompanying legislation dealt with industry, Congress hoped that the **Agricultural Adjustment Act (AAA)** would relieve the plight of millions of American farmers, who had seen farm prices fall even more than those of manufactured goods. The principal purpose of the Agricultural Adjustment Act was to raise the price of farm crops by reducing production. Under the AAA, the federal government rented land from farmers and paid them *not to plant certain crops* on the rented land. Farmers who reduced production of specified crops, such as cotton, corn, rice, and tobacco, earned "benefit payments." Most farmers eagerly agreed, because they received money directly from the government and because fewer farm products meant slowly increasing the crop prices.

In order to pay the farmers the rent money, the federal government charged a "processing tax" to the businesses that processed the farmers' produce for public consumption, in other words, the middle man. For example, the cotton planter sells his cotton to a factory that turns the cotton into cloth or shirts. The factory sells the shirts to a store that sells them to the public. The government began charging the factory a "processing tax."

The Farm Credit Act of 1933, passed on day 100, made it possible for many farmers to keep their farms by offering them short-term loans for agricultural production as well as extending them low interest rates if their farms were threatened with foreclosure. Twelve district banks, called **Banks for Cooperatives**, were established to enable small farmers to refinance their mortgages. Local **Production Credit Associations** made short-term "seasonal" loans to farmers, thus ensuring that farmers would not lose essential harvests.

Farmers were not the only group that needed help during the depression. Many homeowners did as well. Many faced the loss of their home because they could not pay their monthly home loan or mortgage. Consequently, Congress created the **Home Owners' Loan Corporation (HOLC)**. Through the HOLC, home owners could arrange longer-term mortgage loans to save their homes from foreclosure.

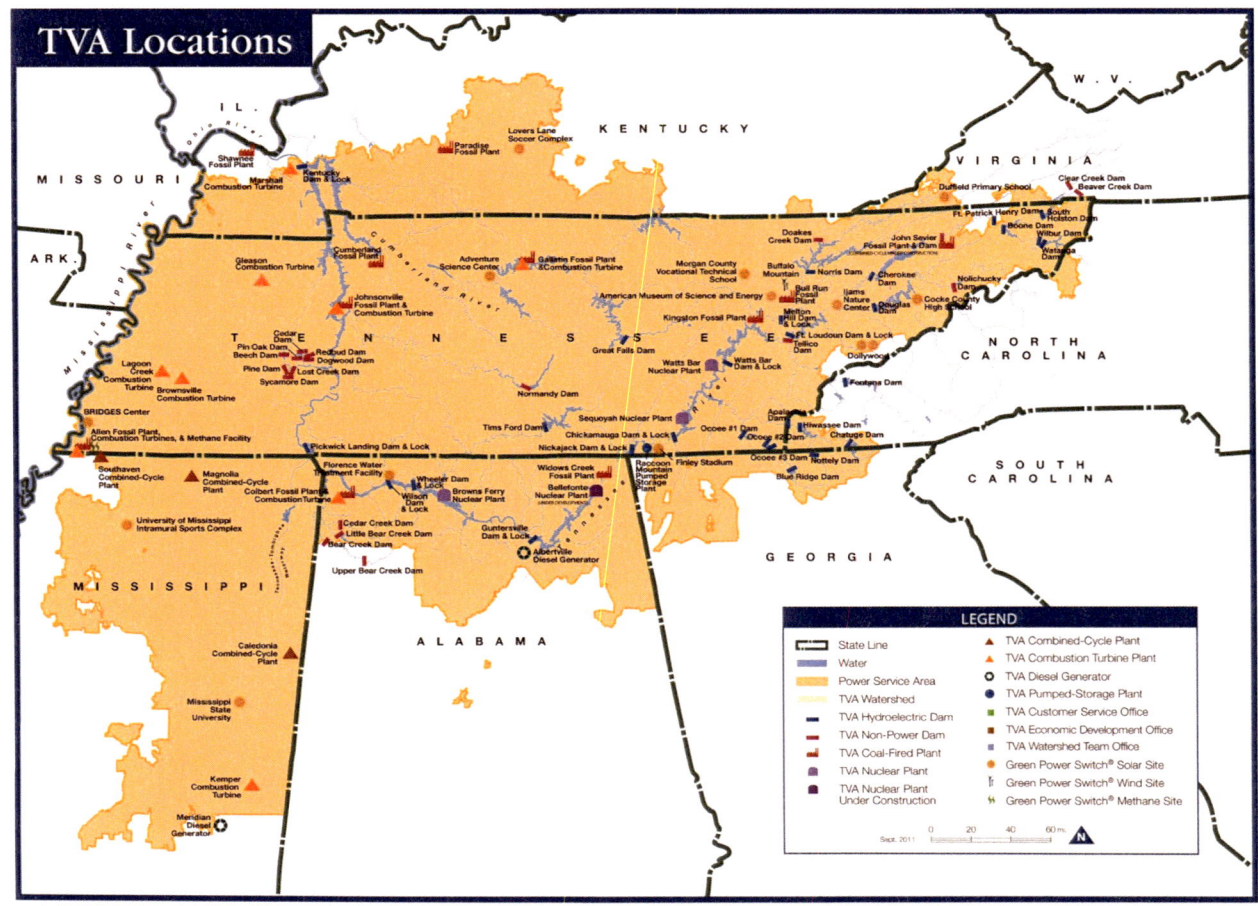

The **Tennessee Valley Authority** (TVA) was another agency Congress created during Roosevelt's first 100 days. By the beginning of the Roosevelt Administration, five giant utility companies controlled and provided about half of the electric power produced in America. High electric power rates limited people's use of electricity. Many poor families could not afford electricity. President Roosevelt decided that since the states could not regulate power production at a lower rate, the federal government would. The TVA is a vast government project designed to generate and sell electricity at a very low rate to private companies. It also sets the rates at which the private companies can resell electricity to consumers.

The Tennessee Valley Authority provided electricity for the entire Tennessee River region. This region includes parts of Tennessee, Kentucky, North Carolina, Virginia, Mississippi, Alabama, and Georgia. Since the TVA is a land developer, it also has the right to control flooding, improve river navigation, and irrigate land. The various TVA projects greatly improved the economy and social welfare of the people who resided in the Tennessee Valley. Its marvelous success caused the TVA to become a model for similar river projects around the world. The big power companies bitterly opposed the TVA project, which they saw as government interference in private enterprise. They challenged the TVA in court. The Supreme Court ultimately upheld the legality of the TVA.

In his Inaugural Address, Roosevelt had spoken of helping the poor and the unemployed. Unlike Herbert Hoover, Roosevelt believed that the federal government *should be involved* in charitable work. As governor of New York, Roosevelt had created a Temporary Emergency Relief Administration in October 1931 to aid the unemployed. Therefore, it came as no surprise when Congress quickly created the **Federal Emergency Relief Administration** (FERA), which was led by Harry Hopkins, who had spent his life as a social worker and was a close personal friend of both Franklin and Eleanor Roosevelt. During its

Members of the Civilian Conservation Corps in Connecticut

existence, FERA distributed hundreds of millions of dollars to state government organizations that aided the poor. Later, in order to help people get through the winter of 1933-34, FERA created the **Civil Works Administration** (CWA) which created short-term manual labor jobs. Under Harry Hopkins' leadership, the CWA created four million jobs for unemployed workers. The CWA ended on March 31, 1934.

Another agency of particular interest created during the 100 days is the **Civilian Conservation Corps (CCC)**, which Congress established to care for, employ, and train jobless youths. Under the sponsorship of the CCC, unemployed young men were employed, housed in camps, clothed, fed, and paid a salary of one dollar a day. These young men blazed forest trails, dug fire breaks, planted trees, controlled plant infestation, and built dams on public lands. Congress passed the law creating the Conservation Corps on March 31, 1933. By July, over 300,000 young men were working in 1,300 camps across the United States. The Corps gave thousands of young men a new outlook and a suddenly brighter future, and re-established their faith in America.

Not part of the 100 days, but related to the CCC, was the **National Youth Administration (NYA)**. By 1935, unemployment among young people between the ages of 16 and 25 had risen to 30%. Many of them could not afford to attend college. In June 1935, President Roosevelt created the NYA to help protect the futures of young Americans. The NYA paid poor students between the ages of 16 and 25 to work part time, while they continued their high school or college educations. For example, a college student's part-time job might be grading papers. The NYA operated from June 1935 to 1939 and, unlike the CCC, it included young women.

In his first hundred days, Franklin Roosevelt achieved much of what he promised. Millions of men and women had been put back to work. The banks had been made more secure. Millions of poor people had been given aid. People had hope.

The New Deal is Extremely Popular

Although somewhat controversial today, in 1933 the New Deal was extremely popular. In 1934 midterm elections, the Democrats increased their majority in Congress. When Roosevelt ran for re-election in 1936, he won by an even greater landslide than he had in 1932. He defeated **Alf Landon** of Kansas with almost 61% of the popular vote. Roosevelt won 46 states, losing only Maine and Vermont, and winning almost 99% of the electoral college vote.

Roosevelt won re-election despite failing to end the Depression and despite high unemployment. However, to many people it *seemed* that the New Deal had made conditions slightly better – and actually they were. For example, in 1933, unemployment stood at almost 25%; by 1936 it had declined to about 17%. Industrial production had also slightly increased. However, although unemployment had declined, federal spending had increased. In 1933, the federal government had spent about $5 billion. In 1936, that amount had ballooned to about $8.5 billion. So why had so many Americans voted to re-elect Franklin Roosevelt? Part of the answer is *charisma*.

Unlike Woodrow Wilson, who *believed* he could charm people into accepting his positions, Franklin Roosevelt *could* charm almost anyone into accepting his position. Roosevelt had a remarkable affinity for connecting with people, whether in person, in a crowd, or over the radio. One of his most successful means of communication was his "fireside chats," which he delivered via the radio. Between 1933 and 1944, Roosevelt delivered 30 of these evening addresses. Through radio, he came into the home of every American and appeared to speak directly to each of them. In his calm, optimistic tone, he explained the problems that faced the nation and what he intended to do to fix them. He also told his listeners what they could do to help. His fireside chats allowed Roosevelt to communicate directly to the public as television and social media do today. As a result, people loved him.

The New Deal was also popular because most Americans believed that the government was doing *something* to fix the problems that faced the nation. Most Americans realized that the Depression was a massive problem that would not be solved overnight but would take time. They felt that as long as Roosevelt made progress, they would continue to give him a chance. They also saw that people were going back to work. The Civilian Conservation Corps, the Civil Works Administration, and the National Youth Administration had created jobs for millions of unemployed men and women, even if they were mostly manual labor construction-type jobs. These jobs did improve America's infrastructure by building roads, subways, airports, and bridges.

Alf Landon

Roosevelt delivers a "fireside chat."

Critics of the New Deal

Despite Roosevelt's widespread popularity, both he and the New Deal had several critics. Among these critics were small-government conservatives who feared that the New Deal had granted vast new powers to the federal government in general and the president in particular. They pointed to all the New Deal legislation which contained language like "the President is authorized to..." and "the Secretary of the Interior shall have the power to..." Herbert Hoover strongly criticized the New Deal and President Roosevelt, calling much of the New Deal "socialism." During the campaign of 1936, Hoover gave several speeches supporting Alf Landon and attacking the New Deal.

Small government conservatives pointed out that the Constitution gives the federal government limited powers, which means that the Federal government has only the powers that are expressly given to it, or are implied as being necessary to carry out those express powers. They became alarmed during the Great Depression and the New Deal Era as they saw many of their fellow Americans reject the explicit dictates of the Constitution. These Americans wanted the government to take more responsibility, especially for the many improvements they said were needed in society. These people were not concerned whether the Constitution granted the federal government the power to make these "improvements." Often in a difficult situation, the government assumes power to deal with a crisis, but later, when people realize that the government has taken too much power, it is doubly difficult to return to basic democratic principles. Many of these Constitutional opponents to the New Deal recalled the words of Ben Franklin who said, "Those who would give up essential liberty, to purchase a little temporary safety, deserve neither liberty nor safety."

In addition to those opposing the New Deal on Constitutional grounds, businessmen also came to oppose the New Deal. They objected to government interference in their affairs and the regulation of free enterprise. They believed that vast government control over so much of society effectively limited the opportunities for private initiatives and development. Other business leaders believed that much New Deal legislation exceeded the federal government's authority and was unconstitutional. As a result, they filed several lawsuits seeking to have such legislation declared unconstitutional.

In May 1935, with only one month remaining for the NIRA, the Supreme Court declared it to be unconstitutional. The Court said the NIRA, which attempted to regulate wages and hours within the individual states, exceeded the powers of Congress. Congress responded by enacting the **National Labor Relations Act**, which actually was more favorable to labor and withstood constitutional challenge.

In January 1936, the U. S. Supreme Court declared the Agricultural Adjustment Act unconstitutional. In response, Congress passed the **Soil Conservation Act**. Under this act, the government paid farmers for planting crops that conserved natural sources, rather than paying them not to plant at all.

In addition to constitutional conservatives and businessmen, Roosevelt and the New Deal also found critics in those who believed that his policies were *too conservative*. One such critic was flamboyant Louisiana Senator **Huey Long**, who had given himself the nickname "the Kingfish." Though Long originally supported Roosevelt, by the mid-1930s he felt that Roosevelt no longer had the best interests of the poor at heart, but was instead working for the enrichment of the wealthy and powerful businessmen. Long, claiming to represent every poor person in the country, proposed that the federal government establish a "Share Our Wealth" program that would annually pay $2,500 to each family. In order to finance his giveaway program, Long proposed that every American who earned over $1 million be heavily taxed. Then he could give every family the money they needed to live decent lives with a home and car. Long's **socialist** message resonated with many. By 1935, over 3.6 million people had joined his "Share Our Wealth" movement.

Another former Roosevelt supporter was popular, but controversial, radio personality and Catholic priest **Charles E. Coughlin**. One of the first clerics to employ the radio as an evangelization tool, Coughlin's broadcasting career lasted from 1926 to 1940. At his peak, 30 million people listened to his weekly broadcast and he received thousands of letters every day. His popularity came from his message, which was Catholic, anti-Communist, reassuring, and hopeful. In some ways, Fr. Coughlin provided an optimistic faith-based message similar to Franklin Roosevelt's secular message. However, over time, Coughlin's calls for social justice became overtly anti-Semitic.

Coughlin began his broadcasting career in October 1926, broadcasting from a station in Detroit, Michigan, with the approval of the Detroit bishop, Michael Gallagher. Coughlin, with his Irish lilt, had a voice perfectly suited for radio and quickly became successful. By the early 1930s, Fr. Coughlin may have been the most well-known American Catholic. In 1932, he supported Roosevelt for president and threw his weight strongly behind the New Deal. However, by 1934, he began to speak out against the New Deal. Fr. Coughlin began speaking about monetary policy, wealth redistribution through taxation, and government ownership of banks, natural resources, and public utilities. As the Depression worsened, his Catholic radio sermons became more political and occasionally devolved into personal attacks on Roosevelt and other business leaders. These attacks upset the Church hierarchy both in the United States and in Rome. Church leaders pressured Coughlin to moderate his attacks and focus on his message of social justice as found in *Rerum Novarum* and *Quadragesimo Anno*, which Pius XI had just promulgated in 1931. He refused and, with the support of Bishop Gallagher, continued his broadcasts. However, over the next years, both the Roosevelt administration and the Catholic hierarchy continued to push for his silence.

In January 1937, Coughlin's protector, Bishop Gallagher, died and was replaced by Bishop Edward Mooney, who began asserting more control over Fr. Coughlin. By 1940, with World War II raging in Europe, the National Association of Broadcasters *self-imposed* a ban on controversial speech. Fr. Coughlin was taken off the air. He returned to his job as a parish priest in Royal Oak, Michigan, where he served until his retirement in 1966, living in almost total obscurity. He died in 1979 at the age of 88.

The "Dust Bowl"

No one was hurt by the Depression more than farmers, especially those on the Great Plains. The Great Plains does not normally receive much rainfall. However, in the early 1930s, it received far less than normal. In his book *The Grapes of Wrath*, author John Steinbeck described the terrible suffering of the western

Fr. Charles E. Coughlin

John Steinbeck

Farmer and sons walking through a dust storm in Oklahoma in 1936

farmers and their families when he wrote, "*Our people are good people; our people are kind people. Pray God some day kind people won't all be poor. Pray God some day a kid can eat.*"

During the Depression, prices for agricultural products tumbled sharply. Most farmers could not pay their taxes, mortgages, or the interest on loans. A majority of farmers had invested heavily in expensive machinery for the production of the additional crops needed to meet the war effort. Many farmers had enlarged their farm's cultivated areas and invested in larger herds of livestock. Overproduction and surplus crops virtually paralyzed the marketplace. Between 1929 and 1933, thousands of farmers lost land that several generations of family members had owned and farmed because they were unable to make their mortgage payments. Farms were auctioned off to satisfy taxes and debts, usually at a fraction of their true value.

To add to the nation's suffering, a severe drought in 1930 devastated the farmland and dehydrated many regions of the nation. So many dust storms blew over the land between Texas and the Dakotas that the area was named the "Dust Bowl." Anxious to utilize every square foot of their farms for planting crops, farmers had unwisely neglected to create essential windbreaks between their plowed fields. Without these wind breaks, roaring winds blew across hundreds of miles of plowed ground, picking up the topsoil and carrying it away. As one farmer described it, "I used to have a farm in Colorado, but it's in Nebraska now."

Reciprocal Trade Agreements

In 1934, Congress passed a **Reciprocal Tariff Act**. This act empowered President Roosevelt to execute special trade arrangements with other countries without the consent of the Senate. The Reciprocal Trade Agreement also permitted the president to lower tariff rates between the United States and any nation that lowered their tariffs on American products. These reciprocal trade agreements vastly increased American exports and greatly improved friendly relations with other nations. Of course, no one could foresee how this would affect future presidents' power regarding upcoming trade agreements.

The Federal Housing Administration

In June 1934, Congress passed the **National Housing Act** in an attempt to make home mortgages more affordable. The Act created the **Federal Housing Administration (FHA)**, which helped make it possible for a greater number of people to own their own homes. The FHA insures part of the loss that banks and loan associations *might incur* if clients, new homeowners, to whom they have loaned money, cannot repay their loans. FHA insurance made it possible for many people to buy homes who otherwise would have been unable to do so. The Act successfully stopped the flood of bank foreclosures on family homes during the Depression and improved the standard of living for many Americans.

The Federal Communications Commission

On June 19, 1934, President Roosevelt signed into law one of the most important and far-reaching pieces of federal legislation in American history. This was the **Communications Act of 1934**, which created the **Federal Communications Commission (FCC), one of the most powerful federal government agencies.** The Act was created "*for the purpose of regulating interstate and foreign commerce in communication by wire and radio so as to make available, so far as possible, to all the people of the United States a rapid, efficient, nationwide, and worldwide wire and radio communication service with adequate facilities at reasonable charges, for the purpose of the national defense...*" To affect these goals, the act created a central authority known as the "Federal Communications Commission," which had the power to enforce the provisions of the Act.

Under this act, the FCC has the power to regulate foreign and domestic communications by telephone, telegraph, cable, radio, television, and internet. In other words, if something can be used to communicate, the FCC claims the right to regulate it. Since its creation, the FCC has licensed radio and television and recently attempted to license the Internet. Many Americans fear that the FCC can become the federal government's instrument of **censorship**, by choosing *not to license* radio and television stations that disagree with the federal government. Even the Internet, which, despite many evils, provides an opportunity for open political discourse, can be regulated or even blocked by the FCC.

Sign outside the FCC building in Washington DC protesting government over-regulation of the Internet

Even the strongest businesses cannot stand before the might of the FCC. For example, decisions of the FCC eventually led to the creation of the **American Broadcasting Company (ABC)**. The FCC issued rulings which sought to regulate the national radio networks. In 1943, NBC appealed these rulings to the U. S. Supreme Court. The Court upheld the FCC's ruling. This forced NBC to sell its "Blue Network," one of its two national networks. The new ABC network launched on October 12, 1943 as the successor to the Blue Network.

The Second New Deal

President Roosevelt delivered his annual State of the Union Address to Congress on January 4, 1935. This speech signaled the beginning of what is commonly known as the "Second New Deal." The president clearly stated that the federal government had to assume greater responsibility for the economic welfare of the American people. Part of that responsibility, he declared, included better housing and significant financial aid for the sick, the elderly, and the unemployed, all of whom had little or no income. Roosevelt declared that the government must help these victims of the Depression by giving them a way to purchase goods and services and elevate their standard of living. This would stimulate the production of goods and stimulate the economy. The Second New Deal would create two pieces of incredibly powerful and life-altering legislation.

The National Labor Relations Act of 1935

The first of Roosevelt's new laws was the **National Labor Relations Act of 1935 (NLRA,** also known as the **Wagner Act** after its chief sponsor), which Congress passed after the Supreme Court declared the National Industrial Recovery Act to be unconstitutional. The National Labor Relations Act provided incredible power to the nation's labor unions. It guaranteed them the right to organize and engage in collective bargaining. Moreover, when a majority of the workers in a business voted to join a union in a NLRA election, that **union would represent all the workers in that business, even those who had not voted to join the union!** Additionally, these objectors would also have to pay union dues to be members of an organization to which they chose not to belong. Also, the Labor Relations Act created a National Labor Relations Board which oversaw and ran these union elections and assisted in settling disputes.

The National Labor Relations Act ushered in an era of ever stronger unions. Over the next forty-five years, unions grew in strength, becoming not only labor organizations, but also political organizations, almost always working on behalf of and supporting Democratic candidates. As repayment for the NLRA, unions overwhelmingly supported Roosevelt for his re-election in 1936.

In response to what many saw as the unfairness of the NLRA, in future years, several states passed "**right-to-work laws.**" Right-to-work means that employees are legally allowed to work in unionized workplaces without being compelled to join the union or pay union dues. Although pro-union advocates claim that right-to-work laws are "anti-union," defenders of right-to-work laws stress that the point of the laws is individual freedom. Workers in right-to-work states have the right to join or not join a union as they choose.

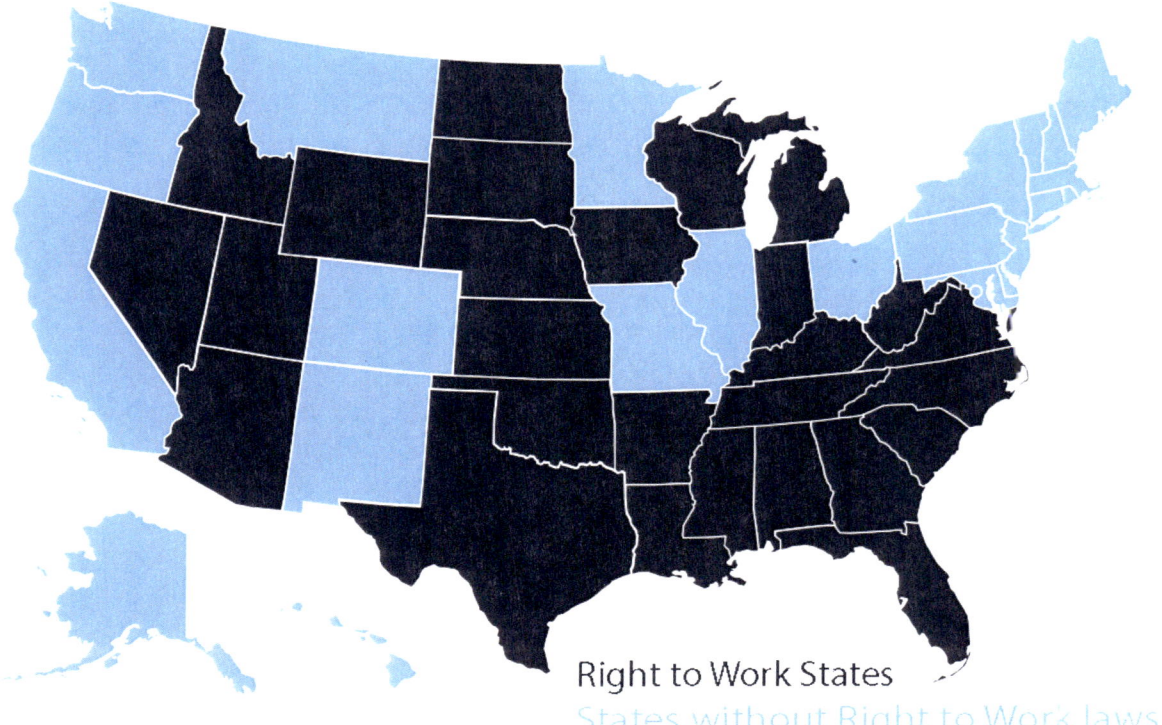

Right to Work States

States without Right to Work laws

The twenty-eight Right to Work states as of January 2022

Social Security

The most far-reaching and beneficial legislation of President Roosevelt's second new deal was the **Social Security Act**, which he signed into law on August 14, 1935. The Act created the **Social Security Administration**. President Roosevelt and his advisers agreed that raising America from the shambles of the Great Depression would be a very long, difficult task. However, recovery was only one part of their overall vision. They also sought to create protective legislation designed to guard against future depressions and to *eliminate the possibility of any future wholesale poverty*. They wanted America to become a depression-proof nation with a permanent social program that would be a source of assistance and security for needy, handicapped, unemployed, and elderly citizens.

Financing for this massive "government aid" agency comes from payroll taxes paid by all employees and employers in the United States. The Act has been extended since its original enactment. In 1935, twenty-one workers paid taxes to sustain one Social Security recipient, who tended to receive benefits for only a few years. However, because people live longer in the 21st century, less than two workers' taxes support each Social Security recipient because recipients receive benefits for decades.

Although at the time, the Social Security Act met with objection from many Republican lawmakers, it is now considered a vital part of American society, and – at least in principle – one of the most successful pieces of legislation in American history. America's elderly have little fear of dying of starvation. Today, both Democrats and Republicans agree that Social Security reformation is both urgent and necessary; however, the parties cannot agree on the solution.

President Roosevelt's "Court-Packing Plan"

As the United States Supreme Court declared New Deal laws to be unconstitutional, e.g. the National Industrial Recovery Act, their rulings spawned a bitterly contested struggle for power within the federal government. Many of the conservative Justices felt that much of the New Deal legislation exceeded the powers of the federal government. Even when legislation was upheld, the victory tended to be a narrow 5-4 decision, e.g. *National Labor Relations Board v. Jones & Laughlin Steel Corporation*, which held the National Labor Relations Act constitutional. Because Supreme Court justices are appointed for life, President Roosevelt, despite his popularity with the American people and indisputable dominance over Congress, could not control the nine Supreme Court Justices, nor could he appoint a new Justice until a current one retired or died.

By 1937, the Supreme Court had rejected many of Roosevelt's programs as unconstitutional. However, in November 1936, Roosevelt had won one of the most lopsided elections in history. He felt that the people had elected him to implement the New Deal and that a handful of conservative Justices were standing in the way. Over the next two months, President Roosevelt formally proposed to Congress that they enlarge the Supreme Court to fifteen members by adding a new Justice each time a Justice reached age seventy and failed to retire. Officially known as the **Judicial Procedures Reform Bill of 1937**, it is better known as Roosevelt's **"court-packing plan."** Under the new law, President Roosevelt could appoint six new Supreme Court Justices. Clearly, he would appoint Justices he knew would support his New Deal plans and give him control of the Supreme Court.

For once, Roosevelt had overplayed his hand and misjudged his audience. Even his remarkable charisma failed him in this instance. Many members of Congress realized that his plan would seriously jeopardize the checks and balances among the three branches of government that the Constitution created by threatening the independence of the Supreme Court. Although Roosevelt pushed hard for its passage on various fronts, including a March 1937 Fireside Chat, Congress did not go along with his plan.

However, in the months that followed, the Supreme Court became friendlier to New Deal legislation. They found the National Labor Relations Act and the Social Security Act, among others, to be constitutional.

Shortly thereafter, Roosevelt was able to make his first appointment to the Court when a conservative Justice retired.

Roosevelt's Supreme Court Picks

During his twelve years in office, Franklin Roosevelt appointed *eight* new members to the United States Supreme Court. The only president to exceed that number was George Washington, who appointed ten. On August 12, 1937, Roosevelt nominated **Hugo Black**, a senator from Alabama who had supported all of the New Deal Legislation, to fill the vacancy created when conservative Justice Willis Van Devanter retired. Black would serve on the Court for 34 years before retiring on September 17, 1971. He died eight days later. Although generally very liberal, Hugo Black rendered some conservative decisions. For example, Black did not believe that the Constitution contained a "right of privacy."

Hugo Black

Roosevelt next nominated **Stanley Reed**, the former Solicitor General of the United States. Reed served for nineteen years on the Court and tended to be the "swing" vote on many 5-4 decisions. For example, in the case *McCollum v. Board of Education* (1948), which declared that the state of Illinois had violated the Establishment Clause, Reed supported the Christian group. Reed always disliked Thomas Jefferson's phrase "wall of separation between church and state." His dissent in *McCollum* contains his famous comment that, "A rule of law should not be drawn from a figure of speech."

Roosevelt next appointed **Felix Frankfurter**, a well-known and highly respected Harvard law school professor, who served on the Court from January 20, 1939 until August 28, 1962. Frankfurter is generally considered one of the finest Justices ever to serve on the Court. Although a liberal at Harvard, Frankfurter tended to render conservative Supreme Court opinions.

Stanley Reed

In early 1939, Justice Louis Brandeis retired from the Supreme Court and President Roosevelt nominated **William Orville Douglas** to replace him. Only forty years of age at the time of his confirmation, Douglas was one of the youngest Justices ever appointed. He would serve the longest term in Court history, almost 37 years. He was, arguably, the most liberal Justice ever to sit on the Court. For example, in a 1972 case, *Sierra Club v. Morton*, Douglas argued that "inanimate objects" should be allowed to file lawsuits. In 1973, Douglas voted to create the "right" to an abortion in *Roe v. Wade*. Douglas retired in November 1975 after suffering a stroke.

Felix Frankfurter

Roosevelt next appointed **William Francis (Frank) Murphy**. Generally considered a liberal, Murphy served on the Court for just over nine years before dying suddenly of a heart attack. In July 1941, Roosevelt appointed **James F. Byrnes** to the Court as a political favor. Byrnes served only fifteen months before resigning to serve as head of the Office of Economic Stabilization.

Robert Jackson

In 1941, President Roosevelt appointed another remarkable jurist to the Supreme Court, **Robert Houghwout Jackson.** Jackson served from 1941 until 1954, during which time he established himself as both a brilliant Justice and one of the Court's more conservative members. Following the end of World War II in 1945, Jackson took a leave of absence from the Court and served as the Chief United States Prosecutor at the Nuremberg Trials in Germany. Jackson returned to the Court for the term that began in October 1946 and served until his death in October 1954. In one of his most famous cases, *West Virginia State Board of Education v. Barnette* (1943), Jackson declared that the state of West Virginia did not have the power to force children to salute the American flag if that violated their religious beliefs.

When Justice James Byrnes resigned in the fall of 1942, Roosevelt nominated **Wiley Blount Rutledge** to replace him. Generally considered very liberal in his decisions, Rutledge served only six years before dying suddenly of a stroke in 1949. However, he loyally supported Roosevelt's New Deal legislation during his tenure on the Court.

In choosing his Supreme Court nominees, President Roosevelt sought to appoint Justices who would support his New Deal legislation, which had greatly enhanced the power of the government. With this as the measure, history must grant that he generally succeeded. Four of Roosevelt's eight picks, Hugo Black, William O. Douglas, Frank Murphy, and Wiley Rutledge, were very liberal Justices. Two Justices were conservative or somewhat conservative: Frankfurter and Jackson. Reed was a swing vote and Byrnes did not serve long enough to establish himself in either camp. Thus, Roosevelt succeeded.

The New Deal's Effect on Minorities

In 1936, the African American population was more or less evenly split between the two major political parties, with about 40% belonging to each. However, in the election that year, about 70% of blacks voted for Roosevelt. This swing in black voting had as much to do with Republican apathy as Democratic appeal. Republicans in the South had done very little to keep the goodwill of African Americans after the Civil War, and Southern Democrats, many of whom had supported slavery and opposed Reconstruction, had done nothing at all. As a result, many blacks left the South for better opportunities in the North.

The Great War caused a virtual cessation of European immigration, but northern factories still needed unskilled labor. Therefore blacks, looking for jobs, moved in droves, like the European immigrants before them, into the overcrowded slums of Detroit, Philadelphia, Chicago, and New York. In New York City, the neighborhood known as **Harlem** became a well-known black community. In Harlem, for example, between 1910 and 1930, the African-American population quadrupled from around 50,000 to more than 200,000. Also, like the immigrants, African Americans struggled to find good jobs. Most labor unions, seeking to protect their own members, refused to allow blacks to join.

Yet like European immigrants, African Americans eventually prospered in their communities. They elected local black officials. This allowed them a larger voice in city and state politics. They became more politically powerful.

In the 1920s, the blacks in New York City experienced the **Harlem Renaissance**, a period of intellectual, social, and artistic progress within the black community. Led by poet **Langston Hughes**, artist **Aaron Douglas**, and numerous jazz musicians like Duke Ellington, Harlem became the cultural and intellectual center for Black Americans. Believing that Harlem would give them a chance to improve their lives, ambitious young African Americans from around the nation moved to Harlem. Unfortunately, the Great Depression brought an abrupt end to the Harlem Renaissance.

The Great Depression hurt blacks more than whites. Minorities had always struggled to find employment, usually being the last hired and first fired. For example, in 1932, the African-American unemployment rate climbed to about fifty percent which was almost double the national average.

Thus, in a sense, the New Deal programs benefited blacks more than whites because more blacks were poor and unemployed. However, for most African Americans, simply being treated fairly by the Roosevelt administration earned their loyalty. Roosevelt had ordered state officials not to discriminate on the basis of race when distributing aid. Although this order was not always followed, African Americans appreciated that Roosevelt made the effort.

President Roosevelt also sought to employ competent African Americans in his administration. One of the leading examples of this policy was the appointment of **Mary McLeod Bethune**, a child of former slaves. In 1936, Roosevelt appointed her to head the Office of Minority Affairs, a section of the National Youth Administration. During her lifetime, she worked diligently for the rights of minorities.

Langston Hughes

Mary McLeod Bethune

The Final Years of the New Deal

After Roosevelt's reelection in November 1936, the economy seemed to pick up for the next few months. However, one could argue that the economy had never been strong, only that the federal government had spent so much money that it had artificially stimulated it. In June, with unemployment falling, Roosevelt stopped pumping federal money into the economy. This resulted in the Recession of 1937-1938. Business activity slowed down and unemployment increased to 19%. As a result, Roosevelt again began pushing money into the economy. In addition to new spending on federal works programs, Congress also enacted one last piece of incredibly powerful and far-reaching legislation, the Fair Labor Standards Act (FLSA).

The Fair Labor Standards Act

Passed in 1938, in order to create jobs, the Fair Labor Standards Act (FLSA) affected how employers who were engaged in interstate commerce paid their employees. First, the FLSA created a forty-hour workweek. If an employee worked more than forty hours, the FLSA *mandated* that they be paid "time and one-half" for all work over forty hours. In other words, the employee would be paid 50% more than his or her usual wage for this extra time. Congress believed that employers would rather pay two employees the standard wage, rather than paying one person time and a half. Thus, employers would hire two people rather than one, thus creating two jobs rather than one. The FLSA also prohibited child labor in interstate industries and created a national minimum wage. Since its passage, the Fair Labor Standards Act has deeply impacted American business and people's lives.

Analysis of the New Deal

Economists today disagree about the effects of Roosevelt's policies. Some believe that though these policies were intended to stimulate the economy, they actually deepened and prolonged the Depression. They point out that government cannot create wealth; it merely collects, redistributes, and consumes wealth. In any recession or depression, taxes and tax increases pay for government programs and siphon vital resources away from the private sector, which delays the private sector's recovery.

Economists also note that when there is widespread unemployment, such as in a Depression, labor is inexpensive because workers are paid less. Businesses and industries take advantage of this cheap labor and expand their business. However, government programs during the Great Depression kept wages artificially high. That prevented the private sector from growing as rapidly as it otherwise might have if it could hire more workers. Higher wages means fewer new workers, and consequently, fewer workers who can pay taxes or support their families.

Of course, other economists point to the fact that tens of millions of Americans were out of work. Unemployment was around 20%, which meant that one in five workers was without a job. They note that Hoover's policies clearly had not had an effect. Roosevelt may have gone too far, but something had to be done. Only the federal government had the resources to act to put millions of Americans back to work.

Supporters of the New Deal contend that many of Roosevelt's actions had real positive results. They note that his charitable programs prevented even greater suffering that would have resulted had such drastic measures not been undertaken. However, even supporters agree that these programs resulted in what today is called "**the welfare state**." That is, the government now cares for its citizens in a manner that it never did prior to the New Deal. The New Deal created so many welfare programs, like Social Security, that both Republicans and Democrats eventually realized that it was too late to change these policies without doing irreparable damage to the nation and its citizens.

Many Americans believe this new welfare state came at a high price. The huge New Deal programs massively increased the size of the federal government. According to the Brookings Institute, a Washington "think tank," as of 2020, the federal government employed 2.7 million people, including one half million postal workers, the largest segment. There are an additional 1.4 million active duty military personnel. This huge government increase came at the expense of state and local governments, which lost power, as well as individuals, who also lost some of their rights.

Prior to the Depression, the government and individuals had tried to economize during hard times. America's leaders and her people believed that the nation and its citizens should live within their means. However, Franklin Roosevelt changed that perception. In order to stimulate the economy, he spent more money than was raised by taxes. He spent money that the government did not have. Roosevelt **unbalanced the budget**. Over the next decades, this "deficit spending" would result in higher and higher budget deficits and a higher and higher national debt. Later presidents would try to pass "balanced budget amendments" but all would fail. Congress had become addicted to spending money, and could not stop. Ronald Reagan would describe this uncontrollable spending by saying that "government is like a baby. An alimentary canal with a big appetite at one end and no sense of responsibility at the other."

Unemployment, 1929–1941

Millions of people

Source: *Historical Statistics of the United States*

The New Deal, with its pro-union legislation, created powerful unions. These unions campaigned for more pro-union legislation and more pro-union candidates. Over the next decades, union bosses became more powerful than the politicians they elected. These bosses could bring the country to its knees with calls for strikes.

The New Deal also saw a shift in power from Congress to the president. Much of this was due to the personality and determination of Franklin Roosevelt. However, Congress ceded him much of their authority through the creation of so many New Deal agencies. The NLRB, the TVA, the CCC, and more all expanded the power of the Executive branch. In later years, other agencies would follow to create a president seemingly limited only by the authority of the Supreme Court. With the almost constant, unwavering backing of Congress, Franklin Roosevelt certainly was one of the most powerful and effective presidents in American history.

By 1939, the unemployment rate stood at more than 17%. Many people wondered if the Depression would ever end. It would end, but it would take perhaps the greatest catastrophe in human history to bring that about. It was World War II which actually ended the Great Depression.

Answer the following questions:

1. How was the Great Depression different from other depressions and panics?

2. Why did it seem that Herbert Hoover was an excellent president to deal with the Great Depression?

3. Why did Hoover not succeed in dealing with the Great Depression? What was the basis of his plan to deal with it?

4. What did Roosevelt mean when he said that "the only thing we have to fear is fear itself?" Why was this a good message to give to people?

5. Why was the New Deal popular?

6. What is the Federal Deposit Insurance Corporation (FDIC)? How did its creation affect the Great Depression?

7. What was the Tennessee Valley Authority?

8. Why was Roosevelt able to enact so much New Deal legislation?

9. What were Roosevelt's "Fireside Chats?" How did they help him?

10. Why did some people oppose the New Deal? Name at least two groups who opposed the New Deal and why they opposed it.

11. Who was Fr. Charles Coughlin? How did his position on Roosevelt and the New Deal change? How did the Church react to Coughlin?

12. What is the Federal Communications Commission (FCC)? Why are many Americans concerned about its power?

13. What is the second New Deal? Why did Roosevelt propose it?

14. What is the National Labor Relations Act of 1935? What impact has it had on America? What are right-to-work laws?

15. What is Social Security? How has it helped or hurt the United States?

16. What is the Court packing plan? Did it work?

17. What is the Harlem Renaissance? Name two people involved in it and how they were involved?

18. What is the Fair Labor Standards Act? Why did Roosevelt feel it would increase employment?

19. What was the purpose of the Agricultural Adjustment Act?

Identify the following:

1. The Hundred Days
2. Hoovervilles
3. The Dust Bowl
4. Felix Frankfurter
5. William O. Douglas
6. Welfare state

The Battle for Fox Green Beach, D-Day Normandy by Dwight C. Shepler (1944). The Allies' D-Day invasion of Normandy, France during World War II was the largest amphibious invasion in history. In this painting, the artist depicts American forces fighting for a section of "Omaha" beach codenamed "Fox Green" beach. Its beautiful hills and valleys were a nightmare of crossfire from German guns which raked the beaches and pinned down the American soldiers. By mid-afternoon disabled landing craft blocked the few openings between the obstacles the Germans had deployed to obstruct the beach, making it nearly impossible to land additional troops. Destroyers moved toward the beach into dangerously shallow waters to shell the entrenched German positions. German artillery spotters used the spire of the local Catholic church to direct artillery fire at the American forces. Sadly, the lovely church was destroyed when Americans on the beach called on the destroyer U.S.S. *Emmons* to demolish it. The artist was serving aboard the *Emmons*.

Introduction: The Seeds of War

At the Versailles peace conference, David Lloyd George and Georges Clemenceau demanded revenge on Germany. Clemenceau, furious at Germany for its two invasions of his nation, seemed unwilling to accept anything less than German and Austrian annihilation. Even after the armistice, Germany remained blockaded and without food. British troops in Germany, seeing the starvation of German children, threatened to mutiny if these children were not fed. When Lloyd George learned of this humanitarian crisis, largely of his own making, he realized that he was planting the seeds of future conflicts. He wrote that "... *not a single ton of food has been sent into Germany. The (German) fishing fleet has even been prevented from going out to catch a few herring. The Allies were now on top, but the memory of starvation might one day turn against them. The Germans were being allowed to starve while … hundreds of thousands of tons of food were lying in Rotterdam waiting to be taken up the waterways to Germany.… The Allies were sowing hatred for the future."*

Rarely has a politician been so accurate in his analysis of the future. Yet Clemenceau refused to listen. He had hardened his heart. The suffering continued.

Meanwhile, in Munich, an insignificant Austrian corporal returned to his barracks and awaited orders. In time, this small man, who had shown no signs of any worthwhile achievements, would accomplish evil to rival history's greatest villains. His actions would lead to the deaths of fifty million people, mostly civilians. His name, which has become synonymous with evil, was **Adolf Hitler**.

The Rise of Adolf Hitler

At the end of March 1920, Adolf Hitler was discharged from the army and began working full-time for the *National Socialist German Workers' Party*, the **Nazis**. An effective speaker, Hitler soon gained fame for his bitter speeches ranting against the Treaty of Versailles, Communists, and Jews. Over the next three years, Hitler rose in the Nazi party to the point that by 1923, he attempted to overthrow the German government. However, the attempt failed and Hitler was jailed for fourteen months. Upon his release, Adolf Hitler resumed control of the Nazi Party.

The stock market crash of 1929 affected not only the United States but the entire world, which was thrown into a depression. In Germany, millions of men lost their jobs. This situation created a crisis that Hitler and the Nazis quickly grasped. The Nazis promised the German people that they would abandon the harsh Treaty of Versailles, strengthen the economy, and create jobs. Many Germans remembered how

Adolf Hitler gives a speech at a Nazi rally in Berlin on April 4, 1932.

the Treaty had crushed Germany's pride and believed it caused the nationwide economic depression. They recalled the starvation after the war as food rotted on the docks at Rotterdam. Germans were ready to do anything to make life better.

In his long, riveting, pro-German speeches, Hitler spoke to the German people about their concerns and promised to fix them. Many Germans truly believed that they would have won the Great War if not for Communists and Jews who had "stabbed them in the back." Hitler encouraged hatred of Jews and fierce opposition to Communism. He promised his audiences that he would lead Germany to her former greatness. He assured them that the military, which had long been a source of national pride, would flourish again, more powerful than ever. He promised to restore Germany's prosperity and its place as one of the world's leading nations. Many people responded to Hitler's enthusiasm, promises, and the hope he created, because they were depressed, impoverished, and miserable. In the national elections of 1930, the once-insignificant Nazi party won more than 18% of the seats in the German Parliament, making it the second largest party in Parliament.

Benito Mussolini salutes as troops pass in review before himself and Nazi leader Adolf Hitler.

In 1933, Hitler was elected chancellor of Germany. By August 1934, he had become absolute ruler of Germany. As soon as he gained control of the government, he began to establish a military dictatorship. Hitler then began to assemble the world's strongest war machine. He updated the army, built up the air force, and constructed an incredibly powerful navy. He was preparing to conquer the world.

Hitler also organized Germany's children into the "Hitler Youth" and filled their young, impressionable minds with his beliefs, so his policies would be carried out for years to come. The Nazis forced children to attend semi-military camps on Sundays. Parents were fined if their child did not attend and jailed if a child missed three Sundays. Eventually, the Nazis turned the children against their parents and Christian values.

On May 21, 1935, Adolf Hitler renounced the provisions of the Versailles Treaty.

The Axis Powers

Meanwhile in Italy, another vicious dictator, **Benito Mussolini**, had ruled since 1922. On October 25, 1936, encouraged by the collective weaknesses of other European countries, Hitler and Mussolini formed an alliance by signing the **Rome-Berlin Pact**. A week later, Mussolini gave a speech in which he declared that in the future, all other European nations would rotate around the *Rome-Berlin axis*, thus creating the term "Axis powers." Later in November, Japan, which had been expanding its power in Asia since 1931, signed a treaty with Germany. By the end of 1937, Germany, Italy, and Japan, motivated by a common desire for more land, power, and raw materials, had signed treaties.

America's Neutrality Policy

During the 1920s, America's leaders tried to follow a policy that balanced *isolationism* with *internationalism*. Americans who favored a policy of isolationism recalled the terrible devastation and loss of life caused by the Great War. As time passed, many Americans came to feel that involvement in the Great War had been a great mistake. The United States had entered the Great War "to end all wars" and "to make the world safe for democracy," but neither of those goals had been achieved. For example, in 1917, Russia had fallen to Communism, and in 1922, Josef Stalin, one of the most homicidal rulers in history, had seized control of the Soviet Union. Stalin ordered the murder of millions and obliterated any sense of freedom and democracy in the Soviet Union. That same year, Mussolini had become Italy's dictator and destroyed its democratic institutions. In 1933, Hitler had become head of the German government and had begun his campaign to destroy any semblance of freedom in Germany. By 1935, the world seemed on the brink of war and not safe for democracy. Thus, it

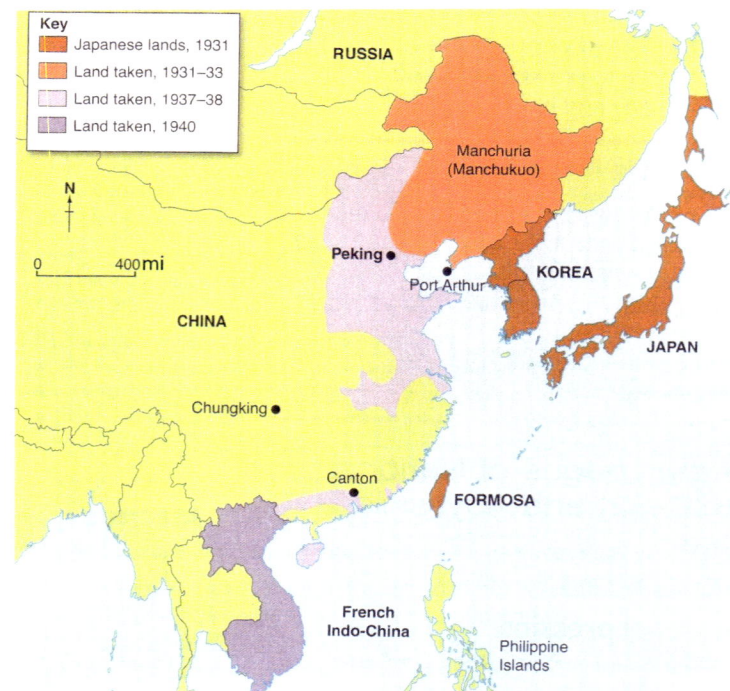

Map showing Japanese aggression against China beginning in 1931 with the invasion of Manchuria. Japan would continue to expand into China for the remainder of the decade.

was not surprising that, according to some polls, by the late 1930s, as many as 70% of Americans believed that the United States had made a mistake by participating in the war.

The situation in Asia mirrored the trouble in Europe. In 1931, the Japanese invaded Manchuria, a province in northern China, in clear violation of the *Open Door Policy*. Americans paid little attention to distant Manchuria's plight. President Hoover took neither economic nor military action against Japan. He simply announced that the United States would not recognize Japan's seizure of Manchuria. Ignoring the problem did not slow Japan's aggression; rather, it likely emboldened their imperial ambitions. In March 1932, the Japanese attacked the Chinese port of Shanghai.

When Franklin Roosevelt became president, his main concern was the American recovery. However, Japanese aggression in China and Hitler's growing influence in Germany troubled him. Yet most Americans wanted to remain isolated from world affairs. For example, on April 6, 1935, the eighteenth anniversary of America's entry into the Great War, 50,000 veterans held a peace march in Washington D. C. Six days later, between 150,000 and 175,000 college students around the country held a one-hour "peace strike," calling for "schools not battleships." Amazingly, some of these students pledged not to fight even in the event that the United States was invaded!

In response to the people's demands, in August 1935, Congress passed the first in a series of **Neutrality Acts** intended to prohibit American involvement in all foreign wars. The first Neutrality Act forbade the sale or transport of munitions and war materials to any warring nation. Another act in 1936 barred loans to any warring nation. In 1937, Congress banned American citizens from traveling on the ships of warring nations. Congress hoped to avoid the causes that had propelled America into the Great War.

Roosevelt Sidesteps the Neutrality Acts

On October 3, 1935, only a few months after the passage of the Neutrality Act, Benito Mussolini's Italian army invaded the African nation of Ethiopia, also known as Abyssinia. Ethiopia promptly declared war on Italy. Although both countries were members of the League of Nations, the League proved powerless to stop the invasion; while Britain and France, who might have intervened, chose not to do so.

Americans sympathized with the Ethiopians, the innocent victims of the Italians' aggression. However, because of the Neutrality Act, Roosevelt could do nothing to aid them. As a result, although the Ethiopians fought hard, the better-equipped Italians eventually defeated them.

However, in 1937, when Japan invaded Manchuria, Roosevelt found a technicality in the Embargo Act. Because Japan had never "formally" declared war on China, Roosevelt declared that the Act did not apply. He allowed the Chinese to purchase American weapons. Roosevelt clearly wished to help nations fight this type of aggression.

In an attempt to persuade Americans to support his position of opposing aggression, in October 1937, Roosevelt traveled to Chicago where he delivered what has become known as his "*Quarantine Speech.*" He called for an international "quarantine" against the lawlessness of aggressive nations, by which he meant Germany, Italy, and Japan. Rather than remaining strictly isolated, America and other peaceful democratic nations would work together to put economic pressure on these nations. In essence, Roosevelt proposed a middle ground between open hostilities and complete non-intervention. However, neither Congress nor the American people were prepared to engage more directly in Europe or Asia. Because the speech was not well received, Roosevelt decided to take a more passive approach to foreign policy. However, events were soon to take matters out of his hands.

Cartoon from Punch, a British magazine of political satire, showing that Britain and France had no more interest in stopping Mussolini's invasion of Ethiopia than just wagging their fingers at him.

Hitler Starts the Second Great War in Europe

Like every British person who had lived through World War I, English Prime Minister **Neville Chamberlain** wanted to avoid another war if possible. Consequently, Chamberlain adopted a policy of **appeasement** toward Adolf Hitler. Hitler wanted to annex the **Sudetenland**, part of the Versailles Treaty-formed nation of Czechoslovakia. Hitler told Chamberlain and French Prime Minister Daladier that if they did not surrender the Sudetenland to him by September 28, 1938, Germany would invade Czechoslovakia. They agreed. Six months later, Hitler annexed the rest of Czechoslovakia.

Neville Chamberlain in 1923

On September 1, 1939, Hitler invaded Poland. England and France had promised to defend the Poles if Hitler attacked them. Two days later, they both declared war on Germany. Although the Poles fought bravely, they were no match for Hitler and his allies, including Soviet dictator Josef Stalin. Hitler and Stalin marched their armies into Poland and divided it between them.

Once German troops had occupied Poland, Hitler's troops quickly subdued Denmark, Norway, the Netherlands, Belgium, and Luxembourg. In June 1940, France fell to the Nazis. To accept France's surrender, Hitler had the railroad car where Germany had signed the 1918 Armistice removed from a museum, placed exactly where it had been in 1918, and sat in the chair where French general Foch had accepted the German surrender.

By September 1939, it was clear that a victory by Adolf Hitler and the Nazis would be a worldwide disaster. The entire free world hoped that England and France would destroy the Nazis. President Roosevelt called a special session of Congress to change the Neutrality Acts. Congress, realizing the global threat, changed the law. Warring nations would now be permitted to purchase arms from the United States if they paid for them with cash and transported them on their own ships. This "cash and carry" policy allowed the United States to sell war materials to England and France.

"This Blessed Plot... this England"

In his play *Richard II*, William Shakespeare describes England as only a man who loves his nation can:

> *This royal throne of kings, this sceptred isle...*
>
> *This fortress built by Nature for herself*
>
> *Against infection and the hand of war...*
>
> *This precious stone set in the silver sea,*
>
> *Which serves it in the office of a wall,*
>
> *Or as a moat defensive to a house,*
>
> *Against the envy of less happier lands,*
>
> *This blessed plot, this earth, this realm, this England...*

Winston Churchill (December 1941)

By June 1940, England stood alone, protected by the English Channel, her "defensive moat." Across the Channel, Hitler's seemingly unstoppable war machine had gobbled up Europe in a matter of months. In late May, England had nearly lost its entire army at Dunkirk. The British army had been trapped on the beach at Dunkirk, but between May 26 and June 4, nearly every British ship that could float had sailed across the Channel to rescue the stranded men. Code-named **Operation Dynamo**, the British navy and civilians rescued nearly 340,000 troops from the Dunkirk beach. Of this miraculous rescue, recently-elected British Prime Minister **Winston Churchill** said that England "must be very careful not to assign to this deliverance the attributes of a victory. Wars are not won by evacuations."

The fall of France, and the other European nations, shocked most Americans and filled them with dread. Everyone feared a Nazi victory. They realized that Hitler was a vicious dictator who ruled through terror and violence, murdering anyone who opposed him. During his rise to power, Hitler had developed certain theories. Among these notions were the idea that Germans, and white people in general, were members of a "master race." Because he believed that Jews had "stabbed Germany in the back" during the Great War, Hitler held a special hatred for Jews. Wherever he gained power, he rounded up Jews and sent them off to concentration camps. Only later, as the Allies entered Germany, would they learn of the Nazis' mass extermination of millions of Jews in the **Holocaust**.

Roosevelt and Congress realized that once Hitler conquered England, America would be next. In a sense, England "served in the office of a wall" to protect America. In July 1940, Winston Churchill appealed to Roosevelt for help. To protect Britain from German U-boats, which were sinking vital supplies, Churchill asked Roosevelt to send England forty or fifty World War I **destroyers**, ships that specifically attacked U-boats. These were older ships that the United States had replaced. In exchange for the destroyers, Britain gave the U. S. free air and naval leases on various Caribbean islands.

Churchill had told Roosevelt that the need for the destroyers was literally a matter of life and death. England was on the verge of surrender. Because Roosevelt felt he could not wait for Congress to act, he issued an executive order, which did not require congressional approval, to send the ships to England. Although his actions probably saved England, anti-war factions in the United States heavily criticized what they viewed as an abuse of power.

The Capture Intact of U-570 by Charles David Cobb. On August 27, 1941, the Nazi submarine surrendered to a British destroyer and the Lockheed Hudson bomber that spotted the sub just below the surface.

The Battle of Britain

On June 18, 1940, Winston Churchill appeared before the British Parliament. He declared, "*the Battle of France is over. I expect that the Battle of Britain is about to begin. Upon this battle depends the survival of Christian civilization…. Hitler knows that he will have to break us in this island or lose the war. If we can stand up to him, all Europe may be free and the life of the world may move forward… But if we fail, then the whole world, including the United States… will sink into the abyss of a new Dark Age… Let us therefore brace ourselves to our duties, and so bear ourselves that if the British Empire…last for a thousand years, men will still say, this was their finest hour.*"

Threatened with a Nazi invasion, the English prepared to meet the invading force in their farms, in their fields, and in their hedgerows. Yet it would not be upon the land where this epic conflict would be waged, but rather, in the air. Fought entirely by air forces, the **Battle of Britain** officially lasted from July 10 until October 31, 1940. During those four months, the *Royal Air Force (RAF)* defended England against

Battle of Britain Aerial Combat by Douglas Ettridge (1927–2009). In this painting a British Spitfire shoots down a German fighter escorting a German bomber squadron.

massive air raids by the *Luftwaffe*, Nazi Germany's air force. Hitler hoped that the air raids would crush British resistance prior to his planned invasion of England. In July, the Luftwaffe began coordinating its attacks with the German navy, which had begun blockading England's ports. However, as the battle turned against the Luftwaffe, it began targeting civilian rather than military targets in terror attacks.

Hitler had underestimated the skill and courage of the British pilots, who were outnumbered five to one by German planes. Although the Luftwaffe inflicted losses on the RAF, the RAF shot down far more German planes – perhaps as many as five times more. Hitler could not continue to sustain such losses. Because of the heroic RAF pilots and millions of bloodied but undaunted British citizens, Hitler could not force Great Britain to surrender. The Battle of Britain marked the first major defeat of Germany's military. In many ways, the victory proved just as important psychologically. The Nazis could be defeated; they were not invincible.

The 1940 Presidential Election

As war raged over Europe, in Philadelphia in June, the Republicans were fighting a conflict of their own. In 1940, the Republican Party had split into two factions: the **isolationists**, who wanted the United States to stay out of the war, and the **interventionists**, who favored aiding Great Britain to stop the Nazis from conquering Europe. Moreover, Republicans could not choose between the two leading candidates, both of whom were isolationists to a certain degree.

The first choice was Senator **Robert Taft** of Ohio, the son of former President William H. Taft. Taft had strong conservative credentials and was from Ohio, a state the Republicans had to carry if they were to win the election. The other leading candidate was **Thomas E. Dewey**, the District Attorney from New York City. Dewey had gained national fame for prosecuting organized crime members. He had won most of the Republican primaries and had the largest number of convention delegates, but not enough to secure the nomination. By June, with the Nazis advancing, the isolationism of both men hurt them among Republican delegates, who came to believe that neither man could win the general election over the Democratic candidate, whoever that might be.

Thus, on the sixth ballot, the Republicans turned to a dark horse candidate. They nominated **Wendell Willkie**, a businessman. Willkie, who had once been a Democrat, headed a large utility company. He had opposed the creation of the Tennessee Valley Authority in 1933. Most important to the Republican delegates, Willkie strongly favored aiding England. The interventionist wing of the party had prevailed.

Meanwhile, the Democrats faced a more interesting problem. George Washington had established the tradition of *two* presidential terms. No president had sought a third *consecutive* term, although Theodore Roosevelt had sought a third *non-consecutive* term. Woodrow Wilson had considered a third term, but chose not to run. During the winter of 1939 and spring of 1940, it appeared that Franklin Roosevelt would not seek reelection. Several items support this contention, including his own campaign manager, **James Farley**, seeking the Democratic nomination. Moreover, Roosevelt signed a contract to write magazine articles starting in January 1941, after he left the presidency.

It seems that in June, as France fell to the Nazis and the Battle of Britain began, Roosevelt had a change of heart. Whether purely out of pride or from deep concern for the nation, Roosevelt came to believe that he was the *one* man who could lead America in the dark days ahead. When the Democrats met in Chicago on July 15, Roosevelt had not even declared himself as a candidate. However, through shrewd political maneuvers, Roosevelt had the committee draft him as the nominee.

Both President Roosevelt and Wendell Willkie campaigned on Roosevelt's record. Willkie lambasted the president for failing to end the ten-year Depression. Willkie also warned that President Roosevelt might

Thomas Dewey

Wendell Willkie. Willkie's unhealthy lifestyle of heavy smoking and drinking caused his early death from a heart attack in October 1944 at age 52.

lead America into the war in Europe. President Roosevelt, fully aware of America's strong isolationist and anti-interventionist sentiments, promised to keep America out of foreign wars if he were reelected. Willkie conducted a hard-hitting, enthusiastic campaign that energized Republican voters in the Northeast and Midwest. However, Willkie could not overcome the strong political base that Roosevelt had built over his two terms. Moreover, Willkie was competing with a president whom most Americans trusted. On November 5, 1940, Franklin Delano Roosevelt amassed 5,000,000 more popular votes than Willkie, won thirty-eight of forty-eight states, and 449 out of 531 Electoral votes.

The Draft

With war raging in Europe, on September 16, 1940, President Roosevelt had signed the *Selective Training and Service Act* which instituted the first peacetime draft in American history. The next month, men between the ages of twenty-one and thirty-six registered for military service. Basic training bases were set up around the country and training began early in 1941.

At the same time, Congress authorized a massive increase in the defense budget. The United States began building world class armed forces. America prepared to fight for "*the survival of Christian civilization.*"

The Lend-Lease Act

Roosevelt saw his landslide reelection as a vote of confidence in his foreign policy. On December 29, 1940, he gave a Fireside Chat explaining how he planned to proceed with aid to Great Britain:

"*This is not a fireside chat on war. It is a talk on national security... Does anyone seriously believe that we need to fear attack while a free Britain remains our most powerful naval neighbor in the Atlantic? Does any one seriously believe, on the other hand, that we could rest easy if the Axis powers were our neighbor there?... The people of Europe who are defending themselves do not ask us to do their fighting. They ask us for the implements of war ... which will enable them to fight for their liberty and our security.... We must be the great arsenal of democracy.... We have furnished the British great material support and we will furnish far more in the future.*" Roosevelt went on to say that America must aid Britain even if it meant becoming involved in the war.

By the end of 1940, Great Britain was running out of gold to pay for material under the "cash and carry" policy. Thus, Roosevelt suggested a change. Under the new "**Lend-Lease**" law, the president had the right to "sell, transfer title to, exchange, lease, lend, or otherwise dispose of" any military equipment to "the government of any country whose defense the President deems vital to the defense of the United States." President Roosevelt signed the Lend-Lease bill into law on March 11, 1941. Though intended primarily for Great Britain, which did receive about two-thirds of the aid under the program, the law was extended to include China in April and the Soviet Union in October.

The Lend-Lease Act did not have full congressional support. Most Republicans, especially the isolationists, opposed it. Senator Robert Taft, who opposed the bill, said, "*Lending war material is like lending chewing gum. You don't want it back.*" One group claimed the bill made the president a dictator because he could involve the United States in foreign wars without congressional approval. However, the policy had the effect of not creating Allied debt as had occurred during World War I. Also, polls showed that most Americans now favored the policy of supporting Britain, even if it meant America was drawn into the war.

Passage of Lend-Lease brought an end to American neutrality. The United States had definitely chosen to be on the Allies' side. All that remained was active participation by American soldiers.

The Battle of the Atlantic

On September 3, 1939, England employed its greatest weapon, the Royal Navy, against Germany, by blockading Hitler's empire as it had Napoleon's over one hundred years earlier. For the remainder of the

A German U-boat attacks a British merchant ship during the Battle of the Atlantic. German sailors on the conning tower of a U-boat watch as the cargo ship they have torpedoed burns and sinks. Survivors are seen in lifeboats. This image was painted in 1941 by German artist Adolf Bock (1890-1968), one of the leading maritime artists of the 20th century.

war in Europe—sixty-eight months—the Battle of the Atlantic would pit the Royal Navy and the U. S. Navy against the U-boats and surface warships of the German navy (*Kriegsmarine)* and the aircraft of the Luftwaffe. The Kriegsmarine and Luftwaffe attempted to starve England as Germany had during World War I.

Because of its massive scale and changes in equipment and tactics, dominance in the Battle of the Atlantic would shift back and forth between the combatants. In the beginning, the balance tilted in Hitler's favor. From June 1940 until about February 1941, German U-boats sank British ships faster than the English could build them. To aid Britain, President Roosevelt permitted U. S. Navy facilities to repair damaged British ships. Roosevelt also gave ten Coast Guard cutters to the Royal Navy.

In April, the U. S. Navy set up bases in Greenland and began to patrol the Atlantic. Because America was not formally at war with Germany, American ships could not engage German U-boats. However, American naval ships could track the U-boats and radio their positions to British ships and planes that could engage and sink the U-boats. Clearly the United States was moving closer and closer to joining Britain as an active combat participant.

Although the U-boats proved the greater threat, the German surface fleet inflicted significant damage and severely disrupted the convoys of ships carrying food and supplies from America to England. In May 1941, the Germans launched their largest raid of the war against Allied merchant shipping. The "invincible" battleship *Bismarck* and heavy cruiser *Prinz Eugen* set out to attack convoys. On May 24, a British fleet intercepted the ships off Iceland. During the *Battle of the Denmark Strait*, the British warship *HMS Hood* was sunk. However, the Royal Navy severely damaged the *Bismarck* and sank it three days later. The loss of the *Bismarck* marked a turning point in the surface action phase of the Battle of the Atlantic. Over the next eighteen months, the Nazis lost more of their surface battle fleet. By the end of 1942, the tide of battle on the surface of the Atlantic finally swung decisively in the Allies' favor.

In early 1943, Allied navies began inflicting massive losses on the U-boats. May 1943 proved to be the turning point in the Battle of the Atlantic, as U-boats inflicted few losses on Allied shipping while absorbing extremely high losses themselves. Although the Nazi submarines would continue to sink Allied shipping until the end of the war, their threat to England had been effectively neutralized.

Hitler Invades the Soviet Union

Despite the secret peace treaty Hitler signed in 1939 with Josef Stalin, on June 22, 1941, Germany launched **Operation Barbarossa**, sending 3,000,000 German troops, 3,000 tanks, and 2,500 aircraft storming into the Soviet Union under the pretense of destroying Communism. In reality, Hitler needed Soviet oil. The invasion took Stalin and his generals completely by surprise. Suddenly Josef Stalin, a Communist dictator as evil as Hitler, turned to Great Britain and became an ally of England and the United States. In October, President Roosevelt extended Lend-Lease aid to the Soviet Union, which ultimately received nearly $11 billion from the United States.

Many Americans hated the idea of helping the Soviet Union and Josef Stalin, a mass murderer, or being allied with the Soviets, in any way. However, Hitler was an *immediate* threat to world peace. Winston Churchill, perhaps the most forceful anti-Communist leader of the century, summed up the attitude of most people when he said, "If I thought that it would injure Hitler, I would give Lucifer himself a favorable mention in the House of Commons (Parliament)." The Soviet military added about thirty million soldiers to the Allied cause – not quite double the number of American troops who served.

During the early stages of the German invasion, it appeared to be another victory for Hitler. For over five months, the Germans advanced eastward, driving the Soviet army back to Moscow. The Germans besieged Leningrad (St. Petersburg). However, with the coming of winter, the tide turned. The German army was forced into defensive positions and the Soviets took the offensive. In November 1942, the German end was in sight, as the Nazis were stopped on the frozen Russian steppes.

The Atlantic Charter

President Roosevelt and British Prime Minister Churchill met on August 9, 1941, aboard the *USS Augusta*, off the coast of Newfoundland. The two men, who had spoken on the telephone, firmed their bond of trust and admiration. On August 14, they signed the **Atlantic Charter.** While not an official document or treaty, it was a statement of eight democratic principles they hoped to achieve in the postwar world.

First, the United States and Great Britain agreed to seek no territorial gains as a result of the outcome of the war. Second, no territorial changes would be made without

President Roosevelt and Prime Minister Churchill seated on the quarterdeck of HMS *Prince of Wales* August 10, 1941. Behind them are American Admirals King and Stark.

the agreement of the affected people. Third, they declared that self-determination was a right of all people. Fourth, both leaders believed that every nation, including the vanquished, had the right to free access to the earth's raw materials and to international trade. Fifth, both nations pledged to work to lower trade barriers. Sixth, they would work to establish freedom from fear and want. Seventh, both nations believed in freedom of the seas. Eighth, both leaders declared that all nations must abandon the use of force to settle international disputes. To this end, they would work towards postwar disarmament of aggressor nations.

The Atlantic Charter proved remarkable in many ways. First, unlike the Versailles Treaty, the Atlantic Charter specifically guaranteed that vanquished nations would have access to markets and raw materials. It thus repudiated what many considered the critical flaw in the Versailles Treaty, that is, its demand for revenge. To spread this message, British planes dropped copies of the Charter in Germany. Secondly, the Charter called for the right of self-determination, something clearly absent in the Soviet Union. Third, it caused the Axis powers, especially the Japanese, to realize that the United States was becoming a greater threat to them. Japanese army commanders began pushing for a more aggressive approach to dealing with the United States. Finally, the Charter served as a foundational document for the future United Nations.

Undeclared War with Germany

On September 4, 1941, a Nazi U-boat fired a torpedo at the *USS Greer*, a destroyer that had been trailing the submarine and radioing its position to the RAF, which had dropped depth charges. Although one could argue that the submarine had attacked in self-defense, President Roosevelt called the attack immoral. On September 11, during one of his famous fireside chats, Roosevelt explained the *Greer* incident and how it would impact American foreign policy. Roosevelt said that the German submarine "deliberately fired a torpedo at the *Greer*, followed by another torpedo attack …that the German submarine fired first upon (the) American destroyer without warning, and with the deliberate design to sink her." As a result of the attack, he ordered naval vessels to escort merchant ships in convoys across the Atlantic and directed the U. S. Navy to "shoot on sight" any German U-boats they encountered.

On October 30, a Nazi submarine sank the destroyer *USS Reuben James*, killing over 100 American sailors. In response, Congress ordered that all merchant ships be armed. Congress also removed all restrictions

The USS *Reuben James* (April 29, 1939). *Reuben James* was the first United States Navy ship sunk by hostile action in the European theater during World War II.

on commerce. For all intents and purposes, the United States was now engaged in an undeclared war with Germany.

By December 1941, the U. S. had abandoned all but a *technical* neutrality. The United States had instituted its first-ever peacetime draft. It had given the British fifty World War I destroyers. The Lend-Lease Act was fully operational. American supply ships in convoys sailing to England were equipped with cannon and manned by U. S. Naval personnel. The United States was mobilizing for war.

America Tries to Curtail Japanese Aggression

In its history, the United States has made mistakes. However, seeking peaceful resolutions has never been one of them. Perhaps no nation in history has desired peace more than the United States. Thus, even as Japan sought to gain greater control of Asia, the United States sought peace.

Chiang Kai-shek in 1943

Since their invasion of Manchuria in 1931, the Japanese had been fighting almost constantly to conquer China. The United States opposed Japanese aggression and recognized **Chiang Kai-shek** as the leader of China. However, in the late 1930s, America gave little military aid to China for fear of upsetting Japan. In September 1940, to cut off supplies to China, Japan invaded French Indochina (present-day Vietnam). On September 27, 1940, Japan joined Germany and Italy and signed a mutual defense treaty, the **Tripartite Pact**, creating what was called the **Rome-Berlin-Tokyo Axis**. Hungary (November 20, 1940), Romania (November 23, 1940), Slovakia (November 24 1940), and Bulgaria (March 1, 1941) would subsequently join the Axis powers.

In an attempt to curtail Japanese aggression, President Roosevelt imposed economic sanctions on Japan. Because Japan is an island chain lacking many natural resources like oil and iron, **in July 1940**, Roosevelt imposed an aviation gas and scrap iron embargo on Japan. Roosevelt specifically did not stop *all oil sales* to Japan, in the hopes of continuing negotiations. However, Japan, which imported 80% of its oil from the United States, realized that it was in a dangerous position. If Roosevelt did stop all oil imports, the Japanese war effort would grind to a halt.

In July 1941, Japan moved more troops into Indochina in preparation for attacking the Dutch East Indies (present-day Indonesia), where there was oil. In retaliation, Roosevelt stopped all oil sales to Japan. Cutting off their oil supplies hit the Japanese military at its most vulnerable point. Japan either had to agree to the United States' demand to withdraw from China and Indochina or find another supply of oil. Japan decided that it would continue its planned domination of Asia and find an independent supply of oil. Because the United States stood in its way, Japan decided to attack it as well.

The Japanese Attack Pearl Harbor

Japan's plan to cripple America's Pacific Fleet was relatively simple. They planned to launch a surprise air attack on the American naval base at Pearl Harbor, Hawaii, where the fleet was stationed. The Japanese military believed that a decisive strike would inflict such massive damage on the American fleet that by the time it had been rebuilt, Japan would have increased its control over Asia and the Pacific. It could then deal with any counter-attack the rebuilt U. S. Navy launched. Japanese planners determined that a Sunday morning, when most Americans slept late or attended church, would be the optimal time to launch their sneak attack. Thus, the planners chose Sunday, December 7, 1941, as the date of the attack.

While the Japanese certainly launched a sneak attack, American commanders should have been more prepared for it. American intelligence, which had broken Japan's secret codes, had intercepted radio transmissions indicating that Japan was planning something very big. During the entire month of November, Tokyo sent messages to its ambassadors in Washington indicating that some type of military action would take place after November 29, 1941. On November 22, a radio message intercepted from Tokyo indicated that unless the United States ceased demanding Japan's withdrawal from China and lifted the oil embargo, something would "absolutely" happen after the November 29 "deadline." While warnings were sent to the American military commanders in Hawaii on November 24 and November 27, they failed to convey the urgency of the "deadline."

Despite these warning signs, most American strategists believed that Japan would attack somewhere in Asia. Most thought that the Philippines were the most likely target. They incorrectly assumed that the Japanese navy could not launch an attack on Hawaii because it was too far from the Japanese mainland.

Admiral Husband Kimmel. Kimmel and Short were both relieved of their commands days after the Pearl Harbor attack. Many historians believe that they were scapegoats for mistakes made by their superiors.

Although the commanders at Pearl Harbor, Admiral Husband Kimmel and General Walter Short, took precautions against sabotage by Japanese agents, they did almost nothing to protect against an air attack. In fact, *their planes and ships were lined up in an almost perfect fashion to be attacked!*

By the early morning of December 7, the Japanese naval force was in position about 200 miles north of the Hawaiian Islands. The first wave of 183 planes left the six Japanese carriers and headed for the sleepy town. At 7:48, the residents of the Pearl Harbor Naval Base were suddenly awakened by the sounds of planes dropping bombs. The surprise was complete. The warships in the American fleet, particularly the battleships, were moored in their berths in **Battleship Row**, side by side, in a neat double line that made it easy for the Japanese bombs and torpedoes to destroy them. The Japanese sunk four of the eight battleships and damaged the other four. Amazingly, six of the battleships were repaired and took part in later World War II battles. Only the *USS Oklahoma* and the *USS Arizona* were destroyed. The attack also sank or damaged three cruisers and three destroyers, and destroyed 188 planes, almost all on the ground. Remarkably, two American pilots took off during the attack and shot down five Japanese planes.

In addition to the loss of ships and planes, the loss of life was staggering. 2,403 Americans were killed, about half on the *Arizona*, and 1,178 were wounded. As the attack occurred before a formal declaration of war, these were technically all non-combatants.

Following the attack, the planes flew back to their carriers. The Japanese task force then sped back to Japan. The attack was the worst defeat in American naval history. However, Japan had made a number of errors.

First, the American aircraft carriers were not at Pearl Harbor during the attack. As the attack on Pearl Harbor showed, aircraft carriers, not battleships, were the key to naval warfare. Second, the attack had not

Destroyer USS *Shaw's* forward magazine explodes in a large fireball during the second Japanese attack wave.

damaged many of the most vital facilities at Pearl Harbor, such as the massive underground fuel storage tanks. If those fuel tanks had been lost, future operations of navy ships and planes would have been drastically curtailed. The electrical power stations, the shipyard maintenance shops, and headquarters buildings, which housed the communications and intelligence units, were not attacked.

Third, the Japanese ignored the submarine base. For months after December 7, American submarines attacked the Japanese merchant fleet, eventually sinking over 75% of it. Fourth, and most importantly, in an opinion popularly ascribed to Japanese admiral **Isoroku Yamamoto**, the Japanese had awakened a sleeping giant and filled him with a terrible resolve. Prior to the attack, America had been a *passive* ally to England, supplying her with ships, food, and weapons. But many Americans demanded the United States not intervene militarily. The attack changed that.

The sneak attack on Pearl Harbor shocked and angered every American. Because Japan attacked without any formal warning in the midst of peace negotiations, President Roosevelt

Isoroku Yamamoto. Yamamoto had been opposed to attacking the United States but had been overruled. He was probably Japan's finest naval commander. Thus, when his plane was shot down in April 1943, it was a serious blow to Japan's war effort and Japanese morale.

proclaimed December 7, 1941, "a date that will live in infamy." On December 8, President Roosevelt asked Congress to declare war on Japan, which it did. Three days later, Germany and Italy declared war on the U. S. and the U. S. declared war on them.

Building the American Military

In the aftermath of the Japanese attack on Pearl Harbor, America's military ranks swelled as patriotic men and women volunteered to fight the Axis powers. By the end of the war, ten million men had been drafted and over six million men and women volunteered for service. By war's end, more than 350,000 women had served in the military, many in very hazardous duty.

Prior to the outbreak of the war, women in the armed forces served exclusively as nurses. With the onset of conflict, the various branches of the armed forces began creating more opportunities for women. In May 1942, the Women's Army Auxiliary Corps was created. In July, women were allowed to join the Navy and Marine Corps. Although technically civilians, another group of courageous women became the Women's Airforce Service Pilots (WASP). They delivered new planes from factories to military bases, towed targets for aerial target practice, taught other pilots, and tested experimental aircraft. For the most part, women in the armed services acted in a support capacity as mechanics, secretaries, and typists, which freed male soldiers for combat. Although the United States prohibited women from engaging in combat, many women did serve very close to the front lines, especially in medical units. As a result, 432 women were killed and 88 were taken prisoner during the war.

Supporting and Supplying the Military

As war loomed on the horizon, President Roosevelt had organized councils to oversee the production and distribution of war-related materials. In January 1942, with the outbreak of the war, President Roosevelt organized the **War Production Board**, whose purpose was to oversee national industries and ensure that the military would be supplied with weapons and other necessary goods. It also sought to decrease the production of non-essential goods. The war also meant government rationing of scarce items like meat, butter, and sugar. Although there was never a gasoline shortage, the government still rationed gas to discourage unnecessary travel and save on rubber. The government issued ration books and ration cards to ensure that everyone received their fair share.

As the United States moved towards war, the Great Depression slowly came to an end. In 1940, unemployment was still over 14%, but had decreased from the previous year as Americans were making war materials for Britain. In 1941, unemployment declined to just under 10%, the lowest it had been since 1930. The demand for weapons, food, and ammunition had brought the Depression to an end. From 1943 through 1945, unemployment would be under 2%, the lowest rate ever recorded, as men and women crowded factories making planes, tanks, and ships for the war.

With the advent of the war, companies switched from producing consumer goods to military ordinance. No industry contributed more to the war effort than the automobile industry which produced approximately 20% of the entire American output of the material manufactured to fight the war. Automobile companies not only built tanks, jeeps, and other military vehicles but also planes, torpedoes, and even anti-aircraft guns. Although it took about 18 months for companies to re-tool completely from automobiles to weapons, by war's end, General Motors (the largest automaker) produced over 200,000 aircraft engines, more than 90,000 bombers, and 854,000 military trucks. Chrysler constructed a factory in Detroit that built more tanks than all the Nazi factories combined. Ford erected a factory complex in Michigan called "Willow Run" that fashioned B-24 *Liberator* bombers. At the height of production, Willow Run produced *Liberators* every 63 minutes! Before the plant closed in 1945, Willow Run produced 8,685 *Liberators*. Donald Nelson, the head of the War Production Board said, "The American war production job was probably the greatest collective achievement of all time."

The nature of the American workforce changed dramatically during World War II. With men away fighting, women took over factory jobs that men had once held. About six million women were employed during the war, many doing jobs that had previously been done only by men. A character called "**Rosie the Riveter**," representing strong working women who did physically demanding jobs, appeared in many images, flexing her arm and saying, "We Can Do It!"

To address the wartime labor shortage, President Roosevelt established a **National War Labor Board** in January 1942. President Wilson had created a similar board during the First World War. The Board regulated wages and worked to prevent labor disputes, thus ensuring that there would be no strikes or work stoppages. America could not afford even to slow down its wartime production.

The end of the Depression affected farmers more positively than most, mainly because the Depression had hurt them so badly. With the advent of war, the demand for food for American

Rosie the Riveter

civilians and soldiers increased, as did the need to feed America's allies. During the war, farmers' income more than doubled. Farmers who had suffered so greatly during the Depression were finally able to pay their bills, buy new and better equipment, and improve their lives. Steinbeck's plea had been answered, "*Pray God some day kind people won't all be poor. Pray God some day a kid can eat.*"

Congress instituted higher tax rates during the war, which affected millions of Americans. In 1939, about 4.5 million Americans paid federal income tax. By 1945, 42 million Americans paid federal income taxes. These high tax rates, in some cases as high as 94% on personal income, had two effects. First, it raised money to support the war. Second, it demonstrated that everyone was contributing as American soldiers risked their lives and died in battle.

To ensure that the federal government received its income taxes, Congress implemented a new *withholding system of payroll deductions*. Under this system, employers withdrew a percentage of their employees' regular pay and sent the money directly to the federal government. This guaranteed that the federal government had a steady stream of income. It also made it extremely difficult for people to cheat on their income taxes.

Soldiers returning home after the Great War had struggled to find jobs, buy homes, and generally assimilate back into civilian life. In 1924, Congress had passed the "Bonus Act," which provided these veterans with money based on their time of service. However, they would not receive the money for twenty years. As a result, the Act served only to infuriate many of them. In 1944, Congress and the president realized that when the millions of veterans returned home from World War II, they would face the same struggles the Great War veterans had. Congress determined to fix the mistakes it had made twenty years earlier. Therefore, in June 1944, Congress and president Roosevelt enacted the **Servicemen's Readjustment Act**, more commonly known as the **G. I. Bill.**

Veterans, furious over the "Bonus Act," marched on Washington DC. In this photo, the "Bonus Army" clashes with police.

Under the G. I. Bill, veterans returning from the war could receive low interest loans for tuition to go to school, buy a home, or start a business, and even receive unemployment pay. According to the U.S. Department of Veterans Affairs, "In the peak year of 1947, veterans accounted for 49 percent of college admissions. By the time the original GI Bill ended on July 25, 1956, 7.8 million of 16 million World War II veterans had participated in an education or training program." Since its inception, tens of millions of veterans, including ones recently discharged, have taken advantage of the G. I. Bill, which has proven a major benefit to America's veterans.

During the war, families and neighbors went on "scrap drives" to collect metal, paper, rubber, and other items useful to the military. Many Americans, including at least one million public school students, planted family **victory gardens** so farmers could send more food to the soldiers. Children visited hospitals, singing, dancing, and reading to wounded soldiers.

The nation's factories operated around the clock, churning out weapons and war materials. They made President Roosevelt's words come true. America quickly became the "great arsenal of democracy."

Poster from the War Food Administration urging families to plant Victory Gardens

Japanese-Americans during World War II

The attack on Pearl Harbor created anger and resentment towards the Japanese. However, on the West Coast of the United States, it also created a fear of invasion. Americans were concerned that Japan might next attack Los Angeles, San Francisco, or San Diego. At the very least, Japanese spies or secret agents might launch sabotage attacks. Part of this concern was probably legitimate. Admiral Kimmel and General Short had taken precautions against sabotage at Pearl Harbor. However, some of the concern was based on the historic suspicion that Westerners had had for the Chinese and Japanese since the time of the Trans-Continental Railroad. Sadly, people who are afraid do not always act charitably nor rationally. Many Americans believed that residents with Japanese ancestry, even those who had been their friends, neighbors, and loyal American citizens, were now untrustworthy. Many believed that unless everyone of Japanese origin were removed from the West Coast, it would soon come under attack.

Therefore, in February 1942, President Roosevelt issued Presidential Order 9066, which ushered in one of the saddest and most prejudicial eras in American history. Because of this cruel order, about 120,000 Japanese, most of whom were U. S. citizens, were forced to abandon their homes and businesses without any warning. Of course, this caused them to suffer financial losses as well as personal hardship. They were taken to isolated internment camps in barren sections of the country, where they remained until the war ended. It is remarkable and highly admirable how calm and forgiving these Japanese-Americans were when they were released back into American society. There is no evidence that Japanese-Americans were less loyal than any other Americans. No Japanese-American was ever convicted of any act of sabotage.

Despite the government's treatment of Japanese-Americans, politicians in Washington thought that it would be a great idea to recruit enough **Nisei**, second generation Japanese-Americans, to form a combat regiment. They put recruiting posters in the internment camps and waited for results. Eventually, 4,500 young Nisei volunteered for duty in the **442 Combat Team**. Most members of the 442 Combat Team were serving in the Hawaii National Guard when the Japanese planes attacked. Loyal Americans, they rushed to join the 442 Combat Team. (In Hawaii, because almost half the population was of Japanese ancestry, internment was virtually impossible; however, the U. S. military did impose martial law and curfews.) Other volunteers had families in the internment camps. During the war, the 442 Combat Team fought in Europe where it amassed an amazing record of bravery and success. In fact, *the 442 Combat Team is the most decorated unit in U. S. military history.*

In 2010, Congress voted to award the Congressional Gold Medal to honor the Japanese-American veterans of World War II. The medal features the 442nd Regimental Combat Team's motto: "Go for Broke."

In 1988, President Ronald Reagan signed the **Civil Liberties Act** as part of the United States government's effort to make restitution to the families of Japanese-Americans interned during the War. The act granted each surviving internee about $20,000. The Act said that the money was being paid because during the War the government had acted out of "prejudice" and "war hysteria," not for any legitimate security reasons.

African-Americans during the War

As it had for women, the labor shortage created new opportunities for African-Americans during World War II. Many learned new skills and had the chance to obtain jobs previously unavailable to them. In June 1940, President Roosevelt created the Fair Employment Practices Committee (FEPC), which sought to ban discrimination by any company engaged in war-related work. The FEPC was also intended to help minorities obtain more skilled and higher-paying jobs, especially in the defense industry. Such actions did not end discrimination; that required a change of heart and mind. The men of the 332nd Fighter Group were changing hearts and minds.

During World War II, African-American men served in segregated military units. Sadly, these brave men were often treated disrespectfully by both officers and enlisted men. However, generally, their situation was an improvement over previous wars. More black men became officers.

Among the most outstanding black officers was **Colonel Benjamin O. Davis Jr.**, a West Point graduate. Davis commanded the **332nd Fighter Group**. Like Colonel Davis, the fighter pilots of the 332nd were all African-Americans. They were popularly known as the **Tuskegee Airmen**, because they had trained at Moton Field, the Tuskegee Army Air Field, and had been educated at the Tuskegee Institute, the school founded by Booker T. Washington. The main mission of the Tuskegee Airmen was protecting Allied bombers from attacks by German fighter planes.

In the beginning, white bomber crews felt nervous entrusting their lives to black pilots. The Tuskegee Airmen's performance,

Captain Benjamin Oliver Davis, Jr. climbing into his plane in Tuskegee, Alabama, January, 1942

The P-51 Mustang fighter that the 332nd pilots flew. The tail was painted red earning them their nickname "Red Tail Squadron."

however, soon changed that. One morning, a few months after the 332nd pilots had demonstrated their ability to protect bombers, several bomber crews were informed that that day's mission was to bomb factories in Berlin. The briefing officer asked if any of the bomber pilots had a question or a request. One young pilot from Alabama, who had been very critical of the 332nd pilots, rose and, in a strong Southern accent, said, "Sir, I request the 332nd be assigned to provide air cover for us. I'll feel a lot more confident of getting back from Berlin with them watching over us."

The 332nd compiled an incredible record. Although for many years it was reported that the 332nd never lost a bomber to enemy fighters, in fact, they did lose twenty-five bombers. However, this record is far superior to those of most other bomber escorts.

The Changing Nature of Warfare

In the twenty years between 1919 and 1939, the nature of warfare underwent incredible changes. Military strategists often say that nations must always be prepared to fight the *next war*. The Nazis had

The Messerschmitt 262, nicknamed "Swallow," was the world's first jet-powered fighter. The Nazis had started work on the plane before World War II began, but various problems delayed production of the aircraft until the middle of 1944. The Me 262 was an incredibly advanced plane. It was faster and better armed than any Allied fighter plane. No Allied plane was a match for it in the sky. The Allies tried to destroy the Me262 on the ground or during take-offs and landings. Had the Nazis been able to build more of the planes the war might have ended differently. However, their technological advantage could not overcome the Allies numerical superiority of planes.

defeated France in six weeks because France had prepared to re-wage World War I. In the 1930s, France had built a line of concrete fortifications called the **Maginot Line**, expecting to fight another "trench war." Germany, using new tactics and weapons, simply went around the Maginot Line. Among Germany's most effective new weapons were the tank and the airplane.

During World War I, the tank had been of little utility and the airplane had served mostly as a reconnaissance vehicle. Since then, the tank had become a powerful mobile offensive weapon. Generals studied tactics for employing tanks and infantry effectively. During World War II, battles would be fought involving hundreds of tanks on both sides. The airplane had also become a weapon of terrible destruction. Bombers could drop tons of bombs on factories, railroads, and other targets. Planes could also transport thousands of men to various locations.

The expanded use of the airplane also created a new type of soldier, the **paratrooper.** These men jumped out of airplanes behind enemy lines. **Operation Market Garden**, launched by the Allies in September 1944, remains the largest airborne assault in history.

The airplane also changed the nature of naval warfare. It caused the creation of a new type of warship, the **aircraft carrier**, basically an ocean-going airport, which began to appear in the early 1920s. Although planes could fly only a few hundred miles, aircraft carriers could move planes into striking range. Then the planes could launch their attacks and return to their carrier, as the Japanese planes had done at Pearl Harbor. Some of the most decisive naval battles of World War II would be carrier battles in which the ships never saw each other.

In the closing days of the war, German inventors developed two incredible new weapons: **rockets** and **jet planes**. Rockets were self-propelled weapons which could hit targets hundreds of miles away. Jet planes were powered by jet engines and were extremely fast. Allied fighter planes were driven by propellers. However, Nazi scientists developed these inventions too late to affect the outcome of the war.

In this new age of technological warfare, scientists developed two devices for detecting enemy planes, ships, and submarines. The first application was **radar**, which stands for "radio detection and ranging." Radar bounces radio waves off objects. The waves are then reflected back, revealing not only the distance to the object but also its shape. The second application was **sonar**, which stands for "sound navigation ranging." Sonar had been invented in 1906 but used sparingly during World War I. It was not until the second World War that scientists developed sonar to the point where it became a truly efficient means of detecting submarines. Sonar works underwater where radar cannot function. Sonar can be *active* or *passive*. Active sonar sends out "pings," which bounce sounds off an object and record its distance. With passive sonar, the sonar operator carefully listens for the sounds of propellers or other noise being made by an enemy ship.

Finally, in the last days of the war, Allied scientists developed the atomic bomb. This weapon changed not only the nature of warfare, but the world. For the first time in history, mankind had the power to destroy incalculable numbers of people and civilization itself.

The War in Europe

The American Military Strategy

At the beginning of 1942, Hitler controlled nearly all of Europe – except for England and a few neutral nations, including Spain, Portugal, Sweden, Switzerland, and Ireland. The Nazis also controlled most of North Africa as well as much of the western, that is, European, parts of the Soviet Union. In fact, the Nazis nearly captured Leningrad (present-day St. Petersburg) and Moscow. America's military leaders believed that the United States should concentrate its strength against Hitler, while at the same time try to restrain Japan from making any additional advances in the Pacific. Thus, America would first defeat Germany and then defeat Japan.

The Supreme Allied Commander: Dwight Eisenhower

Although Great Britain, France, the Soviet Union, China, Canada, and Australia were all Allied nations, the United States led the Allies. America provided the most money and material, and, other than the Soviet Union, the most soldiers to the war effort. In late June 1942, President Roosevelt named General **Dwight David Eisenhower** to be the commanding general of all American troops in Europe. In December 1943, Roosevelt named Eisenhower the Supreme Allied Commander in Europe.

It is difficult to imagine that anyone could have performed better as Supreme Allied Commander than Dwight Eisenhower. Unlike most great military leaders, Eisenhower had never been in combat. Nevertheless, he had gained valuable experience while serving on General

Portrait of Dwight David Eisenhower (1947). Eisenhower was typical of the incredible quality of the American military commanders during World War II. Never in American history has the United States been blessed with so many exceptional commanders in its armed forces.

MacArthur's staff in the Philippines from 1935-1939. General George C. Marshall, the army Chief of Staff, kept close tabs on Eisenhower's career, and, when a strong but tactful commander was needed in Europe, Marshall was convinced that Eisenhower was the best choice for America's top command.

"Ike," as Eisenhower would become affectionately known to millions, had a combination of abilities and personal traits that made people, especially his soldiers, quickly trust and like him. He had a wide, friendly grin, smiling blue eyes, and a cheerful personality. Ike was a first-rate military planner who had enough patience and self-control to respond to difficult situations with a soft word rather than an angry retort. He also had the ability to deal diplomatically with the various military and political leaders from the other Allied nations. Winston Churchill strongly supported Eisenhower's elevation to Supreme Allied Commander.

The Allies Invade North Africa

Although the Allies were anxious to invade Europe, most planners believed that until more troops and supplies had been gathered in England, the invasion would fail. Therefore, the Allies chose to attack North Africa. Planned by Eisenhower, the invasion of North Africa would be the first important campaign that he designed.

On November 8, 1942, the Allies launched *Operation Torch*, a three-pronged attack into North Africa, specifically Morocco and Algeria, in advance of a rapid move on Tunis. The three elements of the task force, about 110,000 men, mostly Americans, accomplished their mission successfully. The Western Task Force, assigned to capture Casablanca in Morocco, did so after a brief siege. The Center Task Force captured Oran in western Algeria and the Eastern Force easily captured Algiers. Morocco and Algeria were soon in Allied hands.

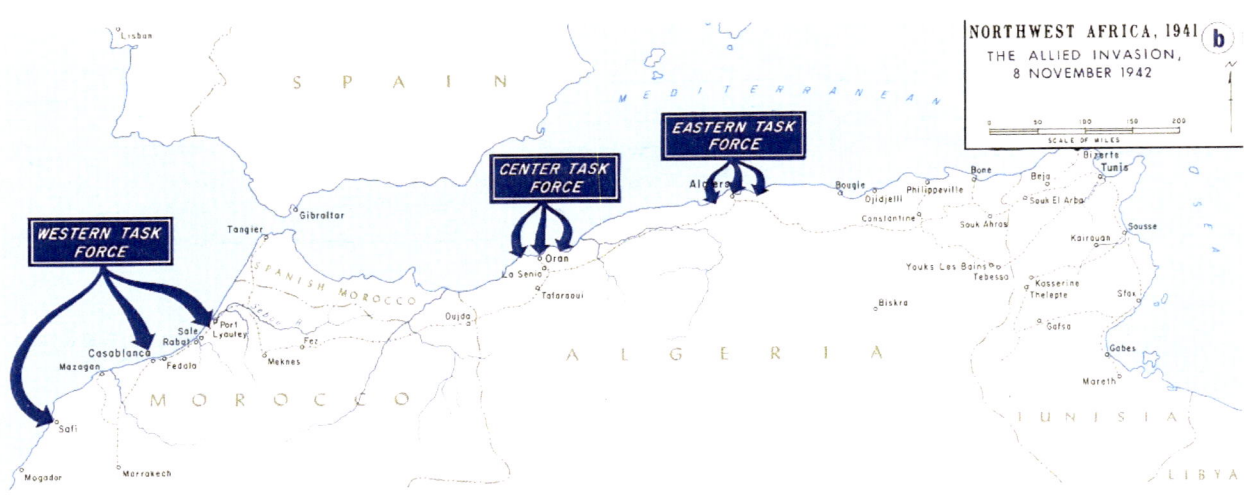

Map of *Operation Torch* created by the U.S. Military Academy at West Point

In early November, Allied forces began the "run for Tunis" with the goal of capturing Tunisia by launching a two-pronged attack. The aim of this twofold Allied attack was to force the German and Italian forces out of North Africa. Once the Axis armies were defeated in North Africa, the Allies could use bases in North Africa to launch an invasion of Europe, starting with Italy.

The campaign for Tunisia flared into a series of fierce battles centered around the **Kasserine Pass**, a two-mile-wide gap in the Atlas Mountains of West-Central Tunisia. In the early hours of February 19, German General **Erwin Rommel**, known as the "Desert Fox," ordered his highly vaunted *Afrika Korps* to attack the Kasserine Pass. For the first time in the war, Germans and Americans met in a full-scale battle. The largely untested American troops suffered heavy casualties against Rommel's tanks and were pushed back over fifty miles.

Despite this humiliating defeat, once the American soldiers were reinforced by British troops, they rallied and took possession of the mountain passes in western Tunisia. The next time Americans met the Germans in battle, they were more efficient and well-prepared. In early April, the British forces from the east joined Allied forces from the west. On May 7, 1943, the last force of 55,000 German soldiers in Africa surrendered.

The Casablanca Conference

As 1943 dawned, Allied troops in North Africa continued to battle German units in Tunisia. However, the numerous Axis victories that had marked the first years of the war were now few and far between. This meant the end of the Allies' defensive tactics and a switch to a more offensive strategy.

President Roosevelt and Prime Minister Churchill decided to meet in Casablanca, Morocco, to plan military strategy in Europe. They met with their top military and civilian advisers for ten days from January 14 to January 24, 1943. President Roosevelt became the first serving president to leave the U. S. in wartime. However, he believed that seeing him in person would increase the morale of the Allied troops.

Roosevelt and Churchill made several important decisions at Casablanca. First, they decided to exert as much force as possible against Germany, to draw German troops away from the Eastern Front. This would allow the Soviet armies to conduct a major offensive against the weakened German forces. Second, they discussed plans for the invasion of Northern France. Third, they discussed the invasion of Sicily, from which the Italian mainland would be invaded. Fourth, they planned to open new supply lines to China to help the Chinese defend themselves against the Japanese invaders. Fifth, Roosevelt and Churchill decided to send several combat units, originally slated to fight in Europe, to the Pacific to fight the Japanese.

Erwin Rommel. Rommel was implicated in the July 20, 1944 plot to assassinate Hitler. Because Rommel was a national hero, Hitler could not execute him publicly. Hitler threatened to murder Rommel's family if he did not commit suicide which he did October 14, 1944. Hitler then announced that Rommel had died from the wounds he had received on July 17 when an Allied fighter plane strafed his car.

Their most startling statement occurred when Roosevelt announced that, going forward, the Allies would accept nothing less than the "unconditional surrender" of the Axis powers. Roosevelt declared that he and Churchill believed that the only way to ensure postwar peace was by adopting a policy of unconditional surrender. However, the president stated that "the policy of unconditional surrender does not entail the destruction of the populations of the Axis powers, but rather, the destruction of the *philosophies* in those countries which are *based on conquest and the subjugation of other people.*"

The Campaign in Italy and Sicily

Following the victory in North Africa, Allied strategists made Italy their next objective. This would solidify Allied control of the Mediterranean Sea, knock Italy out of the war, and force Germany to transfer troops to halt the Allies' northward advance up Italy. To defeat Italy, Allied strategists first planned to capture the island of Sicily. Sicily would act as a base for the Allied invasion of Italy. Sicily fell in only thirty-eight days to the Allied armies led by Generals Bernard Montgomery and George Patton, one of America's more colorful generals. For example, Patton always wore two ivory-handled pistols. However, Patton was an excellent tank commander who possessed a keen mind for military strategy. He also insisted on strict discipline. Everyone in his command wore a helmet and a tie. Although he could be controversial, Patton was the kind of general of whom Abraham Lincoln would have approved. Like General Grant, Lincoln would have remarked, "He wins." By the end of the war, Patton would liberate over 82,000 square miles, capture or kill over 1,000,000 enemy troops, and free over 1,500 cities and towns.

By this point, most Italians had grown tired of the war. In July 1943, they revolted against Mussolini and forced him to resign. Marshal Pietro Badoglio became Premiere and signed a peace treaty with the Allies. On September 3, the Allies landed on the Italian mainland. There was almost no opposition and the Italian troops surrendered almost immediately. On October 13, 1943, Italy declared war on Germany.

However, the Italian surrender had little impact on the Allies' conquest of Italy. The German forces continued their strong resistance to the Allies'

George S. Patton (1945). Like most American commanders during the War, Patton was an excellent general.

northward drive up Italy. Hoping to outflank the Germans in Italy, on January 22, 1944, U. S. troops made an amphibious landing at Anzio, about thirty miles south of Rome. American troops suffered a large number of casualties as a result of the relentless German defense. In addition, the mountainous terrain, heavy rains, and muddy roads slowed down the Allied soldiers.

The Battle of Anzio was followed by battles in Salerno and Monte Cassino. Rome was not liberated until June 1944. The Italian Campaign dragged on and did not end until May 2, 1945, only days before Germany's surrender.

The D-Day Invasion

Since 1942, the Allies had hoped to invade northern France. Finally, **Operation Overlord**, the invasion of France, was about to begin. For months prior to the invasion, Allied planes bombed northern France to knock out German communication facilities, factories, railroad yards, and anti-invasion obstructions. Minutes after midnight on **D-Day**, June 6, 1944, the long-awaited Allied invasion began, as American and British paratroopers parachuted into Northern France.

Simultaneously, it was early evening in Washington D. C. when President Roosevelt spoke to the nation. He asked all Americans to join him in prayer. "*Almighty God: Our sons, the pride of our nation, this day have set upon a mighty endeavor, a struggle to preserve our Republic, our religion, our civilization and to set free a suffering humanity. Lead them straight and true; give strength to their arms, stoutness to their hearts, steadfastness to their faith.*"

Meanwhile, 4,000 landing craft and 600 warships carried 176,000 Allied soldiers across the English Channel to five beaches on the coast of **Normandy, France**, code named Utah, Gold, Sword, Juno, and Omaha Beach. To support the landing, naval guns and about 11,000 planes attacked the German positions.

The Tough Beach by Dwight C. Shepler (1944). The "Tough Beach" is what the American soldiers called the Omaha beachhead. All day soldiers landing on Omaha beach suffered terrible casualties as Nazis in pillboxes and other entrenched positions raked the shore with machine gun and rifle fire. Additionally, the Germans had fortified the beach with underwater obstacles, mines, and tank traps. Shepler, serving aboard a destroyer, provided a first-hand visual account of the deadly landing.

Despite heavy losses, the first precarious footholds at the water's edge were reinforced by succeeding waves of Allied troops as they came ashore. Throughout the day, the determined Allied soldiers slowly gained ground despite the strong German defense. Eventually, late in the day, Allied units linked together. By the time the sun set in the western skies of D-Day, 156,000 men had invaded the five Normandy Beaches and 6,000 had given their lives.

Although the Germans fought hard to dislodge them, the Allied troops clung tenaciously to the Normandy beachhead. During the week after D-Day, hundreds of thousands of troops landed to re-enforce the soldiers already there. By the end of July over a million Allied troops had landed, along with 175,000 vehicles, including 50,000 tanks and half a million tons of supplies. From the beaches of Normandy, the reconquest of Europe would begin. The Allies' next goal was the liberation of Paris.

The Liberation of Paris

Fighting their way off the beaches at Normandy, Allied soldiers were met by determined German resistance. However, the Allied armies' sheer numbers forced the Germans to yield territory. On August 25th, Paris was liberated by Allied troops under the command of General George Patton. After more than four years under Nazi occupation, Parisians greeted Patton's Third Army with hugs, kisses, and a joyous celebration. By the end of November 1944, the Allies had forced all German military units out of France. As Allied soldiers sat in Paris cafes, they knew that the invasion of Germany still lay ahead. For the first time, Germans would be fighting on their home ground.

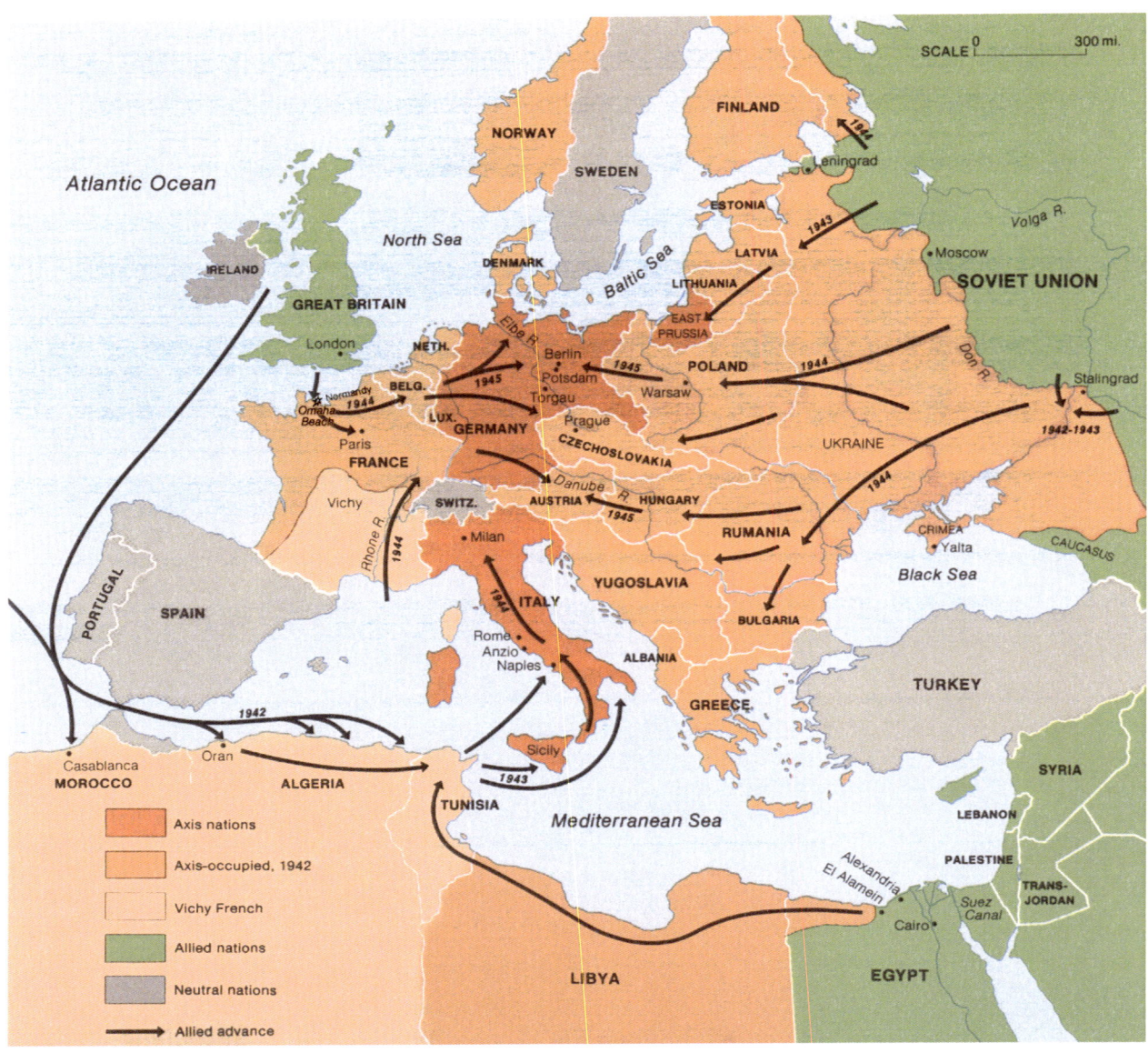

Map of western Europe from 1942 to 1945 showing the extent of Axis control as well as Allied advances. During the war, several countries did remain neutral including Switzerland which historically remains neutral in all European conflicts. Switzerland mobilized its army but, because the Allies defeated Hitler, Switzerland did not have to fight. Although Hitler pressured the Spanish to join him in 1942 at the height of the Nazi's power, Francisco Franco, the ruler of Spain, realized that Hitler was evil and would not join the Axis. As the map shows, in 1942, Hitler controlled most of Europe as well as much of North Africa, an empire that rivaled the ancient Roman Empire.

Vichy France was the nominal government of southern France from June 1940, when the French signed a peace treaty with Hitler until late 1944 following the invasion of France. During this period, 84-year-old Phillippe Petain headed the government which collaborated with the Nazis. A Free French government headed by French general Charles de Gaulle, in exile in London, worked with the Allies. The French colonies in Africa, including Morocco, Algeria, and Tunisia fell under Vichy control.

The Election of 1944

As 1944 dawned, Franklin Roosevelt had a decision to make. Should he seek a *fourth* term? Of course, since no president had ever served three terms, no president had ever faced this decision. On the one hand, Roosevelt had led America through three terrible years of war. Should he not be there at the end to lead the United States to final victory? On the other hand, Roosevelt was dying, something he surely knew. By early 1944, he was suffering from a violent cough, weight loss, and chronic fatigue. On March 28, 1944, Roosevelt saw a cardiologist who diagnosed him with high blood pressure, acute bronchitis, and congestive heart failure. However, Roosevelt was determined to see the war to its conclusion and to find an organization to replace the failed League of Nations. Whether motivated by personal ambition or unselfish dedication, Franklin Roosevelt chose to seek a fourth term. Therefore, on July 11, he sent a letter to Democrat party leaders announcing his intention to run for a fourth term.

However, Roosevelt's obvious health issues caused Democratic leaders, especially Catholics and unions, to oppose **Henry Wallace**, Roosevelt's vice-president during his third term. Most of these leaders realized that Roosevelt's running mate would become president sooner rather than later. The more moderate wing of the Democratic party viewed Wallace as both incompetent and too radical. They privately told Roosevelt that while they would support him, they would not support Wallace. They recommended Missouri Senator **Harry S. Truman**, who had become nationally known as the chairman of a Senate committee that ensured defense contractors charged fair prices for the materials they produced. Although Roosevelt liked Wallace, he reluctantly agreed to accept Truman as his running mate.

The Republicans nominated Thomas E. Dewey, the District Attorney from New York City who had narrowly missed the 1940 Republican nomination. Dewey actually performed better against Roosevelt than any of his other opponents,

Senator Harry S. Truman

winning nearly 46% of the popular vote. However, the still-popular Roosevelt, who had hidden his serious illness from the American people, carried 36 of 48 states, 53% of the popular vote, and won an electoral college landslide, 432 to 99.

However, American voters had elected a dying man. Franklin Roosevelt died less than three months into his fourth term. Harry S. Truman would become America's thirty-third president and see World War II to its conclusion.

The Battle of the Bulge

By December 1944, it seemed that Germany was on the verge of defeat. However, no one had told the Germans. No one expected that they could launch a massive counter-offensive. Thus, when they attacked on the morning of December 16, 1944, they achieved total surprise.

The First Panzer Division, consisting of German Tiger Tanks and 5,000 men, spearheaded the assault. They attacked the Allies' weakest point, a heavily wooded region in the **Ardennes Forest** of Belgium.

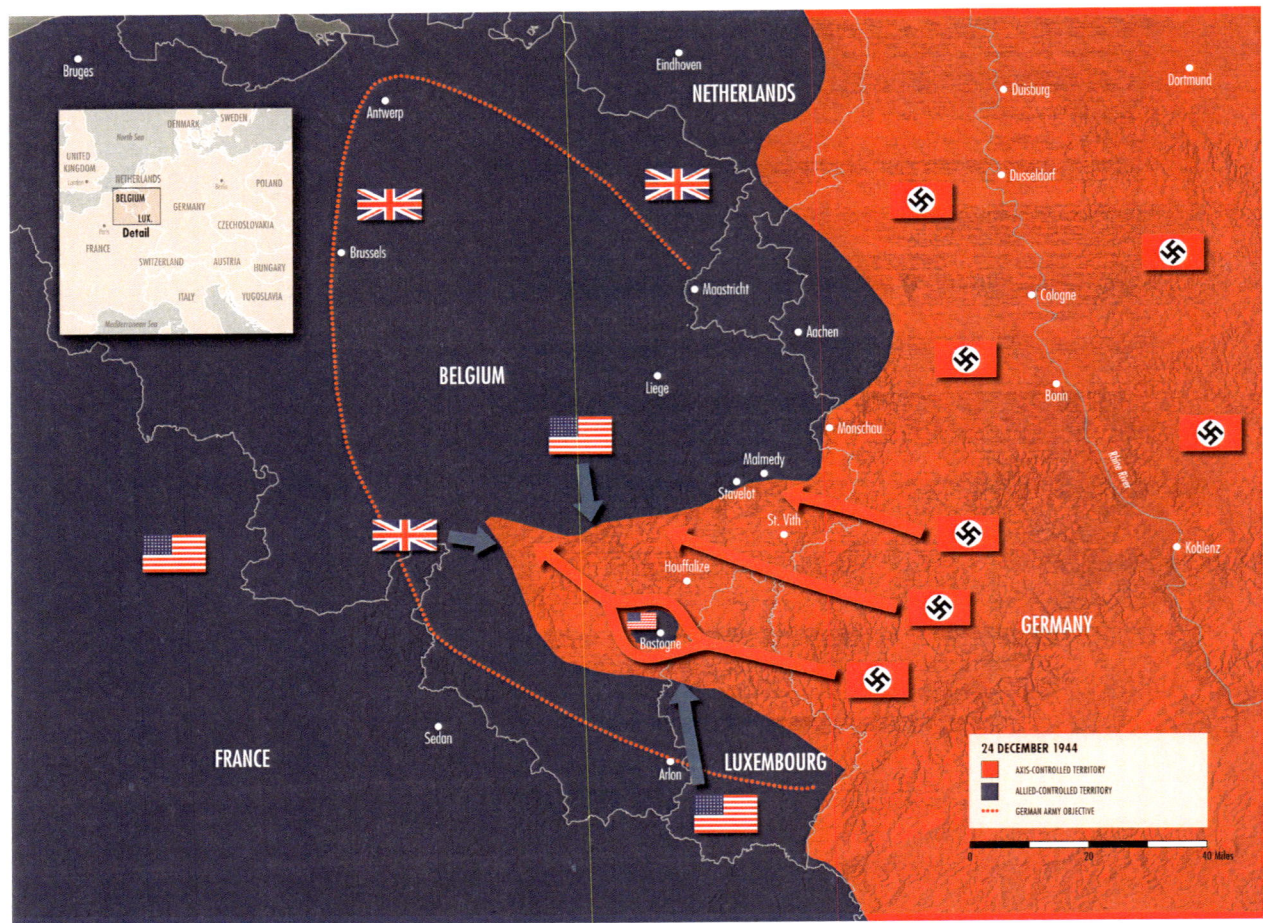

The Battle of the Bulge. (Courtesy of the National World War II Museum)

The German plan was clever. A successful attack would cut the Allied army in half, separating the British armies in the north from the American armies in the south. Then the Germans would charge into France and Luxembourg. The Germans also hoped to capture the strategic seaport of Antwerp, Belgium, through which almost all of the Allies' supplies and troops landed after crossing the English Channel.

The attack slammed into surprised Allied troops across a fifty-mile front and pushed part of the Allied battle line back sixty-five miles creating a "bulge" in the line. The Germans pushed the Allied 101st Airborne Division back, but the paratroopers dug in at **Bastogne**, where the larger enemy force surrounded them. General Eisenhower's Chief of Staff asked various Allied commanders if they could aid the 101st Airborne Division. General Patton replied, "Third Army will relieve them."

Having just defeated one German force, Patton raced his tanks and troops over treacherous winter roads, fighting German opposition, for over a hundred miles to reach Bastogne. Along the way, Patton learned that when the Germans demanded that the 101st surrender, their commanding officer, Brigadier General McAuliffe, replied, "Nuts." Patton smiled and said, "Any man who is that eloquent deserves to be relieved (rescued)." On Christmas Eve, the Third Army broke through the German encirclement relieving the Airborne warriors.

Over 600,000 American soldiers took part in the **Battle of the Bulge,** Germany's final offensive. It was the biggest and bloodiest battle American troops fought in the Second World War. By the end of January, German armies had lost all of the territory they had initially gained in the battle. Allied troops were now advancing on Germany from every side.

The Yalta Conference

In February 1945, President Roosevelt, sick and dying, met Churchill and Josef Stalin in **Yalta** in the Crimea. Roosevelt's seriously poor health likely affected some of the terrible concessions he made to Stalin.

At Yalta's opening session, Stalin demanded that post-war Germany be divided. Although Churchill opposed the idea, Roosevelt agreed to Stalin's demand. When Roosevelt requested that Stalin send Soviet troops to fight in the Pacific, Stalin agreed, but only after Germany's defeat. Stalin agreed that Poland and the other European countries occupied by Soviet troops would have free elections and be free from Soviet domination.

Roosevelt's worst concession was his guarantee that **every Soviet citizen and Eastern European refugee would be sent back to the Soviet Union, by force if necessary.** Many anti-Communist families had fled the Soviet Union during the years of German occupation. Stalin feared they would cause trouble and turn public opinion against him. Consequently, he was determined to return them to his control, together with millions of refugees who had been forced out of their homes during the war.

This plan of forced repatriation of perhaps 2,000,000 Russians was labeled "**Operation Keelhaul**." During the era of sailing ships, keelhauling was a form of punishment whereby a sailor was dragged under the keel (the bottom) of a ship. Since razor-sharp barnacles covered the keels of most ships, keelhauling invariably proved fatal. Operation Keelhaul was the name aptly chosen by American military commanders to demonstrate their fury and disgust for what they were forced to do. For almost thirty years, the American government covered up its shameful participation in Operation Keelhaul. Operation Keelhaul was a dishonorable action that cannot be denied or defended, nor should it ever be forgotten.

Churchill, Roosevelt, and Stalin at Yalta. It does not take a doctor to see that Roosevelt is dying. He is thin and his face is drawn. Stalin certainly recognized his weakness and took advantage of it. However, it was tens of millions of Eastern Europeans who would ultimately suffer for Roosevelt's concessions at Yalta.

Many historians believe that the concessions Roosevelt made at Yalta emboldened Stalin. These concessions allowed Stalin to enslave most of Eastern Europe. They would lead to the forty-five-year-long Cold War.

Goodbye, President Roosevelt

President Roosevelt returned from Yalta totally exhausted. His weakness was visible when he addressed Congress about the Yalta proceedings. Instead of standing at the podium as he always had, he remained seated. In early April, Roosevelt traveled to his favorite retreat in Warm Springs, Georgia. On April 12, 1945, he suffered a massive stroke and died. From the moment he was stricken with paralysis in 1921, he lived in a world of leg braces, pain, and the humbling acceptance of necessary assistance from helping hands in which all physically-challenged people dwell. He overcame these challenges to accomplish incredible feats.

Harry S. Truman, America's New President

Franklin Roosevelt was succeeded by a man remembered as one of America's most humble presidents, Harry S. Truman. Born in 1884, Truman graduated from high school in Independence, Missouri in 1901. He was subsequently employed as a bank clerk before working for ten years on the family farm. In 1917, when the United States entered the First World War, Truman helped establish the Missouri Field Artillery's 2nd Regiment. Before departing for Europe, Truman was promoted to the rank of captain. He saw military action in several battles in France. After the war, Truman returned to Independence and, in 1919, married Bess Wallace, with whom he had one child.

In 1922, with the help of the Kansas City Democratic machine, Truman was elected to public office, beginning his career in politics. In 1934, he was elected to the U. S. Senate and re-elected in 1940. Truman proved to be a hard working senator. As chairman of a Senate committee investigating National Defense, he gained national prominence, and achieved considerable success, ensuring that defense contractors charged fair prices for the goods they produced.

By the time the 1944 Democratic convention began, many of the Party's top leaders believed that Roosevelt would not live much longer. They realized that the man they chose as vice-president would soon be America's president. They picked Senator Truman to run as Roosevelt's vice-president.

On April 12, 1945, Harry S. Truman was sworn in as America's thirty-third president. He said he felt as though the moon and stars had fallen on him. During his first year in office, he would have to make many far-reaching decisions, including, perhaps, the most difficult that any president has ever faced.

President Truman's official White House portrait is considered to be one of the finest presidential portraits.

The Holocaust

During the War, the Allies had received reports of Nazi concentration camps. However, the truth was far worse than anyone had imagined. As Allied troops pushed deeper into Nazi-controlled areas, they

The gatehouse of Auschwitz (a Holocaust museum since 1947). This photograph shows the railroad tracks from outside the camp leading through the gate to an unloading ramp to the gas chambers. Of the 1.3 million human beings the Nazis sent to Auschwitz, they murdered 1.1 million including Maximilian Kolbe (August 14, 1941) and Edith Stein (August 9, 1942).

discovered not only concentration camps, but "death camps" where the Nazis had systematically murdered millions of men, women, and children. Although Hitler murdered several million Catholics, Poles, Russians, Gypsies, and anyone opposed to Nazism, he especially hated Jews who were his primary victims. Before the Allies stopped his murderous reign, Hitler and his supporters slaughtered over 6,000,000 Jews from various European countries. Many died in the gas chambers of these death camps, because of Hitler's need for revenge and his belief that they were racially inferior. The Nazis' mass murder of Europe's Jewish population is known as The Holocaust.

Hitler publicly began expressing hatred for the Jews in 1920. He blamed them for Germany's defeat in the first World War. He also claimed that Jews were racially inferior to other Europeans. As Holocaust historians have stated, "the goal of Nazi propaganda was to demonize Jews and to create a climate of hostility and indifference toward their plight." Sadly, this irrational propaganda inflamed the anti-Semitism of too many Germans. As a result, Jews began experiencing severe persecution once Hitler became Chancellor of Germany.

Beginning in 1933, the Nazis began a methodical campaign of hatred and violence against Germany's Jews, who at the time represented less than one percent of the population. In April, the Nazis began boycotting stores owned by Jews. In 1935, the Nazis enacted a number of laws that forced Jews out of jobs in government, education, the courts, even as art dealers and swimming teachers, in other words, many areas of public life.

Starting in 1937, the Nazis began a more violent stage of anti-Semitism that would eventually lead to the Holocaust. On the night of November 9-10, 1938, the Nazis launched a massive terror attack on Jewish shops and neighborhoods throughout Germany. About one hundred Jews died during the violence. The assault was quickly dubbed *Kristallnacht (Night of Broken Glass)* for all of the pieces of broken glass on the streets from the windows of synagogues, homes, and Jewish-owned businesses that the Nazis destroyed.

In 1939, Hitler ordered the mass arrest and deportation of Jews to forced labor camps. As the Nazis conquered other nations, their populations were subjected to Hitler's anti-Semitic policies as well. In 1941, Hitler ordered that many of the forced labor camps be converted into death camps for the murder of Jews and other "undesirables." Even at the end of the war, as the Nazis were losing, they continued to murder innocents in the camps.

Two notable saints died in Nazi death camps: Maximilian Kolbe and Edith Stein. On February 17, 1941, Maximilian Kolbe, a Polish Franciscan friar, was arrested by the Nazis for sheltering approximately 2,000 Jews in the friary as well as writing anti-Nazi literature. He was ultimately taken to Auschwitz, a death camp the Nazis built in Poland. In July 1941, Fr. Kolbe volunteered to be executed in the place of a married man with young children. Pope St. John Paul II canonized him in 1982.

Born in 1891, Edith Stein was a German Jew who became a Catholic. In 1934, she joined the Discalced Carmelite Order. Edith took the name Teresa Benedicta of the Cross. Because the Nazis considered her a Jew, they arrested her in 1942 and sent her to Auschwitz, where she died in the gas chamber. In 1998, Pope St. John Paul II canonized her.

Maximilian Kolbe

Germany Surrenders

Hitler had gambled his last resources at the Battle of the Bulge. The Nazi defeat meant that an Allied victory in the war was only a matter of time. In March 1945, Allied troops crossed the Rhine River into Germany. With the end in sight, the Allies pushed hard towards Berlin. By the middle of April, American troops were fifty miles west of the city. Soviet troops pushed towards Berlin from the East. On April 25, Soviet and American troops met for the first time at the Elbe River near Torgau, about seventy miles south of Berlin. On April 30, with Soviet troops less than a mile from his bunker, Hitler committed suicide rather than fall into their hands.

World War II in Europe ended on May 8, 1945, called **VE Day**, for Victory in Europe. German General Alfred Jodl, and Admiral Han-Georg von Friedberg had signed an unconditional surrender agreement at Reims, France the previous day. General Eisenhower, who had said he would never shake hands with a Nazi, did not attend the signing.

The War in the Pacific

Japanese Success After Pearl Harbor

In the months after Pearl Harbor, the Japanese had a number of successes. The Japanese seized **Guam** on December 10 and **Wake Island** on December 24. On January 2, 1942, **Manila**, the capital of the Philippines, surrendered to the Japanese. For the next three months, American and Filipino forces heroically defended the **Bataan Peninsula**. The island fortress of **Corregidor,** in Manila Bay, remained the last American-Filipino base.

In early March 1942, with the fall of Corregidor imminent, President Roosevelt ordered **General Douglas MacArthur**, the American commander of the Philippines, to escape to Australia. Roosevelt gave the order for two reasons. First, although Roosevelt personally did not like MacArthur, MacArthur was an American hero and a symbol of the American war effort. The Japanese planned to try MacArthur as a war criminal if they captured him. Second, MacArthur was an acknowledged military genius with an incredible understanding of Asia. His loss would severely damage the American war effort. Therefore, Roosevelt felt that he could not fall into Japanese hands.

On March 11, 1942, MacArthur and his family were evacuated from Corregidor on four PT (patrol torpedo) boats, enduring terrible seasickness and the threat of Japanese warships. They reached Mindanao two days later. From there, MacArthur and his party flew to Australia in a pair of bombers. They arrived in Melbourne on March 21. In Australia, MacArthur made a famous speech in which he promised the people of the Philippines, "I shall return." In early May, General Jonathan Wainwright was forced to surrender Corregidor.

Meanwhile, the British lost the battles for **Hong Kong**, the **Malay Peninsula**, and most of **Burma**. Japanese invaders captured most of the **Dutch East Indies**, one of the richest deposits of raw materials in the world. This victory meant that the Japanese had enough rubber, tin, and oil to wage a long war.

Typical of America's excellent military leaders during the War, Douglas MacArthur was born in 1880. He graduated first in his class from West Point in 1903. During the next years, he served in the Philippines and as an aide to President Theodore Roosevelt. In 1915, he was promoted to major and took part in the Vera Cruz operation. In 1917, he was promoted to colonel. The following year he was made a brigadier general. During World War I, he fought in several campaigns including the Marne and the Meuse-Argonne offensives. Over the next decades, he continued to be promoted and served in various capacities including superintendent of West Point. In 1937, he retired from the Army to become a military advisor to the government of the Philippines, a nation he loved nearly as much as the United States. In 1941, with the outbreak of the War, he was recalled to active duty and given command of the U.S. Army forces in the Far East. He served as Supreme Allied Commander in the Pacific from 1941 to 1945.

The Pacific Strategy

American military leaders believed that Japan would never surrender unless the Japanese home islands were invaded. However, Japan's empire consisted of thousands of tiny Pacific islands, including the *Carolines*, the *Solomons*, the *Marshalls*, and the *Gilberts*. American planners realized that capturing these islands, which the Japanese had had years to fortify, would be a terrible task. It would take years and cost hundreds of thousands of lives. Eventually, the American military developed two strategies.

MacArthur wanted to launch attacks aimed at retaking the Philippines. This would free the Filipino and American soldiers the Japanese held prisoner. The military knew that the Japanese were mistreating both soldiers and civilians under their control.

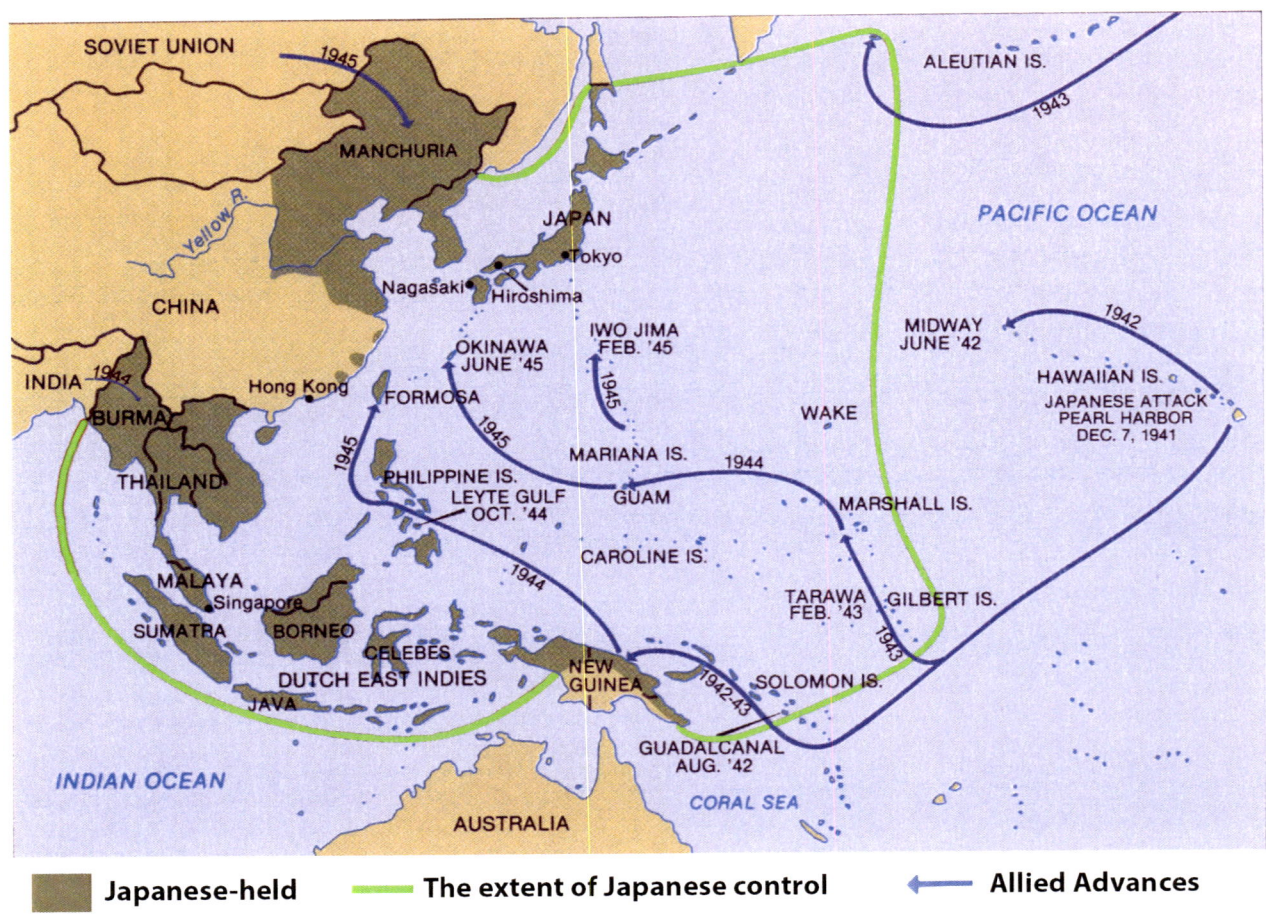

War in the Pacific 1942 through 1945

Admiral **Chester W. Nimitz**, the commander of the Pacific Fleet, favored a more direct attack on the Japanese home islands. This meant attacking the Japanese-controlled islands in the central Pacific. American Marines would then "island hop," or "leap frog," from one island group to another until they were close enough to invade the Japanese mainland. The idea was that instead of clearing the Japanese out of every island on the path to the Japanese mainland, Allied forces would only capture certain strategic islands, e.g. the *Carolines, Solomons, Marshalls*, and *Gilberts*, and bypass more strongly fortified positions. The Japanese soldiers on these islands would be cut off, unable to be resupplied and reinforced. They would eventually have no choice but to surrender. Marines would not need to take the time, nor face the loss of life dealing with these islands. Time and resources would be spent only on the most important island targets. Allied troops would hop over less strategic islands.

America's top commanders, the Joint Chiefs of Staff, decided to implement both plans in a two-pronged attack. MacArthur would go for the Philippines while Nimitz would go for the Japanese mainland. It was a bold and audacious plan. It also meant that American Marines would be fighting in the worst conditions imaginable. Not only would they be fighting an entrenched enemy, they would be fighting in jungles. They would fight the Japanese, constant rain, quicksand, mosquitoes, and tropical diseases. The experience would forge the Marines into the finest fighting force in the history of the world.

American Planes Bomb Tokyo

A few days after the Pearl Harbor attack, President Roosevelt assembled his top military advisers and told them that he wanted to bomb Japan as soon as possible. He believed that Americans needed a victory and that the surest way to raise morale was by bombing Japan. **Lieutenant Colonel Jimmy Doolittle** was ordered to organize and lead the bombing raid. Doolittle believed that medium bombers could fly off an aircraft carrier with enough fuel to bomb Japanese cities and then continue to landing fields in China not controlled by the Japanese.

On the morning of April 18, 1942, the "Doolittle Raiders" took off. The sixteen planes bombed **military targets** in Tokyo and other cities on the Japanese mainland. Although they achieved their goal, their success proved costly. Since the planes had to take off earlier than they planned, none of them had enough fuel to reach the landing fields in China. Seventy-seven of the eighty crewmen survived the initial raid; although the Japanese later killed or captured twelve of them. The last "Raider" died in 2019 at age 103.

As Roosevelt hoped, the Doolittle Raid did raise American morale. However, the most important result of the Doolittle Raid was proving to the Japanese that they were not safe

Chester Nimitz (1944). The background is one of the most unique in all military paintings as it shows the wreckage from the bombing of Pearl Harbor, a military defeat for Nimitz. Yet the painting also displays Nimitz' confidence that he could turn around the disaster, which he did.

from Allied air attacks. As Japan's Foreign Minister Tojo said, "The bombing of Tokyo produced a serious shock in Japan, as it proved the falsity of the military assurances of the inviolability of the Imperial capital."

Battle of the Coral Sea

Following their successes in the Philippines and the Dutch East Indies, the Japanese prepared to invade and conquer Australia. The American Navy met them in the first major sea battle of the war: **The Battle of the Coral Sea**. Waged from May 4 through May 8, 1942, the Battle of the Coral Sea became the first setback that Japanese forces encountered.

In preparation for the invasion of Australia, the Japanese planned to capture **Tulagi**, one of the Solomon Islands, and **Port Moresby** in New Guinea, which is close enough to Australia to launch an invasion. On May 4, the Japanese successfully invaded Tulagi. However, several of the smaller Japanese warships were damaged or sunk by air strikes from the American aircraft carrier *Yorktown*. Aware of nearby American carriers for the first time, the three Japanese carriers committed to the invasion sailed into the Coral Sea, off the east coast of Australia, searching for the American force. In the Coral Sea, American and Australian naval and air forces met the Japanese fleet. For the first time in history, a sea battle would be waged in which the opposing ships neither saw nor fired on each other. It was the **first all-aircraft** sea battle in history.

On May 7, carrier planes from both navies attacked. During the next two days, the U. S. sank one enemy carrier and badly damaged another. The Japanese sank the aircraft carrier *Lexington* and severely damaged the carrier *Yorktown;* however, *Yorktown* managed to creep back to Pearl Harbor for repairs. Meanwhile, the remaining two Japanese carriers sailed back to Japan for repairs.

Tactically, the Battle of the Coral Sea was a draw. However, the Japanese invasion of New Guinea had been stopped. The Allies had finally stopped Japan's southern advance and had protected Australia from invasion.

The Battle of Midway

Following the Battle of the Coral Sea, the Japanese hoped to force a showdown with the American Navy. They planned to lure the American carriers into a trap and destroy them, thus giving Japan control of the Pacific. The Japanese chose **Midway**, an island about 1,300 miles west of Hawaii, as the spot for the trap. However, unknown to the Japanese, American cryptographers had broken the Japanese code and knew the date and location of the trap. Thus, the Japanese trap turned into an American ambush.

In the pre-dawn darkness of June 4, 1942, at a point 240 miles northeast of Midway Island, the first wave of Japanese bomb-laden aircraft, their straining engines screaming in protest, struggled off the pitching decks of Admiral Nagumo's four aircraft carriers – the same four carriers that had attacked Pearl Harbor six months earlier – and clawed their way up into the slowly brightening skies. Their objective was to bomb Midway. The Japanese fleet, unaware of the proximity of an American carrier force, armed its planes for battle against *land installations* that morning.

However, the Japanese were cautious. Concerned that American carriers might be lurking just beyond the horizon, they employed two tactics. First, they sent out scout planes to search for the American carriers. Second, they kept half of their planes in reserve on deck, ready to attack if the American carriers were discovered. When the Japanese scouts finally discovered the American fleet, it had sailed close enough to the Japanese fleet to launch an attack.

The first American planes to attack the Japanese fleet were fifteen torpedo bombers from the carrier *Hornet*. The Japanese destroyed all fifteen planes. Two more attacks closely followed the initial attack. In these three attacks, forty-one American planes attacked the Japanese fleet, but inflicted no damage upon the enemy.

Admiral Nagumo now knew that at least three American carriers faced him. He decided to rearm his planes to attack them. Just as he finished re-arming his planes, the planes that had attacked Midway returned. Many were damaged. All were low on fuel. Nagumo faced a difficult decision. Should he launch the strike against the U. S. carriers immediately, and thus risk losing the returning planes running low on fuel and about to plunge into the sea; or should he postpone the launch against the American ships and recover the returning planes? Nagumo decided to recover his circling planes and launch the attack immediately thereafter. He believed this could be accomplished in five minutes.

Japanese planes bomb Midway Island by John C. Hamilton

Who could have dreamed that the tide of battle in the Pacific would turn completely in just five minutes? Three squadrons of American dive bombers, one from each of the American carriers, which had been launched an hour apart, had had no success up to this point in finding the Japanese fleet. These three flying squadrons, individually groping toward a constantly moving target of unknown position, suddenly saw each other, and at the same exact moment, also sighted the Japanese fleet. Miraculously, it was the most perfectly coordinated air attack in history.

For one frozen moment of time, far below the American dive bombers lay the four Japanese carriers, their decks crisscrossed with gasoline hoses fueling over 250 aircraft waiting to take off. The dive bombers attacked! Five minutes later, only one Japanese carrier remained undamaged. Three were burning, twisted masses of metal, all but hidden by the thick black smoke rising from the wreckage of the once-proud fleet. In five short minutes, Japan's decades-long dreams of conquest had died.

During the final two days of the battle, Japanese planes and a submarine sank the carrier *Yorktown* and American planes sank the last Japanese carrier.

The Battle of Midway proved to be the turning point of the war in the Pacific. It stopped Japanese expansion in the Pacific and allowed the Allies to take the offensive. The Japanese opportunity for victory had been lost forever. Though Japan would continue to fight for more than three bloody years, the loss of its carriers and pilots proved irreplaceable. The Battle of Midway has been called the most stunning and decisive victory in the history of naval warfare.

U.S. Dauntless Aircraft Dive on Japanese Carriers by John Hamilton. After searching in vain for the Japanese fleet and almost out of fuel, the dive bomber pilots saw the entire Japanese fleet below. The Japanese fighter cover, which should have been above the carriers protecting them, were at sea-level destroying the American torpedo-bombers. The dive bombers attacked just at the moment when the carriers were preparing to launch Japan's most experienced pilots. The Japanese carriers Akagi, Kaga, and Soryu were destroyed. Japan could never replace its pilots or its carriers.

The USS *Yorktown* as seen through the periscope of Japanese submarine I-168. *Yorktown* had been seriously damaged at the Battle of Coral Sea but managed to sail to Midway. However, she was critically damaged on June 4. In this painting, the fires burning on board *Yorktown* and its escort the destroyer USS *Hammann* are seen through the periscope of a Japanese submarine. On June 6, the I-168 launched several torpedoes, two of which hit *Yorktown* and one *Hammann*. The destroyer sank in four minutes while the *Yorktown* sank the next day.

Guadalcanal

Japan's defeat at Midway forced the Japanese high command to devise an alternate strategy. They decided to concentrate on the Southwest Pacific. Since they had lost four of their carriers, they needed to replace the ships with island bases. The Japanese thought that when all of their naval and air bases were operational, they could sever Australia's communication and supply lines to the Allied forces. A Japanese airbase in the southern Solomon Islands would make an attack on northern Australia feasible. When the Japanese began building an airfield on the island of **Guadalcanal** in the Solomons, the First Marine Division attacked.

On August 7, 1942, the Marines landed on Guadalcanal for what would be some of the heaviest fighting of the war. The Marines quickly moved inland and captured the Japanese airstrip, but the enemy counter-attacked, trying to recapture the airfield. The tide of the deadly battle over the Guadalcanal airstrip shifted back and forth for several months, with the final verdict very much in doubt. In December, the Japanese decided to withdraw. By February 9, 1943, the United States could claim victory in the Guadalcanal campaign, when the last Japanese troops were evacuated from the island.

The Battle of Guadalcanal was America's first Pacific island offensive. The "island-hopping strategy" had begun. Each island that American soldiers captured became a new base of operations and a stepping stone toward the Japanese home islands.

The Gilbert Islands and Tarawa

The Gilbert Islands were the next Japanese-held island group which the Marines needed to capture. Their main target was **Tarawa**. Japanese strategists, aware of Tarawa's importance, had heavily fortified the atoll with 4,800 soldiers, more than fifty artillery pieces, and over a dozen tanks. During the first hour of the invasion that began at dawn on November 20, 1943, Allied war ships hammered Tarawa with thousands of shells and carrier-based planes bombed and strafed the atoll.

Of the 4,800 Japanese soldiers sent to defend Tarawa, only seventeen survived. The rest died fighting. American losses were 1,009 killed and 2,101 wounded. The huge number of American casualties outraged worried Americans. Clearly, the Japanese would fight to the death for every inch of ground.

The Battles for Saipan and Guam

The Mariana Island chain lies just east of the Philippines in the Philippine Sea. The three principal islands in the Marianas are Guam, Saipan, and Tinian. If Allied forces captured these islands, the Japanese home islands would be within range of American long-range bombers. Knowing this, the Japanese had heavily fortified and garrisoned the three islands.

On June 5, 1944, a fleet of over 500 American warships sailed from Pearl Harbor for Saipan. On June 13, American warships began pounding the island's defenses with a massive naval bombardment.

Despite this "softening up," American marines met very heavy resistance from Saipan's 31,000 defenders when they landed two days later. Nevertheless, American soldiers established and held a beachhead. Over the next few days the marines pushed inland.

Advised of the strong invasion force, Admiral Soemu Toyoda, the Japanese Combined Fleet Commander, ordered an attack on the U.S. Fleet at Saipan with his fleet including nine carriers and five battleships. The Japanese force engaged the American fleet of fifteen carriers and nine battle ships. On June 19-20, the American and Japanese navies met at the Battle of the Philippine Sea, the last great carrier battle of the war. Because the Japanese had lost so many planes, ships, and men in early contests, they were outnumbered, without experienced pilots, and lacked many critical supplies. As a result, the battle was a tremendous victory for the American fleet. In addition to shooting down over six hundred Japanese planes while losing less than a quarter of that number, the American forces sank three Japanese carriers, including the *Shokaku*, the last of the six aircraft carriers that had attacked Pearl Harbor.

The defeat at the Battle of the Philippine Sea meant that the Japanese on Saipan were cut off and could not realistically hold the island. However, they were determined to fight to the last man. On July 7, one of the most ghastly incidents of the war occurred when the Japanese commander ordered a final suicide attack with his last 4,000 men, including his wounded and the Japanese civilians on the island. This horrible attack resulted in the deaths of nearly all the attackers as well as nearly 1,000 dead and wounded Americans. Finally, on July 9, the American commander on Saipan declared the battle for the island to be over. The Allies had lost 3,426 killed and 10,364 wounded. Almost the entire Japanese garrison had perished along with perhaps 22,000 civilians, many of whom had committed suicide.

Once Saipan was secured, Allied forces prepared to invade the other two major islands in the Marianas. On July 21, 36,000 American soldiers came ashore on Guam, where more than 22,000 Japanese prepared to oppose them. The Americans secured Guam on August 10th. However, less than 500 Japanese actually surrendered.

On July 24th, Marines landed on Tinian and gained control of the island after six days, although many of the Japanese soldiers continued to hide in the jungle for several months. U.S. Seabees and other construction battalions (CBs) soon cleared foliage from the three islands and quickly began building landing strips for the American bombers that were destined to attack the island bases that lay closer to the Japanese home islands and the heart of the Japanese Empire of the Rising Sun.

Raising the Flag on Iwo Jima. Six Marines raised the American flag atop Mount Suribachi in the early afternoon after the mountaintop was captured. Sadly, three of the six Marines in the photograph were later killed in action during the battle. The photograph was taken by Joe Rosenthal, reprinted in thousands of publications, and later used in 1954 as the model for the Marine Corps War Memorial which was dedicated to all Marines who died in service since 1775.

Iwo Jima

About 750 miles south of Tokyo lies the eleven-square-mile island of **Iwo Jima**. The highest point on the island is the 550-foot Mount Suribachi, an extinct volcano. In September 1944, General Tadamichi Kuribayashi arrived on Iwo Jima with 21,000 troops and began constructing a labyrinth of tunnels and caves within Mount Suribachi and around the island. He carefully camouflaged his positions and constructed them to allow weapons to be fired in any direction. The Japanese also constructed two airfields and a radar system which could detect approaching American bombers and alert Japanese fighters. Kuribayashi planned to fight to the last man and inflict as many casualties on the invasion force as possible. He told his troops that if each of them killed ten of the enemy before they died themselves, the Americans might be reluctant to invade Japan.

For 74 days before the invasion, Allied bombers carpeted the island with tons of bombs. However, because of the amazing subterranean tunnels and caves, the explosives did little damage. The invasion of Iwo Jima began on February 19, 1945. The first wave of Marines to land on the volcanic ash beach encountered no resistance. However, as the first reconnaissance patrols crept forward, they encountered heavy rifle and machine gun fire from the hidden tunnels and bunkers on Mount Suribachi.

On February 23, six fearless Americans raised an American flag on Mount Suribachi. The photograph of the flag-raising became one of the most famous photos in American history. That photo would become a bronze statue, the **Marine Corps Memorial**.

Committed to die fighting, Japanese defenders made incredible use of their underground network. Popping suddenly to the surface, often in the midst of a Marine unit, they would fire, kill some Marines, then quickly disappear. Most of the 21,000 Japanese were killed during the battle. Only about 200 were captured.

6,821 Americans were killed and 19,217 were wounded. Iwo Jima is the only land engagement where Americans suffered greater casualties than the Japanese.

The Battle for Okinawa

Okinawa, located only 340 miles from the Japanese home islands, was to be the final island captured before the planned invasion of Japan. Therefore, the Japanese military was determined that under no circumstances was it to fall into Allied hands. Because of the intensity of the fighting, some of the bloodiest of the war, and the terrible loss of life, including an incredible number of Japanese civilians, the battle for Okinawa has been called "**the typhoon of steel**."

Photograph from the Department of Defense showing U.S. Marines fighting for control of a ridge on Okinawa in May 1945. Note the complete devastation of the island.

The invasion of Okinawa began on April 1, 1945. The Japanese troops knew they could not win, but they could kill or injure thousands of Americans before they finally were defeated. That would mean fewer Americans to invade Japan in the months that lay ahead. The bitterly fought battles between the Japanese and Americans continued until June 17 when American soldiers officially secured the island.

Okinawa had been captured at a terrible price. About 20,000 Americans had been killed, along with nearly 100,000 Japanese. Perhaps as many as 150,000 Okinawan civilians, almost half the population, were killed. The island had become a vast wasteland.

The Battles for the Philippines

Meanwhile, in the South, MacArthur was carrying out his prong of the American plan: capture the Philippines. General MacArthur's troops had been fighting a jungle war against the Japanese in New Guinea for two years. Because the Japanese were well entrenched, those years were filled with one bloody encounter after another. However, in October 1944, MacArthur turned his attention to liberating the Philippines.

MacArthur's campaign to free the Philippines began on October 20, 1944, when American amphibious units landed on Leyte Island, a strategic Philippine island. The American landing caught the Japanese soldiers by surprise. A few hours later, MacArthur came ashore, fulfilling his promise to return to the Philippines. The landing on Leyte Island was a brilliant tactic. By striking at the heart of the Philippines, the U. S. military succeeded in splitting the 250,000-man Japanese force. That meant the troops under MacArthur would be confronting smaller enemy forces.

Three days later, in an attempt to crush the liberation of the Philippines, the Japanese navy launched a massive attack with almost all of its remaining ships. In a series of battles, generally called the **Battle of Leyte Gulf**, fought between October 23 and October 26, the U. S. Navy destroyed what remained of the Japanese navy. By the end of the battle, the Japanese fleet, once one of the strongest in the world, had virtually ceased to exist.

By the end of 1944, Leyte was under American control. As 1945 began, Douglas MacArthur's troops had destroyed most Japanese communications. The Americans blocked the Bataan Peninsula to forestall a Japanese retreat. On February 3, 1945, the desperate battle for Manila began. The battle proved costly in lives and in property as American troops fought to free the Philippine people. When the city finally fell to the Allies on March 3, the once-beautiful city of Manila was in ruins. On July 5, 1945, MacArthur declared victory in the Philippines. They were free from Japanese control.

The Potsdam Conference

In July 1945, Truman, Churchill, and Stalin met at Potsdam, a suburb of Berlin. During the **Potsdam Conference**, an election was held in Great Britain, and Winston Churchill was defeated. Clement Attlee became the new Prime Minister. At Potsdam, Truman discovered the concessions Roosevelt had made to Stalin. The three leaders, with the approval of Chiang Kai-shek, agreed that Japan had to surrender unconditionally. The Japanese were advised that if they failed to unconditionally surrender, they would suffer massive destruction and loss of life.

Map of the Philippines

The Atom Bomb

With the capture of Okinawa and the destruction of the Japanese fleet at Leyte Gulf the Allied victory was certain. However, Japan refused to surrender. America's military leaders informed president Truman that they believed that Japan would not surrender unless their homeland was invaded and conquered. As American military strategists prepared plans to invade Japan, they began to calculate its incredible cost in both American lives and Japanese civilians. The battles on Tarawa, Iwo Jima, and especially Okinawa had demonstrated that the Japanese military would fight to the last man to defend their homeland. Moreover, they were willing to sacrifice their civilian population as well. **American strategists told Truman that they believed it would take at least eighteen months to conquer Japan during which the United States and its allies could suffer as many as** *one million more casualties*! However, perhaps there was another way to defeat Japan without invading her.

Since late 1941, American scientists had been working on the most secret project of the war. Code-named the **Manhattan Project**, its goal was the creation of a nuclear weapon. **Nuclear fission**, the splitting of the atom, had been discovered by two German scientists in December 1938. Noted physicist **Albert Einstein** wrote a letter to President Roosevelt in 1939 warning him that a new type of bomb, an **atomic bomb,** which utilized the technology of nuclear fission, would be extremely powerful. Fearing that Adolf Hitler would begin researching and producing such bombs, Roosevelt ordered further investigation into and development of nuclear weapons and the stockpiling of **uranium**. Uranium, a highly radioactive element, in its *enriched*, or processed, form is used in atomic bombs. Uranium could also be transformed into **plutonium**, which could also be used in atom bombs.

On July 16, 1945, Manhattan Project scientists tested a nuclear device at Los Alamos, New Mexico. It detonated with the explosive force of 20,000 tons of TNT. The shock wave was felt over 100 miles away.

On July 26, the Allied leaders issued the "Potsdam Declaration" in which they called "upon the government of Japan to proclaim now the unconditional surrender of all Japanese armed forces." They went on to warn that, "the alternative for Japan is prompt and utter destruction." The Japanese ignored this dire warning.

President Truman now faced perhaps the most difficult decision any president has ever had to make. Dropping an atomic bomb would kill thousands of Japanese civilians, but save perhaps 1,000,000 Americans and countless other Japanese civilians. In the end, Truman felt that he had no choice. Far more lives would be lost by not using the bomb than by using it. Truman believed that only by using this terrible new weapon would the proud, militaristic Japanese realize that continued resistance was futile.

Dropping the atomic bomb was highly controversial in America among civilians as well as the military, both then and now. President Truman asked those who objected to his decision what he was supposed to say to American mothers who would ask him why he allowed tens of thousands of American boys to die in battles with Japan, when he could have saved them by dropping a bomb which would end further killing of innocent young American men and women.

On August 6, 1945, the **Enola Gay**, a B-29 bomber commanded by Colonel Paul Tibbets, dropped the first nuclear bomb. Scant seconds later, 80,000 Japanese residents of **Hiroshima** were dead and 90,000 more were injured. Japan still did not surrender. Three days later, on August 9, another B-29 bomber, *Bockscar*, was tasked with dropping a second, more powerful bomb, on **Kokura**, a city of 130,000 people, where the Japanese operated one of their largest munition's plants. However, once the bomber reached Kokura, weather conditions made bombing the munition's plant impossible. With anti-aircraft fire becoming intense, *Bockscar's* pilot turned his plane for his backup target, **Nagasaki**, Japan's most Catholic city. Another 80,000 Japanese perished.

Albert Einstein (1944) by Max Westfield. Einstein realized the terrible force of atomic weapons. He is credited with saying: "I know not with what weapons World War III will be fought, but World War IV will be fought with sticks and stones."

Finally, on August 10, the Japanese offered to surrender, if their emperor were allowed to keep his throne. The Allies agreed, but insisted that the emperor be subject to the orders of the Supreme Allied Commander. On August 14, **V-J Day** (Victory in Japan), Japan accepted the Allied terms of surrender. World War II was finally over.

The remains of the Roman Catholic Cathedral in Nagasaki, Japan. Construction of the original Cathedral began in 1895 and until its destruction in 1945, it was one of the largest Christian structures in Asia. Amazingly, although the atomic bomb detonated less than 2,000 feet from the cathedral and killed everyone attending Mass inside, parts of the cathedral remain standing.

Answer the following questions:

1. How did the Allies' actions in the aftermath of World War I lead to World War II?

2. "Nazi" is a shortened form of what longer name?

3. How did the Nazis appeal to the people of Germany?

4. In what year was Adolf Hitler elected Chancellor of Germany?

5. How did Hitler consolidate his power in Germany?

6. Who was Benito Mussolini?

7. What were the Axis Powers?

8. How did most Americans feel about becoming involved in European affairs during the 1930s? Why did they hold this position? How did Congress respond to Americans' feelings?

9. Describe Japan's foreign policy during the 1930s. How did this policy alarm the United States? How did it bring the two nations into conflict?

10. How did World War II begin in Europe?

11. What was the Battle of Britain? Name two ways in which it was significant.

12. Why did Hitler invade the Soviet Union in June 1941?

13. What two factions dominated the Republican Party during the 1940 Presidential Election? Which faction prevailed? Who was the Republican candidate for president in 1940?

14. What is the Lend-Lease Act? Why did Congress approve it? What were the objections to the Act?

15. What was the Atlantic Charter? Name at least four ways in which it was superior to the Treaty of Versailles.

16. Describe some of the steps the United States took to curtail Japanese expansion in 1940 and 1941.

17. When did the Japanese attack Pearl Harbor? Why did they attack? Why did they attack when they did?

18. Why should American commanders have been more prepared for the attack on Pearl Harbor?

19. Was the attack on Pearl Harbor successful? What could have made it more successful?

20. How were Japanese-Americans treated during the War? How did Japanese-Americans perform in combat roles?

21. Who were the Tuskegee Airmen? How was their combat performance during the war?

22. Name at least four new types of weapons or combat devices developed during the War.

23. How did World War II finally end the Great Depression?

24. Who are Winston Churchill and Neville Chamberlain? What role did they play during World War II?

25. What was the Battle of the Atlantic?

26. What event seems to have convinced Franklin Roosevelt to seek a third term?

27. What was "Operation Dynamo?"

28. Who was the leader of China during World War II?

29. Who was the leader of the Soviet Union during World War II?

30. For what is Colonel Benjamin O. Davis Jr. most well known?

31. What was the American military strategy to win World War II?

32. By 1942, what were the major Allied Powers? Which nation led the Allies and provided the most material and money, and the second most soldiers?

33. Who was the Supreme Allied Commander in Europe? How was he an unusual choice and how was he an excellent choice?

34. Why did the Allies choose to invade North Africa rather than Europe?

35. What happened at the Battle of Kasserine Pass?

36. What was the most important statement that President Roosevelt issued at the Casablanca Conference?

37. What was the date of the D-Day invasion? What was its code name? Where did the Allies land?

38. Name at least four European nations that remained neutral during World War II.

39. What was the Battle of the Bulge?

40. What was Operation Keelhaul? Where was the agreement made for this operation?

41. What was the Holocaust?

42. What was the American strategy for victory over Japan? Who developed the strategy?

43. What was the significance of bombing Tokyo in April 1942?

44. What was the Battle of the Coral Sea? Why was it important?

45. What was the Battle of Midway? Why was it important?

46. What was the Battle of Leyte Gulf? What is its significance?

47. Why did President Truman say he dropped the atomic bomb on Japan?

48. On what two cities were atomic bombs dropped?

49. Where was the photo taken upon which the Marine Corps Monument is based?

50. What was the *Kristallnacht*? From where did the name originate?

Identify the following:

1. Rosie the Riveter
2. G. I. Bill
3. Nisei
4. 442nd Combat Team
5. George S. Patton
6. Douglas MacArthur
7. Chester Nimitz
8. Manhattan Project
9. Battle of Okinawa
10. Battle of Saipan

CHAPTER 31

The Beginning of the Cold War

1945-1960

U.S. Army Breakthrough at Chipyong-ni (Korea). The Cold War was never really "cold." Freedom-loving peoples fought Communist aggression with American help all over the world. In some places, actual wars were waged. The above image depicts the Battle of Chipyong-ni. In February 1951, an American infantry unit, accompanied by some French and Dutch troops, was cut off and surrounded by an overwhelming force of Chinese communist soldiers in the narrow Korean valley of Chipyong-ni. The Communists held the commanding ridges, while the Americans, isolated far from their main force, used a ring of lower hills in the valley as a defensive perimeter. For more than three days the GI's held off the Chinese. The painting shows action from the fourth day when an American armored unit broke through to rescue the trapped Americans. The Americans and their allies were able to break out of the deadly trap and rejoin the main force. The battle was a huge victory for the American forces as they inflicted between 1,000 and 2,000 casualties on the Chinese while suffering only about 300.

America Becomes a World Leader

During the forty-four months American soldiers fought and died for world freedom, the American civilian workforce out-produced every other nation. America became the world's preeminent nation. With the creation of the atomic bomb, the United States had become the world's first "superpower." However, unlike other powerful nations that had sought to build great empires, the United States sought only peace. During the war, Churchill and Roosevelt had espoused certain values which they had enshrined in the Atlantic Charter. The United States now sought to create an organization that would replace the failed League of Nations and, hopefully, work towards world peace.

President Truman signs the United Nations charter on Aug. 8, 1945 as Secretary of State James Byrnes looks on.

The United Nations

During the period after World War I, good leaders of war-torn nations began thinking of ways to build lasting peace. President Woodrow Wilson had decided that a worldwide League of Nations would promote peace and reduce the probability of another world war. However, the League of Nations had failed, largely due to the mistakes Wilson made. Thus, when Roosevelt sought to create a new organization, he was determined to avoid Wilson's mistakes. Most people realized that the League had failed because the United States had never joined. One reason that the United States had not joined was because Wilson had failed to include Republicans in the Versailles Treaty negotiation process.

At the Yalta Conference, in February 1945, Roosevelt, Churchill, and Stalin scheduled a conference to create a "**United Nations**" in San Francisco in April, 1945. Roosevelt died in April, but the San Francisco meeting convened as scheduled on April 25th, attended by delegates from fifty nations. Among the American representatives was a leading Republican senator, **Arthur Vandenburg** of Michigan. In June, the delegates approved a charter that would be presented to every participating nation for approval. Vandenburg's participation led to the U. S. Senate voting 89 to 2, on July 28, to approve the treaty creating the United Nations, the **UN**. President Truman signed the United Nations charter on Aug. 8, 1945.

The UN would not officially exist until the United States, the Soviet Union, England, China, and France had ratified it. A majority of the other forty-five nations which signed the original charter needed to ratify the final Charter as well. On October 24, 1945, everything had been accomplished, and the United Nations officially came into existence.

The UN contains six principal divisions: General Assembly; Security Council; Economic and Social Council; Trusteeship Council; International Court of Justice; and Secretariat. The General Assembly and the Security Council are the two most important divisions. The **General Assembly** includes representatives from every member country, each possessing one vote, but does not pass laws. The General Assembly serves as a forum for discussion. It considers principles of cooperation in maintaining international peace and security.

The **Security Council** is comprised of eleven members. The "Big Five," that is, the United States, Great Britain, Russia (in 1945 the Soviet Union), France, and China are permanent members. The General Assembly chooses the six other members. The Security Council has authority to examine and investigate international disputes, encourage peaceful settlements, and take military action against an aggressor nation. The Security Council can act only if at least seven members, including all of the "Big Five," vote to do so. Thus, the "Big Five" essentially can veto the actions of the Security Council. Because of this veto, some Americans criticize the effectiveness of the UN to stop Chinese and Soviet/Russian aggression. Others believe the UN even hinders good nations from helping nations who need protection.

On the other hand, people note that over its history, the United Nations has played a significant role in feeding starving people, treating the sick, and trying to control the illnesses and disasters that confront the world. Due to these and other various diplomatic functions, these people believe that this type of world organization is necessary in an increasingly interconnected world.

The Beginning of the Cold War: Stalin Seizes Eastern Europe

In the Atlantic Charter, Churchill and Roosevelt declared that no territorial changes would be made without the consent of the affected people and that self-determination was a right of all people. During the war, at various conferences with Churchill and Roosevelt, Josef Stalin had promised to abide by these principles. He promised that Eastern European nations would have free elections and that Soviet troops would withdraw from the land that they had occupied. However, Stalin lied.

Since at least 1919, the start of the Soviet-Polish War, Josef Stalin had wanted to conquer Poland. In August 1920, at the Battle of Warsaw, the Poles decisively defeated the Soviet army and drove them back

The Miracle of the Vistula by Jerzy Kossak. Many Poles believe the Blessed Mother played a role in the Polish Army's 1920 victory over the Red Army at the Battle of Warsaw, known in Poland as "The Miracle of the Vistula," (the River that runs through Warsaw). Poles point out that it was not a mere coincidence that the battle was fought on August 15 the Feast of the Assumption. Thus, Our Lady overlooks the battlefield from a cloud. She commands the Polish army that had saved Europe from the Muslims during the 17th century to rally and save Europe and Poland from the Communists in the 20th century. In the center of the painting, 27-year-old Father Ignacy Skorupka, his Crucifix upraised, leads Polish soldiers and boy scouts into battle against fur-capped Russians.

into the Soviet Union, saving Eastern Europe from Communist oppression for more than two decades. Poland remained free until September 1, 1939, when Germany invaded her.

In 1939, Stalin annexed much of eastern Poland as part of his deal with Hitler. Stalin treated the Poles as brutally as Hitler. In April 1940, Stalin's secret police murdered about 22,000 Polish officers and concealed them in a mass grave in the Katyn Forest. Although Stalin tried to blame the **Katyn Forest Massacre** on the Nazis, the truth came out. Stalin believed that by murdering the Polish army leaders, the Poles would not be able to oppose him. Nevertheless, the Poles assembled an underground army that fought the foreign occupation.

When the Soviet Army reached the outskirts of Warsaw in August 1944, the Polish Home Army was already rebelling against the Nazis. Rather than taking this opportunity to defeat the Germans, Stalin ordered the Soviet army to halt outside of Warsaw and make no attempt to capture the city or aid the Poles. The outnumbered, poorly-armed Poles proved no match for the Nazis. The Soviet army waited for two weeks, watching the Germans crush the Polish rebellion.

Churchill and Roosevelt begged Stalin to intervene, but he refused. The Western Allies tried to drop ammunition, weapons, and food into Warsaw; however, Stalin refused to permit Allied aircraft to refuel at his airbases. Not until Warsaw had been totally destroyed and all its defenders killed did Stalin occupy the city. Stalin used the German army to ensure there would be no Polish military force left to oppose Soviet occupation.

Atlee, Truman, and Stalin at Potsdam. Following the defeat of the Nazis, England's Labour Party demanded that Parliamentary elections be held. Churchill was forced to resign as Prime Minister; however, he fully expected to become Prime Minister in the new government when the Conservatives, his Party, received the majority of seats in the new Parliament following the elections. In one of the most stunning upsets in the history of democratic elections, the majority of candidates elected to Parliament were members of the Labour Party. Clement Atlee, the leader of the Labour Party subsequently became Prime Minister of England.

Meanwhile, in 1920, a Polish boy was born. He grew up during the two decades of Polish freedom. He saw the horrors of the Nazi occupation. The Nazis almost captured him, but he hid in the bishop's palace and escaped. He lived under Communist oppression for decades. His name was **Karol Jozef Wojtyla**. One day he would become **Pope John Paul II** and lead the world in defeating the Communism that enslaved his people.

At the **Potsdam Conference**, Truman and Prime Minister Clement Atlee agreed to give Stalin most of eastern Poland, which would become part of the Soviet Union. In exchange, Stalin agreed that the rest of Poland could hold free elections. However, once again, Stalin lied. In what would become the pattern for Communist-controlled Eastern Europe, Stalin set up a **puppet government** under Boleslaw Bierut. Bierut, a Communist agent, answered to and took orders from Stalin.

Historians have questioned whether Truman could have done more to oppose Stalin's annexation and eventual control of Poland at Potsdam. Sadly, probably not. By 1945, the Soviet army had completely occupied Poland. Stalin was not going to leave peacefully. That meant the only alternative was forcing out the Soviets, that is, war with the Soviets. The United States had just endured the most horrific war in history. Open war with the Soviets was simply not an option at that point. However, the annexation of Poland certainly emboldened Stalin.

Bulgaria, Romania, Hungary, Czechoslovakia, and the eastern part of Germany had surrendered to Soviet armies. Soviet troops remained in each of these "liberated" nations as an occupation force. These Eastern Europeans had exchanged Nazi oppression for Communist oppression. Soviet armies helped

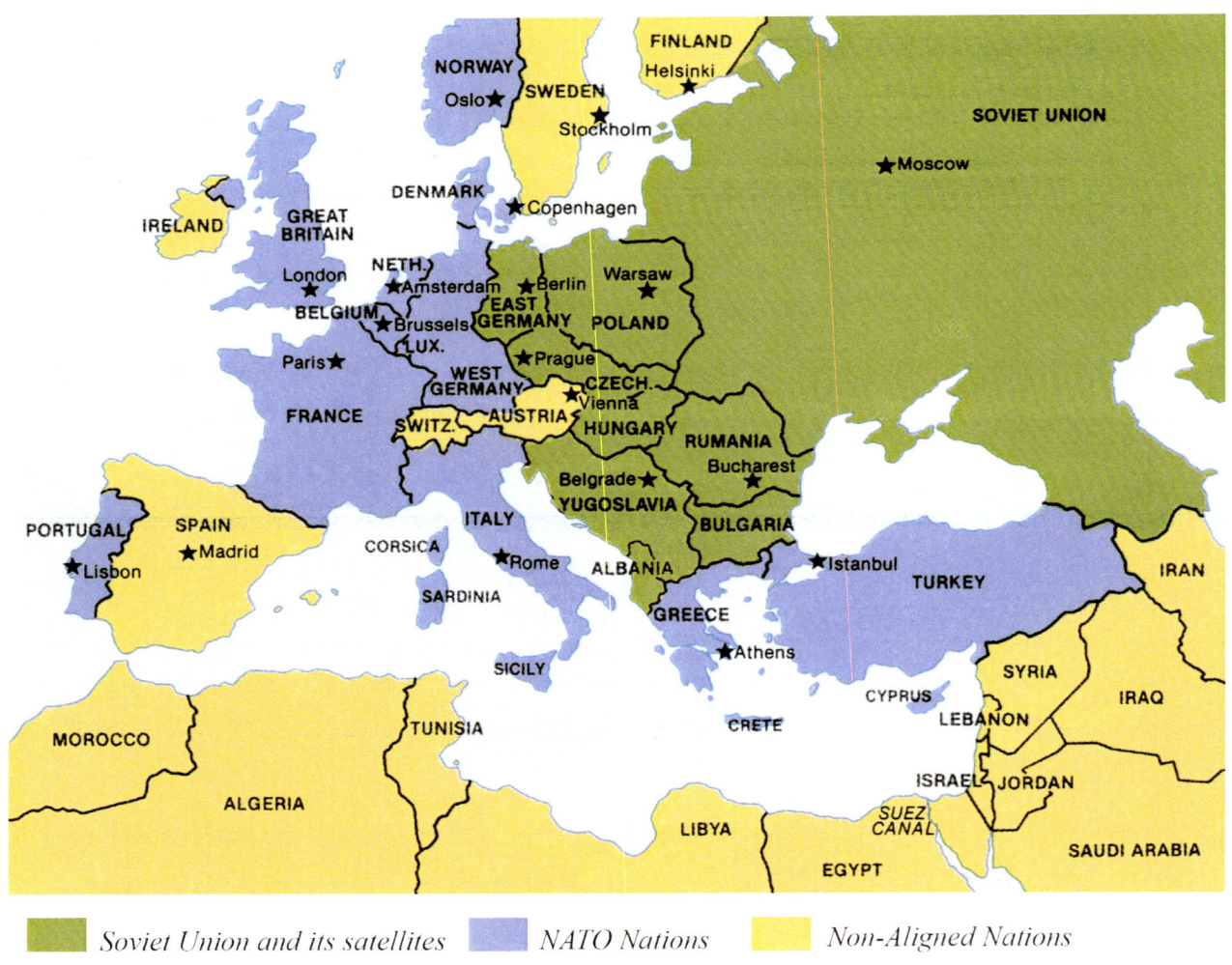

Soviet Union and its satellites *NATO Nations* *Non-Aligned Nations*

establish and grow local Communist parties. By 1949, Communists had taken control of all of these post-war governments. Rigged elections in these nations created the illusion that Communists had legitimately gained power. Communist "victories" resulted from manipulation, force, and fraud. Eastern European countries remained free in name only. Totally dominated by the Soviet Union, they were labeled **Soviet satellites**.

The United States' role as leader of the **free world** meant opposing the Soviet Union, whose leaders were determined to control and enslave the people of the world. For the next four and a half decades, the United States and its allies and the Soviet Union and its puppets fought a "**Cold War.**" Instead of guns and bullets, the Cold War weapons were divergent ideas. The Soviets' political vision consisted of communism, atheism, slavery, misery, torture, and oppression. The United States offered people capitalism, democracy, and freedom. Although the two nations never fought directly, each country engaged in small-scale proxy wars, notably in Korea and Vietnam. However, in 1945, only the Soviets were fighting, but that was soon to change.

A New Day Dawns for Japan

Many months before Japan's surrender, Allied representatives made plans for the occupation and reconstruction of post-war Japan. Their goal was to create a more peaceful and economically prosperous nation. After Japan surrendered, the first segment of the reconstruction plan began. The Japanese would be disarmed and steps to halt any further militarization would be established. The Allies would take control of Japan's former colonies, particularly Formosa and Korea. Efforts to stabilize Japan's economy would begin.

The United States and Great Britain did not seek to punish the Japanese people, but rather to teach them how to create a stable society with some sort of representative government. In September 1945, General MacArthur became the military governor of Japan and began the monumental task of rebuilding and modernizing Japan. Amazingly, this military genius proved to be an even better political leader. MacArthur's first tasks were reshaping Japan's economy and rebuilding Japan as a democracy. He also initiated policies for occupation. He insisted that the Japanese people be treated respectfully. For example, soldiers would get five years in prison if they slapped a Japanese citizen. MacArthur earned the respect of the Japanese people by treating their beloved emperor, Hirohito, with honor.

MacArthur made basic changes in Japan's society and government. He wrote and implemented a constitution which created a Parliamentary System of government. The emperor became only a figurehead without political power. Women received more rights. Japan renounced the right to declare war. Japan's military was dissolved and all former military officers were banned from holding public office. MacArthur worked to create a free market, capitalist economic system. Because of MacArthur's leadership and the hard work of the Japanese, by the 1970s, Japan became an economic and industrial super power.

Mount Fuji, in the background, is the highest mountain in Japan. Located about sixty miles southwest of Tokyo, it is a cultural icon and a symbol of Japan as well as a major tourist attraction. The huge oil refinery in the foreground has also become symbolic of Japan's growing economy and economic prosperity.

The Peacetime Economy

With the successful conclusion of the war, Americans wanted to return to their normal lives. President Truman would be the man most responsible for making this happen. Truman had several qualities that served him well as president. First, he was an honest man and a hard worker. When he became president, he put a plaque on his desk that read, "*The Buck Stops Here*," meaning that he was the one who was ultimately in charge. Secondly, Truman was anti-Communist. Unlike Franklin Roosevelt, Harry Truman did not trust Josef Stalin or the Communists. A famous incident occurred on April 23, 1945, less than two weeks after Truman became president. In a meeting with Soviet foreign minister Molotov, Truman told him off in rather sharp language for breaking agreements that Stalin had made wartime allies. Molotov complained that he had never been spoken to that way before in his life. "Carry out your agreements and you won't get to be talked to like that," Truman responded. Truman believed that the Soviets hoped and expected that the U. S. would fall into a depression as it had after the First World War. Truman was determined that this not happen.

Truman's biggest fear was that in the months following the end of the war, unemployment would be a major problem. The federal government would be canceling its war contracts which meant that people working in factories making war materials would lose their jobs. Also, millions of men returning from the war would need jobs. It seemed that massive unemployment was inevitable. However, the American economy proved incredibly resilient. Unemployment did not become a problem until 1949.

After the War, America returned to normal which meant going back to the movies. By the end of the 1940s over 90 million movie tickets were sold every week -- four times more than the weekly average over the last twenty years. The highest grossing film of 1946 was "The Best Years of Our Lives," the story of three soldiers readjusting to civilian life after serving in the War.

Because there had been fewer consumer goods, like cars or washing machines, to purchase during the war, Americans had saved their money, patiently waiting to buy consumer products when they became available. Post-war demand for consumer goods skyrocketed! People wanted new clothes, new washers, new everything! American car manufacturers had not produced automobiles for consumers since 1941. Millions of Americans wanted new cars. American factories, which had provisioned the "arsenal of democracy," now returned to making consumer goods. America was back in business. Laid-off workers and returning veterans soon found work. As a result, the depression Truman feared never happened.

Unfortunately, while high *unemployment* did not hurt the country, high *inflation* did. In 1946 and 1947, the combined inflation rate was almost 27%! [Historically, inflation tends to be around 3% per year.] By late 1945, Americans faced two competing problems: high inflation and scarcity. Because the extraordinary demand for new consumer goods could not be filled immediately, shortages occurred as demand exceeded production. Whenever demand exceeds supply, prices increase. Price increases caused higher inflation. To pay for the higher priced goods, workers demanded higher wages and when they did not receive them, they went on strike. As 1945 drew to a close, auto workers, steel workers, electrical workers, and coal miners were engaged in crippling strikes. Many of these strikes ended when wages were increased. Of course, to maintain their profits, manufacturers increased the prices of these products. This caused workers and other consumers to decry the price increases. Manufacturers demanded that the government reduce their taxes and remove wartime price restrictions.

In the spring of 1946, the coal strike ended after Truman seized the coal mines. Then the railroad union threatened to close down all railroad operations. Truman threatened the railroad union with a total government takeover, but the union went on strike despite the threat. The Attorney General warned Truman that his actions were unconstitutional. Truman was saved from an embarrassing situation when the union, believing the president would seize the railroads, ended their strike.

President Truman at his desk with its famous plaque

In late 1946, the government did lift most of the wartime price controls. Prices rose sharply and workers demanded higher wages. Employers paid the higher wages. With the additional money, workers purchased more goods, which caused prices to rise and workers to demand higher wages. This cycle of increases in prices and wages has continued to the present day.

The 1946 Midterm Elections

By the time the 1946 midterm elections rolled around, many Americans, including a large number of Democrats, were unhappy with Harry Truman. Many Americans blamed the Democrats, particularly President Truman, for the strikes and the postwar inflation, which meant they were paying higher prices for goods. People at the time commonly joked that "To err is Truman." Republican candidates in the 1946 mid-term elections used the slogan "Had Enough?" to ask voters if they had "had enough" of the Democrats. A majority of voters had *had enough*. For the first time since 1928, Republicans won the Senate and the House of Representatives. With control of Congress for the first time in almost twenty years, the Republicans set out to change some of the more liberal laws passed under Franklin Roosevelt.

Robert A. Taft. The oldest son of President Taft, Robert spent nearly his entire adult life in government. He narrowly missed the Republican nomination for president on several occasions. When he died of cancer in 1953 the Republican Party lost one of its most effective leaders.

Senator Robert Taft of Ohio, known as **Mr. Republican**, believed that the public would embrace more stringent control of organized labor. Senator Taft shepherded the Labor-Management Relations Act through Congress in June 1947. It has always been known as the *Taft-Hartley Act*.

Under the National Labor Relations Act of 1935, employers had been banned from unfair labor practices. The Taft-Hartley Act banned unions from engaging in unfair labor practices. Among its provisions, Taft-Hartley created a **sixty-day cooling-off period** before a contract could be ended by either an employer or a union.

Taft-Hartley **forbade a closed shop**, in which only workers who were already union members could be hired. Unions were forbidden from putting pressure on non-union workers to join the union or charging unusually high initiation or membership fees. Also, unions were prohibited from making contributions to political campaigns.

Under Taft-Hartley, if the president believed that a strike or lock-out threatened the national interest, the president could obtain a court injunction forcing the union to postpone the strike for eighty days. Historically, judges have granted these injunctions to the president. Although Truman vetoed Taft-Hartley, Congress overrode the veto with overwhelming bi-partisan support. During the remainder of his presidency, Truman would rely on Taft-Hartley numerous times.

In addition to Taft-Hartley, the other piece of landmark legislation passed by the new Congress was the **Twenty-Second Amendment** to the Constitution which limited the President of the United States to two terms. The Twenty-Second Amendment was clearly a result of President Roosevelt's four terms. However, Congress has always opposed any legislation which would limit the terms of senators and representatives. The Republican Congress also passed legislation lowering the income tax for certain categories, but Truman vetoed that legislation.

The Truman Doctrine

Although Truman disagreed with Republicans on many domestic issues, they did agree on several aspects of foreign policy. Both Truman and the Republicans, and many Democrats, opposed Communism. Truman determined to resist Soviet expansion, especially in Europe.

Shortly after the war ended, Winston Churchill was voted out of office; however, he did not leave the world's stage. On March 5, 1946, he delivered a memorable speech at Westminster College in Fulton, Missouri. Churchill sought to alert the free world to the dangers of Communism proclaiming that from "Szczecin in the Baltic Sea to Trieste in the Adriatic Sea, an *iron curtain* has descended across the continent." He warned that "the Communists are not going to stop after establishing control of Eastern Europe.... Communist parties are seeking to obtain totalitarian control everywhere."

Under Roosevelt, America had been accommodating towards the Soviet Union. The first evidence of America's change in policy toward the Soviets occurred in Greece. Great Britain had been giving military aid to the anti-Communist government in Greece; however, the vast expense of World War II had nearly impoverished Britain. In February 1947, the British told Truman they would be forced to end their military aid and withdraw their troops from Greece in March. Truman feared that if Greece fell to the Communists, then its neighbor Turkey would also fall under the Communist boot heel.

Churchill speaking at Westminster College. Note the Presidential seal on the podium. President Truman introduced Churchill and attended the speech. Not only was the speech of incredible significance in the West, but the Soviets dated the beginning of the Cold War from this speech.

On March 12, 1947, in response to the situation in Greece, President Truman spoke to a joint session of Congress where he introduced the **Truman Doctrine.** The goal of the Truman Doctrine was to contain Communism. Truman was not going to try to recover lands that the Communists currently controlled. He did not want war. However, he was going to stop them from seizing more nations. Truman told Congress that the foreign policy of the United States is to support free people who are resisting subjugation by armed minorities or external pressures. He said that American help would be "primarily through economic and financial aid."

Harry Truman explained the Truman Doctrine's three basic goals. First, stop Soviet expansion. Second, weaken the influence of Communism around the world. Third, encourage the development of democracies. In response to Truman's impassioned plea, Congress allocated $400 million of military and economic aid to Greece and Turkey to begin building up their armed forces. As a result, Communist expansion was checked in those nations. The Truman Doctrine would serve as a pillar of American foreign policy for the remainder of the Cold War.

The Marshall Plan

The economic situation in Greece and Turkey, and even Britain, demonstrated how devastated most of Europe remained even two years after the war had ended. No matter how strong the United States might be financially and militarily, it could not provide food and money to Europe indefinitely. The nations of Europe needed to rebuild their economies not only to fight Communism and support their own citizens but also to become trading partners with America, as they once had been. America's leaders, realizing this, determined to implement a plan to provide short-term aid with long-term benefits.

George C. Marshall in 1949

In June 1947, Secretary of State George C. Marshall delivered a speech at Harvard University, in which he outlined a plan to rebuild a free Europe. Secretary Marshall proposed that the United States extend twenty billion dollars of credit over four years. These funds would help restore economic independence to European nations. It was imperative for Europeans to rebuild their farms and factories and recover from the terrible effects of the war, and thus be able to fight Communism. Amazingly, in its generosity, the U.S. offered the aid to the Soviets. Marshall said that the purpose of the plan was to fight "hunger, poverty, desperation, and chaos." The Soviet Union and its puppets rejected Marshall's plan. However, eighteen Western European nations gladly accepted the aid.

On April 2, 1948, Congress passed the European Recovery Program, or **Marshall Plan** as it was commonly known. Over the next four years, America sent more than $12 billion to Europe, about half to Britain. By 1951, the economies of the Western European nations that had participated in the Marshall Plan were booming. The threat of Communism in Europe had been reduced. However, when Czechoslovakia and Poland hinted that they might also accept Marshall Plan funds, the Soviets cracked down, and refused to allow it. Almost everyone agrees that the Marshall Plan proved an unqualified success. In fact, some historians consider it the greatest triumph in the history of American diplomacy.

The Berlin Airlift

After World War II, the Allies divided Germany into four sectors. Each sector was occupied by one of the leading Allies, that is, the United States, Great Britain, France, and the Soviet Union. Berlin was in the Soviet-controlled sector, but the Western Allies were unwilling to allow Berlin, Germany's capital and most important city, to fall under the control of Stalin and the Communists. So, Berlin itself was divided into four sectors. The Western Allies controlled three sections and the Soviet Union controlled one.

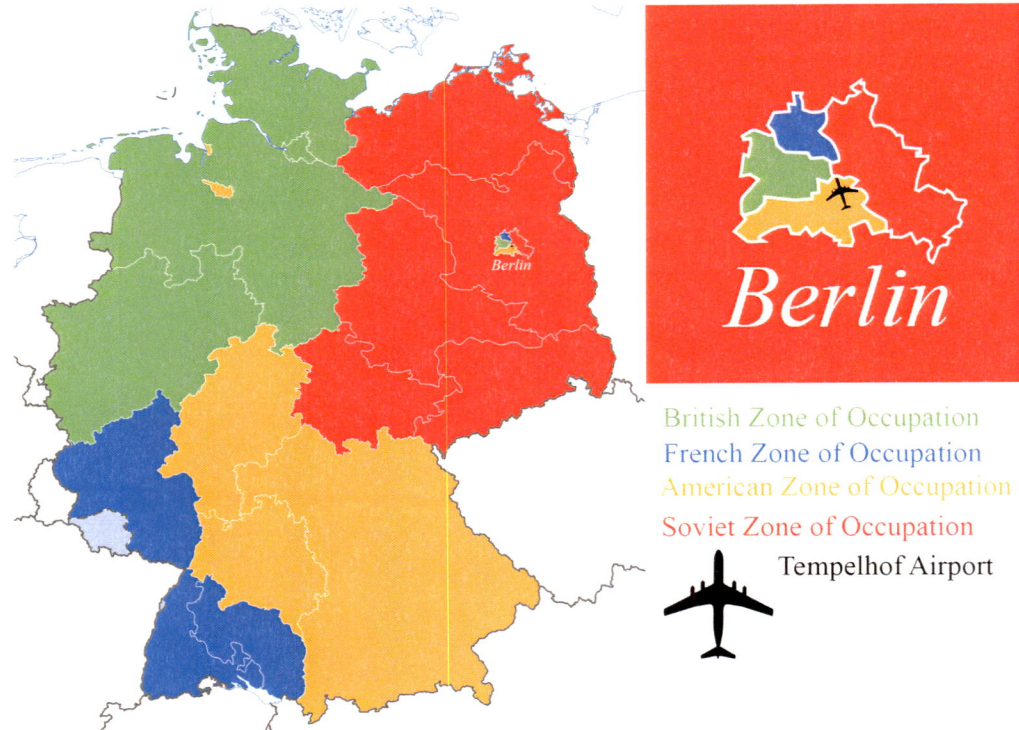

British Zone of Occupation
French Zone of Occupation
American Zone of Occupation
Soviet Zone of Occupation

Tempelhof Airport

Post-war Germany. Berlin is completely in the Soviet zone of occupation but Tempelhof Airport is in the American zone.

However, the western Allies, who had no ambitions for territorial gains, wanted the Germans to have their nation back and become part of the international community. In spring 1948, the United States, Great Britain, and France announced that they were going to return the areas of Germany that they occupied back to the Germans to resume self-rule. This would have the effect of creating a new independent nation, the **Federal Republic of Germany**, or as it came to be called, **West Germany**. The Allies only insisted that West Germany be a democracy.

At the same time, Stalin was adamant that first Berlin and then all of Germany become Communist. The Soviets were convinced that if Germany fell to Communism, the rest of western Europe would eventually follow. The notion of a democratic West Germany infuriated Stalin and stood in the way of his plans of Communist domination of the world. He simply would not stand for it!

Although Stalin could not stop the western Allies from creating West Germany, he could try to force them out of Berlin. Therefore, in the summer of 1948, Stalin decided to heat up the Cold War. To force the western Allies out of Berlin, thus leaving him in total control, Stalin established a blockade around Berlin that stopped all railroad, river, and road traffic. Stalin was basically telling the Western powers to get out or let the Germans in their sectors of Berlin starve.

The blockade seemed like a brilliant plan. If the Allies tried to send supplies by the normal river, road, or train routes, they would run into the Soviet blockade. They would either have to turn back or fight their way through the blockade, which would mean war with the Soviet Union. However, Stalin had not imagined the incredible power or resolve of America. Tempelhof Airport, Berlin's international airport, lay within the American zone of control. Truman decided that rather than going through the blockade, the Allies would simply fly over it! Thus, the Allies established the "**Berlin Airlift**."

Now the Soviets faced a choice. Would they allow American planes to fly into Berlin or shoot them down, thus starting a war with the United States? The Soviets chose to do nothing. Stalin probably believed that the United States could not possibly fly enough supplies into Berlin to feed a city of two million

West Berliners watch an American cargo plane delivering vital supplies during the Berlin Airlift.

people. However, Stalin had underestimated the resolution of the United States and the abilities of the United States Air Force.

For the next eleven months, the U. S. Air Force and the RAF flew almost 300,000 missions into Berlin carrying unimaginable amounts of materials ranging from food to coal! The airlift proved the former Allied nations would oppose every Communist effort to control the German people. The Allied countries' defiance elevated their prestige throughout Europe. Eighty percent of voters in western Berlin rejected communist candidates for office in the 1948 elections. After maintaining the blockade for nearly a year, on May 12, 1949, the Soviets agreed to resume normal traffic to Berlin. The blockade had been lifted, but Berlin remained divided.

In response to the creation of West Germany, the Soviets formed the **German Democratic Republic** on October 7, 1949. Commonly known as "East Germany," it was one of the most repressive regimes in Europe. Soviet troops remained in East Germany throughout the Cold War.

America's Surprise Election

As the presidential election campaign of 1948 began, the Democratic Party was in disarray. President Truman was unpopular. The Berlin Airlift was ongoing but no one knew if it would succeed. His policy in China (discussed below) seemed to have failed. Inflation was high. Consequently, most Democratic leaders did not even want to nominate him, although he was the incumbent president. As a result, the Democrat Party splintered into three factions.

One faction of Democrats supported **Henry Wallace**, Truman's former Secretary of Commerce, who was running as the candidate for a new Progressive Party. Wallace, who was practically a Communist himself, trusted the Soviets and believed that the Truman Doctrine would lead to outright war with the Soviet Union. When Wallace attacked the Truman Doctrine, Truman had to force Wallace to resign as Secretary of Commerce. Wallace subsequently attacked the Marshall Plan, one of the few American politicians to do so.

Meanwhile, Southern Democrats, who felt that Truman was moving too fast on civil rights legislation, especially laws ending segregation, opposed him as well. When the national Democratic party finally did nominate Truman, the Southern Democrats, who called themselves *Dixiecrats* formed another party, the **States' Rights Party**. They nominated **Strom Thurmond**, the governor of South Carolina, as their presidential candidate.

The Republicans once again nominated Thomas E. Dewey. Dewey had done well in 1944 against Roosevelt, winning almost 46% of the popular vote. Republicans believed that if Dewey could do as well in 1948, he would win the election because he was running against *three* Democrats. If they split the remaining 54% of the vote, Dewey would win with a plurality of the vote. Therefore, Dewey's campaign strategy was simply not to make any mistakes and let the Democrats beat themselves. It seemed like a smart plan. However, one of Harry Truman's best qualities was that he was a hard worker. He started working hard on his campaign.

Truman began an energetic campaign that took him by railroad to small towns across America. He made "whistle-stops" where he spoke to rural voters from the platform of a highly decorated train caboose. Voters saw and heard a working class, down-to-earth man, confiding in down-to-earth voters who might have been a bit uneasy about a new president from the "big city." In his speeches, Truman attacked the Republicans who, he said, if elected would overturn New Deal legislation, civil rights' advances, and the union gains. His strategy worked. Unions supported him for his opposition to the Taft-Hartley Act. African-Americans supported him for his stand on civil rights. New Dealers supported him for backing the New Deal.

Nevertheless, it seemed that the mathematics worked against Truman. How could he overcome Dewey when two other Democrats were siphoning off his voters? Public opinion polls gave Dewey a fifteen-point lead over Truman one week before the election. On election night, an early edition of the

Chicago Tribune newspaper hit the street with the election results in a banner headline: **Dewey Defeats Truman**. However, the *Tribune* had published the edition before all the votes had been counted.

In one of the biggest upsets in American political history, Harry Truman defeated Thomas Dewey. Once again, Dewey won about 46% of the popular vote. But Truman won nearly 50% of the popular vote. He carried 28 of 48 states and won 303 of 531 electoral college votes. The Democrats regained control of both houses of Congress.

It has been theorized that many Republican voters, confident of the predicted Dewey landslide, failed to vote on Election Day. However,

In one of the most iconic photographs in American history, Harry Truman gleefully holds up the newspaper incorrectly proclaiming his loss to Thomas Dewey.

this seems unlikely, as the total number of voters in the 1944 and 1948 elections are nearly the same, about 47 million; and the number of people who voted for Dewey in both elections is about the same, about 22 million. More likely, Dewey lost because he failed to respond to Truman's attacks on the Republicans. His inaction, as much as Truman's action, caused his defeat.

The election of 1948 proved a number of items. First, polls are not always correct. Second, hard work and energy in a campaign are incredibly important. Both of these factors would be demonstrated again in the 2016 election. Third, the New Deal was still very popular. Fourth, America remained staunchly anti-Communist. Wallace won just over 1.1 million votes.

The *Fair Deal*

His surprise re-election encouraged Harry Truman to advance an ambitious domestic agenda. In his January 1949 State of the Union Address, Truman announced a series of proposals he called the "**Fair Deal.**" Many of these ideas expanded on New Deal legislation. For example, Truman called for the repeal of the Taft-Hartley Act, a higher minimum wage, an increase and expansion of social security benefits, national health insurance, and an expansion of low-incoming housing. However, he also asked Congress for more "bi-partisan" measures such as funds for rural electricity expansion, a stronger military, and civil rights legislation. As with most presidential "wish lists," Congress had mixed feelings. Republicans disliked expansion of the New Deal, but were willing to enact certain legislation. As a result, Congress refused to pass most of his Fair Deal legislation. However, social security was expanded, the minimum wage was increased, and funds were allocated for the construction of low-income housing. Congress did not enact civil rights legislation at this time.

The North Atlantic Treaty Organization

The Berlin blockade convinced western leaders that they needed a defensive alliance against Soviet aggression. On April 4, 1949, during the Berlin Airlift, the United States, Great Britain, Canada, Iceland, France, Portugal, Belgium, the Netherlands, Denmark, Norway, Italy, and Luxembourg signed a treaty creating the North Atlantic Treaty Organization (NATO). Greece and Turkey joined NATO in 1952 and West Germany joined in 1955. [The United States, England, and France officially ended their military occupation of West Germany on May 5, 1955. West Germany joined NATO four days later.] NATO members rely on a strategy of "collective defense." This means that NATO nations consider an attack on one member as an attack on all members. Under Article V of the NATO treaty, members pledge to aid each other in the event of such an attack. The Soviet Union called this defensive pact "aggressive." On May 14, 1955, in response to West Germany's admittance into NATO, the Soviet Union formed the Warsaw Pact, a military alliance between the U.S.S.R. and its Eastern European satellites, including East Germany.

Since its creation, NATO has worked well to defend Western Europe. Under NATO's protection—mainly American protection—Western Europe has generally maintained its democratic governments and prevented Soviet/Russian incursions. Thankfully, the threat of America's military has mostly deterred Soviet/Russian aggression. In fact, more than fifty years elapsed before Article V was invoked for the first time. On September 12, 2001, after the terrorist attacks on the United States, NATO invoked Article V and took eight steps to support the United States including sharing intelligence; granting clearance to Allied airspace, ports, and airfields; and deploying naval and airborne units to support operations against terrorism.

China Falls to the Communists

While Truman acted wisely in his dealings with the Communists in Europe, he dealt foolishly with the Communists in China. His mishandling of the situation in China ultimately caused it to fall into the hands of the Communists. Today, China, which retains much of its Communist nature, ranks among America's greatest adversaries. Harry Truman bears much of the blame.

By 1945, the leader of China's Nationalist government, Chiang Kai-shek, had been at war with the Chinese Communists, led by **Mao Zedong**, for nearly twenty years. Ironically, when Japan invaded China,

Chiang Kai-shek and Mao Zedong both fought the Japanese, but they also fought each other. On August 14, 1945, Japan surrendered, ending the war between Japan and China. However, Japan's surrender failed to bring peace to China because of the civil war between Chiang and Mao.

In the final days of World War II, the Soviets declared war on Japan and invaded Manchuria. At that time, a million Japanese troops remained in China. The Soviet army captured most of these well-armed Japanese soldiers and turned all of their equipment and weapons over to the Chinese Communists. As a result, the Chinese Communists emerged from World War II much better off than before the war.

In December 1945, under orders from president Truman, General George C. Marshall went to China and asked Chiang Kai-shek to accept Communists in his government. Chiang knew that if he agreed, Communists would eventually rule China. So, Chiang rejected Marshall's request. Consequently, Marshall regarded Chiang as a totally uncooperative leader – a huge mistake by Marshall.

Mao Zedong, the greatest mass murderer in history. Although no one will ever know how many people died and were murdered because of his policies, estimates range from 45 million to 65 million.

In March 1946, the Soviet Army withdrew from Manchuria, the richest and most industrialized section of China. Following the withdrawal, the Chinese Communists moved into much of northern Manchuria, including **Changchun**, one of the largest and most important cities in Manchuria. Chiang, realizing that he had to drive the Communists from Manchuria, launched an offensive which managed to capture Changchun on May 23. The fall of Changchun infuriated General Marshall, who, speaking on behalf of President Truman, ordered Chiang to accept a cease-fire with the Communist and stop his offensive in Manchuria. The two-week cease-fire enabled the Communists to regroup.

After the cease-fire concluded at the end of June, Chiang Kai-shek decided that he needed to renew his offensive against the Communists. He may not have believed that America would stop providing aid; however, he knew that the only way to win was to attack and destroy the Chinese Communists while he still had a strong army. Without discussing his plans with the Americans, he decided to launch nearly his entire army against the Communists, not only in Manchuria, but throughout northern China.

On July 20, 1946, Chiang attacked the Communist army in north China with over one and a half million troops. Marshall responded by asking Truman to institute a total *arms embargo against Chiang's Nationalists*. Truman agreed, ending American aid.

Chiang's campaign initially proved very successful. His Nationalist forces drove the Communists back and liberated immense areas of Communist-controlled China. However, in March 1947, Chiang's offensive ground to a halt. After ten months without any outside aid, the Nationalists ran short of ammunition and other supplies. Then, when all seemed lost, a flicker of hope appeared.

In March 1947, the Truman Doctrine was unveiled. The arms embargo on Chiang was partially lifted but no new arms arrived until November. Truman and Marshall, determined to allow Communists into China's government, refused to provide the assistance to Chiang that was being provided to anti-Communists in Europe. Because Truman failed to give Chiang the support and supplies he needed, the military balance shifted decisively in favor of the Communists.

In May 1948, the Communists reached Changchun and began to besiege the city. In order to starve the Nationalist soldiers faster, the Communists refused to allow any civilians to leave. As a result, as many as 200,000 civilians starved to death during the 150-day siege. On October 19, the remaining Nationalist soldiers surrendered.

During the final months of 1948, the last great battles of the Chinese Civil War were fought. Communist victories in these battles sealed China's fate. In August 1949, realizing that the war was lost, Chiang Kai-Shek assembled the remnants of his army and his supporters, about two million people, and began transporting them to the island of **Formosa** (Taiwan). On December 7, he declared the Republic of China. Meanwhile, on Mainland China, on October 1, Mao established a Communist regime he called the **People's Republic of China**. Most Americans called it **"Red" China**, because China, the world's largest nation, with its hundreds of millions of people, was now a Communist country.

The Soviet Union Develops an Atomic Bomb

As the Cold War began, the United States had an advantage over the Soviet Union: America had nuclear weapons and the Soviets did not. The threat of those weapons was the only deterrent Stalin respected. American leaders believed that our nuclear superiority would last for many years. Unfortunately, Soviet spies had been working on the Manhattan Project almost from its inception. One such agent was a brilliant German theoretical physicist named **Klaus Fuchs**. Fuchs gave the Soviets detailed data on atomic bomb research, probably as early as 1943. Aided by secret information from Fuchs and others, the Soviets developed a nuclear bomb very quickly. In September 1949, Stalin surprised American intelligence experts by detonating the Soviets' first atomic bomb.

In January 1950, Fuchs confessed to being a spy and a member of a spy ring. He provided information which led to the arrest of fellow spies Harry Gold, David Greenglass, and Julius and Ethel Rosenberg. He was sentenced to fourteen years in prison but served only nine. In 1959, upon his release, he moved to East Germany where the Communists treated him with great respect for all he had done for them.

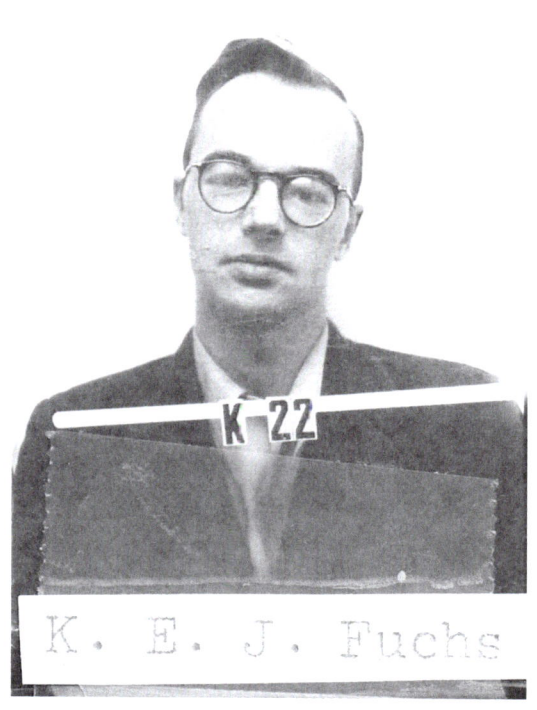

Fuchs' Los Alamos ID badge photo. Interestingly, the photo resembles those taken of recently arrested criminals.

Searching for Soviet Spies

Although some Americans wanted to deny it, there *were* spies in key positions in the United States government. On September 5, 1945, a Soviet spy named **Igor Gouzenko**, who worked in the Soviet embassy in Canada, defected and exposed Soviet efforts to steal nuclear secrets. Gouzenko brought 109 documents with him that proved the existence of a large Communist spy ring in North America and Great Britain. Gouzenko described the Soviet technique for planting *sleeper agents*, agents who would not act right away but would wait for suitable opportunities, in vital positions where they could steal atomic secrets and pass them on to the Soviets. Gouzenko's defection, and the information he produced, proved to be a wake-up call for the United States government. It would eventually lead to the arrest of Klaus Fuchs. In fact, some historians point to the date of Gouzenko's defection as the beginning of the Cold War.

An investigation designed to ferret out hidden Communist agents in high government positions was put in motion. The House of Representatives set up the **House Un-American Activities Committee (HUAC)** which questioned people whose actions were suspect. Among those HUAC charged with spying was a trusted government official named **Alger Hiss**. **Whittaker Chambers**, a former Communist, identified Alger Hiss as a Communist. Hiss had been an influential assistant Secretary of State who had gained President Roosevelt's trust. The evidence against Alger Hiss included testimony and secret documents that Hiss had given to Whittaker Chambers. The overwhelming evidence resulted in a conviction of perjury and a prison term for Alger Hiss.

Senator Joseph McCarthy

One of the foremost leaders attempting to discover Communist agents was Wisconsin **Senator Joseph McCarthy**. Joseph McCarthy, a Catholic, had been elected in 1946. Senator McCarthy probed Communist influence in the U. S. government, especially the State Department. Known and suspected Communists were called before his Senate committee and asked about their activities. In the beginning of his investigations, Senator McCarthy enjoyed widespread support, but before long, the liberal media and the Democrats harshly attacked him. They alleged that he accused people of being pro-Communist without concrete evidence. The media discredited McCarthy by calling him foolish and dangerous which led many people to question the validity of his claims.

McCarthy's support had always been among Catholics, most of whom were Democrats, and blue-collar Republicans. But he never created a national organization to support his position or formed political alliances with other national organizations outside of the Republican Party. As a result, McCarthy was basically a one-man show.

Whittaker Chambers

Senator Joseph McCarthy

By January 1954, McCarthy was at the height of his popularity; however, he then made a crucial error. He had previously aimed his attacks and investigations at Communists in the State Department; however, he shifted his attacks to the U. S. Army. While there probably were Communists in the Army, in 1954, the president was Dwight D. Eisenhower, who loved the army and would not abide anyone attacking it. In the spring of 1954, the **Army-McCarthy** hearings were televised. On television, McCarthy seemed to be ill-prepared and a bully.

In the 1954 midterm elections, the Democrats won control of the Senate. In December, the Senate voted 67 to 22 to censure McCarthy. Because McCarthy had failed to build a national network, his ability to fight Communism evaporated overnight. Although he remained in the Senate until his death in 1957, he was largely forgotten. The prejudiced media and Senator McCarthy's political opponents coined the new term "McCarthyism," which denotes *unfounded* attacks on innocent individuals' characters by questioning their loyalty to the nation.

After the collapse of the Soviet Union, secret documents from the **KGB**, the Soviet spy agency, became available to the public. These documents proved that McCarthy had been correct in his assertion that a Communist conspiracy did exist in the United States. Based on these documents, **Hayden Peake**, the curator of the Central Intelligence Agency's Historical Intelligence Collection, stated, "No modern government was more thoroughly penetrated" than the U. S. government.

The Korean War

Japan ruled Korea from 1910 until the end of World War II when American and Soviet armies occupied Korea. Communists ruled Korea north of the 38th parallel and American forces occupied Korea's southern section. The Soviet Union agreed to establish a unified government with the United States in Korea, but shortly after the war ended, Stalin reneged on the agreement and established a Communist government in North Korea led by Kim Il-sung. In 1948, elections were held in South Korea, which created the **Republic of Korea** with Seoul as the capital city. In North Korea, the people lived under Communist tyranny, while in the south, people enjoyed freedom in a democratic government. In June 1949, the United States and the Soviet Union withdrew their military forces from Korea, leaving the two Koreas to defend themselves.

On June 25, 1950, North Korea invaded South Korea without warning. The United Nations condemned North Korea's unprovoked assault on South Korea. The United States asked the Soviet Union to cooperate in ending the assault and restore peace. However, the Soviet Union and Red China supported North Korea.

Applying the Truman Doctrine's containment policy, Truman asked the United Nations Security Council to pass a resolution allowing UN forces to intervene in the conflict. The Soviets could have vetoed the resolution; however, it seems that they wished to have a proxy war in Korea to test American resolve. Consequently, the resolution to intervene in Korea passed the Security Council. However, other than South Koreans, the vast majority of the soldiers who fought to defend South Korea were Americans.

With the advantage of surprise, North Korea's very large army forced the American and South Korean soldiers to retreat during the summer of 1950. By August, the American and

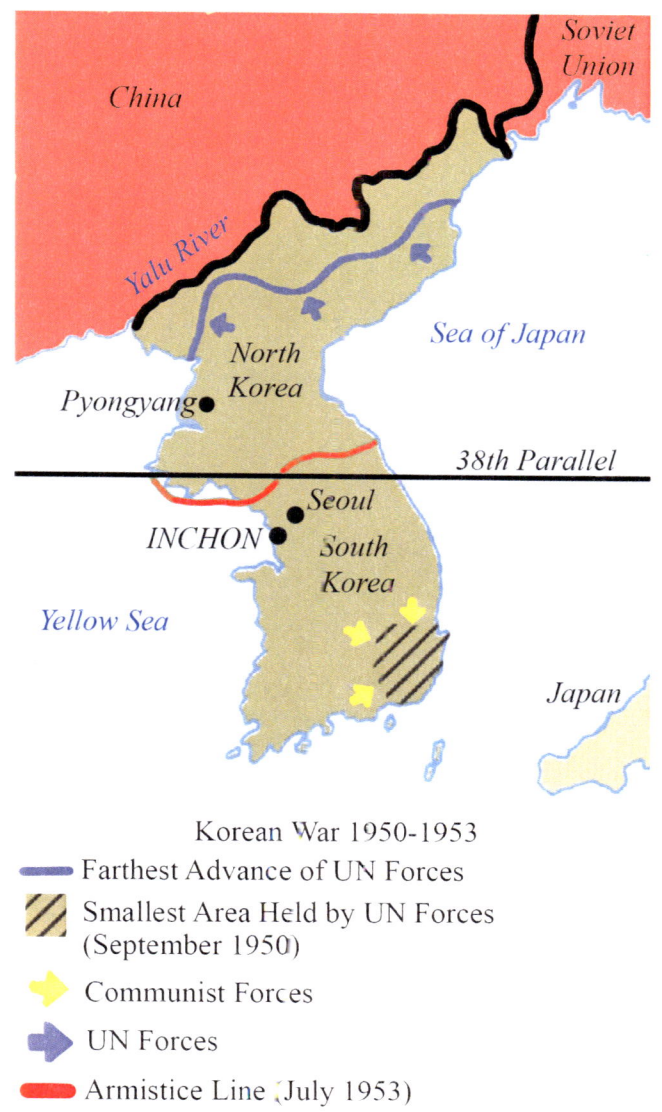

Korean War 1950-1953

— Farthest Advance of UN Forces

▨ Smallest Area Held by UN Forces (September 1950)

➤ Communist Forces

➤ UN Forces

— Armistice Line (July 1953)

UN forces held only a small area around Busan (formerly Pusan) Harbor, the so-called "Busan Perimeter." Clinging to this tiny plot of land, the Americans and their allies waged a bitter six week-struggle from August 4 to September 18, 1950. Despite determined attacks by the North Koreans, the perimeter held.

On September 15, American Marines under the command of General Douglas MacArthur made a daring amphibious landing at **Incheon** harbor, far behind the Communist battle lines. The Incheon landing quickly shifted the tide of battle. The Marines soon re-captured Seoul and cut the Communist forces in two.

By October 1950, Americans had recovered all of South Korea. Then, with the permission of President Truman, MacArthur turned north to destroy the Communist forces and reunite the country. By November, MacArthur's troops had taken most of North Korea and were approaching the **Yalu River**, the boundary between North Korea and China. Victory appeared to be near, when Mao Zedong suddenly and unexpectedly ordered a massive Chinese army to invade North Korea.

On November 25, more than one hundred thousand Chinese soldiers flooded across the border. They swarmed over the UN forces, taking them completely by surprise. The Marines, who had spearheaded the American advance, were surrounded by the Chinese at the Chosin Reservoir in the mountains of central Korea.

The **Battle of Chosin Reservoir** began on November 27, 1950, and lasted seventeen days. The First Marine Division totaled 25,000 troops. However, they were surrounded by 150,000 Chinese soldiers. The entire battle was fought in cruelly frigid temperatures that dropped as low as -36 degrees! Veterans of the battle, known as "The Chosin Few," would later say that "If you stopped moving, you froze." Most of the Marines were career soldiers who had served in World War II. They were arguably the world's finest warriors. Surrounded, outnumbered six to one, the Marines attacked! They fought their way out of the Chinese trap. When they finally emerged from the mountains, they had defeated eight Chinese divisions. By the time the Marines, along with thousands of North Korean refugees, reached the evacuation beaches, nearly 6,000 Americans were dead or missing and thousands more were wounded. However, the communists had lost more than 50,000 soldiers, including Mao's oldest son.

Band of Brothers by Charles H. Waterhouse (The USMC Museum). Marines make their way down Funchilin Pass on their way from Chosin Reservoir to the port of Hungnam. Not only did the Marines not leave behind any dead or wounded, they cleaned up their own trash and burned it so that the Chinese were not able to use it in any way!

In the weeks after the Chosin Reservoir success, the Chinese pushed MacArthur's forces back down the Korean Peninsula into South Korea. In the spring of 1951, the line of battle stabilized along the original borders between the two Koreas. MacArthur then asked Truman for permission to blockade the coast of China and bomb their supply lines in Manchuria. However, **General Omar Bradley**, one of Truman's closest military advisers, told the President that he opposed MacArthur's plan. Truman sided with Bradley believing that bombing the Chinese directly would expand the war, rather than resolve it. Consequently, Truman would not allow MacArthur to bomb the bridges between North Korea and Manchuria that the Chinese used to bring supplies and troops into North Korea. Truman told MacArthur he wanted to fight a limited war aimed only at protecting South Korea from North Korea and the Chinese.

General Omar Bradley by Guy Rowe (1950). The symbol in the back resembling a parachute alludes to Bradley's work in creating America's first Airborne division shortly after the US entered WWII.

MacArthur was furious. He publicly criticized Truman in the newspapers for pursuing a "no-win policy" in Korea. Truman decided that MacArthur had exceeded his authority by publicly criticizing him and his policy decisions. On April 11, 1951, Truman fired MacArthur and replaced him with General Matthew Ridgway.

In June 1951, with the war at a stalemate, the Communists indicated that they would be willing to begin truce talks. The talks began in July. One of the most difficult issues confronting delegates at the talks was the issue of the North Korean and Red Chinese *prisoners of war* (POWs). Communist negotiators demanded that all captured POWs be returned. However, the majority of those POWs did not want to return to live under Communism. America favored honoring their wishes. Probably most of the American negotiators remembered *Operation Keelhaul*. Peace talks dragged on for months. Then, on March 5, 1953, Josef Stalin died. Following Stalin's death, the United States threatened to end the stalemated talks by using atomic weapons. Faced with the American ultimatum, the Communists agreed to the American position on the POWs. A neutral commission would decide which POWs did not wish to return. 75% of the Chinese prisoners and 50% of the North Korean prisoners chose not to return.

The Election of 1952

In 1952, the Democrats again seemed to be in disarray. Harry Truman was eligible to seek the presidency because the newly-enacted Twenty-Second Amendment did not apply to him. However, he had become incredibly unpopular as inflation and unemployment were both on the rise. Also, a number of scandals had touched his administration including one that led to his firing the Attorney General. Third, the war in Korea seemed to be stalemated with no end in sight. It appears that Truman considered running for a third time until he lost the New Hampshire primary. Less than three weeks later, on March 29, 1952, he declared that he would not seek a third term. Ultimately, Truman convinced **Adlai Stevenson** to become the Democratic nominee.

In any other election, Stevenson might have had an excellent chance at victory. He had a tremendous amount of experience in the federal government. He had helped found the UN. He was governor of Illinois, a state that the Democrats needed to carry to win the election. He has been described as witty and cultured. However, in American history, it has proven almost impossible to defeat a war hero who has chosen to run for president. In 1952, the Republicans nominated America's most beloved war hero, Dwight D. Eisenhower.

Dwight D. Eisenhower earned the gratitude and the respect of millions of Europeans and American soldiers while serving as the Supreme Allied Commander in Europe. Many of them owed their lives to him and the gallant officers that he commanded. American hearts were filled with pride and love for this steadfast leader.

Unlike the vastly experienced Stevenson, Eisenhower had never been involved in, nor even shown much interest in, politics. In fact, before choosing Adlai Stevenson, Democratic leaders had asked Eisenhower to run on their ticket. He declined, saying he had no interest in politics. A few weeks later, a group of leading Republicans approached him. They said that they were concerned that the Republican front runner, Senator Robert Taft of Ohio, would probably try to take America out of NATO if he were elected president. As a result, Eisenhower, who strongly supported NATO and had served as commander of NATO forces, agreed to run for president as a Republican. As Eisenhower's running mate, the convention chose thirty-nine-year-old, anti-Communist California Senator **Richard Nixon**, who had played a prominent role in the Alger Hiss trial.

At the Republican convention, the delegates all repeatedly shouted, **"I like Ike."** The phrase swept across the nation, and during the late summer and fall of 1952, it seemed as if everyone was wearing a button that proclaimed "I Like Ike." And Americans did like Eisenhower's easy-going personality.

America seemed ready for a change. Voters had not elected a Republican since 1928. When Eisenhower promised to go to Korea to negotiate a settlement to the war, it seemed to clinch his victory.

Voters elected Dwight Eisenhower with 55% of the vote. Soon after his inauguration, he warned the Chinese that they had better sign a peace treaty and end the war in Korea; otherwise, he threatened, he might order the use of atomic weapons. The Chinese complied six months later. There can be no doubt that the United States' protective action saved South Korea from Chinese Communist aggression. Communists still rule North Korea which remains one of the world's most brutal regimes.

Eisenhower and Stevenson faced off again in the presidential election of 1956. In 1956, Eisenhower, a popular incumbent, was re-elected by an even greater margin. Even more Americans liked Ike in 1956!

Eisenhower Wages the Cold War

During his presidency, Eisenhower tended to follow Truman's containment philosophy. Eisenhower's Secretary of State, **John Foster Dulles,**

Eisenhower campaign button. Historians generally agree that "I Like Ike" is probably the finest presidential campaign slogan in history. It's short, it's simple, it fits on buttons, and it rhymes – an unbeatable combination!

Painting of John Foster Dulles. Dulles traveled extensively on behalf of the United States. Dulles airport, in Northern Virginia, is named in his honor.

spoke of liberating the people of Eastern Europe suffering under Communist oppression. Although Eisenhower had many opportunities to intervene and help liberate these people, as well as others in Asia and the Middle East, perhaps fearing escalation caused by intervention, Eisenhower chose not to intervene.

Early in 1954, a Communist force in **Vietnam**, a nation in southeast Asia, isolated the French military base at **Dien Bien Phu**. Knowing that if Dien Bien Phu fell to the Communists, it would end French involvement in Southeast Asia, President Eisenhower announced that he opposed the Communist encroachment. The French asked the United States for air support. However, Eisenhower chose not to bomb the communist positions. A short time later, Dien Bien Phu fell to the Communists and the French withdrew from Vietnam. The country was split in two. Communists controlled the North, while anti-Communists established a government in the South. With the departure of the French troops and the division of Vietnam in 1954, the United States became South Vietnam's protector. Millions of people, including many Catholics, fled from the North to the South seeking freedom. The wretched people in the North suffered horribly under the Communist dictator **Ho Chi Minh**.

Two years later, in 1956, Eisenhower faced a crisis in the Middle East involving the nation of **Israel** and the Suez Canal. On May 14, 1948, the nation of Israel, which for decades had been part of the British colony of **Palestine**, declared its independence. President Truman immediately recognized Israel's existence. Early the next day, a coalition of Arab nations invaded Israel to prevent what they considered an invasion of their territory. Despite being vastly outnumbered, the Israelis prevailed. The war officially lasted until 1950 when a truce was declared. However, the truce was hollow. The Arab nations continued to launch raids and terror attacks on Israel.

In 1952, Gamel Abdel Nasser, a pro-Soviet leader, took power in Egypt. In July 1956, Nasser seized the **Suez Canal** which coursed through Egypt but was owned by a private company. Nasser expelled all foreign employees and announced that no Israeli ships would be given access to the canal. This violated international law. The French and British, fearing that they also might be denied access, demanded that Suez Canal traffic be unimpeded. Nasser ignored their demands. England and France then asked President Eisenhower to join them in retaking the canal. However, Eisenhower refused to involve the United States in the dispute.

The already critical situation mushroomed. On October 29, 1956, Israel attacked Egypt. Two days later, England and France joined the Israelis to forcibly seize the canal. The United States refused to support Britain and France since they had acted without consulting the UN. In fact, Eisenhower demanded that Britain and France withdraw. So did the Soviet Union. Without American support, England and France were forced to withdraw their forces. Eisenhower's actions caused resentment and disappointment in England and France. Egypt kept control of the Suez Canal. It would be many years before every nation had open access to the canal.

On October 23, 1956, in the midst of the Suez crisis, brave Hungarian freedom fighters challenged their Communist rulers. They insisted that Soviet troops be withdrawn, that free elections be held, and that a democratic government be established. Since the Soviet Union seized Hungary in 1947, the Catholic Church had suffered terrible persecution. More than 400 priests and 3,000 other religious had been imprisoned or condemned to slave labor camps. Catholic seminaries, schools, and hospitals had been closed or taken over by the government.

The Soviets moved quickly to suppress the Hungarian freedom fighters. Four Soviet tank divisions roared down the streets of the Hungarian capital, Budapest. But the Communists did not send infantry support. The Hungarians pelted the tanks with flaming bottles filled with gasoline, known as "Molotov cocktails" in honor of the Soviet foreign minister. Soviet tanks were forced to withdraw from Budapest less than a week after they arrived.

Hungarian freedom fighters stand on top of a Soviet tank outside parliament during the Hungarian Revolution. Because Cleveland, Ohio had a large Hungarian community, many refugees who escaped Hungary during the Revolution came to Cleveland. Our relative, Mary Lynch, worked for the Red Cross where she tried to find housing for the refugees. On one occasion, a Hungarian family of four stayed with the Lynch family for two months.

The Hungarians appealed to the West and the United States for help. They watched the western skies for American supply planes. But America never sent military help to the Hungarians. The Soviets then assembled a stronger military force to subdue and ultimately destroy the Hungarian rebellion.

Eisenhower's Domestic Policy

The Eisenhower years saw welcome changes for most Americans, as the average family's income rose. Consequently, manufacturers began turning out irresistible products on which consumers could spend their money. Television sets could now be found in most American living rooms. Radio broadcasts still had listeners, but quite often they were sitting in shiny new automobiles. During the 1950s, more families purchased a car.

Because Eisenhower had never been in politics, no one really knew whether he was politically conservative or liberal. Voters might have expected that as a former army general, he would have followed a more conservative foreign policy and strongly opposed Communism. However, his opposition to Communism was rather passive, as evidenced by his failure to support the French in Vietnam and Suez and his failure to support the Hungarians.

Domestically, Eisenhower also seemed to favor a more "middle of the road" approach. He wished to reduce government spending, encourage capitalism, and grow private businesses. But at the same time, during his administration, 11 million more people signed up for social security and unemployment. The minimum wage was increased. Eisenhower created the federal Department of Health, Education, and Welfare.

Eisenhower's single most important domestic accomplishment was passage of the **Federal Highway Act** of 1956. During World War II, Eisenhower had seen how dependent Europe was on railroads. Allied bombers had crippled Nazi movement by bombing railroads and rail yards. Eisenhower determined that America should never be so dependent. Thus, he favored creating a national system of super highways. Automobiles, trucks, and, in times of war, mechanized vehicles could travel quickly virtually anywhere in the United States. Today, America's interstate highway system is the finest in the world.

Earl Warren

Eisenhower also championed the construction of the **St. Lawrence Seaway**. The Seaway deepened the St. Lawrence River to allow ocean-going ships to sail directly into the Great Lakes. Eisenhower also saw the commercial and military benefits of this waterway.

During his presidency, Eisenhower appointed five men to the United States Supreme Court, one of the highest numbers of appointments by any president. In 1953, Eisenhower appointed **Earl Warren** as Chief Justice. Although a Republican, most historians consider Warren a liberal in his decisions. Under his leadership, the *activist* Warren Court created a **right to privacy**, which ultimately became the "right" to an abortion, and outlawed school prayer. In 1954, Eisenhower appointed Justice **John Marshall Harlan II** to the Court. Interestingly, Harlan II was the grandson of former Justice John Harlan, who served on the Court from 1877 to 1911. Harlan is generally considered to be a conservative justice. In 1956, Eisenhower appointed **William J. Brennan** to the Court. At the time of the appointment, Eisenhower was in the middle of the 1956 election. His advisers thought that appointing a Catholic Democrat from the Northeast would help him in the election. Apparently, the archbishop of New York, Francis Cardinal Spellman, had asked Eisenhower to put a Catholic on the Court at the first opportunity. With the exception of William O. Douglas, William Brennan proved to be the most liberal justice in Supreme Court history! Moreover, he served on the Court until 1990, authoring more opinions than anyone but Douglas. The following year, Eisenhower appointed **Charles Evans Whittaker**. Whittaker apparently was not suited for the High Court, never really developed a judicial philosophy, and in 1962, retired after a nervous breakdown. He seemed

John Marshall Harlan II

William J. Brennan

to lean towards a conservative viewpoint. In 1958, Eisenhower made his final appointment, **Potter Stewart**. Most experts consider Stewart a *moderate*. He did not believe that there was a constitutional "right" of privacy, but he did believe in the "right" to an abortion.

If one gauges a president's Supreme Court appointees *solely* on their positions on the issue of the right to life, Eisenhower failed miserably. Of the seven justices that voted in favor of the *Roe v. Wade* decision, Brennan and Stewart had been appointed by Eisenhower. Justices Harlan and Warren left the Court before *Roe* was decided.

Finally, America's last two states joined the Union during Eisenhower's presidency. Alaska became the 49th state on January 3, 1959. Hawaii became the 50th state in August.

Potter Stewart

School Desegregation

According to the 14th Amendment to the Constitution, all Americans must be treated equally under the law. In 1896, in *Plessy v. Ferguson,* the Supreme Court ruled that the 14th Amendment meant that facilities for blacks and whites could be "separate" as long as they were "equal." "Separate but equal" seemed fair, but was never fair in practice. In practice, it meant inferior facilities for African-Americans. For example, public schools with mostly black students received less money than schools with mostly white students.

In 1954, the U. S. Supreme Court handed down a landmark decision in ***Brown v. Board of Education of Topeka, Kansas,*** in which it declared that it was unconstitutional for states to maintain separate public schools for black and white students. *Brown* explicitly overturned the "separate but equal" standard established in *Plessy.* The Court in *Brown* ruled that a separate education was "inherently" an unequal education even if the conditions in the schools were absolutely identical "with respect to buildings, curricula, qualifications and salaries of teachers, and other 'tangible' factors." The Court asserted that by keeping African-American children out of the white school, that is, segregating them, the school system is stating that they are inferior and injuring them mentally and emotionally "in a way unlikely ever to be undone." Thus, segregation, even in "equal conditions," harms the entire community of both black and white children by teaching that black children are inferior to whites.

The *Brown* decision had far-reaching implications. It was easy for the Court to abolish the "separate but equal" doctrine and insist that schools be integrated, but desegregating the schools would not be easy. In 1954, all southern public schools were segregated. There were literally two school systems: one for black children and one for white children. A year later, the Court, recognizing that desegregating the schools would be time-consuming and costly, ordered that the schools proceed with "all deliberate speed." This sensible order allowed the public school systems to desegregate in an orderly manner. Unfortunately, it also allowed school districts that did not want to change to drag their feet.

In the mid-1950s, segregation had become incorporated into the southern states far more than any other part of the country. Many Southerners were unwilling ever to accept desegregation. A crisis arose in 1957 in Little Rock, Arkansas when a local school board, *under a federal court order*, voted to allow nine African-American students to attend an all-white high school. Arkansas Governor Orville Faubus called out the Arkansas National Guard to *prevent* the black students from attending classes.

Eisenhower felt like most Northerners. He believed it was "just plain nuts" to *force* white parents to send their children to integrated schools. However, Governor Faubus had directly challenged the power of the federal government. That Eisenhower could not allow. He swiftly sent 10,000 heavily armed paratroopers to Little Rock to escort the nine African-American students to class.

The Civil Rights Movement

African-Americans had been working for equality long before the *Brown* decision. However, in the months following the end of World War II, the civil rights movement gained a new momentum. The war itself had exposed a great irony in American society. Well-known World War II historian Stephen Ambrose, commenting on this irony, would later write that, "The world's greatest democracy fought the world's greatest racist with a segregated army." Many other Americans of the time noted this irony and determined to end segregation in America.

In 1947, **Jackie Robinson** broke baseball's color barrier when he became the first African-American athlete to play for a major league baseball team, the *Brooklyn Dodgers*. Despite animosity from both players and fans, Robinson became a star second baseman. In 1949, he was the National League batting champion.

Once Jackie Robinson had broken the color barrier, other African-American athletes were given opportunities to play professional sports. The *Cleveland Browns* led the National Football League in hiring black players. With Hall of Famers' Bill Willis and Marion Motley, the Browns would win *five championships* in the late 1940s.

By 1960, black and Hispanic athletes were playing in all the professional sports leagues, although some owners continued to refuse to hire African-American players. The smarter owners hired athletes based on their abilities rather than the color of their skins. These athletes gave hope to black and Hispanic communities and filled them with pride.

In June 1941, President Roosevelt had issued an executive order banning discrimination in the defense industries. On February 2, 1948, Truman followed up on Roosevelt's order by sending a "Special Message to the Congress" calling for stronger civil rights legislation. He asked Congress to enact legislation with ten specific goals, among them strengthening existing civil rights statutes; providing better protections for the right to vote; and eliminating discrimination in interstate transportation facilities.

Jackie Robinson (1949). Although the term "hero" is overused to describe sports figures it does apply to Jackie Robinson. In 1947 he transformed professional sports by becoming the first African-American to play major league baseball. During his first season with the Brooklyn Dodgers he endured abuse from players and spectators who taunted and heckled him. Robinson responded by becoming baseball's Rookie of the Year and helping the Dodgers win the National League championship. Over the next ten years, this Hall of Fame player led the Dodgers to six pennants and one World Series title. He continued working for civil rights after he retired from baseball.

On July 26, 1948, President Truman, made a dramatic change to America when he issued an executive order which ended segregation in the armed forces. As a result of Truman's order, African-Americans served in all combat units during the Korean War and fought in all major battles. In October 1951, the all-black 24th Infantry Regiment, which had been created in 1869, was disbanded, basically ending segregation in the Army. Desegregation also meant more black officers and more black soldiers in special units.

The *Brown* decision energized and empowered African-Americans to seek equality not only in public schools but everywhere. In December 1955, a brave African-American woman named **Rosa Parks** was arrested and jailed in Montgomery, Alabama for refusing to give her seat on a city bus to a white man. The next day, 50,000 African-Americans in Montgomery began boycotting the city's buses until the rule changed that mandated the blacks sit in the back of the city buses. Of course, losing so many riders cost the city bus company a great deal of money.

The Montgomery Bus Boycott lasted for almost a year. It ended when the Supreme Court ruled that Alabama's segregation laws were unconstitutional. Although the struggle for civil rights continued, the African-Americans had won this battle.

The man who had led the boycott was a young black Baptist minister named **Martin Luther King Jr.** Reverend King was destined to become the principal leader of the Civil Rights movement. He favored direct action, such as **sit-ins** and

Martin Luther King Jr. by Boris Chaliapin (1957) (Commissioned by Time Magazine, National Portrait Gallery). The portrait shows King and the Montgomery bus boycott (bottom left). The success of the bus boycott made Dr. King a national figure. In February 1957, Time Magazine featured his portrait on its cover and published a lengthy article on the twenty-eight-year-old pastor. In the article, King said that his beliefs came from Christ and that his methods of passive resistance came from Gandhi.

boycotts, that often caused clashes with police. However, King believed in non-violence. Regardless of the violence perpetrated against them, Martin Luther King told his followers not to fight back. Although he believed in non-violence mainly for religious reasons, he had practical reasons as well. King believed that, to win the civil rights conflict, African-Americans needed to appeal to their white neighbors' better natures, rather than working through violence. King was confident that eventually black Americans would win the support of white Americans.

The sit-ins, especially at segregated lunch counters and restaurants, are a good example of the kind of peaceful protest in which King's followers engaged. A group of African-Americans would enter a restaurant that served only whites. They would sit quietly but would not leave until they were served or arrested. Whatever happened, they drew attention to the policy of segregation and their demand for simple fair treatment.

A New Frontier

By 1960, America stood on the brink of a new frontier. A new generation of Americans stood ready to face a new set of challenges. America stood ready to boldly go where no one had gone before.

Answer the following questions:

1. What is the UN General Assembly? What does it do? What nations are represented in it?
2. What is the UN Security Council? What does it do? What nations are represented in it?
3. What is the Katyn Forest Massacre?
4. What are Soviet satellites? Name at least five Soviet Satellites.
5. What is the Cold War?
6. Why did the depression Truman feared not materialize after World War II?
7. What is the Taft-Hartley Act?
8. How and why did Japan become an economic superpower after World War II?
9. What was the Truman Doctrine?
10. What was the Marshall Plan?
11. Why did China fall to the Communists? What role did the US play in the fall of China to the Communists?
12. What was the Berlin Airlift? Why was it necessary? Was it successful?
13. What is NATO? Why was it started? Was/Is it successful?
14. How did the Soviet Union develop an atomic bomb so quickly?
15. Why did Truman order troops into Korea?
16. Why did Truman relieve MacArthur of his command?
17. Describe some of the actions President Eisenhower took to fight the Cold War. Mention his actions in at least two nations.
18. What two major transportation programs did President Eisenhower initiate?
19. What is the significance of the Supreme Court decision in *Brown v. Board of Education*? What did the Supreme Court direct in the decision?
20. How did Martin Luther King Jr. become the leader of the Civil Rights movement in America during the late 1950s? What methods did he use to win civil rights for African-Americans?

Identify the following:

1. Rosa Parks
2. Joseph McCarthy
3. Alger Hiss
4. Iron Curtain
5. Jackie Robinson
6. William J. Brennan
7. Earl Warren
8. Klaus Fuchs

The Vietnam War Era
1960-1974

Dawn of a New Era or *Whistler's Mother Watches the 1960 Presidential Debate* (after *Whistler's Mother* by James McNeil Whistler) (created 2020 by Ken Clark). Although the period from the late 1940s to the present day has many names, e.g. Cold War, Vietnam Era, Reagan Era, War on Terrorism, nothing has had such an impact on America and the world as television. Television has changed the world in a way that almost nothing else has. Thus, unlike eras that have come and gone, the Television Era seems here to stay. In the photoshopped image above, Whistler's mother watches the 1960 Presidential Debate on her black and white television. Behind her, a blue curtain has been pulled back to reveal a bright orange background. Television will be color, bright, brash, and vulgar soon enough.

Introduction

The 1960s were a time of great unrest in the United States. For the first time since the Civil War, Americans seemed more concerned with their differences than their similarities. Sadly, this attitude would worsen over the coming decades. It seemed like the catalyst for this confrontation involved America's participation in the war in Vietnam. Many Americans opposed the war but many supported it. Many did not understand it.

The 1960s were also a time of unparalleled achievement in the United States. America achieved something that humans had dreamed of for thousands of years. Americans traveled in space and walked on the moon.

The 1960s were a time of great cultural and social change in the United States. Americans began to lose faith in God and faith in their country. They began to drift away from the moral values that they had embraced for hundreds of years. The 1960s saw a decline in the traditional family structure and an increase in drug use.

For the first time in history, Americans saw all these events unfold in their living rooms. The 1960s saw the rise of perhaps the most influential social media tool in all of history: television. Television affected presidential elections, American culture, and American foreign policy. In short, television changed everything.

Television

From the development of the printing press until the advent of the Internet, no other media tool has had such an impact on society, especially American society, as **television**. Television, the ability to transmit moving images with sound the same way sound is transmitted by radio, began in the late 1920s when **Philo Farnsworth** developed the first functioning television. Regularly scheduled television broadcasts began to appear in the early 1930s, but the quality of the black and white pictures was very poor. Over the next years, technology improved. RCA and CBS began producing regular television programming, but it could only be seen in New York City.

Philo Farnsworth

By the late 1940s, manufacturers began producing reliable TV sets that almost everyone could afford. By then, NBC, ABC, and CBS all had television networks and everyone wanted a TV. During the 1950s, about seven million sets were sold every year. By 1960, almost every family had at least one TV. Because television sets came in a variety of price ranges, even relatively poor families could afford a television. Color television emerged in the early 1950s. However, color sets were very expensive and most networks continued to broadcast in black and white.

The 1950s became the "Golden Age of Television." Many radio stars moved their shows to TV. *Jack Benny* and *Burns and Allen*, who had hit radio shows, became TV stars. However, television, unlike radio, required that a performer be physically attractive, not simply have a "good voice." Many radio actors did not make the switch to TV because they lacked the physical attractiveness.

One of the leading types of shows in the early days of TV were dramatic series called **soap operas** because they were sponsored by manufacturers of soap products. Sports were among the top programs as well; then, as now, Americans loved watching football and baseball on TV. Nightly news programs were also extremely popular. TV became more influential in people's lives during the 1950s and 1960s.

In 1960, for the first time in American history, a presidential debate was televised. The entire nature of political campaigns changed as a result. From that point on, television would play a central role in the electoral process.

The 1960 Presidential Nominees

In 1960, a war hero once again ran for president. This time, however, the hero was a Democrat. His name was **John Fitzgerald Kennedy**.

John F. Kennedy was the scion of an established Irish Catholic family from Boston. John's father, **Joseph P. Kennedy**, was one of the richest men in America, friends with President Franklin Roosevelt, and had served as ambassador to Great Britain. Joseph, in addition to being one of America's leading Catholics, was also one of its most influential Democrats.

Joseph ensured that his sons had every advantage. John attended the most prestigious preparatory schools, then Harvard University. During World War II, when John Kennedy received a commission in the Navy, he requested combat duty. He was assigned to a patrol torpedo

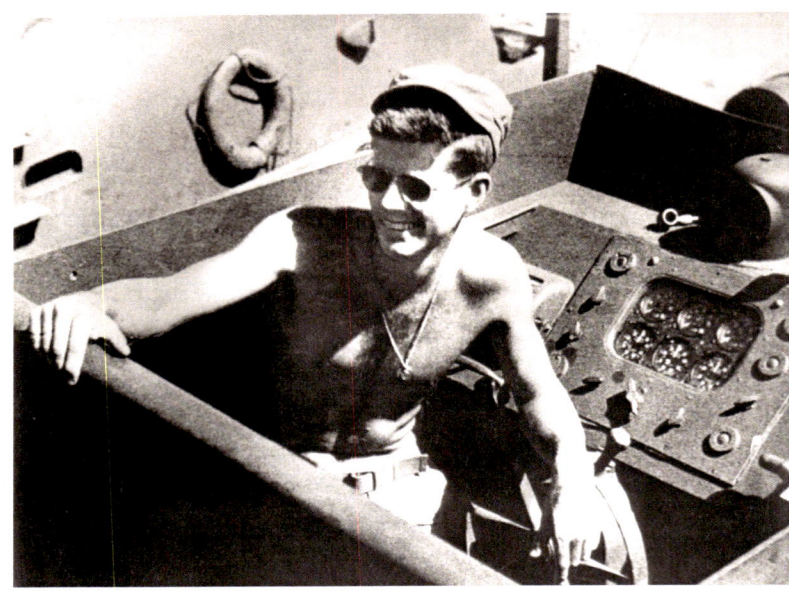

Lieutenant Kennedy at the helm of the PT 109. After the PT 109 was destroyed, Kennedy, who had been on the swim team at Harvard, swam more than three miles towing an injured man by a belt clamped in his teeth.

(PT) boat squadron in the Philippines. On August 2, 1943, while he and his crew were on a routine night patrol, a Japanese destroyer rammed his boat, the *PT 109*, slicing it in two. Despite a severe back injury, Kennedy led the survivors on a swim to a small nearby island. Shortly thereafter, fearing discovery by the Japanese, they swam to a larger island. For his bravery and ingenuity in preventing his crew's capture until they were rescued, John Kennedy received the Navy and Marine Corp Medal. Kennedy returned to combat but his back injury continued to be a problem. He was honorably discharged in 1945.

In 1946, war hero and Democrat John F. Kennedy was elected to the House of Representatives, one of a number of veterans elected to that Congress. In 1952, Kennedy was elected to the U. S. Senate, defeating a three-term Republican incumbent. At the 1956 Democratic Presidential convention, Kennedy gave the speech that nominated Adlai Stevenson. This brought Kennedy into the national spotlight. Four years later, he decided to run for president.

In 1960, a number of Democrats, including Adlai Stevenson, sought their Party's nomination. However, John Kennedy possessed several advantages over them. First, Kennedy was a decorated war hero who had been wounded in battle. Second, in the age of television, Kennedy was **telegenic**. He was quite good-looking and incredibly charismatic, so necessary for election. Also, he was married to a very pretty wife, Jacqueline, who campaigned with him. Third, Kennedy had a good political organization run by his younger brother **Robert Kennedy**. The Kennedy political organization would elect numerous members of the family to office. Also, people viewed Kennedy as being particularly intelligent. In 1956, he had written a prize-winning book, *Profiles in Courage*, about U. S. senators. Finally, Kennedy had *broad voter appeal*. He seemed liberal on social issues, but not too liberal. He was anti-Communist, so he appealed to conservatives. When he chose **Senator Lyndon Johnson** of Texas as his vice president, it clinched the nomination for him.

In his speech accepting the nomination, Kennedy maintained that the economy was not growing fast enough and that the nation needed new ideas. Unlike President Eisenhower's administration, a Kennedy administration would be imaginative and vigorous. Kennedy set forth his vision of the future which he called the "**New Frontier**." Kennedy said, "... *the New Frontier of which I speak is not a set of promises – it is a set of challenges. It sums up not what I intend to offer the American people, but what I intend to ask of them.*"

During the campaign, Kennedy attacked Eisenhower's record. This made great sense because his opponent was Eisenhower's vice president. In 1960, the Republicans nominated **Richard M. Nixon** for president.

Unlike the wealthy John Kennedy, Richard Nixon was the son of middle-class parents who operated a small grocery store in Whittier, California. During the War, Nixon enlisted in the Navy, performing his duties well, and received a number of commendations. In 1946, he was elected to the House of Representatives and re-elected in 1948. Nixon gained national prominence exposing anti-American activities during the Alger Hiss trial. In 1950, Californians elected him to the United States Senate. Two years later, Party leaders selected Nixon to serve as Eisenhower's running mate. After eight years as Eisenhower's vice president, Nixon's experience, especially in international affairs, made him the early favorite to win the election, as the two candidates launched their campaigns.

The 1960 Presidential Campaign

Historically, incumbent presidents campaign on behalf of their Party's nominee. However, President Eisenhower did not help Nixon. It seems that during their eight-year association, some type of friendship might have developed between Nixon and Eisenhower. Yet, in one of America's most interesting relationships, it did not.

Nixon had been chosen as Eisenhower's running mate by the Party's leaders, not Eisenhower, who was not involved in politics. So, the two men had no relationship to begin with. During Eisenhower's campaigns, Nixon attacked his opponent so that the public could continue to like the likable Ike, but Nixon was seen as aggressive. During his time as vice president, Nixon remained totally loyal to Eisenhower in public. However, in 1954 when the Communists were driving the French out of Indochina, Nixon wanted Eisenhower to help the French and gave a public speech in support of helping them. Privately, Nixon disagreed with Eisenhower on desegregation, which Eisenhower thought was "nuts," but which Nixon completely supported.

During the campaign, a reporter asked Eisenhower if he could name a "major contribution" that Nixon had made to Eisenhower's Administration. Eisenhower half jokingly responded, "Well, if you give me a week I might think of one." Kennedy used that line against Nixon in a TV commercial.

Interestingly, after Eisenhower left office, the two families began to socialize. Nixon's daughter Julie began dating Eisenhower's grandson David. In 1968, they married. After that, Eisenhower began supporting Nixon's political campaigns.

Even without President Eisenhower's public support, Nixon still had several advantages over John F. Kennedy. Americans were enjoying a thriving economy and a comfortable lifestyle. Most voters wanted to continue the good times and saw no reason to change. Sadly, Kennedy's biggest obstacle was his Catholic faith. When Party leaders recalled the smashing defeat that anti-Catholics had engineered against Al Smith in the 1928 presidential election, Democratic leaders feared that the upcoming election would become a Republican landslide.

To allay fears that his Catholic Faith would affect his decisions if elected, on September 12, 1960, Kennedy spoke to the Greater Houston Ministerial Association. He declared, "*I believe in a president **whose views on religion are his own private affair**, neither imposed by him upon the nation, or imposed by the nation upon him .... I am not the Catholic candidate for president. I am the Democratic Party's candidate for president who happens also to be a Catholic. I do not speak for my Church on public matters, and the Church does not speak for me.*"

In the speech, Kennedy presented himself as a **religiously neutral politician** who treats his religion as a purely "private affair." However, in the words of America's leading Catholic political thinker, John Courtney Murray, S. J., "To make religion merely a private matter was idiocy." Kennedy sought to place his conscience

After his speech to the Greater Houston Ministerial Association, Senator Kennedy took questions from the audience.

in a box and take it out only when dealing with "private" matters. But what for a politician, especially a president, is a private matter? Presidents and legislators impose policies on American citizens every day. On what do they base their votes if not their consciences? Whether or not Kennedy intended in the speech to avoid Catholics being marginalized, he ultimately created terrible problems. Since then, too many Catholic politicians take positions contrary to Church teachings and the moral good, claiming that one's religious views should not have any role in the public square, because faith is nothing more than a "private affair."

Despite his Houston speech and his excellent campaign, Kennedy still trailed Nixon, who was foolishly campaigning in every state, including many he could not win and others that had too few electoral votes to matter. Nixon seemed the likely victor. However, on September 26, the first of the four Kennedy-Nixon debates was held. It proved to be the turning point of the campaign.

The TV networks had provided the televised debates with an enormous amount of publicity, so as many as 70 million Americans watched the first debate. Nixon made several errors before he even arrived at the studio. First, he campaigned almost until the start of the debate, so he looked tired. Also, he had been hospitalized with an infection and had lost almost twenty pounds, so he looked sick. He refused makeup to cover his heavy facial stubble, which showed very poorly on black and white televisions. Also, his face seemed to be covered in sweat, perhaps from the hot TV lights, much of the time. On the other hand, Kennedy, who had just returned from vacation, looked tanned, handsome, young, and vigorous. When surveys about the debates were tallied, most TV viewers believed Kennedy had won, while most radio listeners, who had heard but not seen him, thought Nixon had prevailed.

Nixon would go on to win the second debate, gaining back the lost weight and wearing makeup. The third and fourth debates are considered draws. However, fewer people watched the last three debates. The first debate had made an impact. The race was now too close to call.

The 1960 Presidential Election

Sixty-eight million people voted in the 1960 presidential election. When it was over, the margin of victory was less than 113,000 votes—0.17% of the total votes. It is the second closest presidential election

Kennedy slaps his hands as he makes a point. Kennedy did almost everything right at the debate while Nixon did almost everything wrong. Nixon was tired, he banged his knee getting out of his car as he entered the TV studio and was in pain. He had been sick and spent much of the debate wiping sweat from his face because of his illness and the heat from the studio lights. His constant sweating and his facial stubble, visible in this image, created a poor impression among TV viewers. Sadly, even the color of suit he chose, light grey, was wrong because it blended into the background. Interestingly, neither Lyndon Johnson, in 1964, nor Richard Nixon, when ran again in 1968 and in 1972, would debate their opponents. The next televised presidential debate would not occur until 1976.

in American history. [In 1880, Garfield had defeated Hancock by 1,898 votes out of roughly 9.2 million cast, a .09% margin.] Kennedy won 303 electoral votes to Nixon's 219.

The tightness of the election caused many to speculate that there had been election fraud. Kennedy won Illinois on the strength of the votes in Chicago where **Richard Daley**, a Democrat, was mayor. Daley was close friends with Joseph Kennedy, who owned the largest building in Chicago. Kennedy also won Texas, the home state of his running mate, Lyndon Johnson. Johnson had a strong political machine in Texas. Some Republicans claimed that Johnson had forged votes. Had Nixon won Illinois and Texas, he would have had the 270 electoral votes needed for election.

However, Nixon did not pursue recounts and asked that others not pursue them either in order to avoid a constitutional crisis. It seemed that Nixon had accepted the results with equanimity. However, something had changed in Richard Nixon. It would be years before America saw the change, but the change would rock America.

On January 20, 1961, John F. Kennedy took the oath of office and became America's thirty-fifth president and its first Catholic president. He set forth his worldview in his Inaugural Address: "*Let the word go forth from this time and place, to friend and foe alike, that the torch has been*

Official portrait of President John F. Kennedy by Aaron Shikler. Jacqueline Kennedy told Shikler that she wanted the portrait to be a unique presentation of her husband. Thus, unlike all other presidential portraits, Shikler's image features Kennedy with his eyes downcast and his face obscured. Shikler said he sought to show the president in contemplation.

passed to a new generation of Americans, born in this century, tempered by war, disciplined by a hard and bitter peace, proud of our ancient heritage, and unwilling to witness or permit the slow undoing of those human rights to which this nation has always been committed, and to which we are committed today at home and around the world. Let every nation know, whether it wishes us good or ill, that we shall pay any price, bear any burden, meet any hardship, support any friend, oppose any foe, to assure the survival and the success of liberty."

President Kennedy's first chance to assure the success of liberty was in Cuba.

The Bay of Pigs Invasion

In 1952, **Fulgencio Batista** seized power in Cuba. Batista's regime was corrupt, but Cuba's overall economy remained stable. Less than ninety miles from Florida, Cuba was a tourist paradise for many Americans because of its gambling casinos, swank hotels, and beautiful beaches. Many American corporations opened businesses in Cuba because of the favorable tax and working conditions.

In an effort to overthrow Batista, a young Communist revolutionary named **Fidel Castro** assembled a band of followers. By November 1956, he had eighty-two followers. However, bad weather and other hardships caused most of them to leave until only fifteen remained. Most men, faced by such wholesale desertion, would have given up, but Castro was determined to achieve his goal. Deciding that good publicity would attract recruits, Castro contacted a liberal American journalist and invited him to Cuba to write a story about him. The journalist came and listened to Castro enumerate all of his "virtues." Completely hoodwinked, the journalist wrote a series of stories for the *New York Times*, praising Castro as a brilliant leader who could save Cuba from disaster. The journalist's flattering evaluation spread from New York to Havana, where it was heard by many discontented Cubans who joined Castro.

Fidel Castro on a visit to the United States in 1959

Castro did not admit he was a Communist, but there was ample evidence of his political persuasion and his ruthlessness. The American ambassador to Cuba, Earl Smith, called Castro an "unstable terrorist" and said that Castro taking power it would be the worst thing that could happen to Cuba. However, Smith's superior **refused** to pass any of his reports on Castro to his superiors at the State Department. As a result, the State Department proposed an arms embargo against the Batista regime in March 1958. Ambassador Smith strongly objected, but he was ignored and President Eisenhower approved the embargo. Batista, realizing that his life was in jeopardy because of Castro's increasing strength and vicious intentions, fled Cuba on New Year's Day 1959.

Once in power, Castro's true colors surfaced very quickly. He established close ties with the Soviet Union. He murdered his political enemies and any military officers who opposed him. Castro seized millions of dollars of American assets and businesses. Members of Castro's regime tortured those who did not support him. The Catholic Church suffered persecution. Thousands of Cubans fled and sought asylum in the United States.

Principally due to Vice President Nixon's urgent insistence, President Eisenhower approved a plan to overthrow Castro's regime. The **Central Intelligence Agency (CIA)**, America's foremost spy organization, began to train a small force of Cuban refugees. They would return to Cuba to depose Fidel Castro. Because the plan was secret, *Senator* Kennedy was unaware of it.

When *President* Kennedy learned of the planned invasion of Cuba, he hesitated. President Kennedy wanted the United States to be seen as a "helper" nation, rather than appear to be an aggressive nation, even against a Communist dictatorship. For example, in early 1961, Kennedy had created the **Peace Corps**, an organization of volunteers who traveled to poor countries to help the people. Kennedy wanted to raise the standard of living in Latin American nations through economic aid and the Peace Corps. He did not like the idea of invading other nations.

Thus, Kennedy inherited the Castro problem and the Cuban freedom fighters' operation; however, he was reluctant to support an invasion. At the same time, he was unwilling to cancel the invasion which might remove a vicious dictator. Ultimately, Kennedy reluctantly approved the CIA plan.

On April 17, 1961, the exiled Cuban freedom fighters were put ashore at the **Bay of Pigs** in western Cuba. The invasion was doomed to fail when President Kennedy suddenly abandoned his promise to provide enough air support for the Cubans in their landing. Consequently, shortly after the Cuban patriots reached the shore, Castro's aircraft attacked the expedition's ships. The brave Cuban exiles fought as long as their ammunition lasted. The survivors were captured and imprisoned. The Bay of Pigs fiasco not only affected Cuba and the United States, but also emboldened the Soviet Union.

The Berlin Wall

Following Josef Stalin's death, **Nikita Khrushchev** became the leader of the Soviet Union after a brief power struggle. Khrushchev, often called "The Butcher of Budapest" for his vicious repression of the 1956 Hungarian Uprising, met with President Kennedy in Vienna, Austria, in June 1961. President Kennedy was shocked when Khrushchev spoke of ending the American presence in Berlin. Kennedy flatly told Khrushchev that he would not allow the Soviets to take West Berlin. Both men had taken the measure of the other. Based on the Bay of Pigs debacle, Khrushchev believed that Kennedy was a weakling who would not fulfill his commitments.

In August 1961, in an effort to stop East Germans from escaping to the West, Khrushchev suddenly began building a very high wall across Berlin which cut the Soviet zone off from the western zones. Since the

The Brandenburg Gate. Originally built in the center of Berlin by Prussian king Frederick William II in 1791. For centuries it was one of the best-known landmarks in Germany. During the Cold War it took on a sadder and more sinister meaning as it become a symbol of oppression as it stood at the boundary of East and West Berlin. The Berlin Wall passed directly by the western side of the gate. The sign warns, "Attention! You are leaving West Berlin."

end of the War, thousands of East Germans had fled to Berlin and then flown to the West seeking freedom. **The Berlin Wall** had the desired effect. Almost no East German could escape to the West. Those that tried did so secretly. Anyone who was caught was killed or imprisoned. *The Berlin Wall became the symbol of the Cold War.* It reminded everyone that the people of Eastern Europe were the prisoners of Communist regimes.

Some historians have wondered whether Kennedy could have stopped the construction of the Berlin Wall. American bulldozers *could have demolished the Wall* as it was being constructed. In that event, would Khrushchev have escalated the situation, or would he have backed down? Was he testing Kennedy's resolve? Future events seem to indicate that Khrushchev was testing Kennedy, because when America let the Wall stand, Khrushchev took events a step further.

The Cuban Missile Crisis

In the late summer of 1962, the Soviets began building bases in Cuba from which nuclear missiles could be launched into the United States. Castro, fearing another U.S. invasion, saw the Soviet bases as a useful deterrent, while Khrushchev, though he cared little for Castro and Cuba, saw the missiles as a bargaining chip. If he placed missiles in Cuba, he could trade their withdrawal for America's withdrawal from West Berlin.

Since the failed invasion at the Bay of Pigs, American intelligence agencies had been spying on Cuba using high-flying U-2 spy planes. However, due to bad weather, spy missions over Cuba had been canceled for several weeks, during which time the Soviets had secretly begun construction of their missile bases. On October 14, a U-2 mission took photographs that clearly indicated the construction of a missile base and objects that were identified as medium range ballistic missiles capable of striking targets deep within the United States with nuclear warheads.

President Kennedy now faced the very real probability of World War III. Albert Einstein, knowing the devastation that nuclear weapons would cause, is reported to have said that he did not know what weapons would be used to fight World War III, but World War IV would be fought with sticks and stones. If Kennedy destroyed the Cuban missile bases, it might trigger a third world war, or an attack on Berlin. If Kennedy did nothing, nuclear weapons would sit less than 100 miles off America's shores, a constant threat of nuclear destruction, and a ready blackmail tool for Khrushchev and his successors.

For the next week, Kennedy met with his top advisers and discussed his two main options: an air strike against the Cuban missile bases or a naval blockade of Cuba. On October 22, 1962, having reached

A US Navy destroyer intercepts a Soviet cargo ship on its way to Cuba.

a decision, President Kennedy appeared on national television to show photos bolstering his position and inform America of the **Cuban Missile Crisis**. He demanded that the Soviets remove all offensive weapons from Cuba and close the missile bases. He informed the Soviets that he was establishing a naval "quarantine" around Cuba. In his address, he said, *"All ships of any kind bound for Cuba, from whatever nation or port, will, if found to contain cargoes of offensive weapons, be turned back.... We are not at this time, however, denying the necessities of life as the Soviets attempted to do in their Berlin blockade of 1948."* Kennedy went on to say that it would be American policy that if any nuclear missile was launched from Cuba against any nation in the Western Hemisphere, it would be considered as an attack by the Soviet Union on the United States. In that case, the United States would launch a full retaliatory strike upon the Soviet Union.

For the next several days the world teetered on the brink of nuclear war. Pope St. John XXIII begged the Soviets not to start a war. On October 27, a U-2 plane flown by Major Rudolf Anderson was shot down over Cuba, resulting in Anderson's death. When Kennedy and his advisors learned of the incident they believed that war was imminent, but they also believed that Khrushchev did not order the attack. Realizing the incredible danger the world faced, Kennedy was finally able to negotiate a deal with the Soviets. Khrushchev agreed to remove the missiles if Kennedy promised not to invade Cuba. War had been averted. For his heroism, Major Anderson was posthumously awarded the Air Force Cross. Many historians believe that his sacrifice averted one of history's greatest catastrophes.

Following the crisis, a "hot line" between Moscow and Washington was established which let the leaders of the Soviet Union and the United States speak directly to each other, rather than through intermediaries as had occurred during the missile crisis.

The Space Race

One of the less confrontational aspects of the Cold War was the **Space Race**, the competition between the United States and the Soviet Union to be the first nation to put a man in space and walk on the moon. Winning the Space Race meant achieving an ideological victory by sending a "free" man into space rather than a Communist. Also, scientists saw national security implications with "controlling" space. Space was the new and the final frontier.

The Mercury 7, America's first astronauts, in 1960. Back row (Left to Right: Alan Shepard, Gus Grissom, Gordon Cooper; front row: Wally Schirra, Deke Slayton, John Glenn, Scott Carpenter. All seven eventually flew in space. Shepard became the first American in space in 1961 and later walked on the Moon as part of Apollo 14 in 1971. Grissom died in 1967 in the Apollo 1 fire. Schirra flew Apollo 7, the first manned Apollo mission. Slayton, grounded because of a medical issue, flew on the Apollo–Soyuz Test Project in 1975. Glenn became the first American in orbit in 1962 and in 1998 flew on the Space Shuttle Discovery becoming at age 77, the oldest person to fly in space at that time. He outlived his fellow Mercury Seven heroes when he died in 2016 at the age of 95.

Neil Armstrong walking on the moon. "We came in peace for all mankind."

In October 1957, the Soviets took an early lead in the Space Race when they launched *Sputnik I* (Russian for "traveling companion"), the first man-made satellite, into space. The United States responded by sending the first American satellite into orbit the following month. Less than four years after the launch of Sputnik, the Soviets surged ahead once again when Soviet cosmonaut (astronaut) **Yuri Gagarin** became the first man to travel in space. In May 1961, **Alan Shepherd** became the first American into space. In February 1962, **John Glenn** became the first American to orbit the Earth.

On September 12, 1962, at Rice University, President Kennedy explained America's ultimate goal in the Space Race. He told the Rice students that, "*We choose to go to the moon in this decade and do the other things, not because they are easy, but because they are hard, because that goal will serve to organize and measure the best of our energies and skills, because that challenge is one that we are willing to accept, one we are unwilling to postpone, and one which we intend to win ...*"

On July 20, 1969, America won the Space Race when **Neil Armstrong** and **Edwin "Buzz" Aldrin** became the first humans to walk on the moon. Live television showed Armstrong descending from his *Apollo 11* capsule. As he descended the stairs and took mankind's first steps on another world, he declared, "*That's one small step for man, one giant leap for mankind.*" Armstrong and Aldrin placed an American flag and a commemorative plaque on the Moon which ended with the words "We came in peace for all mankind." (**Note**: According to NASA, Armstrong was supposed to have said "That's one small step for *a* man..." In the excitement of the moment he flubbed his line. NASA maintains that he did say "a" but static covered the transmission.)

The Space Race was massively expensive, and people then as now questioned its value. However, it seems that the cost has been more than recouped as a result of the products created directly or indirectly from the space race. The most obvious item to be developed as a result of space exploration is the computer and all the computer-related items generated from it. From giant, room-sized computers, geniuses like **Steve Jobs** and **Bill Gates** revolutionized the world with personal computers, cell phones, iPads, etc. Further developments led to the Internet, digital movies, and digital cameras. The list is almost endless. This does not mention the advances computer technology has made in medical science and micro-technology. The cost of the Space Race was massively expensive, but the return on that investment has been many times greater.

President Kennedy's Domestic Agenda

After the Cuban Missile Crisis, President Kennedy began to focus more on domestic affairs. In 1963, he proposed a large tax cut. He argued that cutting taxes would stimulate the economy. People would have more money to spend on consumer goods, which would cause businesses to produce more, which would cause businesses to hire more employees who could buy more goods and so forth. Unemployment would decrease and personal and business income would increase. In time, the government would actually receive *more income because more people were paying taxes and businesses were paying taxes on more money.* In other words, Kennedy proposed stimulating a normally strong business cycle.

Sadly, both the Democrats and the Republicans in Congress failed to see the wisdom in this plan. They objected to cutting taxes when the federal government had a **deficit**. Of course, had the government reduced its spending and lived within its means, like normal Americans, the deficit would have been reduced. However, Congress seems unable to do that. Thus, Congress refused to pass Kennedy's tax legislation.

The Growing Civil Rights Movement

During his election campaign, John F. Kennedy pledged to end racial discrimination. As president, he did his best to fulfill his promise. In 1962, he banned racial and religious discrimination in federally financed housing. He ordered the Interstate Commerce Commission to end segregation on interstate buses, trains, and planes. He appointed the first black justice to the U. S. Supreme Court, **Thurgood Marshall**, the attorney who had won the *Brown v. Board of Education* case. However, Kennedy's main action occurred as a result of work done by Martin Luther King Jr.

After leading the Montgomery Bus Boycott, Dr. King became a national figure and the leader of the Civil Rights Movement in America. In June 1957, in recognition of his leadership role, Vice President Nixon invited King to Washington, D.C. to discuss civil rights and how congressional Republicans could help.

In 1963, in an attempt to involve President Kennedy more in the Civil Rights movement, King led a campaign in Birmingham, Alabama against segregation. King chose Birmingham because he believed that it was the most racially divided city in the United States. King planned to stage a non-violent protest, as he always did, to draw attention to the

Justice Thurgood Marshall. Along with William Brennan and William Douglas, Marshall would be one of the most liberal Justices on the Court most notably joining the majority in Roe v. Wade to create a "right" to abortion. When Marshall retired from the Court in 1991, he was replaced by another African American, Clarence Thomas, who was as conservative as Marshall was liberal.

situation and to force business owners and city leaders to end segregation in public facilities and schools. Sadly, the peaceful sit-ins and marches became violent when the local police turned fire hoses on the marchers to drive them from the streets. Even more horrific, the police used attack dogs on the marchers. King was thrown in jail where he wrote his famous "**Letter from Birmingham Jail**."

When photographs of the police confronting the protesters appeared, millions of Americans, both black and white, were shocked. They were also impressed by the courage of the black Americans, many of whom were teenagers. When Reverend King was released, he had gained even more support for the civil rights movement.

As a result of the Birmingham incident, in June 1963, President Kennedy proposed a sweeping civil rights bill. It prohibited racial segregation in schools, employment, and all public accommodations. However, the bill stalled in the Senate.

To publicly demonstrate their support for President Kennedy's proposed legislation, Reverend King asked people to join him in a massive **March on Washington**. On August 28, 1963, more than 250,000 people came to Washington to lend their support. They heard one of the most riveting orations ever delivered in America. In his famous *I Have a Dream Speech,"* Dr. King said that he dreamed that one day, his four children *"would live in a nation where they would not be judged by the color of their skin, but by the content of their character.… From every mountainside, let freedom ring. And when we let it ring from every village, from every hamlet, from every state and every city, we will speed up the day when all God's children, black men and white men, Jews and Gentiles, Protestants and Catholics, will be able to join hands and sing the words of the old Negro spiritual: 'Free at last. Free at last. Thank God Almighty, we are free at last.'"*

During the early 1960s, President Kennedy issued several executive orders banning segregation in federal housing projects, as well as on any public vehicles, like planes and trains, engaging in interstate travel. Yet, probably the greatest victories civil rights advocates won during this period occurred when two amendments they had promoted were added to the Constitution. In 1961, the states ratified the Twenty-Third amendment which permits residents of the District of Columbia, the overwhelming majority of whom are African-Americans, to vote in presidential elections. In his 1948, "Special Message" to Congress, Truman had called for an anti-poll tax law. On January 23, 1964, the Twenty-Fourth Amendment to the Constitution, which prohibits any poll tax in federal elections, was ratified.

From the steps of the Lincoln Memorial, Martin Luther King, Jr. waves to the more than 250,000 people who have just heard him deliver his "I have a Dream Speech," his most memorable and moving oration.

Judge Sarah T. Hughes administers the oath of office to Lyndon B. Johnson aboard Air Force One two hours after the assassination of President Kennedy. Jackie Kennedy (right),clearly in shock, still in her blood-soaked clothes, looks on. Johnson's wife, new First Lady, Lady Bird Johnson (left), observes her husband in this moment of national tragedy. While the murder of President Kennedy was horrific, the orderly transition of power from one president to another demonstrates the exceptionalism of American democracy. Other nations following such an assassination might fall into civil war.

President Kennedy is Assassinated

On November 22, 1963, President Kennedy flew to Dallas, Texas, to gain support for his 1964 re-election campaign. As he rode in an open limousine through the downtown streets of Dallas, Texas, shots rang out and bullets struck the president in his head and throat. He was rushed to Parkland Hospital where he was pronounced dead. While the country mourned in shock, Vice President Johnson was sworn in as the thirty-sixth president aboard Air Force One, the president's airplane.

The Dallas police searched the city for the assassin. Less than an hour after the death of President Kennedy, a veteran Dallas police officer named J. D. Tippit was shot and killed. Minutes later, police charged **Lee Harvey Oswald** with the murder of Officer Tippit and took him into custody. Oswald, a former Marine, now a deranged Communist and a supporter of Fidel Castro, denied any part in the murder. However, subsequent investigation uncovered evidence against Oswald who was charged with the assassination of President Kennedy. Two days later, while in police custody, Oswald was shot to death by **Jack Ruby**, a local nightclub owner with connections to organized crime.

Numerous investigations have been conducted into the Kennedy assassination and many theories have been developed to explain it. However, no evidence has been introduced that Oswald, a trained Marine sniper, could not have acted alone. Historians likely will never know the full truth.

President Lyndon B. Johnson

After the assassination of President Kennedy, Vice President **Lyndon Baines Johnson** became America's thirty-sixth president. President Johnson promised to continue the policies that President Kennedy had favored. However, Johnson was unlike Kennedy in many ways. First, Johnson had served for many years in government. He was first elected to Congress in 1937. He was the first member of Congress to volunteer for active military duty on the day after the Pearl Harbor attack. In 1948, he was elected to the U. S. Senate, where he developed a reputation as a man who got things done. Thus, it was not surprising when President Johnson approached Congress and asked the members, his old friends, to approve the most liberal sweeping social welfare programs since the New Deal. Johnson sought to approve Kennedy's programs both as a legacy to the assassinated president and to advance his own career. Using a combination of charm and pressure, Johnson convinced Congress to enact much of his legislative agenda.

Lyndon Johnson's official White House portrait. Johnson was known throughout his career for his domineering personality and his aggressiveness in advancing legislation he supported. From 1955 to 1961, he served as majority leader in the Senate where he helped enact a number of Civil Rights laws.

In 1964, Congress adopted the Civil Rights Act that Kennedy had proposed but had been stalled in the Senate. The **Civil Rights Act of 1964** was one of the most comprehensive laws that Congress ever passed. It prohibited discrimination in most public places, such as restaurants and hotels. The Act ordered states to provide identical voting requirements for blacks and whites, and it prohibited discrimination on the basis of race or gender by companies or individuals engaged in interstate commerce. It denied federal funds to public school districts that were segregated, but offered funds to public schools working to desegregate.

President Johnson tried to abolish poverty in the United States. In his State of the Union Address in 1964, Johnson declared a national **War on Poverty**. Congress endorsed his plan and passed the **Economic Opportunity Act** of 1964, a massive spending bill to try to end poverty. Congress created numerous programs to aid poor Americans. These included programs that provided federal funds to help provide public housing; to start training programs to assist the poor to find employment; and to provide food stamps and other welfare benefits for poor families.

The Election of 1964

In 1964, the Democrats nominated Lyndon Johnson for president, whom most Democrats saw as the heir apparent to John Kennedy. Democrats especially approved of his handling of the Civil Rights Act and his War on Poverty. Thus, he easily won the nomination.

The Republicans nominated Arizona Senator **Barry Goldwater**, whom most historians still consider the founder of the modern conservative political movement. Senator Goldwater believed the federal government was usurping powers granted by the Constitution to the states, not to the Federal government. Senator Goldwater decried Johnson's massive new federal regulations that, though sounding beneficial, restricted individual liberty.

Some people labeled Goldwater as "too conservative." However, in his speech accepting the Republican nomination for president, Senator Goldwater addressed the issue of his "extremism." He said, "Extremism in the defense of liberty is no vice, and moderation in pursuit of justice is no virtue."

During the campaign, Johnson painted Goldwater as not only extreme but dangerous. Johnson ran one of the most controversial, but most effective, political ads in history. Known as the "Daisy" ad, it ran only once, but had a massive impact. The ad showed a little girl standing in a meadow picking the petals off a daisy and counting them. When she reaches "nine," she pauses. Then a male voice says "ten." It is the start of a missile launch countdown. The picture zooms in on her eye until the blackness of her pupil fills the screen. Suddenly the blackness is replaced by the flash of a nuclear explosion and footage of a mushroom cloud. At the end of the spot the announcer says, "Vote for President Johnson ... [because] the stakes are too high for you to stay home."

Though Goldwater is never mentioned, the implication was clear: Goldwater will start a nuclear war.

Johnson convinced millions of Americans that, as President Kennedy's heir, he still had important work to finish. He easily defeated Barry Goldwater. The Democrats increased their majority in Congress.

A rather clever portrait of Barry Goldwater (1964). The artist depicts the elephant, the symbol of the Republican Party wearing the same kind of glasses as Goldwater. The sign the elephant carries reads "AuH20." "Au" is the chemical symbol for the element gold while H20 is the symbol for water. Thus, AuH20 reads "Goldwater."

The Great Society

Lyndon Johnson considered his landslide victory a *mandate*, and he had many other ideas for social changes. In his Inaugural Address, Johnson asked Congress to pass laws that would create his "Great Society" programs. The Democratic Congress approved almost everything he asked for. Congress created **Medicare**, which provides health insurance to people over the age of sixty-five. It passed a Housing Act which helped poor people pay their rent. Congress also passed two highway safety acts in 1966 which created the Department of Transportation and empowered the federal government to set and administer new safety standards for motor vehicles. The Acts decreased highway fatalities dramatically.

The Great Society and the War on Poverty were noble dreams. They did achieve many of their goals. Lives were saved when seat belts were required in cars. More blacks did gain the right to vote. However, the programs were terribly expensive. Also, many Americans objected to the federal government taking power reserved to the states and local governments.

The Selma to Montgomery Marches

The right to vote had always been at the heart of the civil rights movement. In January 1965, Martin Luther King launched a voter registration campaign aimed at registering African-Americans in the South, where, despite federal laws encouraging blacks to vote, local white leaders continued to hinder black voting. King chose to start his campaign in Selma, Alabama, a city with a majority black population, but less than two percent black voter registration.

During the first weeks, King and his supporters registered many African-Americans without serious incident. However, in February, the peaceful registrations and protests encountered violence as police attacked the protesters. Sadly, one man died during the violence. In response to the death, King called for a march from Selma to Montgomery, the state capital to protest the violence.

On March 7, the protesters, led by **John Lewis** because King was in Atlanta, began marching from Selma. However, as they crossed the Edmund Pettus Bridge, state and local police attacked the marchers with clubs and tear gas when they refused an order to disperse. Television coverage from the march, which became known as "Bloody Sunday," shocked Americans around the nation.

President Johnson spoke to Congress in support of the marchers on March 15. He declared that their cause was his cause and Congress's cause. He called upon Congress to pass a stronger voting rights act.

On March 21, King led a final march from Selma to Montgomery. This time the marchers had the protection of FBI agents and the Alabama National Guard who President Johnson had ordered to protect the marchers. Four days later, over 25,000 marchers arrived in Montgomery.

On August 6, 1965, as Dr. King and other civil rights leaders looked on, President Johnson signed the **Voting Rights Act of 1965** which he had encouraged Congress to enact back in March. The law appointed federal officials to oversee elections in districts where local white officials were refusing to allow blacks to register to vote. Within a year, over a million blacks, mostly in the south, had registered to vote. Five days later, King would declare, "Montgomery led to the Civil Rights Act of 1957 and 1960; Birmingham inspired the Civil Rights Act of 1964; and Selma produced the voting rights legislation of 1965."

The Vietnam War

The Domino Theory

During the Eisenhower Administration, many congressmen became increasingly concerned about the situation in Southeast Asia. Their concern involved what President Eisenhower called the **Domino Theory**. In 1954, Eisenhower had spoken of nations falling like a row of dominoes to Communism. Once the first one fell, the others would fall in quick succession. According to the Domino Theory, if South Vietnam fell, then its neighbors, Laos and Cambodia, would fall. The effect would continue with all of Southeast Asia falling. The Domino Effect might spread as far as India, one of the world's most populous nations, which could also fall to Communism. Based on the Domino Theory, the United States had to ensure that the first domino, South Vietnam, did not fall. However, that was proving difficult to accomplish.

In October 1955, South Vietnam had established a pro-Western, anti-Communist government, under the presidency of **Ngo Dinh Diem**, a Catholic. Although Diem's government had some corruption, as all governments do, Diem did not murder his people nor enslave them. Since 1954, **Ho Chi Minh**, the Communist leader of North Vietnam, had been supplying aid to guerrillas in South Vietnam, known as the **Viet Cong**. The Viet Cong had been fighting to conquer South Vietnam, make it a Communist nation, and unite it with the North since the country had been divided in 1954. When the Viet Cong attacks began, Diem requested American military aid, but not American soldiers. He feared that the presence of American troops would play into the hands of the Communists who would declare that the American government was interfering in a simple "civil war."

Eisenhower had sent a small number of American military advisers and special forces troops, known as **Green Berets**, to train the South Vietnamese army. The Green Berets' motto is *To Liberate the Oppressed*. In addition to advisers, Eisenhower also provided South Vietnam with economic aid and military supplies. President Kennedy continued this policy when he was elected.

In 1960, ten percent of the population of South Vietnam were Catholics, including President Diem and his closest advisers. The Communists hoped to use Diem's Faith against him. **Tri Quang** was a

Buddhist priest and a "former" member of the Communist party. On May 8, 1963, he addressed a crowd of Buddhists, claiming that the Diem government was persecuting Buddhists. The crowd grew larger and larger, until soldiers were called to keep control. Two explosions erupted in the audience, causing chaos and killing nine. Diem's soldiers were accused of firing into the crowd. This allegation was accepted as "proof" that Diem's government was persecuting Buddhists. Tri Quang continued organizing demonstrations against the alleged government persecution.

On June 11, a Buddhist monk named Quang Duc saturated his saffron-colored robes with gasoline and committed ritual suicide by setting himself on fire. The photo of the burning monk spread around the world like a poisonous wind. Many viewers assumed that the persecution by Diem's government must be terrible if men were willing to burn themselves alive. The United Nations investigated and determined that there was no persecution, but the report came too late to stop the worldwide headline news that the suicide had created.

Quang Duc's suicide, as well as their personal dislike for president Diem, caused certain members of the State Department and the CIA to begin plotting a coup to overthrow a friendly government in the middle of fighting a war against America's greatest enemy, the Communists. Representatives of the American government, notably CIA agent Lucien Conein, informed certain South Vietnamese generals unhappy with Diem that the United States would support his overthrow.

Despite warnings that Diem was the only one who could lead South Vietnam against the Communists and musings of how "leaders of other underdeveloped countries (would) … view (American) assistance if they … believe the same fate lies in store for them," President Kennedy allowed the coup to move forward. On November 1, 1963, South Vietnamese troops stormed the presidential palace. However, Diem and his brother escaped. Several hours later, the two men agreed to

South-East Asia in 1965

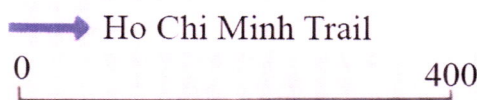
Ho Chi Minh Trail

0   400

On May 8, 1957, President Diem arrived at Washington National Airport where President Eisenhower and Secretary of State Dulles greeted him.

surrender at St. Francis Xavier Catholic Church where they often attended Mass. Although they had been promised safety, soldiers murdered President Diem and his brother.

In the aftermath of Diem's assassination, the South Vietnamese government and army fell into confusion. Many of the high-ranking officers in the Vietnamese military who had supported Diem were dismissed. Communists quickly took advantage of the absence of strong military leaders in the South by increasing the frequency and violence of their attacks. Eager to keep the pressure on the South, Ho Chi Minh asked Red China and the Soviet Union for more men and supplies. President Johnson's advisers urged him not to abandon the South Vietnamese people. They believed the U. S. should take immediate action that demonstrated a commitment to stop the Communist aggression in South Vietnam.

The Gulf of Tonkin Resolution

On August 2, 1964, three North Vietnamese gunboats attacked the American destroyer *Maddox* while it was patrolling off the coast of Vietnam, in the **Gulf of Tonkin**. On August 7, at the request of President Johnson, *Congress overwhelmingly passed the Gulf of Tonkin Resolution*, which gave the president the power to take any steps that he felt were necessary to prevent further attacks against U. S. forces. By the end of the day, President Johnson had ordered retaliatory air strikes against the Communists in Vietnam. The Gulf of Tonkin Resolution became America's legal authorization for its military involvement in the war in Vietnam.

During the 1964 election, Johnson had assured voters that he would support South Vietnam, but would not send American troops into combat. He promised he "would never send American boys to do the fighting that Asian boys should do themselves." However, continued Communist successes in Vietnam made President Johnson believe that expanding America's role was the only way to assure ultimate and final victory. That meant more ground troops – more "American boys to do the fighting." By the end of 1964, Johnson had increased the number of advisors in Vietnam to 23,000.

Johnson believed, as did Eisenhower and Kennedy, that based on Korea and Cuba, the Communists only respected force. If America left South Vietnam, it would, according to Johnson, "just whet the enemy's appetite for greater aggression and more territory, and solve nothing." Johnson accepted the Domino Theory. He felt South Vietnam *had to be defended*.

The War Escalates

In February, 1965, Johnson ordered the Air Force to begin bombing raids targeting Communist supply lines and military bases in North Vietnam. The goal was to stop North Vietnam from aiding the Viet Cong and destroy the morale of the North Vietnamese. About two-thirds of the supplies coming from the Soviet Union and Red China were destroyed before reaching their destinations. However, China and the Soviet Union sent more and more supplies. The bombing never seriously hurt North Vietnam's ability to wage war nor damaged their morale.

In March, Johnson sent 3,500 Marines to Vietnam to protect the Da Nang air base from which the bombers launched their missions into the North. The Marine's arrival changed the nature of American involvement in Vietnam from that of advisors to defenders and combatants. The following month, the Marines were authorized to fight the Viet Cong guerrillas and North Vietnamese soldiers. By the end of 1965, nearly 185,000 American troops were serving in Vietnam, and many more were on the way.

At Christmas 1965, Johnson had called for a "peace offensive," which meant stopping all the bombing. However, the Communists were unwilling to talk about peace as long as American troops remained in Vietnam. The Communists knew that once American troops left, they could defeat the South Vietnamese military and take control. Instead of leaving Vietnam, President Johnson decided to increase the pressure by resuming heavy bombing after Christmas and sending more troops. Over the next three years, the war

A Navy F-4 Phantom fighter-bomber drops its bombs on an artillery site in North Vietnam.

continued to escalate, as more and more American troops were sent to Vietnam. By the end of 1966, the number of troops in Vietnam had doubled. By the end of June 1967, American forces in Vietnam had risen to 448,800, but the Communists had increased their forces as well.

Unlike other wars America fought, Vietnam was broadcast nightly into people's living rooms. Images of soldiers fighting and dying in a faraway land began to impact the country. Although American troops launched numerous successful campaigns, in 1966 for example there were 18 major offensives, it seemed that ultimately victory was not within reach. After years without victory, people began to wonder if involvement in Vietnam really was good for the United States. An ever-growing number of Americans believed the United States should get out of Vietnam. However, many others thought President Johnson needed to pursue victory more vigorously. Americans who wanted to fight until the Vietnam War was won were called *hawks*. At the war's inception, most Americans and most people in Congress were hawks. They wanted to defeat Communism and defend South Vietnam; a country America had promised to protect. However, as the war dragged on, it became less popular. Americans needed assurance that it was almost over.

In November 1967, **General William C. Westmoreland**, the commanding general in Vietnam, tried to provide that assurance. At a speech in Washington D. C., Westmoreland said that the war had come to a point "where the end begins to come into view." He also told reporters that he was "absolutely certain that whereas in 1965 the enemy was winning, today he is certainly losing." However, Westmoreland had not calculated on the utter ruthlessness of Ho Chi Minh.

Ho was willing to sacrifice thousands of lives to make all of Vietnam a Communist nation. While American leaders in Vietnam and Washington were preparing for North Vietnam's surrender, Ho Chi Minh was organizing the biggest Communist offensive of the war. He planned to launch a countrywide attack against the Americans and the South Vietnamese. The attack would coincide with the Vietnamese New Year's Holiday, called Tet.

The Tet Offensive

Ho Chi Minh's first step in the **Tet Offensive** was declaring a ceasefire for the holiday. The American military, suspecting that the ceasefire might be a ruse, asked President Thieu of South Vietnam to cancel the holiday celebration and keep his troops on alert. Unfortunately, President Thieu refused the request. Consequently, when the Tet Offensive began, half of South Vietnam's army was at home celebrating.

Just after midnight on January 30, 1968, Viet Cong and North Vietnamese units simultaneously attacked American and South Vietnamese forces in 36 of 44 South Vietnamese provincial capital cities. About 85,000 Communist troops took part in the invasion. During the initial attack, nineteen communist troops actually penetrated the ground floor of the U. S. Embassy in Saigon before being killed. Everywhere that the Communists attacked, they were defeated, and suffered thousands of casualties. Ho Chi Minh had hoped many South Vietnamese would join the Tet offensive. When they did not, the Communists were forced to retreat.

Militarily, the Tet Offensive was a victory for the United States and South Vietnam and a disaster for the North. Total casualties for the Viet Cong and the North Vietnamese Army were estimated between forty and fifty thousand. The Viet Cong's days as an effective fighting force were over. Henceforth, the North Vietnamese Army would fight the war. Although Ho Chi Minh's forces had been decimated, he had won a huge public relations victory. The American media now concluded that it was time for America to begin the withdrawal of U. S. troops, since the Vietnam war could not be won.

On February 27, **Walter Cronkite**, whom many Americans considered the most trusted news anchor in the country, appeared on a special news program after spending several days in Vietnam. For the next hour, he reviewed the history of the war and the recent events of the Tet Offensive, which he declared was a "draw." At the end of the hour, Cronkite, sitting behind his anchor desk, delivered his *opinion* of the state of the war: *"[I]t seems now more certain than ever that the bloody experience of Vietnam is to end in a stalemate … [I]t is increasingly clear to this reporter that the only rational way out then will be to negotiate, not as victors, but as an honorable people who lived up to their pledge to defend democracy, and did the best they could."*

Walter Cronkite had declared that America could not win the war in Vietnam. After Westmoreland had declared that the

William Westmoreland. Westmoreland, a West Point graduate, had seen combat during WWII and in Korea where he commanded an Airborne Division, hence the Airborne badge on his cap. The background image alludes to his overall command of American soldiers in Vietnam.

Walter Cronkite. The portrait shows him as the long-time anchor of the CBS Evening News where he joyfully covered successful NASA missions, note the rocket over his shoulder; as well as breaking the news of President Kennedy's assassination, during which he barely maintained his composure. When Cronkite declared the Vietnam war a "stalemate," Lyndon Johnson told an adviser, "If I've lost Cronkite, I've lost middle America."

war was almost over, North Vietnam had launched a massive attack. These events shocked the American public. They believed Cronkite. The tide of public opinion began to turn against the war.

The invasion of the South by so many North Vietnamese convinced American military analysts that the war's end was far more distant than they had believed. In early March, General Westmoreland asked President Johnson for 206,000 more men. Johnson felt that the nation was discouraged and no longer had the desire or resolve to continue fighting, so he refused. Many historians later claimed that Westmoreland had lied when he said the war was nearly over; however, it is more likely that he was simply wrong in estimating the enemy's strength and resolve.

Peace Talks Begin

Perhaps a strong leader might have restored the nation's will to fight in Vietnam. President Johnson, however, appeared to be a beaten man. On the evening of March 31, 1968, Johnson appeared on national television and outlined his new policy. He announced that all air attacks on North Vietnam had been stopped. He appealed to Ho Chi Minh to enter peace talks to end the war.

President Johnson had been planning to run for a second full term in 1968. However, setbacks in Vietnam and during his re-election campaign caused him to reconsider. Johnson ended his speech by declaring that he would not seek, nor accept, the Democratic nomination for president.

In May 1968, American diplomats began holding peace talks with the North Vietnamese in Paris. Their efforts proved useless since the Communists refused to listen to any proposal. In May 1969, the United States proposed a withdrawal of all foreign troops from South Vietnam. Ho Chi Minh did not even consider it.

The *Pueblo* Incident

Following the end of the Korean War, relations between North Korea and the United States remained strained and distrustful. American troops stationed in South Korea were constantly vigilant because North Korean leader Kim Il-Sung was a cruel, mentally unbalanced tyrant. In January 1968, North Korea seized the U. S. navy ship *Pueblo*. The *Pueblo* was operating in the Sea of Japan, but the North Koreans claimed it was spying in North Korean waters. During the assault on the *Pueblo*, one American sailor was killed. The remaining eighty-two sailors were held hostage for nearly a year, while the U. S. negotiated their release. They were finally released when American diplomats signed a statement "admitting" that the *Pueblo* had been spying. North Korea never returned the *Pueblo*.

Martin Luther King Jr. is Assassinated

On April 4, 1968, Dr. King was talking with friends on the balcony of a motel in Memphis, Tennessee. Suddenly gunshots broke the early evening stillness. Moments later, Dr. King was dead. News of his death flashed around the nation and soon America was aware of the tragedy. In the days that followed the death of a man who had advocated non-violent demonstrations, riots broke out in over one

During his "I have a Dream Speech," Dr. King had spoken to both white and black Americans. He told African-Americans that, "In the process of gaining our rightful place, we must not be guilty of wrongful deeds. Let us not seek to satisfy our thirst for freedom by drinking from the cup of bitterness and hatred. We must forever conduct our struggle on the high plane of dignity and discipline. We must not allow our creative protest to degenerate into physical violence.' Surely the riots after his death would have filled him with sorrow.

hundred cities. Washington and Chicago experienced the most violent rioting. The destruction, burning, and injuries were caused by thousands of rioters who disregarded Dr. King's message of peace.

The 1968 Presidential Election

Early on, Minnesota Senator Eugene McCarthy had announced that he would challenge President Johnson for the Democratic presidential nomination. McCarthy was a leading anti-war candidate but had little support before the Tet Offensive. After Tet, McCarthy almost defeated Johnson in the New Hampshire primary on March 12. Seeing Johnson's weakness, a new candidate threw his hat into the ring.

The memory of President Kennedy's assassination was fresh in the minds of many Americans, when his younger brother, Robert, declared his candidacy. **Robert Kennedy** had the same magnetism as John. Once Robert Kennedy entered the race, Johnson realized that he would face a tough fight for re-nomination, a fight he might not win. On March 31, he announced his decision to withdraw.

It seemed almost certain that the Democrats would nominate Robert Kennedy for president. He had led the fight against the Communists in the 1950s and had served as U. S. Attorney General during his brother's presidency. On June 4, Kennedy won the vitally important California Democratic primary. Late that evening, he delivered a victory speech at a Los Angeles hotel. Minutes after midnight, as he was being escorted to the hotel's exit, a Palestinian radical named Sirhan Sirhan, who hated Kennedy for supporting Israel, assassinated him. As a result of Kennedy's murder, Vice President **Hubert Humphrey** was chosen to be the Democratic nominee.

A clever picture of Hubert Humphrey showing him in Lyndon Johnson's shadow

The Democratic convention of 1968, held in Chicago, proved to be the most violent in American history. Hubert Humphrey had always loyally supported Johnson's Vietnam policy. In a sense, he had to support Johnson's policy if he wanted Johnson's support for his political career. However, the Democratic Party included many anti-war activists. These Democrats supported Eugene McCarthy. They traveled to Chicago to demonstrate in favor of ending the war. These "peace" protests became extremely violent. Mayor Richard Daley called in the police to restore order. The peace protesters attacked the police. Hundreds of people were arrested and hundreds more were injured. Some historians believe that the violence at the convention convinced the American people to vote for the Republican candidate. That man was Richard Nixon.

Nixon had not left politics after the 1960 election. In 1962, he had run for governor of California, but had lost. Nixon campaigned for Barry Goldwater in 1964 and helped the Republicans gain fifty seats in Congress in 1966. By 1966, he had earned the respect and confidence of party leaders and was actually seen as the front-runner for the Republican nomination in 1968. Thus, in 1968, he easily won the nomination from delegates who believed that Nixon could pull the staggering nation back together.

George Wallace, the governor of Alabama, ran as an independent third-party candidate. Wallace had opposed racial integration of the Alabama public schools. However, he was strongly anti-Communist. He was seen as the most conservative of the three candidates.

Norman Rockwell's 1968 portrait of the newly-elected President Richard Nixon.

During his campaign, Nixon criticized President Johnson's Great Society social programs as costly failures. He promised to end the violence on America's streets which was frightening so many people. Nixon said he had a plan to bring an honorable end to the Vietnam War. He did not elaborate on the specifics of his plan because he did not want to upset the ongoing peace talks.

In the election, Nixon received about 43% of the popular vote, less than 1% more than Humphrey. However, Nixon won 32 states compared to Humphrey's 13 and 301 electoral votes to Humphrey's 191. In his Inaugural Address, Nixon said, "We cannot learn about one another until we stop shouting at one another." He also stressed the need to end the Vietnam War honorably.

Nixon's Plan to End the War

Nixon wanted to keep South Vietnam from falling to the Communists but also to withdraw American forces from that country. Shortly after taking office, President Nixon released his *Vietnamization* plan, which would shift the burden of fighting North Vietnam to the South Vietnamese army. American soldiers would be withdrawn as the South Vietnamese troops replaced American combat troops.

Unfortunately, *Vietnamization* ultimately failed. Despite the intensive training that they received, Vietnamese troops seemed incapable of replacing American combat soldiers. After all, America had escalated the war because the South Vietnamese had been unable to defeat North Vietnam on their own. Nevertheless, Nixon slowly began to draw American troops out of Vietnam. By spring 1970, he had withdrawn about 100,000 soldiers and announced that he planned to withdraw another 150,000 within a year.

However, on April 30, Nixon announced that he was sending troops into Cambodia, the nation on Vietnam's western border. Nixon appeared on national television to explain the invasion was necessary because the North Vietnamese were using Cambodia as a sanctuary to launch attacks into South Vietnam. The American troops were going to destroy the Communist bases in Cambodia. Nixon also sent forces into

Cambodia in response to a request from Cambodia's anti-Communist government. On April 17, North Vietnam had invaded Cambodia which appealed to the United States for assistance. During May and June American and South Vietnamese forces launched large-scale offensives in Cambodia.

For years, North Vietnam had moved supplies and soldiers from Cambodia into South Vietnam along the **Ho Chi Minh Trail**. To stop the influx of men and materials, the United States had bombed the Trail. Unfortunately, despite massive destruction of war materials, the bombing campaign did not seem to affect North Vietnam's ability to wage war on the South.

The announcement of the invasion of Cambodia set off a new round of anti-war protests. The protests had diminished during the troop withdrawal, but protesters saw the invasion as an escalation of the war rather than its conclusion. College students began riots on hundreds of campuses. The worst violence occurred at **Kent State University** in Ohio on May 4, 1970. An Ohio National Guard Unit fired into the protesters, killing four and wounding thirteen. Although various courts cleared the guardsmen of wrongdoing, subsequent investigations determined that the guardsmen should not have fired indiscriminately into the crowd.

Another fatal incident occurred eleven days later at Jackson State College in Mississippi. Students clashed with police and firefighters. During the violence, police shot and killed two young black men and wounded twelve others. A twenty-three-member grand jury, which included five African-Americans, failed to indict any of the police officers.

On February 8, 1971, South Vietnamese troops, with American air and artillery support, invaded Laos, the country north of Cambodia. They sought to cut the enemy's supply lines and to destroy enemy bases in Laos. After six weeks of fighting, and significant losses, the Vietnamese withdrew. Though not completely successful, the invasion did delay a Communist offensive set for Spring. The invasion also caused a massive demonstration in Washington DC, where nearly 200,000 people protested American involvement in Southeast Asia.

Over the next months, Nixon continued withdrawing American forces from Vietnam. By early November 1971, only 191,000 troops remained, the lowest level since December 1965. Early in January 1972, Nixon promised to continued drawing down American troops, but also to maintain a force of around 30,000 soldiers in Vietnam until all American prisoners of war were released. By the end of March, less than 100,000 American soldiers remained in South Vietnam.

President Nixon Visits China

In February 1972, President Nixon accepted an invitation to visit Communist China from Chinese dictator Mao Zedong. Since the Communists had conquered China in 1949, the United States had recognized Chiang Kai-shek's Nationalist government (the Republic of China) as China's legitimate government, and refused to recognize Mao's regime. Nixon, as a congressman and senator, had always opposed dealing with Red China. However, by 1972, the world had changed.

By visiting China, President Nixon hoped to establish diplomatic and trade

This picture of President Nixon smiling and shaking hands with Mao Zedong infuriated Conservatives across America who felt that Nixon had betrayed them, a generation of anti-Communists, the United States, and the Republic of China. Congressman John Schmitz, who represented Nixon's former congressional district, summed up the feelings of many Americans when he said that he did not object to Nixon going to China so much as he objected to his coming back!

relations, as well as cultural exchanges, with the Chinese. He also hoped to widen the political gulf between China and the Soviet Union. The Soviet Union and China had been allies since Mao took control of mainland China. However, by the early 1970s, the Soviets and the Chinese were no longer so friendly. Nixon saw this as an opportunity to drive them farther apart. Also, Red China was aiding North Vietnam. Nixon had sent his Secretary of State, **Henry Kissinger**, to Paris to have secret peace talks with the North. He hoped China might assist the U. S. in reaching an acceptable settlement in Vietnam. In exchange, Nixon would support Red China's admission to the UN. (**Note**: The Republic of China, not the People's Republic of China, was the original member of the UN and the Security Council.) China and the United States would begin trade talks and, hopefully, China's markets would open to the United States. In other words, *Pepsi* could sell soft drinks to 800 million Chinese. The Chinese welcomed Nixon with open arms. The visit was a diplomatic triumph.

Nixon Visits the Soviet Union

In May 1972, President Nixon flew to the Soviet Union. The Soviets were "friendly" because they were concerned that America was becoming "friendly" with Red China. During his visit, Nixon negotiated the important **Strategic Arms Limitation Treaty (SALT)** with the Soviets. SALT limited the number of ballistic missiles, which are used to fire nuclear warheads, that each nation could build.

One aspect of SALT was the **Anti-Ballistic Missile (ABM) Treaty**. The United States had been considering developing a defense system against nuclear attack. Some Americans opposed this idea. They feared a defense system would upset the "strategic balance" between the United States and the Soviet Union. They thought that if one or both countries developed a defense system, it would increase the likelihood of war. The final treaties did allow the construction of a small number of Anti-Ballistic Missiles. The Soviets soon violated the treaty by building more than the number agreed upon.

The 1972 Presidential Election

As a result of his diplomatic successes in China and the Soviet Union, as well as his seemingly successful draw-down of American troops, by 1972, President Nixon was more popular than ever. As a result, he easily received the Republican nomination for re-election. However, once again, the Democrats were in disarray.

It seemed as though the Democrats should nominate Hubert Humphrey, who Nixon had narrowly defeated in 1968. Humphrey wished to run, but no other Democrat wanted him to run, because he still carried the stigma of having supported the war as Johnson's vice president. Edmund Muskie, who had been Humphrey's running mate in 1968, also wanted to run, but he lacked sufficient support. Another likely nominee was Senator Edward Kennedy of Massachusetts. Millions of Democrats believed that it was logical to elect Kennedy and let him complete John's and Robert's legacy. Then on July 18, 1969, Kennedy drove his car off a narrow bridge into the water on Chappaquiddick Island. Kennedy escaped from the car, but his passenger drowned while trapped in the car. Kennedy left the scene and waited several hours before reporting the accident to the police. He later pleaded guilty to a misdemeanor and received a suspended jail sentence. The bad publicity kept Kennedy from running for president.

Eventually, the Democratic nomination went to South Dakota Senator **George McGovern**. McGovern ran a very bad campaign filled with mistakes. His first mistake was choosing Senator Thomas Eagleton as his running mate. McGovern's campaign failed to check Eagleton's background and the media revealed that Eagleton had been hospitalized with a mental condition. McGovern declared that he fully backed Eagleton. McGovern made his next mistake by withdrawing his support and forcing Eagleton off the ticket. This made McGovern appear both indecisive and disloyal – bad qualities for a president. Moreover, many of McGovern's ideas appeared to voters to be socialist, ideas that voters in 1972 found very troubling. Nixon soon had an insurmountable lead in the polls.

The final blow to McGovern's election hopes landed less than two weeks before the election. On October 26, Henry Kissinger held a televised news conference during which he announced, "We believe peace is at hand" in Vietnam. Although some questioned the timing of this "October surprise," as it came to be called, most Americans were overjoyed that the seemingly never-ending war was finally coming to an end. McGovern's main campaign issue had been the immediate withdrawal of American forces from Vietnam, but now it seemed that Nixon would bring the troops home and keep his promise to end the war "honorably." On Election Day, President Nixon won a landslide victory with 60.7% of the popular vote and 49 states. Only Massachusetts voted for McGovern.

The End of the Vietnam War

North Vietnam had offered a ceasefire in October which had caused Kissinger to declare "peace is at hand" and Nixon to stop bombing the North. They agreed to stop their attacks on South Vietnam as soon as all American troops were withdrawn. The North agreed to return all American POWs and hold free elections.

However, after the election, the deal fell through. North Vietnam refused to honor the terms of the treaty. South Vietnam's leaders knew the Americans' departure would result in Communist domination and the end of South Vietnam's existence. South Vietnam President Thieu refused to accept a ceasefire under those terms. In an effort to ensure North Vietnam's cooperation, Nixon ordered U. S. planes to begin hourly bombings of **Hanoi**, the capital of North Vietnam. The North Vietnamese finally agreed to a ceasefire. One again, President Thieu refused to sign the treaty, since it allowed Communists troops to remain in the South in the areas they had invaded. Nixon told Thieu that it did not matter whether South Vietnam accepted the truce, because the U. S. was prepared to sign the treaty and withdraw all American troops. With no option, Thieu signed the treaty, knowing full well

George McGovern campaign poster. The poster moves from a crossed-out sketch of President Nixon to a photograph of Senator McGovern suggesting that he could put the country back together. However, his campaign resembled the mixed-up jumble of states more than an orderly system for governing. In the end, voters decided he couldn't put it together.

In this iconic photo taken by photojournalist Hubert van Es, an American helicopter evacuates US government employees atop an apartment building as North Vietnamese Army troops enter Saigon. Tragically, perhaps another 65,000 South Vietnamese fled out to sea in fishing boats, barges, and homemade rafts in hopes of rescue by a U.S. warship or the convoy of 27 South Vietnamese Navy ships that sailed without adequate food or water toward the Philippine Islands. These desperate people risked almost certain death at sea rather than capture by the Communists.

the terrible future to come. In January 1973, the U. S. signed the treaty and began withdrawing the remaining American troops.

In March 1975, hamstrung by lack of aid, the leaders of South Vietnam realized that they could not defend their entire country. They pulled back from their northern borders and committed to defending Saigon. Spearheaded by armored columns, the North Vietnamese Army stormed across the border and raced south, intent upon overwhelming Saigon. By April 29, Communist forces had completely surrounded Saigon. The following day, the Communists occupied Saigon, which they renamed **Ho Chi Minh City** in honor of the victor. For the first time, the United States had lost a war.

The Watergate Scandal

The Break-In

On June 17, 1972, shortly before the Democratic presidential convention, five burglars were arrested breaking into the Watergate Hotel and Office Building in Washington D. C. This arrest would trigger one of the strangest and most controversial events in modern American politics and lead to the resignation of the most powerful man in America, because the burglars were arrested for breaking into the headquarters of the Democratic National Committee.

At the time of their arrest, the five burglars possessed a number of suspicious items. First, they carried a large amount of money in the form of brand-new $100 bills. Second, they had two very expensive, high quality cameras and many rolls of film. Finally, they had a number of sophisticated listening devices, or "bugs." The meaning of these items was clear. The men had been highly paid to photograph documents and install listening devices in the Democratic Headquarters.

Naturally, despite Nixon's massive lead in the polls, suspicion fell on the Republicans. This suspicion was validated when it was revealed that one of the burglars was James W. McCord, who was working for Nixon's re-election campaign. As the evidence mounted against him, both President Nixon and his campaign manager, **John Mitchell**, denied that anyone in the White House had anything to do with the burglary. At the time of the election, everyone believed the President. It seemed ridiculous to think that Nixon or anyone close to him would have been involved in something so foolish, since he was so far ahead in the polls. Based on the election results, the break-in did not affect the election.

The Watergate Hotel complex

The Cover-Up

On January 8, 1973, the Watergate burglars went on trial. They pleaded guilty which meant that the court accepted their plea. It also meant that the court could not question them beyond the facts of the crime, that is, breaking into the building.

One of the burglars, **James McCord** had been convicted on eight counts of conspiracy, burglary, and wiretapping. As he sat in his cell awaiting sentencing, he began worrying about the long prison term he faced. On March 21, three days before sentencing, he cracked. He sent a letter to the trial judge, John Sirica. Two days later, Sirica read the letter aloud in court. McCord claimed that the Watergate defendants had been bribed and pressured to plead guilty, remain silent, and commit perjury during the trial. McCord told Judge Sirica that a number of leading Republicans had helped plan the burglary. (Eyewitnesses stated that after "Sirica finished reading the letter, the courtroom exploded with excitement and reporters ran to the rear entrance to phone their newspapers.") McCord's shocking admissions caused the Senate in February to vote unanimously to establish a committee to investigate his charges. North Carolina Democratic Senator **Sam Ervin** was named committee chairman.

Howard Baker (L) and Sam Ervin (R) listen to testimony during the Watergate hearings.

Over the next month, the Justice Department began investigating the Watergate break-in. One by one, members of Nixon's administration admitted that they knew about the burglary. However, the bigger problem lay not in the burglary, which was bad enough, but in the fact that they had attempted to cover it up. Eleven days after the burglary, FBI Director Patrick Gray had received documents from Nixon's attorney, **John Dean**, relating to the incident. Gray confessed to destroying these documents and resigned.

John Dean, as President Nixon's attorney, had discussed the Watergate affair with Nixon many times. He knew all the details. In early April, he began working with the Watergate investigators, providing them very damaging evidence. On April 30, Nixon appeared on national television and announced resignations of two of his closest advisers, H. R. (Bob) Haldeman and John Ehrlichman. Nixon insisted that both were good and loyal public servants who had done nothing wrong. He also said that Attorney General Richard Kleindienst had resigned and Nixon had named Elliot Richardson to replace him. Although Nixon had fired Dean, once a close friend but now a man he considered a traitor, Nixon said that Dean too had resigned. Throughout the address, Nixon maintained that he personally had done nothing wrong.

Polls conducted after the televised address indicated that about half the voters felt the address helped the President. They felt it restored public confidence. They were willing to give Nixon the benefit of the doubt. However, overall, Americans were somewhat cynical. They felt that both Parties had broken the rules.

After his nomination as Attorney General, Nixon told Elliot Richardson to name a Special Prosecutor to investigate Watergate. In mid-May, Richardson named Archibald Cox, a highly respected law professor. Nixon promised Cox his full cooperation and told him to follow the facts wherever they led.

On May 18, the Senate Watergate hearings began to be televised. Republican Senator **Howard Baker** from Tennessee asked the questions that all America wanted to know about Watergate: "What did the President know and when did he know it?" As witnesses testified, the answers were, he knew a lot and he knew it pretty early.

The most damaging witness was John Dean, who began testifying on June 25. Dean claimed that President Nixon had helped plan the cover-up soon after the break-in. He accused the president of lying in his April 30 broadcast when he denied that anyone at the White House was involved in the break-in. For the first time, someone had directly linked Nixon with the break-in. Dean's testimony was so powerful because he was the president's attorney and confidant. Moreover, he appeared to be telling the truth when his testimony was checked against independent sources. However, President Nixon resolutely denied the charges. There seemed to be no way to prove who was telling the truth.

On July 16, one of Nixon's former aides testified that the president had secretly recorded his Oval Office (the president's private office) conversations. These tapes of conversations between Nixon and Dean would show who was telling the truth. The Senate Committee and Special Prosecutor Cox immediately demanded the tapes.

However, President Nixon refused to comply. He claimed **executive privilege**, that is, the right of the Executive Branch to keep information confidential when it relates to certain national security interests and to protect the privacy of White House deliberations when the public interest requires it. Though the term is not explicitly mentioned in the Constitution, presidents since George Washington had claimed Executive Privilege, so Nixon was not inventing a new doctrine. Within days, the tapes became the center of a national controversy.

From Bad to Worse

When Nixon failed to release the tapes, more and more people began to believe he was guilty. Nixon tried to explain why he was protecting the tapes by saying that "Many people assume that the tapes must incriminate the president, or that otherwise, he would not insist on their privacy. But…Unless a president can protect the privacy of the advice he gets, he cannot get the advice he needs." Meanwhile, the situation went from bad to worse.

On October 10, Nixon's vice president, **Spiro Agnew**, resigned. While serving as governor of Maryland, Agnew had accepted bribes amounting to $200,000. To avoid a public scandal, prosecutors allowed him to plead guilty to one count of income tax evasion, pay a fine, and be placed on probation. Although Agnew's case was unrelated to Watergate, the public viewed it as additional evidence that the Nixon Administration was thoroughly corrupt.

Under the Twenty-Fifth Amendment to the Constitution, which had only recently been ratified in 1967, when the office of vice president becomes vacant, the president is empowered to appoint a replacement. On October 12, Nixon appointed **Gerald Ford**, a leading Republican congressman from Michigan, to fill the vacancy. Ford had a reputation for honesty that Nixon hoped would help defuse the growing Watergate scandal. Congress quickly and overwhelmingly approved the appointment. On December 6, Ford became vice president.

President Nixon Resigns

Under pressure from Cox and the Senate Committee, on October 19, Nixon offered to give them written *summaries* of his tapes as a compromise. The following day, Cox declined the offer insisting on the actual tapes. Nixon then asked Cox to resign, but he refused. Nixon then ordered Attorney General Elliot Richardson to fire Cox, but he refused and resigned. Nixon ordered Richardson's assistant to fire Cox, but he refused and resigned. Finally, Nixon ordered Solicitor General **Robert Bork** to fire Cox which Bork did. Since these events occurred on a Saturday night, the press labeled this remarkable series of firings the "**Saturday Night Massacre**."

The Saturday Night Massacre was incredibly imprudent. Two days later, some members of Congress began calling for the **impeachment** of the president. The official impeachment investigation began on February 6, 1974. To quiet the calls for his impeachment, Nixon released some of his tapes and promised to cooperate with Cox's successor, **Leon Jaworski**. However, public opinion had turned strongly against him. To win back the public's support, on November 17, Nixon held a press conference and urged the nation to move beyond Watergate. He defended himself and declared, "I'm not a crook." Meanwhile, Jaworski began prosecuting others involved in the re-election campaign. Several were convicted of crimes ranging from perjury to obstruction of justice.

In April 1974, Leon Jaworski and the Senate issued a court order demanding President Nixon to give them tapes of conversations dealing with Watergate. Feeling the pressure mounting for his impeachment, in late April, Nixon released edited transcripts of some of the tapes which he claimed proved his innocence. However, there were blank spaces in the transcripts. Nixon claimed that these blank spaces were instances where the tapes were unintelligible. However, many people did not believe him and he refused to allow others to listen to the original tapes to verify his claims. Meanwhile, the Senate Committee and Jaworski still insisted on the actual tapes.

By the end of May, Jaworski and Nixon both decided the Supreme Court had to resolve the issue of the tapes. On July 24, the Supreme Court unanimously denied the president's claim of Executive Privilege and declared that he must surrender the subpoenaed tapes. Hours later, Nixon announced he would hand over the tapes. Three days later, the House Judiciary Committee passed three articles of impeachment against President Nixon. The articles accused him of obstructing justice, misusing the powers of the presidency, and failing to comply with the House subpoenas by refusing to let the committee listen to his tapes.

The Committee's report would next be sent to the full House of Representatives. The House would then impeach the president by turning over the articles to the Senate. The Senate would try the president under charges brought by the House. If two-thirds of the Senate found the president guilty of any of the charges, he would be removed from office.

By the beginning of August, Nixon was in a bad position. The Supreme Court had ruled that he turn over his tapes. If he did not turn them over, he was sure to be impeached and removed from office. He had no choice. On August 5, he released

Amazingly, this iconic photo of Richard Nixon smiling broadly and flashing the "V for Victory" sign with both hands does not take place following a moment of triumph, rather it is the moment when he says goodbye to his staff outside the White House as he boards a helicopter after resigning the presidency! The night before on TV he had told his fellow Americans, "I have never been a quitter… To leave office before my term is completed is abhorrent to every instinct in my body. But as president, I must put the interests of America first."

the tapes. They proved conclusively that just six days after the break-in, he had conversations with H. R. Haldeman in which he obstructed justice. On the tape, Haldeman presents Nixon with a plan to cut off the FBI investigation into Watergate. Haldeman and Ehrlichman would tell the CIA to ask the FBI to stay out of the matter because the FBI was about to unearth some secret CIA activities. Nixon agreed to the plan. After the release of this tape, dubbed the "Smoking Gun" tape, the ten Republicans on the Judiciary Committee who had voted against impeachment announced that they would change their vote.

Nixon now faced the choice of resigning before the House impeached him or hoping that he would win a trial in the Senate. On August 7, Senator Barry Goldwater informed Nixon that he would almost certainly lose a trial in the Senate. On the evening of August 8, 1974, Nixon appeared on national television. He announced that he would resign as president. He admitted he had made mistakes, but refused to admit to any guilt. The next day, President Nixon handed his resignation to Secretary of State Henry Kissinger.

On August 9, Gerald Ford took the oath of office and became the president. Eleven days later, he chose Nelson Rockefeller, the former Governor of New York as his Vice-President. On September 8, Ford granted a full and absolute pardon to Richard Nixon, who accepted. Although Ford's approval ratings declined, he felt that Watergate had torn America apart. He believed that the nation needed to put this part of its history behind it.

Richard Nixon had done many good things for the United States. He had defended America from its enemies, both foreign and domestic. However, it is the Watergate Scandal for which he will be remembered. Nixon's downfall should stand as a lesson to all leaders. He, and they, should recall the immortal words of historian Robert Payne who wrote:

"For over a thousand years Roman conquerors returning from the wars enjoyed the honor of a triumph (a tumultuous parade). In the procession came trumpeters and musicians and strange animals from the conquered territories, together with carts laden with treasure and captured armaments. The conqueror rode in a triumphal chariot, and the dazed prisoners walked in front of him. Sometimes his children, robed in white, stood with him in the chariot, or rode the trace horses. A slave stood behind the conqueror, holding a golden crown over his head, and whispering in his ear a warning that all glory is fleeting."

Chief Justice Earl Warren swears Gerald Ford in as president while Betty Ford watches.

Answer the following questions:

1. What is the "Domino Theory?" How did it cause the US to become involved in Vietnam?

2. Who "invented" television?

3. What did John F. Kennedy do during World War II that made him a war hero?

4. What qualities did John F. Kennedy have that helped him in politics?

5. What feature did John F. Kennedy possess that hurt him among voters? What did he do to minimize this feature? What long lasting impact has this action had?

6. What was the Bay of Pigs invasion? Why was the US involved in it? Did it succeed or fail? Why or why not?

7. What was the Cuban Missile Crisis? How was it resolved?

8. What is the "I Have a Dream Speech?" Who delivered it? From where was it delivered? What was the occasion of giving the speech?

9. What was the "Gulf of Tonkin Resolution?"

10. What was the Space Race? Who was Alan Shepherd? Who was John Glen? Who were the Mercury Seven?

11. What was the Tet Offensive? Who won the Tet Offensive?

12. What was the Pueblo Incident?

13. What was President Nixon's plan of Vietnamization? Did it work? Why or why not?

14. Why did Nixon visit China?

15. What was the Watergate Break-in?

16. What was the Watergate cover-up? How did it cause Nixon to resign as President?

17. How did Gerald Ford become Vice-President and then President of the United States?

18. What was one of Gerald Ford's first acts as President? Why did he take it?

19. Why were the Selma to Montgomery Marches called?

Identify the following:

1. George McGovern
2. Ho Chi Minh
3. William Westmoreland
4. Walter Cronkite
5. Fidel Castro
6. Barry Goldwater
7. The Berlin Wall
8. Thurgood Marshall
9. Lee Harvey Oswald
10. *Letter from Birmingham Jail*

The Reagan Era 1976-2008

Quintessential image of Ronald Reagan. Ronald was a patriot who loved America and believed America could be better. His 1980 campaign slogan "Let's make America great again," summed up his inherent belief in American exceptionalism and his own personal optimism about the future. In his acceptance speech for the nomination for president at the 1980 Republican National Convention, he said, "For those without job opportunities, we'll stimulate new opportunities…. For those who've abandoned hope, we'll restore hope and we'll welcome them into a great national crusade to make America great again." Other presidential candidates would use the line "make America great again," most notably Donald Trump in 2016.

Introduction

As with any historical "era," historians do not always agree on the precise moment of its beginning or ending. However, most historians agree that the "**Reagan Era,**" *the period of American history dominated by Ronald Reagan and his conservative philosophy*, started about 1976, when Ronald Reagan narrowly failed to obtain the Republican presidential nomination. It continued until at least 2008, when Barack Obama was elected president. Some historians believe that the Reagan Era continues even today.

Like most men who initiate "eras," Ronald Reagan led a movement that was greater than he was. Franklin Roosevelt's "New Deal" survived long after he did. Much of it, like Social Security, remains ingrained in American life. Likewise, the "**Reagan Revolution**" fundamentally changed American society because of Reagan's conservative beliefs about the Cold War; national defense; the federal Judiciary, especially the Supreme Court; and the economy.

President Gerald Ford

Following the resignation of Spiro Agnew, Richard Nixon faced a serious problem: finding his replacement. Many Republicans would have been excellent choices. For example, Barry Goldwater or one of his followers, like Ronald Reagan, seemed like logical candidates. However, the choice had to be approved by the Democrat-controlled Congress. They were never going to approve Goldwater or any other staunch conservative. In fact, they were not going to approve anyone who was not a moderate *or* who had a good chance of being elected president in 1976. When Nixon asked Congress whom they would approve, their advice was unanimous. As Democrat Speaker of the House Carl Albert later said, "We gave Nixon no choice but (Gerald) Ford."

Gerald Ford was the perfect candidate for the Democrats. Ford had been elected to the House of Representatives from Michigan's 5th congressional district in 1949. By 1974, he had served in Congress for 25 years. During

Gerald Ford's official White House portrait. With his relaxed posture and his pipe, the artist has portrayed Ford as an intellectual; however, Ford was not an original thinker.

that time, he had failed to write a single piece of major legislation. He was known in both Parties as a moderate. He was virtually unknown outside of his own congressional district. Thus, *Gerald Ford was an unknown moderate congressman,* that is, the perfect candidate for the Democrats. As a result, Congress voted overwhelmingly to elect him vice-president. When Richard Nixon resigned on August 9, 1974, Gerald Ford became the only man ever to become president who had never been elected either president or vice-president by the American people.

Interestingly, Gerald Ford did seem to understand his own limitations. He realized that he was not an original thinker or a visionary. But he was a hard worker and he was honest. In making a clever comparison of presidents and automobiles, he would famously quip, "I'm a Ford, not a Lincoln."

President Ford was acutely aware that the Executive branch had to undergo sweeping changes if he, or any occupant of the Oval Office, were to recover the people's trust. Fortunately, Ford made friends easily. People described him as "a helpful next-door neighbor who could be trusted." Despite the difficult problems that marked the early days of Ford's presidency, millions of Americans began to believe that he was "one of us," rather than "one of them."

The Economy

In addition to the still-lingering Watergate Scandal, Republicans had to face serious economic issues during the 1974 midterm elections. The nation was beset by recession, inflation, and a sinking economy. To find answers to fix America's economic troubles, President Ford held meetings with some of the nation's wisest economists. Based on the meetings, Ford decided to cut back on federal spending.

The Democrats, however, blamed Nixon and Ford for the poor economy. The Democrats wanted to increase government spending in hopes of stimulating the economy. However, the Republicans said that spending more money would not stimulate the economy, but would only cause prices to rise.

In the 1974 midterms, Americans voted against the Republicans and Richard Nixon, who many Americans felt had betrayed the nation. As a result, the Democrats increased their majorities in both Houses of Congress. The Democrats passed bills increasing aid to public housing, education, and health care. President Ford vetoed these bills, explaining that such massive spending would damage the economy, not help it. Although Democrats had a majority, they did not have the two-thirds majority necessary to override a presidential veto. Most of the bills never became laws.

The economic situation worsened in early 1974 when OPEC (Organization of the Petroleum Exporting Countries) announced they were *quadrupling* oil prices. The price increase was catastrophic because of America's dependence on foreign oil. That increase in oil prices pushed inflation over 11%, three times its normal annual average. The measures that Ford implemented failed to stop the slide in unemployment. During the 1973 to 1975 recession, 2.3 million jobs were lost. By May 1975, unemployment peaked at 9%.

In this caricature, artist Mort Drucker depicts President Ford and Speaker of the House Carl Albert in surgical gowns working desperately to revive a deathly ill patient – the American economy. Carl holds a jar of blood with a dollar sign the idea being that an infusion of cash will help the patient. Ford wears a "WIN" button on his gown. Ford's answer to defeating inflation with a slogan: Whip Inflation Now (WIN). Sadly, it was not a winning strategy. (National Portrait Gallery, Smithsonian Institution; gift of Time magazine.)

In early 1975, Congress sent President Ford a bill that cut taxes, which he signed. The economy began to improve. By early 1976, the recession had ended.

The Mayaguez Incident

On May 12, 1975, just days after the fall of Saigon, the *Mayaguez*, an unarmed American merchant ship, was captured by members of the *Khmer Rouge*, the Communists who controlled Cambodia. The *Mayaguez* was sailing past Cambodia in international waters when Khmer Rouge gunboats attacked it. The Communists demanded that the captain sail the boat to Cambodia where the Khmer Rouge held the crew hostage.

President Ford demanded the Communists immediately release the ship and the thirty-nine Americans on board. When the Cambodians ignored Ford's ultimatum, he ordered an attack. U. S. Marines stormed the ship and Koh Tang Island, where the American government believed the Communists were holding the *Mayaguez* crew. In the poorly managed attack, forty-one soldiers lost their lives. Tragically, the *Mayaguez* crew was not on the island or the ship! The Cambodians had released them just as American military operations began.

Despite the loss of life, most Americans were impressed with President Ford's quick and decisive action against the Communists. Occurring just a few days after the fall of Saigon, it gave people the feeling that

America had achieved at least a small victory in what seemed like the final days of the Vietnam War. Of the *Mayaguez* Incident, President Ford wrote in his memoirs, "*All of a sudden the gloomy national mood began to fade. Many people's faith in their country was restored and my standing in the polls shot up...*"

The Helsinki Accords

In summer 1975, in an attempt to lessen Cold War tensions, thirty-five nations, including the United States and the Soviet Union, sent emissaries to Helsinki, Finland. The delegates sought to make the borders of European nations permanent in the hope that the Soviet Union would not invade and conquer the smaller nations of Europe. The U. S. also asked the nations to pledge to respect and support basic human rights, especially the right to life. Those who opposed the **Helsinki Accords** said it merely helped the Soviet Union maintain its current chokehold over the nations of Eastern Europe. Despite significant opposition to the Helsinki Accords, Ford signed them anyway. However, because the Accords were not a treaty, they had no force of law. In essence, they were a set of noble ideals.

The Accords had little effect on the Soviet Union. Its leaders failed to follow either the letter of the Accords or its spirit. To many Americans, Ford had made a foolish blunder in signing them.

President Ford and Soviet leader Leonid Brezhnev sign the Helsinki Accords

Happy Birthday, America

On July 4, 1976, most Americans celebrated the nation's **Bicentennial**, the 200th anniversary of the signing of the Declaration of Independence. The divided populace came together to celebrate our shared history rather than our political differences. A wave of patriotism washed across the country as Americans staged various celebrations. Every major city unleashed spectacular fireworks displays.

One of the leading events was ***Operation Sail***, a procession of sixteen beautifully decorated, tall-masted sailing ships from around the world. *Operation Sail* launched in New York City, where millions of people lined the harbor or watched from the windows of tall skyscrapers on Independence Day. One week later, the ships paraded into Boston Harbor. In both cities, the public toured the majestic ships.

Less than a year after the Vietnam War, the Bicentennial showed that America had been knocked down, but not knocked out. America remained a nation of generosity, not animosity. As America entered its third century, it did so with hope. The sun was not setting on the United States, it was rising. It was morning again in America.

The 1976 Presidential Campaign

In 1976, sensing weakness in the Republican Party, almost every nationally known Democrat sought their Party's nomination for president. As the primaries began, a number of the leading candidates began to be defeated by the little-known governor of Georgia, James Earl Carter, Jr, or **Jimmy Carter** as he preferred to be called. Unlike the better-known Democratic governors and senators, Carter was a virtual unknown. However, he used that to his advantage. He ran as a Washington "outsider," that is, someone not involved in the "dirty business" of national politics.

Although Carter campaigned as a "good ol' boy," wearing jeans, western shirts, and cowboy boots, he was no fool. For example, Jimmy Carter graduated from the U. S. Naval Academy. During the early days of his campaign, people joked that he was a peanut farmer. However, he ran one of the largest peanut farms in Georgia. He was a successful businessman. In 1971, he was elected governor of Georgia.

Carter began campaigning for the Democratic presidential nomination in 1974, two years before the election. He crafted a well-planned, well-orchestrated, vigorous campaign that successfully recruited supporters who were willing to work tirelessly for him. Slowly but surely, his support crept from one town to another, from one county to another, and eventually from one state to another, until it swept across the nation. This support became clear when Carter won the Iowa caucuses and the New Hampshire primary elections. These early victories vaulted him into a lead he never relinquished. One by one, the more well-known candidates dropped out as Carter won more primaries. By the time the Democratic convention met in July 1976, he had clinched the nomination. Carter chose Minnesota Senator **Walter Mondale**, another relatively unknown politician, as his running mate.

Jimmy Carter dressed as a working farmer. Carter came across as an unsophisticated Southern farmer; however, he was extremely intelligent. He graduated from the Naval Academy in 1946 with distinction, ranking 60th out of 820 midshipmen. He then served in several US Navy posts. In June 1948, he volunteered for submarine duty and may have become a submarine commander, but in July 1953, his father died. Carter resigned his commission to run the family peanut farm. He was honorably discharged from active duty on October 9, 1953.

Unlike the Democrats, in 1976, Republicans had two choices for their nominee for president. On the one hand, Gerald Ford was the incumbent, but had never won a national election or even a state-wide election. Ford was considered a moderate; however, his one nominee to the Supreme Court, **John Paul Stevens**, turned out to be one of the most liberal justices ever appointed. In his two years in office, Ford had had a lackluster presidency marred by a poor economy, the Helsinki Accords, and his pardon of Richard Nixon, which upset many people. However, he was the current president of the United States.

Ford's challenger was **Ronald Reagan**, a two-term governor of California and a popular movie and television actor for almost thirty years. Reagan was born in 1911 in Illinois. After college, he worked as a sports announcer. In 1937, he began acting in motion pictures, appearing in more than fifty. He was successful in television as well, most notably hosting 235 episodes of the *General Electric Theatre* from 1954 to 1962. As a successful actor, Reagan was paying the government 90% of his income. This caused him to begin a lifelong crusade against high taxes, which he believed stifled economic growth.

Two of Reagan's motion picture roles profoundly affected him. One occurred in the film *Kings Row*, when a vindictive doctor unnecessarily amputates the legs of the young man Reagan is portraying. When Drake, the young man, awakes and realizes that he no longer has legs, he screams, "Where's the rest of me?" Ronald Reagan entitled his autobiography *Where's The Rest of Me?* Reagan also played a young Notre Dame football player named "George Gipp" in the movie *Knute Rockne, All American*. In one inspirational speech, the actor playing Knute Rockne tries to encourage his football team. He tells them that as George Gipp lay dying, he asked Rockne to let the players know that one day "*when the team is up against it and the breaks are beating the boys, tell them to 'Go out there with all they've got and win just one for the Gipper.*'" Ronald Reagan's performance was so superb that thereafter, people affectionately referred to him as "The Gipper."

Politically, Ronald Reagan represented the conservative wing of the Republican Party. He was the political successor of Barry Goldwater. In fact, it was during Goldwater's 1964 election campaign that Reagan's political views received widespread national attention. On October 27, 1964, Reagan appeared on television and gave a speech supporting Goldwater, called "**A Time of Choosing**." In the speech, Reagan set forth his political beliefs. He stressed *the need for small government* so that people could enjoy "the ultimate in individual freedom consistent with *law and order*." He stressed *a balanced federal budget* and *control of government spending*. His point, which he would make over and over, was not that the people were taxed too little, but that government spent too much. He warned Americans, "*No government ever voluntarily reduces itself in size. Government programs, once launched, never disappear. Actually, a government bureau is the nearest thing to eternal life we'll ever see on this Earth.*"

Poster for *King's Row* (1942). Most film historians, as well as Reagan himself, consider *King's Row* to be Reagan's finest film.

Although Goldwater lost the election, the "Time of Choosing Speech" launched Reagan's political career. Following the speech, California Republicans urged Reagan to run for governor of California. In 1966, he was elected on a message of smaller government, tax cuts, and greater personal freedom. In 1971, Reagan was re-elected governor. He chose not to seek a third term, deciding instead to seek the Republican nomination for president.

However, President Ford narrowly defeated Reagan and received the Republican nomination. Ford selected Kansas Senator **Robert Dole** as his vice president. Dole, a decorated war hero, had been wounded and lost partial use of his arm during World War II.

The 1976 Presidential Election

Jimmy Carter ran a very smart presidential election campaign based on three messages. First, because the Republicans had been stained by Watergate and Nixon's resignation, Carter ran as an "outsider," someone who was not a professional politician who had been in government most of his life, like Gerald Ford. This led to his second message, which was to run for president as a "man of the people." He campaigned for president like he had for the Democratic nomination, often dressed informally in jeans and open-collared shirts. He ran as a southern peanut farmer who understood the needs of the average voter. Third, Carter embraced his Christianity. In his political ads, he promised not to lie to the voters – something that Nixon, and by extension the Republicans, had done.

Gerald Ford attacked Carter's lack of experience. He pointed to his own twenty-seven years in government compared to Carter's short tenure as governor of a small southern state. However, Ford lacked charisma. He came across as another boring professional politician. He also made a number of silly blunders, including declaring at the second debate with Carter that the Soviet Union did not dominate

This watercolor by Jamie Wyeth shows Jimmy Carter as a typical "man of the people" dressed in a denim jacket and work-shirt. In the background can be seen his farm and a water-tank with "Plains," which references his home in Plains, George. Carter took his disdain for pomp to the White House, starting with his Inauguration where he chose to ride to the ceremony in a Ford rather than a limousine. (Time cover, January 3, 1977 National Portrait Gallery, Smithsonian Institution; gift of Time magazine.)

Eastern Europe. Everyone knew he had misspoken, but the press and late-night comedians poked fun at him. His greatest weakness though was his association with Richard Nixon. Perhaps, had the American people not been so angry at Nixon, Ford might have been elected.

On election day, about 54% of eligible voters cast ballots, down from 55% in 1972. This was less due to lack of interest than disappointment in the political system. The wounds of Watergate were still too raw. When the votes were counted, Carter won by less than 1,700,000 votes. He carried the Solid South, the swing state of Ohio, as well as many of the northeastern states. With the exception of Texas and Hawaii, Carter lost all the states west of the Mississippi River. His electoral victory was also close. He won 297 to 240. Democrats also retained control of both houses of Congress.

President Jimmy Carter

One of President Jimmy Carter's first acts was to give unconditional pardons to 10,000 young American men who dodged the military draft because they did not want to be sent to Vietnam. These men had fled from America and hid, most of them in Canada. President Carter said he hoped his unconditional pardon would dilute some of the bitterness that the Vietnam War had caused. He should not have expected a warm reception from the 404,000 American men who did not run away and were wounded or killed in action. Their families resented Carter's pardons.

President Carter had a lukewarm relationship with the members of Congress. His relaxed manner made it difficult to push through legislation. Moreover, many people in Congress remained wary of any occupant of the White House after the difficult Nixon years. Carter and his staff also tended to try to "go it alone" rather than work with Democrat or Republican members of the House or Senate. As a result, when Carter failed to solve the problems that confronted America, he was quickly labeled a failure.

The Economy and the Energy Crisis

President Carter inherited a weak economy from President Ford. Seven million workers had lost their jobs and unemployment continued to rise. President Carter's solution was creating public work jobs, that is, fixing streets and bridges. In addition to the jobs program, Carter intended to curtail government spending and reduce taxes. By the end of his second year in office, unemployment was decreasing, but the inflation rate had doubled, meaning dollars would not buy as much as before.

Jimmy Carter's official White House Portrait

To address the nation's issues, President Carter and his staff met with various experts for ten days in July 1979. He hoped to make his administration more effective in dealing with the social and economic issues that confronted America. To share the results of the ten-day conference, he gave a nationally televised address on July 15. He said that he had discovered that Americans had a "crisis of confidence." Carter admitted to making mistakes and promised that he would become a stronger leader. As a result of the speech, his popularity increased. However, a few days later he made a colossal blunder when he fired six of his Cabinet officers, including the Attorney General and Secretary of the Treasury, as well as several members of the White House staff. Although he saw the firings as a "reboot" of his presidency and preparation for a re-election campaign, most Americans only saw him giving his staff the boot! If Carter intended to gain the confidence of the American people, he failed. Americans had generally lost hope and he had lost his new-found popularity. However, in fairness to Carter, much of the problem with the economy was due to America's dependence on foreign oil.

Since the time of John D. Rockefeller, Americans had relied on gas and oil for business, industry, and leisure activities. The United States had become a great producer of oil and gas, but over time, Americans began to use more gas and oil than we could produce ourselves. Americans became more and more dependent on foreign oil. By the early 1970s, this dependence had become acute. Most of the imported oil came from the Middle East.

When oil had first been discovered in the Middle East, American oil companies, because they had the technical expertise, found the oil and ran the drilling and refining process. American companies made a nice profit; the Middle Eastern nations, which were poor, became wealthy; and the price of gas for Americans remained low. However, in September 1960, Middle Eastern nations Saudi Arabia, Iran, Iraq, and Kuwait banded together with Venezuela, another major oil producing country, to form **OPEC**, the **Organization of Petroleum Exporting Countries**.

Initially, OPEC had relatively little power. However, during the 1960s the five founding members were joined by Qatar (1961), Indonesia (1962), Libya (1962), the United Arab Emirates (1967), Algeria (1969), and Nigeria (1971). Moreover, the demand for oil increased. As a result, because OPEC controlled more of the world's oil, it became more powerful. OPEC demanded that oil companies pay them more money for their oil. Of course, oil companies passed the price increases on to the American consumer. As long as America had good relations with the OPEC members, it seemed that the economic situation would be fine. However, in 1973, events changed the relationship between the United States and OPEC.

On October 6, 1973, a coalition of Middle Eastern Muslim nations launched a sneak attack on Israel. Israel had been an American ally for decades, so President Nixon quickly began supplying the Israelis with guns and ammunition. This infuriated the Muslim nations, many of whom were OPEC members. As a result, **OPEC imposed an oil embargo on the United States**. The embargo caused an energy crisis in America.

Although the Israeli war lasted less than three weeks, the embargo remained in place until March 1974. By then, the price of oil had quadrupled! It was clear that oil could be used as a strategic weapon.

Over the next years, OPEC realized it had a product that America desperately needed. For the next four years, prices remained relatively stable, but OPEC began producing more and generating hundreds of billions of dollars in revenue. As a result, most OPEC nations became quite wealthy. However, the increase in oil prices had hurt America and the U.S. economy. Americans realized that they had to reduce their dependence on foreign oil.

During the embargo, the government had instituted **rationing**, as it had during World War II. However, Americans found this incredibly frustrating as they waited in long lines at gas stations. Even worse, by February 1974, 20% of gas stations had no gas. Shortages and outages led to short tempers and in some cases serious violence. To help reduce consumption, in 1974, Congress enacted a national maximum speed limit of 55 mph which made only a small impact on consumption although it may have resulted in fewer highway fatalities. In the years after the embargo, the federal government tried three ways to decrease America's addiction to foreign oil.

The government hoped the 55-mph speed limit would reduce gas consumption by 2.2%, the actual savings were less than 1%.

First, the government stressed **conservation**. Politicians told Americans that they needed to change their lifestyle and use less gas and oil. For example, people had to stop driving big cars which had poor gas mileage and drive smaller cars with better mileage. This idea failed to catch on, as many Americans liked the safety and comfort of large cars as they still do.

Second, the government began to expand efforts to increase domestic production of gas and oil. Many Americans wanted to drill for oil "offshore" and in Alaska, especially the area known as **ANWR**, the **Arctic National Wildlife Refuge**, in northeastern Alaska. Unfortunately, such drilling met with opposition from environmental groups, who feared oil spills would destroy the environment. Others argued that it would take decades before the oil from ANWR would reach the pumps. One might note that had the drilling begun in 1975, even if it took 20 years, Americans in 1995 would have had access to that oil. The

Tennessee Valley Authority Watts Bar Nuclear Power Plant. Since 1990 nuclear power plants have supplied 20% of America's energy.

Environmental Protection Agency (EPA), a federal agency which Congress had created in 1970 to protect the environment, also opposed almost all drilling and exploration. Conservative politicians quickly began looking for ways to defund the EPA.

Finally, Americans sought to use "alternative" forms of energy. One of the most efficient of these new forms of energy was **nuclear energy**. Nuclear power plants create energy by slowly splitting uranium atoms. When the atoms are split, they create an enormous amount of heat which turns water into steam to turn turbines to produce electricity. Unlike fossil fuels, e.g. coal, oil, natural gas, there is no limit to nuclear power. Because **it does not deplete, it is a** *renewable* form of energy. Although nuclear plants have proven safe over the decades, people still fear the possibility of a **meltdown**, which would release dangerous radiation.

Other forms of renewable energy were also investigated and remain popular with environmentalists. One form, **solar energy**, uses the sun's energy and converts it into electricity. Another form, **wind energy**, turns giant windmills which produce energy. However, solar and wind power, while helpful in relieving the energy crisis, have never proven effective enough to replace fossil fuels.

Despite conservation measures, increased drilling, and new energy sources, America remained at the mercy of OPEC, which could raise or lower its prices as it wished. In 1977, Congress created the **U. S. Department of Energy**, which would be responsible for improving America's energy programs and policies. Congress passed laws which gave incentives to American oil companies to explore for oil and natural gas in America. Finding and using other sources of energy was rewarded. Congress enacted penalties to curb gas and oil consumption.

Despite the good intentions of these measures, their ultimate failure came to light in 1979 during a second oil crisis. In late November 1979, conditions in the Middle East caused oil production to drop slightly but the price of oil to double! Barely six years after the last energy crisis, Americans once again faced high prices, long lines, and gas shortages at the gas pumps. The energy crisis would be the reason that Carter delivered his "crisis of confidence" speech in July.

In the speech he set forth six points which he believed would solve the energy crisis and make America energy independent. In his first point he insisted that America "never use more foreign oil than (it) did in 1977…." In fact, oil imports did stay below 1977 levels for the next 16 years, but not because of Carter's policies. A massive increase in oil prices coupled with a recession simply reduced American demand for oil.

Carter's Foreign Policy

In some ways President Carter's Christianity formed his foreign policy. He believed that everyone was entitled to be free of poverty, disease, and political oppression. He criticized nations that failed to adhere to his beliefs about the proper role of government. He even threatened to stop American aid to nations that failed to use it to improve the lives of their citizens.

During the 1976 presidential campaign, there was a great deal of concern about the future of the **Panama Canal**. President Carter pledged to keep the Panama Canal under American control. However, in 1977, he negotiated two treaties with Panama. The first turned full control of the Canal over to Panama by December 1, 1999. The second treaty gave the United States the right to defend the canal from those who might want to destroy or control it. Many Americans opposed releasing the Panama Canal, especially since Americans had built it at great sacrifice.

President Carter's greatest diplomatic triumph occurred on September 17, 1978. The 1973 war between Israel and her Muslim neighbors had caused great hardship and loss of life. Carter worked diligently to forge a peace treaty between Israel and Egypt. In November 1977, Egyptian President **Anwar Sadat** flew to Israel to meet with **Menachem Begin**, the Israeli prime minister. The two men talked for several days but could not agree on a peace deal. In September 1978, President Carter invited them to meet with him at the presidential retreat known as Camp David. The three men spent twelve days in secret negotiations before the two Middle Eastern leaders agreed on a "framework" for a peace treaty, the **Camp David Accords**. The following year, both nations signed the Egypt-Israeli Peace Treaty. President Carter received credit for conjuring up a diplomatic miracle.

Egyptian President Anwar Sadat (left), President Carter, and Israeli Prime Minister Menachem Begin (right) shake hands at the conclusion of the Camp David Peace Accords signing ceremony in the White House on September 17, 1978. Many historians feel the Accords succeeded because Begin and Sadat personally trusted each other.

President Carter had less success dealing with the Soviet Union. A serious diplomatic crisis arose in December 1979 when the Soviet Union invaded Afghanistan, seized control of the government, and installed a puppet leader. The Soviets quickly drove the Afghan forces out of **Kabul**, Afghanistan's capital, and began hunting down "rebels" in the surrounding countryside. In response to the invasion, President Carter imposed sanctions on the Soviet Union. Grain shipments to the USSR were cut back. The United States also boycotted the 1980 Olympic Games in Moscow. Nevertheless, the Soviets sent many more soldiers into Afghanistan. However, the Soviets had very little success against the Afghan freedom fighters and ultimately withdrew from Afghanistan in 1989. (**Note**: In retaliation for America's failure to attend the 1980 Moscow Olympics, the Soviets declined to participate in the 1984 Games which were held in Los Angeles.)

The Hostage Crisis in Iran

While many people questioned Carter's handling of the Afghanistan situation, especially his decision to boycott the Olympics, most Americans believed that he completely bungled the horrific situation known as the **Iranian Hostage Crisis**.

Shah (King) Mohammad Reza Pahlavi assumed the throne of Iran in 1941 and became a friend to the United States. Iran's location made it an important buffer between the Soviet Union and Saudi Arabia. Also, Iran is an oil-rich nation and a member of OPEC. Over time, Shah Pahlavi worked to modernize Iran by instigating a program of land reform and granting more freedom to women. Many Iranians supported his changes, but Muslim fundamentalists claimed that modernization violated their religious beliefs. During the 1970s, Muslim religious leaders, called *mullahs*, gained power in Iran. Pressure from the mullahs forced the Shah to leave Iran. In early 1979, a mullah named **Ayatollah Ruhollah Khomeini** took control of Iran and demanded that the Shah be put on trial. In October 1979, President Carter allowed Shah Pahlavi to enter the United States to receive treatment for cancer. This infuriated the Iranian government.

In retaliation, and to force America to expel the Shah, Iranians overran the American embassy in **Tehran, Iran** on November 4. They took the fifty-two Americans in the embassy hostage. For several months, President

Iran provided a strategic buffer between the Soviet Union and the Middle East including the Persian Gulf through which much of the world's oil traveled.

Carter used diplomacy and sanctions against Iran but failed to secure the hostages' release. On April 24, 1980, Carter ordered the U. S. military to free the hostages. Eight American helicopters filled with Marines attempted a rescue. Sadly, as the helicopters flew across the desert, several of them malfunctioned. The mission was canceled. As the helicopters returned, two of them collided, killing eight Marines and wounding five others. Carter's Secretary of State, **Cyrus Vance**, resigned because he had opposed the rescue mission. Many Americans saw the tragedy as another example of the incompetence of the federal government. The ongoing hostage crisis would be a major issue during the 1980 presidential election.

The 1980 Presidential Election

Historically, it is almost unthinkable that a sitting president be challenged for his Party's nomination for a second term. Yet, in 1980, that is precisely what happened to Jimmy Carter. With a struggling economy and the hostages in Iran, Carter was being criticized not only by the Republicans, which was to be expected, but also by Democrats, particularly Massachusetts Senator **Edward Kennedy**, President Kennedy's younger brother, and Jerry Brown, the governor of California. These Democrats claimed that Carter had failed to provide leadership and would continue to fail if reelected. Kennedy forced Carter into a bruising re-nomination campaign which many people believed left Carter very weak politically. Nevertheless, the Democrats renominated Jimmy Carter and Walter Mondale.

The Republican nominee seemed rather straightforward. Ronald Reagan had narrowly missed being nominated in 1976. Consequently, he was the early front runner. However, he also faced strong opposition in his quest for nomination. Reagan's principal opponent was **George H. W. Bush**. Bush possessed an impressive record of government service. He had

Ronald Reagan's official White House portrait was painted by Everett Raymond Kinstler in 1991. Unlike prior, and most future presidents, Reagan is smiling. Uniquely, he is posing outside, sitting against a pillar rather than behind a desk or in a chair.

been a fighter pilot during World War II, had served as a congressman from Texas, Ambassador to the United Nations, Director of the Central Intelligence Agency, and a special envoy to China. Bush ran an excellent campaign, but Reagan won easily. However, he chose Bush to be his running mate.

During the campaign, Reagan relentlessly hammered Carter for failing for four years to solve social and economic issues. He said Carter's failures could be measured using a **"misery index,"** which referred to the high inflation and high unemployment. Carter talked about his foreign policy experience, especially his role in the Camp David Accords.

Prior to the election, experts predicted a close race for the White House. The close race never materialized, as Reagan won in a landslide. Reagan received about 51% of the popular vote and won 44 states. In the Electoral College, Reagan won 489 to 49. Republicans won many congressional seats and won the majority of the Senate for the first time in almost thirty years. It was a mandate for Reagan and the Republicans and a rejection of Carter and the Democrats' fiscal policies.

On January 20, 1981, as Ronald Reagan was taking the oath of office as America's 40th president, a plane left Iran for America. After 444 days, the hostages were coming home. It appears that Iran's leaders feared that Reagan would take a much stronger approach to freeing the hostages than Carter had. That fear likely led them to release the hostages.

The Reagan Economy

As president, Ronald Reagan had three principal concerns: high unemployment, high taxes, and the growing Soviet military. Reagan felt that a robust and growing American economy would solve all three problems. Thus, he announced an economic policy aimed at reducing four factors: government spending, federal income tax, government regulation, and inflation. People referred to Reagan's economic plan as **Reaganomics**, **supply-side economics**, or **free-market economics**, depending on how they felt about it.

Basically, *Reagan planned to increase government revenue by having more people pay taxes.* For example, if fifty people pay $1 in taxes, the government earns $50. But if one hundred people pay 75 cents in taxes, the government receives $75. Although each person pays less, because more people are paying taxes, the government actually receives more tax revenue.

The key to Reaganomics lay in the implementation of his four-pronged economic policy. It worked like this: When business owners pay lower taxes, they can invest the tax money they save back into their business. This allows the business to grow and hire more employees. Income taxes on these formerly unemployed workers more than offset the tax relief granted to the business owner. High taxes and government regulation stifle growth and result in high unemployment. Thus, Reagan cut both. He convinced Congress to lower taxes. **As a result, the United States treasury took in more money than ever before**. An era of plenty began in 1982 and lasted until 2007. Federal revenue increased while unemployment decreased.

However, no matter how much money the federal government obtains, it can always spend more than that. Reagan was determined that he would increase the amount spent on the military to oppose Soviet military growth, but at the same time cut all other federal spending. Although the Republicans controlled the Senate, the Democrats controlled the House of Representatives. They opposed cuts to their social welfare programs and to education. Nevertheless, after about 18 months in office, Reagan had cut the overall budget but increased defense spending.

President Reagan believed that the nine scariest words in the English language were "*I'm from the government and I'm here to help.*" He believed that the government over-regulated people and businesses, which made people's lives miserable and made it difficult for businesses to grow. Therefore, part of Reagan's economic plan was to cut government regulation. He began cutting government regulations almost the minute he became president. By the end of his first term, he had cut about half of all the regulations that existed when he became president. He also reduced the number of government employees who enforced these burdensome regulations.

Thus, in relatively short order, Ronald Reagan achieved most of his major economic goals.

The Assassination Attempt

On March 30, 1981, Reagan showed the courage and humor that caused so many Americans to love him deeply. As he came out of a hotel lobby, an assassin shot him in the chest. A secret service agent was also wounded. As Reagan was wheeled into an operating room for emergency surgery, he showed his courage with a bit of humor. He quipped, "I hope all of you doctors are Republicans." One doctor immortally replied, "We're all Republicans today, Mr. President." When Reagan's wife Nancy arrived later at the hospital, he joked, "Honey, I guess I forgot to duck." The "Gipper" was back in the White House two weeks later, more popular than ever.

Reagan's Foreign Policy

Ronald Reagan's foreign policy was based on his belief that the Soviet Union was "an evil empire" that only respected strength. Therefore, Reagan determined to stand up to the Soviets and help any group who sought to overthrow Soviet-backed, pro-communist governments. This policy of granting assistance to anti-communist freedom fighters came to be known as the "**Reagan Doctrine**." Reagan's overall goal was not merely to free nations held in the thrall of communist oppression, but to win the Cold War. He began his campaign in Poland.

As the Reagan Presidency began, the Soviet Union had a stranglehold on Eastern Europe. However, many nations struggled against their Communist oppressors, most notably Hungary and Poland. Poland, because of its strong Catholic Faith and the leadership of prelates like **Cardinal Stefan Wyszynski**, refused to accept Communist domination. When the opportunity presented itself to help the Poles reduce Communist control, Reagan brought diplomatic and monetary pressure to bear.

Cardinal Stefan Wyszynsk

During Reagan's early weeks in office, Polish workers requested their union leaders to ask the Soviets for a voice in government. By the end of 1998, leaders of a labor union called **Solidarity** began demanding a voice in national policies. Solidarity proposed a referendum to decide on Poland's type of government. In response, the Communists declared martial law and shut down Solidarity. To protect their puppet

Lech Walesa, the leader of Solidarity. An electrician by trade, in 1990 he became the first democratically-elected President of Poland, a position he held until 1995.

government, the Soviet Union sent troops to patrol the Polish border. Martial law remained in effect in Poland until 1984. During this time, the United States quietly sent aid to Solidarity.

Reagan also provided weapons to the people of Afghanistan who were fighting the Soviet Union's invasion of their nation. America's supply of weapons is generally considered the main reason for the Soviet Union's ultimate failure to win the Afghan war. In February 1989, the Soviet Union withdrew the last of its troops from Afghanistan. Sadly, while America had helped to win the war, it failed to win the peace. The freedom fighters became the **Taliban** and **al-Qaeda**, terrorist organizations that eventually attacked America.

Reagan dealt with Communist forces closer to home when he sent American troops to Grenada, a Caribbean island. In 1983, pro-Communist forces seized the government of Grenada. Cuban workers began building an airstrip, which America believed could be a staging location for Cuban and Soviet aircraft. President Reagan sent Marines to dislodge the Communist government and rescue American citizens in Grenada's medical school. The locals welcomed the Marines, who took the island after two days of fighting. The Grenadians held elections and installed a democratic government. Grenada remains a peaceful and beautiful island favored by the cruise ship lines.

Reagan also dealt with Communists in Central America. In July 1979, Communists in Nicaragua called **Sandinistas**, led by Cuban-trained Communist **Daniel Ortega**, seized control of the government. The U. S. discovered that Nicaragua was supplying weapons to a Communist guerrilla group that was planning to take over neighboring El Salvador. To oust Ortega and the Sandinistas, Reagan began secretly supplying money, arms, and training to an anti-Communist rebel group, called **Contras**. Reagan also placed a trade embargo on Nicaragua. When Congress discovered the secret aid to the Contras, they denounced it and halted it temporarily. In 1990, it appears the Nicaraguans held free elections which voted Ortega out of office.

In October 1981, the Camp David Accords suffered a serious setback when a Muslim extremist group assassinated President Sadat of Egypt.

In 1982, Lebanon became a Middle Eastern powder keg, when the **Palestine Liberation Organization** (PLO), a terrorist group, threatened to destroy Israel. Unfortunately, for many years, Lebanese leaders had

Grenada. One of the most idyllic islands in the Caribbean. The Catholic Cathedral of the Immaculate Conception in St. George has managed to survive several hurricanes since its construction in 1884.

been unable to control the PLO, which had military bases in Lebanon. In June 1982, Israeli military forces invaded Lebanon. Israeli leaders said they would stay in Lebanon and stop PLO aggression until international peacekeepers were sent into Lebanon. In August 1982, peacekeepers from Italy, France, and the United States took over and forced some PLO members to leave Lebanon. The peacekeepers then left, but the PLO was still strong. At Lebanon's request, the international force, which included American Marines, returned. On October 23, 1983, a terrorist drove a truck loaded with high explosives into the Marines' barracks. In the subsequent explosion, 220 Marines were killed and more than one hundred were wounded. On February 7, 1984, President Reagan ordered the Marines home.

The 1984 Election

As the 1984 presidential election approached, Ronald Reagan was incredibly popular and easily won the Republican nomination. A number of Democrats sought their Party's nomination, including **Jesse Jackson**, the first African-American to seek the White House. The Democrats eventually chose former Vice-President Walter Mondale as their presidential nominee and Representative **Geraldine Ferraro** from New York as their vice-presidential candidate. She became the first woman to be so honored.

Reagan and Mondale had two televised debates. During the first debate, Reagan seemed tired. His age suddenly became an issue. Thus, at the second debate, the question of his age, 73, came up. His response to the moderator's question has become legendary: "*I will not make age an issue of this campaign. I am not going to exploit, for political purposes, my opponent's youth and inexperience.*" At this, perhaps the greatest line in all presidential debates, the entire audience erupted with laughter and applause. Even Walter Mondale could not help laughing.

During the campaign, Reagan ran one of the most effective political ads in history. Known as "**Morning in America**," the ad began by declaring that "*It's morning again in America.*" The ad showed images of happy Americans going to work in a peaceful, successful nation. The message to the viewers was clear: Reagan had made America a better place to live and work. As it turned out, most Americans agreed with him.

One of the images from "Morning in America." Over pictures of happy Americans, the announcer declared: "It's morning again in America. Today more men and women will go to work than ever before in our country's history. …nearly 2,000 families today will buy new homes…This afternoon 6,500 young men and women will be married, and…they can look forward with confidence to the future. It's morning again in America, and under the leadership of President Reagan, our country is prouder and stronger and better…."

The 1984 election was the greatest landslide since George Washington. Reagan won every state but Mondale's home state of Minnesota, 59% of the vote, and 525 electoral votes, the highest number in history. The Senate would be Republican, but the House remained under Democratic control.

Tragedy in Space

Space travel is inherently dangerous. Since President Kennedy began America's conquest of space in the early 1960s, more than two dozen astronauts have died as part of the space program. On January 27, 1967, the crew of Apollo 1, which included "Gus" Grissom, one of America's first seven astronauts, died along with two other astronauts when a fire swept through their space capsule.

In the decades since Neil Armstrong walked on the moon, NASA had been working on a vehicle that could go into space and return: a **space shuttle**. In April 1981, the space shuttle *Columbia* completed 36 orbits of Earth and landed perfectly back on Earth. It became the first orbital craft to land safely.

On January 28, 1986, the space shuttle *Challenger* readied for launch. It was to be an ordinary flight like the last two dozen launches. Seven people were on board: five astronauts and two civilians. One civilian was a teacher who planned to tell her students what it was like to travel in space. Her name was **Christa McAuliffe**.

As the seven voyagers walked toward their space craft, they laughed, waved, and gave the "thumb-ups" sign. As the nation watched, seventy-three seconds after leaving the launching pad, *Challenger* exploded when a booster engine failed. That evening President Reagan spoke to a grieving nation. He announced that America was committed to the continued exploration of space. Of the crew of *Challenger*, he said, *"We will never forget them, nor the last time we saw them, as they prepared for their journey. They waved goodbye and smiled, 'then slipped the surly bonds of earth to touch the face of God.'"*

Sadly, this was not the last shuttle disaster. On February 1, 2003, the space shuttle **Columbia** broke apart as it returned from a two-week mission. All seven astronauts on board died, including two women and an Israeli astronaut.

The Challenger crew on January 9, 1986 taking a break from training. From left to right are Christa McAuliffe, (civilian) Gregory Jarvis, Judith Resnik, Dick Scobee, Ronald McNair, Mike Smith, and Ellison Onizuka.

Reagan's Supreme Court Nominees

During his presidency, Ronald Reagan appointed three new Justices to the United States Supreme Court. His first appointment was **Sandra Day O'Connor**, the first woman ever appointed to the Court. Reagan appointed her in 1981, as part of a campaign promise to name a woman to the Court. She replaced Potter Stewart, who is generally considered a moderate. Most historians consider O'Connor a "moderate conservative." She tended to write conservative opinions but tried not to expand the law. For example, she believed a state could limit abortions but did not overturn *Roe v. Wade*. Justice O'Connor served until 2006.

When Chief Justice Warren Burger announced his retirement in 1986, Reagan elevated Associate Justice William H. Rehnquist to Chief Justice. Reagan then chose **Antonin Scalia** as new Associate Justice. Justice Scalia proved to be a brilliant Constitutional scholar and defender of the Constitution. A staunch conservative, and a devout Catholic, Scalia became the benchmark by which conservatives measured every future nominee. Although he was eighty years old when he died in 2016, most people felt his death was sudden and unexpected. Antonin Scalia was Reagan's finest appointment.

In June 1987, Lewis Powell retired from the Court, giving Reagan a chance at a third appointment. Although some people consider Powell a conservative, his voting record on social issues was very liberal. For example, he voted in the majority to uphold *Roe*. In July, Reagan nominated **Robert Bork**, a well-respected conservative much like Antonin Scalia, who the Senate had easily confirmed. At the time of his nomination, Bork had served six years as a federal Court of Appeals judge, a position to which the Senate had unanimously confirmed him. However, the liberal senators, especially the Democrats, were utterly determined that Bork never be confirmed to the Supreme Court!

The problem with Bork, as far as liberals were concerned, was that **he was the key to overturning *Roe v. Wade***. In 1987, with the retirement of Powell, the Court consisted of four votes to overturn *Roe* – Rehnquist, White, Scalia, and (probably) O'Connor – and four votes to uphold it – Brennan, Marshall, Blackmun, and Stevens. Bork represented the fifth vote to overturn *Roe*. From the perspective of the liberals and most Democrats, Bork had to be opposed and defeated at all costs!

Sandra Day O'Connor

Official portrait of Justice Scalia. Although perhaps not the best likeness of Antonin Scalia, the image is otherwise quite revealing. First, unlike the normal Justice whose robes are closed and who sits behind a desk with his hands folded, Scalia sits with his robes open, in a comfortable, relaxed position. He looks out humbly, a little smile on his face. Second, the picture on the desk in the lower left is of St. Thomas More, the patron saint of lawyers. Scalia never lost sight of his Catholic faith during his years on the bench. Personally, he and his wife had nine children, one of whom became a priest.

Within forty-five minutes of the announcement of Bork's nomination, Senator Edward Kennedy made a speech on the Senate floor, declaring that if Bork became a Justice, there would be an end to all civil liberties in America. These absurd attacks continued for months. Ultimately, the Senate voted not to put Robert Bork on the Court.

The Bork hearings and nomination began the current era when Supreme Court nominees now essentially "run for office." Nominees are attacked personally, almost always by liberal senators and the media. Their qualifications no longer matter. Judge Bork was smeared in the press and by the Senate. Although he was an eminently qualified candidate, fifty-eight senators voted against him, including six liberal Republicans. Judge Bork's name has since become a verb. To "bork" someone means "to obstruct (someone, especially a candidate for public office) through systematic defamation or vilification."

On November 11, 1987, Reagan nominated **Anthony Kennedy** from California, who was serving on the Ninth Circuit Court of Appeals. Kennedy, who was seen as a moderate and not a threat to *Roe*, was quickly confirmed. During his time on the Court, Kennedy proved to be a "swing" vote, deciding many 5-4 decisions. While statistically Kennedy voted more conservatively than not, his votes on social issues, like abortion, tended to be more liberal.

Thus, *overall*, Reagan's nominees to the Court must be judged *as good but not great*. Scalia ranks among the all-time best. However, O'Connor and Kennedy were average on the important social issues. Still, Reagan should be credited with trying to put Bork on the Court. Had he succeeded, the impact of Bork and Scalia would have changed the face of America for decades.

Bork is sworn in for his Senate hearing. All six Republican Senators who voted against Bork's confirmation were pro-abortion.

Anthony Kennedy

The End of the Cold War

While Reagan may have failed fully to achieve his goals on the Court, he succeeded in ending the Cold War. Less than two months after President Reagan began his second term, 54-year-old **Mikhail Gorbachev** became leader of the Soviet Union. Gorbachev seemed more open to change than his predecessors had been. He also believed that the Soviet Union needed to reform, both economically and politically.

Gorbachev and Reagan planned to meet in Geneva in late 1985 to discuss reducing nuclear weapons. However, a potential problem existed. Two years earlier, Reagan began research to build a space-based defense system known as the **Strategic Defense Initiative** (SDI). If it worked, SDI would shoot down nuclear ballistic missiles in space before they reached their targets. Reagan, who earnestly sought to abolish nuclear war, felt that SDI, which was purely defensive, would make nuclear war impossible. In fact, at one point, Reagan even mentioned giving SDI to the Soviets. However, the idea of SDI upset Gorbachev and the Soviets. Nevertheless, at their meeting in Geneva, Reagan and Gorbachev issued a statement saying that neither nation would seek to achieve military superiority over the other. (**Note**: SDI was canceled in 1993 because of cost concerns.) After Geneva, Reagan and Gorbachev continued to negotiate privately to reduce weapons.

In October 1986, Reagan and Gorbachev met in Reykjavik, Iceland. No agreement was reached because Gorbachev opposed Reagan's development of SDI. Despite their disagreement, the nations continued to negotiate the reduction of nuclear weapons.

On June 12, 1987, Reagan gave one of the finest speeches in American history. As he stood before the Brandenburg Gate in front of the Berlin Wall, he spoke not only to those present but to Mikhail Gorbachev. To Gorbachev he said, *"There is one sign the Soviets can make that would be unmistakable, that would advance dramatically the cause of freedom and peace. General Secretary Gorbachev, if you seek peace, if you seek prosperity for the Soviet Union and Eastern Europe, if you seek liberalization, come here to this gate. Mr. Gorbachev, open this gate. Mr. Gorbachev, tear down this wall!"*

A few days before he wrote the Brandenburg Gate speech for President Reagan, speechwriter Peter Robinson spent some time in West Berlin. One evening he joined a dozen West Berliners for dinner. These men and women had different professions and political views. After a bit of small talk, Robinson asked them, "Have you gotten used to the wall?" The Germans looked at each uneasily. Then one man raised an arm, pointed, and replied. "My sister lives twenty miles in that direction, I haven't seen her in more than two decades. Do you think I can get used to that?" Another man related how every morning on his way to work he walked past a guard tower where a soldier watched him through binoculars. "That soldier and I speak the same language. We share the same history. But one of us is a zookeeper and the other is an animal, and I am never certain which is which." Another woman spoke up, suddenly angry. She pounded her fist on the table. "If this man Gorbachev is serious with his talk of glasnost and perestroika (openness and reform) he can prove it. He can get rid of this wall." With this background Robinson wrote his magnificent speech and Reagan delivered it brilliantly.

Such an impassioned plea would have fallen on the deaf ears of previous Soviet leaders. However, Gorbachev truly seemed interested in peace and change. In 1987, Reagan and Gorbachev met in Washington, where they signed a treaty agreeing to eliminate their short- and intermediate range nuclear missiles. It was the first time that the United States and the Soviet Union had agreed to eliminate nuclear weapons. Reagan signed the treaty because it could be verified. As he said, "Trust, but verify."

In December 1988, Gorbachev renounced the Soviet policy that had held Eastern Europe enslaved for more than forty years. His announcement signaled to the people of Eastern Europe that they could establish truly democratic governments in their nations. In June 1989, the people of Poland and Hungary quickly chose freedom from Communism. On the evening of November 9, 1989, ten months after Ronald Reagan had left office, East Germans gathered at the Berlin Wall, the symbol of the Cold War. They began smashing it with hammers. Over the next few days, the hammers became bulldozers. Soon the Berlin Wall had fallen. The Cold War was over.

Ronald Reagan's Legacy

During his presidency, Ronald Reagan created wealth and freedom for the United States of America. He created freedom for Eastern Europe. In short, his legacy is one of freedom and prosperity. Ronald Reagan accomplished what every truly great leader wishes. He left the world a better place than he found it.

President Reagan and Soviet leader Gorbachev in Reykjavik, Iceland.

Answer the following questions:

1. Why was Gerald Ford the Democrat's perfect choice to be Nixon's vice-president?

2. What qualities did Ford have that gave him an opportunity to be a good president?

3. What was the Mayaguez Incident? How did Ford handle it?

4. What were the Helsinki Accords?

5. What is the "Time of Choosing" Speech? Who gave it? Why was it given?

6. What was Ronald Reagan's political philosophy?

7. Why did Carter pardon the draft dodgers?

8. What is OPEC? How did OPEC add to America's energy crisis?

9. What steps did the federal government take to address America's energy crisis?

10. What is ANWR? Why did it become controversial?

11. What forms of renewable energy did the federal government promote?

12. What are the Camp David Accords? What nations and leaders signed the Accords?

13. What caused the Iranian hostage crisis? What did President Carter do to end the crisis? How did the crisis end?

14. What were Ronald Reagan's three main concerns as President? How did he plan to address them?

15. What was Reagan's basic economic plan?

16. What is the Reagan Doctrine? Where was it first applied? Was it successful?

17. What was the Strategic Defense Initiative?

18. Why was Reagan's nomination of Robert Bork to the Supreme Court so controversial?

19. What was Solidarity? How did it help end the Cold War?

Identify the following:

1. Mikhail Gorbachev
2. Sandra Day O'Connor
3. Walter Mondale
4. Antonin Scalia
5. Geraldine Ferraro
6. Operation Sail

CHAPTER 34 Modern Times 1988-2008

One of the most important moments in modern history – the fall of the Berlin Wall, November 9, 1989. Following an announcement from East German officials allowing free passage from East to West Germany, East Germans swarmed into West Berlin where they were joyously greeted. Before long, West Germans climbed onto the Wall outside the Brandenburg Gate where they were joined by East Germans. The crowd milled about but soon began hammering and destroying the hated symbol of their oppression. The evening of November 9, 1989 will forever be remembered as the night the Berlin Wall came down.

Introduction

In 1989, the nations of Eastern Europe finally broke free of Soviet control and peacefully overthrew their Communist governments. In the Soviet Union, the openness known as *glasnost* began to cause it to break apart. Beginning in August 1991, the fifteen nations that comprised the Soviet Union, including Russia, all voted to leave. On Christmas Day 1991, Mikhail Gorbachev resigned as the last leader of the Soviet Union, which then ceased to exist.

With the collapse of the Soviet Union, the United States entered a new age. Sadly, it was not an age of peace as most people expected. Although war with the Soviets was no longer a concern, Russia and China continued to challenge America militarily. Additionally, China presented America with economic challenges as China sought to become the world's leading economic power.

America also had to deal with the growing threat of international terrorism, as on September 11, 2001, America endured the greatest attack ever on American soil. The *War on Terror* would dominate American foreign policy until the present day. It might very well be the main foreign policy issue for decades to come.

With the end of the Cold War and the fall of the Soviet Union, the period from 1988 to 2008 must be considered a period of lost opportunities. A time that had begun with such promise failed to achieve its expectations. Yet Americans never lost hope.

The Election of 1988

In 1988, the most popular politician in America was Ronald Reagan. If the Twenty-Second Amendment to the Constitution had not prohibited him from a third term as president, he almost certainly would have won re-election. In his place, the Republicans nominated the next best thing, his vice-president, **George Herbert Walker Bush**.

George H. W. Bush was born on June 12, 1924, in Milton, Massachusetts and raised in Greenwich, Connecticut. Bush was attending Yale University when the Japanese bombed Pearl Harbor. He interrupted his studies to enlist in the U.S. Navy Reserve and, at eighteen, became one of the Navy's youngest pilots. In 1944, Bush was assigned to an aircraft carrier in the Pacific where he flew a torpedo bomber. He flew his first mission in May. Eventually Bush was shot down in combat. His combat record earned him the Distinguished Flying Cross for bravery. By the time the war ended, George Bush had flown fifty-eight missions in the Pacific theatre of operations.

After the war, Bush re-enrolled in Yale. When he graduated, he was offered a place in his father's law firm, but chose instead to move to Texas with his wife and young son. In Texas, he prospered in the oil business. In his early thirties, Bush became active in the Republican Party. In 1964, Bush ran for the U. S. Senate, but was defeated. However, he was not discouraged, and in 1966 he was elected to Congress as the representative from Houston's congressional district. He served two terms and came to the attention

Photograph of George Bush being rescued by the submarine, USS *Finback*. On September 2, 1944, Bush piloted one of four aircraft that attacked the Japanese installations on Chi Chi Jima. During the attack the planes faced heavy anti-aircraft fire. Bush's plane was hit and his engine caught on fire. He managed to complete his attack and drop his bombs, severely damaging his targets. With his engine on fire, Bush flew away from the island and bailed out of his burning plane. Bush anxiously waited four hours in his life-raft until he was rescued.

of Presidents Nixon and Ford, who named Bush Ambassador to the United Nations (1971), Special Envoy to China (1974), and Director of the Central Intelligence Agency (1976).

In 1980, George Bush ran for president but lost the Republican nomination to Ronald Reagan. Reagan's choice of Bush as his vice-president was quite clever. First, it unified the Party. Second, Bush was one of the most qualified men ever to run for president. His broad range of both domestic and foreign policy experience would be vital to the new president. Third, many "centrist" voters liked the idea that while Reagan was very conservative, Bush was a moderate. As his running mate, George Bush chose **Dan Quayle**, a young conservative senator from Indiana.

To oppose George Bush, the Democrats nominated **Michael Dukakis**, the governor of Massachusetts. Dukakis ran a remarkably poor campaign filled with gaffes and blunders. In one famous photo, Dukakis, who was only five feet eight inches tall, is shown riding in a tank with only part of his head showing out of a port hole in the tank. The photo made him look foolish and comedians made fun of him. He lost the election badly. Bush won forty states, more than

Official White House portrait of George H. W. Bush by Herbert E. Adams. Bush stands in front of a painting of Lincoln meeting with his generals.

fifty-three percent of the popular vote, and 426 Electoral votes compared to Dukakis' 111. In a bit of irony, Dukakis' vice-presidential choice, **Lloyd Bentsen**, had defeated George Bush for the U. S. Senate 18 years earlier.

George Bush Oversees the End of the Cold War

When George Bush took office, his biggest foreign policy concern was the collapsing Soviet Union. The economic and military pressure that Reagan had exerted on the communist system had brought the Soviet Union to its knees. Mikhail Gorbachev had made overtures of peace and had been willing to negotiate. However, Bush, unlike Reagan, did not trust Gorbachev.

When Bush took office on January 20, 1989, the situation in Eastern Europe was still precarious. No one was certain how Gorbachev would react to the growing freedom movements in Eastern Europe, especially in Poland. Thus, the diplomatic position that Bush inherited was delicate and the stakes were high, that is, the freedom of hundreds of millions of people.

The situation *within* the Soviet Union complicated negotiations. The first issue Bush had to resolve concerned Gorbachev's *sincerity*. Bush feared that Gorbachev might be attempting to lure the U. S. into a false sense of security to buy time to rebuild the Soviet Union before renewing hostilities. However, even if Gorbachev sincerely wished to negotiate, he had powerful enemies in the Soviet Union. It was possible that America might begin negotiations with Gorbachev only to see radical communists overthrow him and seize control of the country. Bush even feared that if he were too openly friendly with Gorbachev, he might give Gorbachev's enemies more incentive to oppose him violently. Despite these concerns, Bush recognized the need to act. Gorbachev's apparent openness presented an opportunity for peace that could not be ignored. However, before Bush could act, history overtook him.

In February, Poland began the process which would lead to its eventual freedom from Communism. Pro-democracy movements also erupted in Hungary and Czechoslovakia. By late 1989, most of Eastern Europe was demanding to be free of Soviet domination. Although many radical Communists demanded that Gorbachev crush these freedom movements, he refused.

Meanwhile, the poverty and suffering caused by communism made the government of East Germany increasingly unpopular. Many East Germans demanded democratic elections. In an effort to regain support, the government began to relax some of its harsher laws, including its travel restrictions. Finally, at a press conference in November 1989, a spokesman for the East German government relayed a confusing account of the new travel regulations. In a matter of hours, media outlets around the world picked up the story. They announced that the East German border was open.

Soon crowds gathered on the East German side of the Berlin Wall. They had come to test the new regulations for themselves. Would they be allowed to pass through? The border guards were not sure what to do. They had seen the news, but had received no orders from their superiors. Eventually, they opened the gates. People began passing from East to West, a trickle at first, quickly increasing to a flood. Crowds had gathered from the West, too. Germans embraced in the streets. Young people climbed onto the wall and began to chip away at it while the guards stood by. The Berlin Wall fell, not to the sounds of guns and shouts of anger, but to the sounds of laughter and shouts of joy.

The fall of the Berlin Wall caught world leaders off guard. It had happened so suddenly that they were unsure of its significance and how to react. President Bush responded to the news with restraint, making a conscious effort not to appear to be gloating over what seemed a Soviet defeat. However, that Gorbachev had not sent the Soviet military to crush the East Germans, something that all his predecessors almost certainly would have done, eased some of Bush's fears about dealing with him. By allowing the destruction of the wall, Gorbachev had shown that he sincerely wished to reform his nation. For his part, Gorbachev saw Bush's restrained response to the fall of the wall as a sign that he could trust Bush. Bush would not try to cause him political embarrassment at home.

The Berlin Wall fell to shouts of joy, laughing cheers, champagne toasts, and fireworks.

Bush meets with Gorbachev in Malta.

As Eastern Europe finally emerged from behind the Iron Curtain, Bush and Gorbachev made plans to meet. They met in Malta in December 1989. Bush specifically requested that the meeting be private and without a formal agenda. He did not want this meeting to come under the pressure of world expectation or wide publicity. The Malta meeting was typical of Bush's diplomatic style. He established trusting relationships with foreign leaders before pushing for results. Though certain issues remained unresolved, the Malta meeting established the willingness of the two leaders to cooperate. For many historians, the Malta Summit marked the "official" end of the Cold War. Gorbachev later said as much. The cooperation of the Soviet Union and the United States would be tested during the Gulf War, which broke out the following year. In the meantime, American soldiers went to war in Panama.

Bush Defends Panama

Since America built the Panama Canal, she had always had a good relationship with Panama. Although the United States operated the Canal, Panama received money from ships transiting the Canal. Thus, Panama became enriched.

Sadly, the relationship between the two nations began to fall apart when **Manuel Noriega** became dictator of Panama in 1983. Noriega used force, intimidation, and fraudulent elections to stay in power. He also became a drug dealer. American authorities sought to arrest him for smuggling illegal drugs into the United States. On December 15, 1989, Noriega declared that a "state of war" existed between Panama and the United States. The following day, some of Noriega's thugs murdered an unarmed American Marine. President Bush responded swiftly. Four days later, American forces invaded Panama. The Marines gained control of Panama in just nine hours, at the loss of only twenty-three soldiers. Noriega surrendered himself ten days later.

The invasion of Panama was very popular in the United States because it was quick, successful, and resulted in the loss of few American lives. However, the UN and other countries condemned the invasion. For America's next conflict, Bush sought to form a coalition of international support.

The Gulf War

The most significant military conflict of George Bush's presidency was the **Gulf War**, also known as the **First Iraq War**. In 1979, **Saddam Hussein**, a brutal dictator, became ruler of Iraq. To maintain power, he employed vicious tactics, including the use of chemical weapons against civilians, that resulted in the deaths of hundreds of thousands of men, women, and children. On August 2, 1990, Hussein invaded the neighboring country of Kuwait, an oil-rich nation, arguing that it had historically been a part of Iraq. In Bush's view, as well as that of most of the international community, Iraq's invasion of Kuwait was wholly unjust. Bush compared Hussein to Hitler and his actions to the Nazi invasion of the Rhineland at the beginning of World War II. Bush argued that the way to prevent the conflict from escalating was to meet it promptly with strong opposition.

In addition to believing in the justice of driving Iraqi forces from Kuwait, Bush also felt that the action of a united world against Iraq would set an important precedent. He worked with the UN in order to present Saddam Hussein with a unified coalition of nations that opposed his aggression. The Gulf War was significant because even the Soviets, although they did not provide troops, supported America's opposition to Iraq's invasion.

On September 11, 1990, Bush addressed a joint session of Congress. He had just returned from a summit with Gorbachev and the two leaders had issued a joint statement calling for Iraq's withdrawal from Kuwait. With this diplomatic triumph in mind, Bush enthusiastically proclaimed a "New World Order" of peace and cooperation. He believed that presenting a united front against Saddam Hussein's aggression would not only stop the injustice of the present situation, but would ultimately make the whole world a more peaceful place. Bush said that, "*We stand today at a unique and extraordinary moment. The crisis in the Persian Gulf, as grave as it is, also offers a rare opportunity to move toward a historic period of cooperation. Out of these troubled times...a new world order can emerge: a new era – freer from the threat of terror, stronger in the pursuit of justice, and more secure in the quest for peace.*"

The United Nations gave Saddam Hussein until January 15, 1991 to withdraw from Kuwait voluntarily or be forced to leave. Once the deadline passed, Bush ordered American troops into action early in the morning of January 17. The first phase of the combat consisted of air strikes against the Iraqis. On February 24, because Saddam Hussein still refused to withdraw, Allied ground troops advanced into Kuwait. By that afternoon, the Iraqis began asking for peace. The ground war officially ended after exactly one hundred hours with Iraq's withdrawal from Kuwait. The military action in Kuwait was popular with the American people because Kuwait had been liberated in a short war during which few Americans were killed or wounded. Bush seemed to have ushered in a new period of world peace and cooperation.

The Collapse of the Soviet Union

Although Gorbachev had permitted the nations of Eastern Europe to break away from Soviet control, he had not yet shown a willingness to grant that freedom to the approximately fifteen nations that formed the Union of Soviet Socialist Republics (USSR). In fact, in early 1987, he was working diligently to keep the Soviet Union intact. However, Gorbachev's policies of openness and restructuring had brought him face-to-face with increasing pressure not only from the member Republics of the Soviet Union but also in Russia. The Russian people, especially the young people, demanded full democracy. During 1987, the three Baltic Republics that had fallen under the power of the Soviet empire openly asked for independence. Although Gorbachev replaced the Communist leaders in those nations with more tolerant leaders, it was not enough. By 1988, the Baltics were mostly independent.

Meanwhile, the desire for freedom spread like wildfire across the Soviet Union. In the Soviet Republics of Armenia, Georgia, Ukraine, and Belarus, the people began demanding democracy and independence. Gorbachev now recognized that he could no longer hold the Soviet Union together. On December 25,

1991, Gorbachev officially resigned. The Russians lowered the *Hammer and Sickle* flag for the last time. The national flag of Russia replaced it. The nations that had fallen under the power of communism were given the freedom to decide their own affairs. In his Christmas address, Bush told the American people it was "*a victory for democracy and freedom.*"

Ronald Reagan's determination to end the Cold War and defeat Communism weakened the Soviets and strengthened the freedom-loving people of the world, especially in Europe. However, once Reagan left office, the diplomatic situation remained delicate. George Bush deserves credit for his careful handling of the final months of the Cold War and the collapse of the Soviet Union. There are reasons to believe that his restraint significantly affected the peacefulness of this final outcome. A more impetuous president might not have been blessed with such a successful conclusion and may well have triggered an unfortunate series of events.

Bush's Supreme Court Appointments

During his presidency, George Bush appointed two new Justices to the U. S. Supreme Court. In July 1990, William Brennan, one of the two most liberal Justices ever to sit on the Court, retired. Bush had an opportunity to shift the balance on the Court to a more conservative judicial philosophy. Instead of choosing a well-known conservative, Bush chose virtually unknown New Hampshire judge **David Souter**.

Apparently, Bush chose David Souter for two reasons. First, no one knew much about him, so the Senate could not smear him like they had Robert Bork. Moreover, liberal senators were not sure how Souter would vote on important social issues like abortion, so *they were not sure they should smear him.* His anonymity made his confirmation more likely. Secondly, Bush's Chief of Staff, **John Sununu**, had appointed Souter to the New Hampshire Supreme Court. Sununu assured Bush that Souter was a conservative. The Senate quickly confirmed Souter.

Initially, David Souter seemed to be a conservative Justice. However, before long, he began to vote consistently with the Liberal wing of the Court. For example, in 1992, Souter provided the fifth vote to uphold abortion in *Planned Parenthood v. Casey*. To his credit, Bush regretted the decision to appoint Souter who served until 2009.

Conservatives agree that Bush did much better with his second nominee: **Clarence Thomas**. In 1991, Thurgood Marshall, another very liberal member of the Court, resigned. Once again, Bush had the chance to shift the philosophy of the Court to a more conservative one. He nominated Clarence

David Souter

Clarence Thomas. One of the most interesting individuals ever to serve on the Court, Thomas considered becoming a priest before entering law school. At sixteen, he fought to enter St. John Vianney seminary to pursue his dream of becoming a priest. He was the first African-American admitted to St. John Vianney and felt the pressure of being the only black student. In 1967, he entered Conception College Seminary but, after the assassination of Dr. King in 1968, he abandoned his dream of becoming a priest because he felt a stronger passion for the growing Civil Rights movement. He enrolled at College of the Holy Cross and graduated in 1971. He then attended Yale Law School. Upon graduating, Thomas began working for various state and federal agencies. In 1990, President George H. W. Bush nominated him to the U.S. Court of Appeals for the District of Columbia. The following year, Bush nominated him to the Supreme Court.

Thomas, an African-American. Like Bork, Thomas faced terrible opposition from the Liberals in the Senate because they feared he would overturn *Roe v. Wade*. Nevertheless, despite the vicious Senate hearings, which Thomas described as a "high-tech lynching," the Senate confirmed him 52-48. Thomas proved to be an excellent choice, and a strong conservative Justice, voting almost 90% of the time with Justice Scalia. Thomas has consistently maintained that "Roe (v. Wade) was wrongly decided, and that it can and should be overruled…" (*Planned Parenthood v. Casey* (1992)). Like Justice Scalia, Justice Thomas is a practicing Catholic. As of January 1, 2022, the seventy-two-year-old Thomas is still on the Court.

The 1992 Presidential Election

For the 1992 election, the Republicans re-nominated George Bush. At the beginning of 1991, Bush was incredibly popular. In fact, had the election been held during the spring instead of autumn, he almost certainly would have defeated any Democrat. However, the election was held in November.

Following America's success in the Gulf War and the dissolution of the Soviet Union, Bush's approval rating was very high. However, he seems to have become a victim of his own successful foreign policy. The newfound peace and stability caused Americans to become less concerned about international affairs. They turned their attention more to domestic matters. Here, Bush had made some critical mistakes.

Bush's domestic problems actually began during his 1988 presidential campaign. After eight years of Reagan, people wondered whether the then-vice-president really had the strength to lead the country. There was widespread concern that Bush lacked backbone and vision and would profess whatever position might be most politically advantageous. When he had become Reagan's running mate, Bush had changed his opinion seemingly overnight on important issues such as the economy and abortion. This led conservative Republicans to become concerned that Bush would not truly represent them. In an effort to counter these perceptions and project strength and conservative values, Bush had made an important promise at the Republican National Convention in 1988. He declared, "*My opponent won't rule out raising taxes. But I will. The Congress will push me to raise taxes, and I'll say no, and they'll push, and I'll say no, and they'll push again, and I'll say to them, 'Read my lips: no new taxes.'*"

Though Bush won the 1988 presidential election, the Democrats gained control of both chambers of Congress. They were determined to make Bush break his "*no new taxes*" promise. Congress refused to pass a budget without a tax increase. In 1990, Congress compelled Bush to approve a tax increase. When Bush campaigned for reelection in 1992, he paid dearly for his broken pledge.

In 1992, most Democrats believed that Bush, because he was so popular, would almost certainly win re-election. As a result, the more well-known Democrats decided not to run. As a result, the Democrats chose the little-known Arkansas governor, **William Jefferson (Bill) Clinton**, as their nominee. Most voters considered Clinton a moderate Democrat. He ran a smart campaign which focused on the economy, which was in recession, and rising unemployment. Clinton capitalized on the situation. He painted Bush as a wealthy and elite politician who had lost touch with the concerns of ordinary Americans. He told Americans that he "felt their pain." He blamed the recession on the policies of Reagan and Bush. Despite Clinton's campaign, some historians believe that Bush still might have won the election if a third party candidate had not entered the race.

Arkansas governor Bill Clinton

Historically, third party candidates have had *interesting, but not decisive,* effects on presidential elections. In the one hundred years preceding the 1992 election, only four independent candidates had made any impact at all on the presidential election. In 1924, Senator Robert La Follette won 16.6% of the vote. In 1948, Strom Thurmond won four states and about 2% of the vote. In 1968, George Wallace won five states and 13.5% of the vote. Finally, in 1980, John Anderson received 6.6% of all the votes. With the exception of Truman's election in 1948, where he received just under 50% of the popular vote, and Nixon's election in 1968, where he received only 43.4% of the popular vote, the other two Presidents received more than 50% of the vote, so the presence or absence of the independent candidate would not have affected those outcomes.

Harry Truman was elected because he carried California, where Strom Thurmond did not even appear on the ballot. However, **Henry Wallace**, a liberal third party candidate, likely siphoned away almost 200,000 votes from Truman, who won California by only 18,000 votes. Wallace hurt Truman but almost certainly did not decisively affect the outcome.

The presence of George Wallace certainly hurt Richard Nixon in 1968. Wallace, who was seen as more conservative than Nixon, won five southern states and 9.9 million votes, almost 25% coming from those five southern states. Had Wallace not been in the race, Nixon likely would have won those five southern states as well as seven or eight million more votes, giving him a popular majority.

Thus, independent candidates had made some presidential races more interesting, but their presence does not seem to have modified what would have been the outcome had they not run. In 1992, a third party candidate once again entered the race. His name was **H. Ross Perot**.

Perot ran as a fiscal conservative and social liberal. Thus, he favored cutting certain taxes, balancing the federal budget, and reducing the national debt. He also opposed gun control but supported abortion. During his campaign, he focused on fiscal policies rather than social issues. Most of the people who eventually voted for him described themselves as moderates.

Ross Perot was the most successful independent candidate in American history. However, despite conventional wisdom and the anger of Bush's supporters, it appears that while he made the election interesting, he did not affect the inevitable outcome. Perot received about 19.6 million votes. However, in 1992, thirteen million more votes were cast than in 1988. One might posit that many of those new voters voted for Perot and had no interest in voting for either Bush or Clinton. Although Clinton received 3 million more votes than Dukakis had in 1988, Bush received almost 10 million fewer votes than he did when he was elected in 1988! Additionally, of those who did vote for Bush or Clinton,

Ross Perot. National Portrait Gallery, Smithsonian Institution; gift of Time magazine.

about 53% voted for Clinton. Even if Perot had not been in the race, and all the people who voted for him voted for Bush or Clinton, they would have had to vote for Bush by a margin of 58% to 42% to affect the race – almost the exact opposite of the way people were voting.

At the end of election day, Bill Clinton had received only 43% of the popular vote, the smallest in history for a winning candidate. He won 32 states in the Electoral College compared to Bush's 18. Perot had received almost 19% of the popular vote.

President Bill Clinton

Bill Clinton won the presidency by convincing voters that he was the champion of the average voter and the right person to solve America's domestic and economic woes. Bush had been born into a wealthy New England family, but Bill Clinton had a more humble background. He grew up in a small town in Arkansas. As president, Clinton planned to invest in government programs that he thought would help ordinary people by stimulating economic growth, such as education and transportation. In order to raise funds for these programs, he needed to reorganize the federal budget.

In the month following his inauguration, Clinton laid out his economic plan. He would reduce the budget deficit by raising taxes and cutting spending. Rather than raise taxes on all citizens equally, however, Clinton proposed raising the taxes of only the wealthiest and most successful individuals and businesses (those that Reagan showed were the job and income creators). Clinton called for significant cuts in government spending, especially large cuts in military spending. He felt that, with the end of the Cold War and the coming of what appeared to be an era of peace, the United States no longer needed such a large military.

Clinton's budget proposal met with strong opposition, particularly from the Republicans. Many people worried that his proposed heavy tax on the wealthy and successful would ultimately inhibit economic growth. Businesses could not use the money to expand and hire more workers, it would be in the hands of government bureaucrats. Many feared that Clinton's new taxes would increase unemployment and harm the very middle-class citizens that he wished to help.

President Clinton's official portrait. The artist, Nelson Shanks, stated that he placed the shadow on the left side of the painting as "a bit of a metaphor in that it represents a shadow on the office he held, or on him" because of his impeachment and the scandal he brought to the office of President.

Though Congress enacted much of Clinton's proposed budget, his first two years as president were not particularly successful. The economy failed to show signs that it was recovering. Clinton's promised universal health care bill, which his wife Hillary championed, failed in Congress. The 1994 midterm elections saw a stunning rejection of Bill Clinton and the Democrats. The Republicans took control of both chambers of Congress for the first time in forty years.

The Republican takeover of Congress limited Clinton's ability to pursue his agenda. Over the winter of 1995-1996, the government partially shut down, as the president and Congress failed to reach a budget agreement. The Republican Congress wanted a balanced budget, but they also wanted to repeal Clinton's tax increases. To balance the budget without a tax increase, Republicans called for spending cuts in programs Clinton favored. As public discontent mounted, Clinton and the Republicans blamed each other for the shutdown. The president and the media convinced the nation that the Republicans were being unreasonable and causing the shutdown because of their heartless disregard for the suffering of the general public. The Republican Party became the focus of people's anger on the verge of the 1996 presidential election.

The 1996 Election

As the 1996 election rolled around, Bill Clinton's popularity was very high. The Republicans needed to nominate someone with energy and charisma. Instead, they nominated **Robert (Bob) Dole**. Bob Dole had represented Kansas in Congress since 1961. He had been Gerald Ford's running mate in 1976. However, Dole lacked charisma. In fact, he tended to speak in a dull monotone. Moreover, as one of the oldest men to run for president, at seventy-three he lacked energy. His campaign never really got going.

Ross Perot again sought the presidency. This time he ran as a member of the **Reform Party**, which he had founded in 1995. Although it still exists, the Reform Party has had very little impact on American politics since 1996.

Clinton again ran a very intelligent campaign. He continued to portray himself as a moderate. For example, he said he supported abortion but wanted to make it rare. In the end, he won re-election but once again failed to obtain more than 50% of the popular vote. Clinton won 49.2% of the popular vote, 31 states, and 379 of 538 Electoral College votes. However, while people seemed to like Bill Clinton, the Democratic Party did not enjoy the same popularity. Republicans retained control of the House and the Senate. During Clinton's second term, Congress and the president would have many unpleasant confrontations.

Domestic Terrorism

During Bill Clinton's presidency, a new threat to the American people began to emerge: **terrorism**. Rather than engage in open warfare, America's enemies began to commit unpredictable acts of violence against noncombatants. Their goals were to avenge wrongs that they believed America had committed and to inspire fear in the general population. As Lenin is credited with saying, "*The purpose of terrorism is to terrorize.*"

During Clinton's presidency, two acts of **domestic terrorism**, that is, acts of terror committed by Americans against Americans, occurred. In 1995, two former soldiers carried out the deadliest terror attack in American history up to that point. Their hatred for the federal government caused them to launch this cowardly attack. They parked a rental truck containing a bomb outside a government office building in

The Oklahoma City National Memorial. This somewhat unusual memorial honors those murdered on April 19, 1995 when domestic terrorists attacked the Alfred P. Murrah Federal Building. The memorial encompasses the hallowed ground upon which the Murrah Building once stood, as well as the surrounding area devastated by the bomb blast. Each chair in the Field of Empty Chairs represents and memorializes a person killed in the bombing.

Oklahoma City. When the bomb exploded, it killed 168 people and injured an additional 680, including children in the building's daycare center.

The following year, another domestic terrorist planted a bomb at the Olympic Games in Atlanta. Thankfully, this bombing proved less deadly than the attack in Oklahoma City. Sadly, it killed one person. However, it introduced a new reality into American life: innocent Americans enjoying a public event had become a target of violence.

The War on Terror

Even as the threat of domestic terrorism worsened, international terrorism cast its even darker shadow on the United States. While domestic terror attacks were usually carried out by so-called "lone wolf" bombers who were often mentally unstable, international terror attacks were executed by groups of Muslim fundamentalists who were well aware of their intentions, well trained, and well-funded.

Since the time of Mohammad, Muslims have historically used violence to spread Islam. The Middle Ages saw repeated Muslim attacks on Christian Europe. While some modern Muslims condemn such violence, others still consider it "Holy War" and a part of their religious duties. American involvement in the Middle East, especially American support for Israel, had inflamed the hatred of these Muslims. They believed that the presence of American troops in Saudi Arabia during the Gulf War was a particularly serious affront. Some particularly fanatical Muslims imagined that America's intervention was the beginning of a plot to conquer the Muslim world. Unable to respond with a conventional war, they chose to launch terrorist attacks against the United States.

Just after noon on February 26, 1993, a massive explosion ripped into New York's World Trade Center. Muslim terrorists had left a rented van filled with bombs and hydrogen gas in an underground parking garage below the World Trade Center. When the bomb detonated, it killed six people and injured over 1,000. **The 1993 World Trade Center Bombing marked the first attack by Islamic terrorists against American civilians**. Sadly, it would not be the last.

In addition to bombing the World Trade Center, Muslim terrorists also targeted American military bases and embassies abroad. In 1996, Muslim militants bombed a U. S. Air Force base in Saudi Arabia. That same year, a terrorist leader named **Osama Bin Laden** officially declared a holy war on the United States. In the late 1980s, Bin Laden had established a terrorist network called **al Qaeda**. On August 7, 1998, al Qaeda carried out simultaneous bombings at American embassies in Kenya and Tanzania. The coordinated attacks hundreds of miles apart took 224 lives. They revealed that Bin Laden's terror network was extensive.

In response to the embassy attacks, President Clinton ordered the navy to fire cruise missiles at suspected al Qaeda bases in Afghanistan. Many Americas saw this response as ineffective and criticized Clinton for appearing weak on terrorism. However, Clinton had never been an expert on or particularly interested in foreign policy matters. His strength was on domestic issues. In fairness to Clinton, neither he nor his foreign policy advisers fully grasped the severity of the threat that Bin Laden, al Qaeda, and terrorism posed to American lives. Also, in 1998, Clinton had become embroiled in a personal scandal which certainly distracted him from his responsibility to defend America. This scandal captured the attention of both the president and the general public far more than bombings in two distant embassies.

Clinton is Impeached

In early 1998, news reports surfaced that President Clinton had been conducting an adulterous relationship with a young intern named **Monica Lewinsky**. Clinton denied the reports, both publicly and under oath. As irrefutable evidence of his guilt emerged, Clinton admitted that he had made misleading statements, but maintained, based on legal technicalities, that he had done nothing criminal. The House of Representatives voted to impeach him on the charges of perjury and contempt of court. However, the

Senate acquitted him, deciding that Clinton's offenses, though reprehensible, did not fall into the category of "high crimes and misdemeanors."

The embassy bombings of August 1998 occurred in the midst of this scandal. Many thought that Clinton's response to the bombings was more of an effort to distract the public from his own troubles than a sincere attempt to counter the threat of al Qaeda. Despite the scandal, Clinton left office in 2001 with high approval ratings, evidence that America's moral standards were no longer as high as they had been or should be.

Pro-Abortion Actions

Although Bill Clinton claimed that he wanted to make abortions "rare," he did little legislatively to achieve this goal. In fact, Clinton promoted one of the most brutal abortion procedures. Twice during his presidency, Congress passed a ban on **partial birth abortion**, a procedure that involves partially delivering a viable baby before killing it while it is still in the birth canal. On both occasions, Clinton vetoed the ban, single-handedly allowing the savage procedure to continue. He also allowed federal funds to go to abortions and overturned several other pro-life policies implemented by Reagan and Bush.

Clinton's Supreme Court Selections

Clinton's support for abortion shaped the choice of his two Supreme Court nominees. In 1993 and 1994, Byron White, a conservative, and Harry Blackmun, the author of *Roe v. Wade*, retired. Clinton appointed **Ruth Bader Ginsburg**, the second woman, to the Court. Ginsburg had served as an Appeals Court judge for almost thirteen years. Ginsburg became one of the most liberal Justices ever to serve on the Supreme Court. After 1999, Ginsburg was treated for various serious illnesses, including cancer. However, despite her declining physical and mental condition, she refused to retire from the Court. She died on September 18, 2020.

Following the retirement of Harry Blackmun, Clinton appointed **Stephen Breyer**, who had been a Circuit Court judge for almost fourteen years. Clinton chose Breyer because of his support for abortion, and during his tenure on the Court, Breyer has consistently voted to support abortion. Although Breyer has tended to hold a liberal judicial philosophy, he will occasionally vote with the conservatives. For example, in **Van Orden v. Perry** (2005), a 5-4 decision, he voted to allow a Ten Commandments display

President Clinton and Monica Lewinsky in the Oval Office

Ruth Bader Ginsburg

on public property, although the other liberal Justices voted to disallow it. Breyer retired in 2022.

In general, from a conservative point of view, Clinton's two nominees rank among the worst, with Ginsburg being one of the five most liberal Justices in all of American history.

New Technologies

Though Clinton took credit for the improvement of the economy during his presidency, the technological development of the nineties played a significant role in the boom. During the early 1990s, the **Internet** became publicly available and its use quickly spread. In 1995, just fourteen percent of Americans had access to the Internet. By 2000, the percentage had grown to forty-six. In addition to helping the economy, the Internet affected American life in other significant ways. It was a powerful tool that encouraged new forms of business, so-called **e-commerce**, and made massive amounts of information instantly accessible. However, as people began to depend on it more and more, it also led to isolation and loneliness, as people replaced real-life relationships with **virtual** ones.

Stephen Breyer

The 2000 Presidential Election

In 2000, one of the most controversial presidential elections in American history took place. The Democratic candidate was Clinton's vice-president, **Al Gore**. The Republican nominee was **George W. Bush**, eldest son of George H. W. Bush. Bush was the governor of Texas but otherwise had no political experience. However, he had been a successful businessman and even owned a baseball team. Bush campaigned on a platform of various domestic reforms, including improving education and making tax cuts. He had a record of working with Democrats as governor of Texas and claimed he could heal some of the bitterness that had characterized government affairs during the Clinton years.

On the other hand, Al Gore had spent almost his entire adult life in politics. Since 1977, he had served as a member of the House of Representatives and Senate from Tennessee and as Clinton's vice-president. Gore wisely campaigned as an extension of the peace and prosperity that America had enjoyed during Clinton's presidency. At the same time, he tried to distance himself from Clinton's scandals.

When Election Day arrived, polls indicated that the race would be close. By the end of the day, there was no clear winner. As the results came in, it became apparent that the state of Florida would decide the election. Whichever candidate claimed Florida's 25 electoral votes would receive the 270 electors necessary for victory.

On the morning after the election, Bush held a razor-thin lead in Florida of about a thousand votes out of six million. The margin was so close that Gore legally demanded the votes be recounted. For five weeks, the election remained undecided, until the Florida Supreme Court ordered a manual recount of the votes. At this point, Bush appealed to the U. S. Supreme Court, arguing that there was no fair way to conduct the tedious task of a manual recount before the fast-approaching meeting of the Electoral College. On December 12, the Supreme Court ruled in Bush's favor and stopped the recount. George W. Bush won Florida by 537 votes and became the forty-third president of the United States.

However, Bush and Gore were not the only candidates running for president in Florida. For the first time in American history, a third party candidate did affect the outcome of a presidential election. **Ralph Nader**, the Green Party candidate, also appeared on the ballot in Florida. Nader represented a very liberal position, much closer to Gore's than to Bush's. He received over 97,000 votes, about 2.3% of the total. Had Nader not run, it is almost certain that a large number of his votes would have gone to Gore.

The 9/11 Attacks

George Bush had not been in office for eight months before America experienced the worst day in its history since the bombing of Pearl Harbor on December 7, 1941. On the morning of September 11, 2001, Bush visited an elementary school in Florida to promote his education reforms. By the end of the day, he was taking shelter in an emergency bunker below the White House. That morning, Muslim terrorists had hijacked four passenger airplanes, which they used as weapons in suicide missions. Two planes slammed into the twin towers of New York City's World Trade Center, killing all on board. The jet fuel in the airplanes caused the buildings to burst into flames. Within two hours, the impact of the planes caused both towers to collapse, killing hundreds of workers who were trapped inside, as well as heroic firefighters who had entered the burning buildings. A third hijacked plane crashed into the Pentagon.

Official White House portrait of George W. Bush. Unlike the portrait of his father, this George Bush appears much more relaxed. Even the painting in the background reflects the different moods. In this portrait we see cowboys on horseback, a relatively innocuous scene. Recall that George H. W. Bush posed in front of Lincoln and his generals discussing matters dealing with the Civil War.

The take-off of the fourth plane was delayed. Before it left the ground, passengers learned about the other attacks. When they realized that their plane had also been hijacked, they knew that cooperating with the hijackers would not save their lives. Instead, they bravely attacked. They forced the hijackers to crash the plane in a field in Pennsylvania. Though they all died, their heroic sacrifice saved countless lives. Investigators never determined the intended target of the fourth plane. Suggestions include the White House and the Capitol building. However, it is clear that the hijackers intended to commit mass murder.

The attacks of September 11 transformed George Bush from a president focused on a domestic agenda to a war leader. As the ruins of the World Trade Center smoldered, he developed his war plan. While no specific nation was directly responsible for the attacks, Bush characterized any nation that gave sanctuary to terrorists as an enemy. Bush also stated that he saw the attacks as a declaration of war. In articulating what came to be known as the "Bush Doctrine," President Bush declared that the United States had the right and responsibility **to preemptively attack** nations that harbored or aided terrorists in order to defend itself from future plots. This war came to be called the "War on Terror."

The Tower of Voices is a monumental, ninety-three feet tall musical instrument holding forty wind chimes which represent the forty passengers and crew members of United Flight 93 who sacrificed their lives to save the lives of their fellow Americans. Constructed at the sight of the crash, the Tower serves as both a visual and audible reminder of the heroism of the brave men and women on Flight 93. The Tower is part of a larger memorial which includes a "Wall of Names" which lists the names of the forty passengers and crew who wrested control of the plane from the four hijackers.

The War on Terror

On September 14, the Congress almost unanimously agreed that America's response should be war. They authorized Bush to use any means necessary to bring the terrorists to justice and prevent additional attacks. As Bush led the nation's response to the terrorists, he faced the same fears as other Americans, along with the heavy responsibility of trying to prevent further attacks.

The first military response to the 9/11 attacks occurred in Afghanistan. Investigators quickly determined that al Qaeda was responsible for the 9/11 attacks. Several al Qaeda terrorist training camps were located in Afghanistan. Moreover, Afghanistan, which was ruled by the Taliban, an extremist Islamic group, had provided Osama Bin Laden with a safe haven and refused to turn him over to American authorities. Bush and his advisers hoped that a military victory in Afghanistan would prevent future terrorist attacks. An occupying American force could destroy the al Qaeda training camps, remove the Taliban, and install a democratically elected government. Bush believed that these measures would bring peace and order to Afghanistan, which would no longer be a refuge for terrorists.

In March 2003, the War on Terror expanded into Iraq. Relations between Iraq and the U. S. had only deteriorated since the Gulf War of 1991. A condition of the ceasefire at the end of the Gulf War was that

Saddam Hussein destroy any Weapons of Mass Destruction (WMDs) in his possession and allow UN inspections to ensure his compliance. Over the years, the inspectors continued to find forbidden weapons, and, in 1998, Hussein stopped complying with the inspections. As a result, intelligence agencies throughout the world strongly suspected that Hussein was developing WMDs. Though Iraq was not directly involved in the 9/11 attacks, the attacks made the Iraqi threat seem more immediate to many Americans, including President Bush. After several diplomatic attempts to ensure that Iraq possessed no WMDs, Bush concluded that Hussein's resistance meant that he had something to hide. Bush knew that Hussein had used WMDs against the Kurds, his own people, in the past. A large majority of congressmen, both Democrats and Republicans, agreed with Bush's reasoning. American military forces entered Iraq.

The American military quickly *appeared* to defeat the Iraqis and the Taliban. On May 1, 2003, after less than two months of fighting, President Bush boarded an aircraft carrier to announce the end of major combat in Iraq. The same day, the secretary of defense announced that major combat was over in Afghanistan. The Taliban and Saddam Hussein were ousted from their respective countries. The new task of the occupying forces was to stabilize the countries and put democratically elected governments into power before withdrawing. Many American leaders assumed that democracy would solve all problems. They were wrong.

The newly elected governments of both Afghanistan and Iraq faced unexpectedly serious difficulties. In Afghanistan, the Taliban and al Qaeda continued to disrupt American efforts and the new government. In 2005, from secret bases in the mountains and in neighboring Pakistan, they began to disrupt the new democracy with suicide bombings, which greatly increased American military casualties. The new Afghani government proved incapable of maintaining control.

The war in Iraq also dragged on. Violence erupted between different Iraqi religious groups, which cost many American and Iraqi lives. Meanwhile, investigators failed to find the Weapons of Mass Destruction whose presence had been a major reason for Bush's decision to go to war. These factors all contributed to making the war extremely unpopular with many Americans. By the time Bush left office in early 2009, both countries remained unsettled and American troops remained in both. The Middle East remained unstable and Christians in the area faced severe persecution.

In addition to direct military intervention to combat terrorism, President Bush authorized several other measures. In October 2001, Congress passed the **PATRIOT Act,** which allowed American intelligence agencies to spy on suspected terrorists, including U. S. citizens. While the PATRIOT Act was intended to make it easier for investigators to detect and stop terrorist plots, many Americans in both Parties felt it violated the Fourth Amendment right to protection from unlawful searches.

The Bush administration also established a prison for captured terrorists in Guantanamo Bay, Cuba. Some people felt that the conditions at Guantanamo were inhumane. However, others pointed out that the terrorists received the same health care that the army provided its own troops, as required by international law. Since it opened in 2002, fewer than 800 terrorists have been held at the Guantanamo Bay detention camp.

Hurricane Katrina

In late August 2005, *Hurricane Katrina*, one of the worst natural disasters in American history, struck New Orleans, Louisiana. New Orleans, which lies below sea level, employs a system of **levees** that protects it from flooding. However, locals live with the nagging fear of a big storm that would overwhelm the levees and inundate the city. As Hurricane Katrina strengthened in the Gulf of Mexico, weather forecasters predicted that it would hit New Orleans. The mayor ordered the city evacuated, but *only one day before the storm hit*. Many residents were unable to find their way to safety. Katrina made landfall early on the morning of August 29th, and passed east of New Orleans. At first, people thought the city had escaped the

Water spills over a levee and floods New Orleans.

worst of the storm. However, it soon became clear that the flooding resulting from the storm had caused the levee system to fail. Water poured into New Orleans, flooding about 80% of the city.

The failures of various local and federal officials worsened the effects of the storm for the people of New Orleans. Flood victims whose homes had been destroyed took shelter at the New Orleans Convention Center and the Superdome. However, neither shelter was prepared to support a large number of refugees for an extended period. With tens of thousands of people inside, shortages of food and water, along with high temperatures, became serious problems. It took almost a week to evacuate the refugees. Meanwhile, law enforcement authorities lost control of the city. As images of the chaos reached the rest of the country, Americans vented their anger on government officials. Although local officials, especially the mayor, bear much of the blame, the news media placed the majority of their criticism on George Bush because they felt federal agencies had not responded quickly enough.

The "Great Recession"

As a presidential candidate, Bush had promised to cut the taxes that Clinton had raised. Bush signed tax cuts into law in 2001, but before the tax cuts could affect the economy, the 9/11 attacks threw the nation into shock. The war on terror also led to two expensive wars. Finally, in 2008, the worst economic crisis since the Great Depression struck, the so-called "Great Recession."

In the early 2000s, the value of homes had been rising steadily for some years. This steady increase prompted lenders to approve mortgages for people who were unlikely to be able to repay their loans. Both lenders and borrowers reasoned that their money was safe, since homes were increasing in value. Large investment companies bought up hundreds of mortgages from banks, planning to profit from the homeowners' interest payments. Eventually, because so many people had bought houses, buyer demand decreased, and the value of homes started to decline. Both homeowners and banks lost money.

This crisis triggered the failure of several major banks. Panic broke out and people stopped investing in other areas. As people had less, they spent less, impacting the overall economy. Many businesses closed and people lost jobs, further worsening the situation. In an effort to stem the crisis, the government provided loans to some of the banks in danger of failing. While total catastrophe was averted, many people suffered, losing their jobs or years of savings. When Bush left office, the economy was showing signs of recovery but still stood on unsteady ground.

The Supreme Court

In late 2005, President Bush was able to name two new members to the Supreme Court when Chief Justice Rehnquist died and Associate Justice O'Connor resigned within a few months of each other. Rehnquist had been a strong conservative voice on the Court and O'Connor had tended to vote with the Conservatives. Bush sought nominees who would also be conservatives.

John Roberts

Bush's first choice was **John Roberts**, whom he had made an Appeals Court Judge. Roberts seemed to be a conservative based on his opinions on the Court of Appeals. However, once he replaced Rehnquist as Chief Justice, he began to write more liberal opinions. Conservatives have been very disappointed in Roberts. He is now considered a moderate and the Court's "swing vote."

On the other hand, Bush's second choice, **Samuel Alito,** has proven to be a staunch conservative. Confirmed in 2006, as of 2022, he is one of the most conservative members of the Court. A Catholic, Alito seems to have taken up the mantle of Antonin Scalia. Alito has voted to protect religious liberty and the unborn.

The Bush Legacy

George W. Bush came to office at a time of peace, but by the end of his term, the United States was involved in two drawn-out wars. While the crises of his presidency were not of his making, he received criticism for them—perhaps unfairly. His unpopularity would be a major issue in the 2008 campaign, which would lead to the Democrats winning a sweeping victory.

Samuel Alito

Answer the following questions:

1. Why was George H.W. Bush very qualified to be president?

2. Why did Bush not trust Mikhail Gorbachev?

3. What event marked the "official" end of the Cold War?

4. Why did Bush become involved in the First Gulf War?

5. Why did President Bush order the invasion of Panama?

6. Why does Bush deserve some credit for the end of the Soviet Union?

7. What is "domestic terrorism?" Where did the two worst cases of domestic terrorism occur?

8. Why was Bill Clinton impeached? Was he convicted? Why or why not?

9. What act launched the war on terror against the United States?

10. Who were the Republican and Democratic candidates in the 2000 presidential election? How did a third party candidate affect the election?

11. What were the targets of the 9/11 attacks?

12. What is the Bush Doctrine?

13. Why did President Bush go to war with Iraq?

14. What is the Patriot Act? Why did Congress enact the Patriot Act? Why is it controversial?

15. Where did Hurricane Katrina do the most damage? Why did so many people suffer because of it? Why did President Bush receive so much blame for it?

16. What is the Great Recession? Why did it happen? What did the government do to try to solve the problem?

17. Who did President George W. Bush nominate to the U.S. Supreme Court?

18. When did the Berlin Wall fall?

19. When did the Soviet Union officially cease to exist?

20. What was the first attack by Islamic terrorists against American civilians?

Identify the following:

1. Michael Dukakis

2. Manuel Noriega

3. Saddam Hussein

4. Clarence Thomas

5. H. Ross Perot

6. Osama bin Laden

7. Ralph Nader

8. Ruth Bader Ginsburg

9. Al Gore

10. Stephen Breyer

11. Samuel Alito

The Church in the Twentieth Century

1901-2000

CHAPTER 35

Pentecost by Jean Restout. The story of the Church in America during the 20th century is a microcosm of the Church of the past twenty centuries. The Church faces threats from enemies without and heretics within. Despite these dangers, great leaders emerge who stand in the breach and fearlessly declare, "you shall not pass!" Finally, despite times of trouble and hardship, in our Faith we find peace and joy.

Introduction

The story of the Catholic Church in Twentieth Century America contains a wide range of characters, movements, persecutions, and triumphs. The century began with a time of both persecution and growth. This growth culminated in a period of prosperity around the middle of the century. In the sixties and seventies, the Church in the United States faced serious challenges both internally and externally. Nevertheless, before the end of the century, signs of new growth and a new strength emerged. As the Church entered the first decades of the Twenty-First Century, a new generation of young priests and bishops, burning with the zeal of the first Apostles, answered the call. As the tides of history rise and fall, one lesson remains: The gates of Hell will not prevail against the Church.

The Beginning of the Century: Immigration

During the mid- to late 1800s, the Irish, and to a lesser extent the Germans, had dominated Catholic immigration. However, the turn of the century saw a shift. The greatest numbers of Catholic immigrants began to come from Italy and Poland. The Poles were particularly loyal to their national heritage and established separate Polish parish churches. Many Poles settled in Chicago. Even today, it is possible to attend Mass in Polish inside one of the beautiful Polish churches that fill Chicago's Polish district.

At the beginning of the 20th century, America's Catholics had their highest numbers in the cities of the north. New York, Philadelphia, and Chicago were all Catholic strongholds. A steady stream of Catholic immigrants contributed significantly to the ongoing growth of the Church. There were 12 million Catholics in the U.S. in 1900, making Catholicism the largest religious denomination in the country. By the 1920s, there were close to 20 million, and Catholics accounted for almost 20 percent of the population.

The Church in the United States had grown so much by the early 1900s that it received official recognition from Rome. In 1908, Pope Pius X removed the American Church from the jurisdiction of the Congregation for the Propagation of the Faith. This may seem a small matter, but it had great significance. It meant that the Church in the United States would no longer be considered "mission territory." The Pope was officially recognizing that Catholicism was well established in the United States.

Pope St. Pius X

Catholics in World War I

While American Catholics were rejoicing in their newfound recognition, many other Americans viewed the large numbers of Catholic immigrants with growing concern. They questioned whether Catholics, with their religious allegiance to the Pope in Italy, would be wholeheartedly committed to their new country. When America entered World War I, American Catholics seized the opportunity to prove their patriotism. The American bishops organized a "**National Catholic War Council**," which led Catholic support of the war effort. On behalf of American Catholics, the U.S. archbishops delivered the following statement to President Woodrow Wilson: "*We are all true Americans, ready as our age, our ability, and our conditions will permit, to do whatsoever is in us to do, for the preservation, the progress and the triumph of our beloved country.*" The laity demonstrated the truth of this statement by entering the military in large numbers. In fact, the percentage of Catholics in the armed forces was significantly higher than the Catholic proportion of the nation as a whole: 25% of the army and 50% of the navy were Catholics.

In Times Square, New York, stands the larger-than-life statue of a stern-looking man in military attire. In his hands, he holds not a gun, but a Bible. Behind him towers a Celtic cross. The inscription on the cross reads, "**Lieutenant Colonel Francis P. Duffy**, May 2 1871-June 26 1932, Catholic Priest."

The Statue of Colonel Duffy in Times Square

Fr. Francis Duffy was one of the most beloved Catholics to serve the United States during the Great War. A parish priest in New York, Fr. Duffy traveled to Europe to act as chaplain for the "Fighting 69th," an Irish regiment with many Catholic soldiers. In the grim trenches of World War I, Fr. Duffy inspired and comforted the soldiers. He spent his days offering Mass and hearing confessions on the front lines. He repeatedly put his life in danger in order to bring the sacraments to the dying and often appeared in the heat of battle. He frequently accompanied litter-bearers as they searched for the wounded.

Fr. Duffy's success, of course, cannot be measured in numbers. However, it is likely that there is more than one soul in heaven today thanks to his ministry. His effect on the soldiers' morale did not go unnoticed by his military superiors. His courage won him the Distinguished Service Cross and the Distinguished Service Medal, making him the most decorated military chaplain in American history. Fr. Duffy survived the war and returned to civilian life at his parish in New York. He published his memories of the war in the bestselling *Fr. Duffy's Story*. His book helped to improve the opinion many Americans had of Catholics. However, anti-Catholic prejudice continued to pose a challenge to the growing Church.

The Ku Klux Klan Attacks the Church

On Saturday, May 17, 1924, thousands of travelers descended on the small city of South Bend, Indiana. Many carried white robes under their arms. Seemingly helpful young men offered directions to the visitors as they arrived in trains and cars. However, upon following the directions, the visitors found themselves in narrow alleys from whence they emerged without their white bundles and sometimes with a few bruises. The visitors were members of the Ku Klux Klan (KKK), one of the most vicious anti-Catholic groups in the history of the United States. The young men were the "Fighting Irish" students of Notre Dame University, a Catholic stronghold. Hearing that hooded Klansmen were on every street corner of South Bend, 500 students had run the two miles into town to show that they would not be intimidated. The KKK had planned a rally. They got resistance.

Burning crosses in front of the homes of African-Americans as well as Catholic churches was one of the favorite tools of KKK intimidation.

The clash between the Notre Dame students and the KKK was only one event in a larger conflict that occurred throughout the United States in the 1920s. American Catholics had proven their loyalty in World War I, but many Americans still distrusted them. The KKK was at the forefront of American anti-Catholicism. While today, nearly everyone views the Klan unfavorably because of its association with racism, violence, and terrorism, in the 1920s, the KKK enjoyed more popularity. The 1915 film *Birth of a Nation* depicted the group as true patriots, determined to improve American morality and return the country to its pre-Civil War greatness. In addition to the more violent acts for which they are now notorious, the Klan organized social events, such as picnics and parades. They promoted strict Protestant values, including the prohibition of alcohol and reading the Bible in schools. This benevolent facade helped the Klan to gain popularity. From 1922 to 1925, their membership grew from 1.2 million to 5 million. Their large membership enabled the Klan to win elections and gain political power.

For the KKK, a "true" American was a white, Anglo-Saxon Protestant. While they mostly targeted blacks, they also hated other groups that did not fit into their perfect America. They viewed immigrants with distaste. They also discriminated against Jews and Catholics. Since most European immigrants between 1880 and 1920 were Catholic, the KKK had a double reason to persecute Catholics. They feared that, through the growing numbers of Catholics, a foreign power (the Pope) was gaining a strong influence on American soil. The Klan held cross-burnings in front of Catholic buildings and engaged in other forms of violence, intimidation, and vandalism. They feared the presence of Catholic teachers in public schools and worked to have them fired. In Oregon, the KKK helped pass a law requiring that all children attend public schools, thus shutting down Catholic schools as well as all other private schools. Fortunately, in *Pierce v. Society of Sisters* (1925), the Supreme Court declared this law unconstitutional.

In 1925, the decline of the KKK began. David Curtiss Stephenson, a prominent Klan leader, was convicted of abducting and murdering a young woman. His conviction exposed the violent side of the KKK. Membership in the organization quickly plummeted.

The Rise of a Catholic Society in America

While the KKK rose and fell, Catholics in the United States had been quietly growing in strength. Their numbers had grown so much that they were able to develop a system that enabled them to live much of their lives in a Catholic context. While American society in general had decided to keep Church and State separate, Catholics could not so easily separate their Faith from their daily life. In the first decades of the Twentieth Century, they formed what almost amounted to a separate Catholic state within American society. It was possible for Catholics to receive their education in Catholic schools and colleges; join Catholic workers' associations; socialize with and marry other Catholics; and finally die in a Catholic hospital. Many of these separate Catholic organizations had existed for much of the history of the United States. However, they saw great growth in the early 20th century. For example, in 1900, there were only 100 Catholic high schools in the country. By 1920, there were over 1500.

In 1926, Chicago hosted the **International Eucharistic Congress**. This massive event caught the attention of Catholics and non-Catholics alike and showed the strength and influence of the American Church. It was the largest Catholic gathering that the United States had ever seen. Catholics flocked to Chicago not only from around the United States but from countries around the world, including such remote places as China and Africa. Catholics and non-Catholics

A view of the crowd and the altar on the steps of Immaculate Conception Chapel at the University of St. Mary of the Lake on June 24, 1926. About one million people from around the world attended the congress' closing Mass.

of Chicago worked together to ensure the success of the congress. A special train, painted red for the occasion, carried the papal delegation of cardinals from New York to Chicago. On the first day of the congress, 62,000 Catholic school children formed the choir for the outdoor Mass, attended by a crowd of 400,000 at Soldier Field, Chicago's football stadium. Here stood a splendid temporary altar, beneath a gilded, dome-shaped canopy, reminiscent of the *baldacchino* in St. Peter's Basilica itself. For the five days of the congress, the people of Chicago saw their streets fill with pilgrims from all over the world. Meanwhile, Chicago newspapers featured the events of the congress on their front pages.

On the last day of the congress, the attendees made a pilgrimage to the nearby seminary town of Mundelein. The Chicago public transport system flooded with pilgrims, as commuters attempted to make their way to their normal jobs. According to one account, a section of Chicago sidewalk "cracked and sank several inches under the weight of the crowds." The newspapers reported that the number of pilgrims was too large to count, although estimates ranged from 500,000 to one million. Catholics from around the world enjoyed traditional American food. Apparently, nothing was more popular than the good old American hot dog! The Eucharistic Congress showed the people of the United States and the world how strong the Catholic Church had become in America.

On the other hand, two years later, in 1928, Catholicism became a heated political issue when Al Smith became the first Catholic to run for president. Sadly, Smith's candidacy brought anti-Catholic feeling to the surface. Though the KKK had begun to fade away, they gathered their strength against Al Smith. Violent propaganda emerged against Catholics, as Smith's opponents preyed upon the fear and ignorance of the American people. They spread rumors that if Smith became president, the Pope would rule America through him, and he would deny citizenship to Protestants. Smith lost the election in a landslide. The level of prejudice that the election revealed shocked American Catholics. It increased their motivation to develop their own system, and through the 1930s, many began to invest more in their own organizations than in American society as a whole.

Dorothy Day and the Catholic Worker Movement

The 1930s also saw the rise of the *Catholic Worker* movement. The *Catholic Worker* movement was not a major aspect of mainstream Catholicism, but it played a significant role. **Dorothy Day**, the controversial leader of the movement, was a writer and activist. Even before her conversion, this fiery woman would stop at nothing to oppose what she saw as unjust. Dorothy Day possessed the passion for Catholicism of a person who had found a pearl of great price and knew the pain of life without it.

Dorothy Day in 1916.

Day entered the Church after the birth of her daughter, and did so at great personal cost. Her conversion required her to end her relationship with her baby's father, who refused to marry her. A single mother and a new Catholic, Day began her life's work. She established "hospitality houses," or shelters for the poor and homeless, and set up communal farms. A talented writer, she established a newspaper called *The Catholic Worker*, which promoted pacifism and discussed issues such as poverty and workers' rights. *The Catholic Worker* newspaper grew steadily through the 1930s, and before America entered World War II, it had close to 200,000 subscribers. However, Dorothy Day's extreme pacifism caused the newspaper to lose popularity during the War. Although it still exists today, it has never regained the influence that it held in the 1930s.

Dorothy Day is a complex figure, who does not possess the "normal" characteristics of a saint. In some ways, she resembles both St. Paul and St. Augustine. Before her conversion, she embraced Communism and lived a rather immoral life. However, she had a genuine conversion. After her conversion, she became devoted to the Catholic faith. She attended daily Mass and prayed the liturgy of the hours and the Rosary. She was clear in her promotion of Church teaching on the social issues and morality. Nevertheless, some have questioned whether she truly abandoned her communist sympathies. Dorothy Day herself repeatedly maintained that her beliefs and actions complied with Catholic social teaching. She argued that she was promoting the Catholic ideal by calling for individual works of charity, rather than a government-imposed system of wealth redistribution. However, some of her comments on world affairs call these statements into question. She argued against armed opposition to the communists in the Spanish Civil War and she gave limited support to Castro and his communist regime in Cuba. Day died on November 29, 1980.

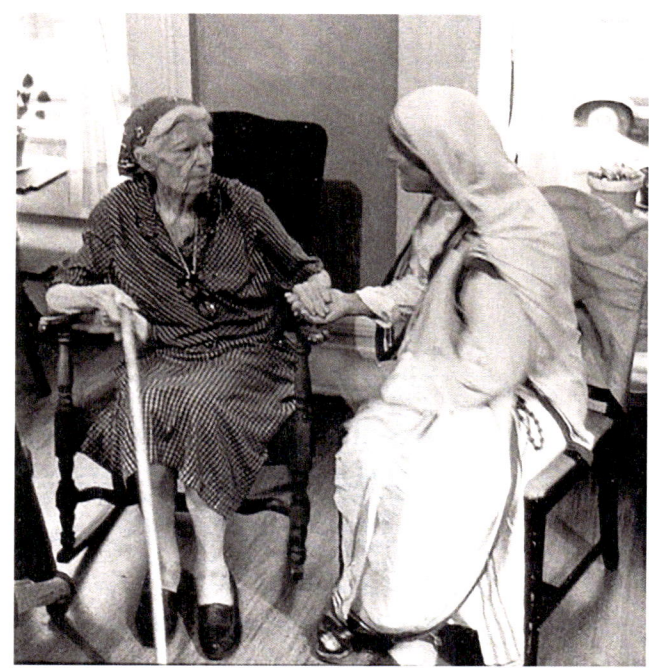

Servant of God Dorothy Day and Saint Mother Teresa met at Mary House, the Catholic Worker soup kitchen in New York City in 1979, shortly before Day's death. In 1970, while Day was in Calcutta, Mother Teresa had asked her to speak to her novices.

Even today, the questions that surround Dorothy Day's life have not been fully resolved. The Church has opened the cause of her canonization, but her life and writings are still under investigation. In 2015, Pope Francis publicly praised Day. Sadly, the movement that Dorothy Day founded has not maintained the level of faithfulness to the Church that Dorothy herself exemplified. While Catholic Worker houses still serve the poor, there are many examples of them engaging in activities that are not in accord with Catholic teaching.

The "Triumphal Era" of American Catholicism

The KKK-led attempts to ostracize Catholics from American society were resounding failures. As Catholics focused on developing their parishes, schools, and societies, American Catholicism blossomed into its "triumphal era" during the 1930s, '40s and '50s. The Church flourished. Funds were plentiful. The American Church became the largest contributor to the Vatican -- a status it still retains. An abundance of men and women generously gave their lives to religious vocations. In the northeast, where Catholicism was strongest, Catholics formed close to 40% of the population by the 1950s while 23% of the entire population was Catholic. These Catholics practiced the faith devoutly. In Philadelphia, for example, 90% of Catholic families attended Mass every Sunday. In addition to these interior strengths, the Church began to exert an unprecedented influence over American culture.

The scene of a First Communion in the 1940s or 1950s provides a snapshot of the Church's strength at the time. Every spring, large groups of children filled the front pews of the parish church. The little girls wore their white dresses and veils while the young boys dressed in their best, usually first, suits. Nuns wearing full habits shepherded the children into place. The youngsters would don their First Communion attire again for the feast of Corpus Christi. On this day, they would process through the streets while the priest carried the Blessed Sacrament in a monstrance. The girls scattered flower petals along the way.

The rituals and traditions of triumphal-era Catholicism were the familiar rhythm of daily life. Mass in every parish was always in Latin. Catholic homes were filled with sacred pictures and statues. Children received a patron saint at baptism and celebrated the yearly feast day of their saint. Catholics lit candles, wore scapulars, prayed the rosary, walked in procession, and abstained from meat every Friday. Homes, cars, and even pets all received special blessings. It was common for people to attend the parish church during the week for daily Mass, special devotions such as adoration or novenas, or social gatherings. Of course, many of these practices continue among Catholics today, but in the 1940s and 1950s, they were particularly widespread.

The large numbers of religious contributed significantly to the flourishing of the Church, especially through their work in Catholic schools. Since nuns and brothers took vows of poverty and did not have families to support, many dioceses could offer an affordable, or even free, Catholic education to all of the faithful. The Baltimore Catechism was the catechetical text of the day. Every Catholic child had its questions and answers memorized. Moreover, Catholic schools kept families close to the parish community.

Priests were plentiful and the people held them in great respect. Most priests lived in community with other priests and there were usually several in a parish. There were so many priests, that a priest would normally not become a head pastor until he was in his fifties. Seminaries could afford to be selective and often had waiting lists. In fact, studying for the priesthood was one of the best opportunities for young men to get an education. Often among the best educated, priests would give advice on all matters, not just spiritual concerns. Sometimes, parishioners would even turn over their personal finances to priests to manage in trust funds.

Catholics Use Mass Media for Conversions

The development of new mass media technology, particularly radio in the 1930s and 1940s and then television in the 1950s, provided the Church with new opportunities to spread the Faith. Now a priest could speak with not merely the several hundred people in the pews, but with millions of radio listeners and television viewers. Two exceptional priests took to the airwaves to bring the Catholic faith to as many Americans as possible. Their names were **Fulton J. Sheen** and **Patrick Peyton**.

Of the two, Fulton Sheen remains the better known. In the 1930s and 40s, he gave weekly talks on the radio show *The Catholic Hour*. However, Sheen is most famous for his TV show, *Life is Worth Living*. Ordained a bishop in 1951, Sheen began the program the same year, always appearing dressed in his episcopal regalia, complete with pectoral cross and scarlet cape. He discussed a variety of topics, ranging from parenting teenagers, to communism, to reflections on the Gospel. Sheen's combination of wit, stage presence, and unabashed proclamation of the truth proved irresistible to the American public.

Fulton Sheen. Sheen's program went head-to-head against *The Milton Berle Show*, one of the most popular shows in TV history, and drew millions of viewers. In explaining Sheen's success, Berle joked "Bishop Sheen had better writers," referencing Sheen's Biblical source material.

Hollywood's biggest stars appeared on Fr. Peyton's radio program, many of whom were not even Catholic. In this photo, Fr. Peyton is shown with Jack Benny, who was Jewish, and Lucille Ball, who was a Protestant Christian.

At its peak, his show had 30 million weekly viewers, including non-Catholics, while more listened in on the radio. Sheen remained humble in the face of his outstanding success, attributing it more to the faith he preached than to his own talents.

Fulton Sheen died on December 9, 1979. During his lengthy career, he had presented hundreds of hours of radio and television shows as well as writing more than seventy books and innumerable magazine and newspaper articles. From 1951 to 1957, during the run of his television program, Sheen may have been the most popular television personality in America. The Church has opened the cause for Bishop Sheen's canonization. As of 2022, he has yet to be beatified.

Fr. Patrick Peyton (1909-1992) was another priest who used mass media to promote the Catholic Faith. Fr. Peyton was an Irish farm boy, whose family prayed the Rosary together every night. As a teenager, he was considering a religious vocation. However, he needed to earn money to help his family when his father became too sick to work the family's farm. Some of his sisters, who had gone to America, sent word that there was work in America for strong young men. Patrick and his brother Thomas decided that they could be more help to the family if they went to America. In May 1928, Patrick and his brother came to America to seek their fortunes.

Eventually both boys discerned priestly vocations and entered the seminary in 1929. Struck with tuberculosis during his years of formation, Patrick miraculously recovered after praying the Rosary. This event instilled in him a deep devotion to Mary. He dedicated his priesthood to her and continued to refer to himself as "Mary's Donkey."

As Fr. Peyton began his priestly work, he realized the importance of helping Catholics build strong and loving families. He promoted daily family prayer, particularly the Rosary, as a keystone of family unity. Wanting to bring the rosary into the homes of as many people as possible, Fr. Peyton eventually went to Hollywood.

In 1947, Fr. Peyton began a weekly radio show called *Family Theater of the Air*. Every week, some of Hollywood's biggest stars participated in his programs, and he coined the famous phrase, "The family that prays together stays together." Fr. Peyton's zeal for promoting the rosary made him tireless in his efforts. In 1948, he began to hold rosary rallies, which led him to travel over the world, attracting crowds of millions. Fr. Peyton realized that through the Rosary, Communism would be overcome and Russia would be converted.

Fr. Peyton died in November 1992, about seven months after the fall of the Berlin Wall. He lived to see the power of the Rosary over Communism. Like Bishop Sheen, the Church has begun the process of canonization for Fr. Peyton. On December 18, 2017, Pope Francis declared him Venerable.

Positive Portrayal of Catholics in Film and Television

The positive image of Catholics in mid-century America is evident not only in the wide audiences that Peyton and Sheen garnered, but also in Hollywood's consistently affirmative depictions of Catholics. Bing Crosby famously starred as Fr. Charles O'Malley in the hit movies *Going My Way* (the highest grossing picture of 1944) and its sequel *The Bells of St Mary's* (the highest grossing movie of 1945). Moreover, there were many other popular "Catholic" movies. These movies portrayed priests and nuns as heroes, outstanding citizens with moral authority and great influences for good. The movies were immensely successful. From 1943 to 1945, Catholic movies received no less than 34 Oscar nominations. One reason for this success was probably the large numbers of Catholics in the U.S. However, their success also indicates that Catholic values were attractive to the average American.

Catholic influence on Hollywood was not limited to movies with strictly Catholic content, but also extended to the moral content of all movies. The large numbers of Catholics, their obedience to their religious authorities, and Hollywood's fear of boycotts combined to give Catholic bishops a considerable influence over movie producers. In the 1930s, the bishops established the **Legion of Decency**, an office that rated Hollywood films based on their moral content. Church bulletins and Catholic newspapers publicized the Legion's ratings so that Catholics were well aware of any movie that had objectionable content. If the Legion gave a movie a "C" rating (for condemned), that movie often failed financially. Of course, some

Theatre poster for *Going My Way*. After World War II ended, Bing Crosby and Leo McCarey, both cradle Catholics, traveled to Rome where they presented a copy of the film to Pope Pius XII.

Bing Crosby, shown with Ingrid Bergman, reprised his role of Fr. O'Malley in The Bells of St. Mary's. Crosby was the most conspicuously Catholic mega-star the United States has ever seen. In addition to playing Father O'Malley, the most well-known priest in movie history, Crosby's recording of White Christmas is the world's best-selling single with estimated sales in excess of 50 million copies worldwide.

C-rated movies were still successful, but many film companies did not wish to risk the objectionable rating and complied with the Legion's moral standards. With the threat of costly boycotts looming over them, it was easier to conform. For the first decade of the Legion's existence, 85-90% of Hollywood productions complied with the Legion's standards to be considered morally unobjectionable. In several years, Hollywood made no movies that earned a "C" rating. Protestants admired Catholic success in this area. Many Protestant leaders supported the Legion and encouraged their congregations to follow the Legion's ratings.

Hints of a Troubled Future

In many ways, the 1940s and 1950s were the Golden Age of the Catholic Church in America. The Church had more influence on American culture and society than ever before, or ever since. Young men and women vigorously sought the priesthood and the religious life in record numbers. In the election of 1960, America would elect a Roman Catholic president.

Francis Cardinal Spellman. From 1939 until his death in 1967, he served as the Cardinal Archbishop of New York. During that time, he was probably the most influential Catholic in the United States.

However, there are temptations associated with such great strength. Some men and women began to see the priesthood and religious life as paths to power and respect, rather than as positions of service to the people of God. With large numbers of children to educate, the memorized formulas of the *Baltimore Catechism* were efficient, but many did not receive the deeper formation that they needed. Some Catholics who grew up in this era have complained of a rigidity that did not foster in them a loving relationship with God. With the large numbers of lay faithful, priests, and nuns, there must have been great differences in the Catholic experience from place to place. Nevertheless, the extent of the decline that would occur over the next twenty years suggests that internally, the Church may have begun to experience a corruption that left it ill prepared for the challenges to come.

The Decline of American Catholicism

A time-traveling visitor from the fifties who stepped into a typical Catholic Mass in 1970s America would certainly be confused. He would not see many of the external rituals that had long characterized Catholicism. For example, the prayers and hymns of the Mass were no longer in Latin. Mass was now said in English. The priest faced the people instead of standing with his back to them. In some churches, parishes had chosen to remove altar rails. Some more "liberal" parishes had even chosen to remove statues of the saints. Guitars and electric keyboards took the place of the organ. Nuns, no longer wearing full habits, were either totally absent or indistinguishable from the rest of the congregation.

These *external* changes marked a deep upheaval that had taken place in American Catholicism. Many Catholics had flagged in their faithfulness to Sunday Mass. Many religious had left their orders. In place of the *Baltimore Catechism*, children received a religious formation that emphasized emotions and failed to convey the fullness of Catholic teaching. At the same time, the Church lost much of its influence on popular culture.

A primary reason for the decline of Catholicism during the sixties and seventies was the rise of a heresy called **modernism**. Modernism had first appeared in the late 1800s. The modernists claimed to

Vatican Council II

be 'modernizing' or updating the Church's teachings and practice. Small things do sometimes change in the Church, but **the modernists sought to change everything**, including fundamental doctrines. They presented religion as a matter not of objective truth but of personal preference, and thus argued that it should change to fit the tastes of the times. The modernists believed that it was impossible for human beings to know the truth about God. Instead, they believed that religion was simply a matter of sentiment and feelings. As a result, they denied the objective truth of many important Church teachings. They said that these teachings were simply attempts to express religious feelings, that they were not really true, and that they could change over time. It followed that there was no reason to believe that the Catholic Church was the one true Church, or any different than any other religion.

In 1907, Pope Pius X officially condemned modernism and temporarily silenced the modernists. However, the modernists did not leave to form their own religion. One of their beliefs was that the Church must change her teachings to appeal to the feelings of the time. Thus, the modernists believed that it was their duty to "reform" and "update" the Church. They waited for a more favorable time to promote their teachings within the Catholic Church.

The modernists found an opportunity in the Second Vatican Council, which met from 1962 to 1965. The documents that the council released *did not teach modernism*. However, most ordinary Catholics never read the Council documents. Instead, they depended on the clergy, and, foolishly, on the press, to let them know what the Council said. Modernists taught that the council had called for radical changes and sweeping innovations in the Church. For example, they claimed that the Council had suggested that monks and nuns abandon their habits. Of course, the Council had never said that.

When modernists were accused of not telling the truth, they justified themselves by invoking the so-called "spirit of Vatican II." They claimed that this "spirit" embodied what the bishops at the council had really *intended*. In fact, it was simply an excuse to promote their ideology, which ran contrary to Catholic teaching.

Over the next decades, the infiltration of the modernists devastated the Church. As they attempted to make Catholicism "relevant" to modern culture, they discarded many of its beautiful traditions. Although most Catholics knew the basics of the Faith, that is, the prayers, the catechism, the Sacraments, most Catholics were not theologians. They did not possess a deep understanding of the *philosophical foundations* of the faith. Moreover, and most importantly, *Catholics trusted their priests and bishops to teach the truth.* Thus, modernist teachers and shepherds led the flock astray. The results were shocking.

Catholic Mass attendance fell dramatically. In 1955, 75% of Catholics regularly attended Sunday Mass. By 1975, the number had fallen to 54%. Some left because of the radical changes in the liturgy, e.g. guitar Mass, liturgical dancing. Others grew lukewarm because the teachings of the modernists undermined their motivation to stay faithful. Modernism made Catholicism no better than any other religion. If the Eucharist is not truly the Body and Blood of Christ, and if Jesus did not really rise from the dead, there is no compelling reason for people to center their lives on their faith. Instead, it becomes little more than a hobby, or a cultural event that one celebrates at Christmas and Easter when there is a good choir. Religious orders discarded their habits. Some changed the focus of their mission. Many religious abandoned their vows. As a result, the stream of new vocations dwindled to a trickle and in some cases dried up completely.

Modernism had particularly negative effects in Catholic higher education. The Church teaches that both faith and science lead to the same truths because God is the Author of Science. However, modernists believe that faith and science contradict each other. They argued that when the two seem to be in conflict, faith must give way, since faith is only emotion while science is rational. As science moved further away from Church teachings, Catholic colleges in the United States faced an identity crisis. At the time, the Jesuits ran most of the Catholic colleges in the United States. Rather than defending the Faith as they had since the time of Ignatius of Loyola, and working to reconcile Faith and Reason (science), the Jesuits took the lead in conforming their institutions completely to *worldly* standards. They replaced priests with lay teachers and their curriculum became increasingly secular. At times, teachers would even challenge official Church teachings in the name of academic freedom. With higher education in a state of disarray, the future looked bleak.

Yet modernism cannot be blamed for all of the problems in the Church. American culture in general was in a state of upheaval in the sixties and seventies. The legalization of the birth control pill caused a massive rise in sexual immorality and marital infidelity. Most devastatingly, in 1973, the Supreme Court decision in *Roe v. Wade* made abortion legal. The influence of the Legion of Decency waned and movies became increasingly immoral. Riots in opposition to the Vietnam War damaged property and showed a lack of respect for legal authority. As the nation became wealthier, many people turned away from God and religion and embraced material things. In addition to problems within the Church, the collapse of the Judeo-Christian society that had existed in America for more than 350 years affected Catholics. They could not live within the society and not be somewhat touched by it.

The forties and fifties had been the Golden Age of the Catholic Church in America. However, during the next two decades, the Church had experienced a tragic decline. As with most such declines, no single event is solely responsible. Nevertheless, modernism and the decline of the overall culture contributed greatly.

Roe v. Wade

In 1970, *Jane Roe* (a fictional name used to protect the plaintiff's identity, later revealed to be Norma McCorvey) filed a lawsuit against *Henry Wade*, the district attorney of Dallas County, Texas, where she resided, challenging a Texas law which criminalized abortion unless a doctor determined it was necessary to save the mother's life. In her lawsuit, McCorvey (*Roe*) alleged that the Texas law was unconstitutional.

The Supreme Court Justices who decided *Roe v Wade*. Only William Rehnquist (standing far right) and Byron White (sitting far right) voted to protect the unborn. Blackmun, who wrote the opinion, stands beside Rehnquist.

The Supreme Court initially heard oral argument on the case on December 13, 1971 and issued its opinion on January 22, 1973.

Justice Blackmun, writing for the Court, began his opinion by detailing the history of the medical, philosophical, and theological positions on abortion beginning with ancient times and concluding with the 1970s. All so he could declare, "*We need not resolve the difficult question of when life begins. When those trained in the respective disciplines of medicine, philosophy, and theology are unable to arrive at any consensus, the judiciary, at this point in the development of man's knowledge, is not in a position to speculate as to the answer.*" This is the judicial equivalent of an umpire recalling the history of baseball so that he does not need to call balls and strikes. By failing to decide when life begins, the Court is able to determine that the "right to privacy," which the Court has recognized since at least 1965, contains a right to an abortion.

However, the Court declared that the "right to an abortion" was not absolute but needed to be balanced against other interests, including the state's interests in protecting the health of pregnant women and the "potentiality of human life." These interests vary during the pregnancy and the law must account for this variability. Thus, during the first trimester of pregnancy, the state may not regulate abortion. In the second trimester, the state may regulate abortion to protect the mother's health. In the third trimester, once the unborn child reaches "viability," a state may regulate abortions or prohibit them entirely, so long as exceptions exist to protect the life or health of the mother. [**Note**: the decision becomes more problematic as the point of viability moves closer to conception.]

Justice Rehnquist, in his dissent against the *Roe* decision, noted that the Court relied on the Fourteenth Amendment to bolster the right of privacy. He points out that by "the time of the adoption of the Fourteenth Amendment in 1868, there were at least 36 laws enacted by state or territorial legislatures limiting abortion." Clearly the Framers of the Fourteenth Amendment did not have abortion in mind when they enacted the Amendment. The other dissenting justice, Byron White, was even more blunt in his dissent: "*The Court simply fashions and announces a new constitutional right for pregnant mothers and, with scarcely any reason or authority for its action, invests that right with sufficient substance to override most existing state abortion statutes….As an exercise of raw judicial power, the Court perhaps has authority to do what it does today; but, in my view, its judgment is an improvident and extravagant exercise of the power of judicial review that the Constitution extends to this Court."*

In 2022, the Supreme Court overruled *Roe* in *Dobbs v. Jackson Women's Health Organization*, returning the abortion issue to the states.

A Renaissance in the Church in America

A forest fire is an awe-inspiring and terrifying event, difficult to stop and intensely destructive. Today, scientists understand that despite their devastation, these fires do have some positive consequences. Though the landscape after a forest fire looks dead and ghostly, new shoots soon push their way through the scorched earth, and young saplings thrive in the open spaces cleared by the flames. Diseased plants and destructive insects, eliminated by the fire, pose no threat as the forest re-grows. In a similar way, the trials that the Church suffered in the sixties and seventies, though they may have seemed catastrophic, were not the end. Like a forest fire, the decline in the Church in those decades also cleared away some of the temptations associated with power and prestige. The eighties and nineties saw new beginnings springing up throughout the United States. Of course, these organizations started out as tiny shoots, but they continue to grow vigorously. As truth, goodness, and beauty naturally draw people in, the future remains hopeful.

John Cardinal O'Connor was a great defender of human life both born and unborn.

John O'Connor, the archbishop of New York, led the way in addressing the widespread problems in the Church and in secular culture. Before being ordained bishop, O'Connor visited the former site of the Nazi concentration camp at Dachau. This visit inspired him to dedicate himself to protecting human life, which he realized was under serious threat in the United States. He became a leader in America's pro-life movement. In 1990, he wrote a newspaper column in which he explored the idea of a religious community dedicated to the pro-life cause. The response was so enthusiastic that in 1991, he founded a new *religious order, the* **Sisters of Life**. The Sisters dedicate themselves to promoting the dignity of every human life, especially those at risk of abortion. In addition to the normal vows of poverty, chastity, and obedience, they take a fourth vow, "to protect and defend the sacredness of human life."

In founding the order, as he did throughout his ministry, O'Connor incorporated the authentic teachings of the Church. He emphasized the traditional monastic life, with a central focus on Eucharistic Adoration and the liturgy of the hours, and with the requirement of religious habits for the sisters. While many religious orders that had lost their identity struggled for vocations, the Sisters of Life became a flourishing young order.

Like the Sisters of Life, other religious communities that promote orthodox Catholic teaching and a traditional religious way of life have continued to thrive. Young Catholics are willing to answer the call to a life of radical love, and each year these faithful orders see an intake of new postulants. This new generation of dedicated religious gives hope to the whole Church. Similarly, dioceses that remain true to orthodox Catholicism attract men to the priesthood in record numbers.

In August 1993, Pope John Paul II visited Denver for **World Youth Day** and sowed the seeds for a further renewal and rebirth for American Catholics, especially young Catholics. At the time, Denver was an unlikely venue for a religious event. Fresh from the "summer of violence," crime had been a serious issue for the past few months. However, the Holy Father chose Denver deliberately. He wanted to bring the Gospel to the secular world. Local authorities were apprehensive as thousands of young people descended on the city. Miraculously, crime came to a standstill. During the event, the police did not make a single felony arrest. The fruits of the Pope's visit continue to blossom today, as various influential Catholic organizations credit their inspiration to World Youth Day Denver. The city of Denver itself is slowly becoming a home to more and more Catholic organizations.

Mother Angelica, the founder of EWTN

Perhaps the most important organization to benefit from World Youth Day was the **Eternal Word Television Network** (**EWTN**). Although the network had begun broadcasting in 1981, its live coverage of World Youth Day marked a turning point in its popularity. The network, which broadcast World Youth Day into homes throughout the nation, became the national leader of authentically Catholic programming. Devout Catholics, poorly educated Catholics, and even non-Catholics began to tune in. Many Catholics developed a deeper knowledge of their faith, supplementing what had been lacking in their religious education during the upheaval of the sixties and seventies. Others returned to the faith. Some became Catholics.

The eighties also saw new efforts emerge in the area of Catholic education. Many parents, disappointed by what they considered an insufficient religious education in the Catholic schools, took matters into their own hands. They started private, parent-run Catholic schools. Other parents decided to take a more direct approach and teach their children themselves. Thus, the Catholic homeschooling movement was born. Courageous laymen founded new Catholic colleges as alternatives to the secularized Jesuit universities. One of the most prominent of these is **Christendom College** in Virginia, the alma mater of one of the principal authors of the textbook. These institutions, and others like them, provide authentically Catholic academic life, where faith and reason work together. Meanwhile, FOCUS, an organization that had its roots in World Youth Day 1993, began to bring Catholicism to college students across in the country.

In 1999, Pope John Paul II returned to the United States, this time to St. Louis. The seventy-eight-year-old Pope was frail, and clearly ill. Yet, as he stood before the youth of America, they gave him their strength. The aged pontiff told 20,000 young people at a youth rally that "tonight the pope belongs to you." He went on to tell them that Christ wants them "to be light to the world, as only young people can be light.

The future of the Catholic Church in the United States. Above are eight of the forty-four seminarians studying for the priesthood in the Diocese of Arlington in 2020. Many of the seminarians are graduates of Christendom College. These will be the leaders of the Church in the coming decades. Since this photograph was taken, they have been ordained.

It is time to let your light shine!" Later in his homily at Mass, he emphasized the importance of the family, which is the "primary and most vital foundation of society," a renewal of Christian marriage, and support for a culture of life.

In 1984, Ronald Reagan had declared that it was "morning in America." He had said that it was a time of optimism. It was a time to look forward because the new day would bring hope and prosperity. The eighties and nineties were also morning in America for the Church. The ideas of Modernism had caused problems, many that remain, but the future looks brighter. The next decades for the Church in America are a time of hope and optimism as new young leaders embrace orthodoxy and tradition.

And the Gates of Hell Shall Not Prevail...

In 1969, Fr. Joseph Ratzinger (the future Pope Benedict XVI) commented on the problems in the church:

> "It seems certain to me that the Church is facing very hard times. The real crisis has scarcely begun. We will have to count on terrific upheavals. But I am equally certain about what will remain at the end: not the Church of the political cult, which is dead already, but the Church of faith. She may well no longer be the dominant social power to the extent that she was until recently; but it will enjoy a fresh blossoming and be seen as man's home, where he will find life and hope beyond death."

The story of the Church in America during the Twentieth Century contains both triumph and tragedy. The losses that the Church sustained in the sixties and seventies are great tragedies. The Church no longer has the dominant influence on American culture that she once held. However, God continues to be with His people. The beauty of authentic Catholicism generates an irresistible attraction on the human heart.

In considering the history of the Catholic Church in the United States during the last 100 years, it might help to ponder the words of William Barclay: "Jesus promised the disciples three things -- that they would be completely fearless, absurdly happy, and in constant trouble."

The past contains nostalgia, but we can also look to the future with hope.

Answer the following questions:

1. During the mid-to-late 1800s, from which nations did most Catholic immigrants come?

2. During the early 20th century from which nations did most Catholic immigrants come? Where did these new immigrants tend to settle?

3. What is the significance of Pope Pius X removing the American Church from the jurisdiction of the Congregation for the Propagation of the Faith?

4. During World War I, how did American Catholics show their patriotism? Why was it important that Catholics in the United States be patriotic?

5. Who was Lieutenant Colonel Francis P. Duffy? Why is he a heroic figure not only to Catholics but to all Americans? How has the United States honored Colonel Duffy?

6. What is the KKK? Why did/does it hate Catholics?

7. Why was the KKK popular in the early part of the 20th century?

8. What did the KKK do to intimidate those it hated?

9. Why was the 1926 International Eucharistic Congress in Chicago so important to the Church in the United States?

10. Who was Dorothy Day? What is the name of the movement she started? Why is she a controversial figure in the Catholic Church?

11. What is modernism? Why is it so destructive?

12. How did modernism affect Catholic higher education?

13. Who are the Sisters of Life? What is their mission? Who is their founder?

14. What was World Youth Day Denver?

15. What is EWTN?

16. Who is Fulton J. Sheen? What was the name of his TV program?

17. What argument did Justice Rehnquist make against the majority's position in *Roe v. Wade*?

18. What decision overturned *Roe v. Wade*?

19. What are some of the events that occurred in the 1960s and 1970s that led to the decline of American Catholicism?

20. What role did Bing Crosby play in *Going My Way* and *The Bells of St. Mary's*?

Identify the following:

1. Legion of Decency

2. Hospitality houses

3. Patrick Peyton

4. John O'Connor

End of Volume Two

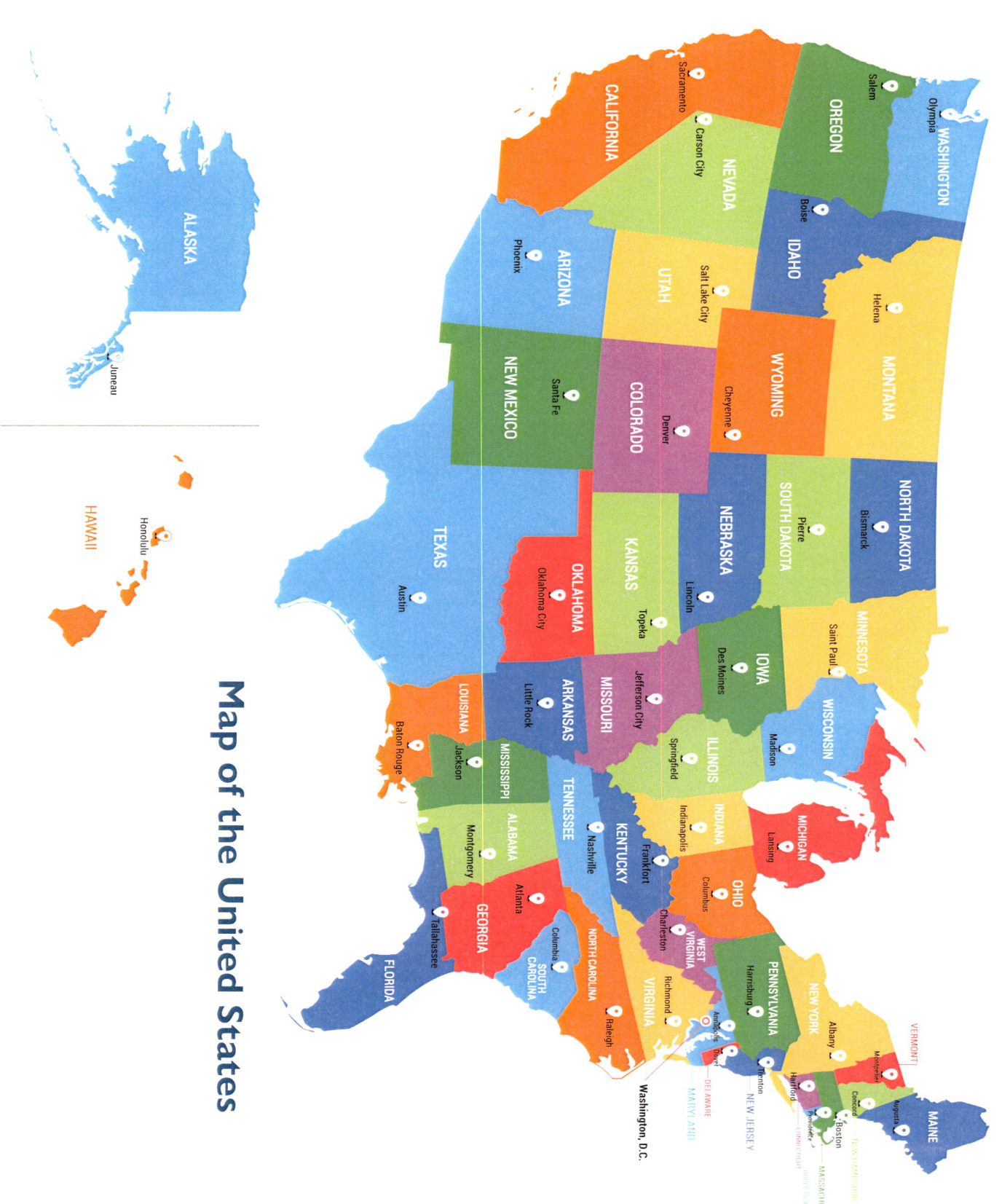

Map of the United States

List of Presidents and Vice-Presidents

YEAR	PRESIDENT	VICE PRESIDENT
1789-1797	George Washington	John Adams
1797-1801	John Adams	Thomas Jefferson
1801-1805	Thomas Jefferson	Aaron Burr
1805-1809	Thomas Jefferson	George Clinton
1809-1812	James Madison	George Clinton
1812-1813	James Madison	office vacant
1813-1814	James Madison	Elbridge Gerry
1814-1817	James Madison	office vacant
1817-1825	James Monroe	Daniel D. Tompkins
1825-1829	John Quincy Adams	John C. Calhoun
1829-1832	Andrew Jackson	John C. Calhoun
1833-1837	Andrew Jackson	Martin Van Buren
1837-1841	Martin Van Buren	Richard M. Johnson
1841	William Henry Harrison	John Tyler
1841-1845	John Tyler	office vacant
1845-1849	James K. Polk	George M. Dallas
1849-1850	Zachary Taylor	Millard Fillmore
1850-1853	Millard Fillmore	office vacant
1853	Franklin Pierce	William R. King
1853-1857	Franklin Pierce	office vacant
1857-1861	James Buchanan	John C. Breckinridge
1861-1865	Abraham Lincoln	Hannibal Hamlin
1865	Abraham Lincoln	Andrew Johnson
1865-1869	Andrew Johnson	office vacant
1869-1873	Ulysses S. Grant	Schuyler Colfax
1873-1875	Ulysses S. Grant	Henry Wilson
1875-1877	Ulysses S. Grant	office vacant
1877-1881	Rutherford Birchard Hayes	William A. Wheeler
1881	James A. Garfield	Chester A. Arthur
1881-1885	Chester A. Arthur	office vacant
1885	Grover Cleveland	Thomas A. Hendricks
1885-1889	Grover Cleveland	office vacant
1889-1893	Benjamin Harrison	Levi P. Morton
1893-1897	Grover Cleveland	Adlai E. Stevenson
1897-1899	William McKinley	Garret A. Hobart

List of Presidents and Vice-Presidents, continued

1899-1901	William McKinley	office vacant
1901	William McKinley	Theodore Roosevelt
1901-1905	Theodore Roosevelt	office vacant
1905-1909	Theodore Roosevelt	Charles W. Fairbanks
1909-1912	William H. Taft	James S. Sherman
1912-1913	William H. Taft	office vacant
1913-1921	Woodrow Wilson	Thomas R. Marshall
1921-1923	Warren G. Harding	Calvin Coolidge
1923-1925	Calvin Coolidge	office vacant
1925-1929	Calvin Coolidge	Charles G. Dawes
1929-1933	Herbert Hoover	Charles Curtis
1933-1941	Franklin D. Roosevelt	John N. Garner
1941-1945	Franklin D. Roosevelt	Henry A. Wallace
1945	Franklin D. Roosevelt	Harry S. Truman
1945-1949	Harry S. Truman	office vacant
1949-1953	Harry S. Truman	Barkley, Alben W.
1953-1961	Dwight D. Eisenhower	Richard M. Nixon
1961-1963	John F. Kennedy	Lyndon B. Johnson
1963-1965	Lyndon B. Johnson	office vacant
1965-1969	Lyndon B. Johnson	Hubert H. Humphrey
1969-1973	Richard M. Nixon	Spiro T. Agnew
1973-1974	Richard M. Nixon	Gerald R. Ford
1974-1977	Gerald R. Ford	Nelson Rockefeller
1977-1981	Jimmy Carter	Walter F. Mondale
1981-1989	Ronald Reagan	George Bush
1989-1993	George Bush	Dan Quayle
1993-2001	Bill Clinton	Albert Gore
2001-2009	George W. Bush	Richard Cheney
2009-2017	Barack Obama	Joseph R. Biden
2017-2021	Donald J. Trump	Mike Pence
2021-	Joseph R. Biden	Kamala Harris

Bibliography

Catholic Encyclopedia. New York: Robert Appleton Company, 1909.

Carroll, Warren. *A History of Christendom* (Six Volumes). Christendom Press. Front Royal

Carroll, Warren. *Seventy Years of Communist Revolution*. Christendom Press. Front Royal

Fuchida, Mitsuo, and Okumiya, Masatake. *Midway: The Battle That Doomed Japan, the Japanese Navy's Story*. United States Naval Inst. (1992)

Garraty, John. *American History*. Harcourt Brace Jovanovich. (1986). Orlando.

Goebel, Edmund J. *A History of the United States*. Laidlaw Brothers. (1959) Chicago.

Goebel, Edmund J.; Richard, Mary; O'Loughlin, John. *United States History.* Laidlaw Brothers. (1966). Chicago.

Graf, Henry. *America: The Glorious Republic*. Houghton Mifflin (1990). Boston.

Guilday, Peter. *A History of the Councils of Baltimore 1791-1884.* New York (1932).

Index